D1611733

*Citizen, State, and Social Welfare
in Britain, 1830–1990*

Citizen, State, and Social Welfare in Britain 1830–1990

GEOFFREY FINLAYSON

CLARENDON PRESS · OXFORD

Oxford University Press, Walton Street, Oxford OX2 6DP
Oxford New York
Athens Auckland Bangkok Bombay
Calcutta Cape Town Dar es Salaam Delhi
Florence Hong Kong Istanbul Karachi
Kuala Lumpur Madras Madrid Melbourne
Mexico City Nairobi Paris Singapore
Taipei Tokyo Toronto
and associated companies in
Berlin Ibadan

Oxford is a trade mark of Oxford University Press

Published in the United States by
Oxford University Press Inc., New York

British Library Cataloguing in Publication Data
Data available

Library of Congress Cataloging in Publication Data
Finlayson, Geoffrey B. A. M.
Citizen, state, and social welfare in Britain 1830–1990 / Geoffrey
Finlayson.
p. cm.
Includes index.
1. Public welfare—Great Britain—History. 2. Welfare state
—History. 3. Great Britain—Social policy. I. Title.
HV245.F56 1994
361.941—dc20 93-28926
ISBN 0-19-822760-4

3 5 7 9 10 8 6 4 2

Printed in Great Britain
on acid-free paper by
Ipswich Book Co. Ltd.
Ipswich, Suffolk

Preface

We are very conscious that there are individuals and institutions whose help and advice, particularly with regard to the early stages of his research, the author would have wished to acknowledge. We greatly regret that, owing to his untimely death, it is possible to offer thanks on his behalf only in very general terms.

In the work of preparing the completed manuscript for publication, we are deeply grateful for the assistance of friends and former colleagues in the University of Glasgow, who have been most generous in offering their time and scholarly expertise.

Professor and Mrs A. G. R. Smith of the Department of Modern History have supported us with unfailing kindness and encouragement. Dr Richard H. Trainor, Dean of the Faculty of Social Sciences, Dr M. Anne Crowther, both of the Department of Social and Economic History, Dr Marguerite Dupree of the Wellcome Institute for the History of Medicine and Mr Irvine Tait—all scholars in the field of social and economic history—have provided invaluable help in very many ways, particularly in checking footnotes. We are also indebted to Miss Patricia Ferguson, a colleague and friend for many years, for the high quality of her work in typing and word-processing.

It is a pleasure, too, to record our thanks to Dr Tony Morris, Ms Anne Gelling, and Mrs Dorothy McCarthy, of Oxford University Press, for their kindness and courtesy, and for their patience over the past several months.

Pre-eminent among our helpers, however, is Mrs Felicity Strong. Our debt to her is immeasurable. She has worked tirelessly in reading the manuscript, in proof-reading, in preparing the index; her professionalism and scholarship in these areas have been invaluable. In personal terms, she has been a constant source of reassurance and encouragement to us.

It is with love and pride that we present this book.

Elizabeth F. Finlayson
E. Jane E. P. Finlayson
Laura A. M. S. Finlayson

September 1993

Contents

Introduction   1

1. Citizen and State, 1830–1880: Providence,
   Paternalism, and Philanthropy   19
2. Citizen and State, 1880–1914: Challenge,
   Collectivism, and Convergence   107
3. Citizen and State, 1914–1949: War, Want, and
   Welfare   201
4. Citizen and State, 1949–1991: Participation,
   Perception, and Pluralism   287

Conclusion   401
Bibliography   424
Index   449

Introduction

Richard Titmuss wrote that 'when we study welfare systems we see that they reflect the dominant cultural and political characteristics of their societies'.[1] It is also true that studies of welfare systems reflect such 'dominant cultural and political characteristics'; and this may be illustrated by the fact that books which have been written on the history of social welfare provision over the past twenty to thirty years have, almost without exception, linked the word 'welfare' to the word 'state'.[2] The overwhelming tendency to work 'Welfare State' into the titles of books might well suggest that the approach of their authors reflected a 'dominant cultural and political characteristic': the existence and acceptance of a settled, established, and seemingly permanent Welfare State, the origins and development of which required to be explained. One book, indeed, used the title *Before the Welfare State*;[3] this seems to illustrate the tendency to look on other forms of welfare, which predated the Welfare State, as somehow deviating from the norm: the norm being that welfare was inextricably associated with the state.

This may attach too much importance to the title of a book, which can reflect the preference of the publisher as much as that of the author. Yet even this point is not without significance in the present context. The fact that 'Welfare State' is used so frequently in the titles of books on the history of social policy and

[1] For an edn. of Titmuss's work on these subjects, see Brian Abel-Smith and Kay Titmuss (eds.), with an Introduction by S. M. Miller, *The Philosophy of Welfare: Selected Writings of Richard M. Titmuss* (London: Allen & Unwin, 1987).

[2] See e.g. David Roberts, *Victorian Origins of the British Welfare State* (New Haven, Conn.: Yale University Press, 1960); Maurice Bruce, *The Coming of the Welfare State* (London: Batsford, 1961, 4th edn. 1968); Gertrude Williams, *The Coming of the Welfare State* (London: Allen & Unwin, 1967); Maurice Bruce (ed.), *The Rise of the Welfare State: English Social Policy, 1601–1971* (London: Weidenfeld & Nicolson, 1973); R. C. Birch, *The Shaping of the Welfare State* (London: Longman, 1974); Pat Thane, *The Foundations of the Welfare State* (London: Longman, 1982); Derek Fraser, *The Evolution of the British Welfare State* (London: Macmillan, 1973, 2nd edn. 1984).

[3] Ursula R. C. Henriques, *Before the Welfare State: Social Administration in Early Industrial Britain* (London: Longman, 1979).

provision could be taken to suggest that publishers consider the state to be something which the reading public recognizes without difficulty, and with which it readily identifies. It is an accepted part of its political vocabulary.

Another feature of this approach is a tendency to see the history of welfare in terms of the development or evolution of the Welfare State. 'Evolution', 'coming', 'rise', 'shaping': these are words which appear in the titles of the books to which reference has been made. The impression which such words give is of a process of fairly smooth and steady growth in the activities of the state. The point at which that process began is a matter of dispute. A. V. Dicey, writing in 1905, saw the phenomenon of 'collectivism' as beginning in the years after 1870; thereafter, Dicey argued, there was a 'willingness to extend the authority of the State . . .'[4] Moreover, this tendency, in Dicey's view, could only become ever stronger; by 1900, he wrote, it was evident that 'the feelings or the opinions which had given strength to collectivism would continue to tell as strongly upon the legislation of the twentieth century as they had already told upon the later legislation of the nineteenth century.'[5]

Other writers, however, discern the presence of the state at an earlier period. Dicey's views were subjected to considerable criticism in the 1960s and 1970s by scholars who traced statutory activity in the period from 1820 to 1880: a period which Dicey, with some qualifications, had characterized as one of 'individualism'. There was, indeed, disagreement as to the forces which had brought this about—but virtual unanimity among Dicey's critics that, from at least the early nineteenth century, there was clear evidence of the growth of state regulation and administration.[6] Thus Kitson Clark wrote in 1967 that 'from 1830 onwards

---

[4] A. V. Dicey, *Lectures on the Relation between Law and Public Opinion in England during the Nineteenth Century* (London: Macmillan, 1905, 2nd edn. 1914). Reissued with a Preface by E. C. S. Wade (1962), p. xxxi.

[5] Ibid.

[6] The historical controversy engendered by this point may be traced in P. W. J. Bartrip, 'State Intervention in Mid-Nineteenth Century Britain: Fact or Fiction?' (*Journal of British Studies*, xxiii/1 (1983), 63–83); Valerie Cromwell, *Revolution or Evolution? British Government in the Nineteenth Century* (London: Longman, 1977); William C. Lubenow, *The Politics of Government Growth: Early Victorian Attitudes towards State Intervention 1833–1848* (Newton Abbot: David & Charles, 1971); Oliver MacDonagh, 'The Nineteenth-Century Revolution in Government: A Reappraisal' (*Historical Journal*, i (1958), 52–67); Oliver MacDonagh, *A Pattern of Government*

a formidable governmental machine was being created in Britain which brought much of the conduct of life and the use of property under the control of the state, and provided precedents for more extensive controls when the time of need came'.[7] Some writers, indeed, would date the beginning of the process considerably before 1830—some as early as the beginning of the seventeenth century.[8]

This approach, moreover, could easily merge into a kind of 'Welfare State escalator' which, boarded at whatever departure point was chosen, carried the student of the subject onwards and upwards through different floors until the top—clearly marked 'Welfare State'—was reached in the later 1940s. Another metaphor is the 'collective train'. One writer has commented on the British experience over the years from 1945 to 1979: 'it was', he writes, 'as if society was on a great collective train journey into the future'.[9] In historical terms, it is possible to embark on that train at an earlier stage, to stop at certain 'significant' stations—such as the periods from 1830 to 1850, 1874 to 1880, 1906 to 1911, 1914 to 1918, 1939 to 1945—and, as the historical journey concludes, to see the train brought safely into the terminus by the Labour government of Attlee. Moreover, any further excursions were virtually bound to follow the same route. Thus T. H. Marshall wrote in 1965 that 'There is little difference of opinion as to the services that must be provided, and it is generally agreed that, whoever provides them, the overall responsibility for the welfare of the citizens must remain with the state.'[10] And in 1969 Ralph Milliband commented that: 'more than ever before men now live in the shadow of the State. What they want to achieve,

Growth, 1800–1860: The Passenger Acts and their Enforcement (London: Macgibbon & Kee, 1961); Oliver MacDonagh, *Early Victorian Government, 1830–1870* (London: Weidenfeld & Nicolson, 1977); Henry Parris, 'The Nineteenth Century Revolution in Government: A Re-appraisal Re-appraised' (*Historical Journal*, iii (1960), 17–37); Henry Parris, *Government and Railways in Nineteenth Century Britain* (London: Routledge & Kegan Paul, 1965); Roberts, *Victorian Origins*; David Roberts, 'Jeremy Bentham and the Victorian Administrative State' (*Victorian Studies*, ii/3 (Mar. 1959), 195–210); Arthur J. Taylor, *Laissez-Faire and State Intervention in Nineteenth Century Britain* (London: Macmillan, 1972).

[7] G. Kitson Clark, *An Expanding Society: Britain, 1830–1900* (Cambridge: Cambridge University Press, 1967), 130.

[8] See e.g. Bruce (ed.) *The Rise of the Welfare State.*

[9] Charlie Leadbetter, 'New Times Back to the Future' (*Marxism Today* (May 1989), 13). [10] T. H. Marshall, *Social Policy* (London: Hutchinson, 1965), 97.

individually or in groups, now mainly depends on the State's action and support.'[11]

It will be noted that Marshall wrote in terms of the welfare of the citizen coming within the 'overall responsibility' of the state. The approach to welfare which puts primary emphasis on the state tends also to see the citizen as entitled to welfare rights which derive from the state. Citizenship, in this sense, implies the enjoyment of 'an extensive, elaborate and generous structure of social policies',[12] which removes responsibility for welfare in various areas, such as provision for unemployment, family, health, or housing, from the individual and vests it in the state. Citizenship is, then, a matter of possessing certain rights, including social welfare rights; these are delivered by the state as the embodiment of all citizens, who share equally in political power by means of the vote: the 'citizenship of entitlement'.

Here it is helpful to consider the definition of a Welfare State offered by Asa Briggs:

A welfare state is a state in which organised power is deliberately used (through politics and administration) in an effort to modify the play of market forces in at least three directions—first, by guaranteeing individuals and families a minimum income irrespective of the market value of their work or their property; second, by narrowing the extent of insecurity by enabling individuals and families to meet certain social contingencies (for example, sickness, old age and unemployment) which lead otherwise to individual and family crises; and third, by ensuring that all citizens without distinction of status or class are offered the best standards available in relation to a certain agreed range of social services.[13]

It is the third point which Briggs considers essential to a Welfare State, which is concerned with optimum, rather than minimal, standards; and this third element deals with 'equality of treatment and the aspirations of citizens as voters with equal shares of electoral power'.[14] All citizens are 'offered the best standards'

[11] Ralph Milliband, *The State in Capitalist Society* (London: Weidenfeld & Nicolson, 1969; Quartet Books, 1973), 3 (of 1973 edn.).
[12] David Harris, *Justifying State Welfare: The New Right versus the Old Left* (Oxford: Basil Blackwell, 1987), 31.
[13] Asa Briggs, 'The Welfare State in Historical Perspective', in *The Collected Essays of Asa Briggs*, 2 vols., ii: *Images, Problems, Standpoints, Forecasts* (Brighton: The Harvester Press, 1985), 183.   [14] Ibid.

by the state as a matter of right and entitlement, since they are an integral part of the state.

Moreover, this approach could also be incorporated within a linear model of development—although Briggs himself was not associated with such an interpretation. Marshall, however, suggested that the eighteenth century witnessed the achievement of rights of individual freedom, speech, thought, and faith; the nineteenth century, rights of political participation; and the twentieth century, those of economic and social welfare.[15] These welfare rights not only were important in themselves, but made it possible for civil and political rights to be fully enjoyed. Ralf Dahrendorf put it this way:

From an early point onwards in our century, more and more people came to believe that civil and political rights are not worth an awful lot unless they are backed up by a certain basic social security which enables people to make use of these rights and makes it impossible for others to push them around in such a way that the rights become an empty constitutional promise without any substance. . . .[16]

Here again, then, there is an emphasis on a progressive enjoyment of rights from the state which eventually included social rights; and this amounted to a progressive enjoyment of citizenship.

Viewed from the perspective of the 1950s or 1960s, such an interpretation was, indeed, justifiable. Even if the starting-point of the process was open to differing views, it could scarcely be denied that the state *did* extend its activities in matters of social welfare, especially in the course of the nineteenth and twentieth centuries. One can well see why Marshall and Miliband reached their conclusions—or why Mencher began the Loch Memorial Lecture in 1954 with the observation that 'The most evident pattern of modern society has been the steady growth of State responsibility in the spheres of social and economic activity.'[17] It is, in fact, arguable that for some thirty-five years after 1945 there was a broad consensus of opinion which accepted the

[15] T. H. Marshall, *Citizenship and Social Class* (Cambridge: Cambridge University Press, 1950), 9.

[16] *Encouraging Citizenship: Report of the Commission on Citizenship* (London: HMSO, 1990), 7.

[17] S. Mencher, 'The Relationship of Voluntary and Statutory Agencies in the Welfare Services' (London: Family Welfare Association, 1954), 1.

Welfare State in Britain, and even sought to expand it to higher standards than those introduced in the late 1940s.[18]

Yet this is a way of studying the subject which always carries with it certain dangers. The first is that a concentration on the state omits reference to other agencies which were involved in the delivery of social welfare. There was always what is now often called a 'mixed economy of welfare';[19] and within that mixed economy, the state was only one element—and, arguably, for much of the nineteenth century and even the·twentieth, it was not the most important element. The other agencies in this area may be broadly categorized under the term 'voluntarism'.[20] This, however, requires further elucidation, since various forms of activity can be conveyed by it. Voluntarism in matters of social welfare may take the form of self-help or mutual-aid, the purpose of which is to promote the well-being of the individual or group choosing to take part in it. Friendly societies, trade unions, and other related organizations come into this category. On the other hand, voluntarism may involve charitable and philanthropic effort, intended—at least overtly—to promote the interests of others; and here, charitable and philanthropic organizations—again formed, or joined, from individual choice—are found.

Further refinements are, however, necessary. Voluntary activity may involve the expenditure of money, effort, and time—but welfare is the objective of such expenditure; it is not concerned

---

[18] See below, pp. 392–3, for further consideration of the matter.

[19] The phrase is used by S. Kamerman, 'The New Mixed Economy of Welfare: Public and Private' (*Social Work* (Jan.–Feb. 1983), 5–10). See also Maria Brenton, *The Voluntary Sector in British Social Services* (London: Longman, 1985), 5, 15–23, 154, and Richard Rose, 'Common Goals but Different Roles: The State's Contribution to the Welfare Mix', in Richard Rose and Rei Shiratori (eds.), *The Welfare State East and West* (Oxford: Oxford University Press, 1986), 13–39. The 'mixed economy of social care' is also examined by Ken Judge and Martin Knapp, 'Efficiency in the Production of Welfare: The Public and the Private Sectors Compared', in Rudolf Klein and Michael O'Higgins (eds.), *The Future of Welfare* (Oxford: Basil Blackwell, 1985), 133 ff.

[20] Brian Harrison notes that 'voluntarism' in the sense of 'the principle of relying on voluntary action rather than compulsion' dates from 1924, according to its 1st cit. in the *OED*. 'Voluntarism' in the sense of 'denoting the involvement of voluntary organisations in social welfare' dates, he notes, only from 1957. But 'the actual practice of voluntarism in Britain dates from much earlier when it was variously described as 'self-help', 'laissez faire', 'self-improvement', 'charity and philanthropy'. ('Historical Perspectives', in *Voluntary Organisations and Democracy* (Sir George Haynes Lecture, 1987, with Nicholas Deakin. London: National Council for Voluntary Organisations, 1988), 1.)

with distributing a profit. Both mutual-aid and charitable organizations come into this broad category. In this sense, voluntary organizations may be defined as 'self-governing bodies of people who have joined together voluntarily to take action for the benefit of the community and have been established otherwise than for financial gain.'[21] Nevertheless, commercial considerations can also be present—where services are paid for, and the distribution of a profit is a major concern of those who provide the services. Included in this type of activity are commercial welfare initiatives, such as insurance companies and insurance pension schemes. Here, then, is a distinction between non-profit-distributing and profit-distributing voluntarism. Another distinction may be made in terms of the degree of organization which is involved in voluntarism. Voluntary activity can be structured and organized within groups and societies—or it can be unstructured and unorganized, and involve relations between individuals or within families, kin-groups, or neighbourhoods.

Voluntarism may, therefore, be defined in various ways. Indeed, it is customary in present-day studies of the subject to divide it into 'sectors'; and—perhaps somewhat confusingly—the term 'voluntary sector' is normally reserved for those aspects which are not concerned with financial gain. The term 'commercial sector' is applied to activity which is orientated towards private profit; and 'informal sector' to activity which is unstructured and unorganized. It should be said that there may well be connections between the 'sectors'; the distinctions are not entirely clear-cut. It must also be borne in mind that these terms were not in use in the nineteenth century, or much of the twentieth; but they will be used throughout this book. 'Voluntarism' will, therefore, be considered under the terms 'voluntary sector', 'commercial sector', and 'informal sector'.

One further point of definition needs to be made. As has been said, charitable or philanthropic activity of a structured kind is located within the voluntary sector; it is not concerned with the distribution of profit. 'Charity' can, indeed, rather generally denote activities which are concerned with the advancement of the interests of others, rather than of self; and this use will be made of the word in the course of the chapters which follow. The word

---

[21] Quoted in Dahrendorf, *Encouraging Citizenship*, 30.

may, however, have a more specific and legal meaning. Historically, it can denote a form of activity which has charitable status conferred upon it by law; and the conditions of such conferment are that it is concerned primarily with the relief of poverty, the advancement of education or religion, or with other purposes recognized by the law as charitable. It must also provide a tangible benefit to the public, or a significant portion of it; and—taking up the points which have already been made—it must not engage in the distribution of profit. This more strict definition of charity, which is bound by charity law, will also be mentioned in the course of the text.

Such, then, are the various aspects of voluntarism within the mixed economy of welfare. Voluntarism itself—and thus the sectors into which it may be divided—indicates activity which springs from individual initiative and choice, is expressed and supported, at least in some measure, by the efforts of those who take part in it, and retains some degree of identity and independence. The word does not necessarily mean doing things without material reward, although it may have that meaning. In the present context, it means doing things from individual choice and in individual, self-governing ways. It does not spring from outward compulsion and does not result in uniform, standardized, and outwardly imposed activity; these features are more characteristic of statutory initiatives. In 1914 an individual who was active in charity wrote that 'the essence of voluntary work is freedom'. The 'natural instinct' of the person who took part in it was 'to do his job singlehanded and to kick at interference'.[22] This quotation captures those elements of choice and self-control which are essential to voluntarism; and it has been echoed by others. Lord Beveridge in 1948 wrote that 'the term Voluntary Action does imply that the agency undertaking it has a will and a life of its own.'[23] In 1990 Nicholas Hinton, director-general of Save the Children, made a similar point when he wrote that 'the most important aspect of charitable giving is its voluntary nature. It is a personal choice made by the individual donor.'[24]

If used in this context, 'citizenship' has a somewhat different meaning from that which has already been examined. Rather

---

[22] *Charity Organisation Review*, NS, xxxv, 93 (Feb. 1914).
[23] *Voluntary Action: A Report on Methods of Social Advance* (London: George Allen & Unwin, 1948), 8.　　　　　　　　　　[24] *The Times*, 1 June 1990.

than implying the enjoyment of a number of rights and entitlements which are bestowed by the state, the word means more
the performance of certain duties and obligations. 'Citizenship'
in this sense implies giving, rather than taking; contribution, rather
than acceptance. It means contributing to one's own welfare or,
more often, to the welfare of others by service to the community.
That service can, indeed, be carried out through statutory
agencies. It is not, therefore, incompatible with the statutory sector;
but it is particularly associated with the voluntary sector, which
depends in very large measure on the exercise of 'citizenship'
in the sense of the performance of what are felt—for a variety of
reasons—to be duties and obligations. Thus when the governors
of the Victoria Infirmary in Glasgow—a hospital founded within
the voluntary sector in 1890 by private donation and public
subscription—met in 1948 for the last time before the absorption
of the voluntary hospitals into the National Health Service, they
minuted that the 'Voluntary Hospital had contributed something
very valuable to the community, and the Governors had ever
given the lead to the ideal of good citizenship'.[25] This meaning of
the word was also clearly implied by the Nathan Committee on
Charitable Trusts, which in its Report of 1952 stated that it was
'essential' that voluntary activity 'in the form of good neighbourliness, voluntary service and financial support should come to be
regarded as a normal part of citizenship in the modern democratic state'.[26] Here, then, is the 'citizenship of contribution': what
Michael Walzer calls a 'positive conception of the citizen's role'[27]—
but one not necessarily expressed through political structures.

The role of individual effort and of agencies within the voluntary, commercial, and informal sectors may be said to be less
well represented within the historical literature on welfare than
the work of the statutory agencies. For the nineteenth century
there is, indeed, work on such institutions within the voluntary

[25] Quoted in S. D. Slater and D. A. Dow (eds.), *The Victoria Infirmary of Glasgow,
1890–1990: A Centenary History* (Glasgow: The Victoria Infirmary Centenary
Committee, 1990), 67–8.

[26] *Report of the Committee on the Law and Practice Relating to Charitable Trusts*
(London: HMSO, 1952, repr. 1974, Cmd. 8710), par. 53. See also below, pp.
288–91, for further consideration of this Committee.

[27] Michael Walzer, 'Citizenship', in Terence Ball, James Farr, and Russell L.
Hanson (eds.), *Political Innovation and Conceptual Change* (Cambridge: Cambridge
University Press, 1989), 211.

sector as friendly societies or charitable organizations; and there are biographies of charitable and philanthropic individuals.[28] Yet this body of work scarcely matches in quantity what has been done on such areas of Victorian statism as the poor law, public health, or factory regulation. The tendency—already noted—of historians of the nineteenth century to concentrate on the growth of the administrative state in the period reinforced this emphasis on statist, rather than voluntarist, agencies in meeting social need.

Further, when the twentieth century is considered, the historical literature is seen to be virtually wholly preoccupied with the state and, with some exceptions, voluntary social action in its various forms disappears from sight. All textbooks written in the past twenty years on twentieth-century Britain contain many references to socialism and collectivism, but few to self-help and charity. There has been a vigorous historiographical debate on the effects of war on social welfare, but this has quite ignored, except by implication, the influence of war on voluntarism and social welfare. Briggs has written of the 'reorganisation of twentieth-century history around the term "Welfare State" ';[29] and this makes the point that historians of the century have been very largely concerned with describing, analysing, and evaluating state welfare. Books which take account of voluntary initiatives have, indeed, tended to be written by students of politics, sociology, and social administration, and to be set in the very recent past, or in the present-day period.[30]

It is true that the source material for statutory welfare is full and relatively accessible, whereas that for the different forms of voluntary welfare is scattered, localized, and patchy. This presents problems in measuring their extent and precise dimensions; and the nature and difficulty of the source material may, in part, explain why the subject has been relatively little pursued. That

[28] See footnotes to Chs. 2 and 3 for cits. of such works.

[29] 'Social Welfare, Past and Present', in A. H. Halsey (ed.), *Traditions of Social Policy: Essays in Honour of Violet Butler* (Oxford: Basil Blackwell, 1976), 4. See also Briggs, 'The History of Changing Approaches to the Welfare State', in E. W. Martin (ed.), *Comparative Developments in Social Welfare* (London: Allen & Unwin, 1972), 9–24. David Cannadine considers the work of Briggs in 'Welfare State History', in *The Pleasures of the Past* (London: Fontana Press, 1990), 172–83.

[30] See e.g. Brenton, *Voluntary Sector*; Norman Johnson, *Voluntary Social Services* (Oxford: Basil Blackwell & Martin Robertson, 1981); Kathleen Jones, John Brown, and Jonathan Bradshaw, *Issues in Social Policy* (London: Routledge & Kegan Paul, 1978); Rose and Shiratori, *The Welfare State East and West*.

neglect, however, may in part also be seen as the other side of the preoccupation with the state, to which attention has already been drawn. Voluntary initiatives have tended to be seen from the perspective of a dominant, and seemingly permanent, Welfare State. What have been perceived as their defects have been pointed out: that they were élitist rather than egalitarian, unreliable, patchy and moralizing, ameliorative rather than curative, amateur rather than professional, overlapping and wasteful rather than properly planned, dependent on suspect goodwill or objectionable ability to pay rather than centred on needs and entitlements. Thus, from the point of view of the historian of the state, voluntary initiatives may be seen as, at best, marginal and, at worst, positively obstructive to the progress of the state.[31]

It may readily be admitted that voluntary social activity was not without the defects which have been ascribed to it; and it is no part of the purpose of this book to ignore them. Yet the book also attempts to consider such activity more in its own right, and, without in any way making a partisan and uncritical case, to consider, where appropriate, the positive contribution of voluntarism within the mixed economy. This may be seen in terms of the opportunities which it gave to varying individuals and groups for active participation in the meeting of needs by self-help, mutual-aid, or charitable service to the community, of its freedom and flexibility, of its pioneering and specialist function, and of its role in drawing public attention to social issues, in exerting pressure—and, more generally, in promoting choice.

If preoccupation with the state model of welfare can very easily lead to the neglect—or distortion—of the voluntary contribution, it can also lead to a failure to recognize a constant interrelationship between voluntarism, in its various guises, and the state in British social welfare. Even a recently published book which is as much concerned with the forces which restrained the expansion of the state in the twentieth century as those which promoted it, and is, therefore, anti-linear in its approach—James Cronin's *The Politics of State Expansion*—virtually ignores the voluntary input and, more pertinently, the ways in which it related to the state.[32]

---

[31] See Pat Thane, 'The Historiography of the British Welfare State' (*Social History Society Newsletter*, xv/1 (spring 1990), 12–15).
[32] London and New York: Routledge, 1991.

It has been noted that Mencher gave considerable prominence to the importance of the 'steady growth' of the state; and yet, somewhat paradoxically, he was also at pains to draw attention to what he called 'one of the striking features of British welfare': 'the complex intermixture of the voluntary and the statutory'.[33] Within the mixed economy of welfare, voluntary impinged on statutory, statutory on voluntary; and this was an enduring process. It was not so much a question of a development *from* voluntarist activity *to* statutory agencies. That could happen; but more often, voluntarist and statutory agencies were in constant relationship within the mixed economy. This does not mean that the relationship remained the same; it changed over time, and such change brought with it a different distribution of emphasis and importance between voluntarism and the state in the delivery of social welfare. But that change should not obscure the fact that there was, more often than not, a continuous, if also a varied, relationship between voluntarism and the state within the mixed economy.

Among voluntarists there was often a strong suspicion of anything but an enabling state, which simply provided the circumstances in which the voluntary agencies could exist properly; here was an attachment to the idea of complementary roles in creating the conditions in which the individual could practise self-help, mutual-aid, or charity. This attitude could, indeed, affect the kind of statutory provision made within the mixed economy, by trying to ensure that it was confined to a minimal role. But where the functions of the state were more positive, there was an impingement on voluntarism; here the relationship worked in the other direction. In that case, voluntarists had to decide whether they should diverge from a more maximal state—or converge with it. Both had their dangers. The first offered the prospect of ineffectiveness and marginalization; the second the possibility of losing that very freedom, independence, and identity which voluntarists held so important, and which was, in fact, essential to their existence.

Equally, the citizenship of entitlement and the citizenship of contribution did not exist in isolation from each other; they were

---

[33] 'Relationship', 1.

also part of the same 'complex intermixture'. An extension by the state of the rights of the citizen into social welfare areas could be seen as enabling the citizen more effectively to undertake responsibility for his or her own welfare and that of others. Yet how far could the citizenship of entitlement be taken without undermining the citizenship of contribution? At what point would collective provision erode individual effort? It was a difficult balance to strike. The idealist Henry Jones, who took a large part in the setting up of the Stevenson Lectureship in Citizenship at the University of Glasgow in 1920, attempted a reconciliation when he wrote that 'the end of the State is the citizen; and the state which exists for the sake of its citizens is safe in their hands.'[34] But such a reconciliation did not altogether resolve the ambiguities. The *Report of the Commission on Citizenship*, published in 1990, recognized some of the difficulties: 'We do not accept', it stated, 'that there is a simple quid pro quo relationship—a bargain— between entitlements and duties for each individual citizen . . . both exist in their own right; the relationship between them is far from simple.'[35]

The 'complex intermixture' between voluntary and statutory, between citizen and state, has, then, been a feature of social policy and provision in Britain: one which excessive preoccupation with the state will not detect. This point has been recognized by various scholars. David Thomson has written of the history of social welfare as 'a series of shifts to and fro between two loci of responsibility'. At one extreme was 'the individual and his or her immediate family'; at the other was 'the wider community of non-kin'. He suggests that 'the location of responsibilities between these two poles changes over time, shifting continually according to a multitude of social, economic, demographic, political, religious or ideological pressures'.[36] There was, Thomson adds, 'recurrent experimentation with the various options lying between the extremes '.[37] Another writer, Graycar, has suggested

---

[34] Quoted in Andrew Vincent and Raymond Plant, *Philosophy, Politics and Citizenship: The Life and Thought of the British Idealists* (Oxford: Basil Blackwell, 1984), 81.　　　　　　　　　　[35] Dahrendorf, *Encouraging Citizenship*, 7.

[36] 'Welfare and the Historians', in Lloyd Bonfield, Richard M. Smith, and Keith Wrightson (eds.), *The World We have Gained: Histories of Population and Social Structure* (Oxford: Basil Blackwell, 1986), 365.　　　　　　[37] Ibid. 366.

that the interrelationship between the various forms—or sectors—of welfare 'is not easily defined, nor is it in any way fixed.
It is open for negotiation and re-arrangement . . .'.[38]

Thus, in addition to concentrating primarily on the contribution of voluntarism to social welfare in the period from 1830 to
1991—and particularly on that of the voluntary sector within
voluntarism—this book will also consider the relationship between voluntarism and the state. It will not examine statutory
developments in any detail in their own right; as has been suggested, that task has already been well done. But it will argue
that any trend towards a 'maximal' state which may be discerned
over the period was not smooth, steady, and clearly defined, but
always subject to the cross-currents of voluntarism which permeated and influenced it. Equally, however, developments in
the statutory sector also posed problems for voluntarism; and
the ways in which it reacted to these—divergent, convergent, and,
somewhat ambiguously, both divergent and convergent—will also
be examined.

Moreover, the book will also consider developments in social
welfare between 1979 and 1991. The ideas and practices associated with the New Right brought into sharp focus the 'non-
statutory' elements in the 'mixed economy of welfare'. The
Welfare State was subjected to criticism for undertaking too much,
and more than it could deliver; and citizenship was defined in
terms more of the exercise of duties and responsibilities than
of the receipt of rights. Mrs Thatcher argued that: 'the sense
of being self-reliant, of playing a role within the family, of owning one's own property, of paying one's own way are all part of
the spiritual ballast which maintains responsible citizenship.'[39]

What, then, had seemed settled was subjected to revision; and,
as this happened, a number of books appeared which, unlike
many of their predecessors, paid considerable attention to
voluntarist agencies. In one such, Alan Ware related this to current
preoccupations: 'rather suddenly', he wrote, 'charities have come
to the forefront of public attention . . . After years in which they

---

[38] A. Graycar, 'Informal, Voluntary and Statutory Services: The Complex Relationship' (*British Journal of Social Work*, xiii / 4 (1983), 379–93). See also Philip
Abrams, Sheila Abrams, Robin Humphrey, and Ray Snaith, *Neighbourhood Care
and Social Policy*, ed. Ray Snaith (London: HMSO, 1989), 150.

[39] Quoted in *Independent on Sunday*, 6 May 1990.

were largely ignored by social scientists and political journalists, they have been "discovered" as interesting, and possibly important social institutions.'[40] For this Ware gives as one reason the fact that after 1979 Conservative governments attempted to cut down on state expenditure and 'to transfer some responsibility for the provision of services to private organisations'[41]—a policy which involved an increased role for charities.

This point may, therefore, be related to the tendency, which has been noted, for studies of welfare to 'reflect the dominant cultural and political characteristics of their societies'. Some studies which emerged were polemical in nature;[42] but many others were more dispassionate.[43] The appearance of such studies dealing with voluntarism in recent years may be related to the political 'climate' in which they were written; and that point no doubt also bears on the fact that the continuing studies of the Welfare State which appeared in the same period did not, like earlier works, trace the origins of an established and seemingly permanent institution, but often dealt with one which was perceived to be under threat.[44]

Moreover, the New Right's emphasis on the citizenship of contribution outside the state provoked a restatement of the case for the citizenship of entitlement from the state. The espousal of what was called the 'active citizen'[45] was seen as excluding large sections of the community from rights to which they were entitled from the state, and as creating an underclass to which individuals were consigned by poverty, race, and gender. 'Active citizenship' was regarded by such critics as an appeal to those who had 'gained from a decade of grossly regressive economic

[40] 'Introduction: The Changing Relations between Charities and the State', in Alan Ware (ed.), *Charities and Government* (Manchester: Manchester University Press, 1989), 1. [41] Ibid.
[42] See e.g. Ralph Harris and Arthur Seldon, *Welfare without the State: A Quarter Century of Suppressed Public Choice* (London: London Institute of Economic Affairs, 1987).
[43] See e.g. Frank Prochaska, *The Voluntary Impulse: Philanthropy in Modern Britain* (London: Faber & Faber, 1988); Anne Digby, *British Welfare Policy: Workhouse to Workfare* (London: Faber & Faber, 1989); Ian Williams, *The Alms Trade: Charities, Past, Present and Future* (London: Unwin Hyman, 1989); Norman Barry, *Welfare* (Milton Keynes: Open University Press, 1990). See also Prochaska, 'Philanthropy', in F. M. L. Thompson (ed.), *The Cambridge Social History of Britain, 1750–1950*, 3 vols. (Cambridge: Cambridge University Press, 1990), iii. 357–93.
[44] See e.g. Peter Wilding (ed.), *In Defence of the Welfare State* (Manchester: Manchester University Press, 1986). [45] See below, pp. 330–51.

and social policies'.[46] The losers in this process became posses-
sors of 'negative citizenship'; they no longer thought of themselves as part of a collective and active state, since the state existed
simply to 'secure a framework of law and rules of order with
which individuals with their own widely different purposes
pursue[d] their own ends in their own way.'[47] The relegation of
the state to this minimal and enabling role, it was claimed, led to
growing social inequalities and a loss of social cohesion, as active
citizens pursued private, rather than public, interests. Thus the
citizenship of active and individual responsibility for self and
others was seen as eroding the citizenship of collective and social
entitlement. The state became an agent for competitive advantage
rather than social morality and the common good.[48]

Thus the events of the years after 1979 revived interest in
voluntary agencies for the delivery of welfare in their own right,
and provoked controversy about the relationship between
voluntarism and the state. In these respects, they provide support
for Thomson's view that social policy involves 'shifts to and fro'
rather than a linear development. Desmond S. King has suggested that the attempts of the New Right to 'roll back the frontiers
of the state' is a 'useful reminder that state welfare is not a

---

[46] Ruth Lister, letter, *Guardian*, 24 Apr. 1990.

[47] Vincent and Plant, *Philosophy, Politics and Citizenship*, 169.

[48] Geoffrey Finlayson, in *Times Higher Education Supplement*, 2 Nov. 1990; Bill
Jordan, *The Common Good: Citizenship. Morality and Self-Interest* (Oxford: Basil
Blackwell, 1989), 68. The issue of citizenship attracted considerable interest from
various of points of view from the later 1980s. See e.g. N. Asherton, 'Citizen Put
on the Active List' (*Observer*, 16 Oct. 1988); J. M. Barbalet, *Citizenship: Rights,
Struggle and Class Inequality* (Milton Keynes: Open University Press, 1988); A.
Brown, 'Cold Charity that Threatens to Usurp the Seat of Justice: The Limits of
Active Citizenship.' (*Independent*, 1 Sept. 1989); R. Dahrendorf, 'Citizenship and
the modern Social Conflict', in R. Holme and M. Elliott (eds.), *The British Constitution 1688–1988* (London: Macmillan, 1988) 112–25; M. Ignatieff, 'Citizenship
and Moral Narcissism' (*Political Quarterly*, lx/1 (Jan. 1989)); David Hild and Stuart
Hall, 'Left and Right' (*Marxism Today* (June 1989), 16–23); Ruth Lister, *The Ex-
clusive Society: Citizenship and the Poor* (London: Child Poverty Action Group, n.d.
[? 1990]); D. Marquand, 'The Subversive Language of Citizenship' (*Guardian*, 2 Jan.
1989); L. Mead, *Beyond Entitlement: The Social Obligations of Citizenship* (New York:
The Free Press, 1986); R. Plant, *Citizenship, Rights and Socialism* (London: Fabian
Society, 1988); Raymond Plant and Norman Barry, *Citizenship and Rights in
Thatcher's Britain: Two Views* (London: IEA Health and Welfare Unit, 1990);
J. Rogaly, 'The Active Citizen for All Parties' (*Financial Times*, 5 Oct. 1988); Bryan
S. Turner, *Citizenship and Capitalism: The Debate over Reformism* (London: Allen &
Unwin, 1986).

unilinear, irreversible process';[49] and Anne Digby has written that, over a long timescale, 'the balance of responsibility laid down in the classic welfare state appears as only one of a number of possible democratic positions'.[50] Thus it may be argued that the 'new' developments since 1979 appeared so only because they were taken against too short a historical background: one in which it was felt that all welfare issues had finally become inextricably linked to the state.

It is, indeed, possible to argue that, even in the period during which a so-called consensus had been reached on such matters, broadly from 1948 to 1979, that debate, even if seemingly settled, had never been entirely stilled. As early as 1961, Briggs wrote of various signs which suggested that 'what only recently seemed to be fixed is far from fixed'; and that 'the post-1945 welfare state was not in itself a final destination'.[51] Norman Barry echoed some of these points when, writing in 1990, he suggested that 'the contemporary welfare debate' is rooted 'both in the historical development of ideas and in the evolution of social institutions'. The expressions of varying and conflicting points of view were 'often replays of familiar debates, involving the same values and propositions and irresolvable disputes . . . The problems of welfare are recurring ones.'[52]

It is, then, with such problems during the period 1830 to 1991 that this book is concerned. It will deal primarily with the contribution of voluntarism, and more particularly with that of the voluntary sector, to social welfare in Britain during these years; and secondarily with the ways in which voluntarism was seen to relate to the state, and the state to voluntarism within the 'welfare mix'. Both themes underwent change in the various periods into which the book is divided; and, it may be argued, the change over the entire period, at least until 1979, is consistent with a broadly Whig interpretation of a developing and expanding Welfare State—which even the Thatcherite attempts after 1979 did not, in practice, disturb. But that approach, to a process which was neither smooth nor easy, and did not necessarily lead to an undisturbed and undisputed resting-place, is much too linear. There

---

[49] 'Voluntary and State Provision of Welfare as Part of the Public-Private Continuum', in Ware (ed.), *Charities and Government*, 51.
[50] *British Welfare Policy*, 66.
[51] 'Welfare State in Historical Perspective', 178.   [52] Barry, *Welfare*, 49.

was 'recurrent experimentation'—and this did, indeed, result in varied solutions at different times; but they were never entirely coherent and clear-cut. Rather, they always contained elements of ambiguity and tension, as citizen intersected with state, and state with citizen. It was not a matter of launching a 'historical trajectory'[53] from voluntarism to state; it was a question of experimenting with 'shifting boundaries' between voluntarism and state. The Whig path to the Welfare State may have its attractions—but it is also beset with dangers.

[53] Thane, 'Historiography', 14.

1

Citizen and State, 1830–1880: Providence, Paternalism, and Philanthropy

I

The practice of self-reliant and provident behaviour in mid-nineteenth-century Britain is often felt to be synonymous with the works of Samuel Smiles.

'Heaven helps those who help themselves' is a well-tried maxim, embodying in a small compass the results of vast human experience. The spirit of self-help is the root of all genuine growth in the individual; and, exhibited in the lives of many, it constitutes the true source of national vigour and strength. Help from without is often enfeebling in its effects, but help from within invariably invigorates. Whatever is done *for* men or classes, to a certain extent takes away the stimulus and necessity of doing for themselves; and where men are subjected to over-guidance and over-government, the inevitable tendency is to render them comparatively helpless.[1]

The sentiments expressed in the opening paragraph of *Self-Help* by Smiles, a book first published in 1859, are, indeed, familiar; and this may also be said of the ideas put forward in his later books of a similar nature, *Character*, *Thrift*, and *Duty*.[2]

The themes of the books are better remembered than their author; for the biographical details of the lowland Scot, born in Haddington in 1812—who first practised there as a doctor and then, in 1838, moved to Leeds, where for four years he was editor of the *Leeds Times*, finding employment in later life in railway administration and insurance—are little known. Samuel Smiles had a long life—he lived until 1905; but it was, and remains, an

---

[1] Samuel Smiles, *Self-Help: With Illustrations of Conduct and Perseverance* (London: John Murray, 1859, 68th imp., 1936), 13.
[2] Pub. 1871, 1875, and 1880 respectively.

obscure life. This is, in fact, much as Smiles himself would have wanted it. He was extremely reluctant to write his autobiography and felt that his books 'such as they are, must speak for themselves, without any biographic introduction'. When he did eventually undertake his autobiography, it was on the prompting of his wife; even then, it did not appear in his lifetime, and remained uncompleted at his death.

The books, however, did 'speak for themselves'—certainly in his own lifetime. Routledge must have regretted its decision in 1855 not to publish the lectures on the general theme of self-help. Smiles had delivered these in 1845 to a group of young workmen in Leeds who had set up an evening school for mutual improvement. He reminded his audience of what other men had done 'as illustrations of what each might, in a greater or lesser degree, do for himself'.[3] When John Murray published the lectures as *Self-Help* in 1859, the book sold 20,000 copies in its first year and 55,000 copies by the end of five years. By Smiles's death in 1905, it had sold over a quarter of a million copies. It also appeared in every European language and many non-European languages. As Briggs put it: 'The fame of Smiles had travelled far since he first taught his classroom lessons to the group of Leeds workingmen in a dingy hall, which had once been used as a temporary cholera hospital. Cholera itself could have travelled no faster.'[4]

The reasons for this conspicuous success lie partly in the generalized nature of the contents of Smiles's work. The various books were a compilation of homilies, which can easily be read a little at a time, and by no means necessarily from cover to cover, and their moral is easily grasped: the importance of effort and perseverance, hard work and sobriety, self-control and self-improvement—and the need to struggle and to show independence, initiative, and character to develop inner potential. These qualities, rather than brilliance or genius, were necessary for fulfilment. Smiles was at pains to illustrate the benefits which the diligent hand and head would bring; and he preached the doctrine

---

[3] J. F. C. Harrison, 'The Victorian Gospel of Success' (*Victorian Studies*, i/2 (Dec. 1957), 156).

[4] Asa Briggs, *Victorian People: A Reassessment of Persons and Themes, 1851–67* (London: Odhams, 1954; with minor revs., Harmondsworth: Penguin Books, 1965), 126.

that 'excellence in any pursuit is only to be achieved by laborious application'.[5]

Smiles thus stressed universal truths, which might have an appeal almost at any time, and in any place. Indeed, one of his correspondents put *Self-Help* into the same category as the Bible: he would, he said, open it to gain guidance when in difficulty.[6] The book was in fact part of a wide range of literature on similar themes. Earlier examples had tended to stress the need for self-education. This had been done in periodicals such as *The Penny Magazine* and *Chambers' Edinburgh Journal*. Later, in the 1840s, this was broadened into other methods of self-improvement, all of which amounted to the adoption of a provident, sober, and thrifty attitude to life as a means to personal fulfilment and economic sufficiency: a secure basis on which individuals could make arrangements for their own welfare.

Thus, in urging the need for 'help from within', Smiles was by no means striking out in a novel direction; he was, rather, following a well-trodden path. He himself was quite prepared to admit this, and acknowledged his debt to earlier writers, such as George Craik; he later wrote that he knew most of Craik's book *The Pursuit of Knowledge under Difficulties*, published in 1830, by heart.[7] Smiles was, then, a popularizer of ideas already current, and he epitomized many, if not all, of the 'dominant social values of the times'.[8] Yet he did so in a way which was to prove more memorable than the efforts of his contemporaries; he was 'both typical and outstanding'.[9]

The homilies which Smiles did so much to popularize may well have been valid irrespective of time or place; but they should also be seen in their historical context. The social and economic effects of industrialization on the working classes in Britain in the early nineteenth century have been—and to a large extent remain—controversial among historians; and it is scarcely necessary here to rehearse the well-known arguments in favour of the 'pessimistic' and 'optimistic' interpretations of these effects.[10]

---

[5] *Self-Help*, 27.
[6] Kenneth Fielden, 'Samuel Smiles and Self-Help' (*Victorian Studies*, xii/2 (Dec. 1968), 158–9).   [7] Harrison, 'Victorian Gospel', 157.
[8] Ibid. 155.   [9] Fielden, 'Samuel Smiles', 158.
[10] The points are well rehearsed in E. D. Hunt, *British Labour History, 1815–1914* (London: Weidenfeld & Nicolson, 1981), Ch. 3.

What, however, is important is that an emphasis on provident behaviour may be equated with both. A 'pessimistic' interpretation, which stresses the economic and social hardships induced by industrialization, can readily be harmonized with one way of looking at what was being preached: the need for improvement through mutual-aid. This was, indeed, 'help from within'—but from within a group of like-minded persons, who came together to meet common needs and advance common interests. On the other hand, the 'optimistic' interpretation of the effects of industrialization can also be reconciled with another way in which Smiles and his fellow writers may be read; and here the opportunities for individual advancement offered by industrialization may be stressed. Here again, there was 'help from within'—but from within individuals, who sought to take advantage of economic development to meet their needs and advance their interests by their own separate efforts. The literature of improvement, therefore, could be equated with an encouragement to collective activity or individual activity. Both involved the exercise of free choice and initiative, and did not depend on external assistance—and both could, therefore, lead to voluntaristic endeavour, expressed through mutual-aid or self-help. But one might lead to mutual, or common, benefit, and the other to individual advantage.

It is the second interpretation which has tended to be the more prevalent; and, somewhat to Smiles's regret, it led to his being regarded as the patron saint of an acquisitive, thrusting, and aggressive gospel of work and material success—conducted largely through the commercial sector of voluntarism. In the preface to later editions of *Self-Help*, Smiles denied that he had intended to eulogize selfishness, and had been preoccupied only with material success. There were, he wrote, as many lessons to be drawn from failure as from success; and he had been concerned as much with growth in wisdom and knowledge as with more tangible indications of worldly success. It is true that his early efforts in Leeds had been directed at mutual improvement through education; and in *Character*, Smiles wrote that 'a man may usually be known by the books he reads, as well as by the company he keeps ... Men often discover their affinity to each other by the mutual love they have for a book ...'.[11] Moreover,

---

[11] London: John Murray, 1871, 264–5.

as editor of the radical *Leeds Times* in the 1840s, he had shown sympathy with the cooperative ventures of the working classes in the town. In 1846 he wrote in the *People's Journal* that the

> great power which seems yet destined to effect the social improvement of the working classes is the power of co-operation. In this power they now generally recognise the means of their permanent social elevation, and the foundation of all true progress . . . For long enough the working orders have been groping blindly in the dark after the grand principle, and now the light comes beaming upon them from all quarters.[12]

Smiles could, then, be interpreted as an advocate of mutual-aid among the working classes within the voluntary or, indeed, informal, sector. Yet it is not altogether surprising that he was also associated with self-help within the commercial sector. He was not, in fact, consistent. Even in *Self-Help*, he blurred the lines between the group and the individual. 'The whole body of the working classes', he wrote, 'might be as frugal, virtuous, well-informed, and well-conditioned as many individuals of the same class have already made themselves. What some men are, all without difficulty might be.'[13] In *Thrift*, Smiles had much to say about the virtues of cooperation and mutual-aid; and yet he also wrote that 'in all the individual reforms or improvements that we desire, we must begin with ourselves.'[14] He reached some kind of resolution of the ambiguity when he wrote that mutual-aid furnished 'a foundation on which to build up something better. It teaches self-reliance, and this cultivates amongst the humblest classes habits of provident economy.'[15] Mutual-aid—or the 'power of co-operation'—was a means of 'permanent social elevation'; and was thus a route to economic independence and a more individualized form of self-help.

There was, then, some ambivalence in the preaching of providence as a means of voluntary social welfare; and the varied interpretations to which Smiles's work was open no doubt help to explain his popularity. This ambiguity in the practice of provident behaviour was also to become evident among those for whom mutual-aid was most immediately and obviously

---

[12] Quoted by Fielden, 'Samuel Smiles', 168–9. See also Trygve Tholfsen, *Working Class Radicalism in Mid-Victorian England* (London: Croom Helm, 1976), 205–9.
[13] p. 249.
[14] *Thrift* (London: John Murray, 1875), 23; see also pp. 89–109.
[15] *Thrift*, 121. See also R. J. Morris, 'Samuel Smiles and the Genesis of Self-Help: The Retreat to a Petit Bourgeois Utopia' (*Historical Journal*, xxiv / 1 (1981), 89–109).

necessary and, indeed, those to whom Smiles had originally delivered his remarks: the working classes. But, as will be seen, they did not always need the prompting of Smiles to adopt similar measures—and discover similar anomalies.

II

In the context of the economic and social uncertainties induced by industrialization in early nineteenth-century Britain, mutual-aid within the voluntary sector as a path to the achievement of social welfare was widely practised over a considerable range of working-class activity; and a survey of its main areas is necessary at this stage. The most conspicuous institutional evidence lay in the friendly society movement. Friendly societies offered a means of insuring against the vicissitudes which could so easily overtake working-class life, and, in particular, those presented by a period of illness, by old age—or by death itself, with its accompanying funeral expenses and loss of money for dependants. The movement was not, in fact, new in the nineteenth century, but could trace its origin to the seventeenth; the Friendly Benefit Society of Bethnal Green was founded in 1687. But the later years of the eighteenth century saw a considerable increase in the number of friendly societies. Their growth and development may be seen as a consequence of a need to make provision in the face of industrialization, and their geographical concentration tended to be in the industrialized areas of the Midlands and North of England and in the Lowlands of Scotland. A Poor Law return of 1803 for England and Wales suggested that by that date, there were already 9,672 societies with 704,350 members.[16]

During the first thirty to forty years of the nineteenth century, the local society formed the basis of the friendly-society movement. These societies were independent of each other, and had their own funds accumulated from the subscriptions of their members, who also drew up their own rules. They provided two main financial benefits: a weekly allowance for the member when he was ill, and a funeral payment for his widow; and it may be

---

[16] P. H. J. H. Gosden, *The Friendly Societies in England, 1815–1875* (Manchester: Manchester University Press, 1961), 4–5.

noted that almost all societies were exclusively for men—although some were created separately for women. Full sick-pay was usually limited to a specified period, with half pay thereafter for a further defined time. The size of the payment would depend on the contributions paid by the members, and varied from one part of the country to another; and this was also true of the funeral benefit. On occasion, too, societies would provide medical attention, carried out by doctors under contract to them, for an increased subscription. Again, the quality of this would vary greatly from place to place, and from society to society.

Many societies founded in the eighteenth century survived until the twentieth; but many others went out of existence. It was said of the local society that, 'as an organization of thrift it has never been a healthy plant'.[17] Part of the difficulty lay in an inadequate understanding of the actuarial principles which were necessary for the establishment of safe tables to coordinate contributions and payments. It is true that many local societies operated certain safeguards against claims being made on their funds which they could not sustain. Thus new applicants had to enjoy good health before they were admitted, and might have to pay contributions for a minimum period before they were accepted. If a man became ill because of his own fault, possibly as a result of an accident incurred through drunkenness or wrestling, he was excluded from benefit. Some occupations, regarded as especially dangerous—such as coal-mining—were a barrier to membership; it was felt that to admit men in such employment would place too great a burden on the funds of the society.

Various attempts were also made to produce reliable sets of figures by which to judge the possibility of sickness, such as the 'Northampton Tables' produced by Dr Richard Price and the 'Southwell Tables' of Price's nephew, William Morgan. But these and other tables proved to be defective, and it was not until the Royal Commission on Friendly Societies, which reported between 1871 and 1874, recommended that a standard and reliable set of tables should be produced by the government that the position was improved.[18]

In the face of such difficulties, many local societies ran into

---

[17] Quoted in P. H. J. H. Gosden, *Self-Help: Voluntary Associations in Nineteenth-Century Britain* (London: Batsford, 1973), 16.
[18] Gosden, *Friendly Societies*, 94 ff.

serious financial difficulties, and found it impossible to pay the promised benefits. The result would be either the collapse of the society, as happened in the case of the Shipwrights Provident Benefit Society in Kentish London (a collective title for the three towns on the edge of south-east London, Deptford Greenwich, and Woolwich) in 1864, leaving its members unprotected, or an increase in contributions, which almost always meant that fewer young members could afford to join.[19]

Yet this was only part of the problem. There was also mismanagement, which often took the form of improper expenditure of funds. Here, a common failing derived from the double function which many societies performed: conviviality and insurance against misfortune. Money was often spent on drink, a tendency encouraged by the fact that the monthly meeting of the society very often took place in the local inn. Excessive expenditure on drink could cause a society to collapse; and this aspect of the local friendly society attracted considerable criticism. Yet the convivial aspect was important for those who belonged to friendly societies; the monthly meeting—or the annual dinner—was a tangible sign of the mutual trust which bound their members together.[20] When, after 1829, an attempt was made to curb these activities, some societies lost their members—and went out of existence, not because of drink, but because of lack of it.

In the course of the second and third quarters of the nineteenth century, however, the local society, subject as it was to the pressure of financial exigency, tended to be overshadowed in strength by the affiliated order. This came about as a result of the grouping of local societies or lodges, a process which underwent a notable expansion from the 1830s and, more especially, the 1840s. The individual lodges of an affiliated order retained a considerable degree of independence, and kept control over their sick-funds and management expenses. The affiliated orders, moreover, did not eschew the convivial aspects of their activities, nor did they escape criticism. It was, indeed, in reaction to this that the Independent Order of Rechabites was set up in 1835 as

[19] Geoffrey Crossick, *An Artisan Elite in Victorian Society: Kentish London 1840–1880* (London: Croom Helm, 1978), 177.

[20] Geoffrey Crossick, 'The Labour Aristocracy and its Values: A Study of Mid-Victorian Kentish London' (*Victorian Studies*, xix / 3 (Mar. 1976), 321–2). See also Crossick, *Artisan Elite*, 178–9.

an affiliated order which catered for those who wished to pledge themselves against drink.[21]

The affiliated orders were not, therefore, free of all the problems which had afflicted the local societies; but they did command a greater financial stability and viability, and were somewhat more efficient, reliable, and businesslike in their organizational structure and financial conduct. In 1872, there were thirty-four societies described as affiliated orders with more than 1,000 members each, with a total membership of 1,282,275.[22] The number of societies in this category was, in fact, a small proportion of the total number of friendly societies recorded as being in existence in that year, but they accounted for a high proportion of the recorded membership; and within the affiliated orders, the Manchester Unity of Oddfellows and the Ancient Order of Foresters were by far the largest. No other affiliated order came near to them in size or organization. The average income of Manchester Unity during the five years before 1874 was £560,000, and the average sickness and death payments amounted annually to some £400,000. In 1874 the current value of the promised benefits of Manchester Unity was estimated at some £11 million.[23]

Friendly societies were, therefore, the most notable and widespread manifestation of providence: of the practice whereby, pooling risks, the working classes—or a proportion of them—made provision for bad times in more favourable periods. Mutuality was embodied in the monthly or annual social occasions, even if these could sit uncomfortably with thrifty behaviour, and also in the quite elaborate ceremonies which characterized many of these societies, especially on the induction of new members. Rituals, such as oaths, regalia, passwords, and secret handshakes, helped to bind the members together in collective activity. Even in death there was solidarity. It was the normal practice—indeed, in some cases, it was a requirement—to attend the funeral of a fellow member of a society, and it was not uncommon for acts of ritual to be performed after the officiating clergyman had carried out his religious role.

The impetus behind the founding of a friendly society could itself be religious. Thus the Loyal Order of Ancient Shepherds

---

[21] Gosden, *Self-Help*, 59. [22] Ibid. 39.
[23] *Royal Commission on Friendly and Benefit Building Societies: Fourth Report* (Parliamentary Papers, 1874, XXIII (C 961)), pt. 1, par. 55.

held its first meeting on Christmas Day 1826 'for the purpose of proclaiming glad tidings to future generations'; and it was agreed to establish a society, 'the intended object of which is to relieve the sick, bury the dead and assist each other in all cases of unavoidable distress, so far as in our power lies, and for the promotion of peace and goodwill towards all the human race, in humble imitation of the great Chief Shepherd and Saviour of mankind'.[24]

It was mutuality, based on active participation, which distinguished the local societies and affiliated orders from other institutions which were often also called 'friendly societies', but which were in effect national societies, based in London, with their members sending their contributions by post and receiving their benefits in the same way. These were described by the Royal Commission as 'ordinary large (or general) societies'; another term was the 'centralised class' of friendly society.[25] They were managed by a board of directors and managers, and the members had little to do with their administration. The largest was the Hearts of Oak, founded in 1842; others were the Royal Oak, the United Patriots, the London Friendly, and the Royal Standard.

If membership of a friendly society was one method of achieving a degree of financial security with which to make provision for welfare, it was not the only one. The general concept of mutual-aid could be expressed in other ways, and through other—related—agencies. There was much in the trade-union and co-operative movements in this period which found common ground with the activities of friendly societies. The initiation ceremonies of many of the early trade unions were very similar to those found in the friendly societies; there tended to be the same quite elaborate ritual, and the same emphasis on secrecy and the taking of oaths, in the interests of brotherhood.

This epitomized mutuality—but it could also be a symptom of suspicion of, and hostility to, the outside world. The view that there was, especially in the trade union and cooperative movements, evidence of a total rejection of industrial capitalism in the 1830s and 1840s—a rejection associated with Owenism—has been

[24] Quoted in 'Conference Service' Of the Loyal Order of Ancient Shepherds (Ashton Unity) Friendly Society, 7 Sept. 1986.
[25] Gosden, *Self-Help*, 62–3.

challenged by historians.[26] It is, indeed, true that the Owenite schemes of the later 1820s and the 1830s did not permeate all unions. Away from the grand visions of large-scale combined activity, local unions were in existence in the early nineteenth century, exercising some of the functions of the friendly society in terms of providing benefits. It is, however, also true that not all militancy died out in the 1840s and 1850s, when, it has been claimed, trade union activity entered a more moderate phase.[27]

It is, then, better to see within trade unionism a continuous thread of mutuality in the interests of its members, which ran in parallel to the efforts of the friendly societies; indeed, it has been suggested that 'collective self-help developed its most powerful potential in trade unionism.'[28] It is, nevertheless, true that this trend became notable in the 1850s. The Amalgamated Society of Engineers (founded in 1851) and the Amalgamated Society of Carpenters and Joiners developed schemes of relief for members who were on strike, sick, or unemployed—thus continuing earlier practices on a larger scale. Unemployment benefit was especially important, for this was not normally available from a friendly society. On the other hand, the centralized system of finance and policy-making tended to remove participation from the ordinary members; and here, the trade unions of the 1850s were more akin to the 'centralised class' of friendly society than to the more localized unit or the affiliated order. Trade union membership in 1872 stood at approximately 500,000—a number considerably lower than that of the friendly societies.

Another area of considerable importance in the world of mutual-aid lay in the cooperative movement. Here too, it is a mistake to see in the 1840s and early 1850s too sharp a break from earlier practices; for the early phases after 1844 of the Rochdale Pioneers—normally regarded as the founding fathers of the movement as it was later to develop—had Owenite associations, and did not wholly repudiate efforts to bring about a large-scale

[26] See e.g. A. E. Musson, *British Trade Unions, 1800–1875* (London: Macmillan, 1972), 34, 49–63.
[27] For further consideration of these points, see Kenneth D. Brown, *The English Labour Movement, 1700–1951* (London: Gill & Macmillan, 1982), 140; Neville Kirk, *The Growth of Working Class Reformism in Mid-Victorian England* (London: Croom Helm, 1985), 1–3, 148–9; Hunt, *British Labour History*, 260–1.
[28] J. F. C. Harrison, *The Common People: A History from the Norman Conquest to the Present* (London: Fontana Paperback, 1984), 271.

transformation of society along cooperative, rather than competitive, lines. But it is also true that, in time, the more idealistic and communitarian objectives, inherited from earlier movements, lapsed; and the procedures which the Rochdale Co-operators introduced in retailing—whereby a trading surplus was distributed in the form of a dividend to those who made purchases, in proportion to the amount of money spent—became the characteristic feature of the cooperative movement, and was widely copied elsewhere. By 1850 there were more than 200 cooperative societies of the dividend-paying type; and it has been estimated that in 1863 the membership for England and Wales was 100,000. In that year the Co-operative Wholesale Society was set up. In 1867, 560 cooperative societies were said to exist in England and Wales, with a total membership of 173,000; and by 1872 the membership stood at between 300,000 and 400,000. As with the friendly societies, the greatest concentration lay in the North of England; the biggest societies were those in Halifax, Leeds, Bury, and Rochdale. The cooperative movement was, therefore, an unquestionably important form of mutual-aid, more especially in the 1840s and thereafter.[29]

Friendly societies, trade unions, and cooperatives tended to be multi-purpose bodies which might cover a variety of provident activity; they were the largest-scale sources of welfare achieved by the pooling of risks on a voluntaristic basis. But their role was mirrored by many other bodies which were rather more specialist in scope. Thus although friendly societies, and some trade unions, offered means whereby provision could be made for a decent and respectable funeral, there were also separate burial societies, the sole function of which was to make such a provision.[30] At their simplest level, burial societies met agreed funeral expenses by means of a levy on members every time a death occurred. Another more elaborate version was to keep a certain amount of money in hand—again raised by levy—to meet a contingency of a number of deaths occurring at much the same time. Sometimes, however, the gathering of subscriptions on a regular basis to build up a permanent fund replaced the levy system.

[29] See also Gosden, *Self-Help*, 180–206.
[30] Ibid. 115–19; Crossick, *Artisan Elite*, 175, 181, 187.

As was the case with the local friendly society, the local burial society could be financially precarious; and it also could run into difficulties through over-expenditure on drink—a frequent accompaniment to funerals. Many local societies quickly went out of existence; but there were exceptions, often associated with infant mortality. One such was the Blackburn Philanthropic Burial Society, founded by workers in a cotton factory in 1839. By 1872 it had over 130,000 members and, for a premium of 1*d*. per week, paid a death benefit of some £4 to £5 if the member was under 10 years old.[31] Another was the Infants' Funeral Friendly Society in Doncaster, which in 1871 had 2,138 members. It enrolled children between the ages of 1 and 14, took in a uniform contribution of 1*d*. per month, and paid out benefit which varied between £1 and £4 according to the length of time a member had served. It was estimated that the total membership of local burial societies in England and Wales in 1872 was some 650,000—although, as in the case of the friendly societies, there were also 'general' burial societies, operating centrally and employing paid staff and canvassers. They developed markedly in the 1850s and 1860s, and by 1872 their membership over the whole United Kingdom stood at 1.4 million, one million of whom were in England and Wales.[32] Here an overlap between the voluntary and commercial sectors was evident.

Other activities related not to preparations for death, but to arrangements for life. House building and purchase came into this category. Such activity was not absent from the cooperative movement. The original rules of the Rochdale Equitable Pioneers Society identified as one of its objectives 'the building, purchasing or erecting of a number of houses, in which those members desiring to assist each other in improving their domestic and social conditions may reside.'[33] House ownership was a theme in the propaganda of cooperatives in Kentish London. John Arnold, the leading figure in Woolwich cooperation in the 1870s, argued that 'we have become capitalists by consuming. We are eating our way into a future; many have already eaten their way into

---

[31] Barry Supple, 'Legislation and Virtue: An Essay on Working-Class Self-Help and the State in the Early Nineteenth Century', in Neil McKendrick (ed.), *Historical Perspectives: Studies in English Thought and Society in Honour of J. H. Plumb* (London: Europa Publications, 1974), 217–18.   [32] Ibid. 218.
[33] Quoted in Gosden, *Self-Help*, 183.

a house.'[34] But, even by 1844, a separate building-society movement was well under way.[35] This enabled individuals to co-operate in the building of houses, until each was supplied with a house; then the society would terminate. Conviviality was not absent from their proceedings; as with friendly societies, meetings were often held in a local inn, although a separate subscription was normally charged to meet the cost of drink. Building societies in their early years were, indeed, subject to the same shortcomings as friendly societies: they were often precarious, over-ambitious, possibly over-convivial—and not without fraudulent officials.

In the 1840s, however, the situation began to alter. The movement expanded considerably; and while it remained consistent in its objective of providing money to build, buy, or lease property, its structure underwent change. The main development was the emergence of the permanent building society, as distinct from the terminating society. Instead of a society coming into existence every time a new group of individuals felt the need for such an initiative, it was felt better to keep the original society in existence, and continue to admit members at any time. Thus individuals could join or leave as they pleased. In 1849 the Leeds Permanent Building Society was founded with the objective of enabling the industrious classes—and 'more especially the working man'—to build or buy a house.

The emergence of the large, permanent building society marked an important transition from the earlier society: a transition from a savings group, designed to finance the building of the houses of its members, to a well-established financial institution, from which individuals might borrow—or in which they might invest. It was estimated that in 1869 there were some 2,000 building societies in England and Wales, with a total of 800,000 members—although subsequent research would suggest that the numbers should, more realistically, be placed at some 1,500 societies with a membership not greatly in excess of 300,000.

Building societies, as they later developed, tended to depart from the mutual-aid principle, in that they were not always run by their members. The development of permanent building

---

[34] Quoted in Crossick, 'Labour Aristocracy', 315.
[35] Gosden, *Self-Help*, 143 ff.

societies, along with the building of suburban estates, was in time to lead away from working-class participation in, and dominance of, the building-society movement. The movement also became more commercial.[36] It was thought that the permanent building societies charged their borrowers more than the old mutual building societies would do, so that they could afford to pay a higher rate of interest to their investors. This problem was recognized by some societies—notably the Leeds Permanent—and steps were taken to meet it. Others, however, held to the belief—expressed by the chairman of the Planet Society—that those who borrowed should not be excluded from the privileges of membership; and the Royal Commission of 1871–4 commented on this tendency when it said that some permanent building societies had become instruments for the investment of capital, rather than for enabling the industrious classes to provide dwellings for themselves by mutual action.[37] Here, indeed, mutuality was giving way to profit; the voluntary sector was shading into the commercial sector.

Building societies could, in fact, become a form of savings bank; but here, too, there were separate institutions, well established in the field. Savings banks owed their origin less to spontaneous mutual-aid activity than to initiative from the richer classes, who encouraged the growth of savings banks to induce habits of thrift and saving. One of the earliest pioneers of the movement was the Revd Henry Duncan, who opened a savings bank in his parish of Ruthwell in Dumfriesshire in 1810.[38] This allowed the depositors some say in its management, but such an arrangement was an exception to the general rule followed in savings banks from a very early period—much earlier than was the case with building societies: the exclusion of depositors from the administration of the bank, which was placed in the hands of managers or trustees. Thus savings banks did not adhere to strict mutual-aid principles in their inspiration and organization; and those who used them were sometimes felt not to share in the full benefits of self-improvement and education offered by more genuine mutual-aid organizations.

Nevertheless, the savings-bank movement was well under way

---

[36] Crossick, *Artisan Elite*, 147–8.   [37] Gosden, *Self-Help*, 155.

[38] Olive Checkland, *Philanthropy in Victorian Scotland: Social Welfare and the Voluntary Principle* (Edinburgh: John Donald, 1980), 133–4.

by 1830, and the 1830s saw a considerable expansion, which was especially notable in the southern agricultural counties. Between 1830 and 1850 the number of banks in the United Kingdom grew from 476 to 573; the number of individual (as distinct from institutional) depositors increased from 400,000 to over 1 million, and their aggregate savings doubled, from £13.4 million to £27.2 million.[39]

Here, then, were further agencies of providence and thrift— even if they departed from strict mutual-aid principles. But the fact that their management was vested in trustees did not mean that they were immune from the kind of mismanagement and fraud which could afflict the friendly societies. There were, in fact, some spectacular frauds and collapses. In the early 1850s the total amount of money lost by fraud was £229,000, and there was almost certainly more than this which was not made public. There was a decline in confidence, as withdrawals exceeded deposits; and the impetus to found new banks declined. Moreover, those in existence offered a somewhat meagre service to depositors. In 1861, 355 of the 638 banks opened only once a week, fifty-four once a fortnight, and ten once a month.[40]

There were, in addition, 'penny banks', designed to attract the money of the poorer sections of the community. Savings banks would not normally accept a deposit of less than one shilling and, on the whole, attracted the funds of the better-off members of the working classes, and even of the middle classes[41]—although manual workers did deposit and retain their savings in the Glasgow Savings Bank and also the Aberdeen Savings Bank.[42] Penny banks were set up in Scotland in the 1840s and 1850s— and involved home visiting and collecting, which, again, was a departure from mutual-aid principles. By 1860, 36 penny banks had been founded in the Glasgow area, and by 1861 this number had grown to 213, with some 60,000 depositors; these penny banks were transferring about £20,000 a year to the Glasgow Savings Bank. In England, similarly, the penny-bank movement

[39] Supple, 'Legislation and Virtue', 219.   [40] Gosden, *Self-Help*, 230.

[41] Ibid. See also Supple, 'Legislation and Virtue', 219, and Albert Fishlow, 'Trustee Savings Banks, 1817–1861' (*Journal of Economic History*, xxi/1 (Mar. 1961), 26–40).

[42] Peter L. Payne, 'The Savings Bank of Glasgow, 1836–1914', in Peter L. Payne (ed.), *Studies in Scottish Business History* (London: Frank Cass, 1967), 152–86.

spread. A notable example was the Yorkshire Penny Savings Bank, which opened in 1859 and which by the end of the century had more than £12 million in the accounts of its depositors.[43] The penny-bank movement, it has been said, 'provided a critical link in the chain of self help.'[44]

There were, too, other links which had to do with more intangible commodities than money—but which were none the less just as critical. As Smiles noted, mutual-aid and self-help often implied self-improvement through education. This also found a place within the multi-purpose organization. The cooperative movement was intended to advance not only the economic and social interests of its members, but also their intellectual development. W. N. Molesworth, writing in 1861, was quite explicit on this subject. Not only did the Co-operative Trading Associations at Rochdale provide members with food, clothing, and other necessities; they also had a library of more than 3,000 volumes. 'The newsroom', wrote Molesworth, 'is well supplied with newspapers and periodicals, fitted up in a neat and careful manner and furnished with maps, globes, microscopes, telescope etc.' Both newsroom and library were open to all members. Molesworth went on to develop the association between material and intellectual wants:

It may, perhaps, provoke a smile to find . . .'social and intellectual attainment' placed in such close juxtaposition with 'groceries, butcher's meat, drapery goods, clothing, shoes and clogs'. But there is a real and very close connexion between these two classes of things. Men must be provided with the necessaries of life, or they will be unable to devote attention to their social and intellectual advancement; and the more abundantly their material wants are supplied, and the more they are released from care and anxiety about these wants, the more time they will have at their disposal to devote to their mental and spiritual improvement: and the greater, as a general rule, will be their intellectual, social, moral, ay, and I would even add, their religious progress. . .[45]

Again, however, education attracted separate institutions. It is true that many of these derived from outside the ranks of the working classes, and were directed at the young. Even among

[43] Gosden, *Self-Help*, 232.   [44] Checkland, *Philanthropy*, 136.
[45] W. N. Molesworth, '7% Co-operation' (*Trans. Royal Statistical Soc.*, xxiv (1861), 107–8).

the adult population, there were Mechanics' Institutes to promote 'educational self-help', where the impetus came from the
middle classes; and very few mechanics found their way to the
managing committees of such bodies. But there was also a tradition of self-culture which came closer to the mutual-aid model.
For the very young—normally between the ages of 3 and 8—
there were working-class private-venture schools—or 'dame
schools', as they were often called. They would normally be held
in the homes of the teachers, who would be unlikely to have any
formal educational training and might, indeed, carry on their
own occupations virtually at the same time as teaching. The
number of pupils might vary between 10 and 30, and there was
no classification by age, sex, or ability. The schools were entirely
'comprehensive' in this respect; but they were not free. Fees,
ranging from three to nine pence a week, would be paid to the
teacher by the parents. Such direct payment, even if not always
made punctually, gave the working classes a control over the
school which they did not have when a school was provided by
outside agencies.[46] Clearly the education provided was rudimentary, although it was quite effective in promoting such basic skills
as literacy; and many writers of working-class autobiographies
looked back on days spent in a dame school with some affection
and gratitude.[47] Thus the working-class private school was
'a part of the culture of the common people . . . an agency of
working-class self-help.'[48]

There was, however, also evidence of self-culture among sections of the adult working classes.[49] This might consist simply of
a haphazard and unsystematic practice of autodidacticism—even
if overcoming the problems in the way of such an enterprise was
far from simple. There were, however, mutual-aid societies, which
typically consisted of a group of persons who joined together to
educate each other, with very small weekly payments made to
allow for the purchase of reading material. Again, the primary

[46] Harrison, *Common People*, 288–92.

[47] See e.g. Thomas Cooper, *Life of Thomas Cooper* (1872), with an Introduction
by John Saville (Leicester: Leicester University Press, 1971). See also John Burnett
(ed.), *Destiny Obscure: Autobiographies of Childhood, Education and Family from the
1820s to the 1920s* (Harmondsworth: Penguin Books, 1984), 136 ff.

[48] Harrison, *Common People*, 292.

[49] David Vincent, *Bread, Knowledge and Freedom: A Study of Nineteenth Century
Working Class Autobiography* (London: Methuen, University Paperback, 1982), 109 ff.

concern was with basic literacy and numeracy, although the societies might extend to other, more ambitious areas. Indeed, in 1849 and 1850 a correspondent of the *Manchester Guardian* expressed admiration at the educational efforts of the workers in the Tonge and Royton districts.[50] In the Tonge area, a considerable variety of manual occupations—bricklaying, weaving, foundry work, and others—were represented in those who took part in such educational activities. In the vicinity of Royton, there were book societies, a mutual improvement society, and a Chartist reading-room, which housed a considerable range of reading material. Although a cold and dismal place, the reading-room was attended every night by thirty members, who met essentially to instruct each other in the three Rs and to discuss contemporary political issues.

All societies such as this were run by the manual workers who attended them, at very low rates of subscription. Thus, as Neville Kirk has written, 'by the 1860s the landscape was peppered with institutions, such as co-operative and mutual improvement societies.'[51] In many cases, indeed, the motivation was that of acquiring skills which could be of use in employment—and thus of achieving personal independence, self-respect, and self-reliance. For those who were politically motivated, however, education also provided a means of understanding—and eventually overthrowing—the capitalist process which, in their eyes, oppressed them. 'Knowledge is Power' was a common radical slogan.

If education might be acquired by means of mutual-aid, the same may be said of another avenue to provident behaviour and self-improvement: temperance or abstinence.[52] It is true that attempts to curb drinking habits—which could stretch the resources of working-class households to breaking-point—were frequently made by those outside the working classes. The temperance movement had its origins in the late 1820s and early 1830s among the middle classes. Yet temperance could be advanced 'from below' as much as promoted 'from above'; and again, it was a cause which often ran through mutual-aid organizations, of both a generalist and a specialist kind. It will be recalled that the Order of Rechabites was founded as a teetotal friendly society,

---

[50] Kirk, *Working Class Reformism*, 208–9.   [51] Ibid. 210.
[52] See Brian Harrison, *Drink and the Victorians: The Temperance Question in England, 1815–1872* (London: Faber & Faber, 1971), *passim*.

and the cause was well represented in a number of friendly societies formed purely for women. These remained fairly small; but the Rechabites expanded rapidly, especially from the 1860s.[53] Within trade unionism, too, temperance made itself felt, although the going was rather harder in those quarters. Attempts made in the 1860s to persuade trade unionists to convene elsewhere than in public houses met with some success—albeit limited. By the 1850s many publicans refused the iron-moulders' trade society access to club rooms, because their members drank so little.[54]

The connection between temperance and the cooperative movement was somewhat stronger. The Rochdale Pioneers had as one of their original aims 'the promotion of sobriety by means of the establishment of a temperance hotel in one of the society's premises'; and it was normal for cooperative societies to avoid connections with drink. A proposal in 1866 to allow the Bolton cooperative society the use of a bar on its premises was described as an 'unnatural union' and led to a considerable dispute. In 1867 Gladstone visited an Oldham cooperative spinning-mill, and was told that 'temperance men were generally co-operators, and that many of the board of directors were such'.[55] Similarly, temperance was to be found in the building-society and savings-banks movements—although here the impetus was often more from outside influences, which saw in such activities a ready means of promoting thrift, property owning, and home.

Nevertheless, there were those among the working classes themselves who came to a similar conclusion. One such was Thomas Whittaker, originally a Preston mill-worker, who in the 1830s was extremely active as a teetotal lecturer. Whittaker was firmly attached to the idea of a decent home: 'the home that had satisfied my wants as a drinker', he said, 'was not in harmony with my self-respect as a teetotaller, and I soon put myself in possession of a house rented at twelve pounds a year.'[56] Teetotalism, indeed, had a wider following than a more moderate temperance stance among the working classes. It was less genteel, and offered much more conspicuous and rapid results in terms of personal improvement.[57] It has been suggested that the total-abstinence movement, initiated by workers and tradesmen

---

[53] Gosden, *Self-Help*, 103 and (on temperance societies for women) 111–12.
[54] Harrison, *Drink and the Victorians*, 336.
[55] Quoted ibid.   [56] Quoted ibid. 321.   [57] See ibid. 137–8.

in the North, 'transformed temperance from a code of social behaviour, prescribed by one class for the elevation of another, to a participatory ethic of self help and self-denial.'[58]

Moreover, in addition to being part of other movements, temperance and teetotalism developed their own organizations. Bands of Hope, founded on a local basis from 1847 to promote the cause among young people, developed a national organization in 1863; and other such organizations were the National Temperance Society (later the National Temperance League), the British Association for the Promotion of Temperance (later the British Temperance League), and the United Kingdom Alliance.[59] It is impossible to be certain of the numbers involved in such movements, nor is it possible to say how many of the 'provident working classes' found their way into them. In the 1840s membership was said to be in the region of 1,200,000, and by the 1860s the estimates had risen to between two and three million. These estimates were, however, almost certainly too high. It would probably be more realistic to say that from the 1860s there were some 100,000 active members of temperance societies, whose activities affected the habits of rather more than one million adults; and to these should be added several thousand juvenile teetotallers in the Band of Hope movement.[60]

Mutual-aid activity was thus expressed through a wide variety of groups and societies to which individuals belonged in order to make material provision for themselves and their fellows—or to 'improve' themselves and their fellows—by acquiring educational skills or habits which could lead to regular employment and a sober, provident way of life. One individual might well belong to several organizations; for the groups and societies, if separate, were often complementary. There were numerous instances in the cotton districts—and elsewhere—in mid-century of men who straddled the cooperative and temperance movements, and who had a stake in building societies, savings banks, and mutual-educational movements.[61] The possible combinations were almost endless. Thus John Bates, for instance, was born in poor circumstances in Bury in 1833, and worked as a child in Pendleton in a calico-printing works. His

[58] Quoted in Brown, *English Labour Movement*, 158.
[59] Harrison, *Drink and the Victorians*, 141.
[60] Ibid. 316–18.   [61] See Kirk, *Working Class Reformism*, 134 ff.

father died in 1843, leaving his mother and five children to be looked after on the earnings of two members of the family. He became active in trade-union activity, and was a member of the Pendleton Mutual Improvement Society. Later he joined the co-operative movement, and in 1870 became president of the Eccles Co-operative Society. In 1873 he was elected to the Board of the Co-operative Wholesale Society. A similar pattern was repeated many times. Tim Pollit was a leading member of the Eccles Co-operative Society, and rose to become grand master of the Eccles district of the Oddfellows in 1884. J. C. Fox, a leading member of Manchester Co-operation, had a poor background and combined a keen interest in temperance with his cooperative activities.

Membership of mutual-aid groups was, therefore, virtually interchangeable; and one institution which very often underlay many of the groups and societies was the Nonconformist—and especially the Methodist—chapel.[62] This was, indeed, a very important form of mutual-aid in itself; and there were clearly strong ideological and structural links between Nonconformity and the practice of voluntarism. John Bates was an active Methodist, and the pattern of membership of both church or chapel and mutual-aid group was very common.

The individual examples of such overlapping membership which have been mentioned could, however, point to that aspect of mutual-aid activity discerned by Smiles: that it could lead to social mobility and entry to a higher station in life, in which self-help could be more readily practised. The appeal of mutual-aid societies was mostly to the better-paid workers. The affiliated orders among the friendly societies catered well for those who were mobile in search of better employment. The Foresters gave grants and offered hospitality to members who were 'tramping' in search of work, and claimed that their branches could give a welcome in every town.[63] A detailed examination of the membership of Manchester Unity showed that the main occupational groupings tended to be drawn from textiles, printing, and assorted trades connected with building. In Kentish London, the membership of the friendly societies was dominated by artisans, even if this was somewhat diluted by the 1860s. The usual age

[62] Harrison, *Common People*, 279.
[63] Crossick, *Artisan Elite*, 181. See also Crossick, 'Labour Aristocracy', 309.

at which men joined such societies appears to have been 24 or 25—by which time they might have sufficient income to qualify for membership; for a large number of societies insisted on a minimum wage and sought to exclude unskilled workers—or workers of dubious character. The Kent Unity of Oddfellows would accept no member 'who bears a bad character, or leads a dissolute life, or frequents bad company'.[64] The leadership of the friendly-society movement, likewise, was firmly in the hands of self-made artisans, who had made their way by their own initiative, hard work, and enterprise.

The same pattern was discernible in building societies and savings banks—and the cooperative movement was of particular importance in enabling working men to rise in the world, whether in economic terms or through social recognition. Co-operative literature made a particular point of stressing this aspect; and, indeed, the Rochdale Pioneers talked of joining together 'the means, the energies, and the talents of all for the common benefit of each'. John Bates left over £2,000 on his death—a large sum considering the meagre circumstances of his birth.[65] Anthony Brelsford, a leading figure in the Foresters, was for many years president of the Stockport Co-operative Society, and became the first working man to be a magistrate of the borough. In Macclesfield, William Barnett, the son of a whitesmith, served an apprenticeship as a bookbinder, and became keenly interested in education. From 1857 onwards he was in turn trustee, secretary, and general manager of the Macclesfield Co-operative Society. He was a director of the Co-operative Insurance Society—and founder and chairman of the Macclesfield Silk Manufacturing Company. He was also an active Congregationalist, and when he died in 1909 he left an estate valued at £4,000. Thomas Whittaker, an active teetotal worker, became mayor of Scarborough.

As in Smiles, so in reality: there was a certain ambiguity in the role of mutual-aid organizations. They were, on the one hand, egalitarian agencies to bind individuals of common interests and needs together and to foster communal interests; yet by their emphasis on qualities such as industry, thrift, and sobriety, they tended to appeal to the more skilled working classes and to be

---

[64] Quoted in Crossick, 'Labour Aristocracy', 316.
[65] Kirk, *Working Class Reformism*, 140 ff.

a means of further advancement. Their egalitarianism was inter-mixed with assumptions and practices which could have inegalitarian results. An Austrian observer noted that friendly societies put great emphasis on personal qualities. 'The best among them', he wrote, 'are not only self-governing bodies, but also real brotherhoods, in which just as much is asked about character and habits of life as about age and health.'[66] Those who took part in such organizations and, in time, became prosperous freely attributed their success to their membership of collaborative and democratic organizations—but also to the fact that they had practised the virtues of industry, restraint, perseverance, moderation, and self-respect which these organizations had preached.[67] A member of the St Cuthbert's Co-operative Association in Edinburgh recalled its early days in a revealing sentence: 'We were all yet working men, but we began to have the feeling that we were something more, and would soon become business men, reaping benefits we have so long been sowing for others.'[68]

Whether or not the achievement of 'something more', or even the aspiration to achieve it, made such men into an élite of respectable artisans—a 'Labour aristocracy'—is a matter of dispute among historians; and also contentious is whether this process amounted to an assimilation of 'bourgeois values'. It can, indeed, be argued that, especially in the 1850s and 1860s, greater economic prosperity became more widely shared—and that these circumstances eased the process by which 'stronger groups of workers, better placed to take advantage of the mid-Victorian boom, [could] pull apart from the weaker groups';[69] and that within a more buoyant economy, mutual-aid working-class activity could shade into a pursuit of providence more associated with the middle classes: self-help.

There is in fact some evidence of this. In 1867 Thomas Wright, an artisan engineer, gave evidence of a change in outlook from what he called a working-class 'crusher' mentality, which attributed all the evils of society to 'the machinations against them of the rich and powerful', to a new outlook, held by 'the more literate, intelligent and energetic workers':

[66] Quoted in Crossick, 'Labour Aristocracy', 316.
[67] Kirk, *Working Class Reformism*, 224.
[68] Quoted in Robert Q. Gray, *The Labour Aristocracy in Victorian Edinburgh* (Oxford: Clarendon Press, 1976), 138.   [69] Ibid. 95.

Hugging themselves in this belief they [the 'crushers'] remain stationary, grumbling at their position, but refusing to 'move on', and are a millstone about the neck of the more literate, intelligent and energetic section of the working class, who have learned, and are striving to carry out the principle that workingmen themselves must be the chief workers in achieving their own elevation, and that self-denial and self-improvement are primary means to the desired end.[70]

It was not, indeed, essential to be a member of a mutual-aid organization to believe in, and practise, self-denial and self-improvement; but such were at the centre of these organizations. In 1863 the Annual Report of the Great and Little Bolton Co-operative Society read as follows: 'Co-operation instils into the people a spirit of self-reliance—that is reliance on the power they themselves possess. It teaches the working classes to look to themselves for the amelioration of their condition, and no longer to be powerless at the feet of the so-called higher classes—the capitalists.'[71]

Yet while this quotation may be taken to suggest a shading of mutual-aid into self-help, it casts doubt on whether such a process amounted to an assimilation of bourgeois values. There is a distinct hint of hostility towards the 'so-called higher classes— the capitalists'. Pride in working-class mutuality and its traditions did not disappear. The friendly societies of Kentish London refused to move away from the public house as a meeting place: all but one of the eighty-five registered societies in that area in the period from 1855 to 1875 met in public houses.[72] There appears here to have been resistance to temperance and teetotalism as something too closely identified with 'improving' middle-class values: values which were resented as being hostile to working-class conviviality and fellowship. Again, in 1854 Samuel Smiles became a resident of south-east London after his appointment to the South East Railway Company; but the apostle of what was popularly, if not always accurately, regarded as middle-class self-help went unnoticed by the artisans of Kentish London, who failed to invite him to a social function in the area or to address a meeting.[73] In 1858 an official summary of the annual meeting of the Oddfellows ran as follows: 'Here we see how working

---

[70] Quoted in Kirk, *Working Class Reformism*, 156.   [71] Ibid. 213.
[72] Crossick, 'Labour Aristocracy', 322.   [73] Ibid. 324–5.

men—we claim no higher title, though we have noblemen, members of parliament, ministers of religion, authors, artists and professors of science working with and among us—can without assistance from the state, and by means of their own money, carry the principles of our association into actual every-day practice.'[74] There was, then, no official suggestion that the working men who practised responsible and industrious habits were other than working men; the Oddfellows was 'essentially a workingman's society'. Identification with the middle classes, or their values, was absent from such statements.

Other working-class mutual-aid institutions also showed a resistance to middle-class domination—perhaps to a greater extent than the friendly societies. Trade unions composed of skilled men were exposed—and vulnerable—to 'embourgeoisement'; and yet, as Trygve Tholfsen has written, 'their continuing battles with the employer class fostered a broader class consciousness . . . Both in theory and in practice the trade unions resisted middle-class hegemony.'[75]

Thus there was, in mid-century, a certain convergence of the mutual-aid and self-help sides of the voluntary sector; and it can be argued that some values were shared by 'both a middle-class and a labour-aristocrat consensus'.[76] But this process was never complete; and to ascribe it, where it did take place, to middle-class permeation and infiltration is to ignore continuing tensions. Mutual-aid activity among the working classes had originated as a barrier against poverty, and it involved collective strength. These aspects were absent from middle-class pursuits within the voluntary and commercial sectors, which were more directed at self-help by individual enterprise. When social and economic circumstances became more favourable in mid-century, the distinction between mutual-aid and self-help became more ambiguous and blurred; but it did not disappear. Mutual-aid activity remained rooted in a 'working-class subculture that prized genuine independence and self-respect.' Thomas Wright provided evidence of a further distinction: one between what he called the 'intelligent artisan', who looked to the improvement of his class, and the 'educated man', who wanted to improve himself and

---

[74] Quoted in Tholfsen, *Working Class Radicalism*, 296.
[75] Ibid. 277.   [76] Crossick, 'Labour Aristocracy', 320.

climb out of his class. In Wright's view, it was the 'intelligent artisan' who was the more frequently encountered and the more influential in working-class institutions.[77] Thus within such a 'Labour aristocracy' as existed, the pursuit of providence did not by any means slither and slide from mutual-aid to self-help—even if some slithering and sliding did take place. Mutual-aid could still be seen as a barrier against poverty, but it might also provide a route to self-help—and the achievement of some degree of financial security and personal welfare.

III

It has been seen that the existence of a variety of activity among the working classes directed at social improvement was not something entirely thrust upon them by other social groups; there were mutual-aid and self-help before, and without, Smiles. And yet, of course, thrusting did go on. The virtues of provident behaviour were constantly preached at the working classes by their social superiors in that 'broad stream of exhortation to the poor'[78] of which Smiles himself was part. Moreover, as has been noted, building societies, savings banks, and temperance societies owed something to the initiatives of those outside the working classes who were anxious to foster thrifty and responsible behaviour. George Porter, writing in his *Progress of the Nation* in 1851, commented on the tendency of those 'whose lot in life has been easy and beyond the reach of want' constantly to bring forward the theme of 'want of providence on the part of those who live by the labour of their hands, and whose employments so often depend upon circumstances beyond their control'. He was critical of this tendency:

it is difficult for those who are placed in circumstances of ease to estimate the amount of virtue that is implied in this self-denial . . . Those . . . persons . . . whose passage through life has been unvisited by the cares and anxieties that attend upon the children of labour, are very inadequate judges of the trials on the one hand, and of the means of surmounting them on the other, which are offered to those who must always form the most numerous class in every community.[79]

---

[77] Kirk, *Working Class Reformism*, 156, 217–18; Crossick, *Artisan Elite*, 156.
[78] Supple, 'Legislation and Virtue', 223.   [79] Quoted ibid.

Nevertheless, if the practice—and preaching—of providence was a much-favoured route to the achievement of social welfare among those 'placed in circumstances of ease', it was not the only one. There was another activity which came into play within the voluntary sector: that characterized by paternalism and philanthropy. These two words are difficult to separate, for both indicate a sense of social concern and conscience felt by the upper and middle classes of society for those who occupied a lesser station in life. Paternalism, however, may be said to have been a form of charity which valued 'face-to-face' relationships. Philanthropy tended to be more generalized and institutionalized. The differences will be more fully explored later; but the two may, for the present, be taken together to indicate responses to social need which, at least in outward appearance, seemed to place more emphasis on 'help from without' than on 'help from within'.

The motivation which led to provident and thrifty conduct may be obvious enough. Among the working classes, there was the spur of dire necessity to make provision in the face of want: the desire for social conviviality and cohesiveness—or, conversely, the desire to escape from too much conviviality, and to embrace sober and responsible habits. The motivation for the practice of provident habits among the middle and upper classes was also clear. It offered a path to individual prosperity and well-being; and the more such habits were adopted by other sections of the community, the more widespread would be that prosperity and well-being—and the less of a burden would be imposed on the 'haves' by the 'have-nots', to the advantage of each. Society as a whole would benefit from individuals practising habits based on self-interest. Here, of course, there was a multitude of ideas, deriving from the classical economists, which provided an intellectual underpinning for the virtues of free enterprise and a market economy as beneficial to the individual and to society at large.

The motivation, however, for paternalism and philanthropy—which appeared to involve some degree of interference with a market economy—may seem rather less obvious and clear-cut. Altruism is, perhaps, less easy to explain than self-interest.[80]

---

[80] For a general discussion of this and related issues, see Ellen Frankel Paul, Fred D. Miller, jun., Jeffrey Paul, and John Ahrens (eds.), *Beneficence, Philanthropy and the Public Good* (Oxford: Basil Blackwell for the Social Philosophy and Policy

Nevertheless, various explanations can be offered. Paternalism and philanthropy were, for the most part, functions of the better-off sections of society—although their existence in the poorer sections should not be overlooked.[81] Where they did proceed from the rich, they might well derive from a sense of obligation and responsibility to those in humble circumstances. Here the term *noblesse oblige* is not inapt. The Earl of Harrowby commented in 1852 that in Britain no idea of charity was allowed to remain barren: 'you have only to cast it on the waters', he continued—mixing his metaphors somewhat—'and it takes root and spreads. Kind hearts were willing to take it up, zeal was not wanting; and the reason was that people were imbued with a deep sense of their responsibilities.'[82]

Often linked closely with this idea was a more specifically religious commitment; and here the influence of evangelicalism was important, although it did not have a monopoly of the motivation to philanthropic endeavour, which could well proceed from religious impulses of a different denominational stamp—and, indeed, from a variety of religions. There was, for example, a very strong Jewish philanthropic tradition.[83] Nevertheless, the evangelical revival at the end of the eighteenth century provided a powerful impetus to Christian philanthropy —even if, as Boyd Hilton has persuasively argued, evangelicalism was as consistent with provident as with philanthropic behaviour.[84] To evangelicals of a charitable disposition and persuasion, however, the temporal disabilities of their neighbours could not be ignored; for that neighbour was made in the image of God, and had an immortal destiny. As one philanthropist, with a lifelong concern for orphans and lunatics, put it; 'the Divine image is stamped upon all'.

Center, Bowling Green State University, 1987). See also Richard Magat (ed.), *Philanthropic Giving: Studies in Varieties and Goals* (Oxford: Oxford University Press, 1989).

[81] Frank Prochaska, *The Voluntary Impulse: Philanthropy in Modern Britain* (London: Faber & Faber, 1988), 27. See also Prochaska, 'Philanthropy', in F. M. L. Thompson (ed.), *The Cambridge Social History of Britain, 1750–1950*, 3 vols. (Cambridge: Cambridge University Press, 1990), iii. 360 ff.

[82] *Ragged School Union Magazine*, 1852.

[83] V. D. Lipman, *A Century of Social Service, 1859–1959: The Jewish Board of Guardians* (London: Routledge & Kegan Paul, 1959). See also Eugene C. Black, *The Social Politics of Anglo-Jewry, 1880–1980* (Oxford: Basil Blackwell, 1988), esp. ch. 3.

[84] *The Age of Atonement: The Influence of Evangelicalism on Social and Economic Thought, 1785–1865* (Oxford: Clarendon Press, 1988), 16.

Thus those distressed in body, mind, or estate demanded the attention of their more fortunate fellows; and, so far as they were able, religious philanthropists had to struggle to remove temporal barriers which impeded spiritual fulfilment. This did not mean the purchase of salvation by good works; rather, good works were a mark of salvation, for faith without works was dead. The religious motive was, then, an extremely powerful force leading to paternalistic or philanthropic activity; and this was, perhaps, especially true of women. The religious impulse among the great number of women who took part in philanthropy in nineteenth-century Britain was extremely strong. The influence of the Bible on the female mind was a constant theme which emerged from the hundreds of memoirs, diaries, and autobiographies written by women in this period—a point well illustrated by the historian of this aspect of philanthropy, F. K. Prochaska. 'If there was a conviction peculiar to nineteenth century philanthropic women,' he writes, 'it was their belief, inspired by Christ, that love could transform society . . .'[85] And they saw themselves as agents of that love, expressed through philanthropic activity.

The churches, moreover, with their parochial system—a much more extensive organization than any other in the country—often provided the structure within which such activity could be carried out.[86] The mission of the churches led them to take the gospel into areas of towns and cities where social problems abounded; parish visitations or mission stations could uncover a vast amount of social need, and the churches could become an agency for social improvement almost as much as one for spiritual instruction. Ragged schools were intended to be instruments of mission to neglected children; but they found themselves undertaking basic educational tasks—teaching the alphabet, so that the Bible could be read, or providing instruction in home-making for girls, on the grounds that they were the wives and mothers of the future. Thus the Revd J. S. Boone, minister of St John's Church, Paddington, and a High Churchman—preaching a sermon in 1844 in aid of the Metropolitan Churches Fund, which provided additional churches and clergy for London—stressed

---

[85] *Women and Philanthropy in Nineteenth Century England* (Oxford: Clarendon Press, 1980), 15.

[86] Brian Harrison, *Peaceable Kingdom: Stability and Change in Modern Britain* (Oxford: Clarendon Press, 1983), 228.

the value of the church in the community. 'A church brings with itself all other forms of good,' he said. It 'becomes the centre for all benevolent designs: it excites and calls into action those unwearied persons . . . who will discover, visit and relieve, physical and temporal, as well as mental and moral necessities. . . .'[87]

There were, then, altruistic, humanitarian, and religious motives for the exercise of paternalism and philanthropy; and it would be hard to make sense of the varied activities in these areas of the Seventh Earl of Shaftesbury—Lord Ashley until his succession to the title in 1851[88]—without taking due account of them. Such impulses are, as Brian Harrison has written, 'easily neglected or depreciated by the secularised twentieth century mind'.[89] And the social hardships which might accompany industrialization in early nineteenth-century Britain—whether in factories, mines, or overcrowded housing—offered ample scope for the expression of such impulses, although, as has been implied, there were also many other areas where philanthropic energies could be spent.

Yet it would be rather simplistic to leave the matter there. Indulgence in paternalistic and philanthropic behaviour could also serve more self-interested motives. *Noblesse oblige* could merge into a way of quieting a conscience troubled by the possession of riches, or of justifying those riches by devoting a proportion of them to the benefit of others. Religious sensitivity to the needs of the deprived could be fuelled by a sense of guilt and sin; and philanthropic activity could become a way of expiating that sin or—despite evangelical warnings against buying salvation by good works—a means of storing up treasure in heaven.

Philanthropy could also provide a means of resolving inner conflicts of personality. Keble once said that 'when you find yourself . . . overpowered as it were by melancholy, the best way is to go out, and do something kind to somebody or other'.[90] Benjamin Jowett asked Florence Nightingale if she had ever observed 'how persons take refuge from family unhappiness in

---

[87] Quoted in B. I. Coleman (ed.), *The Idea of the City in Nineteenth Century Britain* (London: Routledge & Kegan Paul, 1973), 101.

[88] He is referred to here mainly as Shaftesbury. See G. F. A. Best, *Shaftesbury* (London: Batsford, 1964); Georgina Battiscombe, *Shaftesbury: A Biography of the Seventh Earl, 1801–1885* (London: Constable, 1974); Geoffrey B. A. M. Finlayson, *The Seventh Earl of Shaftesbury* (London: Eyre Methuen, 1981).

[89] *Peaceable Kingdom*, 226.   [90] Quoted ibid. 228.

philanthropy'.[91] Equally, philanthropy might fill the space left by lack of occupation. It could absorb spare time—and here the relatively few opportunities for public work afforded to middle- and upper-class women in nineteenth-century Britain provided an additional reason for their involvement.[92] Good works could perpetuate the name of the childless philanthropist after death; many philanthropists were spinsters and bachelors. Philanthropic activity could also be a form of social snobbery by enabling a donor to a charitable cause to rub shoulders with those in a superior station on a charity committee, or at a charity ball.

Lord Hobhouse commented on much of this when, in 1846, he singled out 'love of power, ostentation, and vanity' as the prin- cipal motives which led to charitable activity. To these he added 'superstition'—the belief that charity offered 'advantage after death' or atoned for misdeeds—and 'spite'. He wrote of the 'pleasurable sensation of knowing that the faces of the heirs expectant will look very blank when the will is read.'[93] Philan- thropy could, indeed, be a way of depriving disliked relatives of a hoped-for legacy by diverting it elsewhere. The donation of a legacy to a cat-and-dog home could result from a desire to score off relatives as much as a desire to help cats and dogs.[94]

There could, then, be a considerable variety of individual motives which led men and women to philanthropy; and it can well be argued that 'reciprocity'—whereby donor receives as much as donee—is of great importance.[95] Motives were by no means mutually exclusive, even within one person. The career of Thomas Holloway, who used much of the wealth from the sale of his patent medicines to found a sanatorium at Virginia Water,

[91] Vincent Quinn and John Prest (eds.), *Dear Miss Nightingale: A Selection of Benjamin Jowett's Letters to Florence Nightingale, 1860–1893* (Oxford: Clarendon Press, 1987), 88.   [92] See Prochaska, *Women and Philanthropy, passim*.
[93] Quoted by E. C. P. Lascelles, 'Charity', in G. M. Young (ed.), *Early Victorian England*, 2 vols. (London: Oxford University Press, 1934), ii. 345.
[94] Brian Harrison, 'Victorian Philanthropy' (*Victorian Studies*, ix/14 (June 1966), 361).
[95] Ray Snaith (ed.), *Neighbourhood Care and Social Policy* (London: HMSO, 1989), 33–9, deals with this issue. See also R. M. Titmuss, *The Gift Relationship* (London: Allen & Unwin, 1971); R. Pinker, *Social Theory and Social Policy* (London: Heinemann Educational Books, 1971); R. Pruger, 'Social Policy: Unilateral Trans- fer or Reciprocal Exchange' (*Journal of Social Policy*, ii/4 (1973), 289–302); Stephen Uttley, 'The Welfare Exchange Reconsidered' (*Journal of Social Policy*, ix/2 (1980), 187–205).

and the women's college in London which was to bear his name—housed in a building of bizarre architectural style—showed a not uncommon mixture of altruism, vision, and vanity.[96]

Further, philanthropy might be a means of advancing a particular cause—or, more defensively, of protecting an interest. There was a collective, in addition to an individual, side to philanthropy. Group or class motives could make themselves felt as well as personal ones. And these could easily sit alongside the impulses which have already been mentioned. Thus concern was often expressed about the rough living and working conditions of the railway navvies in the mid-nineteenth century. This was, indeed, partly influenced by a genuine religious or humanitarian solicitude that men should have to live in such circumstances. Another strong consideration, however, was the widespread fear that bands of navvies–whose style of life was, to say the least, robust—might constitute a threat to public order and to property as they moved around the countryside.

Paternalism and philanthropy, therefore, might be a way of upholding law and order, and protecting property from attack. They might also be a means of defending the established social order, to which most philanthropists belonged, against radical criticism. There was a strong authoritarian strain which ran through paternalism.[97] Edmund Burke's *Reflections on the Revolution in France*, first published in 1790, did much to inspire the volume of paternalist writing which was to appear in the 1830s and 1840s. Such ideas had not been absent before 1790, but Burke stated them in a way which was especially cogent in the context of the threat to order and stability posed by the French Revolution. He stressed the need for an ordered, hierarchical society. Society was unequal and should remain so; the poor should be subordinate to the rich, for that was the relationship which a wise Almighty had ordained. Belief in an organic and hierarchical society remained central to the thought of many paternalists who followed Burke. In 1816 Coleridge stressed the necessity for a society in which all classes were so balanced and interdependent as to constitute more or less a moral unity, an organic whole.[98]

---

[96] David Owen, *English Philanthropy, 1660–1960* (Cambridge, Mass.: Harvard University Press, 1965), 395–401.
[97] David Roberts, *Paternalism in Early Victorian England* (London: Croom Helm, 1979), 28–30.   [98] Ibid. 30.

Southey much admired feudalism because it offered 'a system of superintendence everywhere'.[99] Disraeli welcomed the idea of a strong monarchy as an instrument to protect the people.[100]

The idea of the 'protection of the people' was important to paternalists. The people had to be defended from dangerous and seditious ideas which might lead them into movements which were destructive of the social order. This might, indeed, be done by means of repression; and Burke strongly believed in Pitt's repressive legislation of 1795. Equally, Southey was in favour of curbing sedition in the press, and transporting those who indulged in libel or criticism of the established order. Yet alongside this ran the view that the poor might be reconciled to their lot, and diverted from sedition, by the proper discharge of the responsibilities of wealth. Burke wrote of the rich as 'trustees for those who labour for them';[101] and paternalists—and philanthropists—who followed him also preached the necessity of discharging the duties of rank, station, and wealth, so that those in receipt of such sympathy and consideration might be content to remain loyal, deferential, and subordinate, immune from the wiles and weanings of radicals and levellers. Paternalism and philanthropy might, then, derive from a desire to make the world safe for property.

The forces which led to the expression of this facet of the voluntary sector were, therefore, numerous and diverse. And if a variety of individual motives might well reside within one person, so too might a combination of individual and collective motives. As has been mentioned, Shaftesbury's paternalism and philanthropy cannot be explained without reference to his evangelical sense of duty to God and to his fellows; nor, indeed, without taking account of his patrician sense of the responsibilities of rank. Yet it might also be argued that his 'long life spent in the cause of the Helpless and Suffering'—as the inscription on his statue in Westminster Abbey puts it—may have owed something to his inner conflicts of personality; for he was a man given to dark and brooding thoughts. It may be that—unconsciously rather than consciously—he took Keble's advice to 'go out, and

---

[99] Quoted ibid. 44. See also David Eastwood, 'Robert Southey and the Intellectual Origins of Romantic Conservatism' (*English Historical Review*, civ / 411 (Apr. 1989), 308–31).

[100] Roberts, *Paternalism*, 45.   [101] Quoted ibid. 30.

do something kind' as a means of relief to the 'despondency fits', as he himself once described the moods of depression to which he was subject. There may even be some connection between his activity on behalf of others and his own childhood, which was starved of parental affection. These are simply conjectural points, not sustainable by proof.[102]

What, however, can safely be said is that Shaftesbury desired to perpetuate his own order by disarming radical criticism. In 1867 he wrote that his 'whole life [had] been spent in endeavouring to build up the moral, social, political and religious estimation of the Aristocracy'.[103] He did not tire of complaining about those members of the privileged classes who were blind to the dangers of failing to build up such an estimation. When the Commons adjourned in 1848 in order that members might attend racing at Epsom, he commented on the apparent indifference which this showed to the revolutions of that year on the Continent. 'Balls, races, festivals', he wrote, '. . . as tho' nothing had happened in adjacent countries and that we had an assurance of perpetual enjoyment'.[104] Or again, the following month he wrote that the 'dangerous classes' were not the masses, but 'the lazy ecclesiastics of whom there are thousands, and the rich who do no good with their money'.[105]

If paternalism and philanthropy could serve an immense variety of individual or collective aspirations and needs, it would be unduly cynical—and mistaken—to drain out all the altruism by exclusive concentration on self, class, or economic interest. The kind of lifelong attachment to the plight of lunatics, orphans, or chimney-sweeps which many paternalists and philanthropists displayed may possibly have derived from some need, conscious or unconscious. The burden did not always need to be very great to give satisfaction. Lady Violet Greville recalled a poor old man whom she had befriended while visiting him in his slum home— or 'slumming', as the phrase went. On his death-bed, he asked to see her—to her great gratification. 'These little incidents', she wrote, 'make "slumming" a real pleasure. One can give so much

---

[102] See Finlayson, *Shaftesbury*, 603–4.
[103] Quoted in Geoffrey B. A. M. Finlayson, 'Shaftesbury', in Patricia Hollis (ed.), *Pressure from Without in Early Victorian England* (London: Edward Arnold, 1974), 177. [104] Quoted in Finlayson, *Shaftesbury*, 141.
[105] See ibid. chs. 11 and 12, for further consideration of these points.

happiness with so little trouble.'[106] There were, indeed, other aspects of philanthropic work which did involve 'trouble'; and it may have been the case that the greater the burden which was carried, the greater the satisfaction which was derived.

Yet it is rather fanciful to suggest that the pursuit of often disagreeable work, seemingly quite contrary to self-interest, *must* have sprung from some sinister, self-interested compulsion. Further, it is difficult to see how a lunatic, orphan, or chimney-sweep—or a poor old man in a slum—could ever become revolutionary, and a threat to the established order. The historian of paternalism and philanthropy must allow that 'good deeds' *can* be done for good and disinterested motives—although he must, in addition, be alive to the fact that 'good deeds' can also be done for somewhat less than good and disinterested motives; and, above all, he must be aware that the good and the less good can well reside within the one person or group. Prochaska puts it well when he writes of the practice of visiting, so integral to much philanthropic work:

Despite the disappointments, abuses and hypocrisy, visitors from all social backgrounds had reason to be proud of the countless mercies shown to their neighbours. That this work was often so arduous, time-consuming and dangerous to the health of volunteers (many died of disease and some were killed on their rounds) suggests a level of selflessness and commitment which was remarkable. At the level of human contact, in often tragic circumstances, the idea that philanthropy can be reduced to a form of middle-class social control, unresponsive to the genuine grievances of the poor, is not only inadequate but insensitive.[107]

Whatever the motives, good deeds were done. Landowners could be paternalistic towards their tenants. In Sussex, the landowners did not hesitate to display the authoritarian and disciplinary side of paternalism; the sentences meted out at quarter sessions by the Earl of Chichester were harsh. He told the magistrates that 'it was the duty of parents and masters to watch over and endeavour to control all the evil propensities of their servants'.[108] Yet there were also instances where benevolence was shown, and this often took the form of the distribution of coal, clothing, soup, or bread. This activity was in the great majority

[106] Harrison, 'Victorian Philanthropy', 360.
[107] *Voluntary Impulse*, 52.   [108] Roberts, *Paternalism*, 114.

of cases concentrated in the winter months of December and January. Many such 'benevolences' were, indeed, seasonal—part of the ritual of the Christmas season. Thus on New Year's Day the Earl of Arundel and Surrey gave 600 loaves of bread and 200 gallons of beer to the 'necessitous poor'.[109] The winter of 1840–1 was especially severe, and this prompted considerable charitable activity in Sussex. The pattern was repeated elsewhere. In the 1840s great landlords, such as the dukes of Bedford, Northumberland, Devonshire, and Argyll, Earl Fitzwilliam, and the earls of Leicester and Aberdeen, were noted for their paternalistic activity.[110] When Ashley inherited the Shaftesbury title in 1851, he undertook a programme of cottage building and land improvement on the family estates in Dorset—one, in fact, which led him into considerable financial difficulty.[111]

Equally, such activity might be carried out by the clergy. In Chilbolton in Hampshire, the Revd Richard Durnford, sen., and his wife undertook pastoral duties which included the provision of allotments for the poor from his glebe lands, the storing of faggots, which could be sold cheaply to the poor in winter, and the distribution of soup and medicine. The Revd Lord Sidney Godolphin Osborne of Durweston, Dorset, established a considerable reputation for his paternalistic activity, which embraced a coal fund, allotments, cheap blankets, and regular visits to labourers' cottages.[112] This sort of activity was also evident in an urban setting. In the Whitechapel district of east London, the evangelical Rector, the Revd William Champneys, appointed by Bishop Blomfield in 1837, not only built three churches, but also set up schools, including a ragged school, a shoeblack brigade to employ vagrant boys along with a refuge and an industrial home, a local society to provide health and comfort for the working classes, and a hiring office for coal-whippers—who had previously had their wages paid in public houses.[113] Church laity also contributed to the founding and running of soup kitchens and refuges.

Paternalism could find ample scope in an urban and industrial setting—nor was it always church-based. The factory was, in

---

[109] Ibid. 115–16.   [110] Ibid. 133–4.
[111] Finlayson, *Shaftesbury*, 331 ff.   [112] Roberts, *Paternalism*, 156–7.
[113] G. Kitson Clark, *Churchmen and the Condition of England, 1832–1885* (London: Methuen, 1973), 72.

many respects, an ideal setting. Shaftesbury was often attacked for being highly critical of factory owners; but he freely acknowledged that the factory system 'might . . . be made the channel of comforts and even blessings'. In 1844 he said in a speech in Manchester:

When I have contemplated a multitude of twelve or fourteen hundred people, congregated under a single roof, governed by the revolutions of a single engine, all within reach of . . . watchful care, of every happy influence, I have often reflected what prodigious means of doing good had been placed by Providence in the hands of such employers. I do say, when I have contemplated one of these enormous buildings, alive with human beings, and under the authority of a single proprietor, I confess I have often said to myself—'I wish to God I were a factory owner'. I do, indeed, believe that by such an instrumentality as this ancient sympathies might be revived, and ancient habits restored between master and man.[114]

There were, indeed, factory owners—many known personally to Shaftesbury—who showed a paternalistic concern for their employees: the Ackroyds and Crossleys of Halifax, the Ainsworths and Ashworths of Bolton, the Ashtons of Hyde, the Fieldens of Todmorden, the Gregs of Bollington, the Horrockses of Preston, the Salts of Saltaire, the Whiteheads of Hollymount; or in Scotland, Archibald Buchanan of Catrine, James Finlay and James Smith of Deanston. Their paternalism—like that of their urban counterparts—had its strictly disciplinary side: Henry Ashworth fined his factory workers for poor work, swearing, loitering, and lack of punctuality.[115] But there was, too, a more positive aspect in the provision of amenities for the work-force: housing, schools, reading-rooms, churches, Sunday schools, libraries, and lecture halls. Samuel Greg, sen., showed 'genial hospitality' when he met his workers in Sunday school and in the library; his son encouraged exercise for the body through games and gymnastics, and for the mind by means of evening lessons in drawing, singing, geography, and natural history—which he himself taught.[116] Various forms of hospitality and recreation were offered: works dinners and 'treats', boat trips and railway

---

[114] *Speeches of the Earl of Shaftesbury upon Subjects Relating to the Claims and Interests of the Labouring Class* (Shannon: Irish University Press, 1971), 149–50.
[115] Roberts, *Paternalism*, 172–3.   [116] Ibid. 174.

excursions. The firm of Horrockses and Miller sent 1,570 employees to Blackpool in 1850. Such occasions were spectacular affairs, accompanied by brass bands and banners.[117]

All this developed considerably from the 1840s. It was in this decade, as Anthony Howe has written, that 'the scale and intensity of the textile masters' involvement in the patronage of philanthropy and culture changed widely'.[118] In some cases, this took time to show itself; it was not, for example, until the 1850s that Hugh Mason of Ashton—not hitherto known for his benevolence to his workforce—declared himself to be 'far more than . . . mere capitalist'. He regarded himself as a 'father—but yet one of the "brothers and sisters" who made up the mill, marching together for one common end—the mutual welfare of the workpeople and the employer'.[119] Part of this process was the extent to which the cotton master widened his horizon from that of factory paternalist to local philanthropist by becoming 'the patron of the industrial town and its culture'.[120] Mason financed municipal building at Ashton, and the Fieldens at Todmorden spent £54,000 on a town hall.[121] J. H. Ainsworth spent on average £1,000 a year on philanthropic projects, which was a sizeable portion of his income. The development of Saltaire by Titus Salt in the 1850s and 1860s involved a move from Bradford to a specially created factory town in the surrounding countryside; and here, too, provision was made of housing, church, schools, hospital, baths and washhouses, almshouses, an Institute for educational and social functions (incorporating a reading-room, library, rooms for chess and draughts, billiards, a lecture room, a gymnasium, and a rifle drill room), and a park near the river with facilities for boating and swimming, bowls, croquet, archery, and cricket.[122] All this involved considerable expenditure: £106,552 on dwellings, £16,000 on a church, £7,000 on each school, bath, and washhouse.

Saltaire, indeed, became something of a cynosure, attracting

[117] Patrick Joyce, *Work, Society and Politics: The Culture of the Factory in Later Victorian England* (London: Methuen, 1980), 186.
[118] *The Cotton Masters, 1830–1860* (Oxford: Clarendon Press, 1984), 272.
[119] Joyce, *Work, Society and Politics*, 148.
[120] Howe, *Cotton Masters*, 272.   [121] Ibid. 279.
[122] Jack Reynolds, *The Great Paternalist: Titus Salt and the Growth of Nineteenth Century Bradford* (London: Maurice Temple Smith, in association with the University of Bradford, 1983), 279–80.

comment as an exemplar of industrial paternalism and philanthropy. Visitors to Bradford almost invariably made the journey
to Saltaire; when the British Association of Social Science met in
Bradford in 1859 and again in 1874, most of those attending the
sessions visited the new town. After laying the foundation-stone
of the new Wool Exchange in Bradford in 1864, Palmerston in-
spected Saltaire, and said that this was the most memorable part
of his visit. A former prime minister of New Zealand—intent on
establishing his own model village in New Zealand—was warm
in his praise of Saltaire after going there in 1876; four years earlier, in 1872, there had been visits from the Burmese and Japan-
ese ambassadors.[123] Saltaire was in some respects a latter-day
New Lanark in the amount of interest which it attracted; and,
indeed, New Lanark itself had not been without a considerable
measure of paternalism, even if this became intermixed with more
visionary and communitarian projects, not to be found in Saltaire.

The extent to which such activity permeated the industrial districts of Britain is open to dispute. David Roberts does not ignore
industrial paternalism, but he sees it as exceptional, rather than
typical. 'There were not many Saltaires in Britain,' he writes.
'There were not even many Ashworths, Gregs, and Ashtons. There
were, however, in the United Kingdom, 4,800 cotton and wool-
len mills, thousands of collieries, and even more thousands of
workshops and small manufacturers.'[124] For Roberts, paternalism
could exist only in 'spheres in which property was sovereign,
authority and hierarchy secure, and the whole held together
organically by personal relations'.[125] Since 'in smallness lay the
key to paternalism',[126] it was unsuited and inappropriate to the
solution of large-scale urban and industrial problems. Other
writers have drawn attention to the exceptional nature of the
concessions made by the industrial employers—and to the nig-
gardliness of such concessions as were made.[127] Patrick Joyce, on
the other hand, would argue that, far from weakening paternalism, 'the nature of work and of the town after mid-century actively facilitated paternalism'. To Joyce, paternalism *did* suggest
itself as an answer to industrial problems; indeed, he argues that

[123] Ibid. 281–2.   [124] Roberts, *Paternalism*, 180–1.
[125] Ibid. 270.   [126] Ibid.
[127] H. I. Dutton and J. E. King, 'The Limits of Paternalism: The Cotton tyrants
of North Lancashire, 1836–54' (*Social History*, vii (1982), 59–74).

'industrial rather than rural society may have been the chief seat of paternalism in nineteenth-century England'.[128]

As has been seen, 'private' paternalism could easily shade into 'public' philanthropy. Not that private benevolence was ever absent from philanthropy; it was essential to it. And one form of such benevolence which retained an important place in philanthropic endeavour was the endowed charitable bequest left in the will of an individual to assist a particular cause or meet a particular need—or, indeed, to vent spite on a disliked relative. In London, many of these were administered by the City Companies, such as the Mercers' Company, which controlled a very wide range of charitable funds, including those devoted to educational activities, the provision of almshouses, and the distribution of coal and clothes to the poor. The Drapers' Company acted as trustees for funds willed, among other things, for providing bread in prisons and pensions to released prisoners.

Increasingly, however, in the course of the nineteenth century such charitable funds became only part of the whole. Already by 1800 endowed trusts had ceased to be the principal method of giving to charity, either in number or in value. What have been called 'organised donor groups' or 'benevolent societies' had, from the late eighteenth century, become the most popular form of giving.[129] Equally, of course, these societies depended upon individual donations; gifts and lists of subscribers were given considerable publicity in annual reports and in newspapers. But such societies had a corporate identity; they were organized groups to promote a common and a shared interest. They had a committee and officers, elected by those who subscribed at an annual meeting—although elections often went uncontested.

The societies were, for the most part, town-based, and—except for their patrons, who might be drawn from the local aristocracy, gentry, or (if the society was especially well favoured) royalty— they were usually composed of the upper ranks of the middle classes in the district. The president might be a leading industrialist, the secretary a lawyer, and the treasurer a banker.[130] Indeed,

---

[128] *Work, Society and Politics*, 154.

[129] Richard Tompson, *The Charity Commission and the Age of Reform* (London and Henley: Routledge & Kegan Paul, 1979), 68.

[130] R. J. Morris, 'Voluntary Societies and British Urban Elites' (*Historical Journal*, xxvi (1983), 97, 101–2).

it may be argued that whereas friendly societies and other mutual-aid groups were composed of an élite among the working classes, benevolent societies were élite groups among the middle classes. Such voluntary groupings, R. J. Morris has written, 'provided an expression of social power for those endowed with increasing social and economic authority . . .';[131] they may be said to have played a part in 'the continuous recreation of urban élites in conditions of rapid social and economic change'.[132] Thus it is important to see the voluntary association as a powerful instrument for offering the middle classes scope for mutual action over which they had control, and which did not commit them beyond what they themselves desired. Morris has argued that voluntarism in this guise was a vehicle for expressing the 'fragmented and uncertain identity of the middle classes'.[133]

The causes to which these societies devoted their energies and funds were numerous; and the evidence of their activity was clearly discernible in many towns and cities. London churches and chapels took annual collections on one Sunday in June to assist local hospitals; in the 1860s and 1870s these would bring in some £30,000. 'Hospital Sunday' was, indeed, a common feature in the calendar of many churches throughout the country. In Newcastle, which had a population in the 1830s of about 50,000, there was an Infirmary, founded in 1751 but reformed and extended in the early nineteenth century.[134] It provided a twenty-four-hour free casualty service for the poorer classes; but for the longer-term patient, more formal arrangements were necessary. A patient in this category had to present a letter of introduction from a subscriber to the funds for the Infirmary. Anyone who subscribed two guineas could present one in-patient and two out-patients a year—with larger sums bringing an entitlement to more numerous presentations. There was also a Dispensary, mostly for out-patients, founded in 1778 but enlarged in the early

---

[131] Ibid. 113.

[132] Ibid. 96. See also Richard Trainor, 'Urban Elites in Victorian Britain' (*Urban History Yearbook* (1985), 1–17).

[133] *Class, Sect and Party: The Making of the British Middle Class, Leeds, 1820–1850* (Manchester: Manchester University Press, 1990), 197. See also R. J. Morris, 'Clubs, Societies and Associations', in Thompson (ed.), *Cambridge Social History*, iii. 395 ff.

[134] Norman McCord, 'Aspects of the Relief of Poverty in Early 19th-Century Britain', in Arthur Selden (ed.), *The Long Debate on Poverty* (London: The Institute of Economic Affairs, 1972, 2nd imp. 1974), 96–102.

nineteenth century. This provided free medicines and a free service for 'slight casualties'; other cases followed similar lines of presentation to those who used the Infirmary. There was a Maternity Hospital and midwifery service; and in 1814 money was donated to set up a Lock Hospital for the reception of prostitutes. A lunatic asylum, founded in 1767, was improved and extended in the 1820s.

Other institutions in Newcastle catered for various other disabilities: a blind asylum, run by Dissenters, and a deaf and dumb asylum, in the charge of Anglicans. This provision was an example of how denominational differences could be reflected in such work; and, as was the case with mutual-aid societies, local church attachments could well underlie—and affect—involvement in charitable activities. There were also charity schools and a ragged school. In addition to such long-term charitable commitments, public subscriptions were established to meet particular emergencies, such as a fire and explosion in 1854, which laid waste large areas at the riverside in both Newcastle and Gateshead. A total sum of well over £11,000 was raised by a great variety of subscribers, ranging from the Queen to local engineering and shipbuilding firms.

These activities in Newcastle found parallels in many other industrial cities.[135] Manchester, often seen as a place given over to the pursuit of middle-class greed and gain, also had a considerable variety of voluntary provision for the poor. Much of this dated from the early 1860s; it included institutions for orphans, street children, prostitutes, and discharged or juvenile criminals.[136] Sometimes, too, the local bodies which carried out these charitable deeds belonged to a national organization, which would have an annual meeting, normally held in London in May. Shaftesbury was patron of many; and every May he would busily move from

[135] See e.g. Margaret B. Simey, *Charitable Effort in Liverpool in the Nineteenth Century* (Liverpool: University Press, 1951); R. W. M. Strain, *Belfast And its Charitable Society* (London: Oxford University Press, 1961); Neil Evans, 'Urbanisation, Elite Attitudes and Philanthropy: Cardiff, 1850–1914' (*International Review of Social History*, xxvii (1982), 290–323), also has much valuable material on philanthropy in its local context.

[136] Alan J. Kidd, ' "Outcast Manchester": Voluntary Charity, Poor Relief and the Casual Poor 1860–1905', in A. J. Kidd and K. W. Roberts (eds.), *City, Class and Culture: Studies of Cultural Production and Social Policy in Victorian Manchester* (Manchester: Manchester University Press, 1985), 48–73.

the platform of one society to that of another, and address the assembled members. When he died in 1885, the societies with which he had been associated—many embodying an intermixture of evangelicalism and social concern—were represented at his funeral service in Westminster Abbey; they occupy four pages of double columns in Edwin Hodder's biography of him.[137] The descendants of many were present at a service held in the abbey in 1985 to mark the centenary of Shaftesbury's death.

It is, therefore, possible to speculate at some length about the motivation for paternalism and philanthropy in the period; and it is also straightforward to provide evidence of their manifestation. It is, however, extremely difficult to give firm statistics as to their extent. As has been seen, it is possible to give figures for certain acts of paternalism, both in the country and in the town; but, of its nature, much paternalism was private and unrecorded, known only to those who gave and to those who received. It might be thought that public philanthropic activity would be easier to measure; and, while this is true to some extent, there are still formidable problems in arriving at an overall figure. Even to quantify charitable trusts poses very considerable methodological problems;[138] and to concentrate on donor groups or benevolent societies is no easier task. Works which make statistical studies of charities must be approached with care. Sampson Low's directory *The Charities of London*, published in six volumes in 1850, with a second edition in 1861, does, indeed, provide a panoramic view of London's charities at mid-century. In the 1861 edition, Low stated that 640 philanthropic institutions existed in London in 1860. Of these, 103 had been founded before the eighteenth century, 114 during the eighteenth century, 279 between 1800 and 1850, and 144 between 1850 and 1860. He gave the annual income from voluntary contributions as £1,600,594, and the annual income from property or trade in the same year as £841,373, making an aggregate income of £2,441,967.[139]

These statistics are useful in showing the rate of expansion in charitable effort in the nineteenth century; and they broadly confirm a statement, in a letter to *The Times* in 1850, that fifteen to twenty benevolent institutions were added each year.[140] But

---

[137] *The Life and Work of the Seventh Earl of Shaftesbury, K. G.*, 3 vols. (London: Cassell, 1887), iii. 525–8.   [138] Tompson, *Charity Commission*, esp. 55–77.
[139] Owen, *English Philanthropy*, 169.   [140] Quoted ibid. 169–70.

although they include some national charities with offices in London, as well as charities local to the metropolis, Low's figures are most unlikely to be complete or wholly accurate. They almost certainly underestimate the number of causes and institutions to which money was given, and the amount which was raised. An estimate of the sum devoted to charity in London for a slightly later period—about 1870—may be nearer the mark: between £5.5 million and £7 million a year.[141]

There are, in fact, more modern studies which provide some kind of statistical analysis. Prochaska has subjected a number of societies to scrutiny to establish the organizational role and financial contribution of women to philanthropy. Some of his material is presented in statistical form,[142] but again, of course, this does not claim to be comprehensive, and deals with only one aspect of the subject. Equally, Olive Checkland's valuable and detailed study of philanthropic activity in Scotland—a work of which there is no counterpart for England and Wales—cannot be definitive in this respect. She has to admit that 'quantification is almost impossible, at least in any aggregative sense . . . philanthropy as a totality cannot, at least as yet, be measured'.[143] In a more computerized age, there may, indeed, be room for further work along these lines, concentrating on those charities which advertised, were open, and kept good accounts; this would provide a more accurate assessment of at least a 'central core' of philanthropic activity than is at present available. It would, however, still omit many small and local charities, which did not keep good records—or whose records cannot be traced. For the moment, the historian of philanthropy—in all periods—is faced with virtually intractable problems of aggregative quantification; and for this period he is forced simply to say, with David Owen, that the nineteenth century saw the charitable organization 'come to full, indeed, almost rankly luxuriant bloom.'[144]

IV

If the voluntary sector, in its several guises, was much in evidence in Britain in this period, the same may be said of the

---

[141] G. F. A. Best, *Mid-Victorian Britain, 1851–1875* (London: Weidenfeld & Nicolson, 1971), 138.   [142] *Women and Philanthropy*, 231–52.
[143] *Philanthropy*, 1.   [144] *English Philanthropy*, 92.

commercial sector, where considerations of profit were predominant. Thus the commercial insurance societies were active, by far the largest being the Royal Liver, with 550,000 members in 1872, and funds of £264,795.[145] These did, indeed, have some similarities to the mutual-aid friendly societies, in that they were designed to provide funds for various contingencies by the pooling of risks. But unlike the mutual-aid societies, they were purely under the control of their officials, and were dependent on collectors to gather the funds. In this respect, they came closer to the 'centralised class' of friendly society, which has already been considered. Nor were these organizations primarily designed to encourage provident habits for their own sake; they were run for commercial reasons. Here, then, was mutual-aid without participation—but with profit. The collectors were entrepreneurs seeking to build up a large 'book', which yielded a handsome commission of up to 25 per cent of contributions. The collectors personified the society for which they worked. In addition to collecting contributions, they would be the channel for the distribution of rules—or, indeed, the payment of benefit when this became due. Much of the business of the insurance societies was connected with insurance for funerals and death payments.

The societies might—and did—claim that their collectors helped to foster habits of providence and self-reliance among the poorest sections of the community, least able, or likely, to be provident; and such sections did tend to be their particular clients. Nevertheless, although many collectors did build up a relationship with a family by dint of regular visiting, and came to adopt an almost paternalistic role, the real purpose of the visit was a business one; and the regularity of the visit pointed to the assumption that without it, no savings would be made.

Informal arrangements for welfare—the working of the informal sector—were based essentially on the family, which was the fundamental unit of mutual-aid. In times of hardship, help would certainly be looked for from this source.[146] In addition, relatives could provide help in the way of temporary loans or accommodation, or they might assist in finding employment. This was particularly notable among Irish immigrants. As one observer put it in 1836: 'I know that the Irish constantly invite their friends

[145] Gosden, *Self-Help*, 120.   [146] Vincent, *Bread, Knowledge and Freedom*, 53.

and relations in Ireland, and when they come, receive and entertain them in their habitation for a certain period or until they find work.'[147] Kinship was very important in providing immediate assistance; this was another informal mutual-aid grouping,[148] and, in a somewhat extended form, this was also true of the neighbourhood, which could foster a sense of community and interdependence. This might, indeed, underlie and reinforce the more formal expression of mutual-aid through a friendly society or local church. Thus an observer of life in Manchester and other cotton districts wrote in 1841:

In most places, even in large towns of some antiquity, there is such a thing as a neighbourhood, for the poor as well as the rich; that is there is an acquaintance with each other arising from having been born or brought up in the same street; having worked for the same master; attended the same place of worship; or even from having seen the same face, now grown 'old and familiar', though the name and even the occupation of the individual might be unknown altogether, passing one's door at wonted hours, from work to meal, from meal to work, with a punctuality which implied regular and steady habits, and was of itself a sufficient testimony of character.[149]

Again, there were quite frequent references made to the habit of women and children going in and out of each other's houses:

In most cases the doors of the houses stand hospitably open, and younger children cluster over the threshholds and swarm out upon the pavement . . . Every evening after mill hours these streets . . . present a scene of considerable quiet enjoyment. The people all appear to be on the best of terms with each other, and laugh and gossip from window to window, and door to door. The women, in particular, are fond of sitting in groups upon their threshholds, sewing and knitting: the children sprawl about beside them.[150]

It is true that this type of informal 'mutual-aid' group would not always foster provident and thrifty habits. It might well do so; personal self-sacrifice on the part of a wife or mother—or, indeed, on the part of parents—would certainly be necessary if a family budget were to meet the demands that could be made of it. But it is also true that the exigencies of that budget might

---

[147] Quoted in Michael Anderson, *Family Structure in Nineteenth Century Lancashire* (Cambridge: Cambridge University Press, 1971), 155.
[148] Ibid. 161, 171.   [149] Quoted ibid. 103–4.   [150] Quoted ibid. 104.

well prompt a family to have recourse to the local pawnshop or moneylender to obtain credit—and there was a considerable extension of licensed and illicit pawnbroking between the 1820s and 1840s.[151] Here, of course, the achievement of welfare was dependent on agencies located within the commercial, rather than the informal, sector. Nevertheless, the informal sector could also easily display something akin to unstructured paternalism; and here, there were clear links with the voluntary sector—even if the initiative came from the 'have-nots' and was directed at other 'have-nots', rather than from the 'haves' to the 'have-nots'. There was, indeed, a great deal of assistance given to meet particular needs by family, kin, neighbours, and friends: the cooking of meals for, or taking in the washing of, a neighbour who was ill, the whip-round in a public house to help someone in the neighbourhood who was in hardship, the 'handing down' of children's clothes.[152] Clearly a great deal of this—like other acts of personal charity—went quite unrecorded, and is unknown to the historian. But it was, on occasion, commented on by outside observers. Thus the mayor of Clitheroe wrote of the sacrifices of the poor to help their fellows: 'Their charity is unbounded. Let anyone be in want from sickness or any other cause—there are fifty kind Samaritans to comfort and relieve them with both food and personal service.'[153] Even if it cannot be measured, there were, within the informal sector, manifestations of what has been well called the charity 'of the poor to the poor'.[154]

V

The three sectors within voluntarism—voluntary, commercial, and informal—thus provided a considerable network of welfare in the period from 1820 to 1880. As has been noted, the sectors overlapped; they did not operate in separate watertight compartments. It can, indeed, be argued that even if they did differ in important ways, they had certain characteristics in common; and consideration of these helps to shed light on the implementation

[151] Melanie Tebbutt, *Making Ends Meet: Pawnbroking and Working Class Credit* (London: Methuen, University Paperback, 1984), 37 ff.
[152] Prochaska, *Women and Philanthropy*, 42.
[153] Quoted in Anderson, *Family Structure*, 147.
[154] See Prochaska, *Women and Philanthropy*, 42.

of voluntarism as a whole in this period, and on the ideology which lay behind it.

One such characteristic was the large extent to which voluntaristic activities depended on personal initiative and participation. This was particularly true of the voluntary and informal sectors. As has been seen, many, if not all, mutual-aid groupings rested on such attributes. In 1797 F. M. Eden commented on this aspect of friendly societies when he wrote that they did not

owe their origin to Parliamentary influence; nor to private benevolence; nor even to the recommendations of men of acknowledged abilities or professed politicians. . . . The scheme originated among the persons on whom chiefly it was intended to operate: they foresaw how possible, and even probable, it was that they, in their turn, should ere long be overtaken by the general calamity of their times and wisely made provision for it . . .[155]

Historians have also pointed to this aspect of mutual-aid societies. Barry Supple has noted that much of their growth

exemplified an enormously powerful pressure for co-operative self-help, voluntaristic self-government and social and fraternal cohesion. . . . This was illustrated in the extremely democratic methods of government chosen by many societies, in their independence of spirit as well as of organisation, in the essentially local character of various sorts of societies, and in their desire for conviviality and group identification which was apparently such a strong motive for many members.[156]

It is true—as has been noted—that some mutual-aid organizations among the working classes owed their origin to outside influences; that 'social and fraternal cohesion' could give way to personal self-advancement; and that not all societies were run by their own members. But the involvement in the mutual-aid organization of its membership was very often extremely important; Beveridge was later to call the friendly-society movement a 'democratic movement of Mutual Aid sprung from the working

---

[155] Quoted by Gosden, *Self-Help*, 9–10.

[156] 'Legislation and Virtue', 221. See also Brian Harrison, 'Historical Perspectives', in *Voluntary Organisations and Democracy* (Sir George Haynes Lecture, 1987, with Nicholas Deakin. London: National Council for Voluntary Organisations, 1988), 3–4, for a consideration of links between voluntarism and democracy, and ibid. 4–5 on tensions between them.

classes'.[157] Equally, the philanthropic society depended on the
initiative of its members, who also took responsibility for the
conduct of its affairs — although here there was less 'democracy'
and more 'hierarchy' than might be found in the friendly society.
If participation within a group or society was important in the
voluntary sector, the informal sector clearly depended entirely
on it, even if not in a structured setting.

Here, then, was an exercise in citizenship, in the sense of an
active contribution to one's own welfare and that of others
through voluntary methods. Those who took part in it were often
not themselves 'citizens' in the more formal sense of belonging
to the political community; large sections of the working classes,
and, of course, all women were, indeed, excluded from that kind
of citizenship during this period. There were, however, certain
links between the citizenship of contribution within voluntary
agencies and the citizenship of entitlement to political rights. If
mutual-aid or self-help among the working classes led to personal advancement, this could bring with it the possession of
property—and if this were at the requisite level, the qualification
to vote. In this way, the franchise was earned by provident behaviour through voluntary methods. This still excluded women;
but their involvement in philanthropy—while often confined
to a somewhat subordinate and 'domestic' role, reflecting their
political position—could afford experience which might be
carried over into public and political activity. Again, in time,
this was to be one factor contributing to the possession by women
of the citizenship of political entitlement.[158]

Another characteristic of much voluntary activity was a strong
attachment to the separate existence of a particular society or
group. Although it is true that individuals could belong to many
more than one body, the organizations themselves remained
separate—and proudly so, although they were performing similar functions. There might be strong local attachments even within
the one broad organization; indeed, a dislike of London and
London rule was evident among many serving in the provinces.

---

[157] Beveridge, *Voluntary Action: A Report on Methods of Social Advance* (London:
George Allen & Unwin, 1948), 300.
[158] It can, however, also be argued that philanthropic activity reinforced
women's subordinate role in society. See Prochaska, *Woman and Philanthropy*,
222–9, for a consideration of this issue.

There were, as has been seen, numerous friendly societies—and numerous different types of friendly society. Their historian P. H. J. H. Gosden has emphasized the 'complete independence' of the local friendly societies; this, he has written, was their 'most important feature'.[159] The movement to establish affiliated orders could, and did, lead to suspicions, when local lodges felt that their independence and control over their funds were endangered by the central body. There were schisms; thus the National Independent Order of Oddfellows broke away from Manchester Unity,[160] and became independent in 1845. The formation of the Nottingham Ancient Imperial was the result of another such schism from Manchester Unity. The movement towards the more highly organized and permanent building society, too, was not always welcomed, and the older form of terminating society remained in existence. It was reported that even in 1870, terminating societies were being founded in great numbers in some Lancashire towns, in Sunderland, and in South Wales;[161] and one was established in Deptford as late as 1890.

The same sense of independence, leading to profusion of effort, was to be found in philanthropic activity, which was sometimes regarded as being too diffuse and all-embracing, lacking the kind of specific focus of personal, paternalistic acts. Richard Oastler, who was active in pressing for a ten-hour day in factories, castigated those 'benevolent factory owners', as he called them, who would enthusiastically attend meetings to protest against slavery abroad, and 'sign everlasting petitions' on that subject— and yet refuse to remedy the hours and conditions of their own work-force.[162] The writer of an article published in the *Westminster Review* in 1869 commented that 'it seems now that the public mind is not able to arrive at correct conclusions upon any rule of private conduct or any measure of public policy, without some large committee to conduct the work of instruction. Thus we have Leagues, Associations, Societies, Brotherhoods, etc. etc. without stint or limitation.'[163]

---

[159] *Self–Help*, 14.   [160] Ibid. 40.   [161] Ibid. 159.

[162] C. Driver, *Tory Radical: The Life of Richard Oastler* (Oxford: Oxford University Press, 1946), 131.

[163] *Poverty in the Victorian Age: Debates on the Issue from 19th Century Critical Journals*, with an introduction by A. W. Coats, 4 vols., iii: *Charity 1815–1870* (Westmead, Farnborough: Gregg International, 1973), 271.

The author strongly deplored this aspect of philanthropy. Many of the oldest philanthropic institutions were, he freely admitted, beneficent in intention, and played an important public role in providing 'hospitals for the sick and helpless'. But, he continued:

the acknowledged value of such institutions furnishes a plea for the formation of others, weakening the resources of the older institutions ... [T]he majority of them have either survived the uses to which they were designed, or they have degenerated into rank abuse, existing for the purpose of paying salaries to a staff of officers and servants...[164]

The validity of the criticism that impulses which were benevolent and well intentioned could, once organized, be diverted into maintaining a swollen bureaucracy is one which is not, perhaps, strictly relevant to the present issue; but the comment that such impulses were directed at specific issues, and thus resulted in a great number of separate societies, all jealous of their independence, was a fair one on much philanthropic activity.

These points about the independence and multiplicity of voluntary bodies are closely related to two other aspects: that they overlapped each other, and were often in competition with each other. Clearly the great variety of bodies in the world of mutual-aid meant that there was considerable overlapping of role and function. The same was true of the other side of the voluntary sector—philanthropy—and of the commercial sector. David Owen has drawn attention to both the overlapping and competitive aspects of the charitable world: 'The costly duplication and institutional rivalry of the charities ... were reflected in their money-raising practices. Collectors, paid and voluntary, were crossing and recrossing each other's trails ... frequently calling on the same individuals on behalf of identical varieties of charitable endeavor. ...'[165] The system of commission on contributions which were collected was not peculiar to the agents of commercial friendly and insurance societies—who, of course, were in direct business competition with each other. Paid collectors for charitable societies might receive some five to seven and a half per cent of their takings; and this might apply even to hospital secretaries on the money which they raised. On one occasion, the demand of a professional agent for his commission on a large

---

[164] Ibid. 447.　　　[165] English Philanthropy, 480.

bequest to a hospital—for which he had canvassed—resulted in a somewhat unseemly lawsuit between him and the charity which had engaged his services. Again, the system employed by some charities whereby beneficiaries were selected by the votes of the subscribers to the charity could lead to practices which sat ill with the relief of need: canvassing for votes, public polls, trading of votes. 'Charity electioneering' was, indeed, quite widely criticized, but it remained deep-seated, and was defended on the grounds that it encouraged donations. As Prochaska has put it, fund-raising was 'an obsession' with voluntary institutions; charity organizers 'put the public under unrelenting pressure'[166] to subscribe to the activities which they represented—many of which duplicated and overlapped with causes canvassed by others.

It was partly to try to rationalize and tidy up the charitable world that the Charity Organisation Society was set up in 1869. It was not intended to add yet another charity to the multiplicity already in existence. Rather, its purpose was to act as a coordinating body, so that particular needs could be met in appropriate ways, and not indiscriminately by large numbers of overlapping and competing agencies. Its attempts to match needs with appropriate relief resulted in the development of 'casework', by which individual situations were carefully studied before referrals were made to suitable bodies.

Such characteristics of voluntarism—individual initiative, attachment to independence, a marked tendency to overlapping and competitive activity—led to a further feature: patchiness and lack of uniformity. There could, in some areas, be what many observers thought to be over-provision; in others, under-provision. Where individual initiative was lacking, gaps in provision were evident. It was into such gaps in mutual-aid activity that the collectors of commercial insurance companies often directed their energies. With respect to rural paternalism, everything depended on the inclination of the local landowner. Thus the Sixth Earl of Shaftesbury was far from being paternalistic, and, in a speech at Sturminster in 1843, reacted furiously to the promptings made by his eldest son for landowners to show concern for the tenants on their estates. When he died in 1851, and the estates passed to

---

[166] *Voluntary Impulse*, 59.

his eldest son, their condition offended the new earl's paternalistic conscience. 'Filthy, close, indecent, unwholesome; many . . . dangerous, many more disgraceful, all unsatisfactory': these were some of the comments which the Seventh Earl made in his diary about the cottage accommodation which his father had provided for his estate workers. It was these conditions which led to his improvement schemes.[167]

Even paternalistic landowners were not always consistently so. The Duke of Norfolk gave to charities and hospitals, supported schools in Arundel, and kept labourers in employment in winter—something which by no means all landowners did. Yet he could be very sparing with money. He refused to improve the Horsham House of Correction, although this was his responsibility.[168] When the Duke of Richmond's son came of age, he entertained his tenants quite lavishly; yet he did not give money to complete his own parish's school. Similarly, by no means all clergy were infused with pastoral zeal for the temporal needs of their flocks; it will be recalled that Shaftesbury wrote of the 'lazy ecclesiastics'—and those who were not lazy often did not have enough resources at their disposal to feed the hungry and clothe the naked—or felt that their task lay with the soul, rather than with the body.[169]

In an industrial setting, it is, indeed, possible to point to paternalistic employers—as has been done above; but here too there was lack of uniformity and consistency. Paternalistic and philanthropic activity was more characteristic of the large or medium-sized than of the small firm. The owners of the latter sort —possessing a workforce of under about 150—could scarcely afford to be philanthropic on any large scale; they operated on too small a margin to be generous.[170] The role of the City Companies as trustees for charitable endowments in London has already been noted, and various other older towns, such as Lichfield, also had such endowed charities. But there was no consistency in how well such trusts were administered. The City Companies' conduct was often lax and open to abuse; and charity administration in other towns, especially where the funds were vested in the municipal corporation, might well be used for

[167] Finlayson, *Shaftesbury*, 199–200.   [168] Roberts, *Paternalism*, 117–19.
[169] Ibid. 166–7.   [170] Howe, *Cotton Masters*, 303–9.

political and electoral malpractice—even after the reform of the municipal corporations in 1835. On the other hand, the conduct of the Lichfield trustees, both civil and ecclesiastical, appears to have been satisfactory.[171] 'Newer' and more industrial towns and cities were unlikely to possess any such endowed charitable money at all. There was, then, a wide spectrum; and, of course, the degree of mutual-aid and charity shown in the informal sector depended entirely on individual circumstances, which makes any overall pattern impossible to establish.

If these were some of the features of the implementation of voluntarism in its various sectors, certain characteristics of the ideology which underlay that implementation may also be discerned. Here again, an overall characteristic was a strong belief in freedom and independence. This was clearly evident in the side of voluntarism which placed emphasis on provident and thrifty behaviour: on 'help from within'. It has been seen that the theme of independence and self-reliance was stressed in many statements made from the ranks of mutual-aid societies. Equally, paternalists and philanthropists were often at pains to insist that the 'help from without' which they offered was designed to increase the power of self-reliance among those at whom it was directed. This was the way in which any tension between 'help from within' and 'help from without' was resolved, at least in theory. Thus in 1831 the Society for the Improvement of the Working Population in the county of Glamorgan—a philanthropic organization—issued a pamphlet on friendly societies. It appealed to the notion of the independence of the individual as the main advantage which such societies could offer. The ideal labourer was one who could say: 'Poor as I am, I am obliged to no man for a farthing and therefore I consider myself as independent as any gentleman or farmer in the parish.'[172]

Similarly, landowning paternalists encouraged the establishment of friendly societies, savings banks, and schools in their rural districts; and their wives and daughters often founded, and attended to the running of, such institutions, especially those in the interests of women and children. They wished to inculcate useful domestic skills, and to develop habits of tidiness, diligence,

---

[171] Lascelles, 'Charity', 331–2.
[172] Quoted in Gosden, *Friendly Societies*, 163.

and punctuality in village girls, who later might be employed in service in their own—or their neighbours'—country houses. Meetings were held on how to instruct mothers in bringing up their children and managing their households. Clergymen and their wives also attended to such tasks. It was a clergyman's wife who, in 1876, founded the Mothers' Union, devoted to the 'sanctity of marriage' and the instruction of children 'in obedience, purity, and morality'.[173] Such endeavour, far from being designed to undermine self-reliance, was intended to promote it.

The same was true of much philanthropic and paternalistic work in an urban setting. Octavia Hill's efforts over housing were designed to instil habits of self-reliance and sobriety. In 1869 she read a paper to the London Association for the Prevention of Pauperization and Crime, which was entitled 'The Importance of Aiding the Poor without Almsgiving'.[174] The paternalism of the cotton masters was shot through with a belief in provident behaviour. Joyce has commented that employer paternalism was the 'logical outcome of *laissez-faire* ideology and not its logical opposite'. Much paternalist practice, he argues, 'developed within the matrix of strongly held *laissez-faire* notions of what the relations of employer and worker should be'. Thus the Halifax Crossleys spent great sums on the town—and yet insisted that the Crossley Institute and Works Canteen should be self-supporting, paid for by the operatives who used it. The journal of the employers' federation, Joyce notes, 'constantly lauded schemes that stressed self-reliance and promoted the entrepreneurial virtues of thrift and hard work.'[175] Employer paternalism was, therefore, he concludes, 'refracted through the lens of *laissez-faire* ideology'.[176]

Again, the range of philanthropic effort in the area of education and training was directed at increasing self-sufficiency. Ragged schools were seen as a means of providing training for children to look after themselves. It is significant that the Ragged School Union only very reluctantly gave money to refuges and night shelters, on the grounds that such institutions would

---

[173] Jessica Gerard, 'Lady Bountiful: Women of the Landed Classes and Rural Philanthropy' (*Victorian Studies*, xxx/2 (Autumn, 1986), 199).

[174] See Nancy Boyd, *Josephine Butler, Octavia Hill, Florence Nightingale: Three Victorian Women who Changed their World* (London: Macmillan, 1982), 132 ff.

[175] *Work, Society and Politics*, 138.   [176] Ibid. 145.

encourage a sense of dependence and undermine the will to work. It much preferred placing children in employment, and gave prizes for good conduct in that employment. It encouraged emigration to America, Canada, and Australia, giving only the best-behaved children the chance of such a new start in life. In the same vein as its rural counterparts, it ran classes to give children an idea of the 'dignity of labour', and mothers' meetings to give instruction in domestic economy and family duties.

The same ideas ran through the activities of the industrial brigades. These were often designed to complement the ragged schools by providing rudimentary employment opportunities for young persons, such as cleaning shoes or delivering parcels. Largely on the initiative of William Quarrier, the Glasgow Shoe Black Brigade was founded in 1864, and this was followed by News and Parcel Brigades.[177] A similar effort was made in Edinburgh in 1876. The *Scotsman* reported that:

The chief object of the movement is to reclaim these boys as quickly as possible from an idle street life, and those who give promise of improvement are only employed as shoe blacks until better, more constant, and more skilled work can be procured for them. Thus two of the boys have got situations in chemists' shops, where they have every prospect of advancement, others have been sent to grocers, others to bakers, one has gone to the drapery business, another is a clerk, another a blacksmith, another a painter . . . and one—spoken of as a remarkably fine fellow—has gone to sea.[178]

In no sense, then, did support for ragged schools or industrial brigades imply any lack of belief in provident behaviour; rather, they were held to be a spur to such behaviour. In evangelical and philanthropic ragged schools, the works of Smiles were regularly drawn upon to teach the virtues of self-improvement. Equally, philanthropic provision of baths, washhouses, and drinking-fountains could be justified on the grounds that such facilities gave the working classes the means of cleanliness, health, and self-respect, and enhanced their capacity for self-improvement. Public parks, donated by philanthropists, gave space for recreation in an environment which was infinitely preferable to the public house. 'I am sure,' said Richard Marsden in 1851, '. . . [a

[177] Checkland, *Philanthropy*, 253.   [178] Quoted ibid. 253–4.

park] tends very much to civilise the working classes and to keep them from Beer-houses'.[179]

Voluntarism, in its various aspects, was, therefore, directed to encouraging and sustaining independence and self-maintenance. This may be seen in terms of two individuals who feature prominently in this chapter, Smiles and Shaftesbury. Smiles, the apostle of providence, wrote in 1859 that 'the highest . . . philanthropy' consisted 'in helping and stimulating men to elevate and improve themselves by their own free and independent individual action.'[180] Shaftesbury, the apostle of paternalism and philanthropy, wrote in 1858 that 'all society can do it ought to do to remove difficulties and impediments; to give every man, to the extent of our power, a full, fair and free opportunity so to exercise all his moral, intellectual, physical and spiritual energies, that he may, without let or hindrance, be able to do his duty in the state of life to which it has pleased God to call him'.[181]

Another example may be cited of complementary beliefs and activities, this time coexisting within one person. Joseph Sturge, who became associated with innumerable voluntary movements in Birmingham from the 1820s onwards, combined a belief in self-help with one in charitable endeavour. As a young man in Gloucestershire, he joined the Bristol Endeavour Society and remained a firm adherent of self improvement.[182] He also became active in philanthropic work. There was, he wrote, 'scarcely any species of misery but there is some charity open to relieve it; and may these charities continue to increase until misery and want are driven from our happy shores'.[183] Thus Sturge, as Alex Tyrrell has put it, combined 'the ideals of self-help and Christian fellowship';[184] and he immersed himself in numerous philanthropic causes, directed towards the improvement and elevation of the working classes and the fostering of responsible behaviour. More anonymously, a Manchester observer in 1844 wrote that there was 'no charity more profound than that which habituates the working man to rely on his own resources, and which enables him to be independent of the charity of others'.[185]

---

[179] Quoted in Howe, *Cotton Masters*, 278–9.   [180] *Self-Help*, 14.
[181] Quoted in Finlayson, *Shaftesbury*, 410.
[182] Alex Tyrrell, *Joseph Sturge and the Moral Radical Party in Early Victorian Britain* (London: Christopher Helm, 1987), 13–14.   [183] Quoted ibid. 25.
[184] Ibid. 26.   [185] Quoted in Norman McCord, 'Aspects', 91–2.

This aim was also evident in the various agencies which have been considered above—and achieved its most notable expression in the Charity Organisation Society. As has been noted, the Society was, in part, intended to rationalize the implementation of charitable endeavour; but it was also concerned to ensure that its ideology was firmly directed at encouraging self-help. This was, indeed, the basic thrust of the activities of its leading spirit and secretary, C. S. Loch, who was strongly influenced in this respect by the ideas and practices of the Revd Thomas Chalmers, Minister of the parish of St John's in Glasgow in the early 1820s. Chalmers had been much concerned to improve what he called 'the frugality and provident habits of our labouring classes', and organized the members of the Kirk Session of St John's to investigate the circumstances of the needy in their districts before appropriate assistance was given.[186] Loch wrote of charity as 'a social regenerator . . . We have to use Charity to create the power of self help.' This was one reason why the Society did not itself seek to become an agency of direct relief; it issued the sombre warning that 'a penny given' resulted in a 'child ruined'.[187] Rather, it would arrange for individuals to be given the means whereby they could earn their own living: a widow in need might be supplied with a sewing-machine, a washerwoman with a mangle, a costermonger with a donkey.

The theme of independence thus ran through both the implementation and the ideology of voluntarism: independent agencies concerned to foster independent conduct. It must, however, be said that such a simple formula was not achieved without difficulty—and was sometimes not achieved at all. There were, indeed, tensions and conflicts, which in practice were difficult to resolve. As has already been seen, the tendency of mutual-aid organizations to indulge in conviviality and good fellowship could well impede the achievement of provident conduct; and the behaviour of fraudulent officials, who might disappear with the funds of the society, was a further barrier to the pursuit of 'help from within'. The provision of 'help from without' by the vast number of charitable agencies in existence might also erode the capacity for self-help—whatever the intentions of their sponsors

---

[186] See Kathleen Woodroofe, *From Charity to Social Work in England and the United States* (London: Routledge & Kegan Paul, 1966), 46.
[187] See ibid. 25 ff. for a consideration of these points.

to the contrary. There is certainly evidence that those in receipt of charity often 'played the system' by relying on as many charities as possible to eke out a bare living. Thus housewives in London who received charity seldom used it as it was intended; clothes and boots often found their way into the pawnshop to pay for food.[188] What were regarded as the harmful effects of excessive philanthropy were often commented upon. In his investigations of the London poor, published in volumes between 1851 and 1854, Henry Mayhew expressed sympathy for those who were badly paid and poorly housed—and wondered whether self-help was within their reach. Yet he felt that he must not be misled by 'morbid sympathy', for at least some of their misfortune was, he suspected, caused by their 'want of providence, want of temperance, want of cleanliness'. He acknowledged the role of charity, and wrote that the 'fuller and more general development of human sympathies' towards the poor was the main distinction of the period—more notable than the steam engine or railway. He felt, however, that its extent said more about the needs of the poor than about the generosity of the rich, and he was doubtful whether, in fact, it could meet those needs. Yet he did not feel that the generosity should be extended further. There was, he wrote, only one way of benefiting the poor, and that was 'by developing their powers of self-reliance, and certainly not in treating them like children'. Philanthropists, he felt, 'always seek to do too much, and in this is to be found the main cause of their repeated failures'.[189]

The tendency of philanthropists 'to do too much' was also the subject of more severe comment and criticism. It was often thought to result in fraud, deception, laziness, and disinclination to work. The writer of the article in the *Westminster Review* quoted above (p. 69), who objected to the multiplicity of charities, was concerned not only with the duplication and swollen bureaucracies which, he felt, were the result; he argued that the

---

[188] See Peter Mandler (ed.), *The Uses of Charity: The Poor on Relief in the Nineteenth-Century Metropolis* (Philadelphia: University of Philadelphia Press, 1990), chs. 3 and 6.

[189] Quoted in Gertrude Himmelfarb, *The Idea of Poverty: England in the Early Victorian Age* (London: Faber & Faber, 1984), 343. See ibid. 312–46 for a consideration of Mayhew.

existence of so many charities, subscribed to by those who made it a 'part of their religion to be good to the poor',[190] simply encouraged imposture and an erosion of the capacity of self-help. C. S. Loch believed that charity 'infects the people like a silent pestilence', as he put it. It had become an 'endowment to the hypocrite and a laughing stock to the cynic'.[191]

It was, however, difficult to rationalize both the implementation and the ideology of voluntarism. There was resistance within the voluntary sector to any attempts to exercise centralized control over it; and the competitive nature of the commercial sector, and disorganized character of the informal sector, clearly also placed great problems in the way of any overall integration of practice and principle. The fortunes of the Charity Organisation Society were to be a commentary on these tensions within the voluntary sector. This often found difficulty in ensuring that the charitable world heeded its rationalizing activities—for, of course, the independence of charitable organizations, often fuelled by denominational rivalries, meant that they were under no obligation to do so. Caroline Emilia Stephen found herself 'hampered and bewildered by unanswerable admonitions . . . about the danger of pauperizing', even to the extent that she scarcely dared to offer 'a cup of beef-tea to a sick neighbour for fear of demoralizing him and offending against the canons of political economy and the organisation of charity'.[192] There was, however, little that the Charity Organisation Society could do if others saw fit to offer the beef tea without worrying if the sick neighbour was thereby demoralized, and the organization of charity breached; and to those involved in charities concerned with physical or mental handicap, such considerations were virtually meaningless. Even the Society itself was not always able to adhere to its own tenets, and when confronted with actual circumstances, it might become a charitable agency in its own right, thereby adding to the multiplicity already in existence. If, then, it was of the nature of voluntarism to place primary emphasis on free and independent conduct, that very nature often also resisted attempts, through

---

[190] See *Poverty in the Victorian Age*, iii. 437–57, for a full elaboration of these points.   [191] Quoted in Woodroofe, *From Charity* 26.
[192] Quoted in Michael Goodwin (ed.), *Nineteenth Century Opinion: An Anthology of Extracts from the First Fifty Volumes of 'The Nineteenth Century'. 1877–1901* (Harmondsworth: Penguin Books, 1951), 71.

coordination of its activities, to ensure that this emphasis was always maintained. In the last resort, voluntarists cherished the freedom to act and think as they chose, and disliked outside interference — unless they were able to adapt that interference to their own purposes.

VI

The different varieties—or sectors—of voluntarism did not exist in complete isolation in the period from 1830 to 1880; there was a statutory sector within the mixed economy of welfare. The activities of the state aroused contemporary comment. In 1869 the *Pall Mall Gazette* commented that there 'is far more government now than there ever was before. Look, for instance,' it continued, 'at the legislation which has taken place . . . upon matters concerned with public health . . . Look at the Factory Acts, the Acts relating to Mines . . . to lodging houses, the Reformatory Acts, and an immense mass of other laws of which these are only a sample . . .'[193] And, as has already been mentioned, the passage of legislation in areas such as poor law, public health, factories, mines, lunacy, and education has led historians in the past twenty or thirty years to write in terms of a 'revolution in government', as they have discerned a growing role for the central state and the expansion of statutory agencies to implement that role. There has been disagreement as to what brought this about: whether it was the thrust of a systematizing creed like Benthamism, or an undoctrinaire and pragmatic search for solutions to problems in the face of circumstances. There has been, however, little disagreement about the fact that the years from 1830 to 1880 *did* see the growth of an administrative state—nor about the tendency for the agencies of the state, once established, to generate their own administrative momentum, and thus create further growth. It has been recognized that the process might undergo checks and setbacks; but the general direction, it has been argued, was towards growth and development. One writer, J. B. Brebner, wrote of intervention as 'always cumulative, building up like a rolling snowball after 1832 . . . It might be halted, a chunk or two might

[193] Quoted in Evans (ed.), *Social Policy*, 119.

even be knocked off the outside, but almost immediately it was set going and growing again . . .'[194]

It is not intended here to examine this aspect in any detail; that has been fully done elsewhere. Rather, the aim is to consider the relationship between voluntarism and the state, for this had an important bearing on each; and a study of the interplay helps to correct what can readily become a 'Whig' interpretation of the 'cumulative' process of statutory growth. It avoids the 'Welfare State escalator' or 'collective train' approach.

It can, indeed, be argued that the role of voluntarism and that of the state were broadly complementary in this period, and that there was much common ground between them. The liberalization of the state carried out during the period by free-trade policies was intended to promote the circumstances in which the economy would grow, and individual effort flourish. The able-bodied poor would, thereby, be able to provide their own welfare, by mutual-aid or self-help. The report of the Select Committee on Import Duties of 1840 stated the conviction that 'the best service that could be rendered to the industrious classes of the community, would be to extend the field for labour, and of demand for labour by an extension of our commerce'.[195] In 1842 Peel, in his budget speech, spoke of the 'real way in which we can benefit the working and manufacturing classes'; and this was 'unquestionably by removing the burden that presses on the springs of manufactures and commerce'.[196] The Anti-Corn Law League, as Brian Harrison has written, 'aimed at relieving poverty in an up-to-date and "scientific" way: provident and respectable working men, once freed from the Corn Laws, would stand on their own feet'.[197] In repealing the Corn Laws in 1846, Peel did not see himself as surrendering to the pressure of the League; but he would not have disagreed with the sentiments ascribed to it by Harrison. 'Act thus,' Peel told the Commons, 'and you will provide an additional guarantee for the continued contentment, and happiness, and well-being of the great body of the people. Act

---

[194] 'Laissez Faire and State Intervention in Nineteenth Century Britain' (*Jour. Ec. Hist.*, viii (1948), suppl.), 65–6.

[195] Quoted in G. M. Young and W. D. Handcock (eds.), *English Historical Documents, 1833–1874* (London: Eyre & Spottiswoode, 1956), 422.

[196] Complete speech quoted ibid. 422–38; quotation from p. 433.

[197] *Peaceable Kingdom*, 222.

thus, and you will have done whatever human sagacity can do for the promotion of commercial prosperity.'[198]

If 'provident and respectable working men' had to be 'freed' from the Corn Laws, they also had to be disengaged from other hindrances which impeded their progress. One such was dirt and disease; and much of the impetus for the public health movement—as for that which, as has been seen, prompted philanthropic endeavour in this area—lay in the desire to remove impediments to self-improvement and productive capacity. Another area lay in the poor laws; and here, too, the state adopted an enabling role. The concluding paragraph of the Report of the Royal Commission on the Poor Laws in 1834 commented that the measures proposed were intended to 'produce rather negative than positive effects'. These effects were to be achieved by the discontinuance of granting outdoor relief from the poor rate on what were regarded as the very lax and generous lines sanctioned by the Speenhamland system. In its place, there was to be a general implementation of a stricter system—already introduced by some parishes—whereby relief was to be available only inside a workhouse on terms which were less attractive than those offered by independent employment. These measures would, as the Report put it, 'remove the debasing influences to which a large portion of the Labouring Population is now subject', and 'afford a freer scope to the operation of every instrument which may be employed for elevating the intellectual and moral condition of the poorer classes'.[199]

One of these instruments was the mutual-aid society. An assistant commissioner who investigated the unreformed poor law in south-east England wrote that in parishes where the poor laws were most strictly administered, 'the contributions of labourers to savings banks and benefit societies are most numerous'. On the other hand, where 'the most lavish payments are made from the rates, these establishments are neglected'.[200] Henry Bishop found that at Uley in Gloucestershire, a strict system of relief had been in force since 1830. This had had a wholesome effect, since,

---

[198] Complete speech quoted in Young and Handcock, *English Historical Documents*, 451–65; quotation from p. 465.

[199] *Report on the Administration and Practical Operation of the Poor Laws* (Parliamentary Papers, 1834, XXVII), 362.

[200] Quoted in Gosden, *Friendly Societies*, 201.

as he wrote, 'the pauperism existing previously to 1830 had so completely destroyed all providence that the friendly societies of the place had completely sunk under it'.[201]

Further, when attempts were made to introduce a stricter system on a national scale after 1834, there was an increase in the number of friendly societies. The number of lodges in Manchester Unity showed a notable increase. Between 1825 and 1835, 455 lodges were founded; between 1835 and 1845, the number of new lodges was 1,470.[202] The Poor Law Commissioners, appointed to administer the legislation of 1834, complimented themselves on such results; and in 1836 Edwin Chadwick, Secretary to the Commissioners, republished his earlier *Essays on the Means of Insurance* in booklet form, explaining that he was doing this because of the increase in the number of friendly societies encouraged by the administration of the Act of 1834. Certainly, the friendly societies themselves emphasized the gulf which lay between their activities and the receipt of poor relief on the revised terms, which were seen to be degrading and demoralizing. Charles Hardwick of Manchester Unity, in stressing that the function of the friendly societies was to encourage independence, was at pains to add that they were not 'to form a stepping stone, to aid the industrious and provident to pass from the active and manly independence of their days of vigorous labour to the degraded pauperism of the workhouse'. Their function was, indeed, the reverse. The growth of the friendly society among the 'sound-hearted' was the 'honourable substitute for the parish relief of the semi-slave by Act of Parliament'.[203]

Agencies within the voluntary sector were, then, to be encouraged in their activities by an enabling state. Moreover, the state was concerned to take this further by assisting such agencies to work efficiently and effectively. Here, there were parallels with banking and company legislation, passed in the 1840s and 1850s, which sought to ensure that industrial and commercial activity and entrepreneurship rested on a secure financial and legal basis. Relations between the state and friendly societies were initially somewhat ambivalent on both sides. At first the governing classes viewed such societies with unease as potentially subversive organizations, but later they regarded them as having a

---

[201] Quoted ibid. 202.   [202] Gosden, *Self-Help*, 69–70.   [203] Ibid.

certain use and value. Participation in well-managed and stable institutions might integrate the working classes into society, and distract them from radical and reforming activity. On their side, friendly societies were often suspicious of the state as an outside agency, which might well be hostile to their activities. On the other hand, there could be advantages in coming within a system of registration, which brought with it a measure of legal protection against fraudulent officials, and the opening up of favourable opportunities for the investment of funds.

This rather uneasy relationship evolved through a considerable volume and variety of legislation, dating, in fact, from 1793 and stretching through the first three-quarters of the nineteenth century. The Acts offered friendly societies the option of registering with an agent—initially a local one and later a central agent, who in 1846 was formally designated registrar of Friendly Societies, although this office had existed in embryonic form since 1829. The holder of the office, from its inception until his death in 1870, was John Tidd Pratt. He devoted great energy to regularizing and tidying up friendly societies, and kept a sharp eye open for such practices as compulsory levies on members for drink. His actual powers were limited, but his influence was considerable. After the investigations of the Royal Commission on Friendly Societies between 1871 and 1874, in 1875 a further Act was passed which established the office of chief registrar—with assistant registrars for Scotland and Ireland. The powers of the chief registrar were still limited in scope, although wider than those of his predecessor; and the overall intention of the Act was to improve the reliability of the registered societies as insurers by the introduction of more efficient financial arrangements. It was followed by a considerable increase in the membership of registered friendly societies, and in the funds available per member.[204]

Thus friendly societies remained within the voluntary sector; but many of them came increasingly within the ambit of a state agency which was designed to enable them to work effectively. The same may broadly be said of many other mutual-aid organizations, such as cooperatives, trade unions, building societies, and savings banks.[205] The pattern was not, however, the same in

[204] Ibid. 63–76.   [205] Ibid. 147–64, 190–5, 213 ff.

every area. The relationship between the state and trade unions was adversarial and hostile for a longer period than that between the state and the friendly societies—or, indeed, the co-operatives—and did not reach a resolution till the 1870s. The relationship between the state and the savings banks was closer even than that between the state and the friendly societies. The move towards a more centralized form of supervision was taken in 1828, with the appointment by the National Debt Office of a barrister to certify savings banks—the barrister being the ubiquitous Tidd Pratt. Further, in 1861 the state, acting in response to the deficiencies in the arrangements for savings banks which were evident in the 1850s, established the Post Office Savings Bank in order to encourage thrift.

The details of legislation affecting mutual-aid organizations therefore differed—although in many cases there was an approximation to the friendly-society legislation. Behind such differences, however, the principle of a state which enabled and encouraged such voluntary organizations to work effectively was evident; and Tidd Pratt was succinctly, and accurately, described as 'Minister for Self-Help to the industrious classes'. The Fourth Report of the Royal Commission on Friendly Societies, issued in 1874, commented that the state

has to a great extent taken upon itself the task of encouraging, aiding and supervising a work of such high national importance as that of assisting the working classes of this country to provide for their own wants in times of need, sickness, or other casualty, by savings made in times of health and strength, without either throwing themselves upon the system of state aid afforded by the poor laws, or becoming dependent on individual charity.[206]

Here, indeed, was a very clear statement of the role of the state in enabling voluntaristic mutual-aid and self-help methods, which would bring about 'help from within'.

The same pattern may be seen in the charitable aspect of the voluntary sector; for here, too, the state came to play a role designed to ensure that it worked effectively.[207] The misuse and

---

[206] *Royal Commission on Friendly and Benefit Building Societies: Fourth Report*, pt. 1, par. 841.

[207] See Tompson, *Charity Commission*, 78–226; Owen, *English Philanthropy*, 182 ff.

misdirection of endowed charitable trusts had provoked the criticism of reformers since the late eighteenth century and the early nineteenth, and recourse to Chancery for remedy offered a prolonged, expensive, and uncertain path. Henry Brougham turned his attention to the issue in the 1810s; as an enthusiast for education, he felt that a vast number of endowed charities could be reorganized in such a way as to provide educational opportunity for a larger section of the community. His motion in 1816 for the appointment of a select committee on the education of the poor in the metropolis was to lead, by various tortuous twists, to the establishment of the Charity Commission in 1818; and, in a series of four incarnations, the Committee was to last until 1837 and to produce a veritable Domesday survey of charities in almost forty volumes of report and evidence.

Here again, then, an agency of the state—which behaved almost like an office of government, even if it was not such—investigated and reported on the philanthropic and benevolent acts of individuals: acts which might have been perverted from their original purpose, or had outlived their usefulness. Little, it is true, resulted from its efforts—or from its recommendations, which echoed those of a select committee of 1835 to the effect that a permanent board should be established and entrusted with supervisory powers over charitable endowments. It took further years of reforming effort—and, indeed, another Commission, appointed in 1849—before the Charitable Trusts Act of 1853 set up a Board of Commissioners as a form of permanent inquiry. Initially its powers were largely investigatory; and it was not until a further Act of 1860 was passed that it was given powers which went beyond this. Thus the Act of 1860 required that charitable trusts which had become defunct could—under the doctrine of cy pres—be applied only to purposes which came as near as possible to the purpose specified by the original donor.

There remained many limitations on the exercise of the Commissioners' powers. It has been noted by Richard Tompson that 'the vision of a survey which would eradicate abuse and point to a reform solution proved to be an apparition'.[208] It is also true—as has been seen—that the endowed charitable trust, even if it

---

[208] *Charity Commission*, 216. Educational Trusts were exempted from the doctrine of cy pres in 1869 but the great majority of trusts were restricted by it. See below, pp. 289–91, for further consideration of the point.

remained an important expression of philanthropic activity, was becoming less common than the organized donor group or philanthropic society, over which the Commissioners had no control. Nevertheless, the office of the central Commission provided a more accessible, and less expensive, place of recourse for those involved in charitable trusts than the Chancery Judges or the County and District Courts; and the doctrine of cy pres was important for the future. Here, too, the state adopted a role designed to enable this aspect of the voluntary sector to function more adequately.

Education is another area which provides evidence for the argument that much of the legislation of the period from 1830 to 1880 was intended to enable voluntary agencies to work effectively. In 1833 the Whig Chancellor, Althorp, provided £20,000 to be spent on school buildings, to be directed through the two religious voluntary school societies, the National Society and the British and Foreign School Society. This began a long process whereby the state extended its operations through a central government department, an inspectorate, and a teacher-training system. In 1870 the Education Act established a national system of elementary education in England and Wales; it was followed the next year by a similar Act for Scotland. This, however, simply supplemented voluntary educational initiatives already in existence; it did not seek to replace them, and they continued to exist, with increased grants.

A somewhat similar pattern was evident in matters of juvenile crime. In 1854 the Youthful Offenders Act gave authority for the establishment of reformatory schools by private philanthropic groups; and the courts or justices might send offenders under sixteen there for a period of years, the cost of their detention being borne by the Treasury. The same procedures came about in Scotland under legislation passed in 1854. This gave legal status to ragged schools and reformatories, to which courts might send young offenders rather than to prison. Treasury money was provided; but the institutions might still collect subscriptions and were managed by governors, as they had been when they were still purely voluntary institutions.[209]

Thus if the state grew, it often did so in a way designed to

---

[209] Checkland, *Philanthropy*, 251.

enable voluntary initiatives to flourish and function effectively. This was much in the spirit of the precepts of J. S. Mill, who in 1848 wrote that 'a people among whom there is no habit of spontaneous action for a collective interest . . . have their faculties only half-developed; their education is defective in one of its most important branches'. It followed, then, that government 'should not only leave as far as possible to their own faculties the conduct of whatever concerns themselves alone, but should suffer them, or rather encourage them, to manage as many as possible of their joint concerns by voluntary operation'.[210] This was not a recipe for voluntarism alone, but, where need be, for voluntarism encouraged and enabled by the state.

The practice of permissive legislation fitted well into this pattern. As John Prest has put it, it 'offered a happy medium between central control and local initiative'.[211] Public (General) Acts initiated by central government posed the problem of finding an agency to carry them out; Private Acts, where the initiative came from a locality, private body, or even private individual, tended to be very expensive. The Permissive, or Adoptive, Act was, indeed, a Public (General) Act; but it was left to the localities to adopt it if they wished to do so. This saved central government from finding an appropriate enforcement agency, and it enabled localities to undertake particular tasks, such as urban improvement, without having to go to the expense of private bill procedures. The absence of central compulsion, and the discretion left to individual initiative, were an excellent match with the emphasis on participation and the insistence on freedom of action, so characteristic of voluntarism. The neglect by historians of permissive legislation until the publication of Prest's study runs, in a sense, parallel to the neglect of voluntary initiatives and agencies; for not only have statutory agencies been more fully studied than voluntary ones, but it has been *centralized* statutory agencies which have attracted attention. 'For many years, now,' Prest writes, 'it has been fashionable to look at these questions from a centralist point of view.' He is much concerned 'to carry the argument beyond the rim of the Whitehall office desk and

---

[210] *Principles of Political Economy with Some of their Applications to Social Philosophy*, 2 vols. (London: Longmans, Green, Reader & Dyer, 1878), ii. 570–1.

[211] *Liberty and Locality: Parliament, Permissive Legislation and Ratepayers' Democracies in the Mid-Nineteenth Century* (Oxford: Clarendon Press, 1990), 7.

find out what happened on the ground'.[212] Again, that statement might well apply to the aims of the student of voluntarism.

Nevertheless, if much legislation in the period from 1830 to 1880 was designed to enable and reinforce voluntarist practice, this cannot be said of all of it. The *Pall Mall Gazette* of 1869 made this point when it commented that in the legislation which Parliament had passed—resulting in 'far more government than ever was before'—much more had been effected 'than the mere removal of . . . obstructions'.[213] In addition, indeed, to adopting an enabling role, the state undertook a paternalistic and protective function. Paternalists and philanthropists did not always remain satisfied that benevolent and charitable behaviour could safely be left within the voluntary sector. Freedom to behave in such a manner implied freedom not to do so; and in that event, many of them felt, legislation was necessary to ensure that the weak and vulnerable should be protected. Wordsworth wrote that the state should act 'in loco parentis';[214] and in 1830 Southey urged the need for a 'patriarchal, that is to say a parental government',[215] and among the tasks which such a government would undertake, he included the financing of emigration, the promotion of colonization, and the regulation of factories. Michael Sadler called for a 'protective state'; and he was active in supporting the demands for a ten-hour day in factories for children and young persons under eighteen. The cause was taken up after Sadler's defeat at the general election of 1832 by Shaftesbury, who firmly believed in the need for the state to interfere to protect the weak and helpless, who might be overtaken and downtrodden by an unmitigated pursuit of individual gain and profit in the race for industrial growth. In 1843 he told the Commons that 'we owe to the poor of our land a weighty debt. We call them improvident and immoral, and many of them are so; but that improvidence and that immorality are the results, in a great measure, of our neglect . . .'[216]

Such neglect could—and should—be made up by voluntary acts of paternalism and philanthropy; but since these could not always be relied upon, Shaftesbury felt that legislation was necessary. Laws, he said in 1840, should assume the 'proper

[212] Ibid. 46.   [213] Evans (ed.), *Social Policy*, 119.
[214] Roberts, *Paternalism*, 45.   [215] Ibid.   [216] *Speeches*, 86.

functions of protecting the helpless'. He was often to call for the 'vigorous interposition of the legislature' in matters of social policy; and this was echoed elsewhere in the philanthropic world. In 1853 the Ragged School Union stated in its Annual Report that the system of *laissez-faire*—or, as it put it, the 'let alone system'— especially as regards outcasts and the neglected youth of both sexes, was disgraceful to the country and its rulers and would bring a curse on the nation if a remedy were not sought and applied. In 1854 it stated that 'a Christian Government should act the part of a Christian parent and care for its own neglected children'.[217]

Individual paternalists and philanthropists, indeed, played a significant—if by no means exclusive—role in the period from 1830 to 1880 in promoting legislation which was of a protective nature. It was most clearly evident in the large body of legislation which had to do with the regulation of hours and conditions in workplaces, such as factories and mines, or, to give another example, with the regulation and supervision of lunatic asylums.

Here the role of the state was not to enable, but to restrict; not to encourage, but to curtail. And yet it is important to realize that such a role was exercised on behalf of vulnerable groups, who could not be expected to practise mutual-aid or self-help in their own interests. Thus, once again, it tended to complement voluntary initiatives rather than to contradict them. Just as paternalists and philanthropists sought to increase the power of self-help by their efforts in the voluntary sector, so too they wished to use the state—where this was necessary—to achieve the same end. Shaftesbury wrote in 1872 that 'Laws may remove obstacles and sympathisers may give aid, but it is by personal conduct, by sobriety, by order, by honesty, by perseverance, that a man, under God, becomes "the architect of his own fortunes".'[218] Towards the end of his life, indeed, Shaftesbury felt that state interference was in danger of being taken too far. In an article entitled 'The Mischief of State Aid', he wrote: 'Hitherto we have done too little; there is now a fear that in some respects we may do too much . . . It is a melancholy system that tends to debase a large mass of people to the condition of a nursery, where the children look to

[217] *Ragged School Union Magazine*, 1853, 1854.
[218] Quoted in Finlayson, *Shaftesbury*, 410.

the father and mother and do nothing for themselves.'[219] Thus even those who promoted a paternalistic state did not wish that state to undermine individual initiative and to induce a sense of dependency.

Thus what has been called the 'growing reality'[220] of the state cannot be studied in isolation; for it took place within the parameters of voluntarist agencies. The state remained small; it was a minimal and localized state, designed to construct the framework within which individual effort and voluntary and local initiatives could go forward, and to provide safeguards only for those who could not indulge in such pursuits and remained vulnerable. The state also grew within the boundaries of voluntarist assumptions. As in implementation, so in ideology, there was a process of mutual reinforcement, characterized by a common dislike of indiscriminate relief, which carried the danger that the poor would be turned into paupers, dependent on 'help from without', from whatever source it came. Thus in 1853 a reviewer of Sampson Low's survey of London charities wrote critically of what he regarded as the profusion of both private and public provision:

The charities of England in extent, variety, and amount, are something perfectly stupendous. They have long been so. There is scarcely a conceivable form of human want or wretchedness for which a special and appropriate provision has not been made . . . If people are destitute, they are lodged, clothed and fed at the cost of the public by a compulsory Poor-Law. If they meet with accidents, hospitals and infirmaries without number are open to receive them. If they are afflicted with disease, the medical charities are endless and diversified, and easily accessible . . . If maternity comes and finds them unprovided and lying-in-hospitals and cognate institutions swarm around them . . . From the cradle to the grave, they are surrounded with importunate benevolence.[221]

Such benevolence, from voluntary or statutory quarters, could easily turn the deserving poor into undeserving and feckless paupers, who made it their business to depend on others for the livelihood which they should have sought for themselves. Here again there was common ground between voluntarists and

---

[219] Quoted ibid. 590.
[220] Roger Prouty, *The Transformation of the Board of Trade, 1830–1855: A Study of Administrative Reorganisation in the Heyday of Laissez Faire* (London: Heinemann, 1987), 1.   [221] *Poverty in the Victorian Age*, iii. 65.

statists. The social ramifications of a further publication of 1859 were important in this respect; for just as Smiles's *Self-Help* and Mill's *On Liberty* were published in 1859, so too was Darwin's *Origin of Species*. Advocates of Social Darwinism were to come to regard undeserving and maintained paupers as virtually a sub-standard, unfit 'race apart', which posed a threat to the fit and deserving, with whom the future good of the country lay, and in whom it was essential to invest for the sake of that future good.[222] The undeserving had to be separated from the deserving, lest they infect them and pull them down to their level. The deserv-ing should be encouraged to thrive—and here the propertied classes were anxious to promote the citizenship of contribution through voluntary agencies, so that the poor might be safely incorporated within the political nation as citizens by entitlement.

Here too, then, there was a similarity between voluntary-statutory relationships and the relationship which has already been noted between providence and philanthropy within the voluntary sector. In both there was the search for common ground between 'help from without' and 'help from within', which dis-pensed the former without endangering the latter. The best ex-ample of this common search is provided by the way in which *both* charity *and* poor law were 'reformed' in 1869. The rationale behind the formation of the Charity Organisation Society has already been explained as being to tidy up the implementation of charity and to ensure that it was restricted to encouraging self-help. It was matched on the statutory side by a Minute of the Poor Law Board, also of 1869—the Goschen Minute—which attempted to regularize the position over poor relief and ensure that the principles of 1834 would be adhered to. It condemned lax and over-generous practices of poor relief, which, it felt, had crept back over recent years, and stressed the need for the deter-rent workhouse. Voluntary and statutory sectors were, therefore, working on complementary lines. Well-organized charity would assist the deserving poor by encouraging them to maintain themselves; a strict poor law would deal with the undeserving poor in such a way as to try to jolt them into the ranks of the deserving.

---

[222] See Winfried Baumgart, *Imperialism: The Idea and Reality of British and French Colonial Expansion, 1880–1914* (Oxford: Oxford University Press, 1982), 82–90.

There was, then, a certain convergence in social policy and practice around reliance on the formula of well-regulated voluntarism and a minimal, localized state. In many respects, all political parties, Whig/Liberal and Tory, adhered to this formula. It came, in fact, closer to the Whig/Liberal than to the Tory side; as has been seen, Tories such as Shaftesbury favoured a measure of state paternalism, although the paternalistic strain within Toryism was more often a matter of individual than of official opinion. Whig/Liberal and Tory parties in the period as a whole shared much common ground in applauding and upholding the efforts and agencies of the provident and self-reliant individual, pursuing economic independence—and the achievement of the citizenship of entitlement to political rights—untrammelled by over-active charities or an over-protective state. Equally, this convergence could be traced at the local level; indeed, it was there that it was most plainly evident, since local voluntary and statutory agencies fitted well with each other. As Norman McCord has put it:

It would . . . give a misleading impression to suppose that the official Poor Law machinery and unofficial philanthropy existed in two different spheres in the nineteenth century . . . Those who sat as Poor Law guardians would very often be the same people who sat on the committee who controlled schools, hospitals and dispensaries, and the other varied forms of charitable organisations; they would also be among those who took the lead in sponsoring local voluntary efforts in times of disaster or communal celebration.[223]

Thus Joseph Sturge, voluntarist as he was, became a member of Birmingham town council; and many local businessmen were prominent in local charitable pursuits, which were almost an extension of the structure of their firms, and in municipal government. If, moreover, some voluntarists came to appreciate the advantages which convergence with a more centralized state could bring them in terms of legal protection and financial resources, they wanted to do so on terms which suited them, and allowed them to retain their independence. Here again, outside interference had to be adapted to, or seen to be consistent with, their own purposes and kept within their own control.

---

[223] 'The Poor Law and Philanthropy', in Derek Fraser (ed.), *The New Poor Law in the Nineteenth Century* (London: Macmillan, 1976), 100.

The other side of this convergence between voluntarism and a minimal, localized state was evident in a common resistance to outside interference which threatened their ability to act independently. The enabling state may, indeed, have been intended to provide opportunities for the various sectors of voluntarism to thrive; but the process of centralization which could accompany this process often ran into considerable resistance from advocates of voluntarism—and of local government. The Poor Law Commission of 1834 was disliked by voluntarists and adherents of local government alike for its centralizing tendencies. There was a spread of opinion in this respect over many political viewpoints. From a Tory viewpoint, Disraeli disliked the threat which the new poor law offered to the parochial jurisdiction of England; he argued that the great achievements of the English people lay in the local character of government.[224] The Radical Thomas Wakely likewise regarded the centralized poor law as a gross interference with local government.[225]

In the following decade, the appointment of the General Board of Health in 1848 represented, from the point of view of the Whig government, an effort to bring about a measure of central intervention to rationalize the multiplicity of local authorities— which mirrored the similar multiplicity in the sectors of voluntarism. It ran into vigorous opposition for its centralizing tendencies; it was represented as a violation of what Toulmin Smith called the 'great World Tree of Freedom': local government.[226] The Act also encountered resistance from local interests such as vestries and water companies in London; and the decision to abolish the Board was taken in 1854, although it was not formally abolished until 1858.

Thereafter, the progress of the state in public health matters was marked by a more delicate and sensitive touch on the part of central government than had been evident in the 1840s and 1850s. When a Sanitary Commission was appointed in 1869 to look into the whole question of the public health legislation which had been passed in the previous two decades, it came to the conclusion that there was a great need for a process of simplification

---

[224] See William C. Lubenow, *The Politics of Government Growth: Early Victorian Attitudes toward State Intervention, 1833–1848* (Newton Abbot: David & Charles, 1971), 51.
[225] Ibid. 49.   [226] Ibid. 94.

and unification. Nevertheless, reporting in 1871, it clearly recalled the experience of the past when it stated that a new central authority 'must steer clear of the rock on which the General Board of Health was wrecked; so completely is self-government the habit and quality of Englishmen that the country would resent any Central Authority undertaking the duties of the local executive'.[227]

Thus the enabling state could shade into the regulatory state; and where this happened tensions and conflicts with local voluntary bodies could easily arise. As has been seen, the system of registration for friendly societies provided advantages to those societies which decided to register; but it also carried with it a threat to independence and separate identity, and most societies remained unregistered. The Royal Commission on Friendly Societies of 1871–4 admitted that the balance between state and voluntary initiatives was a 'delicate one'.[228] It is also noteworthy in this respect that the working-class venture schools—or dame schools—displayed a remarkable tenacity, despite the fact that they were not well regarded by the increasingly professional educational establishments of the Victorian period. In Bristol in 1875, 4,280 pupils still attended such schools; this was 24 per cent of the number who attended the state elementary schools, established under the Education Act of 1870.

Such attachment to voluntarist initiatives could, indeed, widen into a distrust of the state on the part of those who perceived themselves to be at the receiving end of its attentions, even if these seemed to be well intentioned. The promotion of savings banks was, as has been seen, intended to encourage thrift and independence. Nevertheless, in 1833 Thomas Attwood criticized savings banks 'as a sort of screw in the hands of the Government to fix down the working classes to its system';[229] and in 1839 John Francis Bray complained that, through savings banks, the government 'holds . . . so many golden chains to bind men to it and to the existing order of things'.[230] There was a distinct feeling that the Registrar of Friendly Societies was too close to the government

---

[227] Quoted in Anthony S. Wohl, *Endangered Lives: Public Health in Victorian Britain* (London: J. M. Dent, 1983), 159.

[228] *Royal Commission on Friendly and Benefit Building Societies: Fourth Report*, pt. 1, par. 840.

[229] Quoted in Supple, 'Legislation and Virtue', 224.   [230] Quoted ibid.

for comfort; and thus his recommendations were often looked upon with some suspicion by friendly societies. The Chartists likewise regarded the centralized and directive state with mistrust:

There is little doubt that we should all enjoy better health if the State obliged us to go to bed at ten o'clock and to arise at six; but we believe that there are few who would care for such a life, however healthy, under such restrictions. The liberty of a nation is in proportion to the unfrequency of the interference of the State. Every interference of the State, which is not absolutely necessary, is a palpable act of tyranny.[231]

Such an attitude among the working classes is well worth noting.

Thus the mechanisms used by the enabling state were often unwelcome, and regarded with suspicion if they involved central direction, and were felt to entrench on 'the liberty of a nation'. Similar fears were expressed over education by voluntary groups of a philanthropic nature. The granting of subsidies to church-based voluntary schools, as happened in 1833, did, indeed, enable them to do their work more effectively; but there was an outcry when, in 1839, the Whig government proposed that the distribution of an increased grant of £30,000 would be supervised by school inspectors, answerable to a Committee of Education of the Privy Council. A system of teacher training was to be encouraged by a state Normal School on non-sectarian lines. The Church of England vigorously protested against the secular control which these proposals embodied; and the bishops encouraged the National Society to refuse the grant. The ecclesiastical outcry proved too strong for the Whigs, who dropped the proposal for a Normal School in favour of a grant of £10,000 to the religious school societies to assist them in founding their own training colleges. In 1840 a Concordat was reached which proved highly favourable to the Church of England; church authorities gained control of the appointment of inspectors of grant-aided schools, together with the right, shared with the Privy Council, to receive their reports. Here, indeed, the Church of England secured a considerable victory; and the Nonconformist churches became ever more deeply suspicious of a 'state' system which seemed to be dominated by the Anglican Church.

---

[231] Quoted from the *Chartist* in F. C. Mather (ed.), *Chartism and Society: An Anthology of Documents* (London: Bell & Hyman, 1980), 85.

Voluntarism, then, could prove to be immensely strong and resistant to state interference, even when that interference was designed to enable it to perform its duties; and strongly held denominational positions made it extremely difficult to construct a national state system of education. The Education Act of 1870, designed as it was simply to fill gaps left by the voluntary societies in primary education, was to be accompanied by immense denominational rivalry, as voluntarists feared that an unacceptable variety of religion would be taught in the state schools— or, possibly, no meaningful religion at all. Shaftesbury, for all his willingness to accept a measure of state control in many areas, much preferred ragged schools, which taught religion, to state schools, which in his view taught little or none.[232]

In the activities of the paternalistic state, too, central regulation could be resisted—even if that regulation were exercised on behalf of persons who could not be expected to exercise self-help. Those who wanted the protection of the state to be extended to women and children in factories disliked the centralization represented by the inspectors who were appointed under the Factory Act of 1833 to ensure that the legislation was enforced. They were regarded by such noted advocates of the ten-hour movement as Fielden and Oastler as government spies. Paradoxically, even paternalistic mill owners, such as Samuel Greg, were fined for violating the Act of 1833. Henry Ashworth admitted that he made children work illegal hours, and there were instances of children at Salt's mill beginning work below the legal age. Some factory owners, therefore, wished to be paternalistic on their own terms, not those of the state. Individual paternalists were often particularly attached to local institutions. 'If there is an excellence in the English constitution,' said Richard Oastler, 'it is that it leaves the inhabitants of every locality to manage its own affairs'.[233] Many paternalists felt much more at home in a locality which embraced private, rather than public, agencies. Landowners, ministers of religion, schoolmasters, employers: they were much more acceptable agents than those of a centralized statutory body, with its overtones of interference, compulsion, officialdom, and expense.

It is worth noting, in this context, that the gross expenditure

---

[232] See Finlayson, *Shaftesbury*, 487–90.   [233] Roberts, *Paternalism*, 39.

on poor relief in England and Wales between 1850 and 1880 varied between £4,900 in 1852 and £8,000 in 1872 and again in 1880. This, as Geoffrey Best has commented, was 'certainly less than the amount annually expended by charities'—and possibly 'less than the amount annually subscribed by individuals to charities'.[234] This point provides a good guide to the relative weight which contemporaries placed on voluntary and statutory relief—although it must be said that comparisons of this kind present difficulties, since charities included missionary and educational activities, which were not the concern of the poor law; it was not until later in the period that *some* workhouses—but by no means all—did provide industrial training.

Contemporary solutions to social problems were, therefore, seen to lie in voluntary and local initiative rather than in statutory and centralized agencies. As has been seen, the voluntary sector could not have a blueprint imposed upon it; and nor, indeed, could the informal sector. Such a blueprint was also entirely impracticable for the commercial sector, driven, as it was, by competition and the search for profit. Equally, it is important to appreciate that the statutory sector, if potentially more uniform, was itself subject to local variation. The reformed system of poor law after 1834 was by no means uniformly applied. There were areas—such as Bedfordshire—where eagerness was shown in implementing the principle of 'less eligibility' after 1834; but what have been called 'local initiative and decision-making'[235] remained very important, and these often had to take place in the context of considerable resistance to the implementation of curbing outdoor relief. This was the more marked in conditions of economic difficulty, which made recourse to the poor law more frequent, and the strict application of the workhouse test very difficult to operate. Such was the situation in the later 1830s and early 1840s; and in such circumstances, the application of the Outdoor Labour Test of 1844 attempted to preserve the principles of the 1834 Report; but even this was implemented in only a minority of parishes.

Further, the implementation of the principle of less eligibility

---

[234] *Mid-Victorian Britain*, 140. See also Morris, *Class, Sect and Party*, 204–28.

[235] Anthony Brundage, *The Making of the New Poor Law: The Politics of Inquiry, Enactment and Implementation, 1832–39* (London: Hutchinson, 1978), 105–44, gives a full consideration of this point.

inside the workhouse varied from place to place. There was, indeed, always an ambivalence in poor law administration. The plans of the central commissioners showed an awareness of the particular needs of paupers; and thus, in the large model workhouses which were projected, there was to be internal classification according to sex, age, and condition. Diets were also prescribed, taking account of local eating habits. Yet, if the principle of less eligibility were to be sustained, there had to be hardships which acted as a deterrent to entering the workhouse or remaining in it; and it was difficult to reconcile the building of large, new, and spacious workhouses and proper classification into wards with the saving of ratepayers' money.

The execution of the central plans showed a similar ambivalence and variety. It is certainly true that a deterrent regime—designed to remind paupers that they were maintained at the expense of others, and to encourage them to leave the workhouse—was often applied. This may have been related to—and dictated by—the patterns and routines of an institutionalized life, which applied more widely than to the workhouse alone;[236] and it may also have been particularly associated with vindictive and unsympathetic poor law officials at the local level, and to local ratepayers, insistent on economy. Nevertheless, whatever the reason, strict discipline, pauper uniform, separation of families, refusal of luxuries, and denial of permission to make outside visits were certainly evident. The workhouses at Lambeth, Macclesfield, Fareham, Neath, Swansea—and, most infamously, Andover, where the maltreatment of the inmates caused a public scandal in 1845—were examples of the imposition of severe hardship as the deterrent aspect of relief was stressed.[237]

Yet not all workhouses were of this kind. On special occasions, such as Queen Victoria's coronation in 1838, the inhabitants of workhouses in the North-East were treated to quite lavish supplies of food and drink as they shared in the general festivities associated with the occasion.[238] And there were workhouses, such

[236] M. A. Crowther, *The Workhouse System, 1834–1929: The History of an English Social Institution* (London: Methuen, University Paperback, 1983), 269.

[237] Ursula R. C. Henriques, *Before the Welfare State: Social Administration in Early Industrial Britain* (London, Longman, 1979), 50, 55.

[238] McCord, 'The Poor Law and Philanthropy', 94.

as those at Uckfield and Chatham, which normally provided conditions for their inmates which were not inhumane, but were marked by paternalism and concern. The development of workhouse hospitals and infirmaries indicates a recognition that a 'less eligibility' regime was scarcely appropriate to sick or elderly paupers—just as the distinction between the deserving and undeserving presented problems to charities concerned with physical or mental disability. Both the voluntary and the statutory worlds thus proved difficult to shape according to central direction and control. Centralization was regarded with deep distaste—from whatever source it might come, voluntary or statutory. Mr Podsnap's denunciation of centralization—'No. Never with my consent. Not English'—was by no means an uncharacteristic reaction; and it was one which may be said to have been reinforced by the disasters of the Crimean War. Olive Anderson has written that 'the public disgrace of the state machine during the Crimean War won a decisive victory for a powerful movement which was already gathering momentum— the movement which put backward-looking theories of local self-government and non-interference by the central departments of the state before programmes of public welfare'.[239] Welfare was, indeed, regarded as best achieved, or dispensed, through the various sectors of voluntarism or, if need be, through a complementary *localized* statutory sector.

VII

In many respects, then, the 'welfare system' of the period from 1830 to 1880 did, as Titmuss suggests, 'reflect the dominant cultural and political characteristics' of the society from which it emerged. It was a society which inherited eighteenth-century values of freedom and distrust of a centralized, potentially corrupt, and despotic state; and which laid great store on localism as a counterbalance to such threats. It was also a society undergoing rapid industrialization and economic development, which posed problems calling for mutual effort or charitable endeavour.

---

[239] *A Liberal State at War: English Politics and Economics during the Crimean War* (London: Macmillan, 1967), 182.

Yet it is also true that industrialization offered rich rewards for the free exercise of individual effort; and the cultural and political value attached to such effort was high. Citizenship, in the sense of entitlement to political rights, was to be earned by the acquisition of property; and this could be achieved—at least by some—by the citizenship of contribution, exercised through voluntary agencies.

This dualism was reflected in the 'welfare system'—or 'mixed economy of welfare'—which was developed. Within the voluntary sector, the problems of coping single-handed with social problems resulted in an immense variety of mutual-aid societies; and the equally varied paternalistic and philanthropic side of that sector sought to mitigate the worst aspects of such conditions. And yet both were felt to be compatible with an ideology of self-help; provident mutual-aid might well lead to a more individualized route to welfare, and paternalism and philanthropy were intended to create, and certainly not to impede, the conditions in which providence could be practised. The commercial and informal sectors were also shot through with provision for welfare on an individual or mutual basis. On the statutory side, a degree of paternalism might be exercised to shield those who could not be expected to exercise individual effort and responsibility; but again, this was not intended to interfere with the workings of a state primarily designed to enable individual effort to prosper, and agencies devoted to further such effort to flourish. Central control, with its overtones of compulsion, uniformity, and expense, offended against both the ideology and the implementation of voluntarism and localism.

It can, therefore, be seen that a 'Welfare State' would have been entirely foreign to the 'dominant cultural and political characteristics' of the society of the period; it would have been overprotective in spirit and over-bureaucratic and costly in structure. C. S. Loch wrote that

To shift the responsibility of maintenance from the individual to the State is to sterilise the productive power of the community as a whole, and also to impose on the State . . . so heavy a liability . . . as may greatly hamper, if not also ruin, it. It is also to demoralise the individual. No social system of rewards and punishment . . . will be a substitute for the influence of the social law by which energy, honesty, and ability have their own reward, and failure in these things carries with it its own penalty.[240]

It is a mistake to consider Loch as always representative of the world of voluntarism; as has been indicated, that world could have no official spokesman. But on this occasion his views may be regarded as characteristic of the 'dominant' strain of opinion during the period from 1830 to 1880, from which even those who might have wished to qualify his opinions would not have dissented.

There were, indeed, many strengths and achievements which may be claimed for the proportions of the 'mixed economy' as they prevailed during these years. As has been seen, the implementation of voluntarism in the form of mutual-aid groups performed a useful function for their members, in terms both of welfare provision and of participation in their affairs—bringing with it a sense of identity, and an opportunity for fellowship and conviviality. Equally, those involved in paternalistic and philanthropic activity might find an outlet for abilities which were denied expression elsewhere. Moreover, they dealt with cases of immediate and pressing need, which otherwise might well not have been met. As Morris has written, voluntary societies were 'ideal as a means of innovation, adaptation and experimentation in the face of rapidly changing social demands and relationships'.[241] They had, he further comments, 'a power and flexibility to operate within complexities and respond to the demands of industrial urban society'.[242] Where both mutual-aid and philanthropic organizations exercised selectivity in accepting members or dispensing assistance, this could be defended as a justifiable attempt to protect the interests of their members or clients, and to harbour their resources by countering fraud and imposture. Prochaska has written that 'there was never enough money to go round' for philanthropic activity, and that 'in these circumstances imposters took on a sinister importance. Begging-letter writers, and other ingenious mendicants gave meaning to the term "deserving poor" . . .'[243]

Many of the same points could be made of localist efforts of a

---

[240] Quoted in Woodroofe, *From Charity*, 33.
[241] *Class, Sect and Party*, 168.   [242] Ibid. 197.
[243] *Voluntary Impulse*, 51–2.

statutory kind—linked, as they often were, with voluntaristic agencies of welfare. The poor law, for all the harshness associated with it, was based on the belief that some residual statutory system of support was necessary; and was, in certain areas, implemented with humanity. The growth of civic pride from the 1860s, which incorporated both municipal and voluntary effort, led to considerable environmental improvement, from the installation of drains and pure water supplies to the provision of art galleries. It can also be argued that the efforts of voluntarists and localists brought into prominence and debate many issues which might otherwise have remained hidden, such as the ill-treatment of children; and they put into circulation ideas for improvement. The Manchester Statistical Society, founded in 1833, amassed and disseminated information on social issues, and forged close links with the Manchester and Salford Sanitary Association, founded in 1852. The Association published leaflets on child welfare and had salaried workers. The investigative methods of the Charity Organisation Society, bringing with them the need for careful casework, are often regarded as strikingly modern in professional social work practice.

It would, therefore, be wrong to see the voluntarist-localist system of welfare provision of the period through statist-centralist eyes, and to dismiss it as objectionable and wholly inadequate on the grounds that it did not match up to these 'norms'. And yet, of course, there were limitations, ambiguities, and inconsistencies which must be conceded. The ideology of individualism, with its emphasis on initiative and enterprise, tended to assume that individual character and conduct held the key to the difference between success and failure. Poverty was often explained in terms of personal behaviour—and moralistic and retributive attitudes, evident in many evangelical and utilitarian circles, buttressed such an approach, with its accompanying categories of the deserving and the undeserving poor. This, however, put insufficient emphasis on external circumstances and matters over which the individual had little control. These could be personal circumstances, such as physical or mental disability, which, as has been seen, made nonsense of the distinction between the deserving and the undeserving. Or they could be economic circumstances. When the economy was buoyant, the opportunities for thrifty and provident behaviour among the working classes were greater; and philanthropists and paternalists might exercise their role in such measure as to mitigate residual hardship without eroding self-reliance. Again, in such circumstances, the need for poor relief was diminished, and a deterrent regime might be appropriate to root out the incorrigible pauper. In bad times, however, the pursuit of provident habits became beyond the reach of many among the working classes; and the exercise of too much paternalism and philanthropy always ran the risk of undermining self-help and creating dependency. Equally, in such circumstances, strains were placed on a strict and deterrent poor law.

Thus the individualistic ideology which ran through the voluntarist-localist welfare provision of the period was by no means always appropriate. It was, perhaps, best suited to the situation in mid-century—the 1850s and early 1860s—which have often been seen as a period of economic prosperity for many sections of the community. W. L. Burn has identified this as the 'Age of Equipoise', devoted to

the practice of 'getting on'; it built that art into its system of thought and morality; but (especially from the beginning of the 'sixties) it showed itself sensitive to the anomalies of fortune so created and to the condition of those who never could or never would 'get on'. Its methods for assisting them or disciplining them were under constant discussion but it believed that satisfactory methods could be produced without the sacrifice of certain primary principles. One of these was that people ought to work and maintain themselves by their work and its agents should be residuary and that the initiative should be thrown on the individual, either to 'get on' or to assist those who had failed to do so.[244]

Even in the 'Age of Equipoise', however, it is questionable—as Burn suggests—how far affluence spread down the social scale. Poverty was almost certainly more deep-rooted than some optimistic judgements supposed; poverty which a properly measured and strictly applied formula of providence, paternalism, and philanthropy could not reach, and for which it could supply no answer. In the early 1860s, indeed, the effects of the Lancashire cotton famine, when unemployment affected thousands of factory workers, among whom habits of self-reliance and thrift were deep-rooted, were impossible to accommodate within the formula.

[244] *The Age of Equipoise: A Study of the Mid-Victorian Generation* (London: George Allen & Unwin, 1964), 244.

In these circumstances, the Poor Law Board cooperated closely with charitable efforts and sent a special commissioner, H. B. Farnell, to Lancashire to make common cause with a central relief committee set up to coordinate charitable activities. Thus circumstances could overcome convictions; and the voluntarist-localist welfare agencies were forced to depart from strict adherence to the ideology which their central bodies promoted. It is, perhaps, significant that several attempts had to be made to ensure that the ideology was maintained; the attempt of 1869, manifesting itself in the Goschen Minute and the Charity Organisation Society, was by no means the first. That it was repeated indicates the resilience of the 'primary principles' to which Burn refers; that it needed to be repeated raises the question of how far these principles were sustained in practice. Their future viability remained to be tested.

If the ideology of welfare provision in the period did not always remain unsullied, criticisms may be made of its implementation. Voluntarist and localist agencies could, as has been seen, be patchy, and unreliable: good in some places, bad or non-existent in others. Voluntarism could result in overlapping and uncoordinated activity, and give rise to inefficient and unaccountable administration, which was often open to considerable abuse. This was true of some friendly societies; and charitable and philanthropic societies were not immune from similar defects. Further, the very resistance of voluntarist and localist agencies to central direction and control could prove to be an obstacle to progress. Fierce denominational and sectarian rivalries meant that all schemes for educational reform became entangled in dispute. In public health, localism was often little different from vested interest which refused to move, and was a hindrance to any concerted effort to improve the situation, whether by coordinated voluntary effort or, as more often in this area, by statutory means. Even in the 1860s and 1870s there were powerful local interests which acted as a brake on improvements in public health, such as the Householders' Association in Liverpool.

Further, there were ambiguities and paradoxes common to both voluntarism and statism in this period. Freedom did not come about spontaneously; it had to be created, and this involved interference with freedom and resulted in administrative growth which could further curtail it. Within the voluntary sector, the

Charity Organisation Society was an organized and centralized body—devoted to the achievement of freedom and independence. The enabling and paternalistic state established agencies which, if designed to promote freedom, or to interfere with it to a minimal extent, could easily assume a regulatory and centralized role. A state presence could, indeed, be justified as being perfectly consistent with the creation of circumstances in which free enterprise, whether in economic or in social matters, could properly flourish; but a minimal presence had within it the seeds of a more maximal, quasi-collectivist role. Persistent attempts were made to hold the ambiguities and paradoxes together; but there were often tensions between policy and reality, between convictions and circumstances.

Nevertheless, despite the ambiguities, the balance of the 'mixed economy of welfare' in the period from 1830 to 1880 was, in large measure, weighted towards voluntarism. Through its three sectors, it was extensive in itself, and its ideology and methods of implementation influenced and penetrated the statutory sector. If both favourable and critical historical judgements may be passed on it, it was also seen by contemporaries to have its strengths and weaknesses. Carlyle, Dickens, Ruskin, and Shaftesbury were often critical, but even they tended to write from within what Burn called its 'primary principles'. Charles Masterman wrote in 1901 that considerable progress had been made over the past century—but admitted that 'an amount remains to be done which may well tax the energies of philanthropists and statesmen for years to come'.[245]

That feeling had, indeed, been ever more forcefully expressed since the 1880s. From that decade, the sectors of voluntarism were increasingly open to a series of challenges of an economic, social, political, and intellectual kind, which cast doubt on whether voluntarism could, and should, bear the main weight of the 'mixed economy'. Equally, the complementary role of a minimal, localized state came under critical scrutiny from the same sources. In this context—to which attention will now be given—a new formula had to be devised for the 'mixed economy', and a new point of balance struck; but both formula and balance were to bear many of the marks of earlier principle and practice.

[245] Quoted in Wohl, *Endangered Lives*, 329.

2

Citizen and State, 1880–1914: Challenge, Collectivism, and Convergence

I

In Chapter 1 it was suggested that voluntarism was best suited to a period of relative economic prosperity and social stability, when mutual-aid, self-help, and philanthropic activity, expressed through its various sectors, could make a substantial contribution towards the achievement of social welfare. To regard such features—evident in the 'Age of Equipoise' of mid-nineteenth-century Britain—as suddenly coming to an end towards the close of the century, as 'boom' was replaced by 'depression', is at odds with much historical writing on the subject. The concept of a 'Great Depression', allegedly lasting from 1873 to 1896, is regarded with considerable scepticism by many historians—just, indeed, as is the 'boom' which is often said to have preceded it.[1] Both labels, it may be argued, suggest a unity of economic development within a defined period which, on closer analysis, is hard to justify. As has already been seen, the 'boom' contained within it periods of economic difficulty, such as the mid-1860s; and the 'depression' cannot be said to have witnessed any spectacular slowing up of the economy within the twenty-three years during which it is supposed to have happened. Indeed, such a slowing up was more noticeable in the early twentieth century than it had been before. Thus it may be claimed that there were

<hr>

[1] See R. A. Church, *The Great Victorian Boom, 1850–1873* (London: Macmillan, 1975) and S. B. Saul, *The Myth of the Great Depression, 1873–1896* (London: Macmillan, 1969) for these 2 aspects; more generally, see also John Belcham, *Industrialization and the Working Class: The English Experience, 1750–1900* (Aldershot: Scolar Press, 1990); François Crouzet, *The Victorian Economy*, tr. Anthony Forster (London: Methuen & Co. Ltd., 1982); William P. Kennedy, *Industrial Structure, Capital Markets and the Origins of British Economic Decline* (Cambridge: Cambridge University Press, 1987).

'depressed' periods before 1873, and there were to be such periods later than 1896.

Looked at in this light, there is, then, nothing especially remarkable about the later decades of the century; and, equally, it is possible to exaggerate their significance in social terms. Anxiety about social conditions was not unique to later Victorians. Carlyle's 'Condition of England Question' had gravely troubled the hearts and minds of contemporaries in a much earlier period—and investigations of and comment on, social problems, official and unofficial, statistical and literary, had been carried out in great number at least since the 1830s. There is, as has been seen, a 'pessimistic' interpretation of the effects of industrialization. It was, in fact, on the eve of Queen Victoria's accession in 1836 that the *Westminster Review* stated that 'Poverty in its widest sense, must be understood to mean, the privation of anything tending to physical, moral or intellectual advancement';[2] and early Victorians were acutely aware of its effects on national, as on individual, well-being. The case for self-help, mutual-aid, and philanthropy had already been urged on the grounds that, properly administered, they would not only assist the individual, but also boost the nation's security and wealth; and at the statutory level, Chadwick—to take only one example—urged the necessity for public health partly on the grounds that it would lead to greater national efficiency.

Again, the impression that the later nineteenth and early twentieth centuries witnessed a large-scale deterioration in social conditions is partly a reflection of the fact that this period witnessed an outpouring of social investigation and comment which, in terms of the publicity given to it, eclipsed that of the earlier part of the nineteenth century. Some of this, such as *The Bitter Cry of Outcast London*, published under the auspices of the London Congregational Union in 1883, was, indeed, deliberately sensationalist and propagandist in its portrayal of working-class housing conditions; and the serialization of its more sensational sections in the *Pall Mall Gazette* by W. T. Stead helped to increase the impact of the original publication.[3] General Willam Booth's

---

[2] 'Domestic Arrangements of the Working Classes' (vol. xxv (1836), 450).

[3] See Anthony S. Wohl (ed.), *Andrew Mearns, The Bitter Cry of Outcast London, with Leading Articles from the Pall Mall Gazette of October 1883 and Articles by Lord Salisbury, Joseph Chamberlain, and Forster Crozier* (Leicester: Leicester University Press, 1970).

In Darkest England and the Way Out,[4] published in 1890, drew partly on the problems which the members of the Salvation Army, founded by Booth, had seen in working-class districts; but the presentation was intended to shock contemporaries into a realization that 'as there was a darkest Africa', there was 'also a darkest England'.

Such evidence clearly has to be approached with critical care; and, of course, the same is true of the famous statistical surveys of London, first published in seventeen volumes by Charles Booth between 1889 and 1903,[5] and those of York, compiled by Seebohm Rowntree and published in 1901.[6] Their methodology did, indeed, represent important developments in statistical investigation, but it was not beyond reproach;[7] and, in particular, Rowntree's conclusion that his own work in York, allied to that of Charles Booth in London, suggested that between 25 and 30 per cent of the urban population of Britain were living in poverty, did not rest on any extensive research. Indeed, to be fair to Rowntree, it was put forward as a 'startling probability' and qualified by the phrase 'if this be the fact'.[8]

This point leads to another: that the authors of such differing surveys of social conditions in the later nineteenth and early twentieth centuries did not present such a completely bleak and unrelieved picture of social conditions as is sometimes suggested. It is often claimed that Booth was inspired to set out on his investigations by a desire to discredit an assertion made by H. M. Hyndman in the *Pall Mall Gazette* in 1886 to the effect that 25 per cent of London's population was in distress. It has also been suggested that Booth was driven by his own evidence to adopt conclusions which were even more pessimistic than those of Hyndman. The finding most often associated with Booth's survey, that 30.7 per cent of Londoners were living in poverty, might, indeed, seem to suggest that Hyndman's figure was, if anything, an underestimate. Booth's purpose in launching his great enterprise was, however, more complex than a simple desire to subject Hyndman's conclusions to critical scrutiny; and, of greater

[4] The Salvation Army, 1890; 6th edn., with an introduction by General Erik Wickberg, London: Charles Knight, 1970.
[5] *Life and Labour of the People in London* (3rd edn., London: Macmillan, 1902–3).
[6] *Poverty: A Study of Town Life* (London: Macmillan, 1901, 2nd edn. 1902).
[7] See Karel Williams, *From Pauperism to Poverty* (London: Routledge & Kegan Paul, 1981), 347–8, 356.   [8] *Poverty*, 301.

moment, his figure was an aggregate of various categories which made a distinction between 'poverty', affecting those in Booth's classes D and C, and those in 'want', who were in class B—to whom had to be added a further class, A, incorporating 'occasional labourers, loafers, and semi-criminals'.[9] It must also be remembered that Rowntree's poverty figure, of 27.84 per cent of the total population of York, was reached by adding his categories of 'primary' and 'secondary' poverty together.[10]

These distinctions—often ignored by blanket overall figures—must, then, be kept in mind when assessing the significance of Booth's and Rowntree's findings; and, indeed, Booth himself was much more optimistic about his figures than many commentators, both contemporary and historical, have been. 'Improvement', he wrote in his final volume, 'certainly there has been at every point.'[11] He suggested that temperance was prevalent among those who exercised responsibility in society; and, even among those who did not practise restraint in drinking, there was less drunken rowdiness. There was also 'greater intelligence', even if it was largely devoted to betting; and 'wider interests prevail'—even if they were 'too much absorbed in pleasure-seeking'. Alongside these improvements, Booth concluded, 'the whole level of poverty has been pressed upwards by increasing demands on life—demands which were unthought of forty, thirty, or even twenty years ago'.[12] Booth, in fact, saw the formation of a 'new middle class . . . which will, perhaps, hold the future in its grasp. Its advent seems . . . the great social fact of to-day. Those who constitute this class are the especial product of the push of industry.'[13] Viewed from this vantage point, then, Booth's great survey scarcely belonged to the literature portraying social deprivation with which it is so often linked; and Booth himself commented rather sorrowfully on the fact that his book could be quoted to support points of view with which he disagreed—or which he

[9] E. P. Hennock, 'Poverty and Social Theory in England: The Experience of the Eighteen-Eighties' (*Social History*, i (1976), 73) deals with many of these points. See also the same author's 'The Movement of Poverty: From the Metropolis to the Nation', *Ec. Hist. Rev.*, 2nd ser., xl, 2 (May 1987), 208–27.

[10] See Rowntree, *Poverty*, 86–118.

[11] Albert Fried and Richard M. Elman (eds.), *Charles Booth's London: A Portrait of the Poor at the Turn of the Century, Drawn from his 'Life and Labour of the People in London'* (London: Hutchinson, 1969), 331.

[12] Ibid. 332.   [13] Ibid. 334.

positively disliked. It may also be that the long gap between the publication of his first volume in 1889 and the last, which incorporated his conclusions in 1903, encouraged a selective use of his findings.

Further, if attention is paid to more official inquiries, of which there were many during this period, the situation cannot be presented in terms of unrelieved gloom. The final Report of the Royal Commission on Depression in Trade and Industry in 1886 mentioned the 'immense improvement' in the condition of the working classes over the previous twenty years.[14] The *Report of the Inter-Departmental Committee on Physical Deterioration*, published in 1904, was sceptical of the claims—which had led to its appointment and were in many cases based on Booth's and Rowntree's findings—that there was evidence of progressive national physical degeneration.[15] With regard to such findings, it reprinted as an appendix[16] a Memorandum, drawn up by C. S. Loch of the Charity Organisation Society, which made the point that popular writers and speakers had oversimplified Booth's survey and used his figures 'as in themselves evidence, summary, conclusion, confession, and admission of wholesale want and distress.'[17] Loch also argued that many of the generalizations in the book lent themselves to this treatment; and he felt that in all Booth's 'elaborate classifications, proportions, and adjustments there is an immense liability to error—and the errors cannot be checked in any sufficient manner.'[18] Loch was also critical of Rowntree, arguing that his method was 'extremely speculative', and that the information on which it was based was 'far from sufficient.'[19] Moreover, when Rowntree himself appeared before the Committee as a witness, he was subjected to considerable cross-examination as to how typical his findings in York were of the whole country: 'you would not judge of the whole of England from the conditions of York?', asked the chairman, Almeric Fitzroy, secretary of the Privy Council. 'That would be, surely, unscientific?' Rowntree replied: 'I only said that if they are so. There is just as much reason to suppose that they are as that they

---

[14] Quoted in Donald Read, *England 1868–1914* (London: Longman, 1979), 247.
[15] Parliamentary Papers, 1904, Cd. 2175, pars. 25 and 33.
[16] Ibid. 104–11.   [17] Ibid. 109, par. 28.   [18] Ibid. 108, par. 28.
[19] Ibid. 111, par. 37.

are not'[20]—a response which the chairman, understandably, found less than wholly satisfactory.[21]

Thus the tenor of the Report was not entirely pessimistic. Indeed, on several issues it struck an optimistic note. There had, it argued, been an improvement in living conditions in towns:

> Testimony is almost unanimous as to the improving conditions under which the denizens of large towns are called upon to exist. Rookeries are being dispersed, enclosed yards are being opened out, cellar-dwellings and back-to-back houses are disappearing. One-roomed, two-roomed and three-roomed tenements, with more than two, four and six occupants respectively are diminishing. . . .[22]

The Report also drew attention to the improvements which had taken place in sanitation, water supplies, and public health.[23] In its section on conditions of employment, it likewise stated its view of the 'great amelioration' which had taken place 'in the circumstances of labour.'[24]

Viewed from these varying standpoints, it may, then, be difficult to justify the decision to make a break in 1880, or thereabouts, and to see what followed that date as markedly different from what preceded it in economic or social terms. The old formula of voluntarism, in association with a minimal, localized state, had, indeed, always been shot through with ambiguities and problems; and yet it had received wide support, and had achieved positive results. 'The two chief antidotes to pauperism', wrote T. H. S. Escott in 1879, 'are the organisation of voluntary help and the organisation of thrift.'[25] It might well seem that this primary reliance on voluntarism would remain unscathed in the years to come. This is a point which is worth bearing in mind—and to which further attention will be drawn later.

Nevertheless, there are also grounds for arguing that from the 1880s, voluntarism was operating in harsher economic and social conditions, which presented a stronger challenge to it than earlier periods in the century had done, and when more was expected of it. It is, indeed, true that the blanket term 'Great Depression', applied outside the agricultural sector, is misleading, if it is taken

---

[20] Ibid. 200, Q. 4973.   [21] Ibid. Q. 4974.
[22] Ibid. par. 70.   [23] Ibid. par. 72.   [24] Ibid. par. 140.
[25] *England, its People, Polity and Pursuits*, 2 vols. (London: Cassell, Peter, Galpin & Co., 1881), i. 365.

to mean a general contraction of the economy; industrial output was still growing, and there was no evidence of any notable economic retardation. There was, however, a price decline and a squeeze on profits, and, even if this was not always contained within the 'traditional' period of 1873–96, certain phases in those years were 'depressed': the later 1870s, the mid-1880s, and the mid-1890s. Moreover, while it may be unreasonable to suggest that an economy must maintain its earlier momentum if it is to avoid being labelled 'depressed', there is no doubt that the industrial growth rate did drop by almost a half between the 1860s and the 1890s. There was also a certain lagging behind the growth rates experienced by other, more newly industrialized countries, notably Germany and the USA; and while the significance of this point can also be overemphasized, it was a matter of concern to contemporaries, especially in the 1890s, although it was not absent at an earlier period.

Thus while the 'Great Depression' may have been a 'myth' if judged according to certain economic criteria and taken over a prescribed period, there was evidence of depressed economic activity in the later nineteenth century—and clear evidence, too, of contemporary awareness of economic problems. William Cunningham wrote in 1879 of 'the terrible anxieties of men of business, the harassing struggle against increasing competition'.[26] The appointment of the Royal Commission on Depression in Trade and Industry in 1886 was another such indication of unease, and, even if its conclusions could be optimistic in some respects, its warning of the increased severity of German competition in home and overseas markets did not dispel the anxieties.[27]

Further, an optimistic interpretation of social conditions in these years cannot be accepted without considerable qualification. It is certainly true that, for those in work, standards of living, judged in statistical terms, were rising. The fall in prices and in profit margins, in addition to the import of cheap foreign food, pushed real wages up. Again, environmental improvements—to which, for example, the *Report of the Inter-Departmental Committee* of 1904 pointed—were also evidence of a 'qualitative' improvement in the standard of living. Nevertheless, the economic depressions of

---

[26] Quoted in Read, *England 1868–1914*, 212.   [27] Ibid. 228.

the late 1870s, mid-1880s, and mid-1890s were clearly reflected in the unemployment figures—assembled at the time only for certain unionized and skilled trades. Until 1875 the unemployment rate for the skilled trades remained below 4 per cent, and in a boom year such as 1872 could fall to under 1 per cent. In 1879, however, it rose to 11.4 per cent, and it was 10.2 per cent in 1886. The figures for the great bulk of the working classes, not unionized, must have been considerably higher.[28] There was a greater consciousness of unemployment than there had been in earlier periods of the century; indeed, the term 'unemployed' was first included in the *Oxford English Dictionary* in 1882 and 'unemployment' in 1888. This helped to create a greater awareness of the problem of poverty. William Cunningham in 1879 wrote not only of the 'cares of the rich', but also of the 'miseries of the poor', which, he commented, 'were obvious'.[29]

As in the past, this could be approached from a humanitarian viewpoint, or from a desire to contain a potential threat of disorder—or, again, from an 'efficiency' angle, which suggested that the under-performance of a deprived population was something which the country's economy could not afford. This last approach, moreover, was related with increasing urgency to Britain's economic status at the end of the nineteenth century. Further, in terms of international and military status and security, Britain's position was called in question by the series of setbacks suffered in the Boer War; and this could give rise to doubts about the condition of the people as potential recruits for the army. Thus while the social distress to be found in the later nineteenth century was not new, and comments that the later Victorians were the first to develop a social conscience, or a desire for national efficiency, are inaccurate, it would be true to say that such matters acquired a new urgency in the later part of the century. What was particularly novel was the increased concentration on the need for national efficiency in the light of international developments at a military and economic level. It is, indeed, open to argument whether this phenomenon manifested itself in the 1880s, the decade which historians have often seen as witnessing a waning of the earlier mood of self-confidence and

---

[28] Peter Weiler, *The New Liberalism: Liberal Social Theory in Great Britain 1899–1914* (New York & London: Garland Publishing Inc., 1982), 42.
[29] Quoted in Read, *England, 1868–1914*, 212.

optimism, or in the 1890s, seen by recent historians as a more significant decade.[30] What, however, seems beyond doubt is that the closing years of the century saw the knitting together of a number of strands, leading to a heightened self-questioning and self-criticism on both economic and social matters.

It was in this context that the celebrated investigations of the period were received. A dispassionate reading of them might suggest that social progress was not absent; but the circumstances of the time did not induce a dispassionate reading. Rather, it was their most pessimistic material which was seized upon, and which fuelled yet further pessimism. *The Times* described Booth's survey as 'the grimmest book of the day'.[31] Booth's namesake, William Booth, paid tribute to the work in his own *In Darkest England*.[32] It was published the year after the first volume of Charles Booth's survey came out, and sold 200,000 copies in its first year. Rowntree's survey likewise made a considerable impression—perhaps an even greater impression than Booth's work, owing to the fact that it was relatively brief and more manageable.[33] The journal of the Social Democratic Federation, *Justice*, reprinted Rowntree's conclusions, adding 'all the same the book is for wooden-heads, no other would require it':[34] a remark which well illustrates the point that in many circles the book was regarded as simply reinforcing what was already believed to be self-evidently true. Rowntree's book, it has also been written, inspired 'hundreds of sermons, political treatises and sociological plays and novels'.[35]

Further, if contemporary official reports may be used to present an optimistic interpretation of the social conditions of the period, they can also be cited on the pessimistic side. The *Report of the Inter-Departmental Committee* of 1904 recognized what it called 'acknowledged evils'.[36] These included overcrowding, which, notwithstanding the improvement which was noted, the Report

---

[30] Hennock, 'Poverty and Social Theory', 69, 91.

[31] Hennock (ibid. 79 and n. 48) examines some of the press reaction to Booth's findings. He shows that the *Pall Mall Gazette* commented in 1887 that a paper given by Booth in that year read 'too much like a complacent and comforting bourgeois statement of the situation', but also points out that it 'stood alone in criticising Booth with any severity'.   [32] *In Darkest England*, 21.

[33] See Asa Briggs, *A Study of the Work of Seebohm Rowntree, 1871–1954* (London: Longman, 1961), 30–1.

[34] Quoted ibid. 30.   [35] Ibid. 31.   [36] Par. 426.

admitted to 'stand out most prominent, with its attendant evils of uncleanliness, foul air and bad sanitation'.[37] Despite the improvement in conditions of work brought about by the long-standing factory legislation, there were still 'degenerative agencies' at work, such as long hours, dusty atmosphere, high temperatures; and, especially for young persons, these had harmful physical consequences.[38] The Report also stressed the bad effects created by women working too late into pregnancy, or too soon after childbirth;[39] and it paid particular attention to the lack of supplies of good milk and nourishing food for women and children. The evidence given to the Committee by Dr Alfred Eichholz, an Inspector of Schools since 1898 who had studied medicine at Cambridge and St Bartholomew's Hospital, was reproduced in the Report in edited form—but still at some length.[40] Eichholz made a clear distinction between physical degeneracy on the one hand and inherited retrogressive deterioration on the other. He did not find sufficient evidence to support the existence of the latter; but there was a great deal of evidence of the former, especially in the poorer schools of London and other large towns, where he found poor physique, lack of powers of endurance, and low educational attainment among the pupils. There was, Eichholz conceded, a type 'of child above the lowest even in the poorer districts which were showing an upward tendency'; but in the poorest schools this was still a small percentage. Eichholz singled out Johanna Street Board School in Lambeth as the worst in his experience: there, 94 per cent of the infants and 92 per cent of the older children were below normal physical condition.[41]

Here was yet another source which could be used selectively: to support the sensationalist remarks of *The Bitter Cry* on overcrowding—or to complement the more optimistic sections of Booth. Yet, as was so often the case, it was the more pessimistic aspects of the Report which were given greater prominence. G. R. Searle has commented that the Committee concluded 'in vain' that there was little evidence of a progressive physical deterioration in the population as a whole, 'where standards were

---

[37] Ibid. par. 82.   [38] Ibid. par. 140.
[39] Ibid. par. 251.   [40] Ibid. par. 69.
[41] *Minutes of Evidence Taken before the Inter-Departmental Committee on Physical Deterioration* (Parliamentary Papers, 1904, Cd. 2210), Q. 443.

probably being slowly but steadily raised'.[42] There was a pre-disposition to fasten on the more gloomy aspects of the Report—as on those of all other investigations of the period, whether sensationalist, statistical, or literary. In 1888 H. H. Champion wrote that 'the social condition of the people' was 'attracting an amount of attention in this country which would have been incredible to a man who left England seven or eight years ago, and has ever since been out of reach of English newspapers'. The poor had become 'fashionable'.[43]

They remained 'fashionable' thereafter—especially in the context of the perceived need for national efficiency. In 1908 T. C. Horsfall, a Manchester housing reformer, wrote:

We must remember that already in 1901 we had 77 per cent of our population in towns of considerable size. We must also remember that while we still had a population to a large extent uninjured by town conditions of life, our trade over many parts of the earth met with little dangerous competition, but now when so large a part of our people are enfeebled by the influence of gloomy unwholesome towns, we shall have to struggle everywhere against Germany, whose population has outstripped us in numbers and is far better prepared for the struggle by training both of body and mind than we are. Unless we at once begin at least to protect the health of our people by making the towns in which most of them live, more wholesome for body and mind, we may as well hand over our trade, our colonies, our whole influence in the world, to Germany, without undergoing all the trouble of a struggle in which we condemn ourselves beforehand to certain failure.[44]

The writer may have exaggerated the extent to which, in the past, the population was 'uninjured by town conditions of life'; and, as has been seen, urban problems had been very familiar and well recognized long before he wrote. But Britain's newly perceived international position meant that they were seen in a new and more urgent context. The year after Horsfall wrote, the same points were taken up by another observer of Britain's position—Winston Churchill:

[42] *The Quest for National Efficiency: A Study in British Politics and Political Thought, 1899–1914* (Oxford: Basil Blackwell, 1971), 60–1.
[43] See Weiler, *The New Liberalism*, 43.
[44] Quoted in E. P. Hennock, *British Social Reform and German Precedents: The Case of Social Insurance, 1880–1914* (Oxford: Clarendon Press, 1987), 24.

The greatest danger to the British people is not to be found among the enormous fleets and armies of the European continent ... It is here, close at home, close at hand in the vast growing cities of England and Scotland, and in the dwindling and cramped villages of our denuded countryside. It is here that you will find the seeds of imperial ruin and national decay—the unnatural gap between rich and poor, the divorce of the people from the land, the want of proper training and discipline in our youth, the awful jumbles of an obsolete Poor Law, the constant insecurity in the means of subsistence and employment ... Here are the enemies of Britain. Beware lest they shatter the foundations of her power.[45]

Thus economic and social conditions, taken in conjunction with Britain's international standing, posed what a writer in the *Economic History Review* called 'the problem of the present age': that of 'social reconstruction.'[46] Here, then, was another context in which the agencies of voluntarism had to operate: a context which *did* pose a new challenge to agencies which depended on individual initiative and effort, and were often patchy and uncoordinated.

Moreover, the investigations which made the poor 'fashionable' tended to concentrate on environmental, rather than personal, explanations for poverty. As has been seen. *The Bitter Cry* made a great deal of housing conditions and overcrowding; but it emphasized that it was such conditions which bred bad habits and immorality, rather than bad habits and immorality which produced the conditions. It was 'surely a matter of little surprise' that 'people condemned to exist under such conditions [took] to drink and [fell] into sin'. Who could 'wonder that the public house is the Elysian field of the tired toiler?'[47] Similar points of view were put to the Royal Commission on the Housing of the Poor, appointed in 1884: an inquiry which certainly owed something to the public attention that *The Bitter Cry* had drawn to the problem. Shaftesbury, in what was to be the penultimate year of his life, was the first witness to appear before the Commission. In his evidence he dwelt on the evils of overcrowding, and mentioned the physical and moral effects of the 'one-room' and the 'one-bed' system, which, he said, were especially harmful to young persons. He was asked several times by the Commissioners

---

[45] *Liberalism and the Social Problem* (London: Hodder & Stoughton, 1909), 363.

[46] Quoted in Weiler, *The New Liberalism*, 47.

[47] Wohl (ed.), *Bitter Cry*, 60–1.

whether or not such conditions were the result of the intemperance and carelessness of the people who lived in them; and one such question referred to a recent pamphlet entitled 'Is it the Pig that makes the Stye or the Stye that makes the Pig?'. Shaftesbury answered that it was often the sty that made the pig. It was the poverty of the people that led them to live in wretched conditions, not their habits. Certainly, poverty might be explained in some measure by drink; but even here, he felt that excessive drink might be indulged in as an escape and relief from bad living conditions.[48] Indeed, when supporting the appointment of the Commission, Shaftesbury had told the Lords that it was bad housing which caused immorality, rather than immorality bad housing.[49]

Many of the more statistical inquiries of the period indicated that there was much more to poverty than personal inadequacy, failure, and fecklessness. When investigating east London, Booth discovered the extent of poverty in old age: 38 per cent of all inhabitants over the age of 65 were in receipt of poor relief. Low pay and irregular work were also mentioned by Booth as important elements of poverty; it could not but be admitted, he wrote, that 'the industrial conditions under which we work lead to poverty, or at least poverty follows in their train'; and he included among the contributory factors 'no savings; no opportunity of remunerative work; inadequate pay'.[50] Rowntree was more explicit and exact. His table dealing with the immediate causes of primary poverty indicated that, of the total population of York in primary poverty, 15.63 per cent were so because of the 'death of the chief wage-earner'; 2.31 per cent because the chief wage-earner was out of work; 5.11 per cent because of his 'illness or old age'; 2.83 per cent because of 'irregularity of work'; 22.16 per cent because of 'largeness of family'—that is, more than four children; and 51.96 per cent because of the low wages of those in regular work.[51] Further, Rowntree argued that there was a rhythm in the life of a labourer, marked by 'five alternating periods of

[48] *First Report of the Royal Commission for Inquiring into the Housing of the Working Classes, with Evidence, Appendix and Indices* (Parliamentary Papers, 1884–5, Cd. 4402), XXXI, Qs. 14, 15, 29, 39, 151, 154.

[49] Hansard, *Parliamentary Debates* (House of Lords), 3rd ser., vol. 284, 22 Feb. 1884, cols. 1695–6.

[50] Fried and Elman (eds.), *Charles Booth's London*, 304.   [51] *Poverty*, 120.

want and comparative plenty'—which depended on external circumstances. The labourer was 'in poverty, and therefore under-fed' in childhood—unless his father was a skilled worker; in early middle life, after he had married and had young children to maintain; and again in old age, once his children had married and left home, and he himself was too old to work and was without sufficient savings.[52]

As far as secondary poverty was concerned, Rowntree did, indeed, admit that this might well be due to improvident and careless expenditure. Yet he conceded that this was 'often induced by irregularity of income'; and, like Shaftesbury, argued that improvidence and carelessness were

themselves often the outcome of the adverse conditions under which too many of the working classes live.... Housed for the most part in sordid streets, frequently under overcrowded and unhealthy conditions, compelled very often to earn their bread by monotonous and laborious work, and unable, partly through limited education and partly through overtime and other causes of physical exhaustion, to enjoy intellectual recreation, what wonder that many of these people fall a ready prey to the publican and bookmaker? The limited horizon of the mother has a serious effect upon her children; their home interests are narrow and unattractive, and too often they grow up prepared to seek relief from the monotony of their work and environment in the public-house, or in the excitement of betting.[53]

This kind of argument, too, provided grounds for the environmentalist approach to poverty, rather than the personal approach: for the belief that the problem lay in the conditions in which the individual lived, rather than in the moral or spiritual condition of the individual himself. Here, then, was another challenge, not only to the agencies of voluntarism, but to the ideology which often underlay those agencies. If economic and social circumstances, over which the individual had little or no personal control, did not permit of savings, the whole idea of saving through a friendly society, cooperative, or trade union—or a more specialized agency—was impracticable; and any attempt to encourage thrifty behaviour through well regulated charitable endeavour seemed doomed to fail. Rowntree's line of primary poverty excluded all expenditure except that which was absolutely necessary for keeping alive at a minimal level. Persons living

[52] Ibid. 136–7.   [53] Ibid. 144–5.

below such a line, he said, 'cannot save, nor can they join sick club or Trade Union, because they cannot pay the necessary subscriptions', and 'to expect them to rise of themselves is to expect virtue and powers in them given their station in life far in advance of any other class in the community'.[54]

If social and economic conditions thus posed a challenge to the implementation and ideology of voluntarism in the later nineteenth and early twentieth centuries, so too, it may be argued, did changed political circumstances. Again, the extent of the challenge is open to differing interpretations. It is true that the 'people' did not need to have political rights in order to make their presence felt; that could be expressed in more direct ways. The events of the Chartist years had shown this; the Chartist presence had helped to force social issues more prominently into the consideration of the propertied. In 1886 and 1887, moreover, there were extensive riots in London, caused by hardship and unemployment. Some observers thought this potentially dangerous. Francis Peek wrote that 'it is no time to dream on in blind security while there is an army of more than three quarters of a million of paupers at our gates'.[55] There is no doubt that what Gareth Stedman Jones has called the 'Threat of Outcast London' did bring home to the propertied classes the potential dangers of a situation whereby respectable workers might be swept into direct action by the less respectable; and the demonstrations of the 1880s reached quite formidable proportions, particularly on 'Bloody Sunday' in November 1887. On the other hand—as has already been suggested—such popular disturbances were not in themselves new; and they had taken place in the past without provoking a major change in policy. The Chartist Petitions, after all, had abjectly failed to produce immediate results. Similarly, José Harris has argued that the disturbances of 1886 and 1887 'had little direct influence on the formation of social policies for the relief of the unemployed. They were seen by both Liberal and Conservative governments as a problem of public order rather than of social distress.'[56]

---

[54] Ibid. 133–4.

[55] Gareth Stedman Jones, *Outcast London: A Study in the Relationship between Classes in Victorian Society* (London: Penguin Books, 1971), 224–5, considers these points.

[56] 'The Transition to High Politics in English Social Policy, 1880–1914', in Michael Bentley and John Stevenson (eds.), *High and Low Politics in Modern Britain* (Oxford: Clarendon Press, 1983), 64.

The question of 'direct action' is, however, only one part of the argument, for increasingly in the later nineteenth century, the 'people' acquired political rights; and it may be claimed that this injected a new element—unknown in the years of the Chartists—into the situation. Lord Salisbury's daughter Maud wrote in 1885—just after the passage of the Third Reform Act—that if she were an 'ingenious peasant', she was sure that she would vote for the man 'who promised . . . all sorts of good things, rather than for the man who promised . . . nothing'.[57] In 1892 Sidney Webb, in his evidence to the Royal Commission on Labour, commented as follows:

It appears to me that if you allow the tramway conductor to vote he will not forever be satisfied with exercising that vote over such matters as the appointment of the Ambassador to Paris, or even the position of the franchise. He will realise that the forces that keep him at work, for sixteen hours a day for three shillings a day, are not the forces of hostile kings, of nobles, of priests; but whatever forces they are he will, it seems to me, seek so far as possible to control them by his vote. That is to say, he will more and more seek to convert his political democracy into what one may roughly term an industrial democracy, so that he may obtain some kind of control over the conditions under which he lives.[58]

It is also possible to discern the erosion of the 'consensus' of middle-class and working-class interests of mid-century around a 'Labour aristocracy'—in so far as this had existed—in the later decades of the century, as the incorporation of the unskilled working classes into New Unionism took place. The growth of a more militant Labour movement, to which the growing socialist movement made an appeal, appeared to mark a recognition that the interests of capital and labour were confrontational rather than complementary; and there was a heightened interest among the New Unions in welfare issues, such as old-age pensions, the abolition of the poor law, and measures to deal with unemployment and health provision. The political element was important here too, as the more assertive Labour movement, armed with greater political power, showed itself less inclined than its more

[57] Quoted in F. M. L. Thompson, 'Private Property and Public Policy', in Lord Blake and Hugh Cecil (eds.), *Salisbury: The Man and his Policies* (London: Macmillan, 1987), 236.

[58] Quoted in J. R. Hay (ed.), *The Development of the British Welfare State, 1880–1975* (London: Edward Arnold, 1978), 14.

acquiescent predecessor to follow a Liberal lead. 'The economic side of the democratic ideal', wrote Sidney Webb, 'is, in fact, Socialism itself'.[59]

Yet the importance of the increased political participation of the people—as that of their direct action—is also open to question. The extent to which the parliamentary Reform Acts of the later nineteenth century introduced 'mass democracy' can easily be exaggerated; in 1911 the proportion of adult males entitled to vote still stood at only 60 per cent. Further, it is not altogether clear how far even those of the working classes who had the vote were interested in achieving social reform, which, in itself, never became a major electoral issue.[60] In working-class memory, the state could well be equated with sinister rather than friendly forces, which even the mid-century 'Equipoise' had not erased: poor law, police, punishment. In many working-class circles, there remained an attachment to independence, gained by regular work and higher wages. State welfare could be intrusive—just as philanthropy had been; indeed it could be regarded as simply another form of philanthropy. And, as far as socialism was concerned, it could be seen more as a middle-class phenomenon than as a working-class one: a symbol of middle-class guilt feelings. Where once the middle classes had worn the clothes of philanthropy, now they wore those of socialism and state welfare. There remained a suspicion that the ulterior motive was to hold the working classes in a subordinate position of tutelage.

It is, therefore, possible to mount a strong argument against the case that the extension of the citizenship of political entitlement was bound, ultimately, to lead to the citizenship of social entitlement through the state; and, just as the significance of the closing decades of the nineteenth century may be exaggerated in economic and social terms, it is possible also to exaggerate them in political terms. Yet, as in the economic and social areas, the process of stripping this period of significance can be taken too far. There is little doubt that the politicians of the period *thought* that they were working in an increasingly democratic context, in which social issues would become more prominent in a somewhat different way from that of the past. In November 1867

[59] Quoted ibid.
[60] Pat Thane, 'The Working Class and State "Welfare" in Britain 1880–1914' *Historical Journal*, xxvii (1984), 877–980.

Shaftesbury wrote that the Reform Act passed that year would abate some of his labour; 'for the People', as he put it, 'can now do everything for themselves'.[61] They had no longer any need of an advocate, such as he had been. He felt that the legislation passed by the Disraeli ministry of 1874 to 1880 was dictated by a need to placate the working classes, who were now patrons, rather than clients; anyone, he wrote, who sought to be 'well among them' had to be 'less of a guide than a follower of their opinions'.[62] And as an elderly man he was resentful that, in the new political conditions, others were eager to espouse the causes for which he had long fought when they were less fashionable.

Of considerable importance in this respect was Joseph Chamberlain's Unauthorised Programme of 1885, with its fairly explicit pledges and undertakings on matters of social reform. Chamberlain certainly thought that the recent extension of the franchise was significant. 'The toilers and spinners', he said, 'will have a majority of votes'—and thus could control the government if they so wished. Thus 'social subjects' would require the attention of politicians: 'the centre of power', he wrote, 'has shifted, and the old order is giving place to the new'.[63] Chamberlain acted here as a Liberal—but he was to carry much of this commitment into the Conservative Party after his final departure from the Liberal Party; and his later tariff reform campaign in the early 1900s was, in part, related to the question of raising money for social purposes, such as pensions.

This, in addition to the stirrings of Labour in its political guise with the creation in 1900 of the Labour Representation Committee, was not unimportant in moving the Liberal Party in the first decade of the twentieth century in the direction of 'New Liberalism'. This directed the emphasis of traditional Liberal beliefs in individual effort and achievement more towards the needs of the individual in the community. 'Let Liberalism proceed with its glorious work of building up the temple of liberty in this country,' said Lloyd George in 1903, 'but let it also bear in mind that the worshippers of that shrine have to live.'[64] Or, as Churchill said

---

[61] Finlayson, *Shaftesbury*, ch. 17, develops these points.

[62] Ibid. chs. 19 and 20.

[63] W. H. Greenleaf, *The British Political Tradition*, 2 vols. (London: Methuen, 1983), ii. 227.

[64] Bentley Brinkerhoff Gilbert, *David Lloyd George: The Architect of Change* (London: Batsford, 1987), 355.

in Glasgow in 1906: 'the nature of man is a dual nature. The character of the organization of human society is dual. Man is at once a unique being and a gregarious animal.'[65] Social welfare issues were, then, on the political agenda; the wry comment of Sir William Harcourt to the effect that 'we are all socialists now' touched a sensitive nerve for politicians of all persuasions.

One assessment of the final two decades of the nineteenth and the first decade of the twentieth century might, then, suggest that their economic, social, and political significance can be over-drawn—and that voluntarism could still operate in a reasonably congenial climate. Another, certainly if made from a contemporary standpoint, indicates that new worries and anxieties were present, as social issues made themselves felt in many areas, and the urgent problem of the time seemed to many to be that of 'social reconstruction', to be carried out by an increasingly democratic state. In the light of this background, the question now to be considered is how voluntarism, allied to a complementary minimal, localized state, performed, and was seen to perform by those who were its practitioners—and its critics.

II

It is important to recognize that the voluntary sector was still much in evidence in the years from 1880 to 1914. In parts of his survey which are perhaps less often quoted than those on primary and secondary poverty, Rowntree showed great interest in the various self-help and mutual-aid organizations which he found to exist in York: friendly societies, both registered and unregistered, trade unions, and cooperative societies. He was, indeed, much impressed by the role of the friendly societies.[66] It was, he wrote, 'interesting to note the enthusiasm and interest with which the business of the York Friendly Societies is often conducted. Of this the large number of members is ample evidence.' Many working men's chief interests, Rowntree noted, centred on the friendly societies in the city, the most powerful of which was the Grand United Order of Oddfellows, followed by the Foresters, the National Independent Order of Oddfellows, and Manchester Unity.

---

[65] Quoted in Eric J. Evans (ed.), *Social Policy, 1870–1914: Individualism, Collectivism and the Origins of the Welfare State* (London: Routledge & Kegan Paul, 1978), 216.   [66] *Poverty*, 355–64.

The total number of members of registered and unregistered societies which Rowntree recorded in York was approximately 10,000. In addition to this, some 1,700 men paid for sick and funeral benefits through their trade unions. There was the problem that many men were members of more than one friendly society, and thus Rowntree scaled the male membership of friendly societies, including those who paid for sick and funeral benefits through their trade unions, down to about 7,000. He also drew attention to the fact that often 'the business of the Friendly Societies is carried on with much formality and mystery'—with secret passwords and signs and colourful regalia worn by the office-bearers. Interestingly, too, Rowntree commented on the 'advantageous discipline' which the friendly societies brought to many of their members. Experience of office and responsibility for the orderly conduct of business and the management of considerable sums of money provided 'lessons of high value in the equipment of a useful citizen'.[67]

Here, then, was ample evidence of the mutual-aid side of the voluntary sector in York. Rowntree also mentioned other mutual-aid aspects of the sector: trade unions and cooperatives. The cooperative society in York increased in strength after 1888; and while, as Rowntree conceded, the majority of members belonged to the society because of the dividends, there were 'nevertheless a number who hold to the higher ideals of mutual-helpfulness'. An Educational Committee arranged for lectures, which were given in the society's hall, and provided a library for the use of members. Money was also provided to meet the fees of a member, or member's child, who attended Continuation Classes held under the auspices of the School Board. Rowntree felt that the cooperative society's influence on the life of the city was good. It had cast its influence 'on the side of progressive causes' in York, and its 'absolute insistence on cash payment for all goods purchased, and its general encouragement of thrift, have undoubtedly had a good effect upon the habits of the working classes'.[68]

Rowntree also included comments on the commercial activities of the life insurance companies. He wrote that an impression of the extent of such activities in York might be gauged

----

[67] Ibid. 363.   [68] Ibid. 354–5.

from the fact that there were no fewer than seventy-five full-time agents who collected weekly life insurance premiums from the wage-earning classes of York. There were in addition ten part-time agents. The largest employer of such agents was the Prudential Assurance Company, which employed forty of them; the average weekly payment taken as a premium by the Prudential was about 2*d*., and the average sum insured about £10. Here, then, was evidence of the operation in the city of the commercial sector, and Rowntree's investigations also provided material about the workings of the informal sector, with financial assistance being supplied to their parents by children who were working, but not living at home. It was the normal practice in York for older children living at home to pay their parents the sum which they would have spent on board and lodging if not living there. They saved the remainder for furnishing their own houses when they married.[69]

Rowntree's depiction of the mutual-aid aspects of the voluntary sector in York and those of the commercial and informal sectors could well be extended elsewhere; here the justification for treating York as typical is strong. Self-help and mutual-aid organizations—friendly societies, trade unions, cooperative societies, building societies, savings banks—continued to exist and to exert considerable influence. The membership of Manchester Unity increased from 486,000 in 1880 to 862,000 in 1914, and that of the Foresters from 515,000 in 1880 to 648,000 in 1914. Of particular importance was the growth of organizations such as the Royal Liver, Liverpool Victoria, and Scottish Legal. Although technically non-profit-making, such collecting friendly societies were, in fact, very close to the extremely powerful group in this area which were wholly in the commercial sector: the industrial insurance companies. There were some seventy-five such companies in existence in Britain in the years before World War I, but twelve of these, the largest being the Prudential, monopolized the business, which was mainly concerned with death and burial insurance. The premium income of the Prudential in 1904 was almost £4 million;[70] and the twelve companies together had a premium income of some £20 million per year in the period

---

[69] Ibid.

[70] *Statement of Accounts of Life Assurance and Life Assurance and Annuity Business to 31st Dec. 1904* (Parliamentary Papers, HMSO, 1905), 47, 350.

just before 1914. Industrial Assurance, as it was known, was thus a business of vast proportions.

The largely unseen influence of the informal sector was also pervasive throughout the period as a whole. An Edwardian clergyman noted in 1908 that it was 'largely [the] kindness of the poor to the poor which stands between our present civilization and revolution'.[71] Maud Pember Reeves in *Round About a Pound a Week*, published in 1913 as a result of a study by the Fabians' Women's Group of the daily budgets of thirty families in Lambeth, mentioned help given to families by neighbours in emergencies;[72] and the pages of Robert Roberts's *A Ragged Schooling* and *The Classic Slum* contain episodes which reveal the continuing importance of the informal sector of voluntarism in this period—although, as earlier, the commercial networks of pawnshops and credit facilities were also of great importance in tiding people over spells of hardship.[73] Indeed, the development of pledge shops reached a peak in most parts of the country on the eve of World War I.

If this evidence points to a continuing need for mutual-aid, of varying kinds, to meet economic and social need, it may also suggest that circumstances were still sufficiently buoyant to support such activity among the more prosperous sections of the working classes. The workings of the informal sector which have been mentioned may, however, underscore the more pessimistic interpretation of social and economic conditions in the period; and the same may be said of the philanthropic and charitable activity to be found in the voluntary sector. This side of the voluntary sector was, indeed, also well represented in the pages of Booth and Rowntree. Rowntree stated that there was 'no doubt that the amount of money, food, etc., given in the form of charity is considerable'; but, he added, striking a familiar note in such matters, 'it is not possible to ascertain the extent of such gifts'.[74]

Indeed, the social problems of the later part of the nineteenth century could, and did, evoke a paternalistic and philanthropic

---

[71] Quoted by Frank Prochaska, 'Philanthropy' in F. M. L. Thompson (ed.), *The Cambridge Social History of Britain, 1750–1950*, 3 vols. (Cambridge: Cambridge University Press, 1990), iii. 365.   [72] London: G. Bell & Sons, 1913.

[73] Robert Roberts, *The Classic Slum* (Harmondsworth: Penguin, 1973); *A Ragged Schooling: Growing Up in the Classic Slum* (Manchester: Manchester University Press, 1976).   [74] *Poverty*, 114.

response. As in the past, the motivation was mixed. There could still be a strong religious commitment, or a personal motive, such as that which prompted a leading citizen of Newcastle to provide a new children's hospital in the city as a memorial to his wife.[75] There could be a striving for publicity and status—and a desire to stave off unrest, now threatened by socialist activity, and achieve social stability. In 1881 the *Charity Record and Philanthropic News* commented:

As we all know charity is doubly blessed. It blesseth . . . him that gives and him that takes, and never more is its beneficial effect on the giver more needed than at the present time. To weld together rich and poor; to break down the middle wall of partition between those who have and those who have not; to crush out that class feeling which at times threatens to turn this England of ours into two hostile camps; to make visible that common bond of brotherhood which should exist between all who speak a common tongue and own a common faith is the blessed results of such benevolence as that which it will be our aim to stimulate and record.[76]

A manifestation of such mixed motivation may be found at the personal level—as it had been in the past. The work of Thomas Barnardo among neglected and destitute children owed much to evangelical commitment, and Barnardo worked within, and was supported by, the 'evangelical network'. As a ragged-school teacher driven to engage in wider pursuits, Barnardo saw himself as the successor to Shaftesbury—although relations between the two men were far from being as close and cordial as Barnardo himself wished to suggest.[77] In fact Barnardo's work began long before the revelations of the 1880s and thereafter. It began in the later 1860s, with an East End Juvenile Mission for the Care of Friendless and Destitute Children and a Boys' Home at Stepney Causeway, and grew rapidly in the early 1870s; and Barnardo also worked within the parameters of the temperance movement in his purchase of the notorious 'gin palace', the 'Edinburgh Castle' in Rhodeswell Road, and its conversion into an elaborate temperance coffee-house, with a library, reading-room, and smoking-room—and with the great hall of the former 'Citadel of

[75] Norman McCord, *British History, 1815–1906* (Oxford: 1991), 456.
[76] i/1 (6 Jan. 1881).
[77] Gillian Wagner, *Barnardo* (London: Weidenfeld & Nicolson, 1979; paperback edn. Eyre & Spottiswoode, 1980), 48–9 (of 1980 edn.).

Satan' being used as a Mission Church, in which Barnardo himself would often preach while in London.

Barnardo's work was, therefore, well established *before* the
1880s—and may be said to have belonged to the philanthropic
endeavour of the earlier period. But Barnardo responded to the
revelations made in *The Bitter Cry*, and, indeed, published an
article in reply, entitled 'The Bitter Cry of Outcast Children', in
which he argued that the greatest victims of overcrowding were
children and young persons.[78] It was partly in this context that
he turned his attention to promoting emigration and to extending
the system of industrial training for children; and another innovation of the 1880s was the boarding out of children with foster-
parents in the countryside. By 1886 he announced that this was
a separate branch of his work, and it grew rapidly. Indeed, by
emigration and boarding out, Barnardo increased three-fold the
number of neglected children under the general supervision of
his initiatives.

Barnardo's philanthropic endeavours also owed something to
his traits of personality—although, unlike Shaftesbury's, his was
not a withdrawn personality, seeking, so it may be argued, con-
solation and release in philanthropic activity. On the contrary, he
was extremely assertive and dominant, and sought worldly ac-
claim and recognition. The philanthropic world gave him a stage
on which to display his prowess. Equally, Barnardo was well
aware of the role of philanthropy in staving off social unrest.
What were sometimes called the 'dangerous classes' must not
be allowed to become any more dangerous, and he used this
argument to add to others in his appeal for funds: 'every boy
rescued from the gutter', he said, 'is one dangerous man the
less'.[79] He was, he wrote in 1885, 'deeply convinced' that the time
was approaching 'when this seething mass of human misery will
shake the social fabric, unless we grapple more earnestly with it
than we have yet done'.[80] Thus the founder of what has been
called 'perhaps the most sensational charity success story of the
Victorian Age'[81] amply displayed mixed motivation, as earlier
philanthropists had done; but the 'success story' dates essentially from the later Victorian period.

There were numerous other manifestations of the continuing

---

[78] Ibid. 178.   [79] Ibid. 179.   [80] Ibid. 183.

[81] David Owen, *English Philanthropy, 1660–1960* (Cambridge, Mass.: Harvard
University Press, 1965), 543.

activity of philanthropy and charity in this period. The Salvation Army was founded in 1878—although, in a sense, it had been in existence since 1865 as the Christian Revival Association. The evangelical inspiration here was also obvious; but the Army combined a concern for salvation with a desire to attack social problems by providing food, shelter, and work, and by attempting to heighten awareness of social problems. In the introduction to *In Darkest England*, William Booth acknowledged that he had been on 'active service in the salvation of men' for the past forty years; but it will be recalled that he paid tribute to the work of his namesake, Charles, in attempting 'to form some kind of idea as to the numbers of those with whom we have to deal'. And in 1890 he expressed the hope that 'the upper and middle classes are at last being awakened out of their long slumber with regard to the permanent improvement of the lot of those who have hitherto been regarded as being for ever abandoned and hopeless'.[82]

A similar pattern of activity was discernible elsewhere. The Settlement House Movement, embodying the idea that those with 'social status' and education should live and work in the poorer parts of cities, was by no means new in the 1880s, and the idea and practice of 'slumming' was, of course, familiar to philanthropic ladies in mid-century. In the later 1860s, moreover, the historian J. R. Green made a conscious choice to work in the East End of London rather than in the West End, and became Perpetual Curate of St Philip's, Stepney.[83] In 1872 the Revd Samuel Barnett moved from St Mary's, Bryanston Square, to become Vicar of St Jude's, Whitechapel, at the age of 28. St Jude's was a virtually derelict church; the parish was described by Barnett's bishop as 'the worst . . . in the diocese'.[84] There Barnett and his wife became involved in various community projects, such as a children's country holiday fund; and he developed connections between his parochial activities and his former university, Oxford: connections which emphasized the need for people of education to become identified with the needs of cities and, as Barnett himself put it, 'the duty of the cultured to the poor and degraded'.[85]

---

[82] *In Darkest England*, 282.
[83] Asa Briggs and Anne Macartney, *Toynbee Hall: The First Hundred Years* (London: Routledge & Kegan Paul, 1984), 4.
[84] Ibid. 3.   [85] Stedman Jones, *Outcast London*, 259.

Again, however, the revelations of the early 1880s injected a new urgency into the situation. It was after the publication of *The Bitter Cry* in October 1883 that Barnett—who well knew at first hand the kind of scenes which it depicted, even if he thought their portrayal sensational—visited Oxford and addressed a meeting on 'Settlements of University Men in Great Towns'.[86] This was a different approach from that of the itinerant mission, or from exercises in 'slumming', whereby the rich 'descended' upon poorer parts of the community—and then withdrew to a more affluent area before the next 'descent' took place. It involved a continuous commitment to the life of the community on a personal face-to-face basis, and was intended to be 'fraternal' rather than 'paternal' in approach. Barnett pointed out that large houses were available in the East End. These could be acquired and maintained by colleges and organized under directors, around whom graduates and undergraduates would gather, regarding the house where they lived as their home. They would establish links with the churches and also with the various charitable agencies,[87] clubs and centres of social life—and also local government agencies. It was this initiative which led to the foundation in 1884 of Toynbee Hall, of which Barnett became the first warden. The name illustrated the links with Oxford, for the settlement was named after Arnold Toynbee, the Oxford historian, who had been a pupil and friend of J. R. Green—and who died prematurely at the age of 31 in 1883, just as his long-standing ideas were coming to fruition. By 1900 thirty such settlements had been founded, modelled on Toynbee Hall. About half of these were in provincial cities, for the most part in Liverpool.

Here, too, were manifestations of philanthropic endeavour which incorporated many familiar motivations. Religious concern was evident, although the inspiration in this instance reflected the High Churchmanship then in the ascendancy in the Church of England, and found expression in personal social service, based on empathy rather than charity.[88] The Settlement Movement also attracted the participation of young women studying at university, often under the influence of the wives of academics, such as Mrs Alfred Marshall in Cambridge. This, it has been written, was 'an extension of the kind of part-time, unpaid, non-professional

---

[86] Briggs and Macartney, *Toynbee Hall*, 3.   [87] Quoted ibid. 5.
[88] Olive Anderson, *Suicide in Victorian and Edwardian England* (Oxford: Clarendon Press, 1987), 324.

charitable activity defined as appropriate for married women throughout the nineteenth century.'[89] Further, the desire to heal social divisions was not absent from Toynbee Hall. Toynbee and Barnett have on occasion been described as Christian Socialists, but the term is inaccurate. Barnett always distinguished between 'theoretical socialism' and what he called 'practical socialism'. Toynbee also made a distinction between what he termed 'Tory Socialism' and 'Continental Socialism', and wrote of his 'abhorrence and detestation of the materialistic ideas of the "Continentals" '.[90] As Barnett's thought developed, Toynbee Hall did, indeed, become more closely associated with various working-class and labour issues and movements; and yet, until his death in 1913, he regarded these as being in accordance with his 'practical socialism', and even as a way of staving off socialism of a more doctrinaire variety.

It should also be said that paternalistic activity remained a feature of many rural areas. The dukes of Bedford, Northumberland, Grafton, and Richmond and the Earl of Leicester continued to enjoy a high reputation as excellent landlords; and the Duke of Bedford knew of 'no more satisfactory form of philanthropy possible for the owner of a great estate than the provision of good cottages.'[91] Lord Salisbury showed considerable activity in cottage building on his estates at Hatfield and Hatfield Hyde, and paid attention to community needs at Hatfield.[92] Such activity may, indeed, be quantified in particular cases, such as that of Bedford and Salisbury; but, as is true of the earlier period, it is not possible to quantify the total time and effort put into paternalistic and philanthropic endeavour in the late nineteenth and early twentieth centuries—nor to enumerate the deeds themselves. It also remains extremely difficult to quantify more overt signs of that endeavour, whether in terms of institutions, agencies, or finance, except in individual cases. Thus in 1890 the Victoria Infirmary was opened in Glasgow, financed by public subscription and legacies; and these amounted to some £20,000.[93] More generally, the Charity Commissioners in 1895 recorded very

---

[89] Carol Dyhouse, *Girls Growing Up in Late Victorian and Edwardian England* (London: Routledge & Kegan Paul, 1981), 78.

[90] Briggs and Macartney, *Toynbee Hall*, 7.

[91] Quoted in Thompson, 'Private Property', 272.   [92] Ibid. 272–3.

[93] S. D. Slater and D. A. Dow (eds.), *The Victoria Infirmary of Glasgow, 1890–1990: A Centenary History* (Glasgow: The Victoria Infirmary Centenary Committee, 1990), 16.

considerable sums: the foundation of thirteen new trusts of over £100,000 each over the previous two decades and five hundred new endowments founded on average per year.[94] The reports of the Commissioners, of course, related only to charitable endowments, and not to charities maintained only by subscriptions and contributions. Any attempt to quantify these is—again—shot through with problems, although somewhat better and fuller collections of figures became available in the later nineteenth and early twentieth centuries. In particular, the Charity Organisation Society published an *Annual Charities Register*, and this included information on provincial, in addition to metropolitan, charities. The *Philanthropist* recorded in January 1882 that the approximate income for the past year of the London charities amounted to almost £6.5 million, the bulk of this coming from subscriptions.[95] In 1905 the *Annual Charities Register* began to publish tables of estimated income and expenditure of the London charities and their sources. For the four years from 1908 to 1911, the charities showed an average yearly income of some £8.5 million.[96]

Just as the self-help and mutual-aid side of the voluntary sector remained very active, the same may be said of the philanthropic and charitable side—particularly in the context of the numerous revelations of social conditions. The *Illustrated London News* commented towards the end of 1883 that 'recent revelations as to the misery of the abject poor have powerfully touched the heart of the nation'; and there was 'probably never a time when the desire to alleviate their wretchedness was so widespread.'[97] It is also true to say that the need to bring about greater discipline and efficiency in the face of international competition spurred philanthropic effort, especially among the young. Such considerations were present in the formation of the Boys' Brigade in 1883[98] and the Boy Scouts in 1908.[99] Here, there was considerable emphasis on fostering the citizenship of contribution among boys by means of voluntary agencies.

In all this endeavour, then, the various sectors of voluntarism

[94] Owen, *English Philanthropy*, 469 ff.   [95] Vol. i (Jan. 1882).

[96] Owen, *English Philanthropy*, 478.

[97] Quoted in Briggs and Macartney, *Toynbee Hall*, 3.

[98] John Springhall, *Youth, Empire, and Society* (London: Croom Helm, 1977), 14, 24.   [99] Ibid. 56–60.

showed considerable resilience—and also their customary attachment to independent, localized, and competitive effort. This remained true of the mutual-aid organizations within the voluntary sector; and, of course, the agencies involved in Industrial Assurance were in direct commercial competition with each other as their front-line agents, the collectors, constantly sought to build up more business. The charitable world also presented a familiar scene of effort which was frequently uncoordinated and competitive. The Charity Organisation Society kept up its efforts to try to systematize and rationalize charitable activity. It disliked the work of Barnardo, which it found much too emotional and unreliable; and, indeed, in the mid-1870s Barnardo had been subjected to attack from the Society for alleged financial mismanagement and ill-treatment of children in his care.[100] Barnardo emerged from the court case which followed relatively unscathed, but the Society, and Loch in particular, continued to oppose his activities. Equally, however, Barnardo continued with these activities—with, as has been seen, spectacular results.

Thus, as in the past, attempts to rein in charitable effort met with strong resistance from those who saw the need for more philanthropy, not less. In 1890 Cardinal Manning wrote that he welcomed indiscriminate charity as the 'lightening conductor which saves us. As to waste and wisdom [of donations], I am content that many unworthy should share rather than one worthy case be without help.'[101] Similarly, in Reading, where there was a great deal of philanthropic effort, the Charity Organisation Society, present in the town since 1874, was unpopular and was looked upon with suspicion. It was thought to be too inquisitorial in its methods, and slow and under-financed in its activities. It also ran into the kind of hostile view, expressed by some local clergymen, that any form of organized giving was incompatible with spontaneous kindness and neighbourliness.[102] Philanthropy was, then, too independent-minded—and often too much inspired by personal or sectarian and denominational rivalries—to be

[100] Wagner, *Barnardo*, 121–72.
[101] Quoted in Colin Ford and Brian Harrison, *A Hundred Years Ago: Britain in the 1880s in Words and Photographs* (London: Allen Lane, Penguin Books, 1983), 93.
[102] Stephen Yeo, *Religion and Voluntary Organisations in Crisis* (London: Croom Helm, 1976), 57, 218–20, 227–9.

pruned and trained as a coordinating body such as the Charity Organisation Society would have liked; and even where the Society maintained a strong presence, as in Newcastle,[103] charitable effort often overlapped and duplicated itself. Voluntary activity, in its variety of forms, did not lightly surrender its characteristic belief in freedom and independence of action; and the considerable number of youth organizations which grew up in the context of the need for national efficiency—of which the Boys' Brigade and the Scouts were only two—was a further illustration of the tendency of the voluntary sector to multiply itself.

III

If the agencies of voluntarism were, then, still much in evidence, there remained the question as to how well they were seen to perform. And it is here that the contemporary interpretation of the period as one giving cause for anxiety on economic and social grounds tends to become dominant. As José Harris has written, early and mid-Victorians tended to feel that unemployment was a 'voluntary condition . . . or a predictable hazard for which workers should provide out of their own wages'[104]—and which, it could be added, might be alleviated by the exercise of a properly administered charity and poor law. This interlocking system had come under stresses and strains in the earlier period—for example, in the 1860s; and, as has been seen, part of the reaction to this had been to try to reinforce it in the later 1860s and the 1870s. But this became increasingly difficult to reconcile with the circumstances of the later nineteenth century, when the social problems associated with unemployment, over which the individual might have little control, became especially evident at certain times of 'depression'. The question was whether the old synthesis of providence, paternalism, and philanthropy, of voluntarism and the minimal state, could any longer survive the strains to which it had always been subject, but which were now

---

[103] Keith Gregson, 'Poor Law and Organised Charity: The Relief of Exceptional Distress in North-East England, 1870–1910', in Michael E. Rose (ed.), *The Poor and the City: The English Poor Law in its Urban Context, 1834–1914* (Leicester: Leicester University Press, 1985), 104.

[104] *Unemployment and Politics: A Study in English Social Policy, 1886–1914* (Oxford: Oxford University Press, 1972), 2, 102 ff.

seen to be more severe. Could it cope with the circumstances of the period, which seemed to call for 'social reconstruction'?

Attention may first be given to the mutual-aid side of the voluntary sector. Rowntree's favourable impression of it was somewhat mitigated by a succinct footnote: 'it may be remarked', he wrote, 'that the *very poor* are but seldom members of Friendly Societies. Even if they can be induced to join, they soon allow their membership to lapse.'[105] Paul Johnson has shown that, although the figures indicate an increase in the numbers of men in affiliated or ordinary friendly societies from the turn of the century, the number buying sickness insurance from these societies was declining from that point. There was an increasing tendency to purchase only burial insurance, or other limited cover, from such sources. Johnson thus scales down Bentley Gilbert's estimate that in 1891 almost half the adult male population of Britain were members of friendly societies: but he agrees with Gilbert's assertion that sickness insurance 'made no appeal whatever to the grey, faceless, lower third of the working class. Friendly-society membership was the badge of the skilled worker.'[106] Remarks such as these somewhat underplay a concern often shown by mutual-aid friendly societies for those who did not belong to them, and neglect the commercial activities of the collecting friendly societies and the industrial insurance societies. These had always operated among the poorer sections of the working classes—and, as has been seen, continued to do so with considerable energy, although the problem of lapsing membership was by no means unknown even to them. It will, however, be recalled that their activities related to death and burial rather than health. Thus the traditional mutual-aid societies, associated with cultivating thrift and self-reliance through the initiative of their members, were only dealing with the tip of an iceberg, especially for health insurance—and a narrowing tip at that.

Moreover, such mutual-aid societies were themselves experiencing financial difficulties. This was partly due to the strong competition among societies for new members, which made it very difficult for a society to raise the level of its contributions, or reduce its benefits. A second problem—not unrelated to the

---

[105] *Poverty*, 356 n. 1.

[106] Paul Johnson, *Saving and Spending: The Working-Class Economy in Britain, 1870–1939* (Oxford: Clarendon Press, 1985), 55.

first—was that caused by the increase in longevity in the later part of the nineteenth century, and a correspondingly larger proportion of ageing members on the books of the friendly societies. This made it all the more necessary to recruit new members to help pay for the burdens imposed by the elderly; but it also meant that reduction of benefit to help towards lower contributions was very difficult to achieve. Manchester Unity and the Foresters attempted to run superannuation schemes in the 1880s and 1890s, but the vast majority of their members refused to participate in them. The reason was that the societies had, for many years, effectively used their sickness funds for paying pensions to their older members. As J. Lister Stead, the Foresters' permanent secretary, put it, friendly societies were 'paying as sick pay to members what are virtually pensions for which members have not paid.'[107] Thus there was very little inducement for the individual member to take out separate cover for pension purposes, when his existing contributions for sickness were actually serving that end. Thus voluntary-sector friendly societies were encountering severe financial difficulties in the closing decades of the century, largely as the result of trying to cater for an ageing constituency.

If it now became increasingly open to question how far the practice of mutual-aid or self-help was able to cope with the social problems of the time, this could also be said of the philanthropic and charitable side of the voluntary sector. Once again, a good starting-point is Rowntree—himself a philanthropic employer. As has been seen, Rowntree acknowledged the importance of philanthropic activity in York, and yet he doubted if its effect was more than marginal. He wrote that the recipients of charity were those who were below the poverty line, and that the number lifted above it by charity was likely to be small. It was probable that most of the charity which was given went to those who were ill, unemployed, or widows.[108] Other individuals who were also charitably disposed were coming to similar conclusions. George Cadbury—of similar Quaker background to the Rowntree family, and of similar occupation in a rival chocolate and cocoa business—was, with his brothers, widely known as a

---

[107] Quoted in James H. Treble, 'The Attitudes of Friendly Societies towards the Movement in Great Britain for State Pensions, 1878–1908' (*International Review of Social History*, xv/2 (1970), 278).   [108] *Poverty*, 114.

philanthropic employer; and the creation of the Bourneville factory village—incorporating housing, schools, and recreational facilities[109]—in the late 1870s exemplified that continuing and, indeed, expanding tradition of business paternalism and philanthropy which has already been noted. Like other examples of such ventures, it was not without its 'higher self-interest'; the Cadbury brothers needed space to expand, and the countryside outside Birmingham provided greater opportunities for this than the urban sprawl of the city itself. Cadbury, however, distributed his benevolence in a variety of directions: the China Inland Mission, the London Missionary Society, and—nearer home—the Birmingham YMCA.

Cadbury was also a strong environmentalist. He had since the 1860s taught in an adult school in Birmingham; and his experience there convinced him that it was often insufficient to talk about 'ideals'. How, he asked in similar vein to other philanthropists, can a man 'cultivate ideals when his home is a slum and his only possible place of recreation is the public house? . . . To win them to better ideals you must give them better conditions of life.'[110] However, he came increasingly to doubt if philanthropy alone could do this. It might, indeed, simply divert attention from the underlying social needs. He felt that public attention should be brought to bear on social problems, and in 1891 embarked on the purchase of newspapers. This was not entirely to give prominence to social issues: Cadbury's opposition to militarism and war was also important in making him enter this field. But the newspapers did become vehicles for the advocacy of social reform. 'Much of current philanthropic effort', Cadbury wrote, 'is directed to remedying the more superficial evils. I earnestly desire that the *Daily News* Trust may be of service in assisting those who are seeking to remove their underlying causes.'[111] This was part of the wider purpose of the Trust 'in bringing the ethical teaching of Jesus Christ to bear upon National questions, and in promoting National righteousness'.

Among philanthropists themselves, therefore, there was an awareness of the limitations of philanthropy. Even Barnardo could despair of being able to do enough: 'Experienced as I am', he

---

[109] Owen, *English Philanthropy*, 434 ff.
[110] Quoted ibid. 437.   [111] Quoted ibid. 442.

wrote, 'in the abominations of some of the worst rookeries, I have again and again almost been compelled to give up personal exploration and visitations, heart-sick and stricken as with paralysis of the brain at the sights which I have witnessed, while unable to afford adequate relief.'[112] The disjointed and disorganized nature of charitable effort—to which, paradoxically, he himself contributed—was seen by General Booth as a disadvantage in meeting social problems on a large enough scale. He was dismissive of the sufficiency of what he called 'the miscellaneous and heterogeneous efforts which are clubbed together under the generic head of Charity'. He did not wish to disparage 'any effort that is prompted by a sincere desire to alleviate the misery of our fellow creatures'; nevertheless, he continued:

the most charitable are those who most deplore the utter failure which has, up till now, attended all their efforts to do more than temporarily alleviate pain, or effect an occasional improvement in the condition of individuals.

There are many institutions, very excellent in their way, without which it is difficult to see how society could get on at all, but when they have done their best there still remains this great and appalling mass of human misery on our hands, a perfect quagmire of Human Sludge. They may ladle out individuals here and there, but to drain the whole bog is an effort which seems to be beyond the imagination of most of those who spend their lives in philanthropic work. . . .[113]

If advocates of philanthropy in its widest form—like Barnardo —felt that it was unable to cope with the volume of human need, this increasingly seemed to be the case to those attracted to a more restricted and organized model of charitable effort, such as that provided by the Charity Organisation Society. Samuel Barnett in the 1870s had close associations with the Society—some of which were of a personal kind, since he married one of Octavia Hill's assistants; and, indeed, he was first drawn to social work by the influence of Octavia Hill herself. To some extent, he retained these associations later: thus he was a member of the committee of the Whitechapel Charity Organisation Society from the 1870s to the end of his life. Like the Society as a whole, he had a distaste for what he called 'philanthropic sentiment in

[112] Wagner, *Barnardo*, 178.   [113] *In Darkest England*, 72–3.

London—which loves to give doles no matter how injurious';[114] and, in common with the Society, he was strongly critical of the relief funds for unemployed persons administered by the Mansion House Committees in 1886 and on subsequent occasions; 'every penny', he wrote, 'has eternal issues upon the characters of the recipients, yet pounds are given and scattered without prayer or thought whether those issues end in heaven or hell'.[115]

Barnett was, therefore, concerned with the effect which indiscriminate alms-giving had on individual character. In 1886 he wrote in the *Nineteenth Century* that 'the only test of progress is in the development of character. Institutions, societies, laws count for nothing unless they tend to make people stronger to choose the good and refuse the evil'.[116] In 1912 he developed the same theme when he wrote that 'charities should aim at encouraging growth rather than at giving relief'.[117] The Settlement Movement was in some respects an attempt to substitute a more lasting, continuous, and meaningful relationship between the privileged and non-privileged than was encapsulated in undiscriminating charity, based on impulse.

Yet Barnett was always willing to change his mind, and, as he once put it, 'to lead a revolution against himself';[118] and by the later 1880s he was becoming restive with the Charity Organisation Society, which he saw as too rigid and narrow in its outlook. By the mid-1890s he was, as he described himself, a 'friendly critic' of the Society: he referred in 1895 to the 'chaff of the clumsy methods of the Charity Organisation Society'—and he even posed the question, 'Is thrift always so virtuous?'[119] For such comments, he earned the rebuke of Loch, who wrote of him as 'a declared opponent of the whole policy of the Society'. That probably puts the matter too strongly, and Loch was on firmer ground when he accused Barnett of some degree of inconsistency. Barnett, Loch felt, 'must be in harmony with the current opinion . . . or perhaps just a few seconds ahead of it . . . He sails close to the philanthropic

[114] Briggs and Macartney, *Toynbee Hall*, 6 ff., develops this point.
[115] Quoted in Harris, *Unemployment and Politics*, 111.
[116] 'Sensationalism in Social Reform' (vol. xix, Jan.–June 1886).
[117] 'Charity up to Date' (*Contemporary Review*, Feb. 1912), quoted in Rex Pope, Alan Pratt, and Bernard Hoyle (eds.), *Social Welfare in Britain, 1885–1985* (London: Croom Helm, 1986), 71.
[118] Quoted in Briggs and Macartney, *Toynbee Hall*, 38.
[119] Quoted ibid. 37.

winds . . . having changed once or more he may yet change again.'[120] Certainly, there was a perceptible shift in Barnett's views by 1900, and, in time—displaying his characteristic restlessness— he became increasingly doubtful whether Toynbee Hall itself, at least in its original guise, was relevant to the social problems brought to light, for example, in the course of the Boer War. He wondered if its emphasis on interpersonal relationships was sufficient to cope with issues such as malnutrition and 'physical deterioration'. It was in the context of such a change in mood that Toynbee Hall itself attracted a somewhat different category of 'settler' and, as has been noted, became closer to the nascent Labour movement—even if Barnett himself stopped short of adopting socialist views.

Even some of those, however, who remained firmly within the Charity Organisation Society tended to wilt and weaken in the face of circumstances. The Society itself was not as united in its approach to social issues as Loch would have liked; and the stereotype of an unyielding attachment to individualism is mis- leading. The local committees varied considerably from place to place. Some were, indeed, highly efficient, with a paid staff and dedicated volunteers, anxious to carry out the strict principles of the Society. There were committees of this kind in various parts of London, such as Marylebone, Camberwell, and even Whitechapel. Outside London, they were to be found in New- castle, West Hartlepool, Darlington, Sunderland, Norwich, and Kendal.[121] In other places, however, the Societies were much less efficient and 'rational' in their attitude to social issues—and much less willing to carry out official policy. Although it set its face against distributing relief, and saw itself simply as a clearing- house for other agencies, many local committees *did* dispense relief in substantial volume. The central office of the Society had to recognize the situation, and to leave it open to local committees to provide some form of relief in individual cases—although preferably only in cases where temporary relief was likely to be of permanent benefit, and this could well take the form of relief in kind rather than in money. In 1886 it dropped the category 'undeserving', and put in its place 'not likely to benefit'; and in 1888 even this terminology was altered and the two categories of

---

[120] Quoted ibid.   [121] Gregson, 'Poor Law', 101–5.

'assisted' and 'not assisted' began to be used.[122] Clearly, too much should not be made of this, since those 'not assisted' would be in that category because they were felt to be 'not likely to benefit'—which, in turn, might mean 'undeserving'. Nevertheless, the fact that the Society felt obliged directly to 'assist' in some cases was a departure from its original principles, and thus, even within the ranks of the Society itself, there emerged critics of it and its methods.

Again, then, philanthropy was met by the challenge of circumstances: how well could it cope with them? And this emerged in more detailed form in questionings as to whether the level of giving to philanthropic organizations, considerable as it was, could keep pace with the demands made of it. Like friendly societies, philanthropic organizations were affected by financial worries. In many ways, this was not new; Shaftesbury had often commented on the fact that philanthropic giving tended to be concentrated in a limited number of contributors. Even in the later nineteenth and early twentieth centuries, moreover, there were those who felt that the problem could be overstated. In 1902 the *Philanthropist* commented that the 'annual subscriber [was] the backbone of English philanthropy', and commended those who gave on their achievement in maintaining revenue 'on a fairly substantial basis'. It continued:

English people have for so long looked upon the great charitable institutions of the country as a priceless benefit that they continue the flow of subscriptions with remarkably little variation. The system, in fact, has become a national one, and the public, knowing that they are maintained, take an interest in the hospitals, orphanages and kindred institutions which are the wonder and envy of other nationalities.[123]

In 1908 the *Charity Record*, looking over the past year, commented that 'workers in the fruitful field of philanthropy have much cause for encouragement': and it recorded several extensions in hospital and charitable enterprises, such as a new out-patient and casualty department at St Bartholomew's Hospital, costing some £160,000.[124]

It was, perhaps, to be expected that such journals would point

---

[122] Owen, *English Philanthropy*, 237.   [123] Vol. xxiii (Jan. 1902).
[124] *The Charity Record, Hospital Times, Philanthropic News and Official Advertiser*, 2 Jan. 1908.

up the optimistic side: yet even the *Philanthropist* sounded certain notes of alarm. It admitted that subscriptions were 'a precarious income' and 'uncertain'—and that they were not 'perceptibly diminished'—a rather less than wholly reassuring comment.[125] The gathering of funds for the new Victoria Infirmary in Glasgow was not without its problems. By 1887 the funds in hand and subscriptions promised amounted to some £14,652, and it was decided to delay making a start with the implementation of a limited building plan until £20,000 had been collected by 1890. There were criticisms to the effect that subscriptions for a new hospital in the south side of Glasgow would divert funds from the existing Royal and Western Infirmaries in the city; and a further example of how the competitive element could affect the situation was that the new hospital, with a free out-patient dispensary, posed a threat to the earnings of local general practitioners. In fact, relatively few Glasgow doctors contributed to the new hospital; only eighteen can be identified in the annual reports of the Victoria up to October 1890.[126] This raised the general, and somewhat vexed, question of the relationship between hospital consultants and general practitioners. In 1891 a book written by a doctor, Robert Reid Rentoul, called for a reform of voluntary medical charities on the grounds that they were persistently abused to provide free medicine for those who could afford to pay for it. Rentoul made the point that 'the securing of financial help for charities is becoming more difficult each year'—and that, in these circumstances, there was a 'constant importuning for money' by means of 'cinderellas, charity sermons, raffles, bazaars, street collections, and the selling of charity tickets'.[127]

There is certainly other evidence of philanthropic organizations finding themselves in increasing financial difficulties. Stephen Yeo's investigations of Reading show that the Royal Berkshire Hospital there—founded in 1839—was facing considerable financial problems in the late nineteenth and early twentieth centuries, with an annual loss running at about £2,000 by the end of the century and getting worse.[128] The hospital depended

[125] Vol. xxiii (Jan. 1902).

[126] Slater and Dow (eds.), *The Victoria Infirmary*, 16.

[127] *The Reform of our Voluntary Medical Charities: Some Serious Considerations for the Philanthropic* (London: Balliere, Tindall & Cox, 1891), p. ix.

[128] *Religion*, 212. See also B. Kirkman Gray and B. L. Hutchins, *Philanthropy and the State, or Social Politics* (London: P. S. King, 1908), 232–3, which puts the financial difficulties of charities into a national context and suggests that 'many more

on various local sources of finance: donations, legacies, and subscriptions. These were supplemented from the third quarter of the century by other means: church collections, the Hospital Saturday Fund (which began in Reading in 1886), and the Hospital Sunday Movement—in which, in fact, large numbers of friendly societies participated. Yet the means did not meet the needs, and, indeed, tended to fall away. In 1895 it was said that 'the town of Reading does not support the Hospital as well as it ought to do'. Hospital Saturday was discontinued in 1900; Hospital Sunday survived, but not without problems. Similar difficulties were encountered by other philanthropic organizations in Reading. The Temperance and General Philanthropic Society, founded in 1879 and supported by the local Palmer family of biscuit-makers, stated in 1904 that 'our income had been going down for the past few years'; and the local Guild of Help also found itself in financial difficulties.[129]

Worries about the financial ability of philanthropy to cope with the challenges which faced it were, then, well founded. And this related not only to the volume of demand placed on philanthropy. There was also a growing recognition of the need for increased specialization and professionalism in meeting that demand. In many ways, this grew out of the 'casework' approach used by the Charity Organisation Society and other bodies. This threw up particular, not general, problems—and dictated particular, not general, solutions. Medical advances, such as those necessitating a clinical laboratory for collaboration between research and clinical staff, were also of great importance. Yet such developments were expensive. Extended bed occupancy to treat various illnesses might well prove to be necessary, but voluntary hospitals always wanted to demonstrate a high turnover of patients, which, it was felt, showed efficiency. It was this tension which may have caused a poor response to an appeal launched by the Victoria Infirmary in Glasgow in 1895 to meet an estimated shortfall of £1,700 for the current year; for in previous years the hospital had admitted a high proportion of long-term tuberculous patients.[130] There was, then, always a need for increased giving

people are beginning to question the policy of eleemosynary payment for what is coming to be regarded as a public responsibility'. It also mentions 'the changing habits of the people' as a reason for difficulty in maintaining Sunday collections.

[129] Yeo, *Religion*, 227.

[130] Slater and Dow (eds.), *The Victoria Infirmary*, 38–9.

to provide more equipment or more beds; and it was a gift from the philanthropic shipowner William Robertson which made it possible for the Glasgow Victoria Infirmary to expand its facilities, including the building of a clinical laboratory, in the first decade of the twentieth century.[131]

Another solution to financial difficulty was to stop giving free treatment to various classes of patient—a measure adopted by the Royal Berkshire Hospital. This pattern of finding new sources of income through patients' fees, or small and regular subscriptions, rather than merely from spasmodic and often unpredictable large donations and subscriptions, was, in fact, adopted by many voluntary hospitals and other philanthropic institutions. In Newcastle, the principal hospital benefited to the extent of £2,503 in 1898 from such small sums collected at local works; and nine worker-governors made their appearance on the management committee.[132] Again, as child welfare work became more specialized, philanthropic agencies such as the National Society for the Prevention of Cruelty to Children had also to become more professional and specialized.[133]

Philanthropy thus faced problems of cash, costs—and commitment. For not only was income difficult to maintain at an adequate level, but so too was the offering of time and talents, on which philanthropy had always depended. In Reading, it was found increasingly difficult to keep up attendances at meetings, and to stimulate action; and it may be that other, and more commercialized, forms of 'leisure activity' were becoming more attractive. Further, as far as rural philanthropy was concerned, the agricultural depression depleted the resources at the disposal of landowners for such purposes. Salisbury's paternalism and philanthropy were in large measure financed from urban income— a resource not available to all landowners: and even his activities were tempered by business considerations, amounting to 'an attenuated or parsimonious philanthropy for the benefit of the better-off'.[134]

Thus the circumstances of the later nineteenth and early twentieth centuries posed a challenge to voluntarism in its various

---

[131] Ibid. 42.   [132] McCord, *British History, 1815–1906*, 456.
[133] See George K. Behlmer, *Child Abuse and Moral Reform in England, 1870–1908* (Stanford, Calif: Stanford University Press, 1982), *passim*.
[134] Thompson, 'Private Property', 273.

sectors. Its separate and scattered nature, and its incessant and competitive search for funds, seemed to make it ill-equipped to cope with them. When in 1904 the Inter-Departmental Committee on Physical Deterioration turned its attention to the question of providing nourishing meals for school children, it was, as its Report put it, 'the subject of general agreement that, as a rule, no purely voluntary association could successfully cope with the full extent of the evil'.[135] The 'evil' in this case was the undernourishment of children which its investigations had revealed; but the comment might be applied considerably more widely over an extensive area of newly perceived social need.

IV

Doubts as to the effectiveness and adequacy of social provision based on the sectors of voluntarism were matched in this period by a similar questioning of the provision made by the minimal state in the form of the poor law. This was the more pertinent in the light of the stiffening of poor law principles embodied in the Goschen Minute of 1869—which, it will be recalled, urged a return to the 'less eligibility' terms of the 1834 Report and an abandonment of the looser and more lax administration which, in some areas, had crept in during the intervening period. This stricter formula has to be assessed in the same context as voluntarism—and, indeed, in many respects along with voluntarism, for, as has been seen, it was closely allied to the stricter application of charity envisaged by the Charity Organisation Society. Here, the voluntary sector and the minimal state were intended to act in close cooperation in eliminating overlapping relief and applying appropriate relief only where it was most needed.

Some poor law unions, such as St George's-in-the-East and Whitechapel in London, did adopt strict poor law principles of the '1834' type, and refused outdoor relief; and the same was true of the poor law union in Sunderland, which was 'a model union in the campaign against outdoor relief which was being pressed upon guardians in the wake of the Goschen Minute.'[136] In other places, however, it was exceedingly difficult to adhere

---

[135] Par. 348.   [136] Gregson, 'Poor Law', 103.

to strict principles; this would have placed greater strains on available workhouse accommodation than it could have borne. Thus outdoor relief continued to be given—although usually on the application of a test, such as stone-breaking in the workhouse yard.

This was not, indeed, a new expedient; outdoor tests had been applied in the earlier part of the century at times of exceptional distress. But they brought with them problems for the poor law authorities—and offered no real solution to the problem of unemployment. The authorities often found that those who resorted to relief on these terms were difficult to discipline and control. There were instances of ill-discipline, as at Bermondsey, where the workhouse staff were intimidated by the paupers in the yard. Similarly, at Poplar, a union of paupers was formed, and a strike held in pursuance of a demand for a higher scale of relief.[137] The labour test was often abandoned altogether in such places. Further, although the outdoor labour test—where it was applied—did demand work in return for relief, it often did not appeal to those affected by periods of unemployment; they regarded stone-breaking as harmful to the skills which might eventually lead to re-employment. And where the outdoor labour test was not applied, the prospect of doing nothing was scarcely less objectionable. In one sense, this did, of course, drive such persons on to the labour market in search of work; but at times of exceptional distress, that expedient simply exacerbated unemployment.

Thus, as in the case of the Charity Organisation Society, the poor law offered a scene of considerable diversity and confusion; as in the past, the statutory sector matched the voluntary in its lack of uniformity. There were active poor law unions, prosecuting the principles of 1834, just as there were active branches of the Charity Organisation Society; equally, there were lax poor law unions, offering outdoor relief in return for little or no work—just as there were lax branches of the Society, which actually distributed relief. And this diversity was also reflected in the relationship between the poor law and the Charity Organisation Society, which the Goschen Minute had formulated. The reality of 'reciprocal roles' could never be as neat at the Minute had envisaged—nor as the Society had intended. In some areas,

---

[137] Harris, *Unemployment and Politics*, 266, deals with the situation in Poplar.

indeed, there was active cooperation between poor law guardians and the local Charity Organisation Society branch; this was
true in various areas of London, notably in Stepney, Whitechapel,
Camberwell, and Marylebone. Marylebone, in particular, was
looked upon as a textbook example of cooperation between the
poor law and the Society. Members of the Society served as
guardians and dealt with problems at board meetings. The Society branch itself was highly organized and its members were
trained in poor law methods.[138] On special occasions, too, there
was close collaboration—particularly in opposing the indiscriminate distribution of the Mansion House funds. Elsewhere, there
were instances of cooperation; in Newcastle, Darlington, Dur-
ham, and West Hartlepool, relations between the statutory and
the voluntary agencies grew close.

Yet such collaboration was not evident everywhere. Where a
poor law union was unwilling—or unable—to control outdoor
relief, the possibilities of cooperation with a strict local Charity
Organisation Society branch diminished. Thus in London, a report from the St Olave's committee of the Society complained of
high poor law expenditure; and similar reports were to be found
elsewhere.[139] In North-East England, there were at least as many
instances of *lack* of collaboration as of collaboration. This could
be true even where there was a strong Society in existence—as in
Sunderland; and even in Newcastle, where some collaboration
did take place, the Society, on occasion, criticized the guardians
for undue generosity. In South Shields, too, there was no sign of
cooperation. Whereas in West Hartlepool, there was, as has been
seen, active cooperation, in nearby Stockton there was none, and
the guardians worked without contact with, and in ignorance
of, the charitable organizations.[140] Even in West Hartlepool, cooperation between the statutory and voluntary agencies rested
not so much on the limitation of relief as on the voluntary agency
actually distributing relief, albeit very sparingly, and thereby
saving the statutory authority from doing so. Indeed, in West
Hartlepool, the Charity Organisation Society was by February
1886 no longer able to deal with the manifestations of exceptional
distress, since its funds were exhausted; and thus the burden
was transferred to the poor law union—and its stone-yard was

[138] Gregson, 'Poor Law', 100.   [139] Ibid.   [140] Ibid. 101–5.

reopened. This pattern of the depletion of charitable resources in periods of acute distress was reflected elsewhere; and the corollary was the transfer of the 'deserving' poor to the poor law and the stone-yard—a place where the Goschen Minute had not intended them to be. It is true that when periods of acute distress passed, the burdens on the statutory and voluntary agencies lessened; and the West Hartlepool Charity Organisation Society re-emerged from the problems of the 1880s to play an important role thereafter. Yet the pattern remained confused and far from clear-cut, with great varieties of local practice; and the formula of the Goschen Minute, with its neat synthesis between statutory and voluntary agencies around the principle of self-maintenance, proved impossible to put into effect in all places and at all times.

This situation was, in fact, tacitly recognized by a further Poor Law Minute—that of 1886 issued by Joseph Chamberlain as president of the Local Government Board. This by no means undervalued the principle of self-maintenance; independence, it noted, was 'a quality which deserves the greatest sympathy and respect'. It praised those who wished to retain their independence and avoid the stigma of pauperism by recourse to the poor law. But it did not steer such persons in the direction of the measured charity of the Charity Organisation Society. It stated that local councils should provide work for the unemployed in the form of street sweeping or paving, or in tending municipal parks and cemeteries. Thus a further local force was brought into the relief of unemployment alongside the poor law and charity; and this was extended by the Unemployed Workmen Act of 1905. It is certainly true that the poor law guardians were involved in the work of this further agency. The Chamberlain circular was addressed to local authorities and urged them to establish public works for periods of depression—and to liaise with poor law guardians in 'providing temporary non-pauperising employment for the deserving unemployed'. Similarly, the administration of the Unemployed Workmen Act of 1905 was devolved on borough councils and boards of guardians. But this policy tended to cause still further confusion and disharmony. The Charity Organisation Society in London opposed public work schemes and tended to become a negative influence; in so doing, it might well face the opposition of the poor law, rather than find itself in co-operation with it. The methods of investigation under the Act of

1905 did, in fact, approximate closely to Charity Organisation Society casework; but the Society initially condemned the Act as a 'new pseudo-industrial system of remuneration', which simply concealed the state of economic dependence of the workmen who gained relief under it.[141] Moreover, even these new schemes were themselves of very doubtful adequacy and effectiveness: the Chamberlain Circular, for example, was issued five times between 1886 and 1893—and this very fact perhaps makes the point that, except in certain areas, it was ineffective.

The poor law itself, and its relationship with organized charity, thus presented a scene of considerable confusion; and the further attempt to introduce another localized agency tended to confuse the position even more. Solutions to the problem of poverty which relied on the prized localism of the voluntary and the statutory sectors did not inspire confidence. There was also great variety in the policy adopted towards those who had recourse to workhouses under the poor law. The principle of less eligibility was increasingly difficult to sustain for the inmates of workhouses. For one thing, the much-vaunted 'independent' labourer of the Report of 1834 was felt to be shown by the various social investigations to be something of a myth; or, at least, these investigations appeared to show that the lowest-paid 'independent' labourers were scarcely, if at all, able to maintain physical efficiency. It was, therefore, difficult to devise a regime *inside* a workhouse which was 'less eligible' than the conditions of such 'independent' labourers *outside* it. William Beveridge wrote in 1906: 'It is frankly impossible for any public committee openly to give those dependent on it conditions of life approaching in badness and harmfulness the conditions which . . . public thoughtlessness passes by as "inevitable" for large sections of a free and independent proletariat.'[142]

Thus, if the rigours of the poor law were being somewhat mitigated for those out of doors by the provision of relief in one form or another without tests or stigma, it seemed untenable to retain these rigours for those indoors—especially since these, increasingly, were the old, the young, and the sick. The number of paupers who came within the system of poor relief showed a steady decline in England and Wales throughout the period from

---

[141] Harris, *Unemployment and Politics*, 174.   [142] Quoted ibid. 148.

1871 to 1905—and the number of indoor paupers an increase over the same period. Between 1871 and 1879 the outdoor out-numbered the indoor paupers by 4.5 to 1; between 1896 and 1905, this ratio had dropped to 2.6 to 1. The more the workhouse became populated by the non-able-bodied—or the able-bodied who were temporarily ill or injured by accident—the less appropriate it was to apply the principle of less eligibility; and a feature of workhouse administration in the later nineteenth and early twentieth centuries was an improvement in standards. The general 'mixed workhouse' was discouraged, and the introduction of specialized and separate institutions for different categories of pauper with varying needs—old, young, sick, lunatic—encouraged.[143]

The poor law thus increasingly displayed that ambivalence between deterring the able-bodied, on the one hand, and caring for the non-able-bodied, on the other, which had always been a feature of it. The Local Government Board Circulars of 1895 and 1899 recommended to the guardians that the 'respectable aged' who had no friends or family to look after them should be allowed greater 'comforts', such as the wearing of their own (rather than pauper) clothes, and should receive visits. This new approach—'a change in the spirit of administration', as the 1895 Circular put it—was, indeed, part of the general improvement, specialization, and professionalism in welfare matters which has already been noted in relation to the efforts of charities: an improvement to which, as in the case of hospitals, advances in standards of medicine and nursing, coming in the wake of medical discoveries and changes in nursing technique, contributed.

Here, then, was a challenge to the statutory system of poor relief—and, on the face of it, that system, like the Charity Organisation Society, was undergoing changes within itself. It was becoming much more an indoor than an outdoor system. But this did not mean that expenditure on poor relief diminished—indeed, quite the reverse. In the early 1870s poor relief expenditure in England and Wales diminished, largely owing to the application of the Goschen Minute and the campaign fought against indiscriminate outdoor relief. But from the late 1880s and

---

[143] M. A. Crowther, *The Workhouse System, 1834–1929: The History of an English Social Institution* (London: Methuen, University Paperback, 1983), 54–87.

the 1890s expenditure began to rise—and rose spectacularly in the early 1900s. Most of this increase is explained by the improvements in the workhouses which have already been noted; in 1905/6 indoor pauperism had become approximately four times as expensive, case for case, as outdoor pauperism.[144] This process was accentuated by the practice adopted by some guardians of sending certain categories of pauper to charitable institutions at public expense. Further, although the proportion of paupers in the population showed a decline from the 1870s, that downward trend was slowed and slightly reversed in the first half of the 1900s.

Thus the poor law—like charity—faced increased costs. Expenditure on indoor relief rose by 113 per cent between 1871/2 and 1905/6, although the number of indoor paupers rose by only 76 per cent. Indeed, the raw figures of rising expenditure and the reversal in the trend of the proportion of paupers in the population tended to fuel fears that pauperism was again on the increase—fears which matched those before 1834 and 1869. These apprehensions were heightened by the Unemployed Workmen Act of 1905, which, as has been seen, envisaged an agency of relief other than the poor law. In such circumstances, one reaction was to argue for a return to the stricter principles of 1834 and 1869 to check the progress of pauperism; and the appointment of a further Royal Commission on the Poor Laws in November 1905 has sometimes been seen as having been dictated by the desire to make the poor law more stringent and, in harmony with a well-regulated system of charity, to return to the self-maintenance ideas of 1834 and 1869.

It is true that the Commission was not without such ideas; and its activities gave an opportunity for an expression of them. Its Majority Report stated that, despite poor law expenditure, 'we still have a vast army of persons quartered upon us unable to support themselves, and an army which in numbers has recently shown signs of increase rather than decrease.'[145] But the Commission was appointed more on the grounds that the poor law could not cope with the high unemployment of 1903–5. Rather than being seen as a means of correcting the tendencies of the

---

[144] *Report of the Royal Commission on the Poor Laws and Relief of Distress* (Parliamentary Papers, 1909, Cd. 4499), i (pts. i–vi of the Majority Report) par. 65.
[145] Ibid. par. 152.

Unemployed Workmen Act, it was regarded as complementary to that Act 'as a long-term attempt to grapple with the problems [the Act] was designed to meet immediately.'[146] The Commission was, then, a reaction to what was seen as a challenge to the poor law system: a challenge which was, in fact, more in the nature of a crisis. Further, the scale of the problem is to be seen in the fact that the 'vast army' of paupers which the Majority Report indicated as being 'quartered upon us unable to support themselves'[147] represented some 2.6 per cent of the population. Even a conservative estimate of Booth's and Rowntree's figures suggests a figure well in excess of this for those in 'want' or 'poverty', as distinct from pauperism and dependence on poor relief. The discrepancy is a measure of the extent to which the poor law was failing to meet the challenge of poverty. Even the Majority Report of the Poor Law Commission of 1905–9 did not feel that the existing system could remain as it was, or go back to the model introduced in 1834 and resurrected in 1869.

Thus the formula of voluntarism supplemented by a minimal state in the shape of the poor law was still trying to cope with the circumstances of the period—and often doing so to an extent disapproved of by those who wished to keep a tight grip on the amount of relief dispensed through either source, and who still sought to inculcate thrift and self-maintenance. Seizing on one aspect of charitable relief—medical charities—Rentoul wrote that 'as at present administered, Medical Charities offer one of the greatest obstacles to thrift. No movement has been established by which the working classes might, by self-help, provide themselves with medical aid, without the Medical Charity Managers doing their utmost to destroy it . . . Medical Charities form one of the greatest pauperising institutions in the country.'[148] Yet it was becoming clear to many other observers that attempts to deal with the 'problem of social reconstruction', even in their extended form, were beyond the capacity of the voluntary and statutory agencies of a local and often uncoordinated kind, which were experiencing acute problems in raising enough money to meet the demands made upon them. The old synthesis of providence, paternalism, and philanthropy was breaking down—a point

---

[146] John Brown, 'The Appointment of the 1905 Poor Law Commission', *Bulletin of the Institute of Historical Research*, xlii/106 (Nov. 1969), 241.
[147] *Report of the Royal Commission on the Poor Laws, Part II: Statistical Survey of Poor Law Problems*, par. 152.   [148] Rentoul, *Reform*, p. x.

which even many of those broadly sympathetic to it were coming to recognize.

V

If one source of the challenge to previous principles and practices was that they *could* not cope with the current situation,
another was that they *should* not do so. Intellectual exponents of
the 'New Liberalism' expressed reservations about the justification for providence and thrift. J. A. Hobson's ideas on the relationship between under-consumption and low wages cast doubt
on the value of saving; indeed, in Hobson's view, the practice of
thrift had stifled economic growth rather than promoted it, for
saving had been possible only for a small élite, who had sought
the most profitable return for their money rather than buying
commodities in the domestic market and thus encouraging employment.[149] Hobson was also very conscious of the extent to
which capital in a market economy was derived from unearned
income. In these circumstances, it was quite unrealistic to blame
the poor for lack of thrift; and he questioned why unearned
income was seen to be acceptable for the rich, and yet small gifts
of money were seen to pauperize the poor.

Similar points were made by J. M. Robertson in *The Fallacy of
Saving*, published in 1892. He argued that saving merely withdrew from circulation money which would be better spent in
stimulating the demand for goods. 'Industrial confidence', he
wrote, 'is notoriously commensurate with the activity of demand'—and the creation of wealth could 'obviously be promoted
by the substitution of an ideal of consumption for an ideal of
parsimony'. In his view, to provide for old age and sickness from
savings restricted consumption and demand—and thus helped
to make unemployment worse.[150] L. T. Hobhouse wrote of the
inability of the individual to influence the market and thus to
exercise self-help. An individual workman, he stated, was 'the
last person to have any say in the control of the market'.[151]

---

[149] Michael Bentley, *The Climax of Liberal Politics: British Liberalism in Theory and
Practice, 1868–1918* (London: Edward Arnold, 1987), 94.

[150] See also Michael Freeden, *The New Liberalism: An Ideology of Social Reform*
(Oxford: Clarendon Press, 1978), 131 n. 56.

[151] See also L. T. Hobhouse, *Liberalism* (London: Williams & Norgate, 1911),
160–2: 'In the earlier days of the Free Trade Era, it was permissible to hope that
self-help would be an adequate solvent, and that with cheap food and expanding

To 'New Liberals', then, the traditional liberal belief in removing hindrances to individual effort was based on a mistaken—or at least, misplaced—assumption that there was such a thing as a 'free-standing' individual, independent of, and divorced from, his social environment. And if providence was suspect, and indeed harmful, so too were paternalism and philanthropy. Hobson was critical of philanthropy which concerned itself with individual cases of suffering but was impervious to the idea that anything might be wrong with the general working of the industrial system. The activities of the Charity Organisation Society—in their strictest form—were regarded with hostility. D. G. Ritchie argued that morality limited to the realm of personal help ignored the organic structure of society. Masterman recognized that the 'wide-reaching effect' of charity was 'more extensive than many either believe or desire'. He also realized the possibilities that lie within their power; but felt that they had to come to 'a common conscious recognition of the extent of the general problem, of the conditions that any solution must satisfy, and of the end towards the attainment of which all efforts must be directed'. 'So long', he continued, 'as their strength is not united, so long as men rest content with finding remedies for isolated evils and do not take a broad view of the whole question, so long will the fruit of their labours be scanty, unattractive and scarcely worth the gathering.'[152] Thus to 'New Liberals', philanthropy failed to grasp the element of mutuality which held the community together. At worst it could be harmful; at best it offered only palliatives, and lacked any wider consideration of social justice.

commerce the average workman would be able by the exercise of prudence and thrift not only to maintain himself in good times, but to lay by for sickness, unemployment, and old age. The actual course of events has in large measure disappointed these hopes . . . As a whole, the working classes of England, though less thrifty than those of some Continental countries, cannot be accused of undue negligence with regard to the future. The accumulation of savings in Friendly Societies, Trade Unions, Co-operative Societies, and Savings Banks shows an increase which has more than kept pace with the rise in the level of wages; yet there appears no likelihood that the average manual worker will attain the goal of that full independence, covering all the risks of life for self and family, which can alone render the competitive system really adequate to the demands of a civilised conscience . . .'. See also Andrew Vincent and Raymond Plant, *Philosophy, Politics and Citizenship: The Life and Thought of the British Idealists* (Oxford: Basil Blackwell, 1984), 43–93.

[152] See Greenleaf, *British Political Tradition*, ii. 155–6 for a consideration of Masterman.

If 'New Liberals' were critical of providence, paternalism, and philanthropy, socialists were much more so. Some socialists practised thrift, more or less as a matter of necessity. Ramsay MacDonald in later life recalled that, when he had come to London at first as a young Scotsman, he would buy whatever food he wanted around the slums of King's Cross, but he would receive his staple food—oatmeal—from home, and always paid for it. He could afford tea or coffee, but found hot water as good as tea from the point of view of food—and also that 'it tastes as well when once you have grown used to it'.[153] Similarly, the Webbs— more out of a sense of guilt than from necessity—practised personal austerity and what might be regarded as a thrifty way of life. But to preach the virtues of thrift to the poor was, socialists thought, a means of allowing the rich to evade their social obligations at the expense of the poor. Equally, socialists might well be charitable and philanthropic, and even paternalistic, in their conduct, and many had been active in philanthropy before turning to socialism. Nevertheless, they tended to dislike charitable and philanthropic behaviour on the grounds that it did little, if any, lasting good. A character in *On the Threshold*, a novel written in 1895 by a Leeds feminist and socialist, Isabella Ford, said that philanthropy generally means 'giving away what you don't want to people who would be much better without it';[154] and a writer in the *Socialist*, a Sunderland newspaper, wrote that the working classes required independence and had no need for the 'canting sympathy and foolish patronage' of philanthropists. The Social Democratic Federation was very critical of philanthropy, and William Morris thought of it as a mere palliative.[155]

Socialists regarded philanthropy as an aspect of wealth and privilege which should be abolished. When the future Lord Swaythling told George Lansbury in 1889 that he gave away one-tenth of his income to the poor, Lansbury replied that 'we Socialists want to prevent you from getting the nine-tenths'.[156] The future Earl of Meath was interrupted and heckled when, as a prominent philanthropist, he tried to address socialist audiences

---

[153] Ford and Harrison, *A Hundred Years Ago*, 94.

[154] Chris Waters, *British Socialists and the Politics of Popular Culture, 1884–1914* (Manchester: Manchester University Press, 1990), 65.   [155] Ibid. 72.

[156] Brian Harrison, *Peaceable Kingdom: Stability and Change in Modern Britain* (Oxford: Clarendon Press, 1983), 254.

in London in the 1880s.[157] In Reading, the local branch of the Social Democratic Federation attacked the major employers of the town, Messrs Huntley and Palmer, on the grounds that they financed their philanthropy by paying low wages; and the efforts of charitable organizations there were often subject to socialist attack.[158]

Socialists also disliked what they saw as the hypocrisy and intrusiveness of philanthropy; and the visits of upper-class philanthropists to the homes of the poor were seen in this light. Beatrice Webb was, in fact, initially a member of the Charity Organisation Society, having joined the Soho Branch in 1883; she was also a rent-collector in one of Octavia Hill's housing projects in the East End. She liked the emphasis, encouraged by both pursuits, on saving and self-maintenance, and felt too that personal philanthropy developed moral qualities in both giver and receiver. But she was also aware of the faults and limitations of philanthropy, and felt that it could easily lead to 'pharisaical self-congratulation'. What she called the 'real philanthropist' was 'far too perplexed at the very "mixed result" (even if he can recognise any permanent result) of his work, to feel much pride over it'.[159] And especially after she devoted her energies to taking part in Charles Booth's survey, she began to disengage herself from the ideology of the Charity Organisation Society, and became a more outspoken critic of philanthropy as a cure to social problems.

Beatrice Webb was also very critical of the poor law. Unlike some socialists, she and Sidney Webb did not wish to make the poor law more humane, but to abolish it altogether in the interests of greater efficiency and social planning. Their ideas, foreshadowed in Fabian publications, developed into the strong attack on the poor laws which Beatrice launched as a member of the Royal Commission on the Poor Laws appointed in 1905, and in the Minority Report which she masterminded; and the Commission's sittings were marked by displays of considerable animosity between her and upholders of Charity Organisation Society

---

[157] Ibid.   [158] Yeo, *Religion*, 255–6.

[159] Norman and Jeanne MacKenzie (eds.), *The Diary of Beatrice Webb*, 4 vols. (London: Virago Press in association with the London School of Economics and Political Science, 1982–5), i. 85.

ideas, such as Helen Bosanquet.[160] Beatrice felt that such persons wanted to retain the major role that charity played in the relief of the poor, and she found this unacceptable. Nor could she accept the existing synthesis of providence, paternalism, and philanthropy, and of the mutually supportive voluntary and statutory agencies which upheld it. She wrote of the contribution of Hancock Nunn, a member of the Hampstead Board of Guardians and of the Commission, to one of the Commission's sessions. He had given 'an eloquent defence of a rigid test of destitution *plus* organised charitable agencies, and provident societies'. This was, Beatrice added dismissively, 'quite a sermon . . . on the principles of 1834 *plus* the C.O.S.'[161]

Beatrice Webb was not alone among women as she distanced herself from philanthropic activity. The earlier involvement of women in charitable work—noted in Chapter 1—did, indeed, continue in the later nineteenth century. The activities of university women in the Settlement Movement has already been mentioned, and it was estimated that at least 20,000 salaried women, half a million voluntary women, and thousands of church women were active during the period in assisting the homeless and the handicapped. The habit of 'visiting' remained prominent; and the encouragement of mothers' meetings still yielded spectacular results. Patricia Hollis has described all this as 'a hugely impressive effort in time, money, imagination and benevolence.'[162] Here again, the very circumstances of the time called forth work of this kind. Nevertheless, there were those who angrily rejected philanthropy and saw political activity as much more effective. The Countess of Carlisle said that 'almsgiving [was] such a paltry thing . . . We want no Lady Bountifuls in this last quarter of our nineteenth century; we want Radical women in whatever class they may chance to live giving to people their legitimate rights';[163] and these included proper housing, free education, and better working conditions. The Countess of Warwick, commenting on the plight of hungry children, the

---

[160] See A. M. McBriar, *An Edwardian Mixed Doubles: The Bosanquets versus the Webbs: A Study in British Social Policy, 1890–1929* (Oxford: Clarendon Press, 1987), 368–80, for a consideration of these themes.

[161] *Our Partnership*, ed. Barbara Drake and Margaret I. Cole (London: Longmans, Green, 1948), 358.

[162] *Ladies Elect: Women in English Local Government, 1865–1914* (Oxford: Clarendon Press, 1987), 11.   [163] Quoted ibid. 28.

unemployed, and the aged, asked, 'of what possible use is it to plaster this state of things with philanthropy?'[164] Such comments, moreover, were not confined to radical aristocrats. Ada Chew, a former factory worker, said that she had heard much about the poor needing the assistance of the rich. She disagreed; what they needed was the vote to help themselves. Anything else amounted only to 'methods of alleviation'.[165] This illustrates the point that behind the demand by women for enfranchisement often lay the desire to further wide-ranging social reform rather than remain content with social amelioration.

The closing decades of the nineteenth and the early twentieth centuries thus exposed the limitations of voluntary-sector agencies, supplemented by a minimal and localized state. In ideology, it was criticized as being hypocritical, patronizing, or positively insulting—and another point was to the effect that philanthropic giving actually repressed individual spontaneity and denied personal fulfilment by encouraging the individual to love his neighbour *more* than himself, rather than 'as himself'.[166] Further, the commercial sector was felt by critics to be unacceptable; welfare should not be a matter of profit. In implementation, the agencies of voluntarism—and poor law—were seen to be limited, patchy, and unequal to the circumstances of the time. The solution to social problems, which were perceived as a threat to Britain's standing in an increasingly difficult international situation, seemed quite beyond their capacity to provide.

VI

The defects and shortcomings of the old system called forth the need for new practices. The appropriate agency to fill the vacuum in social provision was increasingly seen to lie in the state—in a more positive and centralized role. The arguments for a more positive state were, in many respects, the obverse side of the arguments against voluntarism intermixed with a minimal state. The state, it was argued, *could* cope with the circumstances of the time—or could be made to cope. It had, or could have, the necessary resources to meet social need on a scale which voluntarism,

[164] Quoted ibid.   [165] Quoted ibid.
[166] Harrison, *Peaceable Kingdom*, 255.

in its limited and patchy way, could never match; and it could develop the necessary professionalism and expertise to ensure that minimum standards of civilized life were universally implemented. From a 'New Liberal' point of view, C. R. Buxton wrote that an appeal to the state was essential to the cause of reform, for 'the power behind all this machinery is enormous. Here at least is an organisation which can grip and grapple with social evils'.[167]

Further, it could be urged that the state *should* intervene in a more positive way in the interests of social justice. T. H. Green, in his *Lectures on the Principles of Political Obligation* delivered in 1879–80, had already begun to modify the views of Mill by allowing the state more authority in creating the conditions for greater 'positive freedom'—although he hedged his views around with many more traditional liberal views.[168] D. G. Ritchie took things a stage further with his *Principles of State Intervention*, published in 1891. The emphasis was less on the individual than on the individual in the community. 'We have', wrote Ritchie, 'come again to recognise with Aristotle, the moral function of the state'; and he also wrote of 'the advisability of immediate state action to secure the health and intelligence of the community and a fair chance for its moral progress'.[169] Hobson argued that the state could bring about a degree of security which no other means could offer, and that there were circumstances in which state intervention was appropriate as a course of first, rather than last, resort. To 'New Liberals', then, the state had a role in setting right the shortcomings of an economic system which had produced poverty on such a scale as would put self-improvement beyond the capacity of the individual.

If the economic and social circumstances of the period strengthened the argument that the state *could* and *should* undertake a more positive role, the same could be said of the political context. The extension of political rights to a greater number of the population meant that those now enfranchised became 'citizens' in the sense of belonging to the political

---

[167] Quoted in Freeden, *The New Liberalism*, 66.

[168] Bentley, *Climax of Liberal Politics*, 49. See also Vincent and Plant, *Philosophy, Politics and Citizenship*, 76 ff.

[169] Vincent and Plant, *Philosophy, Politics and Citizenship*, 76–7. See also Freeden, *The New Liberalism*, 15.

community. It could, then, be argued that just as they were now entitled to political rights, so too they were entitled to social rights. The possession of civil and political rights was, indeed, somewhat empty without social and economic rights; for it was the latter which made full enjoyment of the former possible. 'New Liberals' were acutely aware of this new dimension of citizenship: one to be provided as an entitlement by an active state rather than aspired to by active citizens outside the state.

Such arguments made an appeal not only to 'New Liberals'. From the 1880s the state had a key role to play for socialists. It is true that there was room for considerable disagreement among socialists as to how far the state should go; and, as has been seen, the state was still regarded with considerable suspicion by many socialists as an agency to keep the working classes in a subordinate position. But they also felt that the major causes of poverty were social, rather than personal, and to the Fabian socialist mind it followed that only society, through the state, *could* provide the necessary remedies, which, indeed, it *should* also provide out of a sense of moral fairness and equity. To the Webbs, social reconstruction 'required as much specialised training and sustained study as the building of bridges and railways, the interpretation of the law or the technical improvement in machinery and mechanical progress'.[170] They were also well aware of the political circumstances, and their implications; as has been mentioned, Sidney Webb wrote of socialism as the economic obverse of democracy.[171]

From a very different political perspective, Joseph Chamberlain brought together the 'could' and the 'should' arguments, and put them in a political context which certainly suggested that to the politicians, if not always to the people, social and economic issues were now firmly on the political agenda:

Because state Socialism may cover very injurious and very unwise theories, that is no reason at all why we should refuse to recognise the fact that Government is the only organisation of the whole people for the benefit of all its members, and that the community . . . ought . . . to provide for all its members benefits which it is impossible for individuals

---

[170] Quoted in Tony Novak, *Poverty and the State: An Historical Sociology* (Milton Keynes: Open University Press, 1988), 103.
[171] See Hay (ed.), *Development*, 14.

to provide by their solitary and separate efforts.... It is only the community acting as a whole that can possibly deal with evils so deep seated ... When Government represented only the authority of the Crown or the views of a particular class, I can understand that it was the first duty of men who valued their freedom to restrict its authority and to limit its expenditure. But all that is changed. Now Government is the organised expression of the wishes and wants of the people, and under these circumstances let us cease to regard it with suspicion ... Now it is our business to extend its functions, and to see in what way its operations can be usefully enlarged.[172]

Conservatives of longer standing than Chamberlain also tended to stress what they saw as the heritage of 'Tory democracy'—or, to be more accurate, 'Tory paternalism'—in the Conservative Party. An official Party handbook published in 1909, entitled *The Case against Radicalism*, recognized that Conservatism, if anti-radical, was not opposed to social reform, and, indeed, had a tradition of using the power of the state to better the condition of the people. This point was also frequently made by Lord Milner; and the Tory historian Sir Sidney Low repudiated 'old-fashioned individualism' as a thing of the past, and argued that the state should play an important part in the provision of social services.[173] The Unionist Social Reform Committee was established by Arthur Steel-Maitland, Conservative Party Chairman, who had published a study of unemployment to engender interest in social questions among Conservative MPs; and in 1912 Lord Hugh Cecil argued that there was 'no antithesis between Conservatism and Socialism or even between Conservatism and Liberalism'. Conservatives, he wrote, 'have no difficulty in welcoming the social activity of the state'.[174]

Thus, on all sides, collectivism could be seen to supply the answer to the defects found in providence, paternalism, and philanthropy. Further, there were foreign examples and precedents in the very countries which seemed to threaten Britain's pre-eminence in the area of national efficiency. From the point of view of those who felt that Britain could no longer afford the

[172] Quoted in Greenleaf, *British Political Tradition*, i. 215–16.

[173] Quoted ibid. ii. 232.

[174] See Philip W. Buck (ed.), *How Conservatives Think* (Harmondsworth: Penguin Books, 1975), 130–3, for further aspects of Cecil's thought. See also Greenleaf, *British Political Tradition*, ii. 285–7, for elaboration of these points and a statement of anti-collectivist Conservative thought.

uncoordinated and fragmentary approach to social problems inherent in voluntarism, a more systematic effort was necessary. As Hennock has written, 'more complete organisation became the great desideratum'.[175] Germany provided an example of this in several areas. Thus in education, it could be claimed that Germany and Switzerland had reached a much higher level of achievement by systematic organization than Britain; and that Britain must heed the example if she were to retain her position. The system of compulsory insurance covering various vicissitudes such as industrial accident, illness, and old age, introduced by Bismarck in the 1880s, also had its admirers in Britain, especially after 1907. It was applauded by Beveridge in 1907 for its comprehensiveness in coping with incapacity for work; and he added that such a 'completeness' could not be achieved 'by rough and ready methods. It depends upon organization and the willingness to submit to organization.'[176] Churchill put the whole matter succinctly in 1908 when he commented that Germany was better placed than Britain by being organized 'not only for war but also for peace', and he urged Asquith 'to apply to this country the successful experience of Germany in social organization.'[177] Germany thus seemed to provide proof that an active state could alone provide the degree of professionalism and expertise which could harness national resources and promote national efficiency: a point which gained increasing acceptance in Britain in the first decade of the twentieth century.

The practical application of many of these various strands is, of course, well known to lie in the Liberal legislation after 1906. As has already been mentioned, this is, indeed, always seen by historians as a 'significant' period in promoting the state to a more active and positive role in various areas; and it is unnecessary to do more than mention the measures to deal with the nutritional and medical needs of children in 1906 and 1907, the treatment of children by law in criminal and civil cases in 1908, old-age pensions in 1908, housing and town planning in 1909, the finding of employment through labour exchanges in 1909, and health and unemployment insurance in 1911. The question of family income maintenance in normal times was also raised;

---

[175] *British Social Reform*, 19.	[176] Quoted ibid.
[177] Quoted in Bentley B. Gilbert, *The Evolution of National Insurance in Great Britain* (London: Michael Joseph, 1966), 252.

and the Trade Boards Act of 1909 went some way towards establishing minimum rates in unorganized trades. Fiscal policy also underwent a change, with the introduction of progressive and redistributory taxation in Lloyd George's budget in 1909, finally passed, after vigorous opposition in the Lords, in 1911. Fiscal policy thus became an instrument not only for administrative purposes, but for social policy, based on the principle of collective spending.

To suggest that these developments were wholly new tends to miss the point made in Chapter 1: that in practice, state intervention had been proceeding for a very long time; and that to talk in terms of an age of 'collectivism' replacing one of 'individualism', as Dicey tended to do (in his lectures on the Relation Between Law and Public Opinion in England During the Nineteenth Century, 1905), presents an oversimplified and misleading impression. Some of the legislation passed in the first decade of the century did, indeed, extend areas of responsibility which earlier legislation had already dealt with, such as education, hours of work, and children's rights. It was, in fact, the Conservative government of Balfour which passed the Education Act of 1902—and the 'New Liberals' brought in a national eight-hour day for miners in 1908.

Nevertheless, the measures of the 'New Liberals' may also be regarded as more than simply a continuation of previous principles and practices, and seen to have resulted from a realization that the old synthesis of providence, paternalism, and philanthropy—designed to build up individual character and initiative, and relying heavily on voluntary and local effort—could no longer bear the weight of circumstances and the probing of convictions. The alleviation of distress and, indeed, a more far-reaching assault on poverty seemed to be beyond the capacity of what Chamberlain had called the 'solitary and separate efforts' of individuals as expressed through voluntary and localized statutory agencies, jealous of their independence and often under-funded. The state now seemed to be the more appropriate agency, with its attributes of centralization and uniformity, professionalism and expertise, resources and capacity. And as ever more individuals became 'citizens' in the sense of belonging to the political community, the citizenship of entitlement from the state in matters of social welfare was seen to be more correct and apposite than the citizenship of contribution expressed through voluntary agencies outside the state.

If, then, the period from 1880 to 1914 as a whole did pose challenges to voluntarism allied to a minimal, localized state, the growth of a more collectivist state in response to such problems posed a further challenge; and the reaction of voluntarism in the face of this will now be considered.

VII

One reaction of voluntarism to a growing and more positive state presence was to cooperate and converge with it. This was evident in various areas of the mutual-aid side of the voluntary sector and in the commercial sector. In the friendly-society movement, there was a growing recognition that, in the light of its increasing financial problems, some form of state pension was necessary. In 1895 a delegate conference of friendly societies in the district of Birmingham passed a resolution 'affirming the desirability of enacting a comprehensive system of old age pensions.' In 1896 the annual meetings of Manchester Unity and Hearts of Oak recognized that some form of state grant was necessary to diminish the hardships of old age. In 1896 and 1899 the Grand United Order of Odd Fellows—in considerable financial difficulties—adopted a resolution in favour of a non-contributory state pension of 5s. a week, payable at the age of sixty. Thus within the friendly-society movement, a pro-state-pensions lobby was making progress by 1900. The momentum was retained thereafter; and by mid–1908 even Manchester Unity and Foresters—hitherto opponents of state pensions—had accepted the case for them. Here, then, was a willingness to accept a degree of convergence with the state on pensions on the part of the most prominent mutual-aid voluntary-sector organizations.[178]

In matters of health and unemployment insurance, this convergence may also be detected in the National Insurance Act of 1911. On the latter issue, the trade unions demanded that they should participate in any scheme of unemployment insurance; and the Board of Trade was anxious to involve trade unions in the insured trades within the scheme. Thus a trade union might

[178] Treble, 'Attitudes', 280 ff.

choose to become an administrator for the government, whether or not it had previously offered unemployment insurance. Union members in the insured trades certainly had to contribute to the unemployment fund set up by the Act of 1911, and into which payments of employee, employer, and state were made; but a member might draw his benefit through the union rather than through the newly established labour exchanges, which were to be the government's agency. Smaller unions, which had previously paid their members unemployment benefit, found the administration which was involved in participating in the state scheme somewhat burdensome, and tended to withdraw from it, leaving it to the labour exchanges; but the opportunity for participation was certainly offered. Moreover, the Act made it possible for unions to be reimbursed with a proportion of the cost of the amount which the union paid. Convergence between voluntary and statutory agencies was, perhaps, even more evident in the arrangements made for the administration of health insurance under the first section of the Act. The societies approved to administer the scheme were the mutual-aid friendly societies and trade unions within the voluntary sector, and the collecting friendly societies and industrial insurance societies within the commercial sector. Here, indeed, there was a convergence of voluntary-sector and commercial-sector agencies with the state.

Similarly, those involved in the charitable side of the voluntary sector often welcomed the assistance of the state in areas in which they found it very difficult to make adequate progress by themselves. Thus the authors of *The Bitter Cry of Outcast London*, in a striking statement of the 'citizenship of entitlement' bestowed by the state, came to the conclusion that only the state could achieve results in housing:

We shall be pointed to the fact that without State interference nothing effectual can be accomplished upon any large scale . . . The State must . . . secure for the poorest the rights of citizenship; the right to live in something better than fever dens; the right to live as something better than the uncleanest of brute beasts. This must be done before the Christian missionary can have much chance with them. . . .[179]

The need for better housing—and thus improved health—could also be urged from the angle of 'national efficiency'; and this was

[179] Wohl (ed.), *Bitter Cry*, 69.

also true of the case for improved technical education. Here again, charitable agencies, increasingly anxious about Britain's international standing, could see the need for a greater state presence. Nor was this feeling absent among those involved in industrial or employer paternalism. It is difficult to find a consistent attitude to state welfare schemes among employers; but in the years before 1914, such schemes did have some appeal in the face of foreign competition and labour unrest. They might contribute to social harmony and also to economic efficiency. In 1907 the Birmingham Chamber of Commerce argued the case for a comprehensive social insurance scheme before the Association of Chambers of Commerce. One speaker, J. S. Taylor, claimed that it was 'already admitted that something must be done for the further protection of the industrial classes against the contingencies and uncertainties of their existence'. He spoke strongly in favour of the German system, for, he alleged, 'no scheme had been yet suggested in parliament or out which was equal in any way' to it.[180]

Charities which had to do with the handicapped, or with children—anxious to provide a more specialized, professional, and thus more expensive service—often positively welcomed the prospect of state assistance. The National Society for the Prevention of Cruelty to Children and the State Children's Association had been early supporters of a larger involvement of the state in assisting pauper, vagrant, and delinquent children. George Behlmer has written of the National Society leaders that 'by and large they looked forward to augmenting their resources with help from central government'.[181] The 1908 Children's Act owed much to philanthropic pressure and example. Close relations with a more positive state were also canvassed by those involved with the problem of unemployment. Appeals for state assistance were, on occasion, made by those active in the social work of the Salvation Army. In 1895 Bramwell Booth raised the question of government subsidies for its work in emigration, and outlined the role of the Social Wing of the Army in carrying out pilot

---

[180] Robert Fitzgerald, *British Labour Management and Industrial Welfare 1846–1939* (London: Croom Helm, 1988), 212–25, deals with this area. See also J. R. Hay, 'Employers' Attitudes to Social Policy and the Concept of Social Control, 1900–1920', in Pat Thane (ed.), *The Origins of British Social Policy* (London: Croom Helm, 1978), 107–25.   [181] *Child Abuse*, 217.

schemes which the government itself might adopt for 'all conditions of the unemployed and unfortunate classes'.[182]

The Ragged School Union adopted a largely pragmatic role towards collectivism. By the late nineteenth and early twentieth centuries it had, of course, long become accustomed to the presence of the state in education, and the Education Act of 1870 had made considerable inroads on its educational activities. Thereafter, the Union concentrated on evangelical work with a strong vocational and social content. It was active in industrial training, such as boot-repairing for boys and needlework for girls. It took a great interest in caring for handicapped children, and organized outings and holidays for needy children. In these respects, indeed, the Union provides an example of the continuing role of the voluntary sector in its charitable and philanthropic aspect. In February 1909 it called for a national conference of all workers active 'in social, moral and religious work amongst the neglected child life in British cities outside state Institution'; and this was held in May of that year. Yet it also showed a willingness to cooperate *with* 'state Institution'.[183] At a conference held in 1883, the Chairman of the Union, H. R. Williams, read a paper in which he acknowledged the value of the work of the Hornsey School Board; he was in a good position to speak, since he himself was also its Chairman. Here, then, was an example of cooperation and convergence—although it should be noted that Williams also argued that ragged schools were still necessary to deal with problems with which the state schools could not cope.

There were to be further examples of cooperation in the future. In 1910 and 1911 the Union received requests from the London County Council to finance the feeding of needy children in vacation schools; this could not be financed from public funds during school holidays. The council of the Union was sympathetic in principle; its only reservation was that it would not be able to make full financial provision for the meals. But it made arrangements through the Charity Commission—which, increasingly in the later nineteenth century, diverted various endowed charities to educational purposes, as it was empowered to do under the doctrine of cy pres—for the use of a bequest which had been set

---

[182] Quoted in Harris, *Unemployment and Politics*, 129.
[183] *Minutes of the Shaftesbury Society*, 9 Feb. 1909. (Brighton: Harvester microform, vols. 13–14, Feb. 1905–Sept. 1915).

up to provide free meals; and it made a contribution towards the cost. Here, again, there was a measure of convergence between voluntaristic charitable endeavour and the state.[184]

The emergence of Guilds of Help in the charitable world was also important in this respect.[185] They were coordinating bodies, the model for which lay in the Elberfeld system in Germany, and—significantly—they avoided the word 'charity' in their title on the grounds that 'help' was thought to be less open to misunderstanding and to be more inclusive in its meaning. The reasoning here would seem to be that 'charity' was associated in the public mind with a somewhat condescending, patronizing, and moralistic approach, which laid emphasis on the worthiness—or unworthiness—of the person in need. The Guild of Help in Bradford aimed 'to provide a friend for all in need of help and advice', and 'to secure timely aid for the suffering and needy'. It retained an emphasis on bringing about 'lasting improvement in the condition of each case by patient study and wise methods of help', and sought to prevent overlapping and waste of charitable effort. Nevertheless, the Bradford Guild was critical of the Charity Organisation Society, which, although engaged in similar work, was in its view too narrow and ungenerous in its policy.[186] Here, then, was a certain move away from the self-maintenance ideology of the Charity Organisation Society at its most orthodox and strict.

Moreover, the Guilds of Help sought to coordinate all agencies of relief, charitable and statutory, in their work. Another name by which this movement was known was the 'Citizens' Aid Society'. It sought to cooperate with statutory bodies not on negative principles, such as those which had characterized the cooperation between the Charity Organisation Society and the poor law guardians, but on more positive ones in bringing aid—and in making known to individuals the assistance from the state to which they were becoming increasingly entitled. Here, indeed, was the citizenship of contribution through a voluntary agency

[184] Ibid. 8 July 1910, 13 Jan. 1911, 12 May 1911.
[185] See Hollis, *Ladies Elect*, 24 ff. See also M. J. Moore, 'Social Work and Social Welfare: The Organisation of Philanthropic Resources in Britain, 1900–1914' (*Journal of British Studies*, xvi (1977), 85–104) and Michael Cahill and Tony Jowitt, 'The New Philanthropy: The Emergence of the Bradford Guild of Help' (*Journal of Social Policy*, ix (1980), 359–82).
[186] *Charity Organisation Review*, NS, xxxi (Mar. 1912), 139.

which drew attention to the citizenship of entitlement through the state. Samuel Barnett noticed this tendency of charities to try to integrate their forces internally and externally with those of the state—and approved of it. 'Competition', he wrote in 1912, 'may be the strength of commerce, but co-operation is certainly the strength of charity . . .' He also argued that:

charities should keep in line with State activities. The state—either by national or municipal organisation—has taken over many of the duties which meet the needs of the people . . . State organisations . . . will not, like the charities, be fitful because dependent on subscribers and committees . . . Charities . . . I think, do well when they keep in line with State activities . . . Men and women of good-will may, I believe, find boundless opportunities if they will serve on Municipal bodies or on the Committees appointed by such bodies to complement their work.[187]

All this underlines the dangers, already noticed, of taking the Charity Organisation Society's pronouncements on such matters as representing the views of the entire charitable side of the voluntary sector; other societies and spokesmen were, perhaps, more representative of that side. Even within the Society itself, moreover, there was a growing recognition of the need for co-operative activity of a more positive kind. Indeed, as early as 1886 a Charity Organisation Society Committee on Exceptional Distress admitted that there were 'permanent causes of distress which it is impossible for philanthropy alone to cope with or even in any sufficient degree to palliate by schemes of direct relief'.[188] The Committee therefore suggested that local committees composed of poor law guardians, charities, and local authorities should investigate cases, marshal relief funds, and see to temporary employment for those who were normally independent, but at present unemployed. In 1904 a Charity Organisation Society Committee on Distress Due to Want of Employment recommended that in an emergency, employment on 'public or other works' should be provided by local joint committees of guardians, councillors, and charitable agencies.

The attitude of the Society towards Guilds of Help and Citizens'

---

[187] 'Charity up to Date', quoted in Pope, Pratt, and Hoyle (eds.), *Social Welfare*, 72–3. This comes close to what Cahill and Jowitt have called 'a voluntary welfare state', which was a 'network of charities and organisations which would aid those in distress and intensify the social conscience of the city.' ('The New Philanthropy', 379.)   [188] Quoted in Harris, *Unemployment and Politics*, 108.

Aid Societies was rather ambivalent. Some members resented the activities of such bodies; they felt that the Guilds relied too much on enthusiastic and well-meaning helpers, who lacked the training and professionalism of the Society; and the view was expressed that the Guilds were simply the Charity Organisation Society 'under a more beautiful name'. Nevertheless, others in the Society recognized the limitations of their approach. In February 1908 a speaker from Newcastle at a conference on the future of charity organization societies said that it was 'time for [the Society] to take a wider view of things', and to co-operate with other agencies in a more positive way.[189]

Furthermore, the Charity Organisation Society representatives on the Royal Commission on the Poor Laws (1905–9) were, as José Harris has written, 'prepared to go as far as socialists in recommending anti-depressive public works and industrial retraining for the unemployed'.[190] The Majority Report of the Commission did, in large measure, represent the views of the Society—or, at least, those of its leaders. But, as has been mentioned, it did not defend the pure principles and practice of the 1834 Report, and, as A. W. Vincent has stated, was 'not a manifestation of individualism *simpliciter*'.[191] The Report recognized that 'a study of modern industrial conditions proves that unemployment is often due to influences for which the workman is not responsible'.[192] Nor was it wholly anti-statist. It acknowledged that there was public distrust of the poor law, and that some reform was necessary to regain public confidence in it. It recommended that public assistance authorities should replace the guardians and investigate and award relief; and these should in part be composed of locally elected borough and county councillors. 'The spheres of work of organized charity are wide and manifold', ran the Majority Report; 'but the relief of permanent destitution or of chronic unemployment seems to be more

[189] *Charity Organisation Review*, NS, xxiii (Feb. 1908), 77. In 1909 the Charity Organisation Society changed its name from 'The Society for the Organisation of Charity and Repressing Mendicity' to 'The Society for the Organisation of Charitable Effort and the Improvement of the Condition of the Poor' (Moore, 'Social Work', 97 n. 33).   [190] *Unemployment and Politics*, 109.
[191] 'The Poor Law Report and the Social Theory of the Charity Organisation Society' (*Victorian Studies*, xxvii/3, spring 1984, 345.) See also Vincent and Plant, *Philosophy, Politics and Citizenship*, 94–131.
[192] *Report of the Royal Commission on the Poor Laws*, i. pt. vi, par. 569.

properly the duty of a public authority supported by public funds.'[193] The Report spoke highly of the 'old-fashioned value of thrift', and acknowledged that since 1834, 'the opportunities of husbanding small savings and making insurance against sickness, accident, old age, and death have very greatly increased'. Nevertheless, it admitted that there seemed 'room and necessity for a great extension of insurance against Unemployment', and did not hesitate 'to recommend the encouragement of a State subsidy'.[194]

Further, on a more individual level, Bernard Bosanquet, who claimed that the Majority Report of the Poor Law Commission represented part of the 'social vision' of the Charity Organisation Society, accepted the importance of 'the community', and subscribed to an organic view of society; and, in that respect at least, he may be said to have had something in common with the Webbs. He and his wife also shared the Webbs' distrust of amateurism and 'do-goodism'; thus Helen Bosanquet argued that a 'sound opinion' on social policy was commonly thwarted by a common tendency to ignore 'the fact that scientific principles are as much involved in them, as chemistry or architecture, or any other of the arts of life'. The Bosanquets did not, indeed, object to all aspects of state regulation, and they supported reforms such as compulsory education, state initiatives in housing, the reform of prisons, and legislation to protect children.[195]

There were, then, signs of movement on the part of the Charity Organisation Society itself towards a more accommodating position on the subject of co-operation with a state which had a more positive orientation than that represented by the poor law. By the turn of the century, as John Brown has written, the Society 'was not a monolithic body, united in opposing blanket social legislation'.[196] Brown quotes the case of an attempt by the central body of the Society in 1894 to dismiss C. H. Grinling, Secretary of the Woolwich branch, because he favoured state action. This was met by the rallying of a large section of the Society who came to Grinling's support. Interestingly, the non-contents held a meeting at Toynbee Hall, and passed a resolution

---

[193] Ibid. i. pt. vi, par. 382.   [194] Ibid. i. pt. ix, par. 132.
[195] McBriar, *Edwardian Mixed Doubles*, 371.
[196] 'Social Judgements and Social Policy' (*Economic History Review*, 2nd ser., xxxiv (1971), 111).

that it was not official policy 'to prevent the working together within the society of those who advocated different views as to the limits of state action in relation to poverty'.[197] Even Hancock Nunn—denounced by Beatrice Webb for views expressed in the course of the 1905–9 Poor Law Commission—became Chairman of the Hampstead branch of the Society in 1898 on condition that he came as 'a reformer', and was largely responsible for the founding in 1907 of the Hampstead Council of Social Welfare, which was devoted to community organization.[198]

In March 1912, moreover, the *Charity Organisation Review* published an illuminating exchange of letters between Miss Violet Markham and W. A. Bailward, Chairman of the Administrative Committee of the Charity Organisation Society.[199] Miss Markham was not wholly unsympathetic to the Society; but she felt that it put too much emphasis on the importance of character in causing poverty and too little on environment; and that it took too negative a view of the state. Bailward replied that the Society 'had never denied that economic causes and other avoidable misfortunes play a great part in the problem of poverty'—and had worked hard to mitigate suffering from these causes. Further, he claimed that 'we have never . . . criticised state action *qua* state action but only in so far as it has dealt with poor relief upon which we may presume to have specialist knowledge'. Like the Bosanquets, he argued that the Society had supported the state in housing reform, sanitation, the care of the feeble-minded, the poor law, and the Children's Act of 1908. Even C. S. Loch urged the Society not to get into a groove: and it was quite frequently stated in the pages of the *Charity Organisation Review* that the new statutory agencies created new opportunities for voluntary-sector workers. In July 1913 V. E. Hinks, Secretary of the Leicester branch of the Charity Organisation Society, told his colleagues that there had been an increased demand on charitable institutions since the new legislation had been passed: a point which, he felt, 'upsets the idea that state intervention must mean a decline in the range of voluntary activity'. It was, he concluded, 'not too much to say that upon the number and skill of the

---

[197] Ibid.   [198] See Moore, 'Social Work', 100.
[199] NS, xxxi (Mar. 1912), 129–41.

voluntary workers the working of the different authorities depends'.[200]

It is true that many voluntary-sector workers found their way with relative ease into activity which had a stronger statutory emphasis. In some cases this was a continuation—as further opportunities presented themselves—of the long-standing rapport between the voluntary sector and the localized state. Some women previously active in charitable work saw no conflict whatever between charitable and civic work; the latter was simply an extension of the former. Thus Miss Maud Burnett, who stood for the Tynemouth council at the age of 47, said that she 'did not seek a seat on the council for her own sake, but because she cared for the weak and oppressed, and because she wished to show that women could help.'[201] Eleanor Rathbone of Liverpool became convinced of the merits of elected public office over personal philanthropy, and was active in the Council of Voluntary Aid in Liverpool, which brought together statutory bodies and voluntary agencies, both secular and church-based.[202] But this assimilation could also take place at central government level. The general structure of penal policy for young offenders was laid down in the legislation of the Liberal governments between 1906 and 1914; and persons such as Charles Russell, Arthur Norris, and Alexander Paterson, all of whom had a background of voluntary social work in this area, were in future years to move directly into influential positions in central administration, such as inspectorates of industrial and reformatory schools.[203] Finally, some former philanthropists drifted into a socialist position, as has already been noted. They tended to see socialism as an extended form of philanthropy. Thus John Trevor wrote that 'Socialism of any worthy sort includes philanthropy, but also goes far nearer to the root of our evils than philanthropy alone can do.' Kirkman Gray moved from a philanthropic to a socialist position, and published in 1908 a work which, in a sense, charted

---

[200] Ibid. NS, xxxiv (July 1913), 26. In 1913 the Society agreed to hold a joint meeting with the Guild of Help Movement the following year (Moore, 'Social Work', 98).

[201] Hollis, *Ladies Elect*, 18.   [202] Ibid.

[203] Victor Bailey, *Delinquency and Citizenship: Reclaiming the Young Offender, 1914–1948* (Oxford: Clarendon Press, 1987), 63.

this movement: *Philanthropy and the State, or Social Politics*, 1908.[204] Thus while it is true that tensions between philanthropists and socialists were always present, there was some evidence of merging: doctrinaire socialists were very suspicious of the Bradford Guild of Help, but moderate members of the Independent Labour Party in Bradford were willing to support it.

It may, therefore, be argued that, in the face of a greater state presence in the later nineteenth and early twentieth centuries, the voluntary and commercial sectors reacted by adopting a policy of assimilation to it. Their ideology became less militantly individualistic; their implementation made greater room for professionalism and bureaucracy. This was evident within the voluntary sector itself, for various larger charities, such as the National Society for the Prevention of Cruelty to Children, adopted a degree of organization and professionalism which was little different from, and, indeed, sometimes greater than, that adopted by a statutory body.[205] There was also a greater willingness and, in some cases, an eagerness, among voluntarists to accept a larger state presence—and a greater degree of cooperation with the state in meeting social need directly rather than simply in creating the conditions in which the individual could meet it himself. In 1900 state expenditure on what might be called 'social security' had been confined almost entirely to the poor law, and the figure was £8.4 million; by 1913, the year in which the 1911 National Insurance Act came into operation, it also encompassed old-age pensions, housing, and unemployment and health insurance, and the figure was £43.4 million. What Gladstone had called 'construction', involving a process of 'taking into the hands of the state the business of the individual',[206] had seemed to come about; and responsibility for welfare had become more a matter for an 'active state' which bestowed entitlements on its citizens, and less a matter for 'active citizens' contributing, by voluntaristic methods, to their own welfare outside the state. And with that movement to 'active state', it may be argued, 'active citizens' had cooperated and converged.

---

[204] Benjamin Kirkman Gray, *Philanthropy and the State, or Social Politics* (London: P. S. King, 1908).   [205] Behlmer, *Child Abuse*, 216.
[206] Greenleaf, *British Political Tradition*, ii. 145.

VIII

It would, however, be a mistake to exaggerate the extent of this whole process; the dangers of Whig interpretations of welfare must be heeded. Older ideologies and practices did not disappear from sight—and, indeed, often permeated the new.[207] Thus the themes of 'challenge', 'collectivism', and 'convergence' must be revisited in order to ensure that they are put into an appropriate context.

Even those who challenged providence, paternalism, and philanthropy were themselves almost part of them, in that—even in their criticisms—they did not wholly depart from the values of the past. Charles Booth's survey, as popularly received, did much to lay the basis of the challenge and to discredit the idea that poverty was the result of personal failings; and it has been claimed that Booth 'presents a sympathetic picture of working-class life'.[208] Yet it is also true that his comments were shot through with moral assumptions and overtones close to those examined in Chapter 1.

It will be recalled that Booth's figure for the proportion of Londoners living in poverty, 30.7 per cent, was reached by aggregating his categories from A to D. He admitted that even in class A, some 'gems' were to be found, and that there were, 'at any rate, many very piteous cases'. But class A also contained, in his words, 'occasional labourers . . . loafers and semi-criminals' and indeed, if in small measure, 'barbarians'. Such persons, he argued, were 'a disgrace but not a danger'. Nor were value judgements absent from his remarks about other, somewhat less 'reprehensible', groups. Class B were certainly 'in want': they did not receive, on average, as much as three days' work a week. Yet it is doubtful, Booth wrote, 'if any of them could or would work full time for long together . . . there will be found many of them who from shiftlessness, idleness or drink, are inevitably poor'. Class C—the 'poor'—were often improvident: some did not earn high wages, but often wasted what little they did earn on extravagance and drink. Class D—again, the 'poor'—were

---

[207] Norman Barry, *Welfare* (Milton Keynes: Open University Press, 1990), 41–3, refers to the lack of any '*coherent* philosophy of welfarism' in this period.
[208] Trevor Lummis, 'Charles Booth: Moralist or Social Scientist?' (*Economic History Review*, 2nd ser., xxiv (1971), 105).

somewhat better. They were usually in regular employment, but they owed this in large part to their personal qualities: 'decent, steady men paying their way and bringing up their children respectably'.[209] Thus, as John Brown has written: 'The poorer his classes, the more harshly [Booth] dealt with them.'[210]

Booth reserved his most favourable comments for those in his highest categories, E and F. Those in class E were, indeed, models of providence; they belonged to mutual-aid societies, such as trade unions or cooperatives, and would not take charity. Class F were even better. They were able by careful management to live comfortably and provide for their old age. 'No large business', Booth wrote, 'could be conducted without such men as its pillars of support and their loyalty and devotion to those whom they serve is very noteworthy.'[211] Thus Booth did not entirely abandon the 'personal' approach to poverty for the 'environmentalist' approach; and while his work was often seen as belonging to the latter, it was, in fact, compatible with the former. Indeed, Brown has written that Booth's unflattering descriptions of the poor perpetuated 'a concern for character in the discussion of policy'.[212]

Similar evidence of moralistic ideas may be traced elsewhere among those who helped to lay the foundation of the challenge to older policies and practices. Rowntree, more than Booth, *did* allow for unpredictable circumstances which could lead to poverty; and, as has been noted, he admitted that a poor environment might increase improvidence rather than the reverse. Yet within his category of secondary poverty, Rowntree—as has also been seen—included such causal factors as drink, betting, and gambling; and it was, therefore, possible to reconcile his ideas with those which stressed the distinction between the deserving and the undeserving. The Inter-Departmental Committee on Physical Deterioration claimed that the 'permanent difficulties' which attached to the problem of bad housing 'reside in the character of the people themselves (their feebleness and indifference, their reluctance to move and their incapability of

---

[209] Fried and Elman (eds.), *Charles Booth's London*, 11–18.
[210] 'Charles Booth and the Labour Colonies, 1889–1905' (*Economic History Review*, 2nd ser., xxi, 1968), 352.
[211] Fried and Elman (eds.), *Charles Booth's London*, 19.
[212] 'Charles Booth', 353.

moving)'.[213] William Booth scorned the distinction between the 'deserving' and 'undeserving'—and was criticized by his namesake, Charles, for providing food and shelter at uneconomic prices through the Salvation Army. Yet with his strong evangelical commitment and belief in the sinfulness of man, William Booth could never be entirely clear in his own mind whether social failure was the result of bad habits or bad environment. In his book *In Darkest England*, he wrote of the 'submerged tenth': that 'population sodden with drink, steeped in vice, eaten up by every social and physical malady'.[214] Barnett did, indeed, move away from the strict doctrines held by the purists of the Charity Organisation Society, but, as has already been mentioned, he never quite shook himself free of these associations, and he wrote that the problem of the unemployed was complicated by the presence of the 'unemployable'. Beatrice Webb, who welcomed Barnett's criticisms of the Charity Organisation Society, never entirely rejected the belief that unemployment was as much a personal as an industrial problem.

Thus it remains true that, even among those who *did* depart from a strict view that poverty was a matter of personal failing and were sympathetic to an environmentalist approach, concern for the poor was, in William J. Fishman's words, 'rarely divorced from stern criticism of their life-style, implying that their situation was as much a result of weakness of character as of forces beyond their control'.[215] José Harris has written in a similar vein of 'the new generation of unemployment theorists'; it was 'in some respects no less censorious than its predecessors; and the growth of a scientific analysis of unemployment was paralleled by the growth of a harsher and more pessimistic attitude towards its victims, which was directed primarily against those who failed to support themselves but extended also to those who became unemployed'.[216]

Solutions devised for the 'residuum' or 'unemployable'—which were, in effect, alternative names for the long-standing category of the 'undeserving poor'—were often strikingly authoritarian. Charles Booth believed that the very poorest and most feckless

---

[213] *Report of the Inter-Departmental Committee*, par. 85.
[214] pp. 17–23; see also p. 24.
[215] *East End 1888: A Year in a London Borough among the Labouring Poor* (London: Duckworth, 1988), 39.   [216] *Unemployment and Politics*, 39.

classes—A and B in his categories—posed a threat to the chances of the rest of the poor in obtaining employment, since all were competing in a limited labour market; and he recommended that those in category B should be sent to specially established labour colonies, where they would exchange their idle and unregulated life for a disciplined existence and fixed hours of work.[217] William Booth saw labour colonies as a means of resolving the dilemma between character and environment; they controlled the environment and, at the same time, emphasized the need for personal redemption. A farm colony was begun at Hadleigh in Essex in 1891 by the Salvation Army. A number of colonies were set up; and the Local Government Board allowed poor relief to be paid in cash to the dependants of men who were unemployed and who were willing to attend.

The Webbs were also attracted to the idea of such colonies. The Minority Report of the Poor Law Commission expressed admiration for schemes devised by voluntary bodies to discipline the 'confirmed wastrel and loafer', and to encourage those who could be reclaimed from their idleness by means of emigration under close supervision. The Report recommended that detention colonies should be set up for the wilfully idle.[218] This reflected Beatrice Webb's belief in the need for firm oversight of those in receipt of relief from any quarter. Her dislike of philanthropy was based partly on her view that it offered no real solution to social problems; but it also included a firm belief that too much philanthropy, insufficiently controlled, simply encouraged laziness and dependence. The Fabian Society argued that 'almsgiving of whatever kind—crude, spasmodic, and ill-directed as it generally is—produces all the evil effects of gambling or lotteries upon a race too little inclined by training and hereditary influences to hard work'.[219] There was, here, a strong similarity to the views of the Charity Organisation Society.

The entry of Social Darwinism into social policy—more pronounced in late than in mid-century—also carried with it strong overtones of authoritarianism and control. Britain's attempt to

---

[217] Brown, 'Charles Booth', 353.

[218] *Report of the Royal Commission on the Poor Laws and Relief of Distress. Separate Report by the Rev. Prebendary H. Russell Wakefield, Mr Francis Chandler, Mr George Lansbury, and Mrs Sidney Webb* (Parliamentary Papers, 1909, Cd. 4499), 518–28, esp. 527–8.   [219] Quoted in Novak, *Poverty and the State*, 97.

survive and compete in an increasingly hostile world could not be allowed to be impeded by a large class of unfit labour from an allegedly substandard workforce. Sidney Webb argued in 1910:

The policy of *laissez-faire* is, necessarily, to a eugenicist the worst of all policies, because it implies the definite abandonment of intelligently purposeful selection . . . The question of who is to survive is determined by the conditions of the struggle, the rules of the ring. Where the rules of the ring favour a low type, the low type will survive, and vice versa . . . It is accordingly our business, as eugenicists, deliberately to manipulate the environment so that the survivors may be of the type which we regard as the highest.[220]

It does not take much manipulation of words to substitute 'deserving' for 'the types which we regard as the highest', and 'undeserving' for 'the low type'. The quest for national efficiency led in the same draconian direction, as calls were made for those at the very bottom of society to be prevented from propagating the species.

It is true that the practical application of such ideas was limited;[221] labour colonies were seen to offer an unviable solution to the problem of unemployment when it increased in the years after the end of the Boer War in 1902, and the efforts of the Salvation Army to establish labour colonies, where goods were produced at a cheap rate, ran into opposition from the trade unions. Nevertheless, those rather closer to political power, whose views helped to shape 'New Liberalism', also retained many ideas which carried a distinct and unmistakable echo of the past. They remained firmly attached to the ideals of individual effort, self-reliance, and the improvement of character. There were, indeed, social and economic obstacles in the way of such individual self-fulfilment which had to be removed by a more positive state; but J. A. Hobson argued that each reform of social conditions would be effectual only in so far as it elevated character.[222] Hobhouse wrote that 'the function of the State is to secure the conditions upon which its citizens are able to win by their own efforts all

[220] Quoted ibid. 106.

[221] See Dorothy Porter, ' "Enemies of the Race": Biologism, Environmentalism, and Public Health in Edwardian England' (*Victorian Studies*, xxxiv/2 (winter 1991), 159–78) for a consideration of related themes.

[222] John Allett, *New Liberalism: The Political Economy of J. A. Hobson* (Toronto: University of Toronto Press, 1981), 195.

that is necessary to a full civic efficiency'.[223] Beveridge thought it necessary for the state to 'get hold of its individual citizens, [to] know much more about them, [to] make them consciously and actually part of the social organisation'.[224] But he did not believe in an excessively bountiful state, since this could undermine the will to work, which, if not the sole object of life, was a social necessity. 'It is infinitely better for [the workman]', he wrote, '... that he should not get into the habit of looking to the state as a Lady Bountiful with a Fortunatus purse.'[225]

For 'New Liberals', then, the state did have a role to play in bringing about the 'citizenship of entitlement'; but such entitlements were designed so to moralize the poor that they would be the better able to exercise their own initiative. Here, in many ways, was still a belief in the 'enabling state' mentioned in Chapter 1. It is true that it was now seen to have to do more in economic and social matters than had previously been the case to carry out this role effectively; but not so much that it eroded the impetus to 'help from within', pauperized the poor, and turned the deserving employable into the undeserving unemployable. In extending citizenship entitlements, the 'New Liberals' still thought in terms of 'active citizens' who used such entitlements to better themselves, and who still interested themselves in voluntary-sector agencies such as friendly societies. Vincent and Plant have written as follows about Hobhouse, but their words have a wider application: 'The state had to retain a delicate balance between public centralised government and the self-governing individual, the latter being basic and the former providing the rational conditions for the latter.'[226] The active state was meant to enhance, not to reduce, the efforts of the active citizen; the citizenship of entitlement should enable and enrich, not impede and impoverish, the citizenship of contribution.

It is, therefore, important not to exaggerate the extent of the collectivism of the period. The growth in the scope and scale of government which took place did so within broadly orthodox economic and social parameters. The legislation affecting children that was passed between 1906 and 1908 interposed the state

[223] Quoted in Weiler, *The New Liberalism*, 150.
[224] See José Harris, *William Beveridge: A Biography* (Oxford: Clarendon Press, 1977), 101–2, 106, for an analysis of Beveridge's views.
[225] Ibid.   [226] *Philosophy, Politics and Citizenship*, 64.

into the family relationship between parents and children in a new way—and thus did, in a sense, impinge on the informal sector. The Lord Advocate, commenting on the Act of 1908, which set up juvenile courts and provided for penalties for parents found guilty of neglect, said that fifty years earlier such a step would have been regarded as interfering with individual liberty. On the other hand, the Acts of 1906 and 1907, dealing with the nutritional and medical needs of children, were, although quite widely implemented, still permissive; and they could be seen as simply enabling parents to undertake their responsibilities to look after their children. The Act of 1908, moreover, could be regarded as making it more difficult, under penalty of law, for parents to evade these responsibilities. The legislation could, therefore, be seen as strengthening, rather than weakening, the informal sector.

Further, with regard to the elderly, the Royal Commission on the Aged Poor, which sat between 1893 and 1895, reported that there was a 'strong and prevalent feeling' that there should be discrimination between the 'respectable poor' among the aged and 'those whose poverty is directly the result of their own conduct'.[227] The old-age pensions legislation of 1908 showed evidence of such a feeling. It did introduce the principle of a payment in old age—for those over the age of 70—as a right; and it was one paid from national funds on a non-contributory basis, without the test of destitution, and thus without the taint of the poor law. But the pension was not universal. It was to be paid only to persons with annual incomes below £21; and after the operation of a sliding scale, no pensions were to be payable on incomes over £31 10s. There were various other tests. The pension was restricted to persons who had been resident in the United Kingdom for twenty years and who had not been in receipt of poor relief—other than medical relief—since 1 January 1908; and no person who had been in prison within the previous ten years was eligible. Further, a pensioner must not have 'habitually failed to work according to his ability, opportunity and need'.

It is true that the poor law disqualification did not last beyond two years, and the test of 'seeking work' proved to be unworkable and was abandoned in 1919. Nevertheless, the tests

[227] Novak, *Poverty and the State*, 88.

surrounding the Act of 1908 indicated the intention to limit the pension to the deserving poor; and the scale of state assistance through the pension was unlikely to undermine the principles of self-maintenance and the necessity of saving and thrift in earlier life. Pensions were always justified by their sponsors—from Booth onwards—on the grounds that they would simply supplement private savings and charity, and in no sense replace them. They were, therefore, quite consistent with voluntarist principles, and could be regarded as an incentive to them.

Equally, the establishment of Labour Exchanges was primarily designed not to deal with the needs of the long-term unemployed, but to assist the working of the labour market and improve the prospect for the employable of finding employment. Applicants had to prove 'willingness to work' and 'genuine employability'. Similarly, the practice of insurance was entirely consistent with saving and self-help. It is true that under the Act of 1911, this was to be shared among employer, employee, and the state. But the fact that the employee made a contribution was considered very important. Beveridge regarded the compulsory scheme of social insurance as the most effective way of relieving poverty. Yet, by being contributory, it would not result in entire dependence on the state, nor would it discourage thrift. W. J. Braithwaite, the civil servant who worked closely with Lloyd George in drafting the legislation of 1911, had a firm belief in self-help principles, and felt that the contribution of the worker towards the scheme retained self-respect. Likewise, Churchill argued that the great value of insurance was its emphasis on rights which were *earned* by the insured worker. The contributory principle gave the worker a stake in the system. And there were ways in which that stake could be lost: workers dismissed for misconduct lost their entitlements to unemployment benefit. Such benefits were, in any event, kept low—and applied only to those most at risk in vulnerable occupations.

National Insurance, then, retained strong traces of voluntarist principles of self-help, participation, and responsibility. Further, as Tony Novak has put it, the principle of contribution

ensured that National Insurance automatically discriminated in favour of the deserving sick and unemployed. Only those who had previously been in regular employment, and who had thus built up a sufficient record of contributions, would be eligible for its benefits, while the chronic poor and unemployed, casual workers, most women and many of the unskilled would be excluded. Their destitution was to continue to be dealt with under the Poor Law and the workhouse, where, according to Balfour, they were to receive 'a stern lesson of the necessity of industry, self-exertion, self-reliance and self-respect.'[228]

Hennock has written in rather similar terms. 'The policy of insurance', he comments, '. . . was a bold extension of the circle of the more privileged, intended to give certain deserving categories protection from dependence on the Poor Law.'[229] It is worth emphasizing the point—made by Novak—that such categories were almost entirely confined to men; here again, legislation reflected contemporary attitudes.

Further, if the ideology of the 1911 Act had much to do with voluntarism, so too did its implementation. The original intention was to entrust the administration of health insurance under Part I of the Act to the mutual-aid friendly societies. In examining the relationship between German and British schemes, Hennock has written that the 'really fundamental fact' was that, if there was 'ever a model for the architects of British health insurance, it was not the German scheme, but the practice of the British Friendly Societies.'[230] Braithwaite had a strong regard for the societies, which, he felt, preserved working-class self-respect. He had the opportunity of studying the German schemes and adapting their reliance on bureaucracy to British conditions; but, Hennock writes, he was 'not interested in doing anything of the kind . . . he was orientated towards Friendly Society practices and was not interested in discovering any fundamental alternatives in Germany'.[231]

The administration of health insurance was, therefore, originally envisaged as following the mutual-aid, voluntaristic lines of the mutual-aid friendly societies; indeed, unemployment insurance was, as Hennock also writes, 'undoubtedly constructed on the basis of trade union experience and practice.'[232] Here again, the 'New Liberals' wished to harmonize the agencies of the citizenship of entitlement with those of the citizenship of contribution. There were certainly contradictions in the scheme. The

---

[228] Ibid. 137.   [229] *British Social Reform*, 211.
[230] Ibid. 189.   [231] Ibid. 190.   [232] Ibid.

contributions were compulsory, but the means by which they were collected were voluntary; for a friendly society was at liberty to reject contributors. What of the contributors who were not accepted by a friendly society? Lloyd George relied heavily on the willingness of the societies to compete for members, and made only a minimal provision—a deposit in the Post Office—for the residue not admitted to a friendly society. In a sense, Hennock writes, 'it was impossible to administer a compulsory scheme through voluntary associations. Yet this was exactly what Lloyd George and his advisers wished to do.'[233] This arrangement, too—which foreshadowed various 'agency' agreements whereby the state made use of voluntary organizations to implement its legislation—shows the continuing Liberal preference for voluntarism; and, as will be seen, it was also a measure of the continuing strength of voluntary-sector organizations and, more especially, of commercial-sector agencies. The latter were much in evidence in the whole episode.

Thus the ideology of voluntarism and reliance on voluntaristic methods of implementation were by no means absent from the collectivism of the Edwardian period. Equally, that collectivism might be seen as performing some of the political and social functions of providence, paternalism, and philanthropy by incorporating the respectable working classes into the community, thereby separating them from the residuum and rendering them immune to the advocacy of those who put forward socialist ideas. Churchill put it like this:

The idea is to increase the stability of our institutions by giving the mass of industrial workers a direct interest in maintaining them. With a 'stake in the country' in the form of insurance against evil days, these workers will pay no attention to the vague promises of revolutionary socialism . . . It will make him a better citizen, a more efficient worker, and a happier man.[234]

Or again, the President of the Local Government Board, when inaugurating a local authority housing project in 1910, said that such initiatives were a means of improving personal responsibility and enhancing citizenship—in the sense of making an active contribution to society. 'A good house', he said, '. . . developed

[233] Ibid.   [234] Quoted in Novak, *Poverty and the State*, 138.

certain qualities . . . necessary in these days . . . a good house resisted pauperism, diminished dependence, made for sobriety . . . gave character to the children in a way that nothing else did.'[235] It is statements such as these which have led writers to suggest that the reforms of the period after 1906 amounted to 'marginal ideological concessions in defence of the prevailing value system'—or that the Edwardian solution 'reconstructed, yet retained, the moral assumptions of Victorian welfare'.[236] For J. R. Hay, 'New Liberalism . . . was not an abandonment of individualism, but a re-interpretation.'[237] There is, indeed, no doubt that 'New Liberalism' remained strongly impregnated with the values, and strongly reliant on the agencies, of voluntarism.

Against this background, it is possible to see the 'convergence' of the voluntary, commercial, and informal sectors of voluntarism with the statutory sector in a rather different light. Where voluntarists did merge with the state, they often did their utmost to ensure that their separate identity and interests were protected—thereby displaying that characteristic desire to retain control of their activities and to resist interference which has already been noted. The passing of the Education Act by the Conservative government of Balfour in 1902 was—in common with Education Acts of the past—accompanied by immense denominational controversy. In the view of Nonconformists, it gave church-affiliated schools—mostly Anglican—a public subsidy from the rates in the form of grants which the new educational authorities, the elected county and borough councils, were permitted to award. Here, indeed, 'Old' rather than 'New' Liberalism was much in evidence. Again, there remained in the friendly-society movement a very strong suspicion of the intrusion of the state into their affairs. This has already been seen in relation to registration; and the prospect of state pensions was accepted only with severe reservations by many friendly societies. There was a long tradition of dislike for state pensions in the friendly-society movement. In 1892 the chief registrar of Friendly Societies expressed his opinion that there was no other way of

[235] Quoted in Richard Rodger, 'Political Economy, Ideology and the Persistence of Working Class Housing Problems in Britain' (*International Review of Social History*, xxxii (1987), 132).   [236] Ibid. 139.
[237] *The Origins of the Liberal Welfare Reforms, 1906–1914* (London: Macmillan, 1975), 35.

providing for old age than by thrift, self-denial, and forethought in youth.[238] The assistant secretary of the Foresters was also opposed to state pensions, which were, he wrote in somewhat mixed metaphor:

no doubt considered a very alluring bait to obtain the support of the Friendly Societies; but concealed under the bait, to use an angler's illustration, is an insidious hook, which would drag up out of the free waters of self-dependence and land us on the enervating bank of state control . . . It may be depended upon as a solid truth that the state will not grant us special privileges without wanting a finger in our pie.[239]

This comment was made in response to the efforts of Joseph Chamberlain to promote a contributory pension plan in the 1890s; and, while it may be open to question how far such opposition defeated Chamberlain's proposals, it certainly did not help them. Chamberlain himself was well aware of the need to conciliate the societies, but in the end, he felt that they had warned him off the subject as though he were poaching on their preserve. The societies also felt that state assistance was simply a means by which the demands of the working classes for higher wages and regular hours could be evaded by politicians and employers. Rather than acquiescing in state welfare schemes, many friendly societies urged their members to support trade unions and to press for higher wages, so that the working classes could save for their needs and preserve their independence. This point also found expression in the trade-union movement itself, and in the cooperative movement; and it was felt that it would benefit those outside mutual-aid societies, who could not save systematically.

The friendly societies did—as has been seen—come to accept the need for state pensions; but this was not without a great deal of internal wrangling. This reflected, on the one hand, a recognition of the needs of the elderly—and their own inability to meet them—and, on the other, a desire to perpetuate their own institutions. Chamberlain's proposal had been based on the principle of contributory pensions. As has been noted, the contributory principle was much more in conformity with self-maintenance than the non-contributory, and, as such, it accorded with the views

---

[238] P. H. J. H. Gosden, *Self-Help: Voluntary Associations in Nineteenth-Century Britain* (London: Batsford, 1973), 266.

[239] Gilbert, *Evolution of National Insurance*, 180 ff. See also Treble, 273–5.

of Beveridge and others; Beveridge felt that a non-contributory pension scheme would establish 'the state in the eyes of the individual as a source of free gifts', whereas a contributory scheme 'sets up the state as a comprehensive organism to which the individual belongs and in which he, under compulsion if need be, plays his part'.[240] Yet the Old Age Pension Act of 1908 was based on the principle of non-contribution. This cannot be attributed entirely to friendly-society resistance. It could be argued that the contributory principle was less appropriate to the needs of the elderly, who were beyond the point of being able to work, and thus unable to contribute to their own pensions; and any contributory scheme would take a long time to come into effect.

On the other hand, it is true that a contributory scheme for pensions would have been unpopular with many friendly societies and trade unions. If individuals were compelled to contribute to a state scheme, they would be less willing and able to contribute to friendly societies or trade unions, which would thus meet a formidable competitor. Acceptance of the case for state pensions by the friendly-society movement at a national conference held in 1902 was conditional on the point that the means of raising revenue for a state pension should not entail 'any interference with the funds of thrift societies'.[241] Unpopularity of contributory pensions among mutual-aid agencies in the voluntary sector, and insurance agencies in the commercial sector, was part of the political problem which would have been encountered had pensions based on contributions been introduced: a point which did not escape the notice of Campbell-Bannerman and Asquith.

It is, of course, true that when it came to National Insurance in 1911, the contributory principle *was* invoked. As has been seen, this accorded with self-maintenance principles; and the close association of the original scheme with the friendly societies matched the personal preference of Braithwaite. But it was also a political necessity; and Lloyd George's appreciation of this point was a clear indication not only of the views of the Treasury, which firmly opposed any non-contributory scheme on grounds of cost, but of the continuing strength and importance of the

---

[240] Harris, *William Beveridge*, 98–103, examines Beveridge's views on the issue of social insurance.   [241] Quoted in Treble, 'Attitudes', 289.

societies.[242] Lloyd George thought that he had succeeded in conciliating the societies over health insurance when, in 1908, the first plans for national health insurance were worked out; for these involved the administration of the scheme being vested in the friendly societies. The government plans did, indeed, hold out advantages to the societies, since they would not have to draw on their own funds for sickness benefit, but were to be left at liberty to use these funds to provide additional benefits to their members. The friendly-society movement, moreover, continued to make itself felt by putting the case for consultation and treatment which did not prejudice their interests before the candidates at the general election of 1910.

The collecting friendly societies and the industrial insurance companies were, moreover, also extremely active—indeed, they increasingly came to dominate the situation, to the bitter frustration of the mutual-aid voluntary-sector friendly societies. The commercial-sector companies saw schemes put forward by Lloyd George for widows' and orphans' benefits as a considerable threat to a business in which they had long had an interest; and as a result of their pressure, these benefits were dropped. They also feared that they would lose business to the mutual-aid voluntary-sector friendly societies, once the latter established closer relations with households over health insurance; mutual-aid societies in the voluntary sector might, for example, use the extra funds which they would have available to enter one of the traditional areas occupied by the commercial companies, such as funeral benefits. Thus, in an exercise of intense lobbying, the collecting friendly societies, which were on the border of the voluntary and commercial sectors, and the industrial insurance companies in the commercial sector demanded the right to enter the field of health insurance on equal terms with the mutual-aid voluntary-sector societies. In this they were joined by another powerful lobby, the medical profession, which strongly disliked the constraints imposed on it by contract work to the friendly societies, and did not wish to remain tied to those societies under the proposals of 1911. The doctors wanted to obtain a scheme

---

[242] See Gilbert, *Evolution of National Insurance*, 289–399, for a full consideration of this issue. See also Pat Thane, 'Non-Contributory versus Insurance Pensions, 1878–1908', in Thane (ed.), *Origins*, 84–106.

whereby an insured person could select his physician from a list—or panel—of participating doctors in a district.

Thus both the 'combine', as it was known, of collecting friendly societies and industrial insurance companies and the medical profession strongly attacked the monopoly which Lloyd George's scheme had given to the voluntary-sector mutual-aid societies in the administration of the scheme; and their intense pressure proved to be successful. The Act made it possible for the collecting friendly societies and the industrial insurance societies to be admitted to the scheme as Approved Societies, and instituted the 'panel' system that the medical profession had proposed. This was to result in a considerable weakening of the voluntary-sector mutual-aid friendly societies, which could not compete with the commercial-sector organizations allied to the state; and the spokesmen for the voluntary-sector societies were bitterly disappointed when they saw the powerful position occupied by commercial-sector organizations in the central National Insurance Commission, set up in 1912. Here, indeed, tensions within voluntarism—between the voluntary and commercial sectors— were evident; but the final solution was a recognition on the part of the state of the strength of voluntarism, especially in its commercial sector. As Pat Thane has put it, the societies were 'assured that they would suffer no state intervention in their traditional business.'[243]

It would also be mistaken to exaggerate the extent to which the convergence between the charitable side of the voluntary sector and the state involved a total abandonment by the charities of more traditional attitudes. The view that the state was promoting the citizenship of contribution by creating the citizenship of entitlement was not unanimously held; it was felt by some to be undermining it. While *The Bitter Cry* explained poverty in environmental, rather than personal, terms, and advocated the use of the state, rather than voluntary organizations, to cure it, those who responded to its publication often reversed the emphasis. One clergyman wrote *Sweet Herbs for the Bitter Cry, or Remedies for Horrible Outcast London,* which stressed the need for improved personal conduct, rather than better housing. Forster Crozier's *Methodism and the Bitter Cry of Outcast London* (1885)

---

[243] *The Foundations of the Welfare State* (London: Longman, 1982), 85.

admitted that the original *Bitter Cry* had not been 'altogether overdrawn'. In general terms, it was 'the awful but truthful representation of real life'; but Crozier's emphasis was more on 'life and morals'; and his solution lay not in the activities of the state, but in an increased role for the voluntary sector in the form of the churches and missionary outreach. As things stood, Crozier wrote, the 'insufficiency of religious accommodation [was] not remotely but intrinsically connected with, and largely the cause of, the depraved character of many of the people.'[244] In forming the Boy Scouts, Baden-Powell stressed the importance of fostering character, self-reliance, and self-improvement; all of this was seen as a training in active citizenship. Again, while the question of the nutritional and medical needs of children became a matter of legislation, the view was still expressed that these needs could be met by better motherhood; and advice given to mothers by health visitors, who drew on charitable effort, was much favoured as a means to this end. The family unit, not the state, was the agency for improvement; and here, indeed, was a call for more reliance on the informal sector.

Further, although the stereotype of a rigidly individualistic Charity Organisation Society is misleading, there remained within the Society a strong attachment to self-maintenance and individual responsibility. The assertion of W. A. Bailward that the Society had not opposed state legislation is only partly correct. This could be said of its attitude towards state activity which was reconcilable with, or even conducive to, self-maintenance— as was apparently the case in matters of housing, sanitation, and the legal rights of children. It was, however, a different matter in areas where state intervention could be argued to be a disincentive to self-reliance. Thus there was strong opposition in various quarters of the Society to the Education (Provision of Meals) Act of 1906. It was, the Revd W. G. Edwards Rees told the Society, 'vicious in principle' and relieved 'neglectful and shiftless parents' of their responsibility. The *Charity Organisation Review* called it a 'ready-made panacea which would put the clock back for a hundred years'. Paradoxically, perhaps, it was also regarded as the thin end of a dangerous wedge. The *Review* commented that in certain circles, 'state maintenance for the poorest citizens, or

---

[244] In Wohl (ed.), *Bitter Cry*, 97.

indeed for all', was 'advocated as one of the steps to a more perfect organisation of society'. The measure on school feeding was 'regarded by some as the first step in that direction'. If children were in need of being fed, that could be met—as it was in Glasgow—by charitable agencies. Such a solution, it was claimed, constituted no right on behalf of the recipient, and could be implemented at the discretion of the charity.[245]

Thus the official spokesmen for the Society proved reluctant to associate themselves even with the limited degree of collectivism which came into existence, and continued to adopt a libertarian position. Such a position retained control for the private donor of charity and established no entitlements in the donee. It is also worth noting that provision of school meals encountered opposition, or at least misgivings, from the much less individualistic National Society for the Prevention of Cruelty to Children. This felt that parents who neglected to feed their children could be made to do so by the threat of penalties—and that this would, in large measure, solve the problem without recourse to universal feeding of primary school children. But it did admit that where the cause was poverty rather than neglect, feeding had to be undertaken by any means possible, and thus, as usual, took a less extreme stance than the leaders of the Charity Organisation Society.

Pensions also aroused the opposition of the Charity Organisation Society. In May 1907 the *Charity Organisation Review* published an article on 'The Case against Old Age Pensions'.[246] It argued that the creation of state pensions would destroy all sense of family obligation, and would create a void which the state could never fill; that any scheme could not be final, but would be bound to come under pressure to lower the pensionable age and raise the level of the pension. Further, if pensions were given for old age, why should they not be given for every other infirmity? State pensions were part of other proposals, much favoured by socialists, which involved 'the endowment of life in all its stages': the provision of milk for babies, the foundation of 'scholarships' for successful motherhood, the state feeding of school children, state provision of work for the unemployed. Some of these were,

---

[245] *Charity Organisation Review*, NS, xx (July 1906), 35; NS, xxi (Jan. 1907), 12, 16.
[246] Ibid. NS, xxi (May 1907), 245–50.

indeed, in practical operation already; all were 'socialist schemes', which involved 'state relief and yet more state relief'. Similar libertarian themes ran through later contributions to the *Review*, including an article of February 1909 which stated that 'the great constructive forces of society are not at the disposal of Governments. They are inherent in the individual, in the family and in society as opposed to the state'.[247] And in the view of the strictest upholders of the Society's orthodoxy, such as Loch, G. C. T. Bartley, and Thomas Mackay—and of the Secretary of the Liberty and Property Defence League, Frederick Millar—pensions given by the state would simply encourage wasteful expenditure and discourage prudent and provident conduct.

National Insurance, as has been seen, could be much more readily reconciled with self-help principles—as the comments of the Majority Report of the Poor Law Commission, already quoted, showed. Yet the threats which it posed to the voluntary-sector mutual-aid friendly societies were appreciated by Loch. In June 1913 he wrote that the first section of the National Insurance Act was the 'death warrant of the friendly societies'. He continued:

Insurance against sickness has become a state business, organised in conjunction with what cannot but be larger and larger combinations of Friendly or Industrial Insurance Societies. The older and familiar usages of initiation into Forestry or Oddfellowship can hardly survive or survive in their reality. With the old responsibility must disappear the old interests and the old customs. A sense of responsibility created them—with the loss of it they must pass away.[248]

Thus a continuing distrust of the centralized and positive state within the voluntary sector must be acknowledged. Alongside forces of convergence, which saw a more active state as a means to a more active citizen, ran forces of divergence, which considered a more active state likely to lead to a less active, and more dependent citizen—and, to Dicey, to a loss of freedom, as the active state shaded into the despotic state and stripped the individual of liberty. The *Charity Organisation Review* commented in 1907 that 'voluntaryism and state action cannot co-exist', and in 1914 that the volunteer, surveying the recent social legislation, might 'well feel some anxiety at the prospect before him'. Where charitable agencies agreed to cooperate among themselves, it was

[247] Ibid. NS, xxv (Feb. 1909), 113.   [248] Ibid. NS, xxxiii (June 1913), 328.

often to enhance the prospect of saving the poor from the state and of maintaining the voluntary presence. It was largely in this spirit that the Charity Organisation Society agreed to meet its 'rival', the Guilds of Help, in 1913.[249]

In the same year, Loch, surveying the social legislation passed since 1900, stated his view that it indicated 'very clearly that the spirit of enterprise in social matters [had] passed from the people to the state'. What he called 'state philanthropy' had brought —and would bring—'large numbers of the population to its ministrations'; the state would assume the role of 'caterer in chief for its citizens'. He did, indeed, detect a process of convergence between the voluntary sector and the state—and deplored it:

What the Government has established, be it rightly or wrongly, assumes such large proportions and involves so many interests that the people, or those interested in any branch of relevant work, have, by a kind of social compulsion, to arrive at the conclusion that they must make an effort to back the Government venture and to do their best to make it work well. I notice, too, with some interest, that the most recent proposals for charitable progress are, in the main, proposals to link charity and social work to municipal bodies and generally to Government Departments. Thus the entrepreneurs of charity are running to shelter, like creatures out in a storm. The status of a Government alliance gives them protection and a sense of dignity.

All that was left for charity was 'if it is possible to humanize the action of the state, to keep . . . alive, in spite of it, the initiative of the people, their spontaneity of character and their independence'.[250]

Other observers also noted the continuing extreme reluctance in the charitable world to relinquish a separate identity, in relation both to other charities and to the state. As has been seen, Barnett strongly advocated closer cooperation in both respects, but, while this trend was evident, 'charities . . . are many which do not fulfil it'. 'They seem to wish to establish themselves in permanence,' he continued, 'and to go on in rivalry with the State and with one another. There is a waste of money, which might be used to pioneer work, in doing what is equally well

---

[249] Moore, 'Social Work', 98.
[250] *Charity Organisation Review*, NS, xxxiii (June 1913), 322–30.

done by others; there is competition which excites greed and imposition, and there is overlapping . . .'[251]

Further, the Majority Report of the Poor Law Commission, with its strong representation from the Charity Organisation Society, showed unmistakable signs of a continuing preference for a self-help ideology and for voluntaristic methods—if a somewhat more muted preference than has sometimes been admitted. The Report made allowances for economic factors in causing poverty—but retained a strong belief in moral issues. 'The causes of distress', it commented, 'are not only economic and industrial; in their origin and character they are largely moral.'[252] It also saw a continuing and important role for voluntary effort in meeting the problem of distress, especially for those whose distress was due to temporary unemployment, and where that unemployment could be said to be due to moral causes.[253] In many ways, it called for a return to the reciprocal and complementary roles for poor law and charity laid down in 1869 by the Goschen Minute. 'The principle of Mr Goschen's Circular we accept', ran the Majority Report.[254]

The actual institutions envisaged by the Report were not, in fact, to be those of 1869, but the degree of cooperation between statutory and voluntary bodies was to remain close: between the proposed local Public Assistance authorities on the one hand and, on the other, the Voluntary Aid Councils and Committees— composed of representatives of local charities—which were also to be set up. What amounted to the undeserving poor would be the province of the poor law, while the deserving would be the province of charity. It was, indeed, hoped that the charitable partner would in many cases prevent public assistance from being brought into action at all. One of the members of the Commission who signed the Majority Report, L. R. Phelps, wrote in March 1910 in the *Charity Organisation Review* that 'in the history of the relief of distress you constantly find two things'. One was that the poor law was 'always poaching on the domain of charity', and the other that charity was 'always straying into the field of the Poor Law'.[255] The solution, he wrote, was to keep 'the Poor

---

[251] 'Charity up to Date', quoted in Pope, Pratt, and Hoyle (eds.), *Social Welfare*, 72.

[252] *Report of the Royal Commission on the Poor Laws, and Relief of Distress*, i. pt. VII, par. 86.　　　　　　　　　　　　　　　　　　　　[253] Ibid. pt. VI, par. 382.

[254] Ibid. pt. VII, par. 198.　　　　　[255] NS, xxvi (Mar. 1910), 119.

Law out of Charity and Charity out of the Poor Law'—with only such links as would ensure that, as he put it, 'charity should act as a sieve through which . . . the grain should pass, leaving the chaff to be treated by the state'.[256]

Here, then, was a renewed affirmation of the desirability of self-maintenance—and of the duty, as the Majority Report put it, 'to convert useless and costly inefficients into self-sustaining and respectable members of the community'.[257] There was also a continuing emphasis on the need to keep the agencies of the voluntary and statutory sectors—if remodelled—complementary in maintaining independence, rather than convergent in posing a threat to it.

The Minority Report had much in common with this ideology. Although it subordinated the question of 'personal character' in tracing the causes of unemployment, it felt that personal character was of great importance in treating distress, and it did not wish to encourage laziness by excessive charity or unconditional payments. Similarly, the Minority Report felt that there was an important place for voluntary effort. It wished to make use 'of voluntary agencies and of personal service of both men and women of good will'—and felt that it was not for the state 'to lay its heavy hand on the efforts of the charitable'.[258] But it was essential that the proper sphere of this voluntary effort should be clearly understood—for much of that effort was, at present, misdirected and encouraged dependency. And here lay an important difference of emphasis between the two Reports; for according to the Minority Report, that 'proper sphere' lay under the control of the state. The Minority Report, in putting forward proposals for a complete breakup of the poor law, and the creation of new specialist departments under the local authorities and a new Ministry of Labour to deal with unemployment, put the emphasis *first* on the statutory service and *second* on the voluntary. Provided that this was the order, the voluntary sector could still offer a channel for personal service and opportunities to experiment in ways which a public authority would find difficult.[259]

Thus, as has often been said, the Minority Report suggested

---

[256] Ibid. 125.

[257] *Report of the Royal Commission on the Poor Laws*, i. pt. IX, par. 173.

[258] *Report of the Royal Commission on the Poor Laws and Relief of Distress: Separate Report*, 526.   [259] Ibid. 527.

the role of an 'extension ladder' for the voluntary sector in its charitable aspect rather than the 'parallel bars' role envisaged by the Majority Report. That *both* Reports contained strong elements of a self-maintenance ideology and of a belief in the voluntary sector is noteworthy; that it was the Majority Report which found a greater place for both again shows their continuing strength; and that *neither* Report was implemented, and the Poor Law remained unreformed, is also significant—for this, too, showed the strength of feeling which existed against any reform, even that proposed by the Majority Report, and of institutional vested interests which wished to maintain the status quo.

IX

The period from 1880 to 1914 thus witnessed the emergence of issues and ideas which, while presenting opportunities for a continuing role for voluntary social endeavour of various kinds, also presented a challenge to that endeavour. It saw the development of a more democratic and collectivist state which sought to create what has been called 'a more organic relation'[260] between the individual and society and to establish a citizenship of entitlement. And it provided evidence of a greater willingness on the part of the voluntary and commercial sectors to come to terms with that collectivist state and to operate within it. Voluntarism itself became—almost—collectivized.

Yet the challenge, collectivism, and convergence were all shaped by the past inheritance—and were limited in extent. To regard these years—and in particular the period after 1906—as having seen the birth of the Welfare State is to run the risk of embarking, once again, on the 'Welfare State escalator', or 'collective train', and to ignore the penetration of new ideas and practices by old. The most that the new state which emerged before 1914 can be called is a 'Social Service State', which laid down certain minimal, non-pauperizing standards for certain sections of the population seen to be at risk. It relied on voluntary agencies to a considerable degree and could, indeed, still be said to have been filling in the gaps left by voluntary and local initiatives of various kinds. Churchill wrote to Asquith in 1908 that 'a sort of

---

[260] *The Nation*, quoted in Weiler, *The New Liberalism*, 115.

Germanised network of state intervention and regulation' had to be spread 'underneath, though not in substitution for, the immense disjointed fabric of social safeguards and insurances which had grown up by itself'.[261] This 'fabric' was that provided by voluntary endeavour: and it is significant that Churchill saw it still as having primacy, and not, in any sense, as being superseded by the state.

Nevertheless, the hostile reaction of certain voluntarists to the 'Social Service State' did show that something of significance had happened. The mixed economy of welfare remained mixed, but not in the same proportions; and there can be no doubt that the proportion of the state had grown by 1914. The principles on which that growth had taken place still allowed cooperation between voluntarists and the state on negative, rather than positive, principles: on saving money rather than spending it, and ensuring that the state did not squander its resources and create dependency. At the winter conference of the Charity Organisation Society in 1914, one speaker made the point that while the greater responsibilities undertaken by the state for material relief might 'prejudice the existence of some charities', the voluntary sector still had an 'indispensable' role in ensuring that the relief was properly administered; and in that sense, the need for volunteers would grow rather than decline.[262] On the other hand, if cooperation took place with a more active state on more positive lines, various issues for the voluntary sector were raised. One was the extent to which it would, in future, retain its identity and independence; for if convergence with the state could lead to financial advantage and greater status, it could also lead to loss of identity and control. Loch was perceptive in discerning both developments.

Similar issues were to be raised in the years after 1914. Again, immense economic and social challenges were to be offered to voluntarism—presenting both opportunities and problems. There was to be a further development of the state—but also on ambiguous lines, at once negative and positive; and there was, therefore, once more the question of how voluntarism would react: whether with the negative orientation or the positive. If the

---

[261] Quoted in John Brown, 'Poverty and Social Policy in Britain, 1850–1919', in *Poverty and Social Policy, 1870–1950* (Milton Keynes: Open University Press, 1974).
[262] *Charity Organisation Review*, NS, xxxv (Feb. 1914), 93.

primary movement of frontiers went towards the latter, there would, once again, be issues of identity and independence to face. As Britain entered World War I, voluntarism confronted an uncertain future.

3

Citizen and State, 1914–1949:
War, Want, and Welfare

I

If voluntarism had been exposed to problems and difficulties in the late nineteenth and early twentieth centuries, it might well seem that those of the years after 1914 would prove considerably more formidable. That war was a major feature of the years between 1914 and 1949 is a truism; and it has become a commonplace to dwell on the scale of the domestic problems which war threw up and the extent to which it tested existing practices, of which voluntarism was one. To use the term 'want' to delineate the period between 1914 and 1949 would be to invite considerable questioning and controversy. Even to apply it as a blanket description of the interwar years alone would be to fly in the face of much revisionist work on the 1920s and 1930s which casts doubt on the kind of interpretation which such a word conveys— and which points to progress in various sectors of the economy and various parts of the country for those in work.[1] It is an interpretation which, arguably, is easily derived from the results of the continuing practice of conducting social surveys and investigations which had been such a marked feature of the years covered in Chapter 2. *The Social Survey of Merseyside* was published in 1928; and in 1934 a *New Survey of London Life and Labour* appeared. This described a study carried out in 1929–30, and was in part a repetition of Booth's earlier survey. In 1935–6 Seebohm Rowntree repeated his study of York. In 1937 Herbert Tout's survey of Bristol appeared; and in 1938 *Men without Work*, a report made to the Pilgrim Trust on the subject of unemployment, was published. Also, as in the past, there was a very considerable journalistic and literary output. As Malcolm Muggeridge

---

[1] For a summary and bibliography, see Bernard W. E. Alford, *Depression and Recovery? British Economic Growth, 1918–1939* (London: Macmillan, 1972).

put it—commenting on the great appetite shown in the 1930s for 'facts'—J. B. Priestley 'weighed in with his *English Journey* and Beverley Nichols with his *News of England*'.[2] There was the radio series 'Walks and Talks' by Sir Arnold Wilson, a Conservative MP, and in 1938 *Picture Post* was founded. In addition to portraying more trivial matters, this gave considerable coverage to social issues, such as unemployment. There were also well-known novels, rooted in social distress and unemployment, such as Walter Greenwood's *Love on the Dole*, as well as George Orwell's account of northern industrial life, *The Road to Wigan Pier*.

As with the earlier period, it is, of course, important to approach all this material with care, for it can very easily give a cumulative impression of 'want'—one which revisionist studies seek to question. It must also be noted that the surveys—in common with those of the late nineteenth and early twentieth centuries—often showed evidence of improvement. The *New Survey of London Life and Labour* found that some 14 per cent of Booth's 'East London' were 'subject to conditions of privation which, if long continued, would deny them all but the barest necessities and cut them off from access to many of the incidental and cultural benefits of modern progress'. The figure for the entire county of London was 9.6 per cent. In Poplar it was 24 per cent, compared with 44.6 per cent in the 1890s; in Bethnal Green 17.8 per cent compared with 44.6 per cent in the earlier period. Rowntree's findings in York in the mid-1930s suggested that 6.8 per cent of the working classes of York, judging by the same standards as those used in 1899, were in 'primary poverty'. Using a more generous standard, which allowed for a high level of expenditure on food and a small margin for non-necessities such as newspapers and a wireless, he found 17.7 per cent to be below the line, of whom half were in 'primary poverty'. Here, then, is an 'optimistic' interpretation of social and economic conditions between the wars; and as in the past, this context had a bearing on the fortunes and viability of voluntarism.

Yet if these surveys found evidence of 'progress', their authors were often at pains to state that the improvements should not engender complacency. In his further book, *Poverty and Progress*, published in 1941, Rowntree wrote:

[2] *The Thirties* (London: Hamish Hamilton, 1940; Collins, Fontana Books, 1971), 253 (of 1971 edn.).

It is gratifying that so much progress has been achieved, but if instead of looking backward we look forward, then we see how far the standard of living of many workers falls short of any standard which could be regarded even for the time being as satisfactory. Great though the progress made during the last forty years has been, there is no cause for satisfaction.[3]

It is also fair to say that if the surveys, like those of the earlier period, found evidence of progress, they also found evidence of continuing poverty—and that the main causes of poverty remained much the same as those which had been uncovered in the past—old age, illness, widowhood, large families, low pay, unemployment.[4] Unemployment was, of course, a major issue. From 1921 to 1940 Britain experienced mass unemployment on a scale never known before. In the 1920s it averaged at about 10 per cent of the insured workforce; and from the autumn of 1931 until early 1933 it reached 22 per cent of that workforce, or 2.8 to 3 million. From early 1934 to early 1936 the figure was about 2 million, falling to about 1.6 million by November 1936. And these were figures for the registered and insured unemployed; they did not include a larger number of workers without employment—estimated at about 0.75 million in late 1932—who had not registered or had never been covered by insurance. The problem was most acutely felt in the older-established export industries vulnerable to world recession, in the regions described by Frederic M. Miller as 'outer Britain'—northern England, Wales, and Scotland—where they had been concentrated. Thus, as Miller points out, the rate of insured unemployment for Britain as a whole in June 1932 was 22.4 per cent; but this masked great regional variations.[5] For southern England and the Midlands, the figure for that date was 16 per cent, but for 'outer Britain', 28.5 per cent. In 1936, when recovery had set in, the regional differences were even greater: 12.9 per cent for the whole country, but 7.3 per cent and 18.7 per cent for the two major areas of difference. As Miller also points out, the 'long-term' unemployed were a further feature of the situation, growing from 100,000 in 1931 to 480,000 in 1932 and still at the level of 325,000 in mid-1936.

[3] *Poverty and Progress: A Second Social Survey of York* (London: Longmans, Green, 1941), 476.

[4] John Stevenson, *British Society, 1914–45* (Harmondsworth: Penguin, 1984), 135.

[5] 'The Unemployment Policy of the National Government, 1931–1936' (*Historical Journal*, xix (1976), 455).

This was evident in certain areas heavily dependent on one industry, such as shipbuilding or coal-mining; and among these areas, South Wales was fifty times more depressed than London.

Thus, as *Men without Work* stated in its opening paragraph, unemployment had been 'since the War one of the greatest social problems' of the country—and one which 'on account of the poverty and distress associated with it, and of the effects on character and personality, cannot fail to interest those who care for their fellow men.'[6] The relationship between unemployment and other issues, such as health, in the interwar period has caused some debate, but it cannot be said to have been without effect—whether psychological or physical; and the dependants of those who were without work for long periods suffered from the results of lack of income in various ways, such as malnutrition. 'Want', therefore, may be too general and non-specific a term to serve as a description of economic and social conditions in the interwar years, far less of the period from 1914 to 1948 as a whole; but there were still many vulnerable groups in society, including the old, the young—and the surveys found a high incidence of poverty among children—the widowed, the low-paid, the unemployed, for whom the word is not inappropriate.[7]

War and want were, then, important features of the context in which voluntarism had to work in the period from 1914 to 1949; and they posed considerable problems. Here, indeed, was a further 'challenge'. In fact they did not exhaust that challenge; for there were other issues which presented difficulties, such as—particularly for those in work—increased leisure facilities which might distract attention from voluntaristic pursuits in matters of welfare; and, arguably, a decline in religious commitment and church attachment, already evident before 1914, but more evident thereafter, may have helped to remove some of the traditional impetus for voluntary social work. Nevertheless, war and want provided much of the background of the period from 1914 to 1949—and they may be said to have promoted a further development in the statutory sector, as the exigencies connected with both further exposed the limitations of voluntarism and prompted an increased role for the state. This was clearly another

---

[6] *Men without Work: A Report Made to the Pilgrim Trust*, with an Introduction by the Archbishop of York and a Preface by Lord Macmillan (Cambridge: Cambridge University Press, 1938), 1.　　　[7] Stevenson, *British Society*, 137–8.

matter which was to have an important bearing on voluntarism in its various sectors—and was to raise the earlier question of how far it should converge with—and how far diverge from— a more collectivist state. It is these issues which will now be addressed.

II

One of the most immediate effects of World War I on agencies in both the voluntary and commercial sectors was to put strains on the human resources on which they could call. In the mutual-aid and philanthropic sides of the voluntary sector, there was shortage of personnel. Military service reduced the number of available staff. The number of collectors in the friendly collecting societies and the industrial insurance companies was heavily depleted—although their places were often taken by women collectors. When war broke out, the Act of 1911, involving, as it did, the Approved Societies in health insurance, had hardly gone into effect; and war service added to the difficulties of building up experienced and trained staff.[8]

On the charitable side of the sector, the *Charity Organisation Review* reported in September 1915 that the war was daily reducing the number of workers for charitable agencies; and while new workers were introduced, they tended not to be as experienced as those who had gone. Older charities, in particular, were said to be in difficulties.[9] The war meant that charities were less able than they would have been otherwise to recruit younger men and women to their activities, and it increased opportunities for alternative employment to a traditional 'backbone' of philanthropy—women. It drew the leisured ladies who had once found an outlet in charity into other types of employment; as an agent of the Ragged School Union put it in 1916: 'women and girls were cast from the service of home and class amid the whir of wheels'.[10] Some of this employment was, of course, of a military nature—in the production of munitions, or in uniformed organizations, such as the Women's Army Auxiliary Corps; in

---

[8] Dermot Morrah, *A History of Industrial Life Assurance* (London: Allen & Unwin, 1955), 83 ff.   [9] NS, xxxviii, 290.
[10] Quoted in Frank Prochaska, *The Voluntary Impulse: Philanthropy in Modern Britain* (London: Faber & Faber, 1988), 75.

other cases it was civilian, such as transport. This could, indeed, evoke the same spirit of service—even if it was now paid service —as philanthropy had done. Obviously, this point can be exaggerated; but it seems undeniable that the war, and war service of one kind or another, drained away those human resources on which the voluntary and commercial sectors had been accustomed to draw—or at least redirected them elsewhere into areas connected with the war. This was to be true of both wars; World War II also disrupted traditional patterns of charitable activity.[11]

Further, the circumstances of both war and want posed problems for the practice of saving and contributing to the mutual-aid agencies of both the voluntary and commercial sectors. Indeed, at the outbreak of World War I there were gloomy predictions as to its likely effects on them. It was thought probable that the war would be gravely disruptive in itself, and that it would bring with it a period of industrial depression and social hardship.[12] Claims would multiply and contributions would be difficult to collect. Clearly, the war did bring with it considerable problems for the mutual-aid friendly societies. Some of the affiliated orders and the 'centralised class' of society—for example, the Hearts of Oak—sought to pay the contributions of their members on active service. The funds required to pay for this lapse in income were, on occasion, raised by levies on the civilian members, or by opening subscription lists to which contributions were invited.

This, however, often proved too burdensome to sustain; and many, if not all, societies in this category were forced to adopt the rule that members serving in the navy or army would not be held liable for contributions during their period of service. If they did not maintain them, no sickness benefit would be payable, but death benefit would be paid. Where contributions were maintained—and many members of Manchester Unity and of other societies adhered to this practice—full entitlement to benefit

---

[11] See ibid. 74–5 (World War I). F. Prochaska, 'A Mother's Country: Mothers' Meetings and Family Welfare in Britain, 1850–1950' (*History*, lxxiv/242 (Oct. 1989), 397–9) deals with the effects of both World Wars.

[12] See Morrah, *History*, 83 ff., and also James T. Shotwell (ed.), *War and Insurance*, Economic and Social History of the World War, British Series (London: Humphrey Milford, Oxford University Press, 1927), *passim* and esp. S. G. Warner, 'The Effect on British Life Assurance of the European War (1914–18)' (pp. 101–68) and Sir Alfred William Watson, KCB, 'National Health Insurance and Friendly Societies during the War' (pp. 171–221).

remained; but this could result in payment of sickness benefit for prolonged periods to men who had been wounded, and, with payment of death benefits, could place a considerable strain on finances. There was also the problem of unequal claims for death benefit sustained over different local branches: a comment on the diversity and lack of uniformity in the voluntary sector. To meet this difficulty, Manchester Unity and Foresters arranged to spread over their whole organization a considerable part of the liability of local branches incurred over war deaths. This was achieved by the establishment of a 'War Mutual Liability Fund', maintained by a levy on local funds per head of membership.

There is no doubt, too, that World War I posed difficulties for the commercial sector. The problem over collectors has already been noted; and this, in addition to war service for other sections of the community, clearly put difficulties in the way of capturing new business. Given the much greater risks of war, it was not possible to recruit newcomers to Industrial Assurance on the same terms as those already holding policies. There was, indeed, a fall-off in new business until 1917. There were also, inevitably, heavy claims, since many policyholders were killed in action; and claims amounting to some £10 million were paid. Moreover, there was an increase in actuarial risks, brought about by the high incidence of invalidity among policyholders.

These points must not, however, be exaggerated, for, despite the difficulties, the effects of World War I on voluntary- and commercial-sector agencies in this area were not as bad as had been feared. The Approved Societies, associated with the state over health insurance under the Act of 1911, emerged from the war with much greater strength than had been expected. The war had a favourable effect on employment and wages and kept contributions high—higher, indeed, than would have been expected in normal circumstances. Sickness claims on the domestic front fell considerably. Further, the immense loss of life among young men sustained during the war meant that contributions had been paid by those who would not make any claim in later life, when heavier claims could be expected. Those who survived the war might well lose touch with the society with which they were originally insured, becoming what were known as 'actuarial deaths'. This was also true of women. Considerable numbers of women had entered war work, and paid contributions for three to four years. After the war, they left insured employment, and societies were able to retain a proportion of their lapsed policies. Further, a scheme was devised whereby societies were able to recoup from the Exchequer the proportion of any benefit payment made to men discharged from the services and considered to be directly attributable to war service.

Thus, despite the gloomy predictions that the war would deplete the financial resources of the Approved Societies, it actually helped most of them to build up very considerable reserves. The first valuation of the Approved Societies was taken at 1 December 1918. This showed that in 96 per cent of all societies there were surpluses, amounting, on average, to more than £1 per head. This accumulation—with the high interest rates which it attracted—was to the advantage of the larger societies, and these tended to become ever stronger. Indeed, the war had the effect of thinning out the number of Approved Societies involved in insurance. Of the 2,208 societies granted approval in 1912, 1,192 had ceased to administer insurance under the Act of 1911 by 1922.[13] This in itself was to cause further problems of unevenness in the service provided to members; but certainly for the larger societies, the war did not have the disastrous results which had been predicted. In 1927 Sir A. W. Watson, the chief government actuary, wrote:

Facts have disposed of the gloomy forebodings of those who predicted that to the normal horrors of war would be added a general and permanent lowering of the vitality of the industrial population and a general increase in the claims upon the sickness insurance funds ... There is, indeed, little to be said and no anxiety to be expressed as to the marks of war upon the financial position of the British friendly societies.[14]

Equally, fears that World War I would have serious consequences for unemployment insurance proved to be erroneous. The demands of the war effort, both at home and abroad, led to a fall in unemployment from September 1914, and Beveridge, while acknowledging that unemployment did not entirely disappear during the war, was later to write that for three-and-a-half years the problem of unemployment 'vanished from public

---

[13] Bentley B. Gilbert, *British Social Policy, 1914–1939* (London: Batsford, 1970), 264 n. 1.　　　　[14] Watson, 'National Health Insurance', 220.

sight completely and all but completely in fact'.[15] An Act of 1916 brought workers in munitions and allied trades under the 1911 Act: and while the contributory scheme was abandoned under the 'Out of Work Duration' programme immediately after the war—whereby insurance was granted, without contribution, to ex-servicemen and civilians for a specified period—the contributory principle was reaffirmed under a further Act of 1920, which differed little from the Act of 1911 but enlarged its coverage; thus the scheme included all manual workers and non-manual workers earning less than £250 per year, with the exception of workers in agriculture and domestic service and certain other groups of permanent employees. When the Act came into effect in November 1920, unemployment in the insured trades stood at 3.7 per cent; and the Unemployment Fund, into which the contributions of employee, employer, and government were paid, stood well in credit. It entered 1921 with a surplus of £2 million.

Contrary to expectations, therefore, World War I did not destroy the contributory principle—nor did it deplete the finances of organizations in the mutual-aid side of the voluntary sector and in the commercial sector. Indeed, in many cases it positively assisted them. It is also true to say that the war brought with it increased opportunities for saving through the efforts of the National Organising Committee for War Savings—later the National War Savings Committee—which sought to stimulate savings through savings groups and savings certificates.[16]

The effect of want on the voluntary and commercial sector agencies in terms of saving for, and contributing to, individual welfare was, however, to be more serious.[17] The deteriorating economic situation and the onset of high unemployment did not prove to offer such a challenge to health insurance as it did to unemployment insurance, but it was not without effect. By 1921 sickness and disablement claims among virtually all classes of

---

[15] Sir William Beveridge, 'Unemployment Insurance in the War and After', in Shotwell (ed.), *War and Insurance*, 231.

[16] Paul Johnson, *Saving and Spending: The Working-Class Economy in Britain, 1870–1939* (Oxford: Clarendon Press, 1985), 109 ff.

[17] Relevant literature on this subject includes Morrah, *History*; Sir Arnold Wilson, MP, and Professor Herman Levy, *Industrial Assurance: An Historical and Critical Study* (Oxford: Oxford University Press, 1937); Margaret Barnett Gilson, *Unemployment Insurance in Great Britain: The National System and Additional Benefit Plans* (London: Allen & Unwin, 1931).

contributors began to grow; and what was especially noticeable was a re-emergence of claims among women, which had been a problem before the war but had tended to decline thereafter. Not all societies were affected by these at first, but the largest increases in claims came from areas where unemployment was most serious. The National Amalgamated Society, a large organization which incorporated the health insurance of all the major industrial companies with the exception of the Prudential, was affected very quickly by unemployment. Its records showed that men's disablement increased from 54 per cent of expectation in 1920 to 85 per cent in 1923; and women's disablement increased from 120 per cent of expectation in 1920 to 201 per cent in 1923. The chairman of the National Amalgamated, Sir Edward Neil, suggested that the increase in claims among men, in particular, might well be caused by ill health which attended unemployment, rather than by malingering—which was the other possible explanation. The situation was to become worse in the mid-1920s, and in 1928 a report was commissioned by Sir Walter Kinnear, controller of the Insurance Department of the Ministry of Health and deputy chairman of the National Health Insurance Joint Committee. This was produced by Sir A. W. Watson in January 1930, and showed that claims had increased steeply since 1921. Men's sickness benefit claims were 41 per cent larger in 1927 than in 1921; they had exceeded actuarial expectation in 1926. Disablement claims were 85 per cent higher. Married women's sickness claims had increased by 106 per cent between 1921 and 1927, and claims for disablement benefit by 159 per cent.

The Watson Report, moreover, covered only the period from 1921 to 1927. When it was published in 1930, unemployment was mounting; and the Approved Societies felt ever more apprehensive. At the end of 1931, the third official valuation of the societies appeared. Even it did not cover the worst period of unemployment, since it related only to the period from 1927 to 1929. But it presented a rather disconcerting prospect, especially for the small societies. There had been a fall in disposable surplus of about £7 million since the previous valuation; and among societies in deficit, the total amount of the deficit came to almost £1 million. Moreover, a considerable proportion of the income of societies in profit came from the interest on their surpluses; contribution income had been only 88 per cent of expectation.

Want did, therefore, present problems for the Approved Societies over health insurance—although it should be borne in mind that the figures of 1931, relating to 1927–9, showed that the aggregate surplus of all societies in profit was still £36 million; and the next valuation, published in 1937 and covering the years 1931–4, showed a slight improvement in the position, which was sustained as unemployment fell in the later part of the decade. Various societies were, however, still in a weak position, especially those which included women. Nearly one society in five in this category showed a deficit. This again was to pose problems of unevenness of benefit: one which was to store up difficulties for the whole Approved Society system in the future.

If, however, want put pressure on contributions and claims over health, it proved fatal to those over unemployment as this gathered pace in the 1920s. The surplus of £21 million with which the Unemployment Fund began in 1921 'melted in a moment', as Beveridge put it.[18] It had totally disappeared by July, and, with the exception of a short spell in 1924, the Fund sank more and more into debt. In September 1921 the total deficit reached £116 million. The Scheme of 1911—or 1920—had, indeed, succumbed to the pressure of unemployment. Alan Deacon has used the phrase 'the collapse of insurance' to describe the process;[19] he writes further on the same theme:

In face of whole communities without hope of work, and denied any opportunity to establish a substantial credit of contributions, the foundations of the 1920 scheme collapsed. After March, 1921, no politician could argue that benefits could be supplemented by either trade union schemes or savings . . . The contributory basis of the insurance scheme was abandoned within 6 months of the 1920 Act going into operation.[20]

Deacon's remark about trade union schemes and savings might be taken to suggest that unemployment also depleted these reserves. It is true that unemployment, and stoppages of work, greatly affected trade union membership, which fell rapidly from 1926 to the mid-1930s. The ability of trade unions to pay unemployment benefit over and above the state scheme was also, it would seem, reduced. It has been suggested that the majority of

---

[18] Introduction to Shotwell (ed.), *War and Insurance*, 6.
[19] *In Search of the Scrounger: The Administration of Unemployment Insurance in Britain, 1920–1931* (London: Bell, 1976), 15.   [20] Ibid.

unions which administered state unemployment benefit paid only sufficient funds from their own resources to enable them to carry this out; and these were small additional amounts. There is also evidence to suggest that unions which paid unemployment benefit entirely from their own funds found the burden considerable: in 1928, for example, the Yorkshire Miners' Association had to discontinue such payments.[21] It may also be true that the habit of saving for old age through mutual-aid organizations declined; and that trade unions increasingly saw their role as that of negotiator rather than savings institution.[22] This whole area of the welfare policies of trade unions is, however, one on which it is hard to make any definitive pronouncements. As Paul Johnson has written, 'any generalization ... is sure to be misleading, because ... rates of contribution and benefit varied enormously between industrial sectors, with the established craft unions in printing, engineering, and building levying high membership fees but offering generous welfare benefits'.[23]

Again, the effects of unemployment on saving and maintaining contributions to mutual-aid organizations are very difficult to measure with any certainty. It is true that mutual-aid friendly societies did not expand their membership in the period after 1914 to any marked extent. There was, in Johnson's words, 'a gradual abandonment of those aspects of mutuality and fellowship that had been the hallmark of friendly societies in Victorian Britain'.[24] At the end of World War II the Mass-Observation survey concluded:

The membership of Friendly Societies to-day, judged in terms of attendance at meetings, in lack of interest in the election of officials, in lack of desire for contact with other members of the Society, is very largely a passive one, and, while there have, no doubt, always been a number of purely passive members of Friendly Societies, expression of feeling and opinion among older members suggests that in the earlier days of the societies, there were proportionately far more people actively interested than at present. It is rare to-day to find a Friendly Society which has more than a nucleus of an active membership, or attracts to itself

[21] Mary Brunett Gilson, *Unemployment Insurance in Great Britain* (London: Allen & Unwin, 1931), 98.
[22] Leslie Hannah, *Inventing Retirement: The Development of Occupational Pensions in Britain* (Cambridge: Cambridge University Press, 1986), 32.
[23] Johnson, *Saving and Spending*, 78.   [24] Ibid. 68.

anything like the group loyalty which has in the past characterised such organisations.[25]

How far this development was due to want is hard to say; stagnation in mutual-aid friendly-society membership set in before unemployment got under way—and, indeed, it had been foreseen by Loch in 1911. It could, however, be argued that the traditional pattern of saving offered by the industrial insurance companies in the commercial sector—small sums regularly collected—was better suited to the precariousness of working-class income; and the incidence of low pay and unemployment was clearly one factor in that situation.

Another point which might strengthen this argument is that thrift and saving were still conspicuously practised in the period. They might be carried out by private saving or hoarding, or through savings banks; but other forms of friendly society of a more impersonal, and often more commercial, kind did not suffer the eclipse experienced by the affiliated orders. There was an expansion in the activities of the centralized societies, such as the Hearts of Oak, and a growth in the deposit society, which came somewhere between the centralized society and the savings bank, and involved no mutuality. This was dominated by the National Deposit Friendly Society, the membership of which grew from under 50,000 in 1899 to 1.2 million in 1933.[26] There was also a substantial membership of societies which offered medical or institutional care, without sickness pay; and the collecting friendly societies and the industrial insurance companies in the commercial sector remained extremely buoyant. It is true that, as Johnson shows, contributions to industrial insurance companies could be affected by low pay and unemployment.[27] The onset of depression from the end of 1921 compelled many long-term policyholders of Liverpool Victoria—a friendly collecting society—to lapse on payments; and in 1924 a district manager of Pearl Assurance said that 'there is no doubt that in a general sense, the primary or principal cause of arrears is low paid work or unemployment'.[28]

---

[25] Quoted in Lord Beveridge and A. F. Wells (eds.), *The Evidence for Voluntary Action* (London: Allen & Unwin, 1949), 20.

[26] Johnson, *Saving and Spending*, 68. [27] Ibid. 215.

[28] Quoted ibid. 34.

Nevertheless, the Cohen Committee on Life Assurance reported in 1932 that the money collected in 1930 exceeded the annual cost of the navy.[29] The premium income of the industrial insurance companies increased from £25.3 million in 1919 to £58.8 million in 1939. Rowntree reported that in 1936 life assurance premiums in York were 'paid weekly by practically every family, even the very poorest'; and Tout's survey of Bristol in 1937 reported that 79.8 per cent of all working-class families in his sample had taken out industrial life policies. In the 1940s, moreover, the number of lapses of payments to industrial assurance fell to one-third of the pre-war level, 'quite definitely', as the Industrial Life Offices put it, 'due to the greater economic security of the people in wartime'.[30] By the end of World War II, the Industrial Life Offices announced that industrial life policies of one kind or another were held in nine out of ten working-class homes.[31]

Thus, although the effect of war and want could be disruptive, the repercussions on the mutual-aid side of the voluntary sector and on the commercial sector are hard to measure with any accuracy; and, although the voluntary-sector friendly societies of the mutual-aid variety did suffer a marked decline in these years, other manifestations of thrift and savings—especially in the commercial sector—were amply evident. In one way, this could be regarded as a response to the social needs of the period, especially those of depression—for which, as has been mentioned, the commercial-sector agencies were particularly suitable. In another, it could be related to the relative prosperity of those in work during the period. Johnson notes that the cash value of working-class savings rose by 47 per cent between 1921 and 1931, and their purchasing power by 126 per cent.[32]

What were the effects of war and want on the charitable and philanthropic side of the voluntary sector? The reduction that World Wars I and II caused in the personnel available for charitable work has already been noted; but on the other hand, both war and want could prove to be considerable spurs to charitable activity—and any suggestion that such activity disappeared

[29] Quoted ibid. 14.   [30] Quoted ibid. 34.   [31] Ibid. 22–3.
[32] Ibid. 207. See also Hannah, *Inventing Retirement*, 33: 'the market for voluntary savings was a comfortably expanding one in which the insurance companies . . . were increasing their market share' (see also ibid. 38).

under the exigencies of the period is quite mistaken. As ever, any statistical analysis of the extent of charitable endeavour is fraught with difficulties. It will be recalled that only endowed charities in England and Wales came under the supervision of the Charity Commissioners or, for much of this period, the Board of Education, and had to send annual reports to these bodies. A procedure for registration was extended to war charities in 1916 and charities for the blind in 1920. As in the past, there were publications sponsored by the Charity Organisation Society; and Liverpool Council for Social Service put out similar information. Various volumes of *Whitaker's Almanack* for the period gave figures for, and commented on, the level of charitable giving. In the case of the voluntary hospitals, the Central Bureau of Hospital Information and the King Edward's Hospital Fund for London provided information. But innumerable philanthropic bodies escaped capture by these various gathering nets; or where they were included, their figures were calculated using different gauges. Thus, as always, any firm overall statistical evidence for the dimensions of philanthropic activity remains highly elusive.

This has not, however, deterred certain brave scholars from entering the waters. One such was Constance Braithwaite, who, in her book *The Voluntary Citizen*, published in 1938,[33] attempted an ambitious statistical survey, using sources such as those which have been mentioned. She was careful to hedge her figures and conclusions around with considerable caution, since no one knew better than she the problems posed by the sources. When she contributed a section to *Voluntary Social Services since 1918*, edited by Henry A. Mess and published in 1947, she was likewise cautious. 'Any account of the statistics of charitable finance', she wrote, 'is of necessity very incomplete because of the scarcity of collected information.'[34] Nevertheless, having carried out various local studies, she was bold enough to pose the question as to the magnitude of the total receipts of all charities in England and Wales in the mid-1930s; and she reached the conclusion that if the income of purely endowed charities and purely religious and political organizations were excluded, the total receipts of all charitable organizations in England and Wales were within the

[33] *The Voluntary Citizen: An Enquiry into the Place of Philanthropy in the Community* (London: Methuen, 1938).
[34] London: Kegan Paul, Trench, Trubner, 1947, 195.

range of £35 million to £50 million.[35] She divided this into various categories of receipt and concluded that something like 50 per cent of the total was received in charitable gifts—about £17.5 million to £25 million. Surveying trends in charitable giving over a period of time, for example between 1908 and 1927 in London, she reached the conclusion that changes in giving were relatively small; and, dealing with the interwar years as a whole, she concluded her article of 1947 thus:

There is little if any evidence from the collected figures for the fairly common assumption that the increase of taxation and the greater provision of social services by public authorities have had the effect of decreasing the amount of legacies and of other charitable gifts. The amount given in charity seems to have varied surprisingly little over the period if we consider all the concurrent changes in economic circumstances and public policy which might have been expected to affect it.[36]

This indeed echoes similar remarks made by *Whitaker's Almanack*, which commented in 1934 that 'the flow of charity still shows no sign of serious abatement in volume'. This was 'despite the shrinkage in values due to the general depression, and very high taxation'. The report concluded that the loss of charitable bequests from the very large estates was 'somewhat compensated for by an increasing flow from estates in the medium category.'[37]

Other surveys of this area concentrate less on finance than on organizations and the individuals working within them. The *Report on the British Social Services*, published in 1937 by Political and Economic Planning, noted 'the growth of a salaried bureaucracy' in the voluntary services. It quoted the 1931 Census to indicate that the number of persons employed by social welfare societies in England and Wales had reached almost 10,000:

These voluntary societies by 1931 could offer paid employment to as many persons as the blast furnaces, or as the manufacture of linoleum, of butter and cheese and condensed milk, or of explosives. Evidently, the salaried staff of the voluntary social services is still growing, and its influence is increasing despite the expansion in the personnel of the public social agencies which is also taking place.[38]

---

[35] *Voluntary Citizen*, 168.

[36] H. A. Mess *et al.* (eds.), *Voluntary Social Services*, 202–3.   [37] p. lxiii.

[38] *Report on the British Social Services: A Survey of the Existing Public Social Services in Great Britain with Proposals for Future Development*, 174.

A more strictly organizational approach was used by Beveridge in his book of 1948, *Voluntary Action*. He worked out a classification of philanthropic agencies for the sick and the injured; for children; for youth; for old people; for the blind; for cripples and other physically handicapped persons; for the homeless; for socially handicapped persons; for family welfare; for adult education; for the promotion of the arts; for physical education; service organizations; residential settlements; general agencies. Within each category he listed individual societies which were appropriate to it. The total number of such societies was eighty-one.[39] But this was far from complete; and Beveridge well realized the problems of gathering such information, since no central agency existed to contain it. Also in 1948, the National Council of Social Service, a coordinating body within the voluntary sector founded in 1919,[40] published a much more extensive survey. It had twenty-three categories of society and listed some three hundred organizations. Again, however, the compilers of the survey were careful to point to its incompleteness. With regard to the system of classification which had been used, they commented that 'there is no generally accepted classification of social services in this country'. And as far as the lists of individual organizations were concerned, only national organizations, and no local bodies, were included. Even then, there were omissions. 'Lists of this kind can never be entirely satisfactory', ran the introduction; '... an element of arbitrary choice inevitably enters ... not all organisations could be fitted into the scheme.'[41]

The evidence which has been quoted cannot, indeed, be regarded as definitive; but it does indicate that the charitable and philanthropic side of the voluntary sector was still active. John Stevenson has put the point well when commenting that, between 1914 and 1945, the 'philanthropic traditions of the past' showed 'continued vitality' and 'an ability to command a powerful community response'.[42] That response was not, of course, entirely related to, nor dominated by, war and want; but, as has been suggested, these could present very considerable

---

[39] *Voluntary Action: A Report on Methods of Social Advance* (London: George Allen & Unwin, 1948), 123–4.   [40] See below, p. 302.
[41] *Voluntary Social Services: Handbook of Information and Directory of Organisations* (London: The National Council of Social Service, 1948), 38.
[42] Stevenson, *British Society*, 319.

opportunities for the exercise of philanthropy. As in the past, the motivation could be mixed. In war, philanthropy could be seen as an exercise of national duty, from which the individual gained a sense of patriotism; in want, it could be a means of social reconciliation. These motives, involving some degree of reciprocity, could coexist with more altruistic motives, deriving from a sense of compassion or humanitarian concern—and, indeed, from religion, which, despite evidence of shrinkage, remained a motivating factor. To be involved in voluntary social work could, in fact, be seen as a way of making religion 'relevant': a prime concern of the churches and other religious organizations in the period.

There is no doubt that World War I was marked by a very extensive outpouring of philanthropic effort. One especially urgent problem was raised by the needs of the dependants of men who had volunteered for service. The only semi-official agency responsible for providing allowances and pensions in the early stages of the war was the Commissioners of the Royal Hospital for Soldiers at Chelsea. The rates paid had not altered since the Boer War; and supplementation came from charitable sources, which were fed through the National Relief Fund, set up in 1914 to deal with the emergencies caused by war, and through the Soldiers' and Sailors' Families Association. Founded in 1885, this Association had been active during the Boer War and came promptly into service on the outbreak of World War I. In the weeks before Christmas 1914, between 3,000 and 4,000 voluntary workers under its auspices in London alone were spending between a morning and six hours a week in relief work, either in improvised premises or in visiting the homes of those in need.[43] Financial aid was given; clothing was contributed by organizations such as Queen Mary's Needlework Guild, and special facilities were made available for free meals for invalids. On occasion, too, free medical advice was given and chemists supplied medicine free or at very low cost.[44]

It was estimated that some 65,000 families were assisted in these various ways by the Association during the first months of the war.[45] Elsewhere, too, the Association was active. In Portsmouth, the local branch had a staff of about one hundred

[43] *Conference on War Relief and Personal Service, June 1915* (London: Longmans, Green, 1915), 8.
[44] Ibid. 12–14.   [45] Ibid. 8.

working in and from its offices. A special committee of volunteers visited all expectant mothers and reported to the main committee on their requirements.[46] The Glasgow branch of the Association dealt with some 12,000 applications for relief between 17 August and 15 September 1914.[47] At a special conference organized by various voluntary organizations in London in 1915, Alderman Holt of Manchester said that he thought it 'a disgrace to our country that we should delay in the payments to wives and dependants of our soldiers. It would have been "God Help them" if there had been no Soldiers' and Sailors' Families Association.'[48]

There were numerous other voluntary-sector agencies which worked for the relief of distress caused by the war. The Salvation Army initiated an emigration scheme, whereby help was given to war widows who wanted to go abroad to provide better prospects for their children. The Children's Aid Society placed a large number of children in country houses to give them a change of environment and found families who undertook the care of motherless children while their fathers were on active service.[49] There were many relief funds—especially for the families of officers. And the medical needs of those wounded in the war attracted considerable public support. The voluntary hospitals received the wounded; the London hospitals admitted over 1,300 wounded soldiers by the end of November 1914, and the Norfolk and Norwich hospitals put 250 of their 350 beds at the disposal of the war wounded.[50] The Princess Louise Hospital for Limbless Soldiers and Sailors was founded by public subscription at Erskine, near Glasgow, with particular areas being paid for by the congregational givings of various local churches, who retained an interest thereafter; one such was Newlands South Church in Glasgow. Charities in support of these ventures were, indeed, well supported. In 1918 the Charity Commissioners reported figures which showed the value of new endowments as permanent trusts for investment. Medical charities showed a marked increase: from £153,851 in 1914 to £262,975 in 1917.[51]

---

[46] Ibid. 23.   [47] *Charity Organisation Review*, NS, xxxvi (Oct. 1914), 249–50.
[48] *Conference on War Relief*, 31.   [49] Ibid. 14.
[50] Brian Abel-Smith, *The Hospitals 1800–1948: A Study in Social Administration in England and Wales* (London: Heinemann Educational Books, 1964), 262.
[51] *Sixty-Fifth Report of the Charity Commissioners for England and Wales* (Parliamentary Papers, 1918, Cd. 9008), par. 1.

And there were numerous special appeals. The Red Cross was able to raise very large sums by appeals to the public during the war; these were in the region of £21 million. By September 1916 the National Relief Fund had gathered almost £6 million.[52] The needs of returning ex-servicemen were not overlooked. The Soldiers' and Sailors' Help Society gave assistance to discharged and disabled servicemen; and in 1916–17 three new societies came into existence: in 1916, the National Association of Discharged Sailors and Soldiers, and the following year, the National Federation of Discharged and Demobilised Sailors and Soldiers and the Comrades of the Great War.[53]

If much of the charitable effort of the war years was, inevitably, directed to the needs of servicemen and their families, the problems encountered by refugees were not ignored. Early in the war, on news of the occupation of Belgium, a voluntary body—the War Refugees Committee—was set up in London to give help and advice to those driven to seek refuge in Britain. The committee established several temporary hostels in London and obtained offers of help and hospitality from all parts of the country. Arrangements were made to meet trains arriving at Folkestone and to transport refugees to their destinations. Jews were catered for by the Jewish Community of London at the Jews' temporary shelter.[54] Moreover, the Friends' Emergency Committee for the Assistance of Germans, Austrians and Hungarians in Distress worked in Britain throughout the war in helping the families of *enemy* aliens and in doing such social and educational work as was possible among aliens in internment camps and prisoners of war.[55] In Queens Park in Glasgow, a tree was planted in October 1917 by the Belgian refugees in the city, 'in Remembrance'—as the inscription goes—'of the hospitality and kindness extended to them during their sojourn in Glasgow': another small, but significant, indication of the 'philanthropy of war'.

A great deal of work was undertaken by women—who, despite the increased opportunities offered by public life and

[52] Braithwaite, *Voluntary Citizen*, 94.

[53] Graham Wootton, *The Official History of the British Legion* (London: Macdonald & Evans, 1956), 2–3.

[54] *Report on Special Work of the Local Government Board Arising out of the War* (Parliamentary Papers, 1915, Cd. 7763), 11, 13.

[55] Braithwaite, *Voluntary Citizen*, 48–9.

war-related employment, remained active in voluntary-sector charity. Society ladies were, for example, prominent in welcoming the Belgian refugees and finding them suitable accommodation; and, indeed, many titled ladies began their own charities for families adversely affected by the war. One such group founded the National Milk Hostels committee to supply milk to families in need from their own home farms. And, of course, the role of women in more direct military occupations—sometimes with a 'welfare' aspect—should also be noted: the Women's Emergency Corps, the Women's Volunteer Reserve, the Women's Defence Relief Corps, the Women's Hospital Corps, the Women's Legion.[56]

Young people in voluntary groups, too, played a part in the war effort. The recently formed Boy Scouts resisted efforts to absorb the movement into cadet training, and to make it adopt a quasi-military role. Scouts did, however, guard buildings, bridges, and telephone installations and man the coast; and, in a somewhat more welfare-orientated capacity, they acted as messengers between government buildings and hospitals. In 1917–18, they worked on various harvesting tasks in areas where the male population was in short supply owing to the demands of war.[57]

War, then, provided a focus for a profusion of philanthropic giving and effort. It may have weakened traditional charitable occupations; but it provided the opportunity for new ones. What of peace? In 1926 a Home Office committee noted that 'the circumstances of a great war provide a far stronger appeal to both conscience and sentiment than the conditions of peace'.[58] Yet peace in 1918 brought with it problems on an international scale to which charitable effort could also be directed. Before the war there had, indeed, been various international bodies concerned with social issues, such as public health and child protection: but the Peace Conference established new relief organizations to deal with distress in central and eastern Europe in cooperation with the Red Cross. Much of this work was taken over by the League

[56] Arthur Marwick, *The Home Front: The British and the Second World War* (London: Thames & Hudson, 1976), 132 ff.

[57] Henry Collis, Fred Hull, and Rex Hoglewood, *B.-P.'s Scouts: An Official History of the Boy Scouts Association* (London: Collins, 1961), 73–6.

[58] *Report of the Home Office Department Committee on the Supervision of Charities* (Parliamentary Papers, 1927, Cmd. 2823), par. 62.

of Nations, which, under Article 23, was entrusted with various humanitarian responsibilities. The section of the League which discharged these functions worked in close cooperation with various voluntary organizations. One such was the Save the Children Fund, founded in 1919 by Eglantyne Jebb with the object of relieving child suffering and promoting child welfare on an international scale. This was based on the Declaration of the Rights of the Child, drafted by Miss Jebb—and adopted by the League of Nations Assembly as its 'Charter of Child Welfare' in 1924.[59] The League also prompted the formation of various voluntary groups which, if not precisely welfare agencies, were directed to the promotion of peace and well-being. Thus there were the Women's International League, and the League of Nations Union, founded in 1921 and described as 'perhaps the largest and most universal national voluntary organization of post-war Britain'.[60] Here, then, was the 'internationalization' of charity. Once again, the voluntary sector showed its ability to adapt to new circumstances and challenges—and its tendency to create ever more organizations with somewhat similar objectives.

Moreover, on the domestic front, the problems of war were not long over when they were replaced by the problems of want; and these likewise gave opportunities for charitable endeavour of various kinds. One voluntary organization which linked war and want was the British Legion, founded in 1922. The Legion came into existence as a result of the amalgamation of the various ex-servicemen's societies founded in the course of the war. Certainly one reason for the willingness of those societies to come together was the problem of unemployment after the war and, in particular, the ways in which ex-servicemen were affected by it. Throughout the 1920s and early 1930s the Legion was preoccupied with unemployment among former servicemen.[61] It provided immediate financial assistance, and in 1930/1 spent £258,000 in direct relief. But it was even more anxious to find employment and to place ex-servicemen in it. At its annual conference in 1926 the Prince of Wales, its patron, observed that the most important, but also most difficult, of the Legion's activities was the discovery

<hr />

[59] Beveridge and Wells (eds.), *Evidence*, 281.

[60] Margaret Brasnett, *Voluntary Social Action: A History of The National Council of Social Service, 1919–1969* (London: National Council of Social Service, 1969).

[61] Wootton, *British Legion*, 46 ff.

of employment for ex-servicemen, especially the disabled. The Legion used its funds to set up various employment schemes for its members, and advanced interest-free loans to individuals to enable them to begin new trades. Its factories for the manufacture of poppies for the Poppy Day appeal gave work for the severely disabled. It also set up Employment Exchanges to assist ex-servicemen to take advantage of such employment opportunities as were available. It encouraged and promoted emigration schemes for the unemployed and their families.

Another aspect of the Legion's work lay in campaigning and exerting pressure on issues which were of particular interest to ex-servicemen: pensions, training facilities for the young unemployed, the compulsory absorption by employers of disabled unemployed ex-servicemen. It also had more ambitious long-term aims. It argued for a Work Loan and National Employment Committee to investigate and recommend schemes of public utility. It has been said that it showed signs of 'common-sense Keynesianism before Keynes.'[62] In these larger aims, it was unsuccessful, and in the later 1920s and the 1930s it virtually abandoned them in favour of its small-scale and more specific projects. In Scotland, the needs of ex-servicemen were also tackled by the Earl Haig Fund.

In the context of want, many philanthropic agencies—with no such specific constituency—were active. There was, for example, the work of the large philanthropic trusts. Two of these were especially active in relation to social needs: the Carnegie United Kingdom Trust, founded in 1913, and the Pilgrim Trust, established in 1930.[63] The Carnegie Trust was associated with the provision of libraries and the fostering of music, drama, physical education, and adult education. It set up a committee to undertake educational work among the unemployed in mining areas especially badly affected by unemployment. The Pilgrim Trust, from its inception, was closely involved with the problems of unemployment. It took a wide view of the country's national heritage, which it sought to maintain. These did, indeed, include material and historical possessions—but also the human assets of the country. Its first Annual Report of 1931 noted that the Trustees were concerned with giving help 'in tiding over the

---

[62] Ibid. 77.   [63] Mess (ed.), *Voluntary Social Services*, 172–82.

present distress and to promote the future wellbeing of the country. Their duty is . . . to apply their resources at key points of the present distress and at the same time to help our land to emerge from the crisis with its vigour and its inheritance from the past unimpaired.' Thus between 1930 and the outbreak of World War II, the Trustees divided their expenditure about equally between the preservation of national monuments and schemes for social welfare. They felt under an obligation to respond 'to the repeated appeals which were reaching them to assist agencies which were working to counter-act some of the worst effects of continued unemployment and to prevent many places where moral and intellectual leadership is absent from sinking into despair'.[64]

In similar philanthropic tradition, a gift from Lord Nuffield helped to set up the Upholland Experiment, near Wigan. This involved the employment of some two hundred unemployed workers on four farms which raised pigs, grew vegetables, and produced milk, or, in an industrial centre, were concerned with tailoring, baking, or jam-making. The Nuffield Trust also distributed funds to regenerate industry.

There were numerous other philanthropic initiatives in the Depression. One was the 'adoption scheme', whereby certain well-favoured areas or institutions 'adopted' less fortunate areas. Thus Jarrow was adopted by Surrey, Redruth by Bath, a club in Gateshead by the British Broadcasting Corporation. In 1936 there were ninety-six such schemes in Britain. In Middlesbrough, shelter and occupation were given to the unemployed by voluntary-sector groups: in 1922 the Winter Gardens there catered for 600–900 persons daily. In Stockton, the Personal Service League made similar efforts, and one of its stalwarts, a Mrs Natran, is reported to have said that, to most people she knew, voluntary effort seemed to be the most natural way of dealing with the problem of depression. 'There was a job to do,' she said, 'and we just got on with it.'[65] There was also the work of religious organizations, the Society of Friends being particularly active. This formed a Community Study Council and assisted the work of a cooperative society, which made furniture and woven goods, at Brynmawr; from the former emanated a town development scheme, which

[64] Quoted ibid. 180.
[65] Kate Nicholas, *The Social Effects of Unemployment in Teesside 1919–35* (Manchester: Manchester University Press, 1986), 175.

resulted in the construction of a swimming-pool and park. The Society also organized the Allotments for the Unemployed Scheme, supplying tools, seeds, and fertilizers for the allotments which the unemployed were encouraged to tend. The churches also played their part in providing recreational and other facilities for those without work, and this was true of other kindred bodies: the Boys' Brigade, the Salvation Army, the Young Men's Christian Association and the Young Women's Christian Association.

A case-study of much of this effort was to be found in the voluntary occupational centre movement, for it incorporated, though did not monopolize, much of the voluntary work carried out in areas of unemployment. The centres offered various pursuits to the unemployed: recreation, education, work such as cobbling, joinery, or tailoring. By mid-1935 there were over one thousand such centres in existence for men and more than three hundred for women, with a total membership of over 150,000. There were also unemployed clubs and community service clubs.[66] These provided associational support and facilities for the unemployed—although they were most successful in this respect in areas, such as the Rhondda, where there was an existing associational tradition.[67]

All this was, of course, part of the long-standing traditions of charitable effort intermixed with an element of mutual-aid; some clubs grew out of older working-class clubs and Settlement houses. But they were given a particular spur by want. In January 1932 the Prince of Wales called on the British people to regard the challenge of unemployment as 'a national opportunity for voluntary social service'.[68] The Annual Report of the National Council of Social Service in 1932 commented that the 'spirit of voluntary service . . . [had] been quickened throughout the length and breadth of the land'.[69] The Annual Report of the Pilgrim Trust

---

[66] Ralph H. C. Hayburn, 'The Voluntary Occupational Centre Movement 1932–39' (*Journal of Contemporary History*, vi/3 (1971), 156–71). See also *Men without Work*, 354–77, for an examination of the Wigan Subsistence Production Society and the Lincoln People's Service Club, voluntary initiatives dealing with poverty and isolation respectively.

[67] Ross McKibbin, *The Ideologies of Class: Social Relations in Britain, 1880–1950* (Oxford: Clarendon Press, 1990).

[68] Quoted in Hayburn, 'Voluntary Occupational Centre Movement', 158.

[69] Quoted in Elizabeth Macadam, *The New Philanthropy: A Study of the Relations between the Statutory and Voluntary Services* (London: Allen & Unwin, 1934), 70.

in 1936 noted that unemployment had 'afforded the voluntary agencies an unparalleled opportunity during the past few years'.[70] Braithwaite, in her study of charitable giving in London between 1908 and 1927, found that of the charities supported, those devoted to the categories of 'general relief' and 'social and physical development' were high on the list of favoured causes; and she also found that many charities within the category of 'social and physical development' were of recent origin. In Liverpool, the 'social welfare' group greatly increased its proportion of total income between 1922 and 1933.[71] It is dangerous to draw too many conclusions from this evidence. For one thing, Braithwaite's figures relate to a somewhat different period from that of high unemployment, and for another, the categories mentioned covered a wide variety of endeavour, and were not limited to the effects of unemployment. Nevertheless, the point made by the Prince of Wales and the Pilgrim Trust is a fair one; and even the response of the Trust alone indicates that the opportunities were not neglected.

War, want—and war again: World War II. This brought the servicemen's organizations, such as the Soldiers', Sailors' and—now—Airmen's Families Association, the British Legion, and the Earl Haig Fund to the relief of war problems once again. The Benevolent Department of the Legion was under heavy pressure from applications, and its disbursements on needs such as those caused by chronic illness, permanent incapacity, and orphanage increased by some £60,000 in 1943 and £94,000 in 1944.[72] The Legion also continued to press for legislation on pensions and the employment of the disabled; and in both areas, legislation passed in 1943 met points for which it had long campaigned.[73]

But, of course, World War II gave greater scope for service among the civilian population at home than had been the case in World War I. It was found, for example, that many of the children who were evacuated needed new clothes, and charitable schemes were organized in many districts to raise funds and receive supplies of clothing.[74] In assisting the process of evacuation

[70] *Sixth Annual Report*, 5.
[71] Braithwaite, *Voluntary Citizen*, 105–7 (London), 129–31 (Liverpool).
[72] Wootton, *British Legion*, 272.   [73] Ibid. 265, 270.
[74] Richard M. Titmuss, *Problems of Social Policy* (London: HMSO & Longmans, Green, 1950), 119.

itself in 1940–1, voluntary-sector agencies would often find suitable accommodation in safe areas for mothers and children, the old, and the infirm.[75] Many voluntary organizations were involved in the provision of social centres, recreational clubs for war workers, and family hostels; among them were the churches, the Young Men's Christian Association and Young Women's Christian Association, the Society of Friends War Relief Committee, the Personal Service League, the National Association of Girls' Clubs, and various London Settlements.[76] Again, there was great activity in the setting up of nursery centres for the under-fives in the reception areas. A number of residential nurseries were established by philanthropic agencies in these districts. The Soldiers', Sailors' and Airmen's Families Association was also active in the provision and running of residential homes for the families of servicemen.[77]

A further area which gave opportunities for a great deal of charitable work related to the establishment of rest centres for those made homeless by bombing. Voluntary agencies, such as the Charity Organisation Society, the Society of Friends, Settlement workers, and many others, responded quickly to the problems. The Charity Organisation Society had foreseen the need for blankets and clothing, and, through the agency of the Canadian Red Cross, had acquired stocks of 50,000 blankets, 100,000 miscellaneous garments, and 50,000 tons of food. These stocks were quickly distributed to London rest centres.[78] Next to shortages of blankets and food, insufficient staff was the biggest problem of the rest centres, and here again, many voluntary-sector workers came forward to offer their services. The Red Cross began the experiment in Middlesex of taking over houses in which to provide periods of rest for homeless people and for those suffering or recovering from illness.[79] There were, too, many mobile canteens in the hands of voluntary organizations, such as the Church Army.[80] The needs of servicemen on leave, or with periods of relaxation, were not overlooked; and here the occupational centres for the unemployed of the 1930s often found a new use.

Causes which were war-related almost always evoked a substantial response to the 'Week's Good Cause Appeal' broadcast

---

[75] Ibid. 368.   [76] Ibid. 373–4.   [77] Ibid. 211.
[78] Ibid. 262.   [79] Ibid. 269.   [80] Ibid. 266.

on the wireless. This became a regular feature after the broadcast of the first appeal by the BBC in January 1926. The sums produced by such appeals have—as Beveridge pointed out—to be viewed with some caution, since much depended on the persons making them—and even on the season and the weather at the time that they were made.[81] But the figures for the period from November 1939 to November 1944 show beyond doubt the ways in which appeals which had to do with the war effort produced the maximum support. There were 268 appeals during that period. Of these, thirty-one produced more than £10,000; and the largest responses—considerably in excess of £10,000—were made to appeals such as those for King George's Fund for Sailors in 1939, 1942, 1943, and 1944 (twice), the RAF Benevolent Fund in 1941, and the Lord Mayor's National Air Raid Distress Fund in 1940. By no means all the largest responses, however, were for purely 'British' war purposes; the Finland Fund, appealed for twice in 1940, and the Anglo-Turkish Relief Fund in 1940 also gained very considerable sums. On the other hand, appeals for domestic social issues, which were not primarily war-related, tended to yield fairly small amounts of under £1,000.[82]

World War I, want, World War II: these were great spurs to philanthropic effort. They were not, of course, the only reasons for the vitality of this effort. There was a continuing tradition of charitable effort over a wide variety of need. Thus meeting the needs of the blind evoked what was called the 'persistent energy of voluntaryism'.[83] There were various new developments in the interwar period, such as the establishment of Sunshine Homes for blind babies, which were developed into residential nursery schools; similarly, Chorleywood College, a secondary school for blind girls, was founded, and Worcester College, a public school for blind boys, developed. Voluntary initiatives helped to extend the practice of making 'talking books' available for the blind and, with the cooperation of the BBC, to provide the blind with wireless sets. In this area, too, however, war had its effects. In World War I, the retraining and rehabilitation of the war-blinded was carried out by voluntary-sector activity; and that was extended

---

[81] Beveridge and Wells (eds.), *Evidence*, 219.
[82] Ibid. 221.   [83] Ibid. 172.

in World War II to include civilian war-blinded as well as ex-service personnel.[84]

Charitable organizations, moreover, were by no means indifferent to the international developments of the 1930s which were to have a bearing on World War II. The exodus of Jews from Germany after the appointment of Hitler as Chancellor in January 1930 was more or less immediate, and the number who entered Britain was to be substantial. The Jewish community in Britain was quick to organize a structure to meet them and offer assistance. British Jews created a considerable number of voluntary organizations of varying size and effectiveness in the years ahead, the most important being the Central British Fund and the Jewish Refugees Committee.[85] Relief work was also extensively carried out by non-Jewish organizations in Britain. One active in this area was the Academic Assistance Council, founded on the initiative of Beveridge in 1933 and later to be called the Society for the Protection of Science and Learning. Another was the Society of Friends Germany Emergency Committee, later known as the Friends Committee for Refugees and Aliens.[86] These were only two organizations among many devoted to this cause. It is also true to say that the position with regard to voluntary effort on an international level of the period after World War I found a parallel after 1945. The overseas and international department of the National Council of Social Service forged close links with relevant United Nations agencies on matters of social reconstruction.[87]

If the voluntary sector was, therefore, much in evidence during these years, the informal sector remained an essential unit of support—and within that, the role of the wife and mother was vital. This was particularly true in circumstances of want. Thus Charles L. Mowat has written of the situation in the 1930s:

it was the women who suffered more than the men. Unemployment brought leisure for men, if they chose to regard it so; it brought no rest to the wives and mothers. They must scrape and scrimp to feed and

[84] Ibid.

[85] See Werner E. Mosse (ed.), *Second Chance: Two Centuries of German-Speaking Jews in the United Kingdom* (Tübingen: J. C. B. Mohr (Paul Siebeck), 1991), 453, 579–98, 599–610.

[86] Ibid. 453, 599–610.   [87] Brasnett, *Voluntary Social Action*, 161.

clothe the family, usually on less money than before, even if what there was was now fixed and regular. Very often, the children were well cared-for and healthy. If anyone went short on food and clothes, it was the mother . . .[88]

The Pilgrim Trust's survey of a sample of unemployed men also covered some 170,000 wives; and it was calculated that they ate only 70 per cent of the calories consumed by men, instead of the 85 per cent recommended by dieticians.[89]

Strict economy was one route to the survival of the family, but the assistance of kin and neighbours remained an important informal network of support. Any unusual expense—even the buying of clothes or shoes—usually demanded credit or a loan. There was still reliance on moneylenders and pawnbrokers, although their business was, in fact, declining in the interwar years. There were, however, many other sources of credit. One was simply the corner shop, which would allow credit in bad times to keep custom in good. Francie Nichol gave a description of a general dealer's shop which she ran in a poor area of South Shields in the 1930s: 'poor people make good customers. They can't always pay on the dot, but they're honest if ye trust them. And they can never be bothered to shop around. If they know where they can get all they want handy that's where they'll go.'[90] This kind of 'crisis' credit could be supplemented by longer-term credit arrangements on a more overtly commercial basis. Such was the credit club, which involved payment in instalments in return for goods to a certain value; and this often developed into what was known as 'cheque trading', whereby companies sold cheques on credit, to be redeemed at certain designated stores. Or again, there was the development of deferred payments and hire purchase, which, although distinct in law, were often referred to interchangeably to denote the purchase of quite expensive articles in instalments, with repayments being made over an extended period. Even before World War I, the hire-purchase system was already well established, but it was during the war and after it that the system became widespread.[91]

---

[88] 'The Condition of Britain in the Thirties', in A. V. S. Lochhead, *A Reader in Social Administration* (London: Constable, 1968), 119.

[89] Jane Lewis, *Women in England 1870–1950* (Sussex: Wheatsheaf Books, 1984), 28.

[90] Johnson, *Saving and Spending*, 146.   [91] Ibid. 157.

Thus despite—and, indeed, because of—the scale of the problems which confronted it, voluntarism, in its various sectors, remained very active. In these respects, it might seem that the gloomy predictions as to its future made just before 1914 by the *Charity Organisation Review* were considerably overdrawn. Lord Macmillan, Chairman of the Pilgrim Trust from 1934 to 1952, wrote that the vast number of applications received and considered by the Trust brought home to him 'very vividly the extraordinary growth in modern times of what we designate voluntary social work.'[92] A. J. P. Taylor drew attention to the continuing importance of voluntary effort when he described voluntary workers between the wars as 'the active people of England', who 'provided the groundswell of her history'[93]—and that might also be said of them during the wars. Henry Mess wrote of the 'extraordinary power of survival of voluntary organisations' as 'perhaps the most surprising and interesting feature in the development of our social services'.[94] Here again, then, the citizenship of contribution through voluntary agencies may readily be discerned, and it has attracted favourable historical comment. C. L. Mowat wrote that 'in alleviating the distress of unemployment, the state's efforts were dwarfed by those of a voluntary character';[95] and Gerhard Hirschfeld's verdict on the work of the non-Jewish agencies in assisting German Jewish refugees in Britain in the 1930s is that 'no praise is too high'.[96]

III

Despite such clear evidence of the survival, strength, and valuable service of voluntarism in this period, it would nevertheless be a mistake to think that it remained immune from the kind of criticisms made of it in the period from 1880 to 1914; that it *could* not cope adequately with the problems of war and want, and that it *should* not do so. The scale of the issues which were raised

[92] *A Man of Law's Tale: The Reminiscences of Rt. Hon. Lord Macmillan* (London: Macmillan, 1952), 292.

[93] *English History, 1914–1945* (Oxford: Clarendon Press, 1965), 175.

[94] *Voluntary Social Services*, 10.

[95] *Britain between the Wars, 1918–1940* (London: Methuen, 1955), 488. See also Hayburn, 'Voluntary Occupational Centre Movement', 156.

[96] ' "A High Tradition of Earnestness . . .": British Non-Jewish Organisations in Support of Refugees', in Mosse (ed.), *Second Chance*, 599.

in such circumstances—greater than that of the earlier period—meant that it was virtually inevitable that these criticisms should still be voiced.

In the first place, there remained the criticism that voluntarism suffered from financial uncertainty and unreliability. The practice of self-maintenance was clearly possible for those in work—and as has been seen, voluntary organizations, particularly of a commercial kind, remained strong. For those out of work in the interwar period, however, the option of making any substantial contribution to their own welfare remained a strictly limited one. As has been noted, Johnson does not ignore the extent of working-class savings in the period, but he also acknowledges the 'inevitable chanciness' of working-class income as a deterrent to thrift. He quotes J. B. Hurry, who wrote in his book *Poverty and its Vicious Circle*: 'The uncertainty of the future is one reason why even in prosperous days the working man so often spends his wages as soon as earned. He fears that any small economies within his reach will prove insufficient to save him from misery in the face of unemployment. Uncertainty is the enemy of thrift.'[97] This was published, in the second edition of Hurry's book, in 1921—before the onset of 'mass unemployment'. Johnson himself points to the 'very low average of wealth available to each working-class adult'; and, he writes:

The insecurity of working-class income prevented the adoption of long-term saving plans that might conform to middle-class models of saving over the life-cycle. There was little point in thinking about saving for retirement when there were more immediate calls on funds—payment of the quarterly rent or purchase of new boots. Nor was there much point in attempting to save for a goal beyond the financial means of a typical working-class wage, as, for instance, was the purchase of an old-age annuity.[98]

Even in 1938, when employment had begun to revive, some 17 per cent of all families had no margin at all for savings, and any crisis could push them back into poverty.

Thus, while the route to welfare through mutual-aid organizations in the voluntary sector and through the commercial sector was far from closed over the period of war and want, it does appear that want, in particular, put quite severe obstacles in the

[97] Quoted in *Saving and Spending*, 219.   [98] Ibid. 219.

way of travelling along it. As has already been suggested, one reason for the decline of the affiliated orders may have been that the level of subscription demanded was too high, as compared with the amounts required to belong to commercial-sector agencies.

Again, on the philanthropic side of the voluntary sector, there is evidence to suggest that financial problems were making themselves felt—as they had done before 1914. Employer paternalism, or personnel management schemes, could clearly be difficult to sustain, where the Depression affected the firm in question; and where jobs were scarce, the loyalty of employees did not have to be retained by such schemes. Moreover, Braithwaite's analysis of charitable finance did, indeed, indicate a steadiness in charitable giving; but it also showed that this was insufficient to keep pace with rising prices. Here, of course, the inflationary effects of war were evident. Thus her figures indicated that there had been a rise in the receipts of London charities between 1908 and 1927, but this did not compensate for the rise in prices over the same period. Thus the *real* financial position of the charities was approximately the same in 1927 as it had been nineteen years earlier. She suggested that annual subscriptions of individuals to charities tended to become fixed at certain round sums, which failed to take account of changing price levels. Equally, Braithwaite discovered that there was a considerable change in the relative importance of different sources of charitable income. They tended over the interwar period to depend less than in the past on charitable donations, and more on interest and payments by or from persons to whom the services of the charity were rendered—including the state:[99] a point to which further attention will be given later.

Thus any suggestion that charitable giving survived the period virtually unscathed requires qualification; and the anxiety felt in the charitable world in the later nineteenth and early twentieth centuries about the failure of ordinary income to keep pace with rising costs was still evident. The *Charity Organisation Quarterly* in 1923 reported that there were 'no signs of the drying up of the springs of charity'. It mentioned the rise in prices during and after the war as creating a problem for charities; yet, it said,

[99] *Voluntary Citizen*, 110, 131.

'the aggregate of subscriptions and donations has very considerably increased'—and, of course, this issue became less trouble-
some once prices stabilized and fell, and gifts and givings assumed
a higher value. Nevertheless, the *Quarterly* wrote of a 'common
complaint that charitable funds were becoming increasingly difficult to raise'; and older-established charities, in particular, were
'undoubtedly experiencing difficulty in obtaining support commensurate with their needs'.[100]

The experience of the Jewish Board of Guardians certainly
showed evidence of this pattern. In the years immediately before
World War I, there had been regular annual deficits, as the requirements of the Board had exceeded its normal revenue from
subscriptions and grants. Legacies had been used as part of
normal income, instead of being invested. This trend continued
after 1914. Between 1914 and 1929 some £100,000 was raised
by the immediate realization of legacy money. In addition, the
Board issued regular general appeals, but these tended to cure
the situation only in the short term—until another appeal became
necessary. There was a special appeal in 1921, and another in
1929/30, coinciding with the Board's seventieth anniversary. This
second appeal raised £52,000, and reduced the deficit to £363 at
1 January 1930. Yet there was another deficit—of £5,000—by the
end of 1932, despite the fact that investments to the value of
£12,000 had been realized in the interim. The deficit had reached
£20,000 in 1937. The result was another appeal in 1938 for £80,000,
of which £65,000 was raised. By the end of 1938 the deficit had
been reduced to £2,400.[101]

There was, then, as V. D. Lipman has written of the period
from 1914, a 'monotonous succession of deficits, punctuated by
appeals and realization of investments'.[102] The Board found that
a great deal of its money came from the same core of dedicated
supporters; indeed, it was noted in 1920 that there were some
2,000 names on its subscription lists—and almost half the money
came from 'about 40 fervent individuals'.[103] It was not, however, just a question of difficulty in trying to raise money; it was
also a matter of increased expenditure. The Board developed its

[100] No. 5 (Apr. 1923), 86–7.
[101] V. D. Lipman, *A Century of Social Service, 1859–1959: The Jewish Board of
Guardians* (London: Routledge & Kegan Paul, 1959), 155.
[102] Ibid.   [103] Ibid. 156.

work in convalescence and in caring for the young and old; and the provision of institutions which this involved was extremely expensive. The increasing professionalization of standards of care, moreover, extended a feature which has already been noted with reference to the period before World War I; and this too brought with it increasing costs.[104] The Jewish relief agencies for refugees also found finance a problem: by the end of 1939 the Central British Fund found itself unable to meet demands on its resources.[105]

The finances of the Charity Organisation Society itself were also rather precarious. The Society always insisted that it was not a relief society—although, as has been seen, sums were spent on relief in cases of age or illness and to assist emigration, in addition to administration and training. For some years before 1914, its expenditure was increasing faster than its income; and it made substantial attempts in the interwar years to increase its income from voluntary sources.[106] The district branches of the Society found that unemployment was the most common cause of distress among those who applied for help, and also found it hard to cope with the applications which were made. They limited the services provided, for the most part, to medical, surgical, and convalescent help.[107] In such circumstances, finance remained a difficulty; and the annual reports drew attention to constant deficits, which were repeated in the 1940s. Indeed, after World War II a large-scale reorganization of the Society—by then the Family Welfare Association—took place in the wake of a series of financial crises.[108] Income from subscriptions to the Central Office between 1914 and 1944 fell from £4,803 in 1914 to £3,730 in 1944; and overall receipts were heavily dependent on the unpredictable and variable incidence of donations and legacies.[109]

A not dissimilar pattern may be discerned in the Liverpool Council of Social Service. Since its foundation in 1909, as a coordinating body within the voluntary sector, the Council had not appealed to the public for funds on its own behalf. But one of its

---

[104] Ibid.

[105] Ronald Stent, 'Jewish Refugee Organisations', in Mosse (ed.), *Second Chance*, 582–3, 586.

[106] Madeleine Rooff, *A Hundred Years of Family Welfare* (London: Michael Joseph, 1972), 310.

[107] Ibid. 143–4.   [108] Ibid. 312.   [109] Ibid. 316.

roles was to give grants to charitable organizations; and thus it sought various means of securing funds for distribution. In 1922 it pioneered the scheme of covenanted subscriptions, whereby relief from both standard-rate income tax and surtax was allowed on a seven-year deed covenanted by a taxpayer to a charity. This proved successful, and by 1930 there were 157 covenants, which together were worth £51,114.[110] Later in the 1930s, however, the level of covenanted subscriptions dropped; in 1933 they were worth £34,864. There was also a decline in street collections.[111] The Council's salaried staff took voluntary cuts in salary. In 1938 the financial situation improved somewhat, as the result of the assumption of the Trust conferred on the Council by the will of A. B. Earle;[112] this involved the administration of some £500,000 and enabled the Council to make special grants to a variety of charities. But such sources of money were, by their very nature, unpredictable and unreliable for long-term planning.

Similar problems were felt by the voluntary hospitals. War did, in fact, inject considerable sums of money into hospitals which catered for the wounded during World War I. The War Office between 1914 and 1919 paid some £880,000 to the voluntary hospitals for the care of the sick and the wounded. The hospitals, however, claimed that these payments left the London hospitals alone £530,000 short of the total cost of looking after and treating military patients. When the number of wounded servicemen in hospital fell, voluntary hospitals lost the payments which had previously gone with them, but in 1920 15,000 war pensioners were still receiving treatment in civilian hospitals; and the British Hospitals Association managed to negotiate fairly generous public payments for their maintenance. As has been seen, voluntary hospitals received very considerable charitable support during the war; to put it no more highly, 'wounded soldiers made excellent appeal copy'.[113]

[110] H. R. Poole, *The Liverpool Council of Social Service, 1909–1959* (Liverpool: The Liverpool Council of Social Service (Inc.), 1960), 46. The covenanted subscription, increasingly important to charities, was an unintentional result of the Revenue Act of 1922, which denied recognition to any covenant of less than 6 years. This implied that a covenant of 7 years was valid and the point was exploited in the interests of charity. See David Owen, *English Philanthropy, 1660–1960* (Cambridge, Mass: Harvard University Press, 1965), 337.
[111] Ibid. 52.   [112] Ibid. 62.   [113] Abel-Smith, *Hospitals*, 282.

Nevertheless, despite the ways in which World War I brought the voluntary hospitals increased sources of income, they found themselves in very considerable difficulty at the end of the war. Further, hospitals which were not felt to be vital to the war effort found themselves facing great financial problems. By Christmas 1917 the Chelsea Hospital for Women had a deficit of £16,000 on a new building, and £5,500 on its maintenance account. The East London Hospital for Children claimed support from the public on the grounds that it was 'to the children that we look for our future armies and future mothers of our race'.[114] It was said that the Manchester Royal Infirmary needed £9,000 extra a year to restore its finances; in the mid-1920s it was reported that the London Fever Hospital would be closing and the National Hospital, Queen's Square, was already in process of discharging its patients. Notices were commonly displayed declaring, 'Help us to keep open.' In 1921 the Cave Committee investigated the voluntary hospitals and found them to be in a grave financial position.[115] Whereas the ordinary income of the voluntary hospitals in the London area had risen by 67 per cent since 1913, ordinary expenditure over the same period had risen by 138 per cent. The same situation existed elsewhere; and the overall deficit was of the order of £1 million.

It is perfectly true that some voluntary hospitals expanded as they looked for—and obtained—new sources of income;[116] and the fall in prices assisted them as legacies, gifts, and interest increased in value. Contributory schemes were also developed, and by 1948 there were said to be 10 million members of such schemes. Many hospitals extended the practice of charging their patients. The circumstances of World War II saw a further increase in income from public funds. An overall deficit of some £330,000 in 1938 was turned into a surplus of some £1.8 million in 1940, rising to £2.2 million in 1941 and £3.5 million in 1942. And yet the question remains how far the voluntary hospitals as a whole could

[114] Quoted ibid.

[115] *Voluntary Hospitals Committee, Final Report* (Parliamentary Papers, 1921, Cmd. 1335), pars. 8–12. The situation of the voluntary hospitals in Scotland was somewhat better (par. 11).

[116] It was reported by *Whitaker's Almanack* in 1938 (p. xlv) that hospitals and similar institutions were well supported by charitable bequests and had 'for some years past displaced the church and purposes akin to it as the principal recipient of charitable bequests'.

cope with the problems of costs, exacerbated as they were by the need to repair bomb-damaged buildings. The appearance of overall strength could be deceptive, for by no means all could meet the rising expense involved in looking after patients at the standards which advances in medicine were demanding. As standards were developed further during World War II, higher expenditure would be required to maintain them in future; and it was uncertain whether additional income could be raised by contribution, payment, or charity.

Thus the various sectors of voluntarism, while retaining in certain aspects a great deal of strength in war and want, also suffered from financial precariousness and uncertainty; and this was particularly true of the voluntary—and, indeed, the informal—sectors. A further limitation in meeting the needs of the time lay in the continuing localized and scattered nature of voluntarism. There remained a strong belief in the individuality of voluntarist effort. Friendly societies—and more particularly the agents of industrial insurance—retained their competitive traditions. It was suggested by the Majority Report on National Health Insurance in 1925 that a pooling of one-half of all Approved Society surpluses should be carried out. This would have meant that the wealthier societies would help to pay for new benefits and a wider coverage—such as could not be afforded by the smaller and poorer companies. This was essential if there were to be any extension of benefits; and the money *was* available, since—as has been seen—there were considerable surpluses at the disposal of many of the societies. But this would have meant the breaking down of the competitive, individualistic Approved Society system; and it was resisted.[117]

The Approved Societies were, then, open to the 'could not cope' argument; not that they could not cope with the needs of those who belonged to strong and wealthy societies, but that they could not cope with the needs of the nation *as a whole* in the same way and at the same level. The management costs of Industrial Assurance, moreover, were high. Attempts were made to introduce greater efficiency, but the weekly door-to-door collection of premiums—essential to the commercial success of the whole operation—was in itself expensive, overlapping, and

[117] Gilbert, *British Social Policy*, 278.

cumbersome, and absorbed a considerable proportion of the profit, especially in the case of the smaller societies.[118] Even in 1944 it was estimated that one-half of the small sums paid by contributors went in expenses and lapsed policies. Thus the system was vulnerable to the criticism that it was patchy and wasteful.

With regard to the charitable side of the voluntary sector, there were, indeed, attempts to coordinate charitable activity during the period—to which war and want contributed. This could happen on a local basis. Thus, during World War I, a local fund was established in Bradford to help persons out of work because of the war; and the committee which administered it was widely representative of local philanthropic agencies. In Glasgow, the Charity Organisation Society put its fourteen district offices at the disposal of the Soldiers' and Sailors' Families Association, which lacked such facilities. The conference—already mentioned—in London in June 1915, attended by some six hundred delegates from various voluntary organizations, was an extension of such existing local cooperation to the national scene. F. G. D'Aeth, Secretary of the Liverpool Council of Voluntary Aid, felt that there might come about a 'foundation of voluntary social service on a civic basis which could be one of the greatest events of our day.'[119] Here was a continuing expression of the sentiments which inspired the Guilds of Help. A joint committee on social service was established, including representatives of the Charity Organisation Society, councils of Social Welfare, the National Association of Guilds of Help, the Soldiers' and Sailors' Families Association, and others.

The momentum was kept up after the end of the war. The formation of the British Legion was one such step towards amalgamation, and in 1919 the National Council of Social Service was set up as a coordinating body for the voluntary sector. This was designed to preserve the tradition of voluntary service and to reduce overlapping and duplication. 'Very literally', ran one of the Council's annual reports, 'the council was born out of the experience of these four [war] years.' It referred to the fact that a 'huge army of voluntary workers' had taken part in the relief of war distress, that it was 'natural that this new sense of unity

---

[118] Johnson, *Saving and Spending*, 13–14, 26, 31.
[119] Quoted in Brasnett, *Voluntary Social Action*, 15.

should find public expression'.[120] The National Council, which was incorporated in 1924, was also active in the circumstances of unemployment. It coordinated local schemes, organized conferences for club leaders and members, and published a large amount of literature which contained advice on a variety of topics. It set up a special unemployment committee to foster the creation of centres for the unemployed in various areas, and it handled money donated by the Carnegie United Kingdom Trust and the Pilgrim Trust and from civil service staffs for 'adopted' towns and villages in the areas most affected by unemployment.

Further, there were moves to coordinate the activities of the voluntary hospitals. The Cave Committee reported that lack of coordination was a potential danger—although the warning was little heeded. The Local Government Act of 1929 provided a stronger stimulus to coordination since, in effect, it brought into existence municipal hospitals, which might well be rivals to the voluntary ones. Some steps were, indeed, taken towards a greater degree of internal cooperation. In Liverpool, Manchester, Sheffield, and Oxford, the principal voluntary hospitals initiated a system of joint administration. In 1935 the British Hospitals Association set up a commission under Lord Sankey. This noted that the advent of the municipal hospital had supplied a threat to the voluntary hospitals which had been absent at the time of the Cave Committee. It urged the voluntary hospitals to set up regional councils to coordinate their work, and argued that a central committee should regulate the activities of the regions. This bore some fruit, and the Nuffield Provincial Hospitals Trust, formed in 1939, was designed to coordinate voluntary hospitals in a somewhat similar way to the King Edward's Hospital Fund in London.[121] Again, during World War II the voluntary hospitals participated in the Emergency Hospital Service, which brought about some degree of internal cooperation, and engendered an awareness among medical staff of conditions in hospitals other than their own.[122]

These steps were important and significant—but they had their limitations, as is true of all such attempts to pull the voluntary

[120] Quoted in Macadam, *The New Philanthropy*, 67–8.

[121] J. Trevelyan, *Voluntary Service and the State* (London: George Barker & Son, for The National Council of Social Service (Inc.) and King Edward's Hospital Fund for London, 1952), 25.   [122] Ibid. 26; Abel-Smith, *Hospitals*, 440–1.

sector together. As in the past, there was, of course, no compulsion which the coordinating bodies could use to ensure that all charities took heed of their wishes: compulsion could not coexist with voluntarism. Delegates at the London Conference in June 1915 warned against the dangers of what they called too much 'nationalisation' as something inimical to the spirit of voluntarism.[123] The British Legion was formed in the teeth of attitudes among ex-servicemen's organizations which were warlike rather than harmonious, and which were overcome only with considerable difficulty;[124] and its existence did not prevent the formation of a body such as the Embankment Fellowship (1932), which was designed to assist ex-servicemen and ex-merchant seamen over the age of 45 who were in distress and difficulties.[125] The National Council of Social Service did not replace other coordinating bodies—and, of course, the Charity Organisation Society continued to exist as one such. Others, such as the Christian Social Council, were formed with the object of uniting the efforts of various churches and religious organizations. There were also numerous national bodies of specialized agencies—for example, the National Association of Discharged Prisoners Aid Societies. Thus the National Council added another body to those which already existed—and helped to form yet others, such as the National Association of Boys' Clubs in 1925–6. Indeed, during the period of unemployment, the National Council alienated various other charitable organizations by departing from its coordinating role and acting as a relief agency in its own right—thereby competing with others in the same field.[126] On the eve of World War II a Standing Committee of Voluntary Organisations in War Time was set up. This in itself was an indication that the National Council could not be taken to speak for the whole voluntary service movement—and added yet another body. Equally, the voluntary hospitals were often resistant to any schemes of internal coordination, and despite the various moves to ensure greater cooperation, they were characterized as much by a sense of separate identity and local tradition as by any real desire to work in a united fashion.

[123] *Charity Organisation Review,* NS. xxxviii (July 1915), 138.
[124] Wootton, *British Legion.*
[125] Beveridge and Wells (eds.), *Evidence,* 294.
[126] Brasnett, *Voluntary Social Action,* 70, 89.

Voluntarism thus retained a fondness for separate identity—
as even its adherents freely admitted. Thus in 1927 L. F. Ellis,
Secretary of the National Council of Social Service, wrote that
voluntary social service had qualities of conviction, enthusiasm,
freedom from restraint, and individualism. But it also had the
'defects of its qualities'. It was 'inevitably sporadic, unequal in
quality and unstable'.[127] In 1948 the National Council of Social
Service itself said that 'tidiness is not a major virtue in the field
of voluntary social work'—and added, 'nor can it be so while the
individual remains of primary importance both in the stimulation of voluntary activity and in relations with members or
clients'.[128]

It is not, therefore, surprising that, despite its continuing activity, voluntarism still encountered the criticism that it could not
cope uniformly and adequately with the volume of social need
in the years of war and want. The introduction of conscription in
1916 was, of course, a military issue, and not one of social welfare; but it was also seen in fairly wide and symbolic terms. Thus
the Liberal Home Secretary Sir John Simon, who resigned over
the matter, called it 'the beginning of an immense change in the
structure of our society'. It was, in effect, a recognition that in
such circumstances, voluntarism, based on individual choice and
initiative, was insufficient. That point was also taken up later
in relation to the social issues of the period. In 1937 T. S. Simey
wrote that 'most of the "mass-production" services are entirely
outside the scope of voluntary action and effort, which is unable
to cope effectively with the basic problems of social administration, such as the relief of poverty, unemployment or . . .
sickness'.[129] Simey developed his theme of 'inability to cope' in
terms of the difficulties of ensuring a regular income which could
be used for staff and equipment, and of a general lack of recruitment and training, for which no amount of enthusiasm could
compensate. A report issued by Political and Economic Planning

---

[127] 'The Respective Spheres of Public Authorities and Voluntary Organisations
in the Administration of Social Services' (*Public Administration*, v/4 (Oct. 1927),
391).

[128] *Voluntary Social Services: Handbook of Information and Directory of Organisations*, 38.

[129] *Principles of Social Administration* (Oxford: Oxford University Press, 1937),
136.

in 1937 struck a similar note when it wrote of the 'elasticity, good will, self sacrifice, enthusiastic service' of voluntary provision on the one hand—and 'untidiness and some measure of hypocrisy and "humbug" on the other'.[130] *Men without Work* in 1938 noted that 'improved housing conditions for the whole population, better educational facilities and larger school attendance for the children will lay sounder foundations on which to build, but the problem cannot be left to voluntary agencies alone'.[131] The ways in which war-related charities during World War II tended to dominate charitable giving—to the detriment of charities concerned with more domestic social need—illustrate the point that charity was unevenly spread, and was given to 'bulge' around particular causes which caught public attention at a particular time. Thus, notwithstanding its vitality—or even, because of that vitality, expressing itself through a widespread network of agencies—voluntarism remained vulnerable to the charge that it lacked the depth and reliability of resources and the overall coordination and uniformity to deal with the circumstances of the period. It could still be held to be unequal to the 'challenge of circumstances'.

It also remained open to the 'challenge of convictions': that it *should* not cope with the problems of the period. War and want were unfavourable to any rigid adherence to the values of individualism and self-help, in so far as these sought an explanation for poverty and social distress in personal, rather than structural, factors. In war, those who suffered loss as the result of the death or disablement of relatives or breadwinners, or, particularly in World War II, by bombing and loss of home and livelihood, could scarcely be blamed or held responsible for their difficulties; these could not be attributed to any lack of moral fibre, or a disinclination to provide for themselves. Again, in want, the problems could clearly be seen as more environmental than personal. The unemployed could not easily be regarded as the 'residuum' of the pre-war period; on the contrary, large numbers of the unemployed had worked in skilled trades such as engineering and shipbuilding and lived in communities which had taken pride in their sense of independence and respectability. J. B Priestley's *English Journey*, published in 1934, made this point:

---

[130] *Report on the British Social Services*, 174.   [131] p. 268.

I saw again the older men, who, though they knew they were idle and through no fault of their own, felt defeated and somehow tainted. Their self-respect was shredding away. Their very manhood was going. Even in England, which is no South Sea Island, there are places where a man feels he can do nothing cheerfully, where gay idling is not impossible. But the ironist in charge of our affairs has seen to it that the maximum of unemployment shall be in those very districts that have a tradition of hard work and of very little else . . .[132]

Men without Work gave prominence to age as a determinant of unemployment:

Even in Leicester it was suggested to us by some of those well qualified to know that in a comparatively light industry like the boot and shoe trade, once a man over 50 is unemployed for more than a few weeks, he may find it exceedingly hard to get back, and their view was very fully confirmed by the sample in Leicester. On the other hand, there is a marked increase in the incidence of long unemployment above the age of 60, and it seems that this, partly because the man over 60 gives up more readily, partly because he is refused more roundly by the employer who hears his age, is the most critical age.[133]

Men without Work also noted the tendency among older men to try to maintain membership of a trade union as a symbol of their independence. Again, this was noticeable in Leicester, where those who kept up their membership of the Boot and Shoe Operatives' Union, 'in spite of being out of work for years, were the most respectable; not necessarily keeping up fancy domestic standards, but feeling, as it seemed, that solidarity with those with whom they had once worked, gave them a sort of independent status in relation to the community as a whole'.[134] These men, the report observed, 'were potentially excellent members of the community'. They 'seemed to consider work as something that produces a wage—the wage being, as it were, a mark of the respect and esteem in which they are held'.[135] In such circumstances, it was impossible—or at least very difficult—to hold that unemployment among certain sections of the community was, in some way, an option; on the contrary it was unavoidable.

This was recognized in charitable circles; and adjustments were

---

[132] London: William Heinemann in association with Victor Gollancz, 1934, 407.
[133] p. 212.   [134] Ibid. 195.   [135] Ibid.

made in the spirit which lay behind philanthropic endeavour
—thereby continuing a process which had begun before 1914.
Thus during World War I there was considerable discussion as
to whether assistance should be given to the 'unmarried wife' of
a serviceman. The fact that such women existed was deplored in
many charitable circles; they were natural candidates for place-
ment among the undeserving. Nevertheless, Countess Ferrers,
Vice-President of the North East London district of the Soldiers'
and Sailors' Families Association, told the London Conference in
1915 that investigations into the subject of 'unmarried wives'
needed 'careful and delicate handling'. She said that, although
the investigation of these cases had 'revealed very much to deplore, it has not infrequently shown much to edify'.[136] Alderman
Holt told the Conference that, from the beginning of the war,
help had been given in Manchester to the 'unmarried wife', and
he hoped that this would continue to be the practice. Whether or
not one disapproved of their conduct—and he disapproved—
there *were* such people, and, Holt argued, 'they could not be
allowed to be thrown into the streets'.[137] The circumstances of war,
therefore, made many philanthropists realize ever more clearly
that the concepts of 'deserving' and 'undeserving'—always difficult to apply—were very often unhelpful; in the context of war—
both wars—all became, in some measure, deserving because they
were involved in patriotic duty.

Again, in the circumstances of unemployment, many voluntarists increasingly recognized that whereas, as the Annual Report
of the Pilgrim Trust put it in 1936, the effects of unemployment
were 'social and personal', their cause was 'mainly political and
economic'.[138] This was simply a reaffirmation of a view which
had been increasingly held in voluntarist circles for many years—
even, as has been seen, in some areas of the Charity Organisation
Society. In 1927 William Glen, secretary of the Glasgow Charity
Organisation Society, said that the 'virile individualism of [the]
Victorian Age' was a thing of the past. 'We no longer hold that
it is solely the individual citizen's responsibility as to how he is
housed, kept in health and provided for during periods of unemployment, and in his old age.'[139] Further, the appointment of

[136] *Conference on War Relief*, 10.
[137] Ibid. 30–1.   [138] *Sixth Annual Report*, 5.
[139] *Charity Organisation Quarterly*, NS, 1 (Apr. 1927), 91.

Benjamin Astbury as assistant secretary of the Society in 1930 (he later, in 1936, became organizing secretary and finally, in 1938, secretary) brought a new approach to its affairs. He was much less attached than his predecessors to the virtues of 'virile individualism', and injected new thinking into the Society:[140] thinking which had not been absent in the past, but which had not been prevalent in its upper reaches.

These adjustments in attitude—like those towards greater internal integration—were of considerable long-term importance. As service to the community was stressed—given according to need rather than desert, and recognizing that self-maintenance was not always appropriate or possible—philanthropy was able to shed some of its aura of patronizing and moralistic do-gooding. Nevertheless, like the organizational changes, the adjustments were not complete. More traditional views did not disappear. During World War I, considerable efforts were made by the Soldiers' and Sailors' Families Association to trace servicemen and ask them to make a proper apportionment to their dependants; the Association itself helped to write such letters. If there was suspicion that any money granted by the Association to help in an emergency would be spent on drink, assistance would be given in kind, or rent paid to the landlord.[141] After the first few weeks of the war, it tended to give part-gifts and part-loans—even though loans might prove difficult to recover.[142] Moreover, in the circumstances of want, there was a reluctance to give assistance which might dull the impetus to self-help. Astbury's predecessor as secretary of the Charity Organisation Society, the Revd J. C. Pringle, remained deeply suspicious of any form of aid which might erode self-reliance. He saw himself as the disciple of C. S. Loch, and proclaimed in 1927 that the Society had not changed 'one jot or tittle' since Loch's time.[143] In fact, Pringle lacked Loch's sense of realism and his administrative abilities. *The Nation's Appeal to the Housewife and her Response*, written by Pringle and published in 1933, purported to give the housewife's point of view, which was to the effect that all was much better in the past, when, apart from the poor law—a last resort—every aspect of social need was met by self-help or charity. 'Everything

[140] Rooff, *Hundred Years*, 170.   [141] *Conference on War Relief*, 30–1.
[142] Ibid. 12–13.   [143] Rooff, *Hundred Years*, 125.

else', the housewife said, 'we either paid for by ourselves or got when we needed it, from some charitable institution.'[144]

Even among those who took a more progressive stance, moreover, there was still a marked preference for self-help. Lord Macmillan of the Pilgrim Trust wrote that 'much can be done to bring about a happier way of living for our people'. But, he continued:

Heaven still helps those who help themselves. There will always be calamities in human affairs beyond the control of man. To meet these, charity, whether voluntary through good will, or compulsory through taxation, will always find only too ample occasion. On the other hand, every man ought still to be the master of his fate, the captain of his soul.

Macmillan wanted society to be more concerned with the means by which people, by self-help—'that outmoded Victorian virtue', as he put it—'should be enabled to work out their own salvation, even if in fear and trembling . . . Security [was] a thing to be earned rather than bestowed. It should be the reward of adventure and effort.' And he felt that the Pilgrim Trust should direct itself to giving to the victims of hardship 'the opportunity of attaining by their own efforts, those qualities of character, which are a nation's most precious heritage'.[145] Nuffield likewise regarded his assistance to areas particularly affected by unemployment as boosting confidence in private enterprise, which, he once said, was 'the keystone of National Prosperity'.[146]

Thus, even amidst the opportunities which war and want gave to philanthropists, there remained considerable misgivings in their ranks about the granting of indiscriminate charity which might pauperize. Indeed, those very opportunities carried the danger that they would be met so fully that the result would be to destroy those virtues of self-help and self-maintenance which, in their view, remained pre-eminent.

The continuing existence of such attitudes ensured that there were also continuing criticisms to the effect that voluntarism *should* not cope with social need: that it was inappropriate and

[144] Quoted in Macadam, *New Philanthropy*, 18–19.
[145] *Man of Law's Tale*, 292–3.
[146] Nuffield MS 11/6, Nuffield College, Oxford: commemorative programme of the opening of the Weston Biscuit Factory at Llantaram, Monmouthshire, 1 Nov. 1938.

insensitive, and, in its charitable aspect, rested on the whim of the rich, rather than the entitlements of the poor. The advocacy of thrift by the propertied classes aroused resentment among persons who could scarcely be expected to practise it. The commercial sector was unpopular with the Labour Party. Throughout the interwar years, indeed, the Approved Societies attracted criticism for their orientation towards profit. The Parmoor Committee of 1920 and the Cohen Committee of 1932 commented that business was being too aggressively pushed; high-selling methods used by collectors meant that people who did not really want life assurance—or could not afford it—were being enrolled. The Minority Report of the Royal Commission on National Insurance in 1925 condemned the association—seen to be inherent in the partnership between the state and the Approved Societies—of medical care and private profit. The signatories of that Report argued that the partnership should be dissolved and a system of comprehensive coverage set up.[147] Equally, there was dislike of the practice whereby some voluntary hospitals charged patients to meet their financial difficulties. In 1922 a joint statement from the Trade Union Congress and the Labour Party severely criticized the system of payments by patients. It claimed that 'the purse becomes the criterion of admission, instead of medical and surgical necessity, which is a bad principle'. It also disliked the contributory schemes which were created to meet costs. They were, it said, 'sure to result in the exclusion from hospitals of many of the poorer citizens who cannot afford the luxury of insurance and for whom the hospitals were originally founded'.[148]

Further, while there was on the Labour benches an appreciation of the efforts of charitable societies to mitigate the effects of unemployment, their efforts remained suspect. George Lansbury told the Commons in 1932 that he had received letters from a very large number of people 'who, through various organisations, are trying to palliate this social misery'; and he continued that 'no-one on these benches will pour scorn or ridicule on anything that is done to relieve human suffering . . . we are willing to help every sort and kind of effort to alleviate social misery'.

---

[147] Bentley B. Gilbert, *British Social Policy, 1914–1939* (London: Batsford, 1970), 281.   [148] Abel-Smith, *Hospitals*, 317.

Yet he also said that Labour could not 'accept charity as a substitute for social justice'.[149] Arthur Greenwood argued that everything should not be left to 'the kind hearts of the charitably disposed people'; he called on the nation 'to give until it hurts'—and be forced to give through taxation.[150] In 1937 Simey commented, in more extreme language, that philanthropy was an 'affront to the working classes':

Voluntary associations rely to far too great an extent on voluntary workers who are members of the upper classes and thus find it hard, if not impossible, to deal with the 'lower orders' on the terms of equality which true personal service demands. Voluntary social service has been in the past largely of a patronising coal-and-blanket and Sunday-school-treat type and this has left behind it a bitter feeling of resentment in the minds of many working class people . . .[151]

Charitable activity, for all its efforts, thus retained for Labour politicians and sympathizers elements of upper-class condescension; and the efforts of volunteers to break the General Strike of 1926 hardened the feeling that voluntary activity among the propertied could as easily turn against the working classes as act on their behalf. Justin Davis-Smith has shown how Volunteer-Service Committees were established during the 1920s to rationalize the recruitment and use of volunteers during an industrial emergency. These were composed of representatives of government departments and non-statutory bodies which felt it beneficial to use volunteers during a strike, such as shipping or railway companies. These activities were kept secret until an emergency was proclaimed under the Emergency Powers Act of 1920. During the General Strike, several thousands of volunteers were recruited through the Volunteer-Service Committees. This was to leave bitter memories—and to ensure that voluntary activity among the rich retained its critics on the mutual-aid side of voluntarism, such as trade unionism, and in the ranks of the Labour Party.[152] Thus Richard Crossman, writing in 1973, recalled his activities in the Labour interest in the 1930s:

---

[149] Hansard, *Parliamentary Debates* (House of Commons), 5th ser., vol. 269, 4 Nov. 1932, cols. 2129–30.

[150] Ibid. vol. 270, 7 Nov. 1932, col. 58.   [151] *Principles*, 139.

[152] Justin Davis-Smith, *An Uneasy Alliance: Volunteers and Trade Unions in Britain since 1945* (Berkhamsted: The Volunteer Centre, n.d.), 5–6.

we all disliked the do-good volunteer and wanted to see him replaced by professionals and trained administrators in the socialist welfare state of which we all dreamed. Philanthropy to us was an odious expression of social oligarchy and churchy bourgeois attitudes. We detested voluntary hospitals maintained by flag days. We despised Boy Scouts and Girl Guides. The only volunteers we approved of were volunteers for the struggle against the old oligarchy and their task was to furnish the working class with the knowledge and techniques and intellectual training they needed in order to assume power.[153]

Despite all its adjustments, therefore, voluntarism—especially the charitable side of the voluntary sector and the commercial sector—was still seen by many critics as the preserve of the rich. Even Boy Scouts were felt—with some justice—to make a particular appeal to middle-class boys, whose parents could afford to pay for the uniform and who could comply with Baden-Powell's wish that every Boy Scout should open a bank account, with at least 1s. placed in it, and thus learn how to practise thrift.

IV

The period of war and want may, therefore, be approached from the point of view of the continuing strength of voluntarism on the one hand—and of continuing criticisms of its limitations on the other. It is against this background that the role of the statutory sector in the period may be briefly considered—and its relations with the sectors of voluntarism studied. It is possible to seize on the second aspect—the limitations of voluntarism—and to see the further growth of the collectivist state as an important theme of the period. Yet the continuing strength of voluntarism must also be taken into account—and the way in which voluntarist values still tended to permeate collectivist action noted. And it is, indeed, true, as various historians have pointed out, that social policy, particularly in the years from 1914 or 1918 until 1939 or later, tended to look in both directions: forward to Welfare State collectivism and backward to orthodox economic individualism, of which voluntarism in its most classic form

---

[153] 'The Role of the Volunteer in the Modern Social Service', in A. H. Halsey (ed.), *Traditions of Social Policy: Essays in Honour of Violet Butler* (Oxford: Basil Blackwell, 1976), 264–5.

was part. There was what Anne Digby has called 'Inter-War Indeterminism'.[154]

The aspect of social policy marked by an increasing degree of state intervention during the period may be linked to the points made in Section II above about the perceived limitations of voluntarism. As in the later nineteenth and early twentieth centuries, the very forces which were felt to weaken voluntarism tended to strengthen the case for a more positive and centralized state, able to command sufficient resources to meet social need in a comprehensive and uniform way, and thus satisfy the full entitlements of its citizens. These forces, moreover, also weakened a traditional statutory complement to voluntarism: the localized poor law. As has been seen, the poor law survived the protracted investigations and reports of the Royal Commission of 1905 to 1909, but it ran into increasing difficulties in the 1920s. The cost of indoor relief in what were, from 1913, called 'poor law institutions' rather than 'workhouses' continued to be the heaviest burden on the rates. The circumstances of unemployment and industrial stoppages of 1918–21 and of 1926, however, placed a considerable burden on the rates for the payment of outdoor relief; by 1922 that figure had risen to £1.24 million, and by 1926 to £1.5 million. Where unemployment was high, the cost of relief was also high and the local rating system came under great strain. The central authority, which became the newly created Ministry of Health after 1919, tried to insist on the continuance of the principle of less eligibility, although, like its predecessors, even it showed flexibility on occasion. Thus when the board of guardians of Lichfield declared its intention to withdraw all relief, indoor and outdoor, from striking miners' families—on the grounds that there was work for the miners to do, and it was the duty of the guardians to see that they did it—the Ministry told the guardians that it was *their* duty to relieve destitution, however caused. Even where a stringent administration of relief was carried out—as by the Conservative guardians in Sheffield[155]—heavy debts were incurred, indicating that the burden was beyond the ability of the poor law authorities to undertake.

---

[154] *British Welfare Policy: Workhouse to Workfare* (London: Faber & Faber, 1989), 49.

[155] M. A. Crowther, *Social Policy in Britain 1914–1939* (Basingstoke: Macmillan Education, 1988), 49.

There were, however, local reactions of a different kind which illustrated the attitude that a tightly drawn poor law not only *could* not cope with the situation which confronted it, but *should* not do so. Some guardians were under local pressure from strike committees and political groupings to assert the right to relief in need; and some were sympathetic to them, especially those controlled by Labour guardians, who were increasingly active and prominent in the 1920s. The most famous episode took place in Poplar, in East London, which suffered badly from low pay and casual employment.[156] Some Labour councillors and guardians objected to the fact that high rates were necessary there, while wealthier areas, with low unemployment, had low rates. They demanded subsidies from the wealthier parishes—and were imprisoned for their efforts. There were other episodes where boards of guardians, which had gone bankrupt by generous expenditure of poor relief, were suspended from their duties; this took place at West Ham, Chester-le-Street, and Bedwellty.

These matters helped to highlight the problems encountered by the poor law—and finally, in 1929, the Local Government Act dismantled the poor law unions and guardians and vested their powers in the hands of local authorities, which dealt with various issues through specialist committees, with destitution through a Public Assistance Committee. Later, under the terms of the Unemployment Act of 1934, an Unemployment Assistance Board was set up which took over responsibility for the local Public Assistance Committees, with its funds coming directly from the Treasury, although it was not, in fact, until 1937 that the Act worked smoothly. In 1940 the Unemployment Assistance Board had its name changed to the Assistance Board and took over additional responsibility for those in distress because of war. In 1948 the Board was renamed the National Assistance Board by the National Assistance Act of that year.

Poor relief—like voluntary agencies—did, indeed, give aid and assistance to unemployed families; and help was also forthcoming from municipal authorities. In some towns, free meals were given through schools. Yet again, this tended to be localized and patchy—and could not cope with prolonged and persistent periods of unemployment. This is a further illustration of the ways in which the limitations of the localist solutions of the nineteenth

---

[156] Ibid. 48–9.

and early twentieth centuries—which involved both statutory and voluntary agencies—were exposed by the pressures of circumstances and convictions.

The pressures were, then, towards the assumption by central government of greater social reponsibilities. As in the late nineteenth and early twentieth centuries, one of these pressures may be said to have been political, for, of course, the period after 1918 witnessed an increasing degree of political democracy—although scarcely on a scale which could carry very much weight in this respect. Another may be said to have been a need to ward off the possibility of popular disturbance and unrest in the context of social distress; for this motivation, impelled by a desire for social control on the part of the governing classes, could drive statutory welfare forward, as it could philanthropic initiatives.

Pressures could also be found in the circumstances of war and want. World War I raised issues of health, housing, and education; improvement in all these areas could be urged—as they had been in the past—as matters essential to national efficiency and survival. The unemployment of the interwar years focused attention on issues of poverty as the insurance scheme established in 1911 came under intense pressure. Greater state involvement was required to extend the cover of unemployment insurance, making up the deficiencies in personal contributions. Moreover, poverty and unemployment, if the major issues determining interwar social policy, raised other social problems. Measures already on the statute-book affecting pensions, health, and housing edged their way forward; and the cause of educational reform was advanced with the publication of such documents as the Hadow Report in 1926 and the Spens Report of 1938. By 1939 the state had advanced to a more prominent role in the mixed economy of welfare than it had occupied in 1914—as, indeed, was widely recognized at the time. Active participants in the Labour movement conceded that, despite, or even perhaps because of, the social problems of the period, the 1920s and 1930s were a time of social advance; and historians have likewise commented on the growth of the state in these years. In the view of Gilbert, by 1939 the state had 'committed itself to the maintenance of all its citizens as a matter of right . . .'[157] Here, then, was a growth in the citizenship of entitlement. Crowther suggests

---

[157] *British Social Policy*, 308.

that 'in their tendency to centralise policy, interwar governments moved closer to the Welfare State';[158] and Mowat considers that by 1939 the Welfare State was present 'in scaffolding'.[159]

The process—as historians are also agreed—was largely unco-ordinated and unplanned. Gilbert writes that social policy 'evolved, like the British empire, in a fit of absence of mind'; or, changing the metaphor a few lines later, he writes of the building of an edifice 'shambling and rickety, without an architect'.[160] There had been a period towards the end of World War I when planning was much in vogue. The ideas behind the Ministry of Reconstruction, set up in 1917, implied a commitment to planning; and Seebohm Rowntree wrote in 1918 that he did not believe that, in future, 'we shall allow millions of our fellow-country-men, through no fault of their own, to pass through life ill-housed, ill-clothed, ill-fed, ill-educated'.[161] The belief proved premature, as planning for a reconstructed society was virtually abandoned in the years ahead. But the cause did not die: in the 1930s it attracted considerable support from a wide range of opinion, which expressed itself in groups such as Political and Economic Planning, founded in 1931, and the Next Five Years Group of 1934.[162]

How immediately influential such groups were may be open to question; but, as Paul Addison writes, the idea of planning had 'entered the mainstream of middle opinion'—and was very prominent in the thinking of those to the left of 'middle opin-ion'.[163] It is true that in Labour circles, there was still a residual suspicion of the centralized state. Indeed, the poor law reforms of 1934–7 were—seemingly paradoxically—denounced by Lansbury, who said that local needs were better understood by local people. José Harris has written that even in the mid-1920s there was a 'lurking fear that the growth of the "social service state" was merely an outwork of advanced capitalism'.[164] Yet it

---

[158] *Social Policy*, 73.

[159] *Britain between the Wars*, 495.   [160] *British Social Policy*, 308.

[161] *The Human Needs of Labour* (London: Nelson, 1918), 10.

[162] John Pinder (ed.), *Fifty Years of Political and Economic Planning: Looking Forward 1931–1981* (London: Heinemann, 1981), 6.

[163] *The Road to 1945* (London: Jonathan Cape, 1977, Quartet Books, 1977), 23–52, deals with this issue. See also Arthur Marwick, 'Middle Opinion in the Thirties: Planning, Progress and "Political Agreement" ' (*English Historical Review*, lxxix (Apr. 1964), 285–98).

[164] 'Political Ideas and the Debate on State Welfare, 1940–45', in Harold L. Smith (ed.), *War and Social Change* (Manchester: Manchester University Press, 1986), 251.

will be recalled that Crossman, looking back to the 1930s, wrote of the 'socialist welfare state of which we all dreamed'. This remark may have been coloured by hindsight; but during the 1930s themselves there was—largely under the influence of figures such as G. D. H. Cole, Douglas Jay, Hugh Dalton, Herbert Morrison, Hugh Gaitskell, and Evan Durbin—a significant movement towards the production of Labour policy statements which aimed to transform the capitalist market system into a collectivist state by means of socialist planning within the context of parliamentary democracy. In 1935 Durbin wrote that

the efficiency of Planning depends in the last resort upon the breadth and consistency of the Socialist faith which animates us . . . The interests of the whole are sovereign over the interests of the part. In society we are born: in society we must live. To the centralised control of a democratic Community our livelihood and our security must be submitted. It is the business of society to secure the welfare of all . . .[165]

Labour's *Immediate Programme* of 1937 called for a positive and integrated programme, which involved an increase in old-age pensions, the extension of a health service, and social security. Thus by the late 1930s Labour had committed itself to a greatly increased programme of social welfare through the state, and to the belief that only the state *could* implement this fully, and only the state *should* do so. Again, this was the reverse side of the limitations of voluntaristic methods, which, for all their strength, could not 'secure the welfare of all' through centralized control—nor, in the view of many voluntarists, should it attempt to do so for fear of pauperizing 'all' in receipt of welfare. As has been seen, excessive planning was inimical to voluntarism.

World War II, however, took the impetus towards planning considerably further. In areas of health, housing, and education, the war once again helped to drive the state forward—in a climate of opinion which favoured planning. 'Middle opinion' was once again well to the fore, with *Picture Post* providing a vehicle for it in a popular context. In January 1941 a special issue was published, lavishly illustrated, entitled 'A Plan for Britain'. The year 1942 witnessed a plethora of publications which called for a fairer—and more planned—society. There was, for example, William Temple's *Christianity and the Social Order*, and the 'Nine

[165] Quoted in Elizabeth Durbin, *New Jerusalems: The Labour Party and the Economics of Democratic Socialism* (London: Routledge & Kegan Paul, 1985), 185.

Point Declaration' brought out by J. B. Priestley's '1941 Committee', the ninth point of which demanded preliminary plans for providing full and free education, with employment and a civilized standard for everyone.[166] Moreover, Labour's entry into the Churchill cabinet strengthened its position in attempting to ensure that greater planning was set in the context of greater social justice and equality. In 1942 Labour's *The Old World and the New Society* called for a commitment to full employment, and the organization of the social services at a level which secured adequate provision for health, education, nutrition, and care in old age for all citizens. The Liberals had, indeed, anticipated Labour with the setting up of sixteen committees in the autumn of 1940 on different aspects of postwar planning; and the Conservatives established their Reconstruction Committee in the summer of 1941, under the chairmanship of R. A. Butler, with numerous subcommittees.

The idea of planning through a centralized state was, therefore, much in vogue during World War II; this was the counterpoint to the decentralized and largely uncoordinated nature of voluntarism. The Beveridge Report of 1942 provided the apogee of this drive towards greater planning in the social services. Many of the ideas contained in it had long been present in various quarters; the Report tended simply to pull them together. Sir John Walley, Deputy Secretary in the Ministry of Pensions and National Insurance, pointed out that 'the basic ideas in the Beveridge Report could hardly have surprised anyone versed in current thinking about social security in the 1920s'.[167] The Report did, indeed, provide for a unification of the existing array of piecemeal schemes dealing with pensions, health, and unemployment, and the inclusion of everyone within them, in return for a weekly compulsory payment by all workers, to which the employer and state also contributed. Yet if the Report was a brilliant exercise in synthesis—or what Beveridge himself called 'a natural development from the past . . . a British revolution'[168]

[166] Correlli Barnett, *The Audit of War: The Illusion and Reality of Britain as a Great Nation* (London: Macmillan, 1986), 21 ff., deals with these matters.

[167] Quoted in Novak, *Poverty and the State,* 149.

[168] *Social Insurance and Allied Services: Report by Sir William Beveridge,* 2 vols. (Parliamentary Papers, 1942, Cmd. 6404), i, par. 31. On the other hand, it also stated that 'a revolutionary movement in the world's history is a time for revolutions, not for patching' (i. 7).

—its production at a time when planning for the future was so much in fashion meant that it was regarded in many circles as a kind of blueprint for that future; and its proposals for attacks on the 'five giants', as the Report ran, of 'Want, Disease, Ignorance, Squalor and Idleness' meant that it became, as Marwick has put it, 'the symbol of the aspirations of large sections of the British people for a better society'.[169] Not all politicians welcomed it unequivocally; they saw the winning of what Macmillan called 'this ruinous war'[170] as the first priority. It was disliked, too, by many voluntarists. The extent to which there was a willing consensus on postwar reconstruction can be exaggerated. Nevertheless, its immense popularity with the public meant that it set the political agenda for the future, as was evident in the 'White Paper chase' of 1943–4, all of which involved a chase in the direction of wider state activity in the areas of health, employment, and the social services.

Thus the third 'w' in the title of this chapter, 'welfare', was already firmly on the political agenda *before* 1945 as an answer to the second 'w', 'want'; and it may be argued that this was primarily due to the first 'w' in the trilogy, 'war', and in particular World War II. The fact that 'welfare' in the period after 1945 was introduced by means of the state owed much, it may be held, to the experience of that war. The Education Act of 1944 was, indeed, passed during the war by the Coalition; and much of Labour's social legislation of the later 1940s had been foreshadowed. The Family Allowances Act took up an issue which had, in fact, been advocated long before World War II—and which was incorporated into the Beveridge Report; and the Act of 1945 was passed prior to the 1945 election before being implemented by the new Labour government. The National Insurance Act of 1946, consolidating the existing schemes of insurance against sickness, unemployment, and old age, was seen by Labour as the culmination of virtually fifty years of development—and had most recently been advocated by Beveridge during the war. The National Health Service Act of 1946, implemented in 1948, may similarly be seen as drawing on much previously expressed opinion as to the way in which medical services should be

---

[169] Arthur Marwick, *Britain in the Century of Total War* (London: Bodley Head, 1968), 309. [170] Quoted in Addison, *Road to 1945*, 233.

organized: opinion which received a boost from the wartime arrangements. The National Assistance Act of 1948 bore clear signs of a long past in its underpinning of National Insurance by the provision of assistance for residual cases not sufficiently—or not at all—covered by National Insurance payments. Echoes of the poor law, now finally abolished, could be heard—if as a faint echo of the arrangements of 1834. World War II, then, can be seen on the one hand as finally revealing the shortcomings of voluntarism allied to the minimal state; and on the other as forcing the cause of a more maximal welfare state to the centre of the political stage on grounds of national necessity, by providing a platform for those who advocated the role of planning through the state, and by helping to engender a broad popular commitment to social justice, egalitarianism, and universality of benefit.[171]

Others are more sceptical about the effect of war on welfare, and whether the 'Warfare State' led to the Welfare State. Some historians argue that World War II could, in fact, deflect attention away from welfare issues—or even align opinion against them.[172] Kevin Jefferys suggests that the wartime coalition may have committed itself to considerable advances in social policy; but that its conservative bias meant that this did not 'imply a decisive break in official policy'. Rather, the coalition wished to extend the uncoordinated growth in the state social services which had been proceeding in the interwar period. Rather than travelling, with Addison, on the 'road to 1945', Jefferys feels it necessary to embark on the 'road from 1945'.[173] In his view, it took *new* circumstances and *new* convictions to create the Welfare State: the return of Labour in the general election of 1945, and the distinctive approach of Attlee's Labour administration to social welfare issues.

[171] See Titmuss, *Problems, passim,* and Richard M. Titmuss, 'War and Social Policy', in Brian Abel-Smith and Kay Titmuss (eds.), *The Philosophy of Welfare: Selected Writings of Richard M. Titmuss* (London: Allen & Unwin, 1987), 102–12. Marwick develops these views in e.g. *The Deluge: British Society and the First World War* (London: Bodley Head, 1965) and *Britain in the Century of Total War.* See also Smith (ed.), *War and Social Change.*

[172] See John Macnicol, 'The Effect of the Evacuation of School Children on Official Attitudes to State Intervention', in Smith (ed.), *War and Social Change,* 27–8.

[173] 'British Politics and Social Policy during the Second World War' (*Historical Journal,* 30 (1987), 144).

As is very often the case in the historiography of the state, the reasons for growth are controversial. But there can be little disagreement that the state *did* grow—not, indeed, in a straight, linear development, but towards greater involvement in social welfare matters, and towards a greater fulfilment of the citizenship of entitlement to social rights. Whereas in 1913 the percentage of total government expenditure on social services was 33 per cent, the figure was 37.6 per cent in 1938 and 46.1 per cent in 1950. The percentage of Gross National Product spent on social services in 1918 was 4.1 per cent; in 1938 it was 11.3 per cent and in 1950 18 per cent. These figures have, indeed, to be interpreted with care, but they do suggest that what Sir Richard Hopkins, a leading Treasury official, called in 1932 the 'onward march' of expenditure on social services was a feature of the entire period covered by this chapter.[174] When Beveridge wrote *Voluntary Action* in 1948, in the immediate aftermath of the passage of the Labour welfare legislation, he acknowledged that there had been 'an inevitable development of state action'; and that it was 'clear that the state must in future do more things than it has attempted in the past'.[175] The following year, various speakers in a debate in the Lords, prompted by Beveridge's book, also acknowledged the assumption by the state of a dominant role in social welfare. At its conclusion, Lord Pakenham, speaking for the Labour government, said that the country had moved 'from the era of Laissez Faire'; and various speakers commented that Britain had now entered what they called 'the era of the positive state'.[176]

Nevertheless, if this theme relates to the perceived limitations of voluntarism in the period, the continuing vitality of voluntarism, examined earlier in this chapter, must not be overlooked. Beveridge's book of 1948 was, in fact, largely based on this theme; he was anxious that the voluntary sector, in particular —in its mutual-aid and philanthropic aspects—should not be entirely overshadowed and neglected; and he argued strongly for the continuation of that tradition, even at a time—indeed, especially at a time—of increased state intervention. In the debate

---

[174] Quoted in Crowther, *Social Policy*, 14, and in G. C. Peden, *British Economic and Social Policy: Lloyd George to Margaret Thatcher* (Deddington: Philip Allan Publishers, 1985), 110. [175] p. 10.
[176] Hansard, *Parliamentary Debates* (House of Lords), 5th ser., vol. 163, 23 June 1949, col. 119.

of 1949 he said that 'however much the state has done or may
yet do, there was a perpetually moving frontier for philanthropic
action';[177] and this point was widely endorsed in the debate.
Pakenham went out of his way to state the Labour government's
attitude towards voluntary action, arguing that 'the voluntary
spirit is the very life-blood of democracy'. He continued:

We consider that the individual volunteer, the man who is prepared to
serve the community for nothing, is he whose personal sense of mission
inspires and elevates the whole democratic process of official governmental effort. We are convinced that voluntary associations have rendered, are rendering and must be encouraged to continue to render
great and indispensable service to the community . . .[178]

The fact that Beveridge, who is so often regarded as a quint-
essential bureaucrat, and as an architect of state welfare, should
have accorded such prominence to the voluntary sector in the
late 1940s is significant; the Beveridge Report must not, as has
tended to happen, obscure *Voluntary Action*. That his views should
have received support from Pakenham, speaking for the Labour
government—in whose ranks voluntary effort was regarded with,
to say the least, some suspicion—is also a salutary reminder of
the continuing strength of voluntarism: a strength which, as with
previous periods, exclusive concentration on the state fails to
recognize. That strength, moreover, was not only to be found in
voluntary activity and organizations. As in the period before
1914, it penetrated the statutory sector itself; and here the point
which has already been made about the 'indeterminism' of interwar social policy must be borne in mind.

The 1920s and, to a considerable degree, the 1930s were characterized by economic orthodoxy: a belief in restraint in public
expenditure, a balanced budget, and the preservation of the value
of the currency. This is sometimes referred to as 'Treasury orthodoxy'—although that term has come in for scrutiny from those
who argue that such orthodoxy was not confined to the Treasury, but was shared by the whole Civil Service and by the political establishment of all shades of opinion. It was, indeed,
epitomized by the ending of the 'Reconstruction' of the later
years of World War I with the wielding of the 'Geddes Axe' of
1922 to bring about severe spending cuts—and by Churchill's

[177] Ibid. col. 122.   [178] Ibid. col. 119.

return to the Gold Standard in 1925. Baldwin's 'Safety First' slogan of 1929 again stressed economic orthodoxy and caution. Even Labour was caught up in the orthodoxy. Whether or not the Labour Party could have broken free from it is open to question; but the fact remains that the pressure to adopt deflation drove Labour from office in 1929, and was carried over into the National Government—even if the Party broke up in the process of trying to reconcile its own social priorities with the demand to cut government spending. Thus any edging forward of social services was, as Peden has written, 'done in a way which would minimise interference with the natural working of the market'.[179]

These factors, then, limited the growth of the state. It is true that 'planning' was advocated in the 1920s and, more particularly, in the 1930s, and that Keynes wrote in 1935 that he was preparing a book which would 'largely revolutionise the way in which the world thinks about economic problems.' This was, of course, *The General Theory of Employment, Interest and Money*, published the following year. There was some contact between the followers of Keynes and the National Government's Committee on Economic Information; and this exposed Treasury officials to Keynes's ideas on the necessity for government intervention to stimulate investment, consumption, and demand. Further, as has been seen, the Labour Party was in the 1930s formulating ideas which prescribed a larger role for the state in pursuit of a broadly social democratic programme. Yet none of this should be exaggerated. The planners operated at the fringes of political life, and their activities and proposals were as much a comment on what was not done at governmental level as on what was done. Stephen Constantine has noted the annoyance of the planners at the National Government's 'poor response to the new enthusiasm for state economic planning'.[180] The influence of Keynes on government policy in the interwar years was minimal—certainly before he published his *General Theory*, and even after it.

It would, therefore, be wrong to exaggerate the extent to which the state was adopting a more interventionist role. The various extensions of unemployment insurance of the interwar years went beyond the contributory principle, so strongly regarded as

---

[179] Peden, *British Economic and Social Policy*, 82.
[180] Stephen Constantine, *Unemployment in Britain Between the Wars* (London: Longman, 1980), 75.

consistent with self-help; but the basic theory behind all such extensions was that they remained discretionary payments, and could be withdrawn; to the standard payment alone was there a clear entitlement, since it rested on contributions. A belief in the contributory principle likewise permeated the Beveridge Report of 1942. The Report itself admitted that it was 'first and foremost a plan of insurance—of giving in return for contributions benefits up to subsistence level, as of right, and without means test, so that individuals may build freely upon it.' And it expected individuals so to build:

Social security must be achieved by co-operation between the State and the individual. The State should offer security for service and contribution. The State in organising security should not stifle incentive, opportunity, responsibility; in establishing a national minimum, it should leave room and encouragement for voluntary action by each individual to provide more than that minimum for himself and his family.[181]

Beveridge retained his opposition to the 'Santa Claus' State; and he always preferred the term 'Social Service State' to 'Welfare State'. In many respects, indeed, Beveridge embodied one of the central tenets of the 'New Liberalism' of the first decade of the century: that the active state encouraged, rather than impeded, the active citizen, and that the citizenship of entitlement would be a spur to the citizenship of contribution by voluntary means.

Moreover, access to the extended and uncovenanted National Insurance payments of the 1920s and 1930s was surrounded by various tests, which debarred and disqualified certain categories of people. In many ways, these carried over into official policy the old voluntarist distinctions between the deserving and undeserving. Although it has been suggested earlier in this chapter that the concept of a 'residuum' was difficult to justify in times and areas of mass unemployment which affected highly deserving groups, John Macnicol has drawn attention to the continuing existence of the idea of an 'underclass': a social problem group who swelled the ranks not only of the unemployed, but also of the unemployable. Such an idea, he suggests, was sustained by a small group of eugenicists who applied theories of hereditary causation; and it was supported by those who wished 'to constrain

---

[181] *Social Insurance and Allied Services*, i, par. 9. See also par. 455.

the redistributive potential of state welfare.'[182] There was certainly a desire to root out the scrounger and the parasite; and Peter Golding and Sue Middleton have gone so far as to claim that 'the state remained more interested in the moral than in the social condition of the unemployed'.[183]

Old-style voluntarist ideology was, therefore, easily discernible in the social policy of the 1920s and 1930s. If the frontier of the state moved, it often took traditional voluntarist convictions with it. Various examples of a continuing belief in self-maintenance may be cited among those who might, at first sight, have been expected to disown it. When Margaret Bondfield, on 5 December 1929, grudgingly conceded the acceptance by the Labour government of the Hayday Formula as the sole test of disqualification from benefit, Sir William Jowitt, the attorney general, was considerably alarmed. The Formula denied benefit to a claimant only if he refused an offer of suitable work, and was strongly supported by the trade unions. 'Are we to legislate on the lines that these people should think that they need to do nothing themselves; that they should wait at home, smoke their pipes and wait until an offer comes to them?' Jowitt asked querulously.[184] Working-class reactions to the dole—surrounded as it was with various tests—were not entirely divorced from those of a Wolverhampton local newspaper, which described it as an example of the 'grandmotherly state', encouraging an increase in the 'number of parasites at the bottom end of the scale'.[185] When the Labour government abolished the 'genuinely seeking work' test in 1930, there was resentment about scroungers and malingerers. MacDonald commented that 'there is a very large and growing section of my letters protesting against the way in which unemployment benefit is being used coming from our own people'. He was, he wrote, 'glad to see it'; it was 'very heartening indeed' that those who had helped to build up the Labour movement, and had agitated for unemployment insurance, should write to him of neighbours or fellow workmen who were abusing it.[186] MacDonald also wrote that 'to establish people in incomes which represent no effort to get or to do work is the

---

[182] 'In Pursuit of the Underclass' (*Journal of Social Policy*, 16 (1987), 316).
[183] *Images of Welfare* (Oxford: Martin Robertson, 1982), 43–4.
[184] Quoted ibid. 43.   [185] Quoted in Stevenson, *British Society*, 315.
[186] Quoted in Golding and Middleton, *Images of Welfare*, 43–4.

very antithesis of socialism. The state as Lady Bountiful may be a fatal extension of Toryism but it is not the beginning of Socialism.'[187] Even *Men without Work*, sympathetic as it was to the plight of the unemployed, stressed the 'problem of pauperization'; it warned—in tones reminiscent of the Charity Organisation Society at its most traditional—of indiscriminate charity leading to pauperism. This, however, was something which, it admitted, was very difficult to avoid, since the 'scrounger' type occurred everywhere.[188]

This, then, is the other direction in which the social policy of much of the period pointed—a direction which allowed a great deal of room within collectivism for voluntarist ideology. It may, indeed, partly explain why, as José Harris has noted, even in the 1940s there was scarcely any 'clearly defined perception of welfare and . . . coherent theory of the state'.[189] Social policy at once distanced itself from voluntarist ideas—and absorbed many of them. The Welfare State, as formalized in the later 1940s, may, as Jefferys argues, have owed much to the distinctive contribution of the Labour government; but it was, nevertheless, heir to an ambiguous ideological legacy, which not even Labour entirely disentangled.

V

This raises the question of relations between voluntarism and the state in the period—which, in turn, bears on the themes of 'convergence' and 'divergence' explored in Chapter 2. If the emphasis is placed on the persistence of voluntarist ideas within state activity, convergence with certain aspects of voluntary activity is not hard to find. There was still opportunity for the adoption of complementary roles on the negatives: on the desire *not* to overspend and *not* to pauperize. During World War I, there was felt to be a need to supervise and regulate appeals to cut down on fraud. In 1916 a select committee was appointed to look into war charities. It discovered some evidence of abuse, and recognized the danger that persons holding prominent positions freely and 'almost recklessly' allowed their names to be used as patrons,

---

[187] Quoted in David Marquand, *Ramsay MacDonald* (London: Jonathan Cape, 1977), 525.
[188] p. 280.   [189] 'Political Ideas', 235.

or even agreed to serve on an executive committee, without first satisfying themselves of the bona fides of the promoters of the fund.[190] The War Charities Act of 1916—following the advice of the committee report—made it unlawful to make any appeal to the public for donations or subscriptions for any war charity not registered as such. To qualify for registration, there had to be a responsible committee, keeping minutes and account books; a separate account had to be kept in a bank and all books and accounts had to be open for inspection. The registration authority was to be the appropriate local authority and copies of the register were to be sent to the Charity Commissioners, who would keep a combined register. If registration were refused, an appeal might be made to the Charity Commission. Also in 1916, a further Act empowered police authorities to make regulations about the places where, and conditions under which, persons might be permitted to collect money or sell articles for charitable purposes.

Here, then, was an example of the state regulating charitable activity—and of state and charity cooperating to prevent charitable fraud in war. And this was not absent in want. In 1923 a committee reported on the coordination of the arrangements for the granting of assistance from public funds on account of sickness, destitution, and unemployment. It pointed out that public assistance services were the outcome of 'long years of growth' and were a collection of 'more or less independent units'. The rapid development of public assistance services had brought with it problems of overlapping and fraudulence on the part of those claiming assistance.[191] Thus, at the request of the Ministry of Health, the National Council of Social Service in Reading, Halifax, and Liverpool submitted a report based on a period of four weeks in June and July 1922. This incorporated the findings of a registration of assistance in Reading and Halifax, awarded by various public authorities. The investigation revealed the existence of a number of cases where the authorities, whose explicit duty it was to know the resources of applicants for assistance,

---

[190] *Report of the Committee on War Charities* (Parliamentary Papers, 1916, Cd. 8287), par. 2.
[191] *Report of the Committee on the Co-ordination of Administrative and Executive Arrangements for the Grant of Assistance from Public Funds on Account of Sickness, Destitution and Unemployment* (Parliamentary Papers, 1923, Cmd. 2011), pars. 6 and 7.

were not aware of the grants already made to the same individual or household. The report recommended that there should be local administrative coordination to bring about a greater degree of knowledge. A register of assistance would save public funds by cutting down on the necessity to make grants of assistance in excessive measure.[192]

Here again, there was cooperation on a negative level: the rooting out of fraud and the saving of public funds. Moreover, demands continued to be made for some further regulation of any potential abuse in the collection of money for charity. In 1927 a Home Office committee was appointed, and while it refused to make any recommendations for the overall supervision of charitable work, it did suggest that there should be some tightening up: for example in the minimum age for street collectors and in licensing door-to-door and public collections.[193] This concern to root out fraudulent and irregular charitable activity was to continue until the House to House Collections Act of 1939 achieved many of its objectives.

If, on the other hand, emphasis is put on the perceived limitations of voluntarism in the period and the ways in which the state expanded and developed during these years, the situation is less clear-cut. Here voluntarism and the 'positive' state could, in some instances, find it hard, and even impossible, to coexist; and this was a commentary on the long-standing points of tension which have been mentioned in earlier chapters. The agencies of mutual-aid within the voluntary sector and of insurance in the commercial sector viewed a centralizing state which sought to move towards uniformity with considerable suspicion and as a threat to their cherished traditions of freedom and autonomy. They had, indeed, entered an alliance with the state in 1911 as Approved Societies—but they wished this association to remain on terms which they dictated and over which they retained control. They were suspicious of plans put forward during World War I for a Ministry of Health; and throughout the interwar period, they remained very powerful spokesmen for their position in the face of any possible encroachments by the state.

[192] Ibid. par. 14.
[193] *Report of Home Office Department Committee on the Supervision of Charities* (Parliamentary Papers, 1927, Cmd. 2823), par. 132.

Equally, on the charitable side of the voluntary sector, similar suspicions of the state were to be found among the voluntary hospitals. The Cave Committee Report of 1921 was convinced of the need to preserve the principle of voluntarism and independence. It rejected any form of continuous state funding, but asked for a temporary grant of £1 million to set the hospitals on their feet. In the event, only half this amount was granted. The financial situation remained serious, and in 1925 there was once again talk to the effect that state assistance was essential—although it was recognized that 'any Government grant was to some extent dangerous to the voluntary principle and should be given sparingly and subject to stringent conditions'.[194] The voluntary hospitals were, therefore, placed in the dilemma familiar to many voluntary organizations: that of requiring state funding, but of not wishing to take it—or, more accurately, of being willing to take it, so long as this did not compromise their independence and lead to absorption by the state. On 17 December 1921 the *Charity Record, Hospital Times and Philanthropist*, in what was to be its last issue, expressed the 'fervent hope' that the voluntary hospitals would never be taken over by the state or municipalities.[195]

Here, then, was a mismatch between various agencies of voluntarism and the state. It was to come to a resolution in the 1940s—in favour of the state. Beveridge dealt with the Approved Societies at some length in his Report of 1942. He recognized the contribution which they had made in the past, but argued that

There is growing support for the principle . . . that in compulsory insurance all men should stand together on equal terms, that no individual should be entitled to claim better terms because he is healthier or in more regular employment. With both of these principles, the approved society system, in its present form, is in irreconcilable conflict.

That system, leading as it did to 'inequalities of benefit and . . . substantial inadequacy of benefit, either in cash or of treatment, for those who were not fortunate in their society',[196] could not be reconciled with a planned, integrated, and universal

[194] Quoted in Trevelyan, *Voluntary Service*, 23.
[195] *Charity Record, Hospital Times and Philanthropist*, 17 December 1921.
[196] *Social Insurance and Allied Services*, i, pars. 66, 71.

approach; there had to be what Beveridge called 'a single Approved Society for the nation'[197]—and that lay in the state.

In recommending the abolition of the Approved Society system, Beveridge did not reject the need for voluntary insurance: indeed, as the Report put it, 'voluntary insurance to supplement compulsory insurance is an integral feature of the Plan for Social Security';[198] this was part of the 'co-operation between the state and the individual' of which the Report also spoke. In fact Beveridge suggested that those mutual-aid friendly societies within the voluntary sector which paid substantial benefit from voluntary contributions should be used as responsible agents for administering state benefits to their members. The Report provided details whereby such friendly societies—and trade unions —should administer sickness benefit in place of the system of Approved Societies, thus continuing 'in substance under a slightly different form, the association of these organizations with State insurance.'[199] Beveridge also wanted to see the offices of Industrial Assurance—which was the leading agency of the commercial sector in this area—taken over and converted into a state organ of voluntary insurance, under an Industrial Assurance Board. He thus—characteristically—favoured retaining links between voluntarism and the state. But while the Labour government's National Insurance Act of 1946 abolished the Approved Societies' involvement in National Insurance, it did not accept Beveridge's other proposals to link aspects of the voluntary and commercial sectors in this field to the state. This was much, indeed, to his annoyance. He disapproved of the fact that the state constructed 'a complete and exclusive administrative machine of its own';[200] and it was partly for that reason that he undertook in 1948 to produce *Voluntary Action*, which was written with considerable assistance from the National Deposit Friendly Society[201] and which, to some extent, was an exercise in special pleading for the voluntary-sector friendly societies.

The reasons for the dissolution of the thirty-five-year partnership between the Approved Societies and the state in 1946 can be variously ascribed. It may be held to have been primarily the responsibility of the Societies themselves, and particularly the

---

[197] Ibid. par. 76.   [198] Ibid. par. 73.   [199] Ibid. par. 72.
[200] *Voluntary Action*, 80–1.   [201] Ibid. 10–11.

commercial-sector companies. In much historical writing, they have been treated harshly for what might be called a failure to 'move frontiers' in terms of ideology and implementation. Gilbert has seen them in this light. They were, he argues, competitive, independent, resistant to change; they used their powers and privileges to promote their private business interests and safeguard their profits. They became—through their powerful spokesmen—a vested interest, prepared to use the state for their own purposes, but not to cooperate in the interests of the community at large.[202] Noelle Whiteside, however, feels that this is too strong a judgement. She points out that many of the Societies were willing to expand their services; 'although major differences of opinion', she writes, 'existed over the desirability of pooling and the raising of cash benefits, very little opposition existed among the Approved Societies to raising the quality of medical care available, or even to extending the scope of the scheme'. She suggests that the influence of the Societies on health policy was not, in fact, 'overwhelmingly detrimental'; and that, although 'ostensibly under private management', they 'complied with official regulations and obediently implemented policies formulated by departmental civil servants at central level'. Whiteside, indeed, argues that the Societies were used by governments to save public money.[203] It may also be stated in their defence that certain groups of Approved Societies—the Association of Approved Societies and the Trade Union Approved Societies—*did* accept the abolition of the system as a necessary prerequisite to a national scheme of unified insurance: a point which Beveridge acknowledged.

Not all Societies, however, acquiesced in the termination of their partnership with the state; and many made representations to the Beveridge Committee in favour of retaining the system. Thus the Industrial Life Officers' Association claimed that:

The National Health Insurance Act, 1911, provided for the setting up of Approved Societies and for insured persons to select their own Societies and this provision has continued in force until this day. It has worked to the satisfaction and advantage of the insured person, and it would

---

[202] *British Social Policy*, 270–84.
[203] 'Private Agencies for Public Purposes: Some New Perspectives on Policy Making in Health Insurance Between the Wars' (*Journal of Social Policy*, 12 (1983), 165–93). See also a rejoinder by Frank Honigsbaum (ibid. 515–23).

not only be unjust but unwarranted by any evidence that has yet been produced for the scheme to be amended in such a way as to force all insured people to cease to be insured in the Society of their selection . . . and to compel them to become members of a State society and for the State to enforce a service of its own choosing.[204]

Here, then, was a plea for the choice which the Approved Societies had offered—now to be removed by the creation of a state-run system. But, of course, behind that plea lay the threatened vested interest of commercial-sector voluntarism.

Percy Rockliffe, secretary of the Joint Committee of Approved Societies and National Union of Friendly Societies, was outspoken in his condemnation of Beveridge:

The author of this report is an economist turned spendthrift; having exchanged frugality for thriftlessness, he has no further use for either friendly or approved societies. He would push compulsorily—not a section of the community—but the whole nation back into the days of a glorified Poor Law system, destroying in the process every vestige of self-reliance and self-help which during the past century or more has permeated and strengthened the British character. After 1944, if this scheme were to come to pass, truly might Ribbentrop allege that the Anglo-Saxon race was decadent . . . Under the Beveridge Plan, industry will become a veritable post-war Tom Tiddler's ground.[205]

The statement was, of course, a wildly inaccurate representation of Beveridge's position—but it clearly shows the hostility with which the commercial sector viewed the state over National Insurance. The Approved Societies finally fell victim to the argument that only the state *could*, in the interests of universality, and *should*, in the interests of equity, undertake such matters. Here the path was clearly one of divergence.

There was another noted casualty in the 1940s on the charitable side of the voluntary sector: the voluntary hospitals. As has been seen, they, too, prized their independence and traditions, both within their own ranks—and in relation to the state. They, too, had powerful lobbyists who put their case forward in the various negotiations which took place during World War II about a future hospital service. The White Paper of 1944 on 'A National Health Service' was looked upon as the equivalent of the

---

[204] *Social Insurance and Allied Services*, ii. p. 66.
[205] Quoted in Marwick, *Britain in the Century*, 311.

Beveridge Report: 'a veritable Magna Carta for positive health'.[206] In fact, it was kind to the voluntary hospitals, granting them full independence and autonomy under the proposed scheme; and critics felt that it was too conciliatory. But the spokesmen for the voluntary hospitals regarded the White Paper as threatening to their independence, and in May 1944 a campaign was launched to publicize the case for them: a campaign in which the British Hospitals Association and the King's Fund were active. But Bevan's National Health Service bill of 1946 went much further than the White Paper, for it nationalized both voluntary and local authority hospitals. It was not, indeed, surprising that the bill was fiercely opposed by many in the voluntary hospital lobby; the British Hospitals Association denounced it as confiscation. But Bevan was adamant that there would be no retreat on ownership, which was fundamental to the government's principles.

This aspect of voluntarism too, then, finally fell victim to the 'could not cope' and the 'should not cope' arguments. Bevan stated that the voluntary hospitals already depended to a high degree on state funding—and yet could not offer a national service. They were, of their very nature, varied, uneven, and patchy; there were, for example, too few in the industrial areas. 'A patchwork quilt of local paternalism', Bevan wrote, 'is the enemy of intelligent planning.' What he called 'warm gushes of self-indulgent emotion' were 'an unreliable source of driving power in the field of health organisation'.[207] And he distrusted the control which benefactors tried to exercise with their money.

Thus, as with the Approved Societies, too much was felt to depend on the extent to which the individual was, or was not, 'fortunate', to use Beveridge's word in relation to the Approved Societies. With them, it depended on membership of a particular Society; with the voluntary hospitals, on living in a particular area. In both cases, this might lead to good treatment and service; but it might also lead to poor treatment and service. The difference was largely one of chance; and chance sat uneasily with the control afforded by 'intelligent planning'. Again, the association of the voluntary hospitals with commercial

[206] Charles Webster, *The Health Services since the War, i: Problems of Health Care: The National Health Service before 1957* (London: HMSO, 1988), 57.

[207] See further John Campbell, *Nye Bevan and the Mirage of British Socialism* (London: Weidenfeld & Nicolson, 1987), 169.

considerations—whereby certain hospitals charged their patients—fell foul of the 'should not cope' argument; and Labour
also disliked the connections with charity. In the 1940s Harold
Laski wrote that it was 'better to tackle social problems without
the intervention of gracious ladies or benevolent busybodies or
stockbrokers to whom a hospital is a hobby'. It will be recalled
that Crossman 'detested voluntary hospitals maintained by flag
days'; and Bevan himself told the Commons in 1946 that he believed it 'repugnant to a civilized community for hospitals to
have to rely upon private charity . . . I have always felt a shudder
of repulsion when I see nurses and sisters who ought to be at
their work . . . going about the streets collecting money for the
hospitals.'[208] Thus the voluntary hospitals were seen by Bevan to
be 'a complete anachronism' which must not be allowed to act
as 'historical impediments' to a planned and equitable hospital
system.[209] This was also true of the local-authority hospitals, which
were also incorporated within Bevan's plan to bring about a single
'nationalized' system of hospital provision.

It is true that Bevan's proposals were laced with a considerable number of concessions to the voluntary hospitals, such
as the continuation of private work, the retention of private
pay-beds in hospitals, the granting of special status for teaching
hospitals, and the protection of hospital endowment funds. The
British Hospitals Association remained vocal in its opposition to
the disappearance of the voluntary hospitals; but the King's Fund
and the Nuffield Provincial Hospitals Association were much
less intransigent. As Webster has put it, 'the collective mind was
prepared for such a change because leading planners among the
consultants . . . had been pointing towards this direction for some
time'.[210] The concessions which Bevan made—as elsewhere in
the creation of the National Health Service—did, indeed, point
to the strength of the medical profession as an interested party

---

[208] See Michael Foot, *Aneurin Bevan*, 2 vols. (London: Granada Publishing, 1975),
ii. 132.

[209] See Campbell, *Nye Bevan*, 169.

[210] *Problem of Health Care*, 90. See also S. D. Slater and D. A. Dow (eds.), *The
Victoria Infirmary of Glasgow, 1890–1990: A Centenary History* (Glasgow: The Victoria Infirmary Centenary Committee, 1990), 67, which shows that the income of
the Victoria began to decline after 1945: 'It is hard to avoid the conclusion that
the majority of voluntary hospitals would have found it impossible to survive
without state aid.'

—just as Lloyd George's concessions indicated its strength in 1911. Nevertheless, if the Approved Societies were divorced from the state in 1946, the voluntary hospitals, with some exceptions, were essentially absorbed by the state in 1948. This might be described as a process of convergence—but it was convergence on the state's terms, and meant the disappearance of the voluntary hospitals as separate institutions. Here again, localized voluntary agencies and centralized statutory agencies could not coexist; or, to put it another way, the citizenship of contribution through voluntary organizations was seen to be incompatible with the citizenship of entitlement through the state.

Yet in other areas, the situation was not as clear-cut. The strength and limitations of *both* voluntarism *and* the state engendered a continuation of the process of cooperation and convergence—but not absorption—which was noted in Chapter 2. War and want were, once again, important in this respect. As has been seen, they posed both opportunities and problems for voluntarism; and this was also true of the state. War on a scale even of World War I, let alone World War II, was a new phenomenon, and while it helped to mobilize the resources of the state, it also stretched them to an unprecedented and uncomfortable degree. Moreover, the social problems engendered by unemployment during the interwar years were daunting. Indeed, it might be said that if the issues of the period were beyond the resources of voluntarism to cope with and solve, they were also beyond those of the state. Further, the provision of welfare through the state in the late 1940s also raised the question of the adequacy of the resources at its disposal for the vast tasks which were undertaken. In all these circumstances, there was the making of further convergence, particularly between the voluntary-sector charitable agencies and the statutory agencies. This afforded the charities increased sources of funding; it afforded the state use of agencies long active, and still resilient, in many fields of welfare.

Numerous instances of such cooperation and convergence may be noted—this time on positive, rather than negative grounds. During World War I, the government set up a committee on the Prevention and Relief of Distress. The Local Government Board placed its personnel and offices at the disposal of this committee and a special department was formed at the Board under its direction. The committee channelled relief to the dependants of servicemen through the Soldiers' and Sailors' Families Association, and paid warm tribute to that Association; without its 'unselfish and public spirited efforts', it reported in 1916, 'great suffering must have occurred'.[211] The committee also sent out circulars on the prevention and relief of distress to every mayor and chairman of a local authority in England and Wales, calling for the formation of committees in every authority area with a population of over 20,000. These were to include representatives of the local authority, trade unions—and philanthropic and voluntary organizations.

The National Council of Social Service, set up in 1919, was—as has been seen—an attempt to draw voluntary-sector agencies together; but it was also designed to continue and extend war-time cooperation between voluntary and statutory bodies. One of its stated aims was, indeed, 'to co-operate with Government Departments and Local Authorities making use of voluntary effort'.[212] It acted as a channel through which statutory funding was dispersed to alleviate the effects of unemployment. The Commissioner for Special Areas wrote in his first report of 1935 that he was especially anxious that his appointment should not 'in any way hinder the valuable work or dry up the sources of private assistance'[213]—a clear indication that the state, on its side, was willing to co-operate with charitable effort. Government grants from the Special Areas Fund, fed through the National Council, were used to stimulate and supplement voluntary effort and resources. The first report of the Commissioner showed that £70,000 had been given to school camps for boys and girls; £12,500 for occupational centres for women; £3,125 in capital grants for occupational centres for men; £30,000 for social settlements for adolescents; £12,500 for lecture courses, church societies, and drama groups; £17,000 for the provision of additional district nurses.[214] A further example of the coordination of voluntary and statutory services was evident in the efforts of the National Council to act as a Citizens' Advice Centre, providing guidance

---

[211] *Report on the Administration of the National Relief Fund* (Parliamentary Papers, 1917, Cd. 8449), par. 5.　　　　　　　　[212] Brasnett, *Voluntary Social Action*, 23.

[213] *First Report of the Commissioner for the Special Areas (England and Wales)* (Parliamentary Papers, 1935, Cmd. 4957), par. 131.

[214] Ibid. par. 133.

as to the state benefits which were available—although, interestingly, this idea was first mooted in the course of World War I, when F. G. D'Aeth had foreseen the need for such a service in 1915.[215] And the project was also to be implemented in the course of World War II. Here the citizenship of contribution, expressed through a voluntary agency, gave guidance to the services available through the state in implementing the citizenship of entitlement.

As World War II approached, the national emergency engendered a further substantial degree of cooperation between charitable agencies and the state. The government made it clear that it attached great importance to the contribution which voluntary movements could make at such a time. In 1938 the Women's Voluntary Service was brought into being at the request of the government as part of the preparations carried out in anticipation of war, when the problem was to secure the enrolment of sufficient volunteers in the precautions taken against air raids. Technically, the Women's Voluntary Service—despite its name— was not a voluntary organization: it owed its establishment to government initiative. Yet it well illustrates the close relationship between voluntary and statutory services. It had, at one time, more than a million enrolled members, and in 1948 it still had 900,000. The vast bulk of these gave their services unpaid; in fact, only some two hundred were paid from government or local authority finance. Once established, the purpose of the Service was to assist the statutory authorities in discharging their duties. It was an auxiliary arm to more than twenty government departments and cooperated with local authorities in more than one hundred different occupations. It also worked alongside more genuine voluntary organizations in the enormous variety of tasks which the emergency of wartime threw up: evacuation work, clothing distribution, services following air raids, and many others.[216]

The nursery services already noted also involved close collaboration between bodies of the voluntary and statutory sectors. The majority of residential nurseries for young children whose mothers were ill, or otherwise unable to provide proper care,

---

[215] Brasnett, *Voluntary Social Action*, 15.

[216] Beveridge, *Voluntary Action*, 137–8; Titmuss, *Problems, passim*.

were in the hands of organizations such as the Waifs and Strays Society, which established and ran them for the Ministry of Health; and there were, too, many other organizations which performed a similar agency function, such as the Save the Children Fund, the Invalid Children's Aid Association, and the Friends' Welfare Relief Service.[217] Accommodation for those made homeless by bombing also involved a close degree of cooperation between statutory and voluntary agencies. In September 1940 the government appointed H. U. Willink, a member of the Charity Organisation Society Council, to coordinate, under the Ministry of Health, the services for the homeless of London, and he succeeded in working out a successful partnership between the various bodies, both charitable and governmental.[218] In March 1944 the Ministry of Health commented that experience in bombed areas had shown

the high value of securing in advance the right personnel in the localities, both for organisation and operations and of continuous cooperation both before and after raids between the Ministry's regional office, the local authorities and the voluntary organisations, and between local authorities and voluntary organisations of the target areas and those around them.[219]

Finally, the Citizens' Advice Bureaux may again be mentioned. Some of these were, indeed, set up by the government in the course of the war, but there were also bureaux run by the Charity Organisation Society, the National Council of Social Service, and the London Council for Social Service—to which the government gave grants.

There were, then, numerous examples of a growing convergence between voluntary-sector charitable agencies and a more positive state. That convergence had, of course, been evident in certain areas for many years. By 1944 education had, for over a century, involved a partnership between schools run by voluntary organizations—in particular the churches—and the state. It is true that this had also long been an area where voluntarist sentiments, often fuelled by denominational loyalties, had made the partnership rather uneasy. The Education Act of 1944 was preceded by protracted negotiations between government and the churches to resolve points of conflict—and these were largely

---

,[217] Titmuss, *Problems*, 377.   [218] Ibid. 286–9.   [219] Quoted ibid. 302.

successful. The Act, for example, provided additional finance to the managers of voluntary schools to enable them to comply with minimum Ministry standards. G. A. N. Lowndes has written that these concessions gave the denominations 'not only what they had been promised on the first publication of the Bill but a good deal in addition.'[220] Even given these concessions, the churches certainly had to reappraise their educational provision in the years after 1944; but the Act did represent continuing cooperation between voluntary-sector activity and the state rather than absorption of such activity by the state. Further, the independent schools remained in existence, subject to a system of registration and inspection; and an increasing reliance on fees made their connection with the commercial sector more marked. It is, perhaps, of interest to compare the fate of voluntary and independent schools under Labour after 1945 with that of voluntary hospitals.

The process of convergence was recognized even in the higher ranks of the Charity Organisation Society—always more resistant to change than many of its own rank and file and other such organizations. Lord Macmillan, addressing the Society in 1933, reminded it that

It is wrong to think that nothing ought to be done by the State—for there are many activities which must and can only effectively be undertaken by the State. But it is equally wrong to think that everything must be done by the State and nothing left to private enterprise. Up to what point is State assistance useful; at what point does it become harmful?[221]

Macmillan was later to write of 'an unprecedented state of national affairs . . . when the community must act as a whole to cope with it';[222] and there is no doubt that, under Astbury's leadership, the Society saw itself as part of that whole, working in what he called 'a co-operative partnership' with the state. In 1935 he wrote that

Social service of the future must transcend departments of every kind and one is drawn to declare that its sole object will be that each and

---

[220] *The Silent Social Revolution: An Account of the Expansion of Public Education in England and Wales, 1895–1965* (Oxford: Oxford University Press, 1937, 2nd edn. 1969, repr. 1970), 248.

[221] *Charity Organisation Quarterly*, NS, vii (July 1933), 102.

[222] Ibid. 104.

every citizen shall have life and have it more abundantly . . . Surely this is the answer to those who claim that the day of voluntary service is over. It is something more. It is a vision calling for new hearts, new courage, and a new devotion to an ideal dear to the soul of everyone who would be counted a worthy citizen of the future.[223]

Later, during World War II, a cooperative venture to assist refugees and bombed-out families prompted Astbury to reflect that social workers 'could double their usefulness by working for an official body with public funds behind it'—but that this would not impair 'the flexibility of the voluntary society'.[224]

A significant initiative on the part of the Society was its acceptance of the Beveridge Report, in the belief that in the postwar world, the community 'must accept responsibility for supplying the basic needs of its citizens and this must include the provision of adequate housing, adequate health services and adequate maintenance, when the citizen is unable, through no fault of his own, to provide these services for himself and his family'.[225] The phrase 'through no fault of his own' does, perhaps, reflect a lingering flicker of traditional Charity Organisation Society ideology; but it was no more than a flicker, as libertarian traditions were abandoned. Here, then, was a different reception to the Beveridge Report from that given by the spokesmen of commercial-sector insurance societies. In 1944 Beveridge himself addressed the seventy-fifth anniversary meeting of the Society. In his speech, he recognized the ways in which the Society had changed—and yet the ways in which it might still find a role. It was a speech which shed light on the Society—and also on Beveridge's own inclinations towards 'voluntary-statutory' cooperation:

Today, while you have not departed in any way from your fundamental principle that people should be helped adequately and constructively through careful study of each individual problem, your Society is very far from saying that there should not be any organised general provision to prevent distress . . . Yet, whatever the State does, since that must be the same for all citizens, there will always remain the scope for personal help, individual care of those who for whatever cause need

---

[223] Ibid. NS, ix (Jan. 1935), 33–4.
[224] Quoted in Rooff, *Hundred Years*, 185.
[225] Quoted in Beveridge, *Voluntary Action*, 148.

something more or different. There will always remain the need for such a Society as yours to make charity constructive and healing.[226]

The Annual Report of the Society noted that these words were 'particularly heartening', coming at a time when it was 'engaged in reviewing its whole machinery and functions in order to adapt itself to meet the demands of a new social order'.[227] This review was accompanied by a change of name two years later when, in 1946, the Society became the Family Welfare Association.

It will be recalled that Loch in 1914 had noted a growing willingness of the 'entrepreneurs of charity' to take shelter with the state 'like creatures in a storm'. The process which he discerned then continued in the years thereafter; and, as has been noted, Astbury positively welcomed a development which Loch had foreseen with dread. It was a development which, in her book of 1934, Elizabeth Macadam called the 'New Philanthropy', meaning 'a system of combined statutory and voluntary social service'.[228] It was not, in fact, wholly new, as Macadam herself realized; she traced its growth over the previous forty years—and evidence of it has been discerned in the years from 1880 to 1914, examined in Chapter 2. It is also true that—as has been seen—it did not prove possible to bring about a 'combined' system in all areas. Prochaska has pointed out that Macadam was over-ready to ignore the continuing separate activity of many charities, and 'did not appreciate the resilience of those societies which protected their freedom by shifting their functions into areas where partnership [with the state] was unnecessary'.[229]

But if *The New Philanthropy* did not sufficiently deal with the path of divergence, it did, with much justice, highlight the convergence of the frontiers of philanthropy and those of the state, as both sought to meet social need in a professional manner, and with an increasingly professional staff. As has already been mentioned, Braithwaite's *Voluntary Citizen*, published four years after Macadam's book, showed that a notable feature of charitable finance in the interwar years was the proportion received in payment by the state, or the municipality, for services rendered

---

[226] Quoted in Rooff, *Hundred Years*, 178.   [227] Quoted ibid.
[228] *The New Philanthropy*, 17–18, 44. See also Brian Harrison, 'Historical Perspectives', in *Voluntary Organisations and Democracy* (Sir George Haynes Lecture, 1987, with Nicholas Deakin. London: National Council for Voluntary Organisations, 1988), 7.   [229] *Voluntary Impulse*, 80.

under agency arrangements, rather than by means of voluntary donations.

An example of this is afforded by the provision of welfare for the blind.[230] Under the Blind Persons Act of 1920, a comprehensive statutory system to meet the needs of the blind was set up. The councils of counties and county boroughs were required to make arrangements, to the satisfaction of the Minister of Health, for advancing the welfare of blind persons normally resident in their areas, and to submit a scheme for the discharge of their powers under the Act to the Minister. Local authorities were to arrange for such powers and duties to be carried out by one or more voluntary organizations working within the area of the local authority; and in that event payment would be made by the statutory body. There was, indeed, a tendency for local authorities to take all services for the blind under their control in the years after 1920; but in the years immediately before World War II, this process was reversed in some areas. After 1945 there was a renewed move in the direction of local authority control; this was in accordance with what the National Institute for the Blind called 'the present impulse to planning the life of the community as a whole'. Nevertheless, the National Society also commented that voluntary societies devoted to the welfare of the blind persisted 'in great variety covering the greater part of the country in more or less complex inter-relationships with each other and with Local Government'.[231]

Grants from central funds to a variety of voluntary agencies in 1946/7—not, it is true, all concerned with social welfare—amounted to some £10 million; and this leaves out of account grants from local authorities. Moreover, agency agreements were to be a feature of the years after 1948 in various areas of welfare since the National Health Service Act of 1946 and the National Assistance Act of 1948 empowered the state to make use of voluntary bodies in the meeting of certain statutory obligations.

In a sense, of course, this convergence continued the long-standing tradition of cooperation between voluntary societies and local government; but it did so in the context of a positive social policy, centrally decided by a political party, many of whose members were traditionally hostile to voluntarism, particularly in its charitable and commercial guises. Yet in 1947 Clement Attlee

---

[230] Beveridge and Wells (eds.), *Evidence,* 164.   [231] Ibid. 165.

spoke of a 'tradition of voluntary effort that is not confined to any one class of the community'. He continued:

Alongside everything done by the local authority and by the state there are people who want to do a bit more . . . This country will never become a people of an exclusive and omnipotent State . . . I believe that we shall always have alongside the great range of public services, the voluntary services which humanise our national life and bring it down from the general to the particular. We must keep stretching out to new horizons.[232]

Attlee's remarks become the more understandable when it is recalled that he had once been a resident of Toynbee Hall, and that this speech was made on the occasion of his becoming its President. And yet this was also at the very time that the Welfare State was being created. Other Labour politicians voiced similar sentiments. Herbert Morrison, addressing the London Council of Social Service on the subject of voluntary-statutory relations in the light of the creation of the Welfare State, struck a similar theme:

There are certain services, which, because they are or should be universal, are the special responsibility of the statutory authorities. At the other extreme are what might be called the 'unique' activities of associations and concerns . . . In between are a great variety of other services where statutory and voluntary effort can co-operate effectively.[233]

Thus, although Labour may well—as Jefferys argues—have made a distinctive contribution to the establishment of the Welfare State, the comments of Attlee, Morrison—and indeed Pakenham—suggest that in implementation, as in ideology, the Welfare State had a mixed, and somewhat paradoxical, parentage. Many voluntary welfare agencies remained part of public policy, even as developments took place which might have seemed likely to witness their demise.

VI

Voluntary initiatives in social welfare after 1914 may thus be looked upon as having considerable strength—but also various

---

[232] Quoted in Asa Briggs and Anne Macartney, *Toynbee Hall: The First Hundred Years* (London: Routledge & Kegan Paul, 1984), 135–6.
[233] Quoted in David Owen, *English Philanthropy, 1660–1960* (Cambridge, Mass: Harvard University Press, 1965), 537.

weaknesses. The latter encouraged the growth of the centralized and more maximal state, and this growth was, in certain areas, impossible to reconcile with voluntarist practices. The former, however, ensured that the growth was still quite strongly permeated by voluntarist values—and encouraged the state, even as it did assume a positive role, to ally with many voluntarist agencies, which found in the state a valuable source of funding.

Where the state undertook full responsibility for welfare, as it did over National Insurance, a neat and tidy solution to voluntary-statutory relationships was achieved. The mixed economy of welfare in these cases did not exist, since the state monopolized the situation. Yet even this did not end voluntary initiatives; for a considerable degree of individual voluntary help was given *within* the statutory structure. Not, indeed, that this was new, since voluntary workers had, in the past, worked within statutory systems. Within the nationalized hospitals after 1948, personal voluntary service was still offered. The Labour government claimed that it had never envisaged any other outcome. Bevan told the Commons that, under the National Health Service, 'we are extending the field of voluntary work enormously. What we are doing is to relieve voluntary organisations from the necessity of raising funds.'[234] Further, the Ministry of Health after 1948 constantly emphasized that voluntary societies would have an extremely important contribution to make to the new National Health Service.

Initially, it is true, there appears to have been a decline in the amount of personal service given to hospitals, and some organizations which had previously been active in this area—for example, the Ladies League—were disbanded. But within a short space of time, it became clear that voluntary service was urgently required: an illustration of the fact that the state, even with all the resources at its disposal, found it difficult to meet all needs. Voluntary effort thus provided facilities such as trolley shops, outpatient canteens, library services, flower arranging, visiting, providing transport for visitors, and blood transfusion. Organizations under the name of 'Friends' were formed to provide services for local hospitals—thus, in a sense, maintaining the

[234] Hansard, *Parliamentary Debates* (House of Commons), 5th ser., vol. 441, 7 Aug. 1947, col. 1625.

former link which had often existed between the local community and the local voluntary hospital. 'Friends' could appeal for money for particular needs, provided that they were—and were seen to be—wholly independent of the hospital boards and committees, and that members of these boards and committees did not take part in them. Thus in 1948 the 'Friends of Kelling', which supported the work of the Kelling Sanatoria in Norfolk, was set up by three men patients who had left the hospital at about the same time. The organization was intended to provide a link between the patients of the Sanatoria and the outside world and to raise money to provide for amenities. A film projector was bought, and the children's sanatorium was well stocked with toys and games. This particular development was, indeed, stimulated by a central body—the National League of Hospital Friends. Thus most voluntary hospitals disappeared—but voluntary service, expressed in a variety of ways within the statutory-sector hospitals, did not.[235]

T. H. Marshall commented on this in an article of 1949, which was essentially a review of Beveridge's *Voluntary Action*. He argued in favour of developing the 'special virtues' of voluntary action within the statutory services. There were, he wrote, 'many ways in which citizens could be made to feel that the public services belong to them—especially when vested in a Local Authority.' They could take part in them as voluntary workers. Voluntary service was 'by no means a monopoly of the voluntary agencies.'[236] Here, indeed, was advocacy that the citizenship of contribution should be expressed through statutory agencies which implemented the citizenship of entitlement.

Where that happened, there was little difficulty in reconciling voluntary and statutory roles; they were resolved on an individual basis by the man or woman who, as Pakenham had put it, was 'prepared to serve the community for nothing' through a

---

[235] See Trevelyan, *Voluntary Service*, 71 ff. NHS hospitals serving a local community, even within a large city, could, moreover, still command considerable local affection and support in much the same way as local voluntary hospitals had done. This was to be clear when certain services provided by the Victoria Infirmary in Glasgow, which, as both a voluntary and a statutory hospital, had and has particular links with the south side of Glasgow, were, in 1990, to be transferred elsewhere under rationalization plans. These plans met with considerable local resistance.

[236] 'Voluntary Action' (*Political Quarterly*, xx/1–4), 27.

statutory body. But where the 'new philanthropy' involved combined voluntary-statutory *agencies*—as it very often did—there could be problems. Marshall suggested that when voluntary bodies cooperated with the state, and this involved grants of public money, there would be a tendency for voluntary agencies to amalgamate into large national associations, which brought with them dangers of 'bureaucracy and remote control': characteristics which were inimical to voluntary action.[237] Another difficulty was, in fact, an old one: finding the point of balance between voluntary initiatives and the state. It will be recalled that the Royal Commission on Friendly Societies in the 1870s had described this matter as a 'delicate' one; it was now considerably more so. It was easy to talk in terms of partnership; more difficult to find a way of making it work to the satisfaction of both parties. The problem was one of finding an appropriate link between the flexibility and adaptability—but the patchiness and uncoordinated nature—of the voluntary sector on the one hand, and the uniformity of the state on the other; between the freedom, identity, and independence of voluntary-sector organizations and the grant-awarding function of the state, recognized as necessary to give financial viability to many such organizations—but posing a threat to their leading characteristics. It was even more difficult to find a point of accommodation between universal and free statutory-sector services and partial, profit-making commercial-sector agencies—as the fate of the Approved Societies had shown.

This was, indeed, a matter which exercised the minds of contemporaries. In 1932 Lord Eustace Percy drew attention to the 'enormous volume of private voluntary effort', which, he said, was a matter which had 'never properly been faced by governments before'. But he also mentioned the need for a 'new technique of administration which has never been properly developed in this country' in order to 'secure co-operation between the government and private effort, to mobilise private effort under general government direction'.[238] In 1933 Lord Macmillan used what may be called the 'language of frontiers', when he said that possibly 'the most interesting of all the social problems of the

    [237] Ibid. 32.
    [238] Hansard, *Parliamentary Debates* (House of Commons), 5th ser., vol. 272, 25 Nov. 1932, col. 384.

present day is how to reconcile and adjust the frontiers between the province of the State on the one hand and the province of individual effort on the other'.[239] Macadam in 1934 called for closer coordination by means of a permanent advisory board, commission, or inter-departmental consultative committee.[240] In 1937, however, a Political and Economic Planning Report made the point that existing coordination was untidy; it identified six different variations of voluntary-statutory relations.[241]

The matter was also examined by Beveridge.[242] He cited in *Voluntary Action* the example of the University Grants Committee, appointed in 1919 to distribute central government funds voted by Parliament to the Universities and University Colleges; in 1946/7 more than £6 million, or half the total income of the universities, was distributed in this way. The creation of a body which acted as a buffer between the state and the universities and which had as its members persons from an academic background seemed, Beveridge wrote, 'to have solved the problem of paying away public money without demanding public control'; for, as he put it, universities 'are nothing if they are not autonomous'. He did not, however, think that this machinery would be appropriate in the case of all voluntary agencies. He rejected the idea of a voluntary service grants committee—'allotting resources to voluntary agencies without destroying their freedom'— on the grounds that such agencies were far too numerous and varied in structure, scale, and purpose to be treated in this way.

Beveridge did, however, call for the Lord President of the Council—at present what he called 'Minister-Guardian of Voluntary Action in the academic and scientific fields'—to extend his activities to voluntary bodies; and he argued that the current system of departmental grants should continue, possibly supplemented by an independent corporation endowed by the state for 'social advance by Voluntary Action.'[243] Marshall freely admitted that 'for the proper proportion of the mixture [of voluntary and statutory activity] there is no recipe';[244] but he was forthright in advocating the supremacy of the state within the mixture. Voluntary bodies, he wrote, must appreciate that, although they

[239] *Charity Organisation Quarterly*, NS, vii (July 1933), 102.
[240] *The New Philanthropy*, 33.
[241] *Report on the British Social Services*, 174.   [242] *Voluntary Action*, 315.
[243] Ibid. 317.   [244] 'Voluntary Action', 32.

were 'the first guardians of their own standards', their activities were not 'a guarantee of perfection'. Thus, he continued, 'the state cannot waive its right to inspect and approve a service whose efficient discharge is a matter of public policy'.[245]

These were issues which were not new. There had always been problems in reconciling the tensions between voluntarism and the centralized state. But now that, as Eyre Carter put it, the work of voluntary societies had in many cases 'expanded into state-controlled services without the societies themselves ceasing to function',[246] the problems became the more acute. They were not to disappear in the years ahead, as voluntarism and the state sought to adjust to each other within the new mixed economy of welfare, and in the context of the vast range of social responsibilities which had now been assumed by the statutory sector.

[245] Ibid.
[246] 'The Partnership Between the Statutory and the Voluntary Social Services in Postwar Britain' (*Social Service Review*, 23 (1949), 169).

4

Citizen and State, 1949–1991: Participation, Perception, and Pluralism

I

As social welfare in the later 1940s became predominantly the concern of the state, the various elements in the mixed economy of welfare became somewhat more closely defined. The 'language of the sectors', voluntary, commercial, informal, and statutory, has been used throughout this book; but it now came to be commonly adopted by commentators. This greater formalization into 'sectors' also denoted a realignment of forces within the mixed economy. Some of the functions of the mutual-aid and charitable sides of the voluntary sector were incorporated into the statutory sector; in a sense, the state might be said to have become the mutual-aid and the charitable society of the nation as a whole: the 'caterer in chief for its citizens', as Loch had put it in 1913. The commercial sector kept its characteristic of providing services through the market-place in return for payment. It now operated largely outside the state—but it, too, tended to draw away at least some of the mutual-aid aspects of the voluntary sector. That sector might, therefore, seem to be in danger of suffering some squeezing from both the statutory and the commercial sectors; and relations with the statutory and, in the longer term, commercial sectors were to pose problems of role, identity, and independence. Nevertheless, it retained its mutual-aid and charitable features, dispensed through its own agencies without consideration for the distribution of profit; and indeed, in the 1960s it was to find new expressions of these old traditions. The informal sector also retained mutual-aid and charitable characteristics, expressed without formal structure and without concern for profit.

The predominance of the statutory sector did, then, have clear implications for the others. It is, of course, true that there remained overlapping. The connections between statutory and voluntary sectors have already been noted. Again, in education, schools independent of the statutory sector remained within the voluntary sector, and enjoyed charitable status; but they charged fees, and thus had links with the commercial sector. There were 'pay-beds' in National Health Service hospitals; and here was a certain link between the statutory and commercial sectors. These links were also present in the considerable effect which taxation arrangements had on mutual-aid and charitable organizations in the voluntary sector, and on pension schemes run by commercial-sector insurance companies. The greater use of the 'vocabulary of sectors' did not, therefore, by any means rationalize the mixed economy into rigid, self-contained units; but it did introduce a slightly greater regularity into the nomenclature; and it was symptomatic of the new configuration of the sources of welfare.

In the immediate aftermath of the creation of the Welfare State, the fortunes of the various non-statutory sectors were to be the subject of comment; and this was particularly true of the voluntary sector. Many observations made in the 1950s, however, pointed to the continuing resilience and potential of the voluntary sector, rather than any immediate, or future, demise. Thus in 1952 the Committee on the Law and Practice Relating to Charitable Trusts—commonly referred to as the Nathan Committee, after its Chairman—was lavish in its praise of 'that manifestation of the philanthropic motive which consists in the giving of personal service', which it described as 'the true heart of voluntary action and indeed democracy itself'.[1] It claimed that 'the same essential desire to improve the lot of one's fellows lies behind both voluntary and state social action' and that 'so far from voluntary action being dried up by the expansion of the social services, greater and greater demands are being made upon it. Tens of thousands of voluntary workers have been enlisted to operate the statutory services in a manner in which Parliament has laid down that they should be operated.'[2] Here, indeed was

[1] *Report of the Committee on the Law and Practice Relating to Charitable Trusts* (London: HMSO, 1952, repr. 1974, Cmd. 8710), par. 51.

[2] Ibid. par. 54.

the citizenship of contribution being expressed through the state—as Marshall had advocated.

The Report, however, also saw an important role for voluntary agencies, as distinct from individual voluntary service. Voluntary organizations, it argued, were more flexible than state agencies: they could set new standards and undertake new work of their own volition; they could pioneer and make special provision for individuals suffering from certain types of disadvantage or disability. Voluntary organizations could 'stand aside from and criticise state action, or inaction, in the interests of the inarticulate man-in-the-street'. Such attributes provided 'one of the fundamental arguments for interposing this wealth of voluntary associations between the citizen and public authority, however, enlightened and benevolent this latter may be'.[3]

The particular matter with which the Nathan Report was concerned was charitable or endowed trusts, which it described as 'a typical and numerous form of voluntary agency', ranging from 'innumerable small village trusts to the few giants at the top which have a very important part to play in influencing the development of the partnership between public and private services'.[4] It estimated that the assets of the 'some 110,000 such Charitable Trusts' in the country—it could not be more accurate than this—amounted to some £200 million[5] and, to bring the whole matter on to a more orderly footing, it recommended that there should be a central, classified record of charitable trusts, that the Charity Commission be reconstituted, and the practice of cy pres be relaxed.

It will be recalled that this practice had been made binding on the Charity Commissioners by the Charitable Trusts Act of 1860, which had required that trusts which had become defunct could be applied only to purposes which were as near as possible to the purpose specified by the donor. There had been a number of breaches in the cy pres doctrine, the most important of which had been the exemption of educational trusts in 1869; but it still applied to the majority of trusts. The Nathan Committee felt that it should be relaxed for all trusts; this was necessary and urgent in the light of the extension of public social services and 'changes in standards and ways of life and ... shifts of population to

---

[3] Ibid. pars. 55, 56.   [4] Ibid. par. 65.   [5] Ibid. par. 58.

relatively under-endowed areas'.[6] The Committee saw its re-commendations as providing ways in which 'the good will of the past . . . may be more free to serve the changing needs of the present';[7] and it felt that charitable trusts, thus reformed, could perform a useful service in supplementing statutory provision by acting as an agent for public authorities, filling gaps left by those authorities, and pioneering new types of educational, social, and cultural work.[8]

The tenor of the Nathan Report was, indeed, reminiscent of Beveridge's *Voluntary Action* of 1948, and of the House of Lords debate on the subject of 1949. This is not surprising, since the impetus for the setting up of the Committee had, in fact, come from both of these. Beveridge had called for the appointment of a Royal Commission on Charitable Trusts, and this had been proposed in the debate of 1949. The Labour government did not think it appropriate to appoint a Royal Commission, but agreed that the matter could not be allowed to rest as it was; and it was against that background that the Nathan Committee had been appointed. It is also worth mentioning in this context that Lord Nathan himself had originally entered Parliament as a Liberal, but had in the mid-1930s joined the Labour Party; and, as chairman of the Westminster Hospital, had first-hand experience of the impingement of the public services on private philanthropy.

His Committee's Report was, on the whole, well received, al-though the desire which it manifested to tidy up the charitable world encountered the—not unfamiliar—criticism that such a process would involve, as it was put, a 'loss of the grace and spontaneity without which charity, in the Christian sense, is no longer itself'.[9] Despite the fact that the Report was by no means hostile to the voluntary sector in general and to charities in par-ticular, the Conservative government, in office when it was presented, proved slow and reluctant to implement its propos-als. A White Paper, issued two and a half years after the Report was published, went only part of the way towards accepting the recommendations, and there was a further long delay before the Charities Act of 1960 was passed. The Act implemented the Nathan Committee's recommendations in part: a central register

---

[6] Ibid. par. 119.   [7] Ibid. par. 65.   [8] Ibid. par. 642.
[9] Quoted in David Owen, *English Philanthropy, 1660–1960* (Cambridge, Mass.: Harvard University Press, 1965), 590.

of charities was created, the Charity Commission was reconstituted (although not along the lines it proposed), and there was some relaxation of the variation of trusts by cy pres. The legislation also afforded the opportunity to consolidate all the existing statute law on charitable trusts since Elizabeth I. There was to be a further Charities Act in 1985, which made some further modest changes; thus certain charity trustees were to be able to determine their own cy pres arrangements, with the concurrence of the Charity Commissioners. Procedures were made simpler than they were under the 1960 Act, and were designed to make better use of the funds of small-scale charities.

The Nathan Report helped to give prominence to the continuing role of charitable endeavour in the early years of the Welfare State, and it proceeded on the assumption that 'Parliament, so far from wishing to exclude voluntary effort, expected and intended that there should be a close partnership between the charitable organisations and the public authorities'.[10] Similarly, the Charities Act of 1960 also implied a recognition of the continuing contribution of charity. The Lord Chancellor, introducing the second reading, stated that a major aim of the legislation was to set up a statutory basis for cooperation between the public and voluntary welfare services. In the debate of 1960, references were, indeed, made to the earlier debate of 1949. The Earl of Longford—formerly Lord Pakenham—recalled that in 1949 it could not be certain what attitude the Conservative Party would take to the Welfare State, nor how Labour would react to voluntary services. 'To-day', Longford continued, 'the danger of a conflict on Party lines between the principle of the Welfare State and the principle of voluntary action has disappeared.' It was essential, he said—repeating his point of 1949—that there should be a partnership between the two, since 'the Welfare State without voluntary action loses its chance of realising its vision of national welfare in freedom'.[11]

Other Committee reports of the 1950s—and, indeed, the 1960s —also stressed the continuing and important role of the voluntary sector. The Younghusband Committee on social workers in the local authority health and welfare services in 1959 praised

---

[10] *Report of the Committee on the Law and Practice Relating to Charitable Trusts,* par. 633. [11] Quoted in Owen, *English Philanthropy,* 595.

the work of the voluntary sector and stated that voluntary effort 'is still an active and integral part of the health and welfare services and is needed now and in future to supplement statutory provision and to undertake work beyond the scope of legislation'.[12] The Committee—in common with the Nathan Committee—made the distinction between voluntary workers, who might work within the voluntary or statutory services, and voluntary agencies, which worked in cooperation with statutory bodies. This cooperation was closest, it noted, when an agency agreement was in force between a voluntary organization and a local authority to provide a statutory service. It supplied figures which showed that in 1956, 87 per cent of local authorities utilized the services of voluntary organizations for the blind, 83 per cent for the elderly, and 70 per cent for the unmarried mother.[13] It is true that the extent of this usage was unspecified, but, as Maria Brenton has put it, the Younghusband data suggested that in the 1950s, there remained 'a considerable residue of voluntary agency activity utilised and part financed by local authorities'.[14]

Even ten years later, in 1968, the Seebohm Committee on local authority and allied personal services in England and Wales revealed the extent to which voluntary social services were active in various areas. Thus of the 80,000 children in care in 1967, 15,000 were being looked after by voluntary agencies. Voluntary bodies were administering 92 approved schools and two remand homes which were financed from public funds; and the Committee also showed that more children were placed with the registered voluntary adoption societies than with local authorities. There was also a considerable contribution by voluntary organizations to the care of the elderly. Thus some 11,000 of the 95,000 elderly people in local authority residential care in 1967 were housed by voluntary agencies on behalf of local authorities; and some 43,000 elderly and physically handicapped persons were cared for in voluntary and private homes—for the most part in voluntary homes. There were in addition 7,000 social clubs

---

[12] *Report of the Working Party on Social Workers in the Local Authority Health and Welfare Services* (London: HMSO, 1959), par. 152. See also pars. 153–5 and ch. 11 (pars. 1031–62), which deal with the continuing importance of voluntary workers and are warm in praise of them: 'The part played by many different kinds of voluntary worker throughout the health and welfare services has impressed us greatly'.' (Par. 1052.)   [13] Ibid.
[14] *The Voluntary Sector in British Social Services* (London: Longman, 1985), 27.

for the elderly, the majority of which were run by voluntary organizations.[15]

Thus the voluntary sector was far from defunct. Historians of these years have also stressed its continuing vitality and importance. Owen wrote that 'The intervention of the State extended rather than reversed the long tradition of voluntary effort. In no sense a monolithic structure, the Welfare State of the nineteen sixties depended, to a very marked degree, on voluntary resources, human and financial.'[16] More recently, Brenton, writing of the agency role carried out on behalf of many local authorities by voluntary bodies under Welfare State legislation, in particular the National Assistance Act of 1948, has quoted a Ministry of Health circular of this period which stated that

it will clearly be to the advantage of local authorities to make use of voluntary organisations which are providing satisfactory services, and to co-ordinate their work with the authorities' own services . . . The more important voluntary agencies concerned with the care of the aged and infirm and with the welfare of handicapped persons have much special knowledge and experience which would be helpful to local authorities in preparing their schemes.[17]

Thus the previous points of common ground and convergence between much of the voluntary sector and the state, noted in Chapter 3, were to be again evident in the 1950s and 1960s. It was clear that the state—even the Welfare State—had an interest in forging links with the voluntary sector, and exploiting its resources; and it was also true that some voluntary organizations were glad that the state had undertaken a larger role, and were willing to cooperate with it and to accept finance for services rendered. This left them more free to experiment and innovate. It will be recalled that the Jewish Board of Guardians had experienced recurrent financial problems in the interwar period. The Board was quick to realize, as its Report indicated in 1944, that social needs in future would be met by the state. 'But', it continued, 'state relief, whether afforded by benefit or assistance, must of necessity be on mass lines, and there will remain the

---

[15] *Report of the Committee on Local Authority and Allied Personal Social Services* (London: HMSO, 1968), pars. 150, 257, 451. See also Brenton, *Voluntary Sector*, 29.
[16] *English Philanthropy*, 597; see also pp. 531 ff.
[17] Quoted in Brenton, *Voluntary Sector*, 18.

many intangible needs of those requiring some special treatment . . .'[18]

The Board did, indeed, adapt to the changed conditions, with a greater degree of emphasis on the provision of personal help or service than on money, and more attention being given to assistance for particular groups, such as the elderly. One senior official of the Board, recalling the earlier financial struggles, remarked on the position in the 1950s. For him, he said, this was 'a dream come true'.[19] In other areas, too, the same emphasis on specialization was evident. The Nuffield Foundation told the Nathan Committee that its main task was to 'seek out the unique project, and to try out the unique man'; and it gave increasing emphasis to overseas needs. That was also true of many of the activities of the Joseph Rowntree Memorial Trust, created in 1959.[20]

It could also be said that those aspects of employer paternalism and personnel services which have been considered in the preceding chapters survived the creation of the Welfare State. After all, the Welfare State was based, in part, on National Insurance, financed from individual contributions, which guaranteed a minimum income in the event of sickness, accident, unemployment, and old age. There was, however, no intention that the new national standard should adversely affect persons covered by existing private provident schemes, such as those run by companies. The Industrial Welfare Society stated in 1949 that, while National Insurance allowances helped to meet the workers' needs, 'it was never pretended that they eliminated the need for private thrift schemes and assisted saving'.[21] Supplementary company schemes, covering sickness, accident, and pensions, did, indeed, expand considerably after 1945; company welfare was still seen to be in the employer's interest by encouraging loyalty to the company, and this was particularly true at a time of full employment.[22] Peter Townsend wrote of the enormous growth

[18] Quoted in V. D. Lipman, *A Century of Social Service, 1859–1959: The Jewish Board of Guardians* (London: Routledge & Kegan Paul, 1959), 193.

[19] Quoted in Owen, *English Philanthropy*, 542.

[20] Ibid. 572. See also Lewis E. Waddilove, *Private Philanthropy and Public Welfare: The Joseph Rowntree Memorial Trust, 1954–1979* (London: Allen & Unwin, 1983).

[21] Robert Fitzgerald, *British Labour Management, and Industrial Welfare 1846–1939* (London: Croom Helm, 1988), 240.

[22] Peter Taylor-Gooby, *Public Opinion, Ideology and State Welfare* (London: Routledge & Kegan Paul, 1985), 66, notes 'the steady expansion of private pension schemes mainly run by employers'.

of the 'occupational welfare system' since World War II; this entailed provision by employers of pensions, child and educational allowances, health and welfare services, meal vouchers, and medical expenses. Townsend estimated that this cost about £1,500 million a year. 'The term "fringe benefits" ', he wrote, 'is becoming inappropriate.'[23] This comment rightly points to the continuing importance of these schemes, although the 1960s did see a slowing down of the extension of such pension coverage, and this was followed in the 1970s by a decline. Even then, however, those schemes which already existed improved in quality.

What of the other sectors of welfare: the commercial and the informal? Again, it would be quite wrong to regard those as wholly superseded by the state. The commercial sector lost the links of 1911 with the state over National Insurance; but it retained many other aspects of activity, which proceeded in great strength. The occupational pension arrangements were, indeed, partly set in place by company schemes; but these schemes were often closely related to the activities of insurance companies and their agents. Taxation arrangements made a pension fund attractive to both employers and employees; and Hannah has written that there could have been 'few employers whose employees paid income tax and who themselves paid tax who had not encountered an actuary or an insurance salesman who could show that all parties could benefit from an extension of private pensioning at the expense of the Treasury'.[24] Paradoxically, the state could actually assist the commercial sector by its taxation laws.

It is also true that in housing, the commercial sector remained of great importance. The building societies had, by the end of World War II, amassed very considerable assets: the amount advanced to borrowers during 1946 was £187 million compared with £137 million in 1938. The Labour Party was more enthusiastic about the spread of public rented housing than the Conservatives: but by the early 1960s both parties encouraged owner-occupation, at the same time as subsidizing public rental for those who could not afford to buy their houses, or did not wish to do so. In housing, indeed, the private sector was positively encouraged by policies adopted by both parties, such as

---

[23] *Sociology and Social Policy* (Harmondsworth: Penguin Books, 1976), 261.
[24] *Inventing Retirement*, 45.

mortgage-interest relief on taxation; again, the state was a source of subsidy to the commercial sector. As has already been noted, the commercial sector rubbed shoulders with the charitable voluntary-sector activity in education through the independent schools; and, at the other end of the age range, a feature of the 1970s was the considerable growth of residential homes, sheltered housing, and nursing homes—although in some cases these were financed partly by charitable giving and partly by fees. It has, then, been written with some justice that 'over the period of the fully fledged welfare state . . . private welfare . . . continued to flourish and to jostle state provision'.[25] The non-statutory ingredients of the Welfare mix remained of considerable proportions.

Equally, the informal sector retained an important place—even if it is, as ever, difficult to measure with any precision. The role of the family itself had been enhanced by the experiences of World War II; the Ministry of Health, in a survey of the effects of evacuation in breaking up families, acknowledged that it was impossible to find a substitute for the family. Social policy concentrated on building up the family, and keeping the family unit intact; and the Children's Act of 1948, which implemented the Curtis Report on the care of deprived children, instructed local authorities to set up Children's Committees, with specialist and professional officers, to ensure that the situation of children in care should approximate as closely as possible to children in a natural family. Support for the family was, then, entirely consistent with state welfare; and the Wolfenden Committee on the Future of Voluntary Organisations reported in 1978 that the 'informal help of family, neighbours and others . . . continued throughout the period [after 1945] to provide most people with their main line of defence against many kinds of adversity'.[26] Roger Hadley and Stephen Hatch wrote in 1981 that 'most of the care that is provided for dependent people living in their own homes comes not from the state, nor from voluntary organizations,

[25] Elim Papadakis and Peter Taylor-Gooby, *The Private Provision of Public Welfare: State, Market and Community* (Sussex: Wheatsheaf Books, 1987), 7.

[26] *The Future of Voluntary Organisations: Report of the Wolfenden Committee* (London: Croom Helm, 1978), 21. See also Richard Rose, 'Common Goals but Different Roles.' The State's Contribution to the Welfare Mix', in Richard Rose and Rei Shiratori (eds.), *The Welfare State East and West* (Oxford: Oxford University Press, 1986), 13–14.

nor from commercial sources, but from the family, friends and neighbours'. The core of the informal sector, they wrote, 'remains the family'; and they quoted work carried out in the 1950s and early 1960s to indicate that 'in spite of the widely held view that the extended family was rapidly disintegrating under the pressures of industrial society, in a modified form it was alive and well'.[27] Brenton has written of 'a vast hidden iceberg of every day, ordinary helping and caring services rendered by what is nowadays termed "the informal care system" '.[28]

It would, therefore, be quite mistaken to believe that the creation of the Welfare State introduced a monopolistic statutory system of social welfare in all areas; in many, the mixed economy was still amply evident. And yet the predominance of the statutory involvement within the mixed economy did pose problems of adjustment for the others. In the voluntary sector, familiar questions of role and identity were raised in the process of adaptation. While some might welcome the new departures, others were apprehensive. H. R. Poole, Secretary of the Liverpool Council of Social Service, wrote in 1960 that it could not 'be denied that the few years immediately following the end of the [Second World] war were a period of confusion and uncertainty for many . . . voluntary organizations'. One problem which he identified was caused by the very fact that the process by which the central state or local authority took over the work of the voluntary organization was far from clear-cut or precise. It was, therefore, very difficult to know whether voluntary organizations should cease their activities or continue with them until the statutory authorities were ready to take them over—or whether they should try to expand their activities.[29]

This uncertainty was accentuated by the fact that, even if voluntary effort within the statutory services was acceptable to the Labour leadership, there remained in Labour ranks—notwithstanding Attlee, Morrison, and Pakenham—a residue of dislike of voluntary agencies. As has been seen—and as Webb and others have written—'The immediate post-war implementation

[27] *Social Welfare and the Failure of the State: Centralised Social Services and Participatory Alternatives* (London: Allen & Unwin, 1981), 87–8.

[28] *Voluntary Sector*, 31.

[29] *The Liverpool Council of Social Service, 1909–1959* (Liverpool: The Liverpool Council of Social Service (Inc.), 1960), 77–8.

of social policies marked an attempt decisively to move away from social policies that were partial in scope, socially divisive in action, and socially controlling in intent. Voluntary organizations were regarded with not a little suspicion in the process.'[30] This suspicion did not evaporate; and while at the level of central government the talk was of partnership and coordination, and agency agreements brought about cooperation at local level, there was an undercurrent of feeling that these agreements, despite their importance and value, were only temporary arrangements which would, in time, be eliminated. In Liverpool, the talk was of 'allowing the voluntary organizations to continue for the time being';[31] and some persons in local government looked forward to the elimination of what were seen as competitors. It has already been noted that local authorities tended to assume direct responsibility for the blind in the later 1940s; and the Young-husband Committee was

inclined to agree with local authority witnesses that these authorities will increasingly take direct responsibility for providing the services with which we are concerned. This appears to us a logical development of the major changes introduced in 1948. The point has been reached when the greater resources of local and central government are required if the services are to be further developed.[32]

Here, then, was a statement to the effect that, in the long term, only the statutory authorities *could* cope with social need; and the impression was given that voluntary organizations, for all their current usefulness, survived only on sufferance.

A second problem identified by Poole was a familiar one: finance. Many voluntary organizations were, indeed, in a state of financial weakness in the later 1940s and the 1950s; and Poole suggested that the general public—and this included many prominent subscribers to charities—assumed that the new welfare legislation rendered charities redundant or obsolete, and no longer felt obliged to support them. A high level of taxation, he argued, discouraged voluntary giving still further; and he claimed that the disallowance by the Finance Act of 1946 of a payment

---

[30] Quoted in Brenton, *Voluntary Sector*, 20.
[31] Quoted in Poole, *Liverpool Council*, 88.
[32] *Report of the Working Party on Social Workers*, par. 40.

under a seven-year covenant as a deduction for surtax purposes was regarded by charities as 'the unkindest cut of all'.[33]

In expressing these views, Poole was, in fact, echoing comments made by earlier writers. Beveridge himself in *Voluntary Action* wrote that the changes made by the Act of 1946 should have been more widely discussed, and felt that the whole question of taxation policy—which would be of great importance to mutual-aid and charitable societies within the voluntary sector—should be considered by 'some impartial organ of inquiry', possibly the Royal Commission which he advocated for Charitable Trusts.[34] In 1947 Roger Wilson wrote that voluntary social service was likely to be affected by 'the drying-up of traditional sources of money.' The large subscriber, he felt, was 'probably disappearing'; and Wilson extended this argument to what he saw as a diminution in the number of people who would have time to devote to voluntary service. And not only would possessions and time be drained away from voluntary organizations, but so too, in Wilson's view, would talent, which, he felt, would increasingly be recruited into national and local government service and into the service of public corporations.[35] The Nathan Report of 1952 also stressed the financial problems likely to be encountered by charities; here, death duties and general taxation might well deplete the resources of those who had given to charities in the past.[36]

Even amidst the optimism shown by the Jewish Board of Guardians at the shift of many burdens to the state, there remained anxieties caused by financial difficulties. There were increases in administrative costs and in providing trained social workers; and the Board's resources were stretched to meet its new—but far from inexpensive—concerns. Deficits were once again mounting in the mid-1950s, reaching £52,000 in 1957.[37] The Treasurer's Report for 1958 made rather sombre reading. It stated that during the previous five years, the Board's deficits had totalled £167,826. 'The Board just cannot afford recurring deficits

[33] *Liverpool Council*, 88.   [34] p. 312.

[35] 'Notes on the Future of Voluntary Social Work', in Lord Beveridge and A. F. Wells (eds.), *The Evidence for Voluntary Action* (London: Allen & Unwin, 1949), 263–4.

[36] *Report of the Committee on the Law and Practice Relating to Charitable Trusts*, par. 57: 'nearly every voluntary society is experiencing difficulties at the present time.'

[37] Lipman, *Century of Social Service*, 200.

of this size,' it continued. 'Every aspect of the Board's expenditure has been examined and, where possible, pruned. There seems little further scope for economies in this way; on the contrary, demands on the Board increase annually and, with these demands, expenditure is likely to increase.'[38] Over the list of subscriptions and donations ran the repeated caption: 'An Increase in Contributions is Essential. If you have not signed a covenant please do so.'

Clearly, financial problems could be eased by the sums paid by the local authorities to carry out agency work; and a study of the receipts of between 250 and 300 voluntary organizations in the area of Manchester and Salford between 1938 and 1951 confirmed the conclusions which Braithwaite had reached for an earlier period as to the increasing importance of grants from statutory bodies: what helped these charities to survive was not expansion of charitable giving, but government subsidies.[39] But this, of course, brought into prominence the whole question of the separate identity and independence of such organizations— or rather underlined their subsidiary and dependent relationship to the state. Wilson felt in 1947 that the role of voluntary organizations 'as . . . conceiver and executant of the new developments would diminish, although probably not disappear';[40] and the Nathan Committee, for all its praise of charitable endeavour, argued that it was 'one of the magnificent failures of our history'.[41] Reviewing the recent 'revolutionary changes', it acknowledged that

It is now the state which in the Webbs' phrase 'blocks the downward way' by income maintenance and employment services, which meets every normal need of health and education, which seeks to reform the offender, which promotes the welfare of the old and the handicapped, which attempts to provide a substitute home for children who have lost their own, which supplements the housing needs of people, which limits hours of work and makes provision for the enjoyment of leisure in the parks, open spaces, art galleries and museums, and through every kind of formal and informal adult education.[42]

[38] Jewish Board of Guardians, *Annual Report for 1958 of the Board of Guardians and Trustees for the Relief of the Jewish Poor Registered* (1958), 13.

[39] Owen, *English Philanthropy*, 538.

[40] Beveridge and Wells (eds.) *Evidence*, 263.

[41] *Report of the Committee on the Law and Practice Relating to Charitable Trusts*, par. 44.   [42] Ibid. par. 48.

Equally, as has been seen, the Younghusband Committee Report of 1959 saw the future of social welfare in terms of statutory services; the voluntary sector, for all its merits, was still, it argued, tainted with enthusiastic and untrained amateurism, and those involved in it often required greater professional training.[43] Eileen Younghusband herself, in her book *Social Work in Britain 1950–1975*, wrote of tensions between voluntary organizations and statutory bodies in the 1950s, especially at the level of local government; and this too reflects the degree of apprehensiveness, bordering on suspicion, which could characterize voluntary-statutory relations in that decade.[44] It is notable that, while agency agreements maintained the former close association between voluntary initiatives and local government, the relationship underwent a deterioration in the period after the creation of the Welfare State.

Thus, despite the evidence of a strong degree of survival on the part of the voluntary sector in the ten years or so after 1949, many areas of that sector were on the defensive. Certainly, the old mutual-aid friendly societies were in a state of considerable disarray. As has already been seen, they were in decline before the Welfare State legislation of the late 1940s; but that legislation had serious implications, now that they were deprived of their status as Approved Societies. It was estimated by the National Conference of Friendly Societies in 1947 that the loss of administrative income resulting from the divorce from the state would be of the order of £2 million; and a serious immediate difficulty was seen to be the transfer to the government of trained and experienced personnel. It was also felt likely that there would be a reduction of new entrants to friendly societies who would wish to take out supplementary insurance, and an increase in the lapse ratio of those who had made such provision. Material cited by Beveridge and Wells in *The Evidence for Voluntary Action* showed that there was considerable ignorance and apathy among both members and non-members of friendly societies; the whole ethos of participation and group loyalty which had once characterized them had disappeared, and a passive mood prevailed.[45] John A. Lincoln, writing in 1947, argued that such movements had 'lifted

[43] *Report of the Working Party on Social Workers*, par. 1044.
[44] *Social Work in Britain 1950–1975: A Follow-Up Study* (London: Allen & Unwin, 1978), 2 vols, i. 256–7.   [45] pp. 16–26.

the working classes of this country out of the morass of the Industrial Revolution by their own bootstraps'; but, he added, 'the pressure behind the working-class needs which they met in the past has been steadily declining'.[46]

The situation on the charitable and philanthropic side of the voluntary sector was somewhat different. Here, there was much stronger evidence of survival than in the case of the mutual-aid friendly societies—but survival as the result of an increasing degree of convergence with the state. Again, popular perceptions of its place in the mixed economy were not especially encouraging. A *Report on Voluntary Services* issued by the National Council of Social Service in 1947 commented that while voluntary effort retained approval among many sections of the general public, 'fewer people *expect* provision of social services to be left to voluntary bodies in the future, than express *approval* of voluntary organisations now'. Expectations of that kind, the Report felt, might 'militate against the desire to participate in the work of voluntary groups'. Indeed, it concluded that 'it is in keeping with the social climate of our time to *expect* the state to take the initiative in the creation of social services.[47] In *The Evidence for Voluntary Action*, Beveridge and Wells quoted Mass-Observation Reports which indicated that, while certain charities such as those connected with the disabled, children, and old people were regarded as praiseworthy, there was a generally held feeling that 'to an increasing extent personal misfortune is not necessarily the fault of the individual but of the State. As such it is a State responsibility to look after him not as a favour but as a *right*'.[48] Thus the Wolfenden Committee conveyed an accurate impression when it commented in 1977 that in the fifteen to twenty years after World War II, the voluntary sector 'seems in some ways to have been marking time'.[49]

In many respects, too, the same could be said of the commercial and informal sectors. Both were, indeed, also present and important. But, as with the voluntary sector, the predominance of the statutory sector involved an adjustment of role. The informal assistance of family, kin, or neighbour was quite compatible

---

[46] 'Problems of Friendly Societies', in Beveridge and Wells (eds.) *Evidence*, 270.
[47] *Report on Voluntary Services* (London: National Council of Social Service, 1947), 104–5, 109.   [48] p. 59.
[49] *The Future of Voluntary Organisations*, 20.

with the Welfare State; but it often operated within the Welfare State, and was, to some extent, supported by it. Hadley and Hatch have written that 'in a very real sense the provision of almost all informal care in the community relies to some degree on the support of the social security system. Benefits such as those for the retired, the disabled and the chronically sick, and for those who give up their jobs to care for the dependent, are often a precondition of care in the community.'[50] They also suggest that 'the strength and even the very existence of informal caring networks' may well be closely affected by statutory policies not directly related to social care, such as redevelopment, rehousing, or changes in local employment opportunities or in local transport schemes. Here again, the informal sector often operated within—and was affected by—the statutory sector.

With the commercial sector, the situation was somewhat different. As has been mentioned, the delivery of social welfare services on the basis of the ability to pay was regarded as ideologically unacceptable by the Labour Party; and when, in 1951, prescription charges were introduced, this was seen by some in the party as incompatible with the principles of the Welfare State. Equally, the implementation of commercial practice was seen as a breach of the universalism of the Welfare State, since it would lead to the provision of services of unequal quality. Thus there were greater tensions between the statutory sector on the one hand, and the voluntary and informal sectors on the other. The divorce of the Approved Societies from the state affected not only the voluntary-sector mutual-aid friendly societies, but also the commercial-sector insurance companies, and although they remained powerful, it was still to be seen whether they could derive indirect advantages from statutory arrangements, such as taxation, or whether the commercial sector would act as a competitor to the state. It could be, of course, that statutory arrangements would make it into a more powerful competitor. As a manager of Legal and General wrote in 1963, the 'fundamental question' was 'whether we are to regard the State as partner or competitor'. He went on to say that legislation could well provide 'a springboard for new business'.[51]

Thus, whether inside the state or outside it, the non-statutory

---

[50] *Social Welfare*, 91.   [51] Quoted in Hannah, *Inventing Retirement*, 46.

sectors of welfare were reassessing their role for some fifteen to twenty years after 1945. Any 'jostling' of the Welfare State in which they indulged must not be overlooked; and the commercial sector, in particular, had considerable potential in that respect. But, for the moment, the 'jostling' was more at their expense, as the state established itself as the main provider of welfare within the mixed economy. It will be recalled that it was in the early 1950s that Marshall developed his influential model of citizenship—with the final stage of social entitlements through the state newly in place, and, as most observers thought, likely only to become more and more prominent. Any attempts to reduce welfare expenditure and re-examine the objectives of the Welfare State—such as were, indeed, made in the years from 1955 to 1957—came to little or nothing.[52]

There were, however, to be significant developments from the 1960s onwards. From that decade, the voluntary sector underwent a considerable revival; there was what Brenton has called 'an interesting surge of energy and imagination among voluntary groups and organizations.' As she further writes, 'The mushrooming of new forms of voluntary organization and action and the harnessing of energies to new and different causes testifies to a vibrancy and vigour that gained the attention of policy makers and won the voluntary sector a new place in the Welfare State.'[53]

Yet the words 'in the Welfare State' should be noted; for these new activities within the voluntary sector were still seen as being compatible with the Welfare State—and, indeed, were largely concerned with extending it. From the early and mid-1970s, however, increasing attention was given to the voluntary sector —and to the commercial and informal sectors; and the process was taken further after the election of the first Thatcher administration in 1979. All three non-statutory sectors were then seen more as potential alternatives to the Welfare State than as a supplement or stimulus to it; the 'jostling' to the Welfare State, if not entirely new, became more marked—although, even then, the severity of the 'jostling' was questionable. It is to these developments, first in the voluntary sector alone, and then in that sector along with the commercial and informal sectors, that we now turn.

[52] See below, p. 393.   [53] *Voluntary Sector*, 36.

II

In the 1960s the idea and practice of 'participation' was in fashion. As Ann Richardson has put it, there was at that time 'a sudden upsurge of interest in the idea that ordinary citizens might have a part to play in the decision-making process'.[54] This was to be seen in various areas: those who worked in universities in that decade will not forget the mushrooming of joint staff–student committees to ensure that all were given an opportunity to be consulted, and to take part in the making and implementation of decisions. Some of the sources of this lay in the USA, where pressure grew for participation in the 1960s; and there, of course, the whole issue of civil rights was a potent force. With regard to social welfare in Britain, something of the same trend was discernible; indeed, in 1975 Townsend wrote that 'the concept of civil rights should inspire every government action and committee'.[55] This was indicative of a certain waning of the initial optimism that the state alone would solve all the problems of society. This attitude had been held by those responsible for establishing the Welfare State of the later 1940s. Even Beveridge—oscillating as he did between a statist and a voluntarist position—took, as José Harris[56] has put it, a 'highly optimistic view of the nature of the state and of its identification with the interests of the whole of society'. The same point had been made by Douglas Jay from a Fabian angle when, in 1947, he wrote in the second edition of *The Socialist Case*: 'For in the case of nutrition and health, just as in the case of education, the gentleman in Whitehall really does know better what is good for people than the people know themselves.'[57] Thus the state itself had become an agent of paternalism; and the very things which had once commended state planning to those who advocated it—bureaucracy and professionalism—were seen to be making government remote from the people whom it was intended to serve.

The case for participation grew. It grew within the state itself. In 1968 the Seebohm Committee Report suggested that the new

---

[54] *Participation* (London: Routledge & Kegan Paul, 1983), 3.

[55] *Sociology and Social Policy*, 206.

[56] *William Beveridge: A Biography* (Oxford: Clarendon Press, 1977), 142–3, 428–51, considers these issues.

[57] Quoted in Malcolm Wicks, *A Future for All: Do We Need the Welfare State?* (Harmondsworth: Penguin Books, 1987), 34.

departments which it recommended for creation within local authorities to coordinate the social services should consider how clients might become more directly involved in the making of decisions and the delivery of services. Inherent in the 'idea of a community-orientated family service' was a 'belief in the importance in the planning, organization and provision of social services'.[58] In 1969, the Skeffington Report (Ministry of Housing and Local Government) struck a similar theme:

It may be that the evolution of the structures of representative government which has concerned western nations for the last century and a half is now entering into a new phase. There is a growing demand by many groups for more opportunity to contribute and for more say in the working out of policies which affect people not merely at election time, but continuously . . . Life . . . is becoming more complex, and one cannot leave all the problems to one's representatives.[59]

The National Health Service was, in fact, reorganized on more centralist lines in 1974; but, partly to offset this, Community Health Councils were set up to ensure that consumers were better represented in health service administration—although in effect they acted largely as pressure groups to elicit consumer opinion and ensure that those in charge of health administration came to know of it. The participation here was, therefore, indirect rather than direct; but the general idea belonged to the thrust towards greater involvement of the consumer. In 1977 the Taylor Committee recommended greater parental presence on the governing boards of schools; and in the same year, the Housing Review, undertaken by the Department of the Environment, suggested that tenant-participation should be introduced in the management of council housing.[60]

The voluntary sector could readily fit into this increased desire for participation; the involvement of 'active citizens' was, after all, its very essence. The Seebohm Report, although not primarily concerned with non-statutory forms of social care, noted that voluntary agencies could play a major role in developing citizen

---

[58] *Report of the Committee on Local Authority and Allied Personal Social Services*, par. 491.
[59] *Report of the Committee on Public Participation in Planning* (London: HMSO, 1969), par. 7.   [60] Richardson, *Participation*, 33 ff., deals with these issues.

participation. The Aves Committee—an unofficial body which was concerned with the role of volunteers in the social services—noted in its Report of 1969 the point made above about the growing sense of dissatisfaction with the bureaucratic state, and argued that 'the degree of control over parts of our lives and the loss of some of the personal element, particularly at work, have produced a desire to counteract these effects by undertaking activities which give scope for spontaneity, initiative and contact with other people'. The citizen, it said, 'should know about the needs in the community, the services which endeavour to meet them and where he might make some contribution himself';[61] and here the volunteer had a clear role to play. The Wolfenden Committee Report of 1977 argued that 'in the modern industrial state, dominated by the large-scale political, economic and social institutions, most people have little opportunity to shape the society in which they live'. It suggested that the voluntary sector had 'potential as a means of enabling widespread direct public participation' and 'the possibility of direct involvement'.[62] The Report of the Royal Commission on the National Health Service in 1979 received a great deal of evidence from voluntary organizations and others which, it noted, pointed 'to the unique and varied contribution made by the volunteers to the N.H.S.'. It felt that this was 'of major benefit to the service' and recommended that health departments and authorities should continue to encourage voluntary effort within the Service.[63]

'Participation', therefore, gave a considerable boost to the voluntary sector in the 1960s and 1970s; and this was partly the result of a growing sense of frustration at the Welfare State itself, which was felt to be too large, too impersonal, and too inaccessible to the ordinary citizen. Some commentators noted how certain things that had dropped out of fashion in the creation of the Welfare State seemed to be creeping back. In 1977, *New Society* commented that 'in a sense the concept of "participation" is a politically fashionable term for what was once called

---

[61] G. M. Aves, *The Voluntary Worker in the Social Services* (London: Allen & Unwin, 1969), par. 210.

[62] *The Future of Voluntary Organisations*, 29. See also Hadley and Hatch, *Social Welfare*, ch. 3.

[63] *Royal Commission on the National Health Service* (Parliamentary Papers, 1979, Cmnd. 7615), pars. 11, 22, 31–2, 37.

"self-help"'.[64] Thus Marshall's idea that the participation of voluntary workers within the statutory services would engender the feeling that these services belonged to the citizens of the state did not seem to have been fulfilled. Despite such participation, the Welfare State seemed to belong to the professionals who ran it; and the citizenship of contribution through voluntary organizations was seen to be a way of offsetting this development.

Another element in the strengthening of the voluntary sector was what might be called an increased, or heightened, social perception: a perception of needs which were not being met by the Welfare State. Here again, it is pertinent to return to Beveridge. Although he was, indeed, confident that the state could identify with the interests of the whole of society, he had recognized that it was unlikely to be able to meet *all* social and material needs. Basic needs might be so met; but the additional needs of what Beveridge called 'untypical distressed minorities' would still require to be catered for by some form of 'personal service'. What happened in the 1960s was that this became more generally recognized; there was a discovery of Beveridge's 'untypical distressed minorities'—of marginalized groups in the community. The Wolfenden Committee reported that before World War II, virtually the only organizations which existed for persons with particular handicaps were those for the blind and the deaf.[65] The growth of voluntary organizations catering for different needs and disabilities—some medical, some social, and some psychological—was a marked feature of the period after the formal creation of the Welfare State: and the 1960s and 1970s were important decades in that respect. They were, moreover, also important in witnessing the emergence of organizations which espoused the cause of traditionally vulnerable groups in society, the old and the young.

What gave rise to this is a matter of conjecture. One possible

[64] Vol. 42 (24 Nov. 1977), 394. Admittedly, such a comment tends to limit voluntary social action to one area of activity within it. It is also a somewhat misleading analogy, since much of the volunteering of the 1960s and 1970s was devoted to enlarging the state, not replacing it. See below, pp. 316–25. For further consideration of the 'bureaucratic welfare' offered by the Welfare State, see David Vincent, *Poor Citizens: The State and the Poor in Twentieth Century Britain* (London: Longman, 1991), 206.

[65] *The Future of Voluntary Organisations*, 43. See Harris, *William Beveridge*, 458–9, for Beveridge's views.

ingredient was the 'permissiveness' of the 1960s. A society which permitted various forms of behaviour without necessarily attaching praise or blame was, perhaps, more ready to recognize needs which might result from conduct which had previously been regarded as morally indefensible—or 'undeserving'. Thus the problems of the alcoholic, the gambler, the drug-taker, were seen as deserving more of sympathy and understanding than of condemnation. Yet this does not account for the growth of concern for the traditionally vulnerable, whose problems had, indeed, almost seemed to have been solved in the postwar period. Many assertions made in the 1950s had suggested that poverty had been virtually eliminated. In 1950 the Labour government's election manifesto claimed that the government's policies had 'ensured full employment and fair shares for the necessities in life' and that 'destitution has been banished.' In 1951 its manifesto struck a rather similar theme:

Contrast Britain in the inter-war years with Britain to-day. Then we had mass unemployment; mass misery. Now we have full employment. Then millions suffered from insecurity and want. Now we have social security for every man, woman and child. The dread of doctors' bills was a nightmare in countless homes so that good health cost more than most people could afford to pay. Now we have a national health service which is the admiration of the post-war world. Then we had the workhouse and the Poor Law for the old people. Now we have a national insurance system covering the whole population with greatly increased pensions and a humane National Assistance scheme.[66]

This was, no doubt, the stuff of which a party manifesto is made, but it seemed to be confirmed when the third survey of York was published in 1951 by Seebohm Rowntree and G. R. Lavers. This indicated a substantial reduction in poverty since the last survey undertaken by Rowntree in 1936. The proportion of the working-class population in poverty had, it claimed, fallen from 31.1 per cent in 1936 to 2.77 per cent in 1950. It argued that this had been brought about by the postwar policies of full employment, with accompanying rises in wages, and by the welfare legislation of the Labour government. If the welfare provisions had remained as they were in 1936, the percentage in

[66] Quoted in L. J. Macfarlane, *Issues in British Politics since 1945* (London: Longman, 3rd edn. 1986), 52.

poverty in 1950 would have been 22.18 per cent.[67] Such poverty as remained was seen in terms of a minor residual problem, which mostly affected the aged; and it was felt that adjustments to welfare payments could readily overcome this problem.

In fact, the third survey of York was impressionistic; and it should be noted that its findings were not entirely optimistic. They showed that 19.4 per cent of working-class families were 'not far removed from poverty' and that 'unless they concentrate all their spending power on absolute necessities, they will suffer from the evils of hunger and cold.'[68] The York survey also pointed out that the conditions in which families lived could vary considerably over a lifetime; and thus the proportions of those in poverty at some stage of their lives were likely to be much higher than the figures suggested. Nevertheless, whereas in the past the most pessimistic sections of surveys had tended to be stressed, on this occasion it was the most optimistic sections which were more widely accepted. *The Times* exulted in this 'remarkable improvement', which amounted to 'the virtual abolition of the sheerest want.'[69] Crosland, in *The Future of Socialism*, was critical of Rowntree's calculation of the value of welfare benefits, and admitted that there were still areas of hardship; but he was glad to accept credit for the social improvements on behalf of the postwar Labour Government, which, he wrote, 'deserves praise for a very considerable achievement'.[70]

Yet not everyone accepted such optimistic conclusions—even in the 1950s. As so often in the past, 'social-problem' issues emerged in the wake of the publication of further social research.[71] In 1952 Townsend, researching for Political and Economic Planning, cast doubt on the findings of Rowntree and Lavers. He suggested that the list of items which they had deemed to be a

---

[67] *Poverty and the Welfare State* (London: Longmans, Green, 1951), 40.

[68] Ibid. 67.

[69] Quoted in Ken Coates and Richard Silburn, *Poverty: The Forgotten Englishmen* (Harmondsworth: Penguin Books, 1970), 26.   [70] Quoted ibid. 28.

[71] See the following, on which the material in these pars. is based: Keith G. Banting, *Poverty, Politics and Policy: Britain in the 1960s* (London: Macmillan, 1979), 68 ff.; Richard Berthoud and Joan C. Brown with Stephen Cooper, *Poverty and the Development of Anti-Poverty Policy in the U.K.* (London: Heinemann, 1981), 6, 52; David Ball (ed.), *Family Poverty: Programme for the Seventies* (London: Duckworth, 1971), 14–18; and Coates and Silburn, *Poverty: The Forgotten Englishmen*, 29 ff.

'necessary expenditure' needed to be broadened; and, even accepting the findings, he questioned how representative they were of the entire country. In 1954 Townsend criticized the whole process by which poverty was measured, arguing that natural spending patterns were a better guide than the calculations of social scientists and 'experts' as to how money should best be spent. He recognized that spending patterns were not always rational in a purely economic sense, but were subject to the pressures of society, such as advertising and other agencies which shaped opinions and expectations. In 1954 an inquiry by the Ministry of Pensions and National Insurance showed that 54 per cent of men who chose to remain at work until the age of 65 said that financial need was the most pressing reason, and in the same year the Phillips Committee revealed that there was considerable deprivation among the elderly. In 1957 Townsend returned to the attack with the publication *Family Life of Old People*, based on Bethnal Green, which pointed to the existence of considerable hardship among the elderly; and in 1958 he drew attention to vulnerable groups, such as the old, the widowed, the sick, and the disabled, who were unable to take advantage of improvements in the standard of living. These he estimated to be some seven million in number.

There was, then, what may be called a 'rediscovery of poverty'. This process was taken considerably further in the 1960s. In 1960 a Fabian pamphlet by Audrey Harvey, entitled *Casualties of the Welfare State*, attacked the view that, as she put it, 'we have already achieved a Welfare State'. Basing her findings on her experience as a social worker in the East End of London, Harvey argued that there real hardship had not been abolished; and—somewhat in the manner of earlier revelations—stated that insurance was relatively rare even among those whose earnings were higher than average. What made the situation different from earlier periods when this had been true was, of course, the presence of state welfare agencies; but, Harvey argued, they were so bureaucratic and complex that those who were in greatest need often did not get the help which was necessary. She also claimed that there was widespread reluctance to claim National Assistance, which still retained an element of stigma and shame.

The pamphlet caused considerable debate, and was reprinted twice within nine months of its publication. As had happened in the past, the spate of publications on a similar theme continued. In 1962 Titmuss's book *Income Distribution and Social Change* cast doubt on the earlier held view that there had been, as a result of the Welfare State, a substantial redistribution of income to the advantage of the working class. Also in 1962, an essay published by Dorothy Wedderburn dealt with hardship among old people, and a second essay in the same year showed that some 12 per cent of the population was living close to, if not at, the subsistence levels set out by the National Assistance Board. These levels were criticized as being much too ungenerous by Tony Lynes in his paper of 1963, 'National Assistance and National Prosperity'; and the following year, Royston Lambert's paper 'Nutrition in Britain 1950–60' indicated a decline and deterioration in the diet of families with three or more children. In 1973 Frank Field wrote *Unequal Britain: A Report on the Cycle of Inequality*. In this he suggested that most people believed that the Welfare State had had a 'dramatic effect in making people more equal'; and he asked the question whether this had in fact happened. Field concluded that there was a 'cycle of inequality' which persisted from cradle to grave. 'Despite growth in national wealth', he wrote 'the age-old inequalities remain. The position of the poor has improved. But so, too, has that of the rich. It is as if the poor have been placed on an escalator which gradually lifts their position. But the rich, too, are on board their own escalator, which is moving just as fast, if not faster.'[72]

There was, then, no shortage of books and pamphlets which cast doubts on the achievements of the Welfare State; and one of the most influential publications in this whole area appeared in the mid-1960s: *The Poor and the Poorest* by B. Abel-Smith and P. Townsend.[73] Recognizing that the difficulty of finding an objective standard for poverty made the setting of a poverty line arbitrary, Abel-Smith and Townsend sought a standard which would receive widespread support; and they chose the level of benefit paid by the National Assistance Board—to be renamed the Supplementary Benefits Commission in 1966. This level was, by the mid-1960s, fairly generally regarded as a meaningful poverty line. Abel-Smith and Townsend examined the Ministry of Labour's family expenditure surveys between 1954 and 1960

[72] London: Arrow Books, 1973, 62.   [73] London: Bell, 1965.

in the light of this standard, choosing not the basic National Assistance level, but a higher one which covered additional payments often made by the Board to cover various special needs. The survey showed that 3.8 per cent of the population came under the basic level, but 14.2 per cent under the higher level. Poverty, it was claimed, had not been eliminated; and the survey showed that it affected not only the elderly but children. Moreover, the survey claimed that as many as 34.6 per cent of persons in low-expenditure households lived in households where the head was in full-time work; and this upset the idea that full-time employment alone was sufficient to eliminate poverty. *The Poor and the Poorest* appeared just before Christmas 1965 and received a great deal of publicity. 'Many British children living in poverty', proclaimed *The Times*, and the headline was repeated in various forms in many other newspapers, with the proximity to Christmas helping to give it considerable emotional appeal.[74]

Thus poverty re-emerged as an important social issue—and as a political one. The Labour Party adopted a less complacent attitude than it had done in the heady days of 1950 and 1951. The manifesto of 1955 claimed that the Labour government had 'begun to abolish the fear of old age, sickness, and disillusionment which haunted working-class life before the war.' Notwithstanding his satisfaction with the record of the postwar Labour government, Crosland in 1956 called for Labour to 'commit itself to a definite increase in the proportion of national resources devoted to social welfare'. In 1959 poverty in old age was a central issue in Labour's election campaign, and the party promised to increase pensions and other social security benefits. In 1966 it undertook to create a new Ministry of Social Security to alleviate poverty among children and old people. The Conservatives, too, placed social need on their agenda, promising in 1966 to 'give more generous help to children in families where the income is below standard'.[75]

Other social issues re-emerged. In education, reports appeared in the 1960s which pointed to inadequacies and defects. There were, indeed, numerous reports on education in the 1960s: the Robbins Report on Higher Education, the Newsome Report on

---

[74] Banting, *Poverty, Politics and Policy*, 72.
[75] Macfarlane, *Issues in British Politics*, 54–5.

Secondary Education (both 1963), and the Plowden Report of
1967 on primary education, particularly among the disadvan-
taged. As Keith Banting has written, the 1960s 'saw the high
water-mark of the environment perspective and of faith in
the capacity of education to change society'.[76] In housing,
'Rachmanism', following in the wake of the decontrol of private
rents, caused concern; and the Milner Holland Committee on
housing in Greater London came to the conclusion that 'we are
satisfied that abuses are general, and too numerous to be dismissed as isolated instances or in any way insignificant. While
they do occur, their nature is such as to constitute a serious evil
which should be stamped out.'[77] A survey of housing in England
and Wales in 1967 showed that 1.8 million houses—14 per cent
of the total—were not fit for habitation; and 2.3 million were
without one or more of the basic amenities. Homelessness also
caught the attention of the public; the BBC television film *Cathy
Come Home* received wide publicity.

The phrase 'rediscovery of poverty' is, indeed, reminiscent of
the 1880s—although the poverty 'rediscovered' in the 1960s was
scarcely of the same order. In the 1880s, that 'rediscovery' had
pointed to the defects and limitations of voluntarism as a means
of social relief or welfare: it was seen not to be able to cope. In
a sense, as has been suggested, the 'rediscovery' of the 1960s
pointed to the defects and limitations of the Welfare State as
established in the later 1940s. As Banting has written, the efforts
of those who took part in the immense volume of empirical social research in the decade 'revealed the persistence of poverty
and inequality and documented the failures of the welfare state'.[78]
Many of the supporters and creators of the Welfare State had
seen it as a means of attacking economic and social inequality;
Crosland in 1956 wrote of the 'direct and intimate' relationship
between social expenditure and social equality.[79] Yet in the 1960s
and 1970s social scientists were showing that inequality was still
present in wealth and income distribution, and in social conditions. David Donnison, who was closely involved in much of the

[76] Banting, *Poverty, Politics and Policy*, 114.
[77] Quoted in Wicks, *A Future for All*, 31.
[78] *Poverty, Politics and Policy*, 140.
[79] C. A. R. Crosland, *The Future of Socialism* (London: Jonathan Cape, 1956),
519.

research which has been described, wrote that the individuals on whose behalf efforts were made in these years were

often impoverished not so much by basic scarcities of resources as by their exclusion from the services which central and local government provided for the mass of the population. They were newcomers to the city, the furnished tenants who did not get re-housed in slum clearance schemes, the blacks who did not get their fair share of the jobs filled by the employment services, the lone parents who were given a low priority for council housing . . .[80]

Donnison used the term 'poverty lobby'—one which, he admitted, was a journalistic over-simplification—to denote the growth of assorted groups which 'assembled around the causes of the poor' in the 1960s and 1970s: the poor being the 'victims of government and the majorities which gave governments their power'—and the victims, too, 'of the practices of staff in the public services—police, social security, housing and job centre staff—all increasingly strongly represented by trade unions.' The poor, then, were the forgotten and overlooked groups, squeezed out by 'middle England', by which Donnison meant the 'established local citizens with secure jobs and average incomes'.[81] These were the people who had done well out of the Welfare State—but who had left others behind; in a sense, the new 'Labour aristocracy', for whom the state had been the means of upward mobility. Indeed, as Donnison pointed out, they could well be the professionals who administered the Welfare State itself: as early as 1960, Richard Titmuss had attacked the 'welfare professionals', who came between the services which the Welfare State was intended to provide and those who were entitled to receive them.[82] Not only, then, did the professionalization of state welfare services result in a denial of participation; it also put into positions of influence persons who might display attitudes which placed the claimants for state welfare benefits into deserving and undeserving categories—attitudes which had once earned charity a bad name.

Another way of looking at the matter was to claim that the Welfare State had been of considerable benefit to the middle and

[80] *The Politics of Poverty* (Oxford: Martin Robertson, 1982), 126.

[81] Ibid. 127.

[82] Harold Perkin, *The Rise of Professional Society: England since 1880* (London: Routledge, 1989), 475–6.

upper classes—since it was they who had taken most advantage of it—and had helped to co-opt the working classes into the capitalist system. It legitimized the system in the eyes of those who had least need to benefit from it, and deflected them from pursuit of their 'true' interests.[83] Ironically, once again, the same argument which in the past had been deployed against the exercise of charity was now used against the Welfare State: that it was a means of social control for the benefit of the propertied classes.

Within the 'poverty lobby', voluntary organizations could find a ready place. The 'poverty lobby' of the 1880s had tended to look to the state rather than to voluntary organizations as its saviour; that of the 1960s and 1970s remained predominantly collectivist and statist in outlook, but often used voluntary organizations to take up its cause. This was, indeed, recognized and advocated by the reports of the period. Seebohm saw voluntary groups not only as developing citizen participation, but as revealing new needs and exposing shortcomings in existing services.[84] Aves mentioned the role of voluntary effort 'designed to draw attention to unmet needs and to press for effective action to meet them.'[85] Wolfenden believed that one of the key functions of voluntary organizations was to be 'the pioneer of new services with the intention that if successful they should be adopted more widely either by statutory or by voluntary agencies.'[86]

In one sense, then, the impetus to the voluntary sector which came from an increased perception of social need, and was generated by the publication of social research, was a mark of a certain disillusionment with the Welfare State. There was still a great deal of unmet need. Rosemary Marten, writing in *The Spectator* in 1972,[87] made the point that it was remarkable, after almost twenty-five years of the Welfare State, that society was still not near to knowing all the needs that people had for services: the disabled for specially designed equipment, the housebound for meals on wheels, the lonely for visiting. She argued

[83] See John Dearlove and Peter Saunders, *Introduction to British Politics* (Cambridge: Polity Press, 2nd edn. 1991), 395 ff.

[84] *Report of the Committee on Local Authority and Allied Personal Social Services*, par. 495.   [85] *The Voluntary Worker in the Social Services*, par. 27.

[86] *The Future of Voluntary Organisations*, 43.   [87] 12 Feb. 1972.

that the resources of voluntary help were only just being tapped, and should be exploited further. Yet Marten also wrote that *official* interest in caring was at 'an all-time high'; and that central government itself had done much to stimulate that interest and to meet it. An example of this was the Chronically Sick and Disabled Act of 1971, which required local authorities to make their services known to the disabled and to find out the number of disabled in their own areas. It is by no means true that the state was always inferior to the voluntary sector in pioneering and discovering new needs; the state could well set the pace.[88] Indeed, the very presence of the Welfare State had raised expectations and resulted in an increased demand for services. Thus the voluntary sector grew in the wake *both* of the limitations *and* of the achievements of the Welfare State; for it was the achievements which revealed the limitations. These limitations were also the more noticeable in the light of greatly increased aspirations induced by greater affluence; perception of social need became the sharper when judged against the higher expectations of the 1960s.

The potential of the voluntary sector as a provider of personal social services did not go unnoticed by politicians; and if social perceptions assisted the growth of the voluntary sector in those years, so too did changed political perceptions. As has been seen, non-profit-distributing voluntarism—the voluntary sector—was regarded as broadly compatible with statutory services, particularly at the level of central government; but it still attracted some degree of suspicion on grounds of ideology and implementation. It was still felt in some Labour circles to be élitist, patronizing, and amateurish. In the 1960s and 1970s, however, this view changed and there was a growing consensus of political opinion that voluntary-sector workers had a useful role to play within the mixed economy.

This, of course, was simply a strengthening of previously held positions on the Conservative side. In 1969 the Conservative Party, in opposition, set up a working party led by Earl Jellicoe to look

---

[88] See R. Kramer, 'Voluntary Agencies in the Welfare State: An Analysis of the Vanguard Role' (*Journal of Social Policy*, viii/4 (Oct. 1979)), 473–88, and R. Kramer, *Voluntary Agencies in the Welfare State* (Berkeley: University of California Press, 1981), for a critical assessment of the pioneering role of voluntary agencies. The issue is also considered in Brenton, *Voluntary Sector*, 179–85.

at the use of voluntary work by statutory services. The Conservative Party manifesto of 1970 made the following undertaking:

We recognise the important contribution to social welfare that volunteers and voluntary organisations are already making, and we believe there is scope for considerable expansion and development. We are convinced that many of the social problems that now scar society can only be solved through a genuine partnership of effort between statutory and voluntary organisations—between the professional and the volunteer. We will give active support, both financially and legislatively, so that new opportunities may be created in co-operation with the local authorities for all those—and in particular the young people and the retired people—who want to do voluntary work.[89]

In 1971 Edward Heath, Prime Minister of the Conservative Government elected the previous year, spoke to the National Council of Social Service and referred to 'a continuing and developing commitment to the concept of partnership between the Government and the voluntary service movement.'[90]

More significantly, however, the Labour Party increasingly made its peace with the voluntary sector. Again, of course, this was not an entirely new development; but former critics of the voluntary sector in the ranks of the Labour party now changed their position. It will be recalled that in 1973 Richard Crossman looked back to his younger days in the 1930s—when he and his fellow left-wing associates had derided voluntarism, and in particular charity and philanthropy, as an expression of élitist do-gooding. In the 1930s he and his fellows had looked forward to the replacement of the do-gooder by a socialist Welfare State, in which trained professional administrators and experts held the key posts. That had, in large measure, come about, and, as Crossman saw it in 1973, 'in the construction of the huge new social service state we turned our backs on philanthropy'. This, he now felt, had been a mistake. He did not deny 'the need for professionalism and the importance of maintaining the highest

---

[89] Quoted in Brenton, *Voluntary Sector*, 46. See also Brian Harrison, 'Historical Perspectives', in *Voluntary Organisations and Democracy* (Sir George Haynes Lecture, 1987, with Nicholas Deakin. London: National Council for Voluntary Organisations, 1988), 10 for a consideration of the traditions of the Conservative Party in relation to voluntarism.   [90] Quoted in Brenton, *Voluntary Sector*, 46.

standards'; but, he said, the Welfare State had become a vast and, at times, inhuman and faceless bureaucracy. It was dominated by professionals and administrators who were as conscious of career grades as the staff in any other professional organization.

Here again is the criticism which has already been noted about the undue professionalization of welfare—this time from one who had previously been its ardent advocate. The Welfare State, Crossman argued, had cut itself adrift from the altruistic motive which had inspired the old philanthropy at its best. It had alienated the idealism of youth, impatient at the 'blindness of bureaucracy'; and Crossman called for a harnessing of the altruistic motive to the Welfare State, and for a much greater encouragement of voluntary activity, which he recognized as being present in large measure, in society. 'One of the first things I learned as a Minister', he wrote, 'was the staggering extent of voluntary activity in our welfare state.' This was 'increasingly encouraged by some services but tolerated, exploited, and frustrated by the rest.' The case, he argued, for a much greater use of volunteers was 'overwhelming'. Thus to the Crossman of 1973, 'do-good volunteering' was 'as essential to humane social services as highly trained professionalism'.[91]

Very similar themes were explored in debates on the subject of voluntary organizations in both Houses of Parliament in 1975. The debate in the Lords was prompted by Lord Windlesham, who drew attention to 'the continuing need for voluntary service in the community and to the valuable contribution made by voluntary agencies in supplementing the statutory services'.[92] Lord Harris, speaking for the Labour government, said that the development of the Welfare State had not reduced the need for voluntary service, and outlined various ways in which the government was offering positive assistance to the voluntary sector.[93] In a similar debate in the Commons, David Owen, on the Labour benches, matched Norman Fowler, on the Conservative side of the House, in his praise of voluntary effort. The whole House, he

[91] 'The Role of the Volunteer in the Modern Social Service', in A. H. Halsey (ed.), *Traditions of Social Policy* (Oxford: Basil Blackwell, 1976), 269. See also Crossman, 'None so fair as can Compare with the British Volunteer' (*The Times*, 8 Aug. 1973).

[92] Hansard, *Parliamentary Debates* (House of Lords), 5th ser., 25 June 1975, vol. 895, col. 1389.

[93] Ibid. cols. 1410–18. See also *The Future of Voluntary Organisations*, 213.

said, was 'united in its commitment to the value of voluntary effort and to the spirit of voluntaryism that exists in society'. He declared his own belief in a variety of social provision and spoke warmly of the partnership between voluntary and statutory bodies, which he described as 'one of the most encouraging developments in recent years'. 'Previously,' he said, 'there were suspicions that money given to voluntary efforts could always be better spent by being put into statutory efforts. There has now been a marked change in opinion and an increased willingness to work with voluntary people, particularly those who will accept obligations.'[94]

Bruce Douglas-Mann provided evidence of that change. Ten years ago, he told the Commons, he felt that the government and local authorities should be taking on the great majority of the responsibilities fulfilled by voluntary organizations. But his attitude had changed. The flexibility at the disposal of voluntary organizations in areas where government operations had to be conducted within fairly rigid rules provided opportunities to remedy many ills which would otherwise remain unmet. Above all, voluntary organizations provided an opportunity for those who wished to serve the community.[95] Alexander Lyon, Minister of State at the Home Office, admitted to some ambivalence in his attitude to voluntary organizations. He would, he said, like to 'see the time come when the Welfare State would apply resources over such a wide field that there would be no need for the voluntary movement'. But there had been such an expansion of expectation of social services that it would never be possible for the state to meet the need wholly. Thus, Lyon concluded, voluntary work was 'as essential now as it had ever been'.[96]

The Wolfenden Committee Report on the future of voluntary organizations was, on the whole, well received by Labour. Referring to its findings, the prime minister, James Callaghan, said in 1978 that 'there will always be competition for government funds. But there is an almost inexhaustible supply of good neighbourliness, of good-hearted people waiting to help . . .'[97] Merlyn Rees, the home secretary, said that

[94] Hansard, *Parliamentary Debates* (House of Commons), 5th ser., 8 July 1975, vol. 895, col. 360.   [95] Ibid. col. 377.
[96] Ibid. col. 400.   [97] Quoted in Brenton, *Voluntary Sector*, 136.

The special role of the voluntary organisations in a democratic society is to complement the statutory services and to adapt and apply them to individual cases; to innovate and experiment; and, in all that is done, to provide an opportunity for self-development and an outlet for that spirit of altruism which is essential to the well-being and happiness of society.[98]

The voluntary sector thus finally became respectable to Labour. To suggest, as Brenton does, that 'Labour's discovery of altruism as a praiseworthy source of voluntary action in providing social services represents a real turnabout in Labour's ideas'[99] somewhat underestimates the extent to which Labour, even in 1949, had been willing to accept the contribution of charitable activity. Attlee's words of 1947 in praise of voluntary effort should also be borne in mind. But there is no doubt that the fuller acceptance of the voluntary sector by Labour in the 1970s was significant. It was a recognition by Labour of the validity of what may, in one sense at least, be called 'welfare pluralism', if by that is meant a variety and diversity of provision, as opposed to concentration of responsibility and function in a monolithic state. Certainly in the economic circumstances of the mid-1970s, Labour came to realize that the Welfare State did not have unlimited resources at its disposal. Lord Harris commented in 1975 that there had not been a time since 1945 when the statutory social services had been 'under more intense pressure'; thus to cut the 'life-line provided by many dedicated volunteers' would mean that 'many of our most under-privileged people would be the first to suffer'. Yet, he continued, even if the resources were available, 'a society in which all human needs were met by the State would be an absurdity'.[100]

The blessing of the political parties on the voluntary sector did not, as Harris stated, remain merely a matter of words; it was translated into action. In terms of central government, a Minister was appointed in 1973 with responsibility to coordinate government support to voluntary organizations; and also in that year, the Voluntary Services Unit was set up in the Home Office. This was intended to serve as a link between voluntary organizations and government departments, and a liaison officer was appointed

[98] Quoted ibid. 138–9.   [99] Ibid. 136.
[100] Hansard, *Parliamentary Debates* (House of Lords), 5th ser., 25 June 1975, vol. 361, col. 1411.

in each major government department. In 1978 the Home Office announced plans to strengthen the Voluntary Services Unit so that it might be a more effective channel of communication between the voluntary and statutory sectors.

Central government grants to voluntary organizations were increased. According to figures provided by the Wolfenden Committee, the grants—in areas covered by the Committee's research, and excluding money paid under the Job Creation Programme set up in 1975 and through statutory intermediary bodies such as Housing Associations and the Equal Opportunities Commission—amounted to £19.2 million in 1974/5; the following year (1975/6) they amounted to £28 million, and in 1976/7 £35.4 million.[101] A further area in which successive governments funded voluntary organizations was through the Urban Programme,[102] which was set up in 1968 and lasted for ten years; in 1976/7 £1.9 million was given under its auspices. This Programme, involving an integrated and comprehensive concentration of resources and agencies, provided an opportunity for voluntary organizations to make an important contribution to inner-city policy; and under it, projects were set up to deal with urban needs and ethnic problems.[103] There is, of course, also the point that voluntary organizations which are registered as charities benefit from tax exemptions and reliefs. It appears to be difficult, if not impossible, to quantify this relief with any accuracy; but one estimate, based on stamp duty, capital transfer tax, and covenants, but excluding other forms of tax or rate relief, puts the figure at over £200 million in 1980/1.[104]

Cooperation between local government and voluntary organizations was less certain than that at central level. Efforts were made to ensure that it took place. Thus the Community Development Programme was established in 1969 to bring about a co-ordinated approach to assist deprived families and communities. The Urban Programme also brought local authorities into contact with voluntary organizations, which submitted details of projects for which they wished to obtain local authority funding. Forms

---

[101] *The Future of Voluntary Organisations*, app. 6 B, 255–6.
[102] Ibid. 255.
[103] See Joan Higgins, Nicholas Deakin, Joan Edwards, and Malcolm Wicks, *Government and Urban Poverty: Inside the Policy-Making Process* (Oxford: Basil Blackwell, 1983), esp. ch. 5.　　　　[104] Brenton, *Voluntary Sector*, 75.

of communication were, however, complex and varied; voluntary organizations often concentrated on building up points of contact with officials rather than with councillors.[105] The arrival of social works departments in Scotland after the Social Work (Scotland) Act of 1968, and of social services departments in England and Wales after the 'post-Seebohm' Local Authority Social Services Act of 1970, brought about a somewhat variable relationship between local authorities and voluntary agencies. Indeed, the generalist nature of these new departments drove some social workers with specialized interests into voluntary bodies which catered for their expertise. Barnardo's recruited a considerable number of staff in the period immediately after the creation of the new local authority departments—although in time this settled down, and was replaced by a fairly free interchange of staff.[106] Yet the representatives of Barnardo's who gave oral evidence to the Wolfenden Committee in 1975 reported that there was said to be some feeling against voluntary organizations, particularly in certain London boroughs. Here, it appears, there was resentment among those anxious to build up and expand the new departments that money which might be better allocated to the statutory side was given to voluntary organizations.[107] The Urban Programme did, indeed, seek to mobilize all available resources, statutory and voluntary; yet, although partnership between the two did exist and voluntary-sector views were effectively put, the spokesmen for the voluntary organizations were kept at a remove from full membership of key committees; and when the Programme as a whole was affected by expenditure cuts in 1979/80, the voluntary organizations felt that the local authorities had been cushioned against the effects at the expense of the voluntary sector.[108]

The Wolfenden Report recognized the difficulty of finding any

[105] S. Hatch and I. Mocroft, *Components of Welfare: Voluntary Organisations, Social Services and Politics in Two Local Authorities* (London: Bedford Square Press, 1983), 82–3, 89.

[106] Oral Evidence Presented to the Wolfenden Committee on the Future of Voluntary Organisations (Edinburgh University Library, MS Gen. 2034–5), file O.E.2.

[107] Ibid. See also Norman Johnson, *Voluntary Social Services* (Oxford: Basil Blackwell and Martin Robertson, 1981), 116.

[108] Higgins, Deakin, Edwards, and Wicks, *Government and Urban Poverty*, 144, 148, 167.

overall pattern governing the relationships between local government and the voluntary sector, and it acknowledged that
differences of approach to the voluntary sector were far wider in
local than in central government. But it also noted that the most
extreme form of hostility to voluntary organizations on the part
of local authorities—manifesting itself in refusal to grant aid or
cooperate with voluntary bodies—was 'seldom encountered'.[109]
The Committee found it difficult to estimate the level of funding
which local authorities gave to voluntary organizations, since
different local authorities behaved in different ways and few
appeared to collect together information on all the grants given
to voluntary bodies. It estimated, however, that in 1975/6 grants
totalling £7.9 million were made in the field of personal social
services by local authorities in England and Wales, compared
with £5.2 million in 1974/5. In addition to receiving grants—
which might be general or specific—a voluntary organization
often acted as an agent for a local authority in carrying out the
statutory duties of that authority. This, of course, was a continuation of a long-standing role, and happened most frequently in
the provision of specialist services. Or, again, a voluntary body
might supplement scarce local authority facilities. This was particularly common in the use made of places in voluntary residential homes. Where this was the case, the local authority paid
substantial fees to the body concerned; and again, this continued
a well-established practice. The Wolfenden Committee calculated
that in 1975/6 fees and charges in personal social services and
special education paid by local authorities to voluntary bodies in
England and Wales came to £95.4 million.[110] Rent-free accommodation was often provided by local authorities to voluntary
bodies. A mandatory 50 per cent which might be exceeded, in
the form of relief on the payment of rates, operated on all property that was owned by a charity or wholly or mainly used for
charitable purposes.

Clearly, these links with statutory authorities opened up increased sources of finance to the voluntary sector. As has been
seen, these links were far from being wholly new; nor, even as

[109] *The Future of Voluntary Organisations*, 85.

[110] Ibid. 256. See also Johnson, *Voluntary Social Services*, 120; and *Working
Together: Partnerships in Local Social Service* (London: Bedford Square Press, 1981),
4–6.

they were increased, did they succeed in resolving all the financial problems of voluntary organizations. The parliamentary debate of 1975 showed how inflationary pressures were severely affecting the funds of the voluntary sector. Lord Windlesham told the Lords that 'virtually every voluntary organisation shares at present one thing in common—the threat of actual or pending financial crisis'.[111] As in the past, financial difficulties affecting both voluntary and statutory bodies created a common ground for cooperation. For the voluntary sector, government assistance helped considerably in providing much-needed finance. The Urban Programme was, indeed, the most important source of funding for many voluntary organizations and provided their means of survival.

An increased desire for participation, a heightened perception of social need, and an acceptance of a pluralist system of welfare, leading to enhanced state funding for voluntary sector bodies, led to a considerable development of the sector over the period from about the mid-1960s. Lyon in 1975 spoke of a 'burgeoning' of voluntary organizations;[112] and the Wolfenden Committee reported that one reason for its appointment was that the volume and vigour of voluntary activity made it a 'sufficiently important element in our national life to deserve a dispassionate and considered appraisal'.[113] *New Society*, which in 1965 noted the 'volunteer upsurge', and in 1975 carried an article entitled 'A Volunteer Spectrum', wrote in 1986 that 'Defects in the Welfare State as a comprehensive provider, a mountain of unmet social need and the erosion of confidence in traditional institutions— these have led to a renewed wave of interest in . . . "the voluntary sector" '.

It is one thing to note the newly invigorated voluntary sector; it is another to measure it with any accuracy. This is, of course, a familiar problem which has been encountered in the past. As Brenton has put it,

to talk about the 'voluntary sector' is in itself, although a necessary shorthand, to ascribe a homogeneity and unity to this vast range of activities that is totally artificial and misleading. The voluntary sector's pluriformity

[111] Hansard, *Parliamentary Debates* (House of Lords), 5th ser., 25 June 1975, vol. 895, col. 1391.

[112] Hansard, *Parliamentary Debates* (House of Commons), 5th ser., 8 July 1975, vol. 895, col. 400.　　　　　[113] *The Future of Voluntary Organisations*, 10.

and lack of clear boundaries do not lend themselves to the definitions and classifications upon which statistical methods are based.[114]

This reflects the comments of some of the reports which have already been quoted. The Aves Committee of 1969 admitted that it was impossible to describe the extent, range, and variety of voluntary work. It did, indeed, undertake some investigation itself, but this, it wrote, 'effectively highlighted the depth of our ignorance.' The Wolfenden Committee came to much the same conclusions. 'When we began', it commented, 'it was hardly possible even to hazard a guess at the number of organizations and the scope of their activities . . .'[115]

Nevertheless, various attempts were made in this period, as in others, to grapple with the problem. One was to approach it in terms of the number of persons involved in the voluntary sector. This, of course, presents formidable difficulties, as A. Webb, L. Day, and D. Weller freely admitted when they collected data on the basis of a postal survey of a number of voluntary organizations.[116] The survey was, self-confessedly, limited; it was confined to established voluntary organizations which were national in nature—and only forty-four of these. The authors of the findings based on this survey were at pains to stress the fact that they were in no sense a full or accurate representation of the voluntary sector as a whole. They found that in 1975 the forty-four agencies employed between 13,000 and 15,000 paid staff in four main areas of work—field work, day care, residential, and other; and, compared with equivalent areas of work in local authority social services departments, these figures were taken to represent between 15.5 and 18 per cent of the size of the total local authority staffs in England and Wales.

The Wolfenden Committee also tried to arrive at some statistical data, basing this more on the number of hours spent on voluntary work, mostly for an organization, during the previous twelve months. Of the 2,114 respondents to a poll carried out in September 1976,[117] 15.3 per cent said that they had taken part in voluntary work, mostly for an organization, during the previous

---

[114] *Voluntary Sector*, 58.   [115] *The Future of Voluntary Organisations*, 31.

[116] *Voluntary Social Services: Manpower Resources* (London: Personal Social Services Council, 1976). See also Brenton, *Voluntary Sector*, 58–9.

[117] A summary of the findings is given in *The Future of Voluntary Organisations*, 34–5; a fuller version in *New Society*, 40 (7 Apr., 1977), 24–5.

twelve months. To try to make memories more focused, the poll asked how many hours of voluntary work had been done in the week previous to the taking of the poll. The average claimed was 6.1 per cent. These findings have also to be treated with some care—as must the Wolfenden Committee's attempt to translate them into figures for the whole population. It estimated that some 16 million person-hours of voluntary work were given each week—the rough equivalent of 400,000 full-time staff. Some two-thirds of the work was concentrated in the personal social services, where, it was noted, the local authorities employed only 200,000 full-time staff; but here again, it is wise to exercise caution in drawing too many firm conclusions, as the Committee itself recognized. Much of the voluntary work was concerned with fund-raising, and this makes comparison with the work of the statutory sector somewhat misleading. Again, of course, participation in voluntary work could cover a great number of different activities, not all of which were connected with welfare. The same point would apply to the findings of a sample taken by the Volunteer Centre in 1981, which indicated that 44 per cent of the sample had done some voluntary work in the year preceding the inquiry.[118]

The statistical method is, as ever, fraught with difficulties; and this is also true of any effort to examine the voluntary sector in terms of the number of voluntary organizations in existence. As in the past, it is impossible to provide a comprehensive list. All that can be done is to provide exemplar material—and this does, at least, have the merit of illustrating the range of voluntary organizations which originated in the 1960s and 1970s and the variety of roles which they could play. They ranged from self-help or mutual-aid groups to philanthropic organizations (although the word 'philanthropic', with its nineteenth-century connotations, would not be used, and some such description as 'service-giving' or 'caring' was felt to be more appropriate) and pressure groups. Often, indeed, they combined a variety of roles. Mutual-aid groups were represented by the Pre-School Playgroups Association (1961), Mothers-in-Action (1967), Gingerbread (1970), the Spinal Injuries Association (1974), and the National Women's Aid Federation (1975). Philanthropic, or 'service-

---

[118] Brenton, *Voluntary Sector*, 61.

giving', organizations included Help the Aged (1961), the National Society for Autistic Children (1962), Task Force (1964), Elderly Contact (1965), and Age Concern (1971). Other organizations were more concerned with pressure-group activity: the Child Poverty Action Group (1965), which did much to publicize *The Poor and the Poorest*, the Disablement Income Group, and Shelter (1966) come primarily into this category. Shelter, indeed, began as an organization to provide homes, but changed to the role of pressure group for the homeless. In fact, these distinctions between mutual-aid organizations, service-giving groups, and campaigning societies were often blurred; one organization might straddle a variety of roles, a feature which, as will be seen, sometimes posed ambiguities. This was also true of the great number of organizations which came into existence to campaign for the 'distressed minorities', as Beveridge had called them—or the 'socially unacceptable', to use the phrase coined by the Aves Committee. Examples of these were Release (1967) for persons with drug problems; for homosexuals, the Campaign for Homosexual Equality (1969), Friend (1971), and Gay Switchboard (1974); for alcoholics, Alcoholics Anonymous (which began in America in 1935), Alanon (for the relations of alcoholics), and the National Council on Alcoholism (1963); for ex-prisoners, the Circle Trust (1964), and the Griffins Society (1967).

The list could be greatly extended—and could never be complete. It is true that some of the voluntary organizations founded in the 1960s and 1970s were re-formings of earlier bodies; thus the National Association for the Care and Resettlement of Offenders, set up in 1966, took over the work previously carried out by the National Society of Discharged Prisoners Aid Societies. Yet Stephen Hatch, in his study of voluntary organizations in three English towns—which provides a further approach to the problem of definition and focus—shows that, although a few groups in the 1970s could be traced to the nineteenth century, the majority had come into being since 1960; and almost 40 per cent of the organizations surveyed in 1978 had come into existence in the previous eight years. Hatch concluded that organizations which catered for meeting specific handicaps and diseases and those connected with the playgroup movement were the ones with the fastest growths; and also very prominent in this respect were societies which were concerned with advice and counselling, neighbourhood issues, special-need housing, and ethnic and environmental matters.[119]

A further 'institutional' approach to an attempt to define at least the contours of the voluntary sector can be carried out by noting the development of organizers or associates in certain areas. In 1963 two hospitals possessed voluntary-help organizers; in 1975 250 such organizers were at work. In the probation service, voluntary associates had by the mid-1970s become integral to the work in many areas. In the mid-1970s too, it was estimated that there were some 250,000 non-professional helpers in youth clubs.[120] Or again, there was the implemention of the points put forward by the Aves Committee. The Committee recommended that Volunteer Bureaux be set up to act as centres of recruitment, advice, and information and to match individuals and groups with the changing needs of the community.[121] Such bodies were, indeed, set up and spread quite rapidly. In 1969 there were 28, and in 1975, 125. The Committee also recommended the establishment of a Volunteer Foundation at national level to assemble information, promote studies, and pilot projects. The Volunteer Centre was established in 1973. Mike Thomas, its first director, brought together the points which have been made above about participation and perception when he said that increased and more effective community involvement in all the social services, health, social work, probation, and after-care would benefit those who used the services, those who worked in them, and the community as a whole.[122]

Thus the voluntary sector, after a period in the doldrums in the 1950s, came to life in the decades which followed. It had become clear that the statutory services were not allowing sufficient citizen involvement and were falling short of meeting all the needs of all the citizens. Just as it had once been felt that voluntarism alone could not cope with all the problems of society, now it was increasingly recognized that the state could not cope alone. There was a need for active citizens *inside* the state— but also *outside* it.

---

[119] *Outside the State: Voluntary Organisations in Three English Towns* (London: Croom Helm, 1980), 88.   [120] *New Society*, 32 (19 June 1975), 714–15.
[121] *The Voluntary Worker in the Social Services*, par. 296.
[122] Quoted in Kathleen Jones, John Brown, and Jonathan Bradshaw, *Issues in Social Policy* (London: Routledge & Kegan Paul, 1978), 91–2.

III

The development of the voluntary sector after the 1960s has been traced to an increased desire for participation, which the state could not offer, a greater perception of needs which the state could not meet, and a wider acceptance of pluralism, in the sense of a diversified system of social welfare. It might well be said, however, that these features in themselves were scarcely new. Voluntary activity had always depended on the *participation* of individuals and groups who *perceived* needs and responded to them. Equally, it might be said that there had always been some degree of pluralism in the sense of a diversity of welfare systems; the phrase 'mixed economy of welfare' has been used frequently throughout this book.

What may be said to have been 'new' about these developments in the 1960s and 1970s is that they once again became fashionable after a period when they had certainly not disappeared, but had been out of fashion, and had, indeed, seemed to some observers to be on the way to being phased out. Welfare pluralism, as Hatch and Mocroft put it, was 'an ancient reality whose significance [was] beginning to be seen in a fresh light.'[123] The question may now be posed whether the developments of these decades brought with them new dimensions to the voluntary sector, or whether they threw up features which, over a longer perspective, were not new. It is best to relate these points to the ideology of the voluntary sector in these years—which is linked to 'perception'; to the implementation of the activities embraced by that sector—linked to 'participation'; and to its identity—linked to 'pluralism'.

One point which has been noted by various commentators on the voluntary sector at this time is that its ideology showed fewer signs of religious or evangelical commitment than had been true in earlier periods. The Wolfenden Committee stated that voluntary organizations were increasingly 'secular and materialist in outlook rather than inspired by the desire to rescue or evangelise'.[124] This is a point which can be overplayed, since religious perceptions and motivations did not disappear. Voluntary organizations which had long drawn on such motivations

---

[123] *Components of Welfare*, 2.
[124] *The Future of Voluntary Organisations*, 185.

continued to do so. There was still a strong religious dimension to the work of the Shaftesbury Society, and the representatives of the Church of England Children's Society told the Wolfenden Committee that they were attracted to the Society because of its Christian basis. 'Christian motivation', they said, 'is important and the fact that there is a link beyond pure professionalism seems to create an atmosphere and give a certain character to the work.'[125] The same was largely true of Barnardo's. It was felt, said Barnardo's representatives to the Wolfenden Committee, 'that spiritual intervention makes a difference to the quality of our work'.[126] There was also a strong and obvious religious motivation behind the work of the Committee on Social Responsibility of the General Assembly of the Church of Scotland; and the Department of Social Responsibility of the Church of Scotland is, in fact, the largest voluntary-sector welfare agency in Scotland. Even some of the newcomers on the scene of voluntary organizations could claim a religious parentage. The Samaritans were founded—as early as 1952—by the Revd Chad Varah. Thus, as Stephen Hatch has put it, 'a religious inspiration is still present in many voluntary organizations, and more generally voluntary organizations remain a vehicle for the expression of public services and of strong personal commitments and charismatic influences that do not find an easy place in large bureaucracies'.[127]

Yet, if religious motivation did not disappear, it resulted in social work which normally lacked any very clear, or overt, 'religious' or 'denominational' label. The Church of England Children's Society told the Wolfenden Committee that both Christians and non-Christians were attracted to and accepted by it; and that it was the opportunity which the Society offered to the professionally qualified to specialize in work in depth with children which was often the key factor in staff recruitment, rather than any religious or denominational urge. 'In general', the Society's representatives said, 'it can be said that the Society is in the same state of change as the Church itself is in relation to its role.'[128] In

[125] Oral Evidence Presented to the Wolfenden Committee, file O.E.1.
[126] Ibid. file O.E.2.
[127] *Outside the State*, 122. See also Bob Holman with David Wiles and Sandie Lewis, *Kids at the Door: A Preventive Project on a Council Estate* (Oxford: Basil Blackwell, 1981).
[128] Oral Evidence Presented to the Wolfenden Committee, file O.E.1.

time, the Society was to drop 'Church of England' from its title and become 'The Children's Society'. Something similar was true of what Barnardo's representatives told the Committee. Staff were not recruited on any religious basis, and non-believers were accepted. It was more the 'spiritual depth' of an applicant which was explored than any precise religious belief.[129] Stuart Ball, Chief Personnel Services Officer of Barnardo's, and Neena Chauhan, Recruitment Officer, said in 1990 that Barnardo's described itself as 'a Christian childcare organization', and asked those who joined to be aware of this. But not all recruits were practising Christians: 'we welcome people from all world faiths', they said.[130]

Ideology thus became more secular; and it also tended to follow an existing trend, by becoming less élitist, moralistic, and authoritarian—and more permissive. The Aves Committee noted that a 'new . . . characteristic' of current volunteers was that 'unlike most of their predecessors, they start as a rule without social or financial privileges or an assumption that they were entitled to make moral judgements about their neighbours'.[131] Wolfenden noted that, increasingly, voluntary effort was 'based on mutual benefit rather than benevolent paternalism'.[132]

Again, this point can be exaggerated. Joan Cooper has suggested that 'in general the voluntary sector continued to carry the historic legacy of the C. O. S. [Charity Organisation Society] and the tradition of selectivity'.[133] It would also be a mistake to exaggerate the extent to which voluntary work in these years originated from those who were, in the words of Aves, 'without social or financial privilege'. The vast bulk of voluntary social action in the 1960s and 1970s was done by the middle classes; and there was a lack of any real working-class involvement, especially where the voluntary activity had a philanthropic, rather than a mutual-aid, orientation. The evidence produced by the Opinion Survey of 1976 indicated that much the greatest contrast in voluntary work related not to age and sex but to social class. The poll found that 30 per cent of the upper middle class (those defined as AB) claimed to have done voluntary work in the year

---

[129] Ibid. file O.E.2. [130] *Graduate* (24 May 1990), 23.

[131] *The Voluntary Worker in the Social Services*, par. 21.

[132] *The Future of Voluntary Organisations*, 185.

[133] *The Creation of the British Personal Social Services 1962–74* (London: Heinemann Educational, 1983), 81.

previous to the poll, compared with only 9 per cent of the un-skilled and state pensioners. Hatch and Mocroft wrote in *New Society* in April 1977 that voluntary work in the social services 'consists of the well-off helping the less well-off'. They argued that this could be as much a strength as a weakness; but they added, 'in thinking about the future, especially with reference to where untapped potential may lie, there is a case for giving particular attention to voluntary organisations that transcend class differences'.[134]

Nevertheless, the fact that the bulk of those involved in volun-tary social work were themselves propertied did not always mean that socially conservative or paternalistic views prevailed to the exclusion of all others. Cooper qualified her remarks about the lingering legacy of the Charity Organisation Society and selectiv-ity by suggesting that this was based not so much on grounds of moral distinction as responding quickly to particular needs and bringing to bear the altruism and skills of 'ordinary people'.[135] A feature of the voluntary sector which may well be significant in this respect was that, increasingly, it attracted new constituen-cies. One was youth. In 1965 the article 'The Volunteer Upsurge', published by *New Society*, concentrated on the youth of those involved in the upsurge which it detected. The young people doing community work in this country, it suggested, were her-alded less than the school-leavers and graduates who went abroad for 'service' in the developing countries; but they made up an army which, although in the field for some time, had only re-cently 'been gathering a full flood of recruits'.[136] The Aves Report also referred to the involvement of young people, and to 'their increasing interest in and contribution to voluntary work'.[137] The participation of other groups was also noted. The Aves Report recognized some truth in the commonly held view that the typi-cal voluntary worker was the middle-aged, middle-class married woman—and that, of course, was a stereotype inherited from the

[134] Vol. 40 (7 Apr. 1977), 25.
[135] *Creation of British Personal Social Services*, 81.
[136] Vol. 6 (14 Oct. 1965), 18–19.
[137] *The Voluntary Worker in the Social Services*, par. 22. See also Roger Hadley, Adrian Webb, and Christine Farrell, *Across the Generations: Old People and Young Volunteers* (London: Allen & Unwin, 1975), 6–9, and *50 Million Volunteers: A Report on the Role of Voluntary Organisations and Youth in the Environment* (London: HMSO, 1972), 20.

mid-nineteenth century; but it argued that such persons 'no longer constitute an overwhelming majority of the volunteer force'. Men were playing a larger role, as local surveys at Liverpool, Nottingham, and Portsmouth had shown.[138] Opinion research done for the Wolfenden Committee in September 1976 also revealed that women were no more likely than men to say that they were taking part in voluntary work; nor were women not in employment more likely to be doing this work than women in employment—although the evidence also suggested that those who had worked voluntarily for more than ten hours in the week previous to that in which the poll was taken tended to be women not in employment.[139] As in the past, changing patterns of women's employment were obviously important in determining their involvement in voluntary work.

It is, of course, dangerous to equate the involvement of new groups in voluntary work with the adoption of new ideas and attitudes—or any particular new ideas and attitudes. But the increasing part played by young people would be consistent with the point made by the Aves Committee that a characteristic of current volunteers was a lack of social or financial advantage; and might well also be consistent with the Committee's remark that the 'pioneering drive' in voluntary social work tended to come from 'egalitarians and from those who resent social dysfunctioning and individual misery'.[140] Such points are speculative; but what is true is that, even if more conservative political and social perceptions did not disappear from the voluntary sector, the sector did attract a much more radical and populist constituency than it had done in the past. Ken Worpole has, indeed, argued that the voluntary sector shed the old image of privilege, and of patronizing social attitudes; and he suggests that the mutual-aid and campaigning side of voluntarism, always potentially radical, was now more prominent than the more conservative side of charity and philanthropy. Voluntary effort, he wrote, was 'less and less about flag days, "hospital days" and the home visiting of the poor by the leisured religious wealthy'. It was 'much more about self-organization and mutual aid', which, he argued, was to be seen in 'particular groups of consumers

---

[138] *The Voluntary Worker in the Social Services*, par. 37.
[139] *The Future of Voluntary Organisations*, 34–5; New Society, 40 (7 Apr. 1977), 24–5.   [140] *The Voluntary Worker in the Social Services*, par. 21.

politically aware of the shortcomings of state services'. Thus there was a 'proliferation of self-organized community nurseries, disabled mutual-aid groups, allotment societies, black supplementary schools, women's aid centres, gay counselling services, tenants co-operatives, public transport campaigns, community bookshops, cyclists' action groups'.[141]

This emergence of radical activism was, indeed, a new departure even from the old mutual-aid tradition of trade union and state paternalism; and in that sense it could outflank the position held by the Labour Party, not to mention the Conservatives. In voluntary activity of this kind there was, Worpole felt, natural political support for the Labour Party: support which it had once enjoyed, but which had now turned from political to voluntary effort. Worpole's message for Labour was that—in the words of the title of his article—there were here 'Volunteers for Socialism'.

This leads into a consideration of the ways in which such efforts within the voluntary sector were implemented; and here 'participation' comes into play. The increased presence of young people in the voluntary sector was not, perhaps, without significance in this respect. Younger people were on occasion unwilling to join the more established societies—societies which, themselves, did not allow much scope for participation. The Aves Report noted that some young volunteers working alone regretted the lack of communication with their own headquarters and were critical of the lack of interest shown by their central body in their activities.[142] Under this influence, some of the older-established bodies carried out very extensive internal reorganization. Until 1969 Barnardo's was organized entirely centrally, but subsequently there was a great deal of decentralization into divisions, each under a Children's Officer. Control which was once exercised from the centre was now exercised only after consultation with the divisions.[143] Ball and Chauhan of Barnardo's said in 1990 that their aim was to recruit 'people with initiative and imagination, who can contribute.' They continued, 'We need people with good ideas. Different ideas to provide a pluralistic view of the organization . . . As opposed to the private and public sectors . . . all staff have a more intimate involvement with the

---

[141] 'Volunteers for Socialism' (*New Society*, 55 (29 Jan. 1981), 199–200).

[142] *The Voluntary Worker in the Social Services*, par. 53.

[143] Oral Evidence Presented to the Wolfenden Committee, file O.E.2.

purpose of the enterprise. Participation and involvement are intense . . .'[144]

Similarly, the Samaritans in the mid-1970s gradually developed a regional structure, for which the initiative came from the branches themselves. The Spastics Society remained, as it always had been, a parent-orientated body; and it was only to be expected that those suffering from the disease could not take part in the organization. Yet even here there was a development towards the establishment of clubs for spastics which were self-governing and were gradually bringing some influence to bear on the work of the Society.[145] Gingerbread reported to the Wolfenden Committee on the problems that internal organization could pose;[146] and the representatives of Age Concern commented to the Committee that it was 'inherent in the voluntary movement that there should be a love-hate relationship between the centre and the periphery'.[147]

Again, this was by no means new. Voluntary activity always sat uncomfortably with any directives imposed from a central point. As has been seen, in the nineteenth century there had been a tension between an unorganized and spontaneous expression of voluntary activity on the one hand, and an organized, disciplined, and centralized expression on the other. But the popularity of 'participation' in the 1960s and 1970s made the problem more acute. There might well be, on occasion, an extreme hostility to any formal structure at all. The founder and first director of Task Force, Anthony Steen, said that he hated the very label of his organization. The main concern of Task Force was visiting the elderly; but if he wanted to visit an old lady, did he have to call himself a Task Force volunteer? 'Young people don't want to join anything', he said; '. . . they don't want to be classed. In Task Force they join nothing . . . we are not an organization. If we were, we wouldn't exist.'[148] After Steen's resignation as director in 1968—when he moved to the newly established Young Volunteer Force Foundation—the structure of Task Force did become somewhat more formal and bureaucratic; but in 1970 the organization was still characterized by a form of management which

---

[144] *Graduate* (24 May 1990), 22–3.
[145] Oral Evidence Presented to the Wolfenden Committee, file O.E.7.
[146] Ibid. file O.E.22.   [147] Ibid. file O.E.27.
[148] *New Society*, 6 (14 Oct. 1965), 18–20.

gave scope for considerable participation and decision-making at local level. The new director, Marian Would, was faced with the problem of harmonizing the relationship between the central organization and its local staff.[149]

If 'participation' exacerbated an old problem within the voluntary sector, it also led to problems in the area of the recruitment and training of those who volunteered. This was of primary concern to the Aves Committee; and its Report noted that there was a general tendency to accept the majority of those who volunteered, with very few questions asked; some organizations felt that they could not turn volunteers away and tell them that they were unsuitable.[150] The Aves Report strongly recommended the need for preparation; 'preparation', it advocated, rather than 'training', since the latter could deter potential helpers.[151] Some organizations, in fact, had extensive training programmes; examples were the British Red Cross, the St John Ambulance Brigade, and Citizens' Advice Bureaux.[152] In these areas, where technical knowledge was essential, the need for training was obvious enough; but, in others, where the need for training was less obvious, Aves argued that much more should be done to prepare volunteers for their task and to support and supervise them once they were at work.[153]

Thus a loose structure, added to a lack of adequate training or preparation, could lead to difficulties. An examination of Task Force in 1975[154] found that a great deal of good work had been done under its auspices; but it argued that Task Force had suffered from what might be called 'excessive participation'. It had adopted—in the language of the examination—an 'extensive model'. This had the advantage of being able to assist a large number of people by the mobilization of a large number of volunteers, with only a small full-time staff. But there were also dangers: undirected effort without proper selection procedures or training and difficulties in matching needs with help and subsequent support. A more 'intensive' model would—among other things—identify the most needy among the elderly, assess

[149] Hadley, Webb, and Farrell, *Across the Generations*, 15–18.
[150] *The Voluntary Worker in the Social Services*, par. 123.
[151] Ibid. par. 203.   [152] Ibid. pars. 191, 197.
[153] Ibid. par. 229. The theme of 'Preparation and Training' is dealt with in pars. 184–260.   [154] Hadley, Webb, and Farrell, *Across the Generations, passim.*

the kind of help required, and select and allocate volunteers carefully; another possibility was a 'composite' model, which would attempt to incorporate the advantages of the 'extensive' and the 'intensive' approaches. Those who conducted the examination suggested that Task Force should adopt either the 'intensive' or the 'composite' model in the next phase of its development: a recommendation which, it was recognized, implied an increased measure of central control over the organization's activities. Although based on Task Force, the examination did—as its authors suggested—have a wider application; and the whole issue threw light on the problems to which 'participation' could lead if taken to considerable lengths. It could, indeed, be carried to the point where it conflicted with another feature which the voluntary sector had increasingly developed in the twentieth century as a whole: professionalism.

Jeremy Bugler, writing in *New Society* in 1965, quoted a remark to the effect that the upsurge of voluntary activity was 'the transition from the welfare state—structurally dependent on a relatively small cadre of professional experts—to the conception of a participant society, involving the maximum number in the care of the community'. He posed the question whether this was right. Should there be maximum numbers—'the sky the limit'? 'Were experience and professionalism not preferable to enthusiastic amateurism?'[155] Again, however, the problem was not wholly new; the question had been put before. After all, the Charity Organisation Society had sought to bring a more trained and professional approach to voluntary work, which, as others saw it, tended to conflict with the spontaneous initiative of the active citizen.

Another issue raised by the emphasis on participation related to the question of duplication and lack of coordination. This too was by no means new, but the growth of new organizations exacerbated it. As has already been indicated, some of the voluntary bodies which came on the scene in the 1960s and 1970s entered territory which had not been unoccupied before then. Thus Gingerbread admitted to the Wolfenden Committee that it was doing much the same kind of work as that already done by the National Council for One Parent Families—founded in 1918

[155] Vol. 6 (14 Oct. 1965), 20.

as the National Council for the Unmarried Mother and her Child. But, the Gingerbread representatives continued, it was founded in London and so was exposed to greater publicity than provincial organizations.[156] The National Council, on the other hand, felt that to have two bodies in the field working along similar lines was a serious and wasteful duplication of resources, and mentioned steps which it was taking to work more closely with Gingerbread.[157]

Other examples could be cited. Often, however, coordinated effort was resisted—as it had been in the past. When Anthony Steen of Task Force was asked about a central body to avoid duplication, he said: 'Duplication is rot. Any central organization or committee will delay things for a year.'[158] Alec Dickson, of Voluntary Service Overseas and of Community Service Volunteers, said that the gospel according to St Stephen, the Patron Saint of Westminster and Whitehall, was 'I was an hungered and you offered me liaison facilities! I thirsted and you gave me a co-ordinating committee.' 'We don't need co-ordination,' he said; 'we need stimulation.'[159] Nicholas Hinton, director of the National Council of Social Service—later, in 1980, to become the National Council for Voluntary Organisations, and in itself a body which carried out a coordinating role—admitted that 'if voluntary organisations were true to themselves, they would be the last to subscribe to the notion of superimposed blueprints dreamt up by committees'.[160] The Church of England Children's Society told the Wolfenden Committee that its relationships with other organizations were on the whole good and that amalgamation had been considered; but its view was that, although there had to be a minimum size for any organization to make it viable, on the whole it was better that voluntary organizations should work side by side rather than amalgamate.[161]

The Wolfenden Committee itself was ambivalent on this issue. It admitted that there was criticism of the voluntary sector on grounds of duplication and alleged waste; and it recognized that there was 'a clear need for the voluntary sector to keep a close

---

[156] Oral Evidence Presented to the Wolfenden Committee, file O.E.22.
[157] *The Future of Voluntary Organisations*, 153.
[158] *New Society*, 6 (14 Oct. 1965), 19.   [159] Ibid. 20.
[160] *Health and Social Service Journal*, 2 Dec. 1977.
[161] Oral Evidence Presented to the Wolfenden Committee, file O.E.1.

eye on the possibility of wasteful duplication.'[162] But it also argued that the British were, on the whole, specific and particular in their giving to voluntary bodies and that to amalgamate various organizations to one 'faceless' body might lead to a drop in overall giving.[163] This long-standing problem was not, then, resolved by the voluntary sector in these years—although resolution is probably always impossible to achieve. If anything, however, the problem became more acute.

Thus the voluntary sector was still open to the criticism that it was uneven and patchy in its distribution of resources. Hatch, indeed, commented that 'the supply of voluntary workers tends to be in inverse proportion to need.' He found that it was in middle-class suburbs that the Pre-School Playgroups Association was strongest; and that the branches of the Child Poverty Action Group were coincident less with poor families than with the location of universities.[164] The Wolfenden Committee found that 'an old county town' like Bath, Exeter, Oxford, or Reading was rich in voluntary organizations; on average the ten towns in this category had 1.26 branches per 10,000 population. On the other hand, sixteen towns such as Barnsley, Sheffield, and Sunderland—identified as 'traditional centres of heavy industry and manufacturing'—had only 0.44 branches per 10,000 population. Thus, as the Report put it:

This finding conveys an important point about the nature of the voluntary sector, or at any rate about that part of it dependent on voluntary effort. It is of essence unplanned and spontaneous, and it will not necessarily of itself allocate its energies in accordance with abstract criteria of need or equity. Its resources are not deployed in a way that a beneficent deity or social planner, taking all factors into account, would wish.[165]

Thus social policies which relied on voluntary organizations would, as Hatch says, be 'uneven in their impact'.[166]

Again, this point is very familiar; patchiness and unevenness had long been among the most common arguments deployed against voluntarism. It could, however, be regarded as less serious

---

[162] *The Future of Voluntary Organisations*, 154. See ibid. chs. 6 and 7 for a consideration of the roles of intermediary bodies, both local and national, in—among other things—carrying out 'the functions of liaison'. (p. 144).
[163] Ibid. 191–2.   [164] See Brenton, *Voluntary Sector*, 62.
[165] *The Future of Voluntary Organisations*, 58.
[166] Quoted in Brenton, *Voluntary Sector*, 62.

in this period, since social policies did not rest primarily on voluntary organizations, but on the state. And this was, indeed, regarded as inevitable and desirable by the rekindled voluntary sector itself. The 'new' volunteers found the state to be excessively bureaucratic, but it was, nevertheless, to the state that they looked for improvement; convergence was once again evident. The presence of young people within the voluntary sector was important in this respect. Donnison has pointed out that it was during the 1960s that people who had gained their first formative political experience since World War II came to make up a majority of the electorate.[167] The state had played a dominant part in their lives as the provider of education, medical care, subsidized housing. This new generation looked first to the state in the belief that it could do all things, if made properly aware of them. The Wolfenden Committee noted that voluntary bodies were 'concerned to influence the policies and practices of public authorities', and were willing to accept government funding which could provide a welcome lifeline.[168] In its evidence to the Wolfenden Committee, the Family Welfare Association still showed some signs of the strict ideas which had inspired its nineteenth-century parent, the Charity Organisation Society. The director of the Family Welfare Association still felt it 'undesirable to give charity money indiscriminately' and said that the Association aimed 'to increase self helping methods in client families.' It was under no statutory requirement to offer assistance; and thus, although it would do all that was possible to help a family which requested assistance, it could refuse to help a family which did not want—or resisted—help.[169] Yet even the Association, for all its assertion of freedom from statutory obligation, told the Wolfenden Committee that it had a valid claim on government funds.[170]

If a voluntary body which traced its origin to the Charity Organisation Society was willing to look to the state for money—thereby continuing a trend which had long been evident in the Society—this was much more true of the multitude of voluntary organizations which came into existence in the 1960s and 1970s. Often inspired by left-wing thinkers and supported by young

[167] *Politics of Poverty*, 126.   [168] *The Future of Voluntary Organisations*, 185.
[169] Oral Evidence Presented to the Wolfenden Committee, file O.E.33.
[170] Written Evidence Presented to the Wolfenden Committee, file W.E.188.

persons, they were, even if critical of the Welfare State, naturally state-orientated. Organizations such as the Child Poverty Action Group and Age Concern called for radical redistributive measures, financed out of increased and progressive taxation. Shelter —as has been mentioned—was a pressure group directed at the state to provide more housing. Des Wilson, recalling in 1990 his activities with Shelter in the 1960s, wrote that it was enough to say 'look, this is wrong. It was for the government to come up with solutions'.[171] This was also true of the various trusts. Thus Lewis Waddilove has written:

Foundations concerned with social policy—and the Joseph Rowntree Memorial Trust was among the largest and most influential—responded strongly to [the] 'interventionist' philosophy and powerfully reinforced it. 'Foundations like Nuffield, Gulbenkian and the Rowntree Trusts', David Donnison has written of this period [the mid-fifties to the mid-seventies] 'along with their counterparts overseas like Ford, were competing with each other to find innovative proposals for social research and social action to support. Although we prided ourselves on our independence', he writes of a research institution of which he was the head, 'we were in fact closely linked to the development of the public sector of the economy and the professions within it.' David Donnison might equally well have applied the comment to the Foundations to which, in part, he looked for support.[172]

This pattern of convergence, however, as Donnison recognized, raised the issue of identity and independence—again by no means a new one. It was, in part, solved by an increasing tendency for the voluntary sector to adopt an innovative and specialist role; 'increasing', because, of course, the tendency was already well established. The Church of England Children's Society set up an internal working party in 1970 to reconsider its traditional role of running residential homes.[173] They were ever more costly to run; but changes in local government and in social habits also affected their position. There were fewer referrals from local authorities for residential care: 30,000 in 1967, dropping to 20,000 in 1970. Also, the percentage of unmarried mothers who kept their

---

[171] *Sunday Times*, 24 June 1990.

[172] *Private Philanthropy* 220. See also Owen, *English Philanthropy*, 554–72. In considering applications, the Leverhulme Trustees took into account whether they had already been made to statutory bodies.

[173] Oral Evidence Presented to the Wolfenden Committee, file O.E.1.

babies rose from about 30 per cent to 45 per cent in the same period. Information was gathered from workers in the field and from other voluntary organizations, government departments, and local authorities; and this pointed to the need for change. The Society therefore decided that it should move its emphasis from residential to day care. As a result, the number of residential homes dropped from a hundred to sixty-eight; and the remaining accommodation was devoted in large measure to handicapped children.

This involved a reassessment of role. There were no staff redundancies; and although some of the Society's members found it hard to accept the new ideas, on the whole—as the representatives told the Wolfenden Committee—the changes were taken well: 'In general the Society welcomes its freedom and ability to provide new and specialized services and considers this more important than providing an alternative service to that undertaken by the statutory side.'[174] These new services included dealing with the needs of 'latchkey' children, and carrying out experiments with teenage care.

Similarly, Barnardo's—always an organization chiefly concerned with providing residential homes for children—decided in the mid-1960s to reduce this side of its work and to change its emphasis to the provision of day centres and other forms of social work service. This began in 1969/70 and involved the closing of many residential homes. The remaining residential homes offered a specialized service to physically and mentally handicapped children and those who were in some way 'disturbed'. Barnardo's representatives who appeared before the Wolfenden Committee said that running residential homes for 'normal' children was, the Society felt, something which could be done by the statutory side; Barnardo's role had to be a more specialized one, such as caring for maladjusted children or, again, 'latchkey' children—or running day centres in needy areas where the community regularly made visits, rather than the '"old-style" beautifully run nursery'.[175] Lord Windlesham, who was appointed minister of state in the Home Office in the Heath government in 1972 as coordinating minister for voluntary social services, and who had a personal interest in voluntary organizations, commented on

----

[174] Ibid.   [175] Ibid. file O.E.2.

the changes in Barnardo's: 'the management and fund-raising functions also underwent radical overhaul. None of this was accomplished without internal friction and dissent, but the result was to reshape a large and deeply rooted voluntary organization and to re-define its aim in terms of the needs of present day society.'[176]

Here, then, the voluntary sector achieved 'identity' within a pluralist system of social welfare by increasingly concentrating on specialist activities—and not attempting to provide an alternative service to that provided by the state. The representatives of the Royal National Institute for the Blind told the Wolfenden Committee that their society did not see itself as competing with state services, which were mainly channelled through local authorities, but as filling gaps which the state could not deal with locally. These included the provision of cash grants and charitable pensions. They pointed out, indeed, that, as a result of the reorganization of the social services after the Seebohm recommendations, the local teaching and visiting service was abolished by the great majority of local authorities before any effective replacement was provided. This left a real gap in provision for the blind, and the Institute had been overwhelmed with letters about the problem. The situation had improved, but it still gave cause for concern.[177]

Yet, as Donnison clearly realized, this more specialist and limited role did not solve all the problems of identity and independence. There could, indeed, be ambiguity of role and identity, especially where a voluntary organization combined a variety of activities, such as 'quasi-statutory' provider of services and pressure group. Such a combination could make it more effective; but it could also raise conflicts of interest. As has been seen, many voluntary organizations obtained funds from central or local government, in the form both of grants and of fees and charges for services rendered. These funds tended to make up a greater proportion of their income in the 1970s. Judith Unell has calculated, on the basis of sixty-five voluntary organizations, that voluntary giving—in the form of subscriptions, donations, legacies, appeals, and so on—decreased from 51.38 per cent of

---

[176] Quoted in Brenton, *Voluntary Sector*, 40.
[177] Oral Evidence Presented to the Wolfenden Committee, file O.E.1.

income in 1970/1 to 47.15 per cent in 1975/6; whereas government grants, added to fees and charges, increased as a proportion of income from 34.14 per cent in 1970/1 to 40.79 per cent in 1975/6.[178] It is true that voluntary giving under this sample remained at a high level of approximately 50 per cent; and this carried with it freedom of movement and absence of external constraint. Yet this source of income declined as a proportion of the total. More particularly, the total income of Barnardo's between 1969 and 1980 showed a decline in the proportion of income derived from voluntary contributions; from 31 per cent in 1969 to 19 per cent in 1974 and 23 per cent in 1980. The proportion of total income from local authorities increased from 15 per cent in 1969 to 19 per cent in 1974 and 44 per cent in 1980.[179]

This increased dependence on public funding brought in a more assured and reliable income—but also raised familiar problems of identity and independence. If a voluntary organization received a substantial proportion of income from a statutory body, this might compromise its role as a pressure group on government or as a critic of government. The evidence given by Barnardo's representatives to the Wolfenden Committee dwelt on these possible clashes of role. They admitted that their society did not, perhaps, pay enough attention to the role of the critic. But they continued: 'It could be said that an organisation with close links to the statutory side must be careful in how far it went in the direction of critic since so much depended on good relationships. Too destructive criticism could well be counterproductive.'[180]

The Wolfenden Committee also explored this matter. In a 'Note' prepared for the Committee on 'Government Departments and Voluntary Organisations', and published as an appendix, the point was made that most government departments made every effort to ensure that a voluntary organization retained its essential individuality and independence, however great the degree of government funding. Yet it was recognized that 'the increasing extent

---

[178] Quoted in Brenton, *Voluntary Sector*, 65.   [179] Quoted ibid. 77.
[180] Oral Evidence Presented to the Wolfenden Committee, file O.E.2. Ball and Chauhan of Barnardo's observed in 1990 a 'certain irony in the fact that we're still trying to solve some of the problems that (Barnardo) was last century. Now we establish standards for, and share the burden with, the state.' They emphasized the point that campaigning was a 'new avenue'. (*Graduate* (24 May 1990), 21.)

to which voluntary bodies seem to be turning to statutory services, both central and local, for funding does have implications for their independence which cannot be ignored . . . There is . . . a very real dilemma between the need to obtain an assured income and the need to maintain a separate identity independent of government.'[181]

This point was reinforced by the information provided in another appendix to the Wolfenden Committee Report: 'Trends in Voluntary Giving'. The information showed a sharp decline in voluntary giving since 1974. 'Whether this is part of a long-term decline', the appendix ran, '. . . is more difficult to tell.' Thus the Committee saw a 'relative deterioration of the voluntary sector' as 'indisputable'.[182]

It may be that Wolfenden's analysis of trends in voluntary giving was too pessimistic; and it was criticized in these terms. But the point which the Wolfenden Committee made was recognized as posing a dilemma for the voluntary sector, which—yet again—was not new: that of claiming to be independent from the state and yet being dependent on the state for money. Indeed, Colin Ball, who worked in the Voluntary Services Unit between 1975 and 1977 and drafted material for the Wolfenden Committee, wrote in *Community Care* in 1979 that there was no such thing as a 'real voluntary sector'. A very large part of 'so-called voluntary action', he wrote, 'was simply delivering certain services or values . . . as a glorified sub-contractor . . . At best they were "quasi-statutory".' The only distinctive feature of the 'quasis', in his view, was that they were sometimes—but not always—poorer. The less well-off organizations found it difficult to attract and retain staff. In words which were somewhat reminiscent of C. S. Loch's comments in 1913 about charities taking shelter with the state 'like creatures in a storm', Ball wrote that they 'drew ever closer to the government departments, ever further away from their constituents. They jostle and manoeuvre for power and influence, rapaciously self interested in the size, not just of their grant, but of their ascendancy.' He concluded that the voluntary organizations had lost their ability to do things in a distinctively different way from statutory services. 'Pluralism',

---

[181] *The Future of Voluntary Organisations*, 229–30. See also ibid. 148–52.
[182] Ibid. 259–60.

he wrote, is lots of different teams, but all playing the same game.'[183]

Such an argument may be somewhat overdrawn; but it was important, and often repeated. In 1977 *New Society* asked whether voluntary organizations were a 'healthy antidote to the rigidity of statutory services and a central pillar of the pluralist society or a silly appendage which serves merely to relieve the state of a few responsibilities'. It concluded that their recent history showed that they had been increasingly integrated into the statutory services of the Welfare State as 'satellites of it'. The article continued: 'The great proliferation of new groups revealing new needs has in effect overgrown the limited provision of the statutory services, but at the same time rooted itself in the old structure, in seeking financial support. In the future, the distinction between voluntary and statutory may effectively disappear; it's already blurred.'[184]

Thus, despite the revival of the voluntary sector, the old issues of its divergence from or convergence with the state did not disappear; and questions of identity and independence remained. The Wolfenden Committee itself illustrated the ambivalence. It praised the voluntary sector for being spontaneous, flexible, and innovative, with an ability to call on fresh extra-statutory resources in voluntary work and voluntary loyalties. It urged voluntary organizations to 'maintain, improve and extend the vital contribution which they are making to the pluralistic system of social provision'.[185] Yet the Report did not argue for any contraction of the state; indeed quite the reverse. It affirmed belief in a dominant role for the state. 'We believe it to be generally accepted', it ran, 'that statutory bodies have the ultimate responsibility for planning and provision of social services and for looking at the needs of the areas they serve as a whole ...'[186] The state had the advantage of ensuring universal coverage, achieving equity and maintaining standards, and integrating planning; this would offset the unevenness and patchiness of the voluntary sector. The state was, therefore, 'the central strategic [maker] of social policy', and it should take an urgent initiative 'in working out with the variety of agencies which are now operating in this

[183] *Community Care*, 22 Feb. 1979.   [184] Vol. 42 (24 Nov. 1977), 394.
[185] *The Future of Voluntary Organisations*, 193.   [186] Ibid. 95.

field, a collaborative social plan which will make the optimum and maximum use of resources'.[187] Central government should, indeed, through the Department of the Environment, put intermediary bodies in urban areas on to a more secure financial basis. Shared between central and local government, the cost of this might be £2.5 million per annum.[188] *New Society* thought it paradoxical that the Wolfenden Committee should call for an expansion of voluntary effort—and yet call on the state to help finance it.[189]

Other voices were also raised in criticism.[190] Terry Philpot, writing in *Municipal Review* in January 1978, said that the Report, 'major document' though it was, simply recognized, in general terms, the 'conflicts that [might] result from greater official funding', but did not fully deal with them. Shelter's director, Neil McIntosh, argued that the great danger in Wolfenden's request for more state money was the loss of ability to criticize central and local government. More generally, it was felt that, amidst its advocacy of welfare pluralism, the Report lacked any clear definition of the future role and identity of the voluntary sector. Vivien Stern, director of the National Association for the Care and Resettlement of Offenders, criticized the lack of any comprehensive strategy; and she felt that the Committee's report would 'no doubt disappoint those who had expected a set of clear, imaginative, coherent proposals for a new deal for voluntary organizations'. Even those, she said, 'who were looking for no more than a re-definition or clarification of the role of voluntary organizations in the Welfare State will find little to satisfy them'.

The Wolfenden Committee, therefore, tended to fudge the old problem of trying to reconcile the divergent and convergent relationships between the voluntary sector and the state. Age Concern's director, David Hobman, wrote that 'if Wolfenden had anything new to say, it is extremely difficult to find it'. This comment may be rather unfair. The Committee *did* see a role for voluntary organizations as an alternative to statutory services where this was appropriate. It was not appropriate, it felt, in areas such as hospitals or social security; but it already was appropriate, and could be more so, in the residential, domiciliary,

---

[187] Ibid. 193.   [188] Ibid. chs. 6 and 7 and p. 179.
[189] Vol. 42 (24 Nov. 1977), 394.
[190] Those which follow are quoted in *Health and Social Service Journal*, 2 Dec. 1977.

and day-care fields, where the voluntary sector could provide a choice to the client. Equally, the Committee argued that there should be a 'less automatic assumption of statutory responsibility' in the future.[191] Yet the ambivalence remained between asserting a separate role for the voluntary sector and arguing that this should, in some measure, be paid for by the state. Moreover, the problem was not to disappear in the future. In 1984 the Charities Aid Foundation reported that, although charities had increased their income, they were becoming increasingly dependent on non-voluntary sources of funding, including fees and charges for their services, and higher levels of statutory grants. In 1975 it was estimated that charitable contributions from private individuals amounted to almost one-third of charities' total income; in 1984, it was little more than one-tenth. The Charities Aid Foundation concluded that, unless the balance of voluntary funding were restored, voluntarists would come to believe that charity had been 'hijacked' by the state.[192]

There were, indeed, other conflicts and ambiguities of identity. There was not only the point about the dangers of 'biting the hand that fed' voluntary organizations; there was also the question of accounting for the funds which were fed to them. The maintenance of accountability to grant-givers meant ensuring that such grants were properly used for the purposes for which they were given. This could well be an issue governing voluntary-statutory relations, especially at local level; and it, too, raised the question of the independence and autonomy of voluntary organizations.[193] Again, if charities charged fees for their services, this clearly was a divergence from their altruistic and charitable origins; they were, thereby, cutting themselves off from their most needy clients. This was another long-standing problem—and one that was not to recede.

Finally, there was the very large issue of the conflict between charitable status—and the advantages which this bestowed in terms of tax relief—and the obstacles which this posed to indulgence in political activity: or conversely, the bar to charitable status imposed by political activity. Under Charity Law, any activity which has as its purpose the changing of political

---

[191] *The Future of Voluntary Organisations*, 187–8.
[192] *The Times*, 25 July 1984.
[193] See Hatch and Mocroft, *Components of Welfare*, 60–80.

structures or policies by pressure or propaganda is judged to be political—and therefore non-charitable. A Charity Commissioner has been quoted as saying that 'the role of the charity is to bind up the wounds of society. That is what they get their fiscal privileges for. To build up a new society is for someone else.'[194] Thus charitable status can be granted only if the primary purpose of the charity is non-political, non-propagandist, and non-campaigning—although such status can be conferred if political and campaigning activities are ancillary to charitable purposes, and kept in subordination to them. Thus the Child Poverty Action Group and Age Concern, both of which indulge in lobbying, campaigning, and exerting pressure, enjoy charitable status, whereas Amnesty International, an overtly campaigning body acting on behalf of prisoners of conscience, does not.

This too was by no means a new issue; but it became more prominent in this period as voluntary organizations of a radical disposition developed—and as Third-World issues became prominent. Demands for a change in Charity Law were frequently voiced, and recommendations made for such a change. One of these emanated from the Goodman Committee on Charity Law and Voluntary Organisations of 1976, which called for freshly formulated guidelines, setting out the scope of permissible political activity. This was a fairly modest proposal—which did not go far enough for one of the members of the Committee, Ben Whittaker, who submitted a Minority Report in words which were rather reminiscent of those used in the late nineteenth century about the ameliorative, and thus limited, nature of charity:

it is not only the right but in fact the duty of charities in many areas to act as political pressure groups, and . . . legislation must end the present uncertainty about this forthwith. The days of confining charities to pouring soup into faulty old bottles should be consigned to the past; such cosmetic philanthropy can in fact be capable of postponing the more fundamental reforms that may be needed . . .[195]

The Revd Kenneth Slack, then director of Christian Aid—which does enjoy charitable status—complained in 1980 that Christian Aid had been subjected to 'intense and sustained inquiries' over

---

[194] Quoted in Francis Gladstone, *Charity Law and Social Justice* (London: Bedford Square Press, 1982), 88. See also Brenton, *Voluntary Sector*, for a consideration of this area.   [195] Quoted in Brenton, *Voluntary Sector*, 252.

the support which it had given to various human rights projects; and, like Whittaker, said that the law restricted charities to what could be seen as the 'discredited "soup-kitchen" approach' and hindered them from 'tackling the root causes of poverty and distress, such as injustice and social conflict'.[196] Francis Gladstone, writing in 1982, said that 'charity cannot rest content simply to drop pennies in collecting tins, ignoring social injustice and oppression'.[197] Despite such appeals, however, governments have proved unwilling to change the law, influenced in part by the fear that any relaxation would result in the emergence of political parties camouflaged as charities.

Thus while the ideology of the voluntary sector in the 1960s and 1970s did show signs of new perceptions, its implementation betrayed many familiar features. A desire for increased participation could put strains on an organized and disciplined approach, and could conflict with professionalism and training. A heightened perception of social need could lead to the formation of duplicating and overlapping bodies, and by no means always meant that voluntary agencies were in place where they were most needed. An uneven and patchy spread remained a problem. An acceptance of a pluralist system of social welfare could result in the adoption of a more specialist role in meeting social needs, but could also involve ambiguities of identity, especially where such activities were substantially funded by the state.

In its revival, then, the voluntary sector showed, on the one hand, all its familiar characteristics of energy, innovativeness, spontaneity, and flexibility in discovering new needs—and on the other, diffuseness, incoherence, and, in its relations with the state, some degree of ambivalence in meeting them. The voluntary sector still prided itself on its independence and, at the same time, accepted that it required the resources of the Welfare State to realize its potential and, in some cases, even to ensure its survival.

IV

It has been seen that one of the reasons for the revival of the voluntary sector in the 1960s and 1970s was a realization that the

---

[196] *Church Times*, 18 Apr. 1980.　　[197] *Charity Law*, 171.

state *could* not cope with all the demands made on it, and required to make use of the resources of the voluntary sector. As has been shown, one factor contributing to this realization, which made itself felt in both major political parties, was the onset of economic problems in the early and mid-1970s, sparked off, in part, by the oil crisis of 1973 and manifested in high inflation, high unemployment, and slow rates of economic growth. This raised the whole question of the level of public expenditure, which—despite criticisms of the inadequacies of welfare provision—increased markedly in the period. Government expenditure on social security, the personal social services, health, education, and housing increased from 16 per cent of Gross National Product in 1951 to 24 per cent in 1971; and in 1975 it reached 29 per cent, accounting in that year for half of all public expenditure.[198] By 1977, 14 million people were receiving benefits—almost double the figure for 1951. This expansion was paid for mainly through direct taxation and National Insurance contributions; and taxation had, in fact, expanded since 1945 to include, by the 1970s, some 85 per cent of the entire population. Taxation, therefore, bore not only on those with high and average incomes, but on those significantly below this level. Capital, too, made its contribution; by 1975 companies were paying 18 per cent of the state's total tax revenue, exclusive of local rates. A further resource to finance public expenditure was borrowing; and between 1971 and 1975, government borrowing increased to £11 billion per year to cover the gap between state revenues and state expenditure.

This whole process gave rise to a critique of Welfare State provision from the New Right. As has been noted, there was a long-standing belief that increased welfare provision by the state would lead to a fitter and stronger workforce—and a more buoyant economy. By the mid-1970s the belief grew that welfare expenditure was, in fact, a hindrance to economic growth. Wealth production, which was seen as essential to economic regeneration, was being stifled by high levels of public expenditure—and the incentives to wealth production were blunted by the high level of taxation necessary to finance that public expenditure. Not only, moreover, was it a case of the state being unable to

[198] Dearlove and Saunders, *Introduction,* 394.

cope with a level of demand which was virtually without limit; its very attempts to meet that demand were felt by the New Right to be extremely harmful. The idea of 'overload' grew.[199] This was based on a recognition that modern governments had undertaken greatly increased responsibilities—and no longer had sufficient resources to meet the range of activities now expected of them. A considerable proportion of this 'overload' derived from the kind of public welfare provision made since 1945— where, indeed, public expenditure was based not on expectation but on those entitlements seen to be an integral part of citizenship. Moreover, bound up with the process was the existence of interest groups—in particular, trade unions—which increased the pressure on governments and gave them little room for manoeuvre, and virtually no room for retrenchment, as wage settlements mounted in scope. A further refinement of the argument was that governments which could not deliver what they promised, what was expected of them, and what, indeed, they were obliged to deliver, lost mass confidence and support; and were affected by a 'crisis of legitimacy'.

To the New Right, therefore, the state *could* not cope with the growth in its activities which had been engendered by a combination of what were popularly known as 'Beveridgism' and 'Keynesianism'; it had become overloaded to the extent that it was inefficient and ineffective. As welfare had become politicized into a matter of winning or losing votes, the 'political market' operated; it was just as competitive as the economic market, but its effects were felt by the New Right to be disastrous—and especially damaging to the economic market itself.[200] Just as the appetite of charities for funds had always been virtually unappeasable, so too was the appetite of the state; but attempts to satisfy the state's appetite were much more damaging, since the public expenditure involved put immense strains on productive capacity and wealth creation in the nation as a whole.

Furthermore, it was argued that public money itself was being wasted, misdirected, and abused. Concern about 'scrounging' was by no means new and had a long history; it had permeated

[199] A. King, 'Overload: Problems of Governing in the 1970s', *Political Studies*, xxiii (1975) 284–96.

[200] Ramesh Mishra, *The Welfare State in Crisis: Social Thought and Social Change* (Brighton: Wheatsheaf Books, 1984), 29.

the Report of the Royal Commission on the Poor Law of 1834, which gave details of individuals who had claimed poor relief in several parishes and who had developed the practice of 'living off the parish' into an art. Similarly, these ideas were present in the Charity Organisation Society, with its efforts to check on fraudulence, and, as has also been seen, there had been criticism of the dole in the 1930s on the grounds that it led to 'scrounging'. In the 1970s the problem was identified once again—and attracted considerable publicity in the press. The case of an unemployed Liverpudlian, Derek Deevey, was widely reported in 1976. Deevey was charged with obtaining supplementary benefit under false pretences, and, in the course of the trial, estimated that he had fraudulently claimed £36,000. The press seized on the incident and drew particular attention to Deevey's expensive and extravagant tastes. The Conservative MP Ian Sproat constantly repeated the theme of scrounging and sponging on the Welfare State. He claimed that the Deevey case was 'only the tip of the iceberg'.[201]

This, then, caused something of a 'welfare backlash'—directed against the bureaucrats and officials, who seemed to be distributing public largesse with little or no supervision—and against the recipients, clearly labelled as parasitic, malingering, and undeserving. The old classification of 'deserving' and 'undeserving' re-emerged. The point about inefficiency and slackness was also highlighted by other well-publicized incidents. The death of Maria Colwell in 1973, and other similar cases in the years which followed, were seen as exposing inefficiency on the part of social workers and social services or works departments. In 1980 the *Daily Mail* wrote that 'yet another baby had died because of the stupidity and neglect of professional social workers'.[202] In all of this comment, there was evidence of further disenchantment with the 'professionals' of the Welfare State, who were seen to be incompetent or uncaring—or both.

Much of this comment, it is true, was at journalistic level; and the extent to which it symbolized a 'backlash' against the Welfare State is open to question. Yet it tended to strengthen the hand of those who argued that circumstances—the economic

---

[201] Wicks, *A Future for All*, 46. See also Golding and Middleton, *Images of Welfare* (Oxford: Martin Robertson, 1982), 62 ff.

[202] Wicks, *A Future for All*, 47.

problems which beset the country in the 1970s, and the way in which they could be said to be aggravated by public expenditure and its distribution—compelled a reappraisal of the role of the state: a reappraisal which would reduce overload and eliminate waste. This particular wave of disenchantment with the 'welfare professionals' was used not to spur them into being more active and altruistic, as in the 1960s, but to put the case for a drastic reduction in their numbers and powers.

Yet it was not only the pressure of circumstances which compelled some degree of reassessment of the role of the state; it was also the pressure of convictions. To the New Right, indeed, not only *could* the state not deliver all the services expected or required of it, but equally it *should* not do so. Such convictions were not entirely new. As has been seen, there was a long tradition of libertarian, anti-collectivist thought in Britain, evident, for example, in the writings of Herbert Spencer and in the activities of the strictest upholders of the Charity Organisation Society. Spencer wrote in 1868, in words which anticipated the sentiments just mentioned: 'Government is regarded as having unlimited powers joined with unlimited resources; and political speeches make the rustic think of it as an earthly providence which can do anything for him if interested men will let it . . . He does not see that he can have the mess of pottage only by surrendering his birthright.'[203]

The interference by a centralized, planned state with the freedom of the individual was a consistent theme in Spencer's writings; and, at a much later date, this was also true of the writings of F. A. Hayek, Robert Nozick, and Milton Friedman.[204] Even if often expressed from afar, their ideas in favour of the free play of market forces, within the framework of a minimal state which guaranteed and facilitated the proper conduct of the market, gained currency in British New Right circles in the 1960s and 1970s. In a British context, Enoch Powell wrote in 1965 that the market 'was the subtlest and most efficient system mankind has

---

[203] Quoted in John Clarke, Allen Cochrane, and Carol Smart, *Ideologies of Welfare: From Dreams to Disillusion* (London: Hutchinson, 1987), 29.

[204] See e.g. Hayek, *The Constitution of Liberty* (London: Routledge & Kegan Paul, 1960); Nozick, *Anarchy, State and Utopia* (Oxford: Basil Blackwell, 1974); and Friedman, *Capitalism and Freedom* (Chicago: University of Chicago Press, 1962).

yet devised for setting effort and resources to their best economic use'.[205]

Publications of this kind, then, argued that the state not only *could* not, but *should* not undertake extensive duties; nor should it make promises to do so. The tendency in New Right thought was to suggest that the state should concentrate on doing what it did best: creating the conditions and the climate in which the individual could practise self-help. Anything else reduced choice and created dependency. Thus Rhodes Boyson, writing in a collection of articles which he edited in 1971, *Down with the Poor*, commented that:

A state which does for its citizens what they can do for themselves is an evil state; and a state which removes all choice and responsibility from its people and makes them like broiler hens will create the irresponsible society. In such an irresponsible society, no-one cares, no-one saves, no-one bothers—why should they when the state spends all its energies taking money away from the energetic, successful and thrifty to give to the idle, the failures and the feckless? . . . A man will grow to full moral maturity only when he is allowed to take risks, with subsequent rewards and penalties and full responsibility for his decisions. Yet in Britain, the state now decides how half or more of a man's income shall be spent, how his family should be educated, how their health care should be organised, how they shall save for misfortunes and retirement, what library and in many cases what cultural provision they should receive, and where and at what cost they should be housed.[206]

Such sentiments, expressed early in the 1970s, gained converts in the ranks of the Conservative Party as the decade progressed. One of the most notable of these was Sir Keith Joseph, who, indeed, claimed that he had been 'converted to Conservatism' in April 1974; he had thought, he said, that he was already a Conservative, but now he could see that he was not really one at all. The titles of two volumes of his speeches showed evidence of the change. In 1975 there came *Reversing the Trend: A Critical Reappraisal of Conservative Economic and Social Policies*; and this was followed in 1976 by *Stranded on the Middle Ground*, which made play with the title of Macmillan's book of 1938 advocating a 'middle position' between *laissez-faire* and socialism. 'It is clear', wrote Sir Keith, 'that the middle ground was not a secure base

---

[205] Quoted in Rodney Barker, *Political Ideas in Modern Britain* (London: Methuen, 1978), 191–2.
[206] Quoted in Clarke, Cochrane, and Smart, *Ideologies of Welfare*, 133.

but a slippery slope to socialism and state control.' Taking up the issue of the role of government, he wrote: 'When we oppose the kind of interference that socialists advocate, we are not denying the importance of what governments and governments alone can do. We are advocating a particular conception of government as a maker of rules for men who want to fashion their lives for themselves.'[207]

Here again was a plea not for a total absence of the statutory sector, but for such a presence as would allow much greater freedom for individual effort. Later, in 1986, in a preface to an abridged edition of Samuel Smiles's *Self-Help*, Sir Keith wrote that the 'pendulum of welfare—however benignly intended—has swung counter-productively'. The further it moved towards the state, the 'more relevant the philosophy of self-help becomes'. Thus to him, the Welfare State could 'only sensibly aspire to provide a base on which the individual can build. It was not intended to create dependency. Private savings and private provision are crucial still, morally and socially . . .' Smiles's *Self-Help*, if 'deeply expressive of the spirit of its own times', was also 'a book for *our* times'.[208]

The 'New Right', then, wished to get off the 'collective train'. Mrs Thatcher, considerably influenced by Sir Keith's views, became an ever more ardent enthusiast for disembarking. In 1975, the year in which she became leader of the Conservative Party, she told the United Nations that 'amidst our . . . difficulties a vital new debate is beginning, or perhaps an old debate is being renewed, about the proper role of government, the Welfare State and the attitudes on which it rests'.[209] In 1979, the year in which the Conservatives under Thatcher's leadership came to power, she said that it was 'Time to change the approach to what governments can do for people and to what people can do for themselves: time to shake off the self-doubt induced by decades of dependence on the State as master, not as servant'.[210] Later, in 1986, Thatcher ascribed the Conservatives' electoral victory of

[207] *Stranded on the Middle Ground: Reflections on Circumstances and Policies* (London: Centre for Policy Studies, 1976), 70.

[208] Samuel Smiles, *Self-Help with Illustrations of Conduct and Perseverance*, abridged by George Bull, with an Introduction by Sir Keith Joseph, Bt., MP (Harmondsworth: Penguin Books, 1986), 10–11, 16.

[209] Quoted in Clarke, Cochrane, and Smart, *Ideologies of Welfare*, 18.

[210] Quoted in Martin Loney, David Boswell, and John Clarke, *Social Policy and Social Welfare* (Milton Keynes: Open University Press, 1983), 54.

1979 to a sense among the British people that socialism had been leading them into 'a life of debilitating dependency on the state, when what they really wanted was the independence and freedom of self-reliance and responsibility'.[211] And in 1988, addressing the General Assembly of the Church of Scotland, the prime minister said that while Christians might often genuinely disagree on 'what kind of political and social institutions we should have',

what is certain . . . is that any set of social and economic arrangements which is not founded on the acceptance of individual responsibility will do nothing but harm. We are all responsible for our own actions . . . The politicians and other secular powers should strive by their measures to bring out the good in people and to fight down the bad: but they can't create one or abolish the other. They can only see that the laws encourage the best instincts and convictions of the people, instincts and convictions which I am convinced are far more deeply rooted than is often supposed . . . intervention by the state must never become so great that it effectively removes personal responsibility . . .[212]

The New Right in Britain, therefore, placed increased emphasis on non-statutory forms of welfare; and the voluntary sector could well fit into this pattern. As early, indeed, as 1979, Patrick Jenkin told a group of voluntary organization directors that 'As the Government sets about tasks for which it was elected—cutting income tax, cutting public spending and curbing the burgeoning bureaucracies of the public sector, we shall be looking to the voluntary movement to take up more of the running'.[213] In 1980 he stated at the Conservative Party Conference that there was a new consensus on the 'role of the volunteer'. He claimed that for most people in Britain that role was 'honourable and infinitely worth while', and that 'most sensible members of the Labour Party' now took that view. 'It was not always so,' he continued. 'It is not so long since Labour used to talk disparagingly about charity. They saw volunteers as a regrettable necessity, to be tolerated only until the day dawned when the state would take over. The fact that these alien voices are now stilled means that we have won a crucial political argument.'[214]

[211] Quoted in Desmond S. King, *The New Right: Politics, Markets and Citizenship* (London: Macmillan, 1987), 123.   [212] *Observer*, 22 May 1988.
[213] Quoted in Brenton, *Voluntary Sector*, 146.   [214] Quoted ibid. 139.

That kind of statement was, indeed, consistent with a pluralistic viewpoint—in the sense of a diversity of social provision, which encompassed a major role for the state. Jenkin also said that voluntary bodies would be brought 'into a close and continuing partnership with the statutory services so planning, financing, and operations can be undertaken jointly to the great advantage of everyone concerned'.[215] Voluntary organizations were 'not a substitute for state provision' but were additional to them. This theme of partnership between voluntary and statutory bodies was also advanced by the Community Affairs Department of the Conservative Central Office, which issued a paper entitled *We are Richer than We Think*; this gave examples of constructive partnership between the voluntary sector and the state.[216]

Yet this approach tended, under the auspices of the New Right, to harden into a rather different kind of pluralism: one which wished to reduce the role of the state and advance the role of the voluntary sector—not as a supplement to the state but as an alternative to it. That accorded well with the desire to reduce public expenditure. Jenkin's position moved perceptibly in this direction from about 1980 onwards. He saw the future of the statutory services not as 'the main provider of care' but 'rather as a source of enjoyment and stimulus to the community's own resources'.[217] Later, in 1981, he developed this line of argument, which saw the state as performing an 'enabling' or a 'gap-filling' role; and Thatcher, addressing the Women's Royal Voluntary Service, adopted much the same approach. She saw 'the volunteer movement . . . at the heart of all our social welfare provision'; the statutory services were 'the supportive ones underpinning where necessary, filling gaps and helping the helpers'. She told her audience that 'we politicians and administrators must not forget that the state has a limited role' and the 'willingness of men and women to give service is one of freedom's greatest safeguards. It ensures that caring remains free from political control.'[218]

The theme of 'caring' was, indeed, also stressed. Individual responsibility did not necessarily stop at taking responsibility for oneself; it extended to looking after others, and not leaving this

---

[215] Quoted ibid.   [216] Quoted ibid. 140.
[217] Quoted ibid. 143.   [218] Quoted ibid. 143–4.

task to other people. Thatcher spoke glowingly of Victorian philanthropy in 1977—and eleven years later told the General Assembly of the Church of Scotland that 'we simply cannot delegate the exercise of mercy and generosity to others'.[219] Douglas Hurd said that 'individualism is not a narrow or a selfish thing . . . it's not so that we can pile up individual masses of individual wealth, little mountains of wealth, but so that the community as a whole is a more decent place'.[220] Malcolm Rifkind claimed in 1989 that 'freedom of the individual to pursue his career and benefit his family and the community lie at the very heart of Conservative philosophy'.[221]

Here, then, was clear support for the voluntary sector and for charitable activity within it. A White Paper of 1989, *Charities: A Framework for the Future*, stated that the Government was committed

to encouraging a healthy and growing voluntary sector. The impulse to help others in need or distress, or to join with them for some common purpose, is deeply rooted in human nature. Joining in voluntary activity helps to create a sense of belonging and of community, at home, in the work place or at recreation. For many people engaging in voluntary activity is a most important way for people to make a positive contribution to the community and have an influence on it.[222]

The White Paper also singled out the voluntary sector's 'practical grass roots experience, its ability to respond swiftly and flexibly to changing needs and circumstances and, perhaps above all, its capacity to innovate. In this sense enterprise and voluntary activity go hand in hand.'[223]

If the voluntary sector received the blessing of the New Right, the commercial sector was also entirely compatible with its belief in enterprise. Thatcher reminded the General Assembly of the Church of Scotland in 1988 that St Paul had told the Thessalonians, 'if a man will not work he shall not eat'; and that Timothy was 'warned by St Paul that anyone who neglects to provide for his own house (meaning his own family) has disowned the faith and is "worse than an infidel"'.[224] Malcolm Rifkind, addressing the

---

[219] *Observer*, 22 May 1988.   [220] *Guardian*, 23 May 1988.
[221] Speech to the Adam Smith Institute, Apr. 1989.
[222] London: HMSO, 1989, Cm. 984, par. 1.3.
[223] Ibid. par. 1.7.   [224] *Observer*, 22 May 1988.

Adam Smith Institute in April 1989, said that modern Conservatism had dealt the philosophy of state socialism—which had 'subordinated the talents and skills of the individual to a supposedly all-knowing state'—a 'heavy blow' by reviving free market economies and championing the private sector. 'Our radical innovation', he said, 'has been to encourage the private sector in its own interests as well as that of the nation as a whole, to become partners with government and others in achieving progress on social as well as economic objectives.'

Equally, the New Right placed considerable emphasis on the informal sector. In 1980 Jenkin said that 'the first and most natural source of social care' lay in 'the family, friends, neighbours and communities taking action to help those most vulnerable'.[225] Indeed the informal sector, on occasion, received greater praise and attention than the other non-statutory sectors; it could operate without organization and without any public cost. The Family Policy Group advocated policies to give more responsibility for looking after the elderly and the dependent to the family—and more especially to women, who should be encouraged to give up employment and return to the home. In 1977 Jenkin told the Conservative Party Conference that, in his view, mothers did not have the same right to work as fathers. 'If the good Lord', he said, 'had intended us to have equal rights to go out to work, he wouldn't have created men and women. These are biological facts . . . We hear a lot today about social work—perhaps the most important social work is motherhood.'[226] Paul Johnson in 1982 widened the argument somewhat when he claimed that 'the ideal society rests upon the tripod of a strong family, a voluntary church and a liberal, minimum state'.[227] To Thatcher, financial prudence and forethought were encapsulated in the well-regulated family—in which the mother, who supervised the family budget, played a key role. She said in 1988 that 'the basic ties of the family' were 'at the very heart of our society' and were 'the very nursery of civic virtue'. It was, she said, 'on the family that we in government build our own policies for welfare, education and care'.[228] And also in 1988, she told the Conservative Women's Conference in London:

[225] Quoted in Brenton, *Voluntary Sector*, 143.
[226] Quoted in Clarke, Cochrane, and Smart, *Ideologies of Welfare*, 140.
[227] Quoted ibid. 141.   [228] *The Observer*, 22 May 1988.

The state must look after some children in care and those old people who cannot look after themselves. But the family is responsible for an infinitely greater number of children and for more elderly people. However much welfare the state provides, the family provides more—much more. We must strengthen the family. Unless we do so we will be faced with heart-rending social problems which no government could possibly cure—or perhaps even cope with.[229]

Thus the non-statutory sectors of welfare received considerable attention from the New Right. As Norman Johnson has written: 'The neo-liberal vision of the minimum state implies a drastic reduction in the welfare role of the state and a transfer of functions and responsibilities to other institutions.'[230] The term 'neo-liberal' has, indeed, often been applied to Thatcherite Conservatism in addition to the term 'New Right'. In *The Strange Rebirth of Liberal Britain,* Ian Bradley claimed that, in part, Thatcher belonged to the 'British liberal tradition': she was, he argued,

a believer in liberty . . . a voluntaryist and . . . a radical rather than a conservative . . . seeking . . . to transform society . . . [She was] a moral rather than a mechanical reformer, seeing the key to progress as lying not so much in the proper management of the economy or in correct social engineering but in the liberation of human energy and potential and the restoration of the moral values of self-discipline and responsibility.[231]

It is, however, important to appreciate that the New Right's attachment to voluntarism in its various sectors did not imply a total disregard of the state. Far from it; the state had to create the conditions in which the other sectors of welfare could flourish. A state presence—indeed a strong state presence—could be held to be necessary to achieve the objective of minimal government. Thatcher said that the government 'is there to have limited powers'—but added that it should be 'very strong in these limitations'. She went on to itemize the 'limitations':

---

[229] *Glasgow Herald,* 26 May 1988. See also Loney, Boswell, and Clarke, *Social Policy* 55–7 for a consideration of the emphasis on the family.

[230] *The Welfare State in Transition: The Theory and Practice of Welfare Pluralism* (Brighton: Wheatsheaf Books, 1987), 88.

[231] London: Chatto and Windus, 1985, 153.

one of them is to run the finances soundly; another is to make certain that we are always properly defended; a third is to have a firm rule of law; fourth . . . you have got to stop people getting cosy monopolies so that you have got freedom of competition; fifthly, you have got to have a certain fundamental framework of law—civil law—within which your business can operate . . .[232]

Within the field of welfare, there was, indeed, an attempt to break up 'cosy monopolies' and introduce 'freedom of competition' in various areas, of which a few examples may be given. In education, the Assisted Places Scheme, introduced in 1980, was seen as giving parents the opportunity to transfer their children to the independent sector by meeting from public funds a proportion of the fees and other expenses which went with independent schooling. Greater parental involvement and choice within the statutory sector was to be encouraged by setting up school boards, and allowing state schools to opt out of local-authority control. As in education, the 'opting out' of hospitals and the creation of hospital trusts within the National Health Service was introduced. In housing, there was a move to increase the private sector and home ownership by the sale of council houses. The Thatcher governments were also anxious to review pension arrangements. Thus they sought in 1985 to abolish the State Earnings-Related Pension Scheme (SERPS), introduced in 1975, which had supplemented the basic pension. It was argued that the scheme was too expensive and complex, especially in the light of the projected increase in the number of pensioners in the following fifty years; and there was also the point that SERPS reduced the range of choice for pensioners. Were SERPS to be abolished, those involved in it would have to make their own arrangements, either privately or by joining an appropriate occupational scheme. It is, indeed, possible to interpret this as an attempt to transfer pensions in the long term to the commercial sector.

In fact, SERPS was retained, but in narrower form, which involved lower government expenditure and lower benefits.

---

[232] *Sunday Correspondent*, 5 Nov. 1989. See also Thatcher's interview given to the *Independent*, 14 Sept. 1987: 'never let anyone say I am laissez faire. We are a very strong government. We are strong to do those things which government must do and only government can do.'

Although it is certainly true that occupational pensions were widespread before the election of the first Thatcher government in 1979,[233] the Conservative governments after that date sought to expand such pension arrangements in both the private and public sectors. The number of schemes increased, and tax relief on pensions doubled between 1979/80 and 1983/4. Here again, there was an emphasis on breaking up 'cosy monopolies' and on using the state to bring about greater competition—and thus greater choice.

A good example of the Thatcher governments' desire to use the state to enable and facilitate choice was embodied in the White Paper *Caring for People: Community Care in the Next Decade and Beyond,* published in November 1989. This placed considerable emphasis on choice and independence. The signatories expressed their belief that its proposals provided 'a coherent framework to meet present and future challenges'. They would 'give people a much better opportunity to secure the services that they need' and would 'stimulate public agencies to tailor services to individuals' needs'. This, they argued, offered 'the prospect of a better deal for people who need care and those who provide care. Our aim is to promote choice as well as independence.'[234] The 'coherent framework' did, indeed, retain a role for the statutory sector—in this case, the local authorities—in meeting the needs of elderly and disabled persons; and 'social service authorities' would 'continue to play a valuable role in the provision of services.' But community care was 'not to be seen as the prerogative of public services.' The White Paper continued:

People like to take responsibility for their own needs wherever possible. We are fortunate in having a thriving voluntary sector, and a rapidly growing private (i.e. commercial) sector. The Government believes that people welcome this mixed provision of care, and that it encourages innovation, diversity, proper attention to quality and the interests of consumers . . .[235]

The local authority was cast largely in the role of 'the enabling authority', which would stimulate 'the development of

---

[233] Papadakis and Taylor-Gooby, *Private Provision,* 103 ff. 'The post-war growth in occupational pensions was partly because of the vacuum between public welfare and private affluence.' (Ibid. 104.)

[234] London: HMSO, Cm. 849, 1989, Foreword.   [235] Ibid. par. 3, 4.1.

non-statutory service providers'; thus the statutory sector would 'continue to play an important role in backing up, developing and monitoring private and voluntary care facilities, and providing services where this remains the best way of meeting care needs'.[236]

There should, then—as Ian Lang of the Scottish Office put it in a familiar phrase—be a 'mixed economy of care', in which local authorities were to have a 'new role as enablers rather than providers'.[237] Thus the White Paper envisaged a considerable role for 'private and voluntary care facilities', within the 'mixed economy of care'; and, significantly, used the phrase 'independent sector' as a description of their combined efforts. To these efforts, moreover, were to be added those of the informal sector, which also came within the 'independent sector'. The White Paper thus used a new 'vocabulary of sectors': the well-established 'statutory sector' on the one hand, and the newly named 'independent sector' on the other, incorporating the voluntary, commercial, and informal sectors. With regard to the informal sector, the White Paper stated that the 'greater part of care has been, is and always will be provided by families and friends'.[238]

Here, then, was a continuing acceptance of the state; but the state in the role of enabler or facilitator, making it possible to transfer responsibility to the 'independent' sector, and thereby, it was argued, opening up greater choice. Equally, the Thatcher governments did not hesitate to use the state to create a 'coherent framework', within which non-statutory activities could take place. As has been seen, they were well disposed to charities; and the White Paper of 1989 on charities stated that the government was 'keen to encourage innovation and enterprise', and would continue to give selective grants to voluntary bodies. It did not, it said, seek to impose any 'central direction' on the voluntary sector; that would not be possible without damage to its spontaneity and diversity. Yet, it continued, the government 'must help to provide a framework within which voluntary bodies can flourish and their integrity be assured'.[239] The way in which grants were distributed did, of course, constitute an indirect form

---

[236] Ibid. par. 3, 4.3. See *Guardian*, 17 Nov. 1989, for a summary of the White Paper and comment on it.
[237] *Glasgow Herald*, 17 Nov. 1989.   [238] *Caring for People*, Foreword.
[239] *Charities: A Framework for the Future*, par. 1.8.

of influence; and this point will be discussed later. Further, the White Paper proposed new powers to allow the Charity Commissioners to safeguard property and prevent abuse by requiring all registered charities to submit annual accounts to the Charity Commission in England and Wales, ensuring that the register of charities was kept up to date and imposing tighter controls on public charities and fraudulent fund-raisers.[240] Similar schemes were envisaged for Scotland. John Patten, in praising the flexibility of the voluntary sector, said that the charitable world had to put its own house in order. Here, then, the state was being used to provide what was felt to be the the the correct framework within which voluntary bodies could conduct their business.

Thus to the New Right, the state could be a powerful instrument in creating the proper conditions for voluntaristic endeavour; and the historian of the nineteenth century cannot help but notice likenesses between proponents of New Right ideas on this matter and those who, a century or more earlier, had supported the use of the minimal state for similar purposes.

V

The advocacy of a 'neo-liberal' reversion to minimal state interference and an appeal to voluntarist agencies proved controversial in many quarters. At the party-political level, those within the Conservative Party who regarded themselves as being in the tradition of paternalistic Toryism were, indeed, favourably disposed to the voluntary sector, and were often themselves involved in it. On the other hand, such Tories—to be labelled 'Wets', and, in large measure, removed from Thatcher's cabinets—found the New Right's distrust of the state unduly ideological, and the thrust of its policies harsh, unfeeling, and lacking in social sensibility. Sir Ian Gilmour said that 'leaving everything to the market does not work'.[241] Francis Pym formed a very short-lived Centre Group to stress the importance of the moderate and middle ground.[242] The former leader of the party, Edward Heath, is often

---

[240] Ibid.

[241] *Guardian*, 10 Nov. 1989. See also Ian Gilmour, *Britain can Work* (Oxford: Martin Robertson, 1983), esp. chs. 4, 7, 9, 10.

[242] See Francis Pym, *The Politics of Consent* (London: Hamish Hamilton, 1984), esp. 111–30.

regarded as having flirted with New Right ideas in the early 1970s; and John Biffen has written that he, like his successor, was elected leader of the party 'to give a cutting edge to Conservatism'.[243] Heath was, in time, to become a scathing critic of many of his successor's policies, which he condemned as 'divisive, unpopular, authoritarian and unfair'. Giving the inaugural Harold Macmillan Memorial Lecture at Trent Polytechnic in May 1988, Heath said that

It is now fashionable to criticise the upper classes with whom Harold Macmillan was associated. But they appreciated above all that Government is the art of the possible and that if they were not to be violently swept away, as happened everywhere, they had to adapt to the needs of the whole of our society. To-day, such adaptation and moderation is anathema . . .

He called for a return to the Conservative values of 'One Nation' if the Conservative Party were to continue to serve the whole of the British people.[244]

   Michael Heseltine cannot very readily be identified with the other critics of the leadership in the party, and his departure from the Conservative government in 1986 was by resignation. His comments avoided any personal attacks on the prime minister, but in addresses to the moderate Tory Reform Group he stressed the need to 'find a proper balance between individual discretion and public responsibility' and called for policies which were 'hard-headed but not hard-hearted'. As a former environment secretary who had set up a special task force to combat the decline of Merseyside, Heseltine paid particular attention to inner-city problems. In 1986 he defended the enforcement of economy in local government; but he also stated that there was 'no way out of the vicious cycle of decline that is not led by the public purse. The elimination of social stress and the eradication of urban dereliction are not the natural hunting grounds for profit seeking entrepreneurs left to their own devices.'[245] He called for a partnership of 'public and private resource' to address the problem. In 1988 he returned to the matter. 'Let us not allow our faith in the individual and the market to overshadow the reality of inner city life,' he said. 'Only those with no idea of the

---

[243] *The Times*, 8 Mar. 1989.   [244] *Scotsman*, 14 May 1988.
[245] 'Rebuilding the Cities' (speech at Knowsley, 24 Apr. 1986).

conditions found there can believe that the existing communities alone, from their resources, can rescue their environment and reverse their decline.' While tax cuts and wealth creation were welcome and in the national interest, it would, Heseltine said, 'be quite wrong to believe that the Conservative party is unconcerned or indifferent to the quality of life. We certainly are concerned to generate wealth, but wealth is an opportunity . . . among other things to restore and create a better environment.' To Heseltine, then, planning the answers to society's problems was greatly preferable to letting such answers be 'haphazard, imposed by an unfettered market, careless of the longer term, blown by the winds of chance.'[246] He was certainly aware of the paternalistic traditions within the Tory Party, which were in danger of being overlooked in the drive towards self-help, even if that drive had much to commend it.

At the time of his challenge for the leadership of the party in November 1990, Heseltine was once again careful not to distance himself entirely from Thatcherite policies, many of which he regarded as successful. Nevertheless, he called for a fundamental review of the community charge, a local tax which had been perceived to be socially unfair. And he was seen by political commentators as taking a more positive view of the role of the state than Thatcher. The *Observer*, in commending his candidacy, wrote that Heseltine 'genuinely believes that the state has a role—through selective intervention, through better-funded education and training programmes—to get our industries moving again. He has a genuine concern for the plight of our inner-cities'. Once back at the Ministry of the Environment after the whole leadership contest had resulted in the triumph of John Major, Heseltine was, indeed, to be responsible for the review of the community charge which then took place.

If Thatcherism found its critics within the Conservative Party, this was much more true among Opposition parties. The Liberal Party was not, in fact, very happy about its alleged new recruit in the prime minister; David Steel, in his foreword to Bradley's book, argued that Thatcher had embraced 'very small' parts of Liberalism and had quite rejected others, such as Liberal pioneering of welfare measures;[247] and Bradley himself felt that her

---

[246] *Daily Telegraph*, 12 Oct. 1988.   [247] *Strange Rebirth*, pp. ix, x.

Liberal pioneering was too much attached to *laissez-faire* and selfish individualism.[248] To the Labour Party, Thatcherism and New Right ideas and practices were dismantling the Welfare State which the Labour Party had, in the post-war period, created; they were, moreover, putting in its place a society based not on collective care and concern, but on individual greed and callousness. Roy Hattersley, shadow home secretary, called Thatcher's speech to the General Assembly of the Church of Scotland in May 1988 'disgraceful'; it showed she had 'no compassion, no feelings of fairness, no generosity and no sense of community'. She was creating a 'greedy and violent society'.[249]

Gordon Brown, opposition Treasury spokesman, echoed such criticisms, writing that 'to make a few individuals rich, the government has been prepared to make all our communities poor'.[250] Brown focused on the role which the voluntary sector and, in particular, charity were being made to play in the government's social policy. Writing about the social security reforms of April 1988, which set up a Social Fund in place of the system of supplementary benefit, and removed the legal right to emergency help, Brown commented that

we used to rely on charity; it's coming back. We have seen charity pulled from the lumber room of social history, dusted off and, much to the embarrassment and anger of Britain's voluntary organisations, presented to a doubting or indifferent public as a vital component of thoroughly modern Thatcherism. Charity, for the first time since the last war, appears in our social security legislation: those charged with dispensing the new 'Social Fund' must not do so without making sure that charities and benevolent funds have first been considered.[251]

He returned to the earlier Labour idea that charity *could* not and *should* not cope with social need. 'If the N.H.S. is short of £2 billion and the social security system short of £800 million this year alone,' he wrote, 'no gradual spread of payroll-giving and no hospital flag days will bridge the gap.' Charity was being used, Brown claimed in arguments which were strongly reminiscent of those of an earlier period:

as a smokescreen to cover a withdrawal by the state from huge areas of social responsibility . . . Talk of charity . . . helps to distract attention from

---

[248] Ibid. 153.   [249] *The Times*, 23 May 1988.
[250] *Scotland on Sunday*, 23 Apr. 1989.   [251] *The Times*, 3 May 1988.

the basic problems of huge underfunding and provides a useful fig leaf for the more traditional Tory posture of naked self-interest . . . State responsibilities grew because charity became an unacceptable way of dealing with the needs of the sick, the poor and the old in an increasingly complex society. To return to a reliance on charity is to encourage a sad and seedy competition for public pity between the needs of tired donkeys, retired gentlefolk, children with leukaemia and other groups far larger, less spectacular, and every bit as deserving. It is a bleak vision of our future, one that no one voluntary organisation favours, but characteristically Thatcherite . . .[252]

More generally, various critics saw the New Right as posing a grave threat to the citizenship of entitlement. Members of the Thatcher governments were fond of evoking the citizenship of contribution by their advocacy of the role of 'active citizens'. The home secretary in 1988, Douglas Hurd, argued that in the 1990s there should be 'active citizens', who took greater responsibility for their own welfare and that of their families and communities.[253] This was echoed by John Patten, a Home Office minister, who in December 1988 wrote that 'After 40 years during which it was fashionable to exclude or decry individual action in the mistaken belief that government always knows best, we have to come to recognize that there is much room for active citizens to play a part, and sometimes a more effective part than can be played by the state'.[254] Here, then, was a direct challenge to the idea that the state should provide social benefits as of right, and that the citizenship of entitlement would lead to the citizenship of contribution. The citizenship of entitlement had, in fact, led to an overloaded state and a dependent citizen.

The challenge was met by those who argued that the Thatcher governments were eroding the citizenship of entitlement. Ruth Lister conceded that 'charity and voluntary service [had] an important role to play'; but they could not be 'a substitute for the rights of social citizenship guaranteed by the state'.[255] She admitted that citizenship involved 'obligations as well as rights'; but argued that the two had to be in balance. What had happened

---

[252] Ibid. See also Kay Andrews and John Jacobs, *Punishing the Poor: Poverty under Thatcher* (London: Macmillan, 1990), 239–62.

[253] *The Times*, 19 Sept. 1988.

[254] *Sunday Times*, 11 Dec. 1988. See also *The Times*, 11 Sept. 1989.

[255] *Guardian*, 24 Apr. 1990.

under the Thatcher governments was that obligations had been 'emphasised at the expense of rights';[256] and what was needed was a restatement of social citizenship 'as an inspiration to those who want to rebuild the Welfare State on foundations of justice and democratic participation'.[257]

There were, indeed, critics who felt that the New Right was endangering even political citizenship. John Ferris wrote that New Right intellectuals like Hayek and Friedman were 'fond of talking about a minimal state'. But, Ferris continued, 'The state in Britain . . . has never been more intrusive and its representatives so noisily present in our daily lives. It is this growing authoritarianism which is surrounded by an eerie silence by those who claim to love freedom, and it has received insufficient attention from those who are seriously concerned with social policy.'[258] John Mortimer commented on what he saw as the contradiction in New Right practice which sprang from 'the emphasis placed on certain kinds of freedom—the free market, freedom to make money, freedom not to have to join unions' on the one hand, and, on the other, 'an apparently uncontrollable desire to boss the population about, tell them what's good for them and tick them off for not doing it'. The career of Edwina Currie was taken by Mortimer as a case in point.[259]

What of the agents of voluntarism itself: how did they react to the more prominent role which the New Right prescribed for them? It has been seen that the influence of the churches had, historically, been powerful within the voluntary sector; and that, if overt and explicit influence from these quarters had declined in the course of the twentieth century, it had not disappeared. It is, in fact, notable how large a role the churches, or at least their leaders, played in the controversies engendered by New Right principles and policies. Bishop David Sheppard of Liverpool was

---

[256] 'The Exclusive Society: Citizenship and the Poor', in Angus Ersline (ed.), *Social Policy* (London: Child Poverty Action Group, 1991), 68.

[257] Ibid. For issues of justice and welfare, see John Rawes, *A Theory of Justice* (Oxford: Basil Blackwell, 1972); Norman Barry, *Welfare* (Milton Keynes: Open University Press, 1990), 87–8; and Nozick, *Anarchy, State and Utopia*.

[258] 'Citizenship and the Crisis of the Welfare State', in Philip Bean, John Ferris, and David Whynes (eds.), *In Defence of Welfare* (London: Tavistock, 1985) 47. See also K. D. Ewing and C. A. Gearty (eds.), *Freedom under Thatcher: Civil Liberties in Modern Britain* (Oxford: Clarendon Press, 1990).

[259] Review of Edwina Currie, *Life Lines* (London: Sidgwick, 1989) in *Sunday Times*, 19 Nov. 1989.

critical of New Right claims that 'the poor can only be helped towards prosperity by making the nation wealthier.' This simply raised the 'spiral of demand and expectation', and helped those in the front ranks; but rather than advancing the interests of those in the rear, it left them behind, and thus aggravated 'relative deprivation'. Instead, the bishop said, there should be a 'policy of intervention to give those in the back ranks more opportunities'.[260] The president of the Methodist Conference, the Revd Richard Jones, was equally critical of the 'trickle down theory': the idea that, if the rich became richer, the poor would be bound to benefit. He said that anyone who had read and understood the Old and New Testaments would see such thinking as 'a scandalous attempt to put a veneer of respectability over hurtful social injustice'. He argued that 'what might be called the harsh underbelly of capitalism treats the poor with a mixture of contempt and patronising charity'.[261] The moderator of the General Assembly of the Church of Scotland in 1988–9, the Rt. Revd Professor James Whyte, who had occupied the Moderatorial Chair during the prime minister's address of 1988 to the Assembly, said later that he had heard 'much [from the prime minister] about the importance of the individual, a little about the family, but nothing at all about those other communities which give us our sense of where we belong'. There was, then, an absence of a sense of community in the government's philosophy, and this could be called 'the great hole in the theology by which we are governed'.[262]

This, indeed, was a point which the then Archbishop of Canterbury, Dr Robert Runcie, also explored on a number of occasions. In September 1989 he wrote that the government supported the view of society in which the individual's rights and duties were enhanced. That, Runcie admitted, was 'part of the Christian ethic'. But, he continued:

The Church balances this with its understanding of Christians belonging to one another and making up the body of Christ. That gives a corporate dimension to our faith and ethics, bound sometimes to be at variance with a highly individualistic approach. We *are* individuals, but together we make up the community, and it is when we put our

[260] *Daily Telegraph*, 11 May 1989.   [261] Ibid.
[262] *Glasgow Herald*, 18 Feb. 1989.

competitive demands before the needs of others that the structures of our community life break up.

He detected tendencies towards a 'Pharisee society', in which the successful were tempted 'to regard their success as a sort of blessing or reward for righteousness'. This, Dr Runcie felt, could lead to judgements being made 'about the unsuccessful and unemployed, the poor and the unintelligent which [were] both uncharitable and untrue'.[263] In December 1989 a group of prominent churchmen launched a declaration, 'Hearing the Cry of the Poor', which described a society being 'drawn in a direction that contradicts the Gospel'. It did not openly refer to the government, but said that 'many of the social and economic policies currently being pursued cannot be right'. It could not be right, it said, 'to learn from experience that market forces favour the rich and dispossess the poor and yet do nothing about it'.[264]

The leading figures of various Christian churches were, then, critical of New Right ideas and policies, largely on the grounds that the increased reliance on market mechanisms would lead to an unacceptable degree of social inequality. It would, of course, be a mistake to infer from this that all members of these churches followed a similar line; and, indeed, spokesmen for the Jewish community were favourable to Thatcherite principles. A rather similar spread of views was to be found within the voluntary agencies themselves. The opportunities given to the commercial sector did not go unwelcomed; it was acting in a more congenial political climate than it had for some forty years. Spokesmen for the voluntary and informal sectors were, however, somewhat ambivalent in their reaction to New Right policies. In one sense, of course, the emphasis which the Thatcher governments gave to the 'active citizen' was much in accordance with the approach of the voluntary sector, which had always depended on such persons. Alec Dickson, founder of Voluntary Service Overseas and

---

[263] *Sunday Times*, 1 Oct. 1989.

[264] See *Glasgow Herald*, 4 and 5 Dec. 1989. See also Ken Leech, 'Caesar's Religion?' (*New Socialist*, 66 (Apr.–May 1990), 10–12). Leech, commenting on Thatcher's remark that 'there is no such thing as society', wrote: 'Thatcherism comes preaching an individualist gospel at a time when Christians, evangelical and catholic, have rediscovered the importance of social justice and human interdependence.' (Ibid. 11.) See also Raymond Plant, 'The Church and Government', in J. C. D. Clark (ed.), *Ideas and Politics in Modern Britain* (London: Macmillan, 1990), 116–29.

Community Service Volunteers, said that he was unsure exactly what government spokesmen meant by 'active citizenship'—but his reaction was to cry, 'Bravo, let's get started.' He himself felt that 'active citizenship means doing . . . We live in a society where it is still important that the gifted should give.'[265]

The idea of 'citizen contribution' to the good of the community did, in fact, receive quite widespread and non-partisan support. In November 1988 the speaker of the House of Commons, Bernard Weatherill, launched the Commission on Citizenship, an all-party group of MPs and educationalists. The Commission's Report, published in 1990, was warm in its support of voluntary-sector effort as an important element of the citizenship of contribution, and called for greater recognition to be given to it.[266] Equally, such ideas were much in accordance with those long put forward by the Prince of Wales, whose plan to create a volunteer community of up to 100,000 young people was announced in the press in September 1989. This, it appears, was envisaged as a scheme to encourage every young person between the ages of 16 and 25 to spend short periods in full-time voluntary work. The Prince was accorded support from various quarters, including prominent members of the Labour Party. David Blunkett, Labour MP and a member of Labour's national executive, welcomed the initiative. It was not, he said, an attempt to replace paid workers, adding—interestingly—that it was 'something that goes back to the very origins of the Labour movement. It's built on an acceptance of our obligations to others.'[267]

There were, then, grounds for those involved in the voluntary sector to welcome new initiatives which gave it greater prominence. Further, the Thatcher governments increased grants to the voluntary sector. Central government grants to the sector—although it must be borne in mind that these were to all of its aspects, and not simply those concerned with welfare—increased from £93 million in 1979/80 to £150 million in 1982/3 and £267

[265] *Sunday Times*, 21 May 1989.

[266] *Encouraging Citizenship: Report of the Commission on Citizenship* (London: HMSO, 1990), 31–2, 41–2.

[267] *Sunday Times*, 3 Sept. 1989. See also *The Times*, 9 Feb. 1990, where Blunkett's claim is contrasted with the attitude of Conservative ministers who 'see a continuity between what the Prince is trying to achieve and the values of the enterprise culture.' But, the article continues, 'in truth they are not opposites—it is only the necessary dialectic of the British party political debate that makes them so . . .'

million in 1985/6. By 1987/8 the figure was £293 million, an increase in real terms of 91.6 per cent since 1979–80, although figures published in 1989 indicated a slight decline in the previous rapid growth.[268] In 1987, moreover, the 'payroll-giving' scheme was introduced, whereby employers were able to claim tax relief on donations of up to £240 a year to a cause of their own choosing.

Nevertheless, increased funding did not come without a sting in the tail. Under the Thatcher governments, state funding of charities became more centralized and selective—and more in tune with the ethos of enterprise and self-help. Thus certain types of charity were encouraged; others, by implication, discouraged. Among the former were voluntary organizations which could assist with inner-city renewal: thus the 'Action for Cities' campaign of 1988 involved use of the private sector and voluntary effort in the pursuit of a revival of civic pride. Among the latter —those to be discouraged by the cutting off of funds—were voluntary organizations which had been financed by left-wing councils. As Brian D. Jacobs has written, 'Peace groups, gay and lesbian organisations and many politically-orientated ethnic minority organisations came under attack from national and local conservative politicians. Clearly, therefore, no official sanction would be given to blanket support for voluntary organisations.'[269] The abolition in 1986 of the Metropolitan Counties and the Greater London Council, which had often supported various minority voluntarist pursuits, made it evident that undiscriminating support for the voluntary sector would no longer be forthcoming. As Jacobs has put it, this gave 'a clear signal that support was conditional upon organisations being regarded in favourable terms with respect to their attitudes and "good credentials" as potential co-operators within the context of the new enterprise culture'.[270]

There was, moreover, a marked tendency for government to provide funding only on a 'project' and not on a 'core' basis. This reversed earlier practice, whereby a voluntary body, such as the Nuffield Foundation, would 'encourage innovation by giving

---

[268] *Independent*, 7 Nov. 1989. See also *Charities: A Framework for the Future*, par. 1.5.

[269] 'Charities and Community Development in Britain', in Alan Ware (ed.), *Charities and Government* (Manchester: Manchester University Press, 1989), 98.

[270] Ibid. 99.

start-up grants to projects until they proved viable, leaving it to the state to undertake long-term funding. The Thatcher governments tended to be less willing to undertake the long-term core funding necessary to ensure the continuation of the project—and more willing to switch roles and attend to project-funding or, as it was also called, 'pump-priming'. This enabled government to stimulate new initiatives at low cost. It was to be left to the charities to undertake the long-term funding, which was by no means an easy task.[271]

Thus, as ever, the state was by no means a certain and reliable ally; and even if it increased its central funding to the voluntary sector, the cuts which the Thatcher governments imposed on local government spending presented a worrying future for those organizations which had depended on it. Equally, the Conservative administrations were anxious to encourage charities to seek finance from sources other than the state. Timothy Raison said that 'the cornerstone of the voluntary movement is a large degree of financial independence of state'; he also felt that the voluntary ethos would be endangered by too great an availability of government funds, since these would, in his view, encourage too much professionalization and unionization within voluntary bodies.[272] Other critics saw state funding of voluntary bodies as tantamount to an expansion of the Welfare State. Digby Anderson, director of the Social Affairs Unit, argued that there was a good case for 'stopping the hidden expansion of the welfare state through the *permanent* subsidy of "voluntary" bodies by the central and local state'.[273]

There was, then, an encouragement to the voluntary sector to expand its sources of income—from individual donors, from raising money through fees and charges, and from developing links with business and commerce. All these points presented considerable problems for charities—although, as has been seen, the difficulty of raising finance is one which has long beset the charitable world. With regard to increasing the amount of money given by individual donors, the challenge was to reverse a trend which had long been evident in charitable giving. It has already

---

[271] Robert Hazell, 'Role Reversal' (*Trust Monitor and Grant News* (Feb.–Mar. 1991), 14–15).   [272] Quoted in Brenton, *Voluntary Sector*, 148–9.
[273] Quoted in Martin Loney, *The Politics of Greed: The New Right and the Welfare State* (London: Pluto Press, 1986), 137.

been seen that, over a very long period, charities came to depend less and less on money from individual donors. As Alan Ware has written—summarizing a number of points which have already been touched on earlier in this book—'secularization, the break-down of traditional community ties, the influence of advertising in persuading people to spend first on items of personal con-sumption, and the growing expectation that the state should provide for people's needs have all helped to depress contribu-tions to charities'.[274]

The problems of reversing this process were illustrated by a Family Expenditure Survey, which found the average annual household expenditure on charitable donations and subscriptions in 1986 to be £32.67. This was probably a conservative estimate; the Charities Aid Foundation suggested that it might be as high as £103.20 in 1987.[275] This was, in fact, seven times the amount given in central government grants; but it usually represented what was called 'an emotional response to an emotional appeal',[276] rather than any clearly planned system of giving. Some causes—for example, those connected with children, or, indeed, animals—were much better supported than others; the homeless and ex-prisoners would be given a low priority. Public giving was, therefore, highly volatile and capricious. A pessimistic view of such giving was expressed by Michael Brophy, director of the Charities Aid Foundation, who wrote in October 1988—in the wake of the Conservative government's encouragement to 'active citizenship'—that whatever might be said on this subject 'should be set in the context of the way people now give to charity'. He claimed that 'only a handful of people (mostly churchgoers) gave more than £20 per month', and estimated that this was, perhaps, 5 per cent of the population. Some 47 per cent gave £1 per month or less. Those in the 'prosperous South' gave a lesser proportion of their income to charity and less in total than people elsewhere. 'Private giving', Brophy concluded, 'is . . . still light years behind the rhetoric that encourages it.'[277]

---

[274] 'Introduction: The Changing Relations between Charities and the State', in *Charities and Government*, 11.

[275] These figures are given in *Efficiency Scrutiny of Government Funding of the Voluntary Sector* (Submission by the National Council for Voluntary Organisations, June 1989), 7.

[276] Ibid.   [277] *The Times*, 14 Oct. 1988.

A year later, in October 1989, Prebendary Patrick Dearnley referred to this statement, and commented that since it was made, there had been 'no significant rise in the proportion of personal wealth we give to the many excellent charities which deserve our fullest support'. Even if, he continued, these 'derisory rates of giving' were to be increased, 'they could not possibly alleviate the problems which afflict millions of our fellow-citizens'. There remained 'a major role for national government to perform'.[278] The Charities Aid Foundation Report for 1989 confirmed this judgement. A survey of 1,000 homes showed that only 4 per cent gave more than £30 a month to charity, and 40 per cent £1 or less. The average monthly donation was of the order of £2. Those who gave most were churchgoers from Northern Ireland, Scotland, and the North of England: an interesting indication of the continuing importance of religious motivation.[279] And the pattern was the same—or, indeed, had deteriorated—when the Charities Aid Foundation reported in November 1990 that the typical donor to charity in 1990 gave only £1.28 a month, compared with £1.97 in 1989. In 1990, 26 per cent of adults refused to donate to charity at all, compared with 22 per cent in 1989 and 20 per cent in 1988. 'Typical giving', Brophy commented, 'has fallen by a substantial amount'. The situation in 1991 was, if anything, less encouraging, as the prospect opened of money traditionally given to charities being switched to new hospital trusts and grant-maintained schools.[280]

Thus, while arguments were put forward to the effect that there was a growing sense of altruism in Britain—and Nigel Lawson said in 1987 that 'the upsurge of charitable activity over the past few years is . . . very striking'[281]—the figures themselves suggest that such claims should not be exaggerated. There were, it is true, notable successes in tapping sources of income by new methods. The BBC's 'Children in Need' campaigns and ITV's 'Telethons' evoked a considerable response, as did the Band Aid Appeal, organized principally by Bob Geldof; and the newly formed Band Aid Trust became, in 1985, the charity with the largest income. Band Aid was successful in drawing on new sources of giving in the population; and there was an increase of

---

[278] Ibid. 4 Oct. 1989.   [279] Ibid. 12 June 1990.
[280] *The Times*, 15 Nov. 1991. See also *Times Higher Educational Supplement*, 15 Nov. 1991, and below, p. 387.   [281] *The Times*, 22 Nov. 1989.

some 27 per cent in the voluntary income of all charities in 1985/
6 compared with 1984/5. Great publicity was afforded to charities in general, and to charities concerned with international aid
in particular; Band Aid had been especially concerned with famine in Ethiopia.

Yet this very fact tended to siphon off support from other
charities; and medical and health charities, youth groups—and
funds for the arts—were adversely affected. Moreover, it remains
uncertain if the Band Aid venture triggered off a long-term increase in public giving; the increase of 1985/6 was not maintained in 1986/7, and, as Alan Ware has written, 'the ability of
disasters and charity organizers between them to create a perman-
ently more altruistic public seems rather limited'.[282] There is such
a thing as 'donor fatigue'; and this could be accentuated by the
feeling—as in the case of the further Ethiopian famine of 1989—
that aid was not being properly directed as a result of political
unrest and uncertainty in the area in need. The political orientation of a country in which a disaster occurred could affect the
charitable response to that disaster. Wendy Riches, the head of
fund-raising for the Save the Children Fund, said in 1989 that
'more demands are being made on charities and more demands
are being made on donors. Somewhere along the line it is stopping and now there are charities feeling the pinch.'[283] Thus while
particular events abroad, or at home—such as the Penlee Life Boat
Disaster Appeal of 1981[284]—could evoke a considerable response,
the overall effect remained patchy. As Nick Kochan has put it,
'the challenge to the charities is to build a lasting trend from
occasional outbursts of popular enthusiasm.'[285] The same point
about the need for planned and reliable giving was made by
Julia Neuberger.[286]

An appeal for greater giving by individual donors did, therefore, take place—and posed familiar problems for charities. The
same may be said of the practice of charging fees for services and
establishing greater links with commerce and business. The importance of fees to charities is underlined by the fact that in 1985,

---

[282] 'Introduction', in *Charities and Government*, 12.
[283] *The Times*, 28 Nov. 1989.
[284] See Geoffrey Finlayson, 'Penlee's Appeal to Philanthropy' (*Times Higher Education Supplement*, 23 Mar. 1982.)
[285] *The Times*, 28 Nov. 1989.   [286] *The Times*, 28 May 1990.

61 per cent of the income of registered charities in England and Wales was raised in fees and charges.[287] A greater emphasis on commercial considerations in the voluntary sector became evident in a variety of ways. It could involve a tighter and more cost-conscious managerial style, as happened with the Spastics Society. Its chief executive, Ken Young, was appointed in 1988 to bring a more professional attitude to the running of the Society. He denied that his businesslike approach derived from the practices of a market economy; but his methods modernized and introduced a greater sense of commercial reality to the organization and involved the closure of a training centre, disposing of the Society's London Headquarters, and assessing its residential properties.[288] In Scotland, a new Consultancy Service was set up in November 1989 to ensure greater cost-effectiveness in the organization of charities: the Scottish Charities Effectiveness Review Trust. This, in fact, was an equivalent of a similar venture established in England in 1987. Its Scottish organizer, Audrey Milan, said that 'in the voluntary sector we must not only be effective and efficient, but be seen to be so.' One charity which had recently undergone a review was the Glasgow and West of Scotland Institute for the Deaf. Its secretary, Gordon Chapman, said that 'after 125 years we wanted to come up-to-date in order to make the best use of our resources—money, people and buildings'; and the consultants' report listed sixty recommendations which were being considered, or put into effect, by the charity.[289]

A greater reliance on marketing techniques was also evident in raising money for charity. In some cases, these methods of attracting public support were highly reminiscent of nineteenth-century practices. Thus in May 1989 the *Daily Telegraph* reported on various charity balls, stating that those attending the Rose Ball should 'Look out for Lady Grade and lots of Hons in attendance. The place will be bulging with important sounding names.'[290] Other methods made use of advanced techniques of direct mailing. The Save the Children Fund, among many others, used such methods and developed links with business and commerce. Sixteen companies—including IBM, ICI, and Tesco

---

[287] *Efficiency Scrutiny of Government Funding,* 6.
[288] *Sunday Times,* 9 July 1989.   [289] *Sunday Times Scotland,* 12 Nov. 1989.
[290] Quoted in Ian Williams, *The Alms Trade: Charities, Past, Present and Future* (London: Unwin Hyman, 1989), 46–7.

—became corporate members of the Fund, paying a minimum six-figure donation for the role; this, in turn, gave the companies a ready-made promotional platform. In April 1988, Save the Children launched its Trust Card: part of a scheme of 'affinity' credit cards through which, with the co-operation of the banks, a small percentage of the card holder's monthly payment was given to the charity. This proved highly successful in raising money. As Nick Fielding put it: 'Who says charity doesn't pay?'[291] The Imperial Cancer Research Fund, the British Heart Foundation, and MENCAP entered into an arrangement with the Leeds Permanent Building Society, whereby they gained benefit every time a Leeds Visa card was issued and used. All this, then, represented a search by the voluntary sector for new sources of income; and the fact that it was not only a search for public, but also for private, funding tended to blur the distinction between the voluntary and commercial sectors.

Advertising was another feature of this aspect of charitable activity. Charity advertising increased eightfold from 1977 to £16.7 million in 1989; and the Samaritans, the National Society for the Prevention of Cruelty to Children, and the Red Cross were clients of the advertising agency Saatchi and Saatchi. The advent of radio and television advertising for charitable funds was a further dimension—but also posed problems for smaller charities, unable to afford the high cost. Ross Flockhart, director of the Scottish Council for Voluntary Organisations, welcomed the lifting of the ban which permitted television advertising on the grounds that anything which resulted in more money for charities was desirable; but he also felt that there was 'a distinct danger that small charities [would] suffer'. Dr James Minto, general director of Quarrier's Homes in Scotland, commented in October 1989 on Quarrier's decision to undertake radio advertising: 'Although it was always thought that God would provide, costs are escalating and we require labour intensive staffing. Competition is now so fierce that . . . we decided to get into the market very quickly, although in a modest way, to raise our marketing image.'[292]

This shift of emphasis to become more professional and commercial was, therefore, plainly evident in the work of many

---

[291] *Sunday Times*, 21 May 1989.   [292] *Scotland on Sunday*, 22 Oct. 1989.

charities. In a sense, of course, it was not new; as has been seen, charities had always been involved in a scramble for funds—and had always employed varying methods to raise them. Again, it could give rise to criticisms which were not new: to the effect that too much money was being used in fund-raising costs, to the detriment of those purposes for which the money was given. Leaders of charitable organizations were quick to counter such criticisms. In November 1989 Mary Cherry, chairman of Oxfam, wrote that suggestions made that only 55 per cent of the funds collected by Oxfam went in aid overseas gave a misleading impression. She stated that 82 per cent of funds raised for 1988/9 was allocated to the overseas programme, of which 4 per cent was spent on education and campaigning work in the United Kingdom. Only 11 per cent of income was spent on fund-raising costs, 4 per cent on capital investment in shop properties and equipment, and 3 per cent on administration.[293]

Nevertheless, the increased reliance on styles of administration akin to the world of commerce and on marketing techniques did tend to put strains on the altruistic, non-profit traditions of the voluntary sector; and this could give rise to unease. This was evident in the Loyal Order of Ancient Shepherds Friendly Society, which, anxious to arrest the decline inherent in a shrinking and ageing membership, appointed in the early 1980s a consultancy firm, the Moorgate Group, to advise on marketing and sales. The advice was, broadly, to use modern management and sales methods and to offer an updated and streamlined range of policies on the one hand; and on the other to develop a socially orientated club to fulfil the social functions of the friendly society—and thereby to retain a traditional element in its activities. The proposals, however, were felt by some in the Society to be too extreme. The Chief Shepherd at the Annual Meeting in 1983 said that he thought the recommendations to be 'alien to our type of organization'. He continued: 'The Loyal Order of Ancient Shepherds is basically a layman's society, run for the benefit of the members by the members. This assembly [i.e. the annual meeting] is the Governing body of the movement, and if we were to adopt some of the proposals set out in the report, we would be betraying the trust placed in us by the ordinary

[293] *The Times*, 29 Nov. 1989.

members.'[294] A delegate from the Glasgow branch put it this way: 'We are between the Devil and the deep blue sea . . . We have got to change; but we have got to change in such a way that we maintain the inherent part of our Society that has always been with us and God Willing always will be . . .'[295]

The need to change had, of course, been inherent in the situation in which the mutual-aid friendly societies had found themselves since the later 1940s, and was not new in the 1980s; but the greater emphasis on the commercial sector in the 1980s brought the matter into sharper focus in that decade. And, if it tended to blur the distinction between the voluntary and commercial sectors, it also showed up the tensions involved in trying to graft commercial-sector practices on to voluntary-sector traditions.

Another issue raised by an increased reliance of voluntary organizations on commerce was the familiar one of independence and identity. By wooing commerce rather than the state, the voluntary sector might replace one set of paymasters with another; or it might be subject to two sets of paymasters, the statutory and commercial sectors. Here the process of 'squeezing' from two sectors was evident. This could make its cherished autonomy ever more dubious. Thus universities, subject to cuts from 1981 and having the mechanism of their relationship with government altered from the University Grants Committee to the Universities Funding Council, were under pressure to find new sources of income. Dame Mary Warnock wrote that the rhetoric about the independence of universities 'sounded good', but that if they were independent of government, they must be supported directly or indirectly by industry. And, she added, 'the pressures likely to be imposed by industry, demanding instant applicability, overt value for money, and perhaps control over the publication of research, are likely to be far more damaging than any pressure from Government'.[296]

A further issue raised by an increased reliance on the voluntary sector related to the availability not only of money, but of time and talents; and again, this was not a new problem. It was, however, highlighted by the developments of the 1980s. The survey carried out by the Charities Aid Foundation in 1989

[294] The Loyal Order of Ancient Shepherds (Ashton Unity) Friendly Society, *Official Report of the 157th Annual Movable Conference, Torquay, 5 Sept. 1983*, 4.
[295] Ibid. 116.   [296] *Independent*, 6 Nov. 1989.

indicated that two-thirds of the population did no voluntary work for charities. Justin Davis Smith of the Volunteer Centre spoke of a 'crisis in volunteering', caused partly by an ageing population and partly by an increase in the number of women entering paid employment. This, he said, cast doubt on the viability of the government's plan to increase the contribution of the voluntary sector to welfare services.[297]

Moreover, the emphasis placed on the giving of 'time and talents' ran into the problem of obtaining time off work to make this possible. This did happen in some instances. Allied Dunbar Assurance encouraged its employees to do charity work, and from 1987 to 1989, 420 of the 2,500 staff in the company's administrative base in Swindon took part in voluntary activities, ranging from the giving of financial advice to organizing a holiday camp for children from deprived homes. This practice was not, however, so well developed in Britain as in America; and it could cause difficulties and conflicts of loyalty—and dependence on the goodwill of employers or partners.[298] Citizens 'active' at work might well be willing and anxious to be 'active' in the community—but they might lack the time and leisure to be so. This was a point also addressed by the Commission on Citizenship, which reported that the activities for which companies most frequently allowed time off with pay were the Territorial Army, school governorship, blood donation, jury service, and lay magistracy. Charitable work, however, rarely entered the list.[299]

There was also the question not only of time, but of talents, or, to use a more appropriate word, expertise. The complexity and professionalism of late twentieth-century society may suggest that there is room for the contribution of the 'willing amateur'; but they also raise the question whether the 'amateur' has the skills and expertise to make a significant contribution, without a further investment of time in preparing for the task. That was, indeed, a point which the Aves Committee addressed; and it became even more relevant in the 1980s. The running of schools requires specialized knowledge, in the areas both of employment and of education, and there is no guarantee that voluntary and amateur boards of governors possess that knowledge. In 1989 an industrial tribunal involving a redundancy case following financial

[297] See *Independent*, 7 Nov. 1989, and *The Times*, 28 Nov. 1989.
[298] *The Times*, 11 Sept. 1989.   [299] *Encouraging Citizenship*, 40–1, 92–3.

difficulties at Westbourne School for Girls, an independent school in Glasgow, found that the conduct of the Board of Governors was totally at variance with correct procedures in a redundancy; a decision of 'unfair dismissal' was returned on the grounds of lack of consultation and 'positively wrong information' given to the employee in question, which was likely to mislead her as to the reasons for her selection for redundancy.[300] Such a finding did not inspire confidence in the ability of a board to run a school in what is essentially the spare time of its members—even if, as on this occasion, those members included persons with professional experience, such as a solicitor and a professor. In another Glasgow school, Jordanhill College School—a self-governing school in the state sector—the convener of the Board of Governors, Sheona Waldron, questioned, on the basis of the school's experience, whether parents possessed the necessary expertise to run schools under the government's opting-out proposals. In a letter of resignation of October 1989. Waldron wrote:

The ultimate issue is whether a school can be managed like a local voluntary community organisation; whether a disparate group of local volunteers with widely differing abilities, backgrounds and perceptions can realistically take the place of a local education authority. My experiences have led me to conclude that they cannot. The recurring problems of the past 18 months have not simply been teething problems: they are symptomatic of a flawed and inappropriate medium for the management of a school.[301]

It is clearly dangerous to generalize from two cases, where particular circumstances may have applied. And it could be said, on the other side, that many independent, self-governing schools are well run; and that the government's proposals for school boards and opting-out did include facilities for training. Nevertheless, the point remains that the running of schools—or hospitals—requires not only time, but expertise; and it by no means follows that 'active citizens' will be in possession of either, or of both, in sufficient quantity.

Thus while the emphasis on the 'active citizen' might have

---

[300] *Mrs E. F. Finlayson* v. *Westbourne School for Girls Ltd.* (Industrial Tribunal, Glasgow, case no. S/2235/88), 30 Nov. and 19 Dec. 1988. Report RE 74767/2 IM 3/80. TBL 17 Jan. 1989. See also *Glasgow Herald*, 1, 20 Dec. 1988, 24 Jan., 15, 19, 22 June 1989; *Scotsman*, 1 Dec. 1988, 24 Jan. 1989; *The Times*, 1 Dec. 1988; *Times Education Supplement, Scotland*, 23 Dec. 1988, 27 Jan., 24 Feb. 1989.

[301] *Scotland on Sunday*, 22 Oct. 1989.

seemed likely to evoke a favourable response from the voluntary sector, that response has been guarded—and, indeed, often critical—pointing to the problems of this increased emphasis rather than the potential. In November 1989 Usha Prashar of the National Council for Voluntary Organisations put the matter into a perspective which included the 1960s:

Voluntary Organisations have themselves been critical of State provision and its capacity to meet changing needs. But their critique is quite different from that adopted by this government. They have sought to extend the opportunities for choice and the mixed economy within the welfare state and to develop partnership with private and public provision. Their response is exemplified by the wave of advocacy and community-based provision that began in the much maligned 60's and that is based in a collective sense of responsibility for dignity, health, security, freedom, and fair life chances for all people.[302]

The point about 'a collective sense of responsibility' is important, since it relates to the comments made earlier in this chapter about the voluntary sector in the 1960s: that while often adopting a critical attitude to government, it nevertheless looked to government to remedy the problems which it identified. It was, therefore, unhappy in the 1980s about adopting a role which might be seen as doing the government's work for it. Mark Clynder of Age Concern did not feel that receipt of state funding turned a voluntary organization into a government 'lackey'; Age Concern groups, he claimed, continued to criticize government policy even if they were in receipt of government money. But he did think that cuts in public expenditure posed a 'major dilemma for many voluntary agencies. They feel an obligation to those clients "left out in the cold"', he continued, 'by a mean-spirited and thoughtless state, yet also feel that to provide services for such individuals gets the state—and ultimately the taxpayer—off the hook.'[303]

Thus Brown was largely right in his claim, already mentioned, that many voluntary organizations did not welcome the role which they felt was cast for them under the Social Fund of 1988. This role was seen by many to involve them in providing sources of money which the state would no longer provide—and in entering into a partnership with the (then) Department of Health and Social Security in deciding who should receive assistance

---

[302] Quoted in Williams, *Alms Trade*, 179.   [303] *Guardian*, 11 Feb. 1984.

and who should not. Claimants, they felt, were being turned into charity cases. Sixty charitable organizations openly stated their concern at the effect of the Fund on the poor—and on hard-pressed charities. In November 1989 the Spastics Society voiced concern at what it saw as the implications of the White Paper on *Caring for People*: 'We are deeply concerned', it stated, 'about any assumptions that the public provision of care for disabled people can be in the main shifted to the private and not-for-profit sector without serious consequences for disabled people.'[304] ITV's 'Telethon' appeal of 1990, which raised £24 million, was, in fact, picketed by disability groups who protested that such appeals were demeaning to the recipients, and simply encouraged the belief that essential services could rely on this kind of activity.[305] What Nicholas Hinton has called the 'charitisation' of statutory services was, therefore, regarded with acute suspicion by many charities themselves.[306]

This feeling was, moreover, shared by those to whom charities were forced increasingly to make an appeal for funds: the general public and commerce. The report of the Charities Aid Foundation for 1990 stated that there was a growing public resentment that appeals were being made to carry out functions which were regarded as government responsibilities, in particular health and education. It stated that 90 per cent of the public thought that the state had a basic duty to look after those who could not look after themselves; and 83 per cent thought that government should not rely on charity to raise money for such purposes. These figures for 1990 were as high as, or higher than, those for previous years. Brophy of the Charities Aid Foundation said in 1990 that people saw the reliance of public services on charity as 'almost a con trick, the Government offloading its responsibilities'.[307]

The same feeling was to be found among those who provided money for charities from the world of business. In December 1988 Sir Hector Laing, chairman of United Biscuits, told the *Guardian* that:

The charitable giving which was once done by families and the wealthy, which might have devolved on to wealth creating industry, passed

---

[304] *Guardian*, 17 Nov. 1989.
[305] *State of Sector 3: Voluntary Organisations in 1990* (London: National Council for Voluntary Organisations, 1990), 34.
[306] Ibid. 35.   [307] *Daily Telegraph*, 10 Nov. 1990.

instead, in the early 1950s, to government. I think everybody said 'They' will do it. In 1979 a government came in with a wholly different attitude, and took a big step back from industry. It took some time for people to realise that, as government stood back, we, the wealth creators, had to step forward.[308]

Sir Hector founded the Percent Club, the members of which were pledged to give 0.5 per cent of pre-tax profits to charity, inclusive of secondment of staff and donations in kind. He sought to boost its efforts by an appeal to 'enlightened self-interest', claiming that what was at stake was 'a better society, more people in jobs, more entrepreneurial flair in communities, and therefore more chance of making worthwhile profits'.[309]

But the prospect of this 'step forward' opened up rather a daunting commitment. Thus Sir Mark Weinberg of Allied Dunbar, which earmarked 1.25 per cent of its profits for community projects, and, as has been seen, allowed its employees time off work to participate in them, said that the 'fear is that once you start being efficient yourselves, government will say it's reducing its commitment'. Brophy struck a similar note in 1989 when he said that companies were reluctant to allow their gifts to be used by government as an alternative to central funding of essential services. 'At the moment', he said in November 1989, 'people remain suspicious of government intentions. Corporations and individuals feel that if they give a lot more to charity, the Government will withdraw.'[310]

Corporate giving in real terms did, indeed, increase with rising profitability in the years immediately prior to 1989; such donations increased by more than 50 per cent between 1985 and 1988, from about £60 million to £90 million. But this represented a fall in percentage of profit from 0.21 per cent to 0.18 per cent over the same period. The figures for 1989 indicated that only 63 British firms gave more than 0.5 per cent of their pre-tax profits to charity. The figures for 1990 showed a slight upward trend of 3 to 4 per cent, allowing for inflation; but the marked decline in increase from earlier levels, no doubt reflecting the recession of the late 1980s and early 1990s, showed the precarious nature of this source of funding.[311]

---

[308] Quoted in Williams, *Alms Trade*, 189.   [309] Ibid.
[310] *The Times*, 28 Nov. 1989.   [311] Ibid. and *Daily Telegraph*, 10 Nov. 1990.

Thus, as a report of the National Council for Voluntary Organisations put it, the 'trend . . . to try to reduce, or at least confine the contribution of the state and to delegate more responsibility to the private [i.e. commercial] and voluntary sectors' did provoke 'considerable anxiety among those who feel that governments are trying to push too much onto other sectors in society, who can neither be held to account in the same way, nor, in many cases, be expected to carry the load'.[312] It was felt possible that within a 'social economy', the special characteristics of the voluntary sector might be built into a 'third force' between the state and the market;[313] but the report, while recognizing the opportunities for new roles, and confident in the ability of the voluntary sector to adapt to new circumstances, was well aware of the problems of making choices as to where voluntary organizations 'wish to operate within the new welfare market'.[314] Too close a convergence with the commercial sector—as with the statutory sector—ran the familiar risk of loss of identity and independence; too marked a divergence from it might well mean that it became a 'residual sector'.[315]

A similar—and, indeed, more hostile—reception was given to the New Right's eulogy of the informal sector by those who spoke on its behalf. It is quite true that the New Right's emphasis on the informal sector was a simple recognition of current practice. Thus a MORI poll of 1990 showed that 43 per cent of those who had been volunteers in the previous six months had been involved in looking after the elderly.[316] These were not necessarily members of the elderly person's family; but the increasing number of elderly persons in the community did involve families in greater responsibilities in this respect. Yet the New Right's emphasis on family provision tended to assume that the family was constantly the same and able to cope with increased demands made of it, whereas in fact it was subject to considerable change.

This was true of various age-ranges within the family. It has been argued that the reduction of benefits to young persons and the greater governmental emphasis on training schemes made

---

[312] *Directions for the Next Decade: Understanding Social and Institutional Trends* (London: National Council for Voluntary Organisations, 1990), 24.
[313] Ibid. 41.   [314] Ibid.   [315] Ibid.
[316] Quoted in *State of Sector 3*, 39.

those aged between fourteen and eighteen more dependent on their parents. Equally, as has been mentioned, the increase in the number of elderly persons posed problems for those same parents in relation to their own parents. Yet the family itself was less able to withstand these pressures. Rising divorce rates and the increased number of one-parent families—which rose from 8 per cent of all families with children in 1971 to 14 per cent in 1987— in addition to the number of women in paid work, estimated at 60 per cent of the workforce in 1990—meant that the family was not the unchanging unit of support which Thatcherite rhetoric suggested that it was. In 1987, 44 per cent of households conformed to the 'nuclear family' model of a married couple with dependent children, compared with 52 per cent in 1961.[317] There was, then, a demand from family groups not for less statutory support, but for more: to replace lost earnings, to meet costs such as those arising from disability, or to provide day-hospital facilities for those suffering from complaints such as senile dementia, thus giving relief and respite to their carers. According to the director of the National Council for One Parent Families, single-parent families were struggling to survive on 37 per cent of the income of two-parent families.[318] There was also the point that elderly persons kept at home would face increased costs from the community charge, whereas those living in hospitals and residential homes were to be exempted.

Government policies for the family were thus open to the charge of inconsistency; on the one hand urging greater emphasis on family care, and on the other making that care more expensive and difficult to achieve. Sir Ian Gilmour attacked the government's refusal over several years to increase child benefit and suggested that child credit should replace it; 'only then', he said, 'will the claim that we are the party of the family regain some validity'.[319] Roy Parker wrote dismissively of government policies in this area: 'The assumption is that the social obligations are so powerful they are part of the law of nature, but they are rather precarious. The political rhetoric is an effective manoeuvre to deflect attention from other kinds of analyses; it is an effective way of converting public issues into private issues.'[320]

[317] *Directions for the Next Decade*, 18.   [318] *State of Sector 3*, 7.
[319] Speech to Child Poverty Action Group, 5 Nov. 1988.
[320] *Guardian*, 23 Nov. 1988.

If, then, New Right ideology, as has been suggested, 'privatise[d] compassion',[321] spokesmen for those within the informal sector who were expected to shoulder the burden often doubted their capacity to take up the challenge. They also resented the fact that any challenge should be made which might force individuals to make sacrifices to meet it. Thus 'compulsory altruism' was seen as offensive to those forced to be altruistic. This was particularly true of the feminist viewpoint, which saw the Thatcherite thrust towards family and community care as endangering all the gains which women had made in the past century. Thus, as Hilary Land and Hilary Rose wrote, 'the feminist hostility to community care turns partly on the needs and interests of women, who are to be masked once more in altruistic service to others, and partly on the needs and interests of the cared for'. A 'central insight' was cited from Titmuss's celebrated book *The Gift Relationship*, which dealt with the donation of blood by volunteers. This, it was argued, 'demonstrated that for a gift to be safe, that is non-injurious to the recipient', it had to be freely given, without knowledge of the person who was to benefit from it. And, Land and Rose continued, 'What is true for the gift of blood is perhaps even more true for that complex and enduring task of caring for another person. For women to be free not to give as well as to give requires that there are good alternative services. Only then will they not feel that they have no choice except to sacrifice themselves for another.'[322] To those who argued this case, then, the New Right emphasis on the family and the community amounted to an attempt to save public money by forcing the assumption by the informal sector, which often meant daughters of the elderly, of responsibilities which had once been silently borne—but at the cost of career and employment opportunities.

Thus the impact of New Right ideas and policies in the 1980s

---

[321] In *The Times*, 12 Apr. 1989, Brian James wrote on Thatcher's speech to the General Assembly of the Church of Scotland: 'after 40 years' belief in cradle-to-grave welfare, the Prime Minister was proposing the privatisation of compassion'.

[322] 'Compulsory Altruism for Some or an Altruistic Society for All?', in Bean, Ferris, and Whynes (eds.), *In Defence of Welfare*, 93. See also an art. by Sally Brompton in *The Times*, 26 June 1990, on the demands, made on women, particularly those in employment, by caring for ageing relatives, and Pamela Abbott and Claire Wallace, 'The Family', in Philip Brown and Richard Sparks (eds.), *Beyond Thatcherism: Social Policy, Politics and Society* (Milton Keynes: Open University Press, 1989), 78–90.

did appear to mark a significant change in the direction of social policy from that followed in the period from the later 1940s. It is, indeed, often seen as marking the end of a period of consensus on welfare issues, when the primacy of the Welfare State had been accepted by a very broad range of opinion. This may be taken to be a further warning against the 'Welfare State escalator' or 'collective train' approach; the escalator and the train were, seemingly, put into reverse, as older ideas made their reappearance.

This, however, raises two questions. The first is whether there had been a consensus in the period before 1979, or whether the period from 1949 to 1979 was itself intersected by a variety of differing viewpoints. The second relates to the issue of whether the whole New Right episode was more a matter of rhetoric than of reality; and whether the reality was at odds with the rhetoric. These two matters require some brief consideration at this point; and, since they raise issues which are of importance in the context of this book as a whole, they will reappear in the Conclusion.

The 'consensus' view of the period from 1949 to 1979 has strong advocates; and there is no doubt that those writing during the period did feel that there was a broad agreement, which stretched across the parties, that the point of emphasis in the mixed economy of welfare was settled in favour of the state. Donnison argued in 1962 that 'the *development* of collective action for the advancement of social welfare' had been an 'ill-defined but recognizable' feature of British social policy; and he suggested that there was an assumption that the social services would take a large share of the economic growth seen as necessary to uphold them. This was, he wrote, part of 'a widespread consensus within the social administration tradition'.[323] Later, in 1991, he returned to these points. While conceding that 'we should not exaggerate the political consensus of these years'—by which he meant those of the 'generation after the defeat of Hitler'—he argued, nevertheless, that 'the advances made by reforming governments were generally consolidated rather than reversed by their successors'. He continued:

[323] Quoted in Howard Glennerster, 'Public Spending and the Social Services: The End of an Era?', in Muriel Brown and Sally Baldwin (eds.), *The Year Book of Social Policy in Britain, 1979* (London: Routledge & Kegan Paul, 1980), 15.

People drawn from a broad spectrum of society shared reasonably humane and mildly egalitarian hopes for a future in which the state was expected to play a central part. And continuing economic growth gave everyone confidence that these hopes would eventually be realised. Strawberry ice-cream, vanilla ice-cream—did it really matter? Either of them would be nice. And in those days, it seemed that in the fulness of time we'd be able to have both.[324]

There is also no doubt—as has been seen—that the voluntary sector itself was orientated towards the Welfare State; the Wolfenden Committee provided evidence of this in its clear acceptance of the primacy of the state. The political parties, moreover, were broadly united in an acceptance of the Welfare State. The Conservatives were traditionally well disposed to voluntarism, and made efforts to ensure that it survived; but this did not mean that they saw it as a real alternative to the Welfare State. It is true that Macmillan's first chancellor of the Exchequer, Peter Thorneycroft, was anxious about the level of government expenditure and the prospect of inflation; and in 1957 he talked in terms of keeping public expenditure at its existing level. This did seem to offer a challenge to the Conservative Party's acceptance of an expanding Welfare State; but in 1958 Macmillan refused to accept a programme of cuts, whereupon Thorneycroft, along with two junior ministers, Nigel Birch and Enoch Powell, resigned.[325] The challenge receded—as it seemed also to do when, in 1971–2, Heath abandoned the apparently harder face of Conservatism sketched out at Selsdon Park in January 1970 and returned to a more central, consensual position.[326] On its side, the Labour Party remained firmly committed to the Welfare State; and while it did not reject certain manifestations of other sectors—particularly of the voluntary sector—and increasingly came to appreciate their value, this did not mean that it wished to depart from a firm belief in the primacy of the Welfare State. To both parties, it may be argued, 'pluralism' meant a variety of social provision within the mixed economy—but by far the major share of that provision lay with the state.

Nevertheless, it may also be argued that there had always been

---

[324] *A Radical Agenda: After the New Right and the Old Left* (London: Rivers Oram Press, 1991), 47.

[325] David Dutton, *British Politics since 1945: The Rise and Fall of Consensus* (Oxford: Basil Blackwell, 1991), 53.   [326] Ibid. 67–9.

dissentient voices. Charles Carter, indeed, suspects that 'If one could undertake systematic research into the prevailing attitudes in, say, 1950, 1960, 1970 and 1980, there would be evidence of a growing disillusionment with the extension of state provision, whether social or otherwise, and a rising interest in the examination of alternative paths.'[327] Peter Taylor-Gooby has argued that there were always ambiguities in the Welfare State; and, with Hugh Main Bochel, has written that a distinction between the deserving and undeserving persisted throughout the years of the so-called 'consensus', with benefits to the latter being reduced before 1979.[328] It is, indeed, true to say that occupational schemes for private health insurance and pensions were already widespread before 1979, and had been tolerated outside the state; and that home ownership was encouraged by both parties.

Thus it may be held that, from the later 1940s, there were conflicting points of view; and that even those who were anxious to promote the consensus of Welfare Statism were often forced to recognize that there were limitations, often of a financial variety, which could not be ignored. Kenneth O. Morgan has suggested that as early as the late 1940s the Labour Party showed signs of a 'retreat from collectivism'.[329] Briggs—as has been seen[330]—detected evidence of a restlessness with the Welfare State in the early 1960s; and certainly in the later 1970s, the Labour Party was showing signs of a realization that public expenditure could not mushroom for ever, however painful that realization might be. Sir Keith Joseph wrote that 'the seeds of break in the consensus were being continuously implanted by disappointed expectations'.

Put this way, what happened after 1979 was not especially new—and reflected currents which had been present before that date. It has, indeed, been seen that many New Right ideas were present long before 1979. This points up the areas of continuity in social policy rather than those of change; and suggests that, even in the period of so-called 'consensus', it was clear that, to

---

[327] 'A New Direction in Social Policy?', in Brown and Baldwin (eds.), *Year Book of Social Policy, 1979*, 14.

[328] 'Parliament and the Politics of Welfare', in Maria Brenton and Clare Ungerson (eds.), *The Year Book of Social Policy, 1987–8* (London: Longman, 1988), 7, 8, 13.

[329] *Labour in Power, 1945–1951* (Oxford: Oxford University Press, 1985), 489.

[330] *Collected Essays of Asa Briggs*, ii. 178.

quote Briggs, 'policies . . . are never fixed for all time'.[331] All, then, that the election of the first Thatcher government in 1979 did was to re-evoke and to sharpen debate on long-standing issues, which had always been present—even in the immediate past.

Further, the argument can be extended beyond 1979 to suggest that, despite the efforts of the Thatcher governments to change direction, what happened after 1979 should not be exaggerated. Here, many commentators have observed that in various areas there was a mismatch between ideology and implementation— and that despite the rhetoric about self-help and individual responsibility, there was, except in the case of housing, a steady increase in public spending after 1980/1.[332] In education, health, the personal social services, and social security, the sums spent exceeded those planned. In social security, indeed, there was a large increase in expenditure, created mostly by benefits to pensioners and the unemployed.

Just, then, as anti-collectivist ideas had been present in a period of so-called Welfare State consensus, collectivist practices were present in a period when anti-collectivist policies were being widely canvassed. Robert Pinker wrote in 1985 that if the country really wanted to return to the 'Victorian values' held in esteem by the Thatcher governments, it would have to accept the need for deterrence as well as for self-help. That would mean a revival of poor law principles and an increasing reliance on charity and private social services. How far that would be pursued depended 'on the balance between political expediency and the innate conservatism of British institutions and British public opinion'.[333] Harold Perkin suggested in 1989 that the Thatcher

---

[331] 'The Welfare State in Historical Perspective' in *The Collected Essays of Asa Briggs, ii: Images, Problems, Standpoints, Forecasts* (Brighton: The Harvester Press, 1985), 185.

[332] See e.g. Thomas and Dorothy Wilson (eds.), *The State and Social Welfare: The Objectives of Policy* (London: Longman, 1991), 4: 'the fact remains that expenditure in real terms rose substantially under Conservative governments—by almost a third on health and personal social services between 1979/80 and 1989/90, by almost a third on social security and by over a tenth on education and science.' See also Julian Le Grand, 'The State of Welfare', in John Hills (ed.), *The State of Welfare: The Welfare State in Britain since 1974* (Oxford: Clarendon Press, paperback edn. 1991), 338 ff., for a statistical analysis of public welfare expenditure since 1974.

[333] 'Social Welfare and the Thatcher Administration', in Bean, Ferris, and Whynes (eds.), *In Defence of Welfare*, 198.

governments were, in fact, much more cautious than to return to 'Victorian values' in this sense. 'Far from trumpeting the demise of the welfare state,' he wrote, 'government ministers began to boast [at the general elections] in 1983 and 1987 about increased public expenditure on hospitals, schools, pensions and the employment services.'[334] He suggested that this may have been due to public opinion polls which showed that government services like health, education, and welfare enjoyed a great deal of public support, even if they meant that tax increases were necessary to support them. Concentrating on the idea of 'social citizenship', Perkin concluded that 'The aspect of professional society that centred on the social rights of citizenship had survived the onslaught of the New Right and seemed to be entrenched in the national psyche'.[335]

On occasion, indeed, Thatcher was criticized not for going too far, but for going not far enough. In July 1989 John Gray wrote that

After a decade of rule by a Conservative administration dedicated to whittling down the state to its most indispensable functions, government in Britain today remains massively over-extended . . . There is an urgent need to revive the project from which Thatcherism derived whatever philosophical coherence it possessed—a project of limiting government . . .

He argued that the Welfare State in its present form had 'no moral or rational justification', and that everyone would be better off if the institutions of the Welfare State were substantially privatized. There was also a strong case for the wholesale privatization of schooling, with standards being maintained by a 'streamlined National Curriculum designed to foster literacy and numeracy'. Thus resources should be returned to the free market for moral, not economic, reasons. Only the market enabled individuals to 'implement their plans and realise their values'. To Gray, then, there was a need for more Thatcherism, not less.[336]

---

[334] *The Rise of Professional Society*, 486.

[335] Ibid. See also Perkins 'An Untamed Leviathan' (*The Economist* (3–9 Feb. 1990), 53–4).

[336] *The Times*, 1 July 1989. But see also a further art. by Gray in *The Times* (29 May 1990), which argues that Thatcherism in the 1990s 'needs to link the economic liberalism of the free market with a liberal and compassionate approach to social policy'.

The expression of such a point of view ten years after the election of the first Thatcher government might lend support to the view that what had taken place in that period was less spectacular in practice than both its supporters and its critics claimed. Taylor-Gooby has written that, while there was a 'real brake' on welfare spending after 1979, this did not amount to a 'shift into reverse gear'.[337] Indeed, as has been seen, he and Bochel argue that the brake had already been applied to the 'undeserving poor' before 1979—and that government policies after 1979 stopped short even of applying the brake to the major—and popular— welfare services, such as the National Health Service, far less shifted them into reverse gear.[338] Even some of the prime minister's own statements might be taken to imply a continuing commitment to the principles of the 'progressive consensus'. It will be recalled that in her speech to the General Assembly of the Church of Scotland in May 1988, she used scriptural authority for her statement that it was the duty of the individual 'to provide for his own house (meaning his own family)'. But she continued:

We must recognise that modern society is infinitely more complex than that of Biblical times and of course new occasions teach new duties. In our generation, the only way we can ensure that no one is left without sustenance, help or opportunity, is to have laws to provide for health and education, pensions for the elderly, succour for the sick and disabled.[339]

Here, it would seem, was a statement of belief in the state which 'provided', and did not simply 'enable'. Even within a speech which stressed non-statutory welfare agencies, there was a recognition of the presence of—and need for—statutory agencies in certain areas. Here, it may be argued, the prime minister displayed pragmatism rather than principles.

It is, then, possible to argue with Taylor-Gooby that 'the extent to which . . . changes [after 1979] cut across . . . past policy should not be exaggerated', and that it is the 'continuities rather than the cleavages and conflicts' which provide the dominant theme of the Welfare State':[340] continuities to be discerned firstly in the

---

[337] *Public Opinion*, 71 ff., develops these points.
[338] 'Parliament and the Politics', 7–8.   [339] *Observer*, 22 May 1988.
[340] *Public Opinion*, 61 and 92, develops these points.

evidence of 'cuts' in some areas before 1979, as the supposed consensus showed signs of cracks, and secondly in the maintenance of, and indeed increases in, expenditure, particularly on universal services which were popular with the middle classes, after 1979. It was notable that whereas the Barclay Committee Report of 1982 on the role and tasks of social workers had been expected to present a case for contracting the profession, it did not do so; existing social work practices, based on the post-Seebohm local authority arrangements, were broadly accepted. It is also true to say that the community social work envisaged by the Report, involving co-operation among statutory, voluntary, and informal sectors, was, at least initially, widely accepted by the social work profession as a whole.[341]

Such points do, indeed, have some validity. As has been suggested throughout this book, there was always a mixed economy of welfare, in which there was a voluntarist and a statist presence. From that perspective, the period from 1949 to 1991 may be viewed as a whole, as one in which the dialogue over welfare continued—and was not dominated by any one solution to the exclusion of all others. Thus the advocacy and existence of the varied sectors of voluntarism continued after 1949, and the same process in relation to the statutory sector was discernible after 1979. This was all part of the 'recurrent experimentation' with welfare options of which Thomson wrote.[342]

And yet this book has also argued that, while there was always a 'welfare mix', the proportions of that mix did change over time. The 'recurrent experimentations' were not, indeed, characterized by sudden, smooth, or complete changes. Thus to suggest that the expansion of social work during the 1960s and 1970s 'seemed to be constructed on an enormous landmass of consensus', and then after 1980 appeared 'suddenly to be perched on a tidal sandbank',[343] puts the matter too dramatically. Nevertheless, the 'experimentations' did result in a change of balance and emphasis. It is hard to deny that the change in the period from 1949 to 1979 was in favour of the state; and, even if this did not win universal approval—thus detracting from the

---

[341] See Mike Nellis, 'Social Work', in Brown and Sparks (eds.), *Beyond Thatcherism*, 107–8.   [342] See above, p. 13.

[343] Bill Jordan and Nigel Parton (eds.), *The Political Dimensions of Social Work* (Oxford: Basil Blackwell, 1983), 6–7.

completeness of the 'consensus'—it did command a substantial body of support. Equally, it is difficult to dispute that there was a marked change in ideology, at least on the part of the governments in office, after 1979. A different relationship between citizen and state was certainly envisaged. In 1983 Thatcher said of her government that 'we offered a complete change in direction— from one in which the state became totally dominant in people's lives and penetrated almost every aspect to a life where the state did do certain things, but without displacing personal responsibility. I think we have altered the balance between the person and the state in a favourable way'.[344]

The implementation may not have matched the ideology, nor the reality the rhetoric. But both ideology and rhetoric did have some effect. Thus while public expenditure continued to grow in many areas after 1979, there was an attempt to contain the rate of growth of expenditure in real terms. Thus in the health service, for example, an ever-rising level of demand was met by a 'constrained rise in supply',[345] and the higher level of expenditure in social security was explained by an increased demand from pensioners, the unemployed, and single-parent families, rather than any real increase in benefits themselves. Further, as has been implied, there was a real cut—by some two-thirds—in housing. And although the *principle* of state-financed welfare services may be said to have remained, in large measure, intact, the *method* by which those services were delivered and provided—even within these parameters—did witness considerable experimentation with the non-statutory sectors of the mixed economy.[346] The introduction of local management of state-maintained schools and hospitals was, in a sense, an acknowledgement of much voluntary-sector practice; that of 'quasi-markets' within state-financed services involved a greater recognition of, and role for, the commercial sector; and the greater stress on the family and community moved in the direction of the informal sector. The boundaries between citizen and state in matters of

---

[344] Quoted in Peter Riddell, *The Thatcher Government* (Oxford: Basil Blackwell, 1985), 1. In 1979 the Conservative Party manifesto had noted that few could 'fail to be aware of how the balance of our society has been increasingly tilted in favour of the state.' (King, *The New Right*, 120.)

[345] Wilson and Wilson (eds.), *The State and Social Welfare*, 4.

[346] See Le Grand, 'The State of Welfare', 360.

social welfare after 1979 may not have changed as much as those who advocated—or deplored—the changes claimed; but they did move sufficiently to make the period after 1979 different in emphasis from that which immediately preceded it.

Conclusion

This study set out to consider two themes: the contribution of voluntarism to social welfare in Britain in the period since 1830, and the relationship between voluntarism and the state in the same period, as boundaries and frontiers between them moved. The voluntary sector has been given particular attention in both respects. These points were set out in the context of the existing literature in the Introduction. The Conclusion will attempt to draw them together.

One of the strengths of the voluntary sector has been seen to lie in the opportunities which it gave to individual initiative and to participation in what were, for the most part, self-governing societies of a mutual-aid or charitable nature, formed, or joined, from free choice. The voluntary sector did, then, release energies which otherwise might well have remained dormant. This was to be seen in the course of the nineteenth century, in the involvement of the skilled working classes in the great variety of mutual-aid societies which existed; while charitable and philanthropic organizations provided a channel for public service. Those who took part in such initiatives—and they included an immense contribution from women—were involved in 'active citizenship'—in what has been termed in the course of this book the 'citizenship of contribution'—at a time when they were, in large measure, denied access to formal political structures—to possession of what has been termed the 'citizenship of entitlement'. In many ways, too, the experience gained in such voluntary organizations carried over into other areas—and, in time, helped to earn such persons a place within political structures: the citizenship of contribution could lead to the citizenship of entitlement. As a recent report of the National Council for Voluntary Organisations put it: 'through volunteering, many people ... become more involved in public issues and public life and gain the confidence and skills to do so'. This has been true throughout the period covered by this book.

Moreover, even when the political system became more democratic, and the citizenship of entitlement came to embrace not only political but social rights, voluntary agencies remained a vehicle of participation—again often reaching groups which were, or felt themselves to be, marginalized and untouched by the bureaucratic agencies of the state. Even Beveridge, while arguing that the state should do more than in the past, acknowledged the continuing importance of voluntary philanthropic action and welcomed its widening scope. The Wolfenden Committee Report of 1977 commented that 'people are often more willing to give time, energy and money to a voluntary body devoted to a specific cause than to a statutory agency'. As Michael Ignatieff observed, 'passive equality of entitlements' was stressed in the 'citizenship ideal' of social reformers in the period after World War II; but this was 'at the expense of the active equality of the citizenship of participation. The entitled were never empowered . . .'

Participation in voluntary-sector activity could help to remedy this situation; and the mushrooming of voluntary-sector societies, often in the mutual-aid tradition, and drawing on the support of young persons and ethnic groups, in the 1960s and 1970s may, in some measure, be explained in terms of the opportunities which they offered in this respect. Thus, in the work of inner-city regeneration during those decades, voluntary groups, with their strong local base and attachments, played a significant role. There were such agencies as the Groundwork Trust and Project Fullemploy, the latter providing training opportunities for minority ethnic communities. The activities of a charitable organization such as Task Force in the 1960s and 1970s also gave an outlet, while the harnessing of 'pop-star' culture to charitable agencies in such enterprises as Band Aid and Comic Relief, or televisual techniques to the 'Children in Need' and 'Telethon' campaigns, opened up a new, and hitherto largely untapped, constituency to participation, at least in donating to charity. The number of charities greatly increased in the course of the 1970s and 1980s. In 1970 there were 76,000 registered charities in Britain, 65 per cent of which had an annual income of less than £100. By 1976 the number of charities registered with the Charity Commission had risen to 123,000, and by 1986 to 158,000, with an estimated total income of almost £12.7 billion—although, of course, not all of these were orientated towards social welfare.

If voluntarism, and especially the voluntary sector, offered opportunities for participation and the expression of support for and loyalty to a favoured organization, it also had—and has—a role in meeting needs by the provision of services. This was clearly true in the nineteenth century and, indeed, in much of the twentieth. The immense network of mutual-aid and charitable organizations to be found in nineteenth-century Britain delivered a wide variety of what may be called 'basic' services, such as education and health care; and while it is true that statutory services also existed, they were seen more as performing an 'enabling' or complementary role, which facilitated the proper discharge of voluntary initiatives, or a 'residual' or supplementary role, which filled gaps in that provision. Voluntary-sector organizations were also prominent in providing for special needs and 'minority' groups, such as orphans, the blind, and the deaf, where the commercial and statutory sectors made little impact. There was, indeed, in this service-provision often a pioneering role. While it may be conceded that the services provided by voluntary activity were often of an ameliorative kind, it is also true to say that such provision was made when little else was on offer.

The same roles of service-provision and pioneering were fulfilled by the voluntary sector even when the state assumed the provision of 'basic' services. The delivery of 'personal social services' of a specialized nature for certain groups in society was a noted feature of voluntary-sector activity in the period after the formal creation of the Welfare State—and one much praised by Beveridge. The sector's characteristics of flexibility, its specialist activity, and the considerable expertise which it could bring to bear made it well suited to deliver such services; and the pioneering role remained an important and distinctive characteristic in years when the state came to take the major share in the mixed economy of welfare. This was frequently carried out by individual organizations, some of which have remained the sole provider of a service. Examples include the provision of accommodation for the single homeless and refuges for battered women. Cruse was established to secure recognition for the needs of widows. The hospice movement is sustained in large measure by voluntary-sector activity. The highest expenditure was made by charities which provided residential accommodation: thus the Salvation Army's expenditure in 1985/6 was £38.7 million and Barnardo's £36 million—although their activities were far from limited to this particular function. The YMCA was the largest voluntary-sector agency providing training and low-cost accommodation for young people. In other cases, a federation of local voluntary societies provided services. One such was the Abbeyfield Society, which established and managed family-sized houses to accommodate elderly people. By the end of 1986 there were 593 local societies which managed 960 houses and accommodated 7,500 residents. A variant pattern emerged when such services were facilitated by national 'umbrella' organizations. The Charity Organisation Society was one such in the late nineteenth century and the first half of the twentieth century; others, more characteristic of the twentieth century, are the National Council for Voluntary Organisations (formerly the National Council of Social Service), the National Federation of Housing Associations, the Disability Alliance, and the National Council for Voluntary Youth Services.

The provision and pioneering of services could also be considerably facilitated by granting money raised by the voluntary sector. This could take place in the context of notable public emergencies or disasters, which evoked much the same response in the twentieth century as had similar events in the nineteenth century. The Penlee Lifeboat disaster in 1981 is an obvious case in point. The relief of famine overseas depends to a great extent on voluntary-sector activity; and in these emergencies the voluntary sector is able to move more quickly and with greater flexibility than statutory agencies. But this role is not confined to emergencies. It was reported in 1982 that the Scottish public gave more than £10 million a year to medical research in Scotland through voluntary donations: more than the government and its medical agencies. In the United Kingdom as a whole, charitable trusts gave over £566 million to voluntary organizations in 1987/8; and in certain areas, such as medical research, charitable funding is a more important source of income than the government. The 'Telethon' in 1988, which appealed for money for five categories: disability, training and employment, children, special need, and self-help and mutual-aid groups, raised £22 million in twenty-four hours, more than the annual budget of some local-authority social-service or social-work departments.

Such service-provision and pioneering can, however, take rather more intangible forms, such as the provision of public education

—in the wide sense of awareness of social issues—and advice. The work of many philanthropic individuals and organizations in the nineteenth century performed this role. In 1850 Shaftesbury claimed, with some justice, that his work in numerous charitable agencies—such as those concerned with ragged schooling and public health—had 'led to an awakened attention . . . to the wants and rights of the poor: to the powers and duties of the rich.' Similarly, the work of local voluntary agencies (such as churches) in these areas, or of national ones, forced many social issues to the forefront—or at least nearer the forefront—of public attention. The late nineteenth-century awareness of working-class housing conditions owed much to the stimulus provided by *The Bitter Cry*; and the investigative methods of the Charity Organisation Society brought to light much information on poverty which would otherwise have remained hidden. Twentieth-century examples would be the work done by the Pilgrim Trust in the 1930s on unemployment and the needs of new housing estates, and, more recently, Action on Smoking and Health (ASH), Alcohol Concern, and the Family Policy Studies Centre. Again, effort has been expended in highlighting issues such as environmental awareness, international famine, and child abuse—or the plight of hostages and prisoners of conscience, as for instance through Amnesty International or through efforts by family and friends in the informal sector. It would, indeed, be fair to say that the voluntary sector has 'alerted people to numerous issues of public concern since Victorian times'. These have often been controversial issues, to which government could not commit taxpayers' money owing to the fact that they could not command sufficient public acceptance.

There has also been an important advisory and counselling role. Again, the existence of statutory agencies did not inhibit such a role. The Samaritans received 87,000 calls in 1971—and 393,000 in 1986. Alcoholics Anonymous counselled 6,300 persons in 1971, rising to 35,000 in 1986. Indeed, the existence of statutory agencies almost certainly encouraged the growth of voluntary-sector counselling services, for much of it was concerned with the giving of advice on matters of statutory entitlement. The Younghusband Committee report of 1959 noted that a function performed by the voluntary sector—'which may grow in importance as the statutory social services extend'—is to 'assist the citizen who needs help in connection with a statutory service, perhaps in protesting if he thinks his case has not been treated fairly. A voluntary organization may act as a watch-dog in keeping the statutory services up to the mark.' The activities of the Citizens' Advice Bureaux provide an obvious example, and the same would be true of legal advice and law centres; and organizations concerned with the disabled often match volunteers to those with severe disabilities in order to make sure that their point of view is adequately expressed to officials in local or central government. Again, much of this activity, taking place in the informal sector, may remain largely unseen.

Participation, service-provision, pioneering: all these are characteristics of voluntary—and, in particular, voluntary-sector—activity. A final—often related—role is that of the pressure group, urging the attention of governments to the needs of those whose cause is taken up. This too was notable in the nineteenth century: the Ten Hours Movement and the Anti-Corn Law League are two examples. In the twentieth century, the work of the British Legion—or of the Soldiers', Sailors' (and latterly Airmen's) Families Association—urged the interests of service, or ex-service, personnel; and in the 1960s many of the newly created voluntary-sector organizations devoted their energies to the same role. Shelter provides an obvious example. There is, indeed, a long tradition of campaigning within the voluntary sector; and, as has been recently written, 'most organizations feel that campaigning is still an appropriate role within their capacity'.

It is, of course, true that a considerable number of voluntary-sector organizations combine certain of these roles; and taken together, they may be said to be an effective vehicle for what Albert Hirschman called 'Voice', which may be defined as an attempt, through participation in service-provision, to influence and change that provision—or, to move perhaps rather closer to what Hirschman meant by the term, the expression of dissatisfaction with the service which is provided. That dissatisfaction could be directed against the management of the voluntary organization itself; or it could be directed through the voluntary organization at the state. Deacon argued in 1987 that there was potential in the voluntary sector for the provision of 'an alternative voice', which articulated 'as part of a healthy democratic process the case for those whose claims might otherwise be over-looked'.

Again, collectively, the activities of the voluntary sector are often held to offset the danger of dependency and to promote self-reliance. This was certainly true of the voluntary sector in the nineteenth century, when both sides of the sector, the mutual-aid and self-help and the philanthropic, were felt by their prac-titioners to be designed to create the conditions in which self-reliance and self-maintenance could be practised. The strict application of this role was, indeed, questioned in the late nine-teenth and the twentieth centuries by upholders of the voluntary sector itself; but even within this context, it is not absent from present-day proponents of the voluntary sector. Thus a submis-sion made by the National Council for Voluntary Organisations to the Efficiency Scrutiny of Government Funding of the Volun-tary Sector in 1989 stated that voluntary organizations 'excel at getting people to the position where they have enough confi-dence to take up opportunities, or to create them for themselves'. The fuller part which they will thereby play in society helps 'to reduce dependency'.

If many of the functions so far considered are especially true of the voluntary sector, many are shared by the informal sector, which may also be a vehicle for the expression of mutual-aid and/or concern for others in an unstructured manner. The infor-mal sector, in the shape of the family, also carries by far the largest share of care-provision for the young and the elderly. The role of service-provider is, perhaps, most characteristic of the commercial sector, which tends to be less concerned with encouraging participation, pioneering, or pressure-group activ-ity—although the commonly used argument in favour of the commercial sector—that it promotes freedom of choice—does come close to the point about participation, and is certainly akin to the argument concerned with the reduction of dependency and the promotion of self-help. It is also true to say that the contribution of the market to welfare is often seen to consist in the creation of greater wealth which, Barry argues, 'raises the well-being of the worst-off more effectively than welfarist egali-tarianism'. 'Markets', as he further writes, 'maximise welfare and therefore their wide spread would increase individual satisfactions.' This type of argument was, of course, much canvassed by New Right thinkers in their desire to emphasize non-statutory ways of delivering social welfare. To them, the market rather than the state was the enabler to a better life.

The points which have been made about the contribution of the non-statutory sectors have certainly, in recent years, become the more powerful in the light of what have been seen to be the failures of the centralized, bureaucratic, and high-cost state, with its overtones of compulsion rather than choice, officialdom rather than participation, routine universalism rather than flexibility—and, as several American commentators, such as Charles Murray and Larry Mead, have argued, the creation of an underclass, dependent on welfare handouts. Robert Sugden has suggested that, far from political democracy leading inexorably to the delivery of social democracy through an all-powerful state, in a democratic society, 'public morality cannot be something separate from the morality that guides private individuals in the conduct of their own affairs'. People observe such private morality, which may derive from the not disinterested consideration that one should treat others as one would have them treat oneself, in small groups, such as family, friends, and neighbours; and while it is more difficult to observe these conventions when the 'public good game' is played in large groups, 'we may still feel that we *ought* to shoulder our share of the costs of cooperative arrangements—that is if others are doing their part, we ought to do ours'. Thus, Sugden argues, 'even within large groups public goods are sometimes supplied through voluntary contributions'. Here, then, is a statement in favour of public welfare being based on voluntary arrangements rather than through the centralized state: in a sense, a form of 'Exit'.

It is, however, also true that the aspects of the non-statutory sectors which have been seen as contributing to social welfare have attracted criticisms. Participation in voluntary-sector organizations may have arisen from a sense of public service and altruism—but other, less worthy and more self-interested motives might also be at work: self-advancement, vanity, a desire to keep control of welfare, to inculcate values in accordance with the assumptions of those who were spending their money, time, or talents in voluntary activity—although such arguments are themselves also open to criticism. The Younghusband Committee noted that some of the evidence presented to it suggested that voluntary workers 'sometimes fail to appreciate that standards different from their own are not necessarily worse', and that people had 'an equal right to choose their own way of life within the limits of the law'. This suggests that even in the 1950s the categories of 'deserving' and 'undeserving', even if much weakened from the force with which they were often held a century earlier, still existed in some measure within the voluntary sector. As Donnison has succinctly put it, 'charity does not offer rights'. Plant has made much the same point in describing voluntary action as 'inherently discretionary'. Benevolence bestowed can readily be withdrawn if those offering it so choose.

Participation in voluntary-sector activity might, moreover, encourage and reinforce élitism, in that only some sections of the population, endowed with economic or educational advantage, would tend to dominate within such organizations; and their participation would separate them from large sections of society not able, or not prepared, to expend energy in this way. This could also be true of the nineteenth-century 'Labour aristocracy'. While active citizenship could result in 'releasing the community spirit', it could also, especially when shading into pursuit of individual gain through the commercial sector, be erosive of 'the community spirit'. The provision of welfare services through the market could lead to such provision being dependent on ability to pay rather than on recognition of need. It might 'enable' some—but not all.

Participation in voluntary work could also lead to amateurism and a lack of proper professional practice, as all comers were welcomed without questions asked as to their capacity for undertaking welfare work. Once more, the Younghusband Committee noted the dangers here. Visiting the elderly or handicapped—much associated with voluntary-sector work—was 'not the smooth and simple task it may appear to those who have never attempted it'. It could lead to resentment among those at the receiving end. 'Yes, I like visitors,' said one old lady quoted by the Committee, 'but save me from those who show they come only from Christian charity.' This particular problem was also experienced by an organization such as Task Force. It was, of course, true that the voluntary sector itself well recognized the problem. The Charity Organisation Society was early in appreciating the need for more professional training for voluntary social workers; and some organizations, such as the King George VI Social Service Scheme for old people, ran training courses for visitors. The Aves Committee Report stressed the need for adequate 'preparation' for voluntary-sector workers. Nevertheless, it was an issue which gave rise to recurrent problems, and was one which could flaw both the vogue for participation of the 1960s and 1970s and the New Right's enthusiasm for the active—but sometimes ill-informed and ill-prepared—citizen. It should, of course, be said that the professionally trained social worker, employed by a statutory body, was not immune from this kind of criticism, and was on occasion to incur opprobrium, sometimes for a lack of zeal in the handling of individual social welfare issues, and sometimes for too much zeal. The Orkney Inquiry of 1991, following allegations of parental child abuse, raised many such issues.

Participation in voluntary-sector work could also lead to problems of unreliability. It was quite possible, as the Younghusband Committee noted, for voluntary workers, used in this sense— that is, those who contributed effort to a voluntary or statutory organization on an unpaid basis—to lose interest and give up the work on which they were engaged. There was a lack of overall uniformity. Voluntary activity is, of its very nature, dependent on individual effort; as Younghusband put it, 'the winds of voluntary effort blow where they will, and are sometimes most salubrious when least convenient for administrative purposes.' This, of course, makes the provision of welfare services through voluntarism patchy and variable; there is no overall plan. Provision will depend on the willingness of individuals to provide, either for themselves or for others, in the voluntary and informal sectors, and on the ability of individuals to pay in the commercial sector. *The Times* put it thus, with the voluntary sector particularly in mind: 'Inevitably, because it relies on individuals and their enthusiasms, voluntary social service is patchy, non-uniform; there is always an element of chance. Volunteers may do a good job for the elderly in one district, in another, Age Concern and similar groups find it difficult to mobilize.'

If unreliability could be the problem at one extreme, excessive bureaucracy and duplication could be the problem at the other. A large charitable organization might, indeed, differ little from a government department. It was noted in 1949 in *Evidence for Voluntary Action* that when charities turned into 'business propositions', had large offices, and ran advertising campaigns, they 'came to be compared with the Ministries that are also dispensing monetary aid to those in need'. This gave rise to the feeling that the Ministries could 'do the job more efficiently and with less overlap, as well as ensuring that the amounts to be given were as rightly apportioned as the amounts received'. A report based on research carried out for the Royal National Institute for the Blind observed that there was 'considerable suspicion . . . towards the expenditure of charities on administration costs', and that this was especially true in areas where several charities were involved in catering for similar groups.

The voluntary sector, of course, has long recognized these problems, and individual charities have made strenuous efforts to ensure that they cannot be criticized for spending too much on administration at the expense of the people whom they seek to serve. Thus Barnardo's in the mid-1970s spent 80.5p of every pound raised on children in the United Kingdom, with only 3p per pound being spent on head-office administration and 12.5p on fund-raising and educational work. It is also true that numerous 'umbrella' organizations have been formed to rationalize and organize voluntary effort. But with some smaller charities, too *little* money spent on administration can lead to difficulties; and while coordinating bodies can achieve much, there are always limits to the extent to which they can help; in the last resort, they do not have levers of compulsion. Again, of course, the commercial sector is, by its nature, competitive; and any attempts to coordinate its activities are bound to perish on that rock. Thus the various sectors of voluntarism, while they offer freedom, flexibility, and choice, cannot guarantee uniformity and comprehensiveness. They may well embody the citizenship of contribution, and contribution can be offered to statutory bodies; they may well advise on statutory welfare rights; but they cannot implement the citizenship of entitlement.

A further problem—indeed, a basic problem—affecting voluntary organizations, particularly those in the voluntary sector, relates to resources and finance. As has been seen, such organizations were in the nineteenth century characterized by a constant scramble for money; and while this was often forthcoming in large measure, it was of its nature unpredictable, on both the mutual-aid and charitable sides of the voluntary sector. On the mutual-aid side, the contribution of funds by subscription might certainly depend on individual choice; but that choice was often dictated by economic circumstances over which the individual had little control. Choice might dictate the bestowal, either by legacy or by subscription, of substantial sums of money on the charitable side of the voluntary sector; but here, too, choice could depend on economic fortune or ill fortune—and would always be dictated by individual preference. This might lead to the bunching of money around 'fashionable', emotional, or well-publicized causes to the detriment of others. The status of the personnel at the head of a charitable organization can also be of great importance. Royal patronage is of great assistance—and this is true not only of the nineteenth century, but also of the twentieth. When Princess Anne—as she then was—became President of the Save the Children Fund in 1971, she made it clear that she would not become a mere figurehead; nor did she do so. But her patronage of the Fund is unquestionably important in attracting support. As she herself said, 'It is, I think, fair to say that I probably attract slightly more attention than the average.'

It was, moreover, almost always a question of finite resources being set against infinite needs. The very efforts of charitable agencies—even those designed to ensure that charity was 'well' spent, such as the Charity Organisation Society—often uncovered yet more need, which was beyond their capacity to meet. Philanthropists in the nineteenth century, such as Shaftesbury, Barnardo, William Booth, and Cadbury, were well aware of the incessant demands made on charitable giving—and of the limited ability of charity to meet them, or to do more than help individuals. This was to become ever more true in the twentieth century, as welfare services became more expensive in the light of medical and other advances; and charity was often forced to look for assistance outside itself.

This, indeed, leads to the second theme pursued throughout this book, which is the relationship of voluntarism to the statutory sector. In many respects, this involves setting the points already made about the strengths and limitations of voluntarism more firmly into historical context—and also leads back to the quotation from Titmuss with which this book began: that welfare systems 'reflect the dominant cultural and political characteristics of their societies'. A similar point was made by Taylor-Gooby and Bochel: that 'the organization of the welfare state reflects the main current in public opinion'. While it is perfectly true, as Harris has pointed out, that there is a line of continuity between the Poor Law of 1834 and the Welfare State, in that both embodied an 'institutional inheritance of an absolute statutory right to non-contributory public relief', such a judgement masks immense differences in the 'dominant political and cultural characteristics'—or 'the main current in public opinion'—of the societies which produced them. The Poor Law of 1834 was the product of a society which saw the state in minimal terms: as an agency which was primarily designed to enable and encourage voluntary initiatives to proceed, or simply to undertake 'gap-filling' roles when they did not proceed. That could not be said of the society which produced the Welfare State in the twentieth century.

The period from 1830 to 1880 was, then, one in which the merits of voluntarism, as outlined above, were highly prized: the ways in which it embodied individual choice and participation, personal independence and local control, freedom and flexibility. These were the political and cultural norms of the society of the time: ones which were able to embrace statutory initiatives of a localized kind—although even here private initiatives were often preferred—but were highly suspicious of the compulsion and cost seen to go with the centralized state. It is true that, despite this, the centralized state did grow; but it grew by stealth, in the process of promoting economic growth which would lead to greater personal wealth, establishing agencies to encourage or regularize the voluntary initiatives of friendly societies or charitable effort or, in the last resort, to supplement those initiatives. Voluntary and statutory agencies alike were preoccupied with promoting independence—so much so, indeed, that disfranchisement went with receipt of poor relief. The citizenship of entitlement to civic and political rights was, then, cancelled by dependence on poor relief; and there were constant efforts made to ensure that voluntary initiatives in social welfare established, rather than eroded, the capacity for independent mutual-aid or self-help. The pursuit of social welfare in the period was, therefore, permeated by the ideology of voluntarism; it depended heavily on the agencies of the varied sectors of voluntarism, and only minimally on the agencies of the centralized state.

The pursuit of independence—of what Smiles called 'help from within'—had, however, always encountered problems posed by 'circumstances': that in practice, and particularly at times of social and economic hardship, it was difficult to achieve. At such times, 'help from without', whether from a more lax administration of charity or of poor relief, could easily slip into place. When this happened, 'convictions' tried to correct the tendency—as when, in 1869, a stricter application of charity and poor relief was envisaged with the establishment of the Charity Organisation Society and the passing of the Goschen Minute. After about 1880, however, circumstances made such adjustments to the previously tuned balanced formula between 'help from within' and 'help from without' and between providence, paternalism, and philanthropy difficult to retain. The period after 1880 was not, in fact, one of overwhelming depression in economic or social terms; but it did witness an increasing awareness of unemployment and poverty, assisted by the appearance of well-publicized social surveys. These, especially in the context of fears and anxieties about Britain's international and military standing, cast doubt on whether the former reliance on voluntarism and a minimal, localized state could bring about individual well-being in sufficient measure to promote national efficiency. Again, the period between 1880 and 1914 did not witness the establishment of a fully democratic state; but legislation within it did widen the process of political participation and, in that sense, of a wider citizenship of entitlement. In that context—and in the context of the economic hardship of the time—it was difficult to hold to the previous practice of denying civic rights to persons who might now more readily qualify for them but for the receipt of poor relief; and, more generally, the politicians of most persuasions became conscious of a larger electoral constituency which, in their view, might well be swayed by a greater concentration on social issues.

In such circumstances, many of the limitations of voluntarism, as mentioned above, came into prominence: that it was localized, patchy, and unreliable, unable to cope with an environment which made individual effort towards improvement, whether by mutual-aid, self-help, or charity, difficult, if not impossible, to achieve.

It *could not* cope with the situation, the more so since voluntary efforts found themselves in many cases facing increased problems with smaller resources. And in this period, convictions did not come to the rescue; if anything, they reinforced the challenge to voluntarism which, it was felt in many quarters, *should not* cope with the situation. 'New Liberals' became doubtful of its value, and felt that it diverted attention and resources from the need for larger-scale change. Socialists felt that charity was an aspect of the wealth, privilege, and élitism which they wished to abolish; and also that its efforts were not only unavailing but harmful. Thus the citizenship of contribution through voluntary means was open to criticism; and the citizenship of entitlement, now incorporating social, in addition to civil and political, rights, gained an increasing following. That citizenship could, moreover, be implemented only through the state, which seemed alone to have the resources to cope with the task of social reconstruction on a sufficiently large and comprehensive scale. This task was made all the more urgent in the light of Britain's international position. The state alone, as the embodiment of all—or most—citizens could be said to have the moral duty to cater for their needs in a more positive way than the old deterrent and minimal poor law—which, indeed, was equally open to the '*could not* cope' and '*should not* cope' arguments.

The political and cultural characteristics of society thus appeared to be running against voluntarism, and pointing up its defects—and in favour of collectivism. The comment made by Asquith on the problems caused by old age might have a wider application: a 'contingency against which thrift and prudence, however well organized by voluntary effort, are least able to make adequate provision'. There now appeared to be many such contingencies—which also seemed to be beyond the capacity of charity. As Kirkman Gray put it in 1908, 'the State has been forced . . . to take over tasks for which private philanthropy had found its resources insufficient'. Under such influences, the proportion of Gross National Product spent on the social services doubled between 1890 and 1914 as the state assumed a more positive role in social welfare; and a burst of social legislation always seen to be significant in this respect was passed by the Liberal government after 1906.

It may be argued that much the same process was discernible

in the period after 1914. The circumstances of two World Wars and of the unemployment of the 1920s and 1930s further exposed the limitations of voluntarism—and further made the case for a planned and integrated approach to social welfare by means of the state. The citizenship of entitlement through the state could also be advanced on grounds of fairness and equity; and, indeed, it could well be argued that the citizenship of contribution could be expressed through statutory or civic agencies. The Stevenson Lectureship in Citizenship at the University of Glasgow—established in 1920 after a fairly long campaign carried out much in the 'New Liberal' tradition by Sir Henry Jones, Professor of Moral Philosophy at the University—was designed 'to make provision in Glasgow for the instruction in the rights, duties and obligations of citizens in relation to the city, the state, and the commonwealth of nations'. It is of interest that Hugh Gaitskell applied to give the lectures in 1938; of interest, too, that his application was unsuccessful. The lecturer appointed on that occasion, A. D. K. Owen, called in his lectures for social reconstruction which, he said, was 'the major part of Scottish citizenship'. In that reconstruction statutory agencies would play a central role.

It was after what may be seen as the culmination of this process, the formal establishment of the Welfare State in the later 1940s, that Marshall wrote in 1959 that 'voluntary service was in no way a monopoly of the voluntary agencies', and could be channelled through the newly created statutory agencies. It was in 1951 that he developed his progressive model of citizenship with statutory social rights marking the culmination; and it was in the 1950s and 1960s that he and others saw the state as ever more likely to extend its activities; in the 1950s and 1960s, indeed, a much more extensive model of the Welfare State developed than that of the later 1940s, embodying what Harris has called 'the whole complex of social and educational policies and institutions which, in modern societies, bear upon individual and collective socio-economic needs'. Citizenship became ever more closely bound up with the enjoyment of social rights on an optimum basis and with an attack on poverty—which Donnison was later to define as 'the exclusion from the living standards, the life-styles and the fellowship of one's fellow citizens'. As Vincent has commented: 'Properly understood, a poor citizen is a contradiction in terms.'

Viewed in this light, it might be argued that the political and cultural characteristics of society during the century from 1880 to 1979 pointed up the limitations of voluntarism and the strengths of collectivism; and it might also be argued that the efforts of Conservative governments after 1979 did little to stop this process, even if they attempted to do so. For all the rhetoric about 'rolling back the frontiers of the state' in the 1980s, the statutory sector under the Conservative administrations of Thatcher and John Major remained clearly dominant. The other sectors of welfare, voluntary, commercial, and informal, were forced to recognize this and, unwillingly or willingly, to accept it. There was, indeed, a strain within voluntarism which sought to diverge from the growth of the state, which it saw as damaging to its main attributes of freedom and individual choice; but in the end, that libertarian strain lost the battle to the state—and to the other strain within voluntarism, which sought to accommodate to the state and to cooperate with it. This opened up sources of finance and influence which would otherwise be denied to it. Subsequent events were, it might well be suggested, to prove the accuracy of Loch's observation of 1913 to the effect that those friendly societies involved in charity were 'running to shelter, like creatures in a storm', given 'protection and a sense of dignity' by 'the status of a Government alliance'. The development of what Macadam called in 1934 the 'New Philanthropy', involving close cooperation between voluntary and statutory bodies, was an aspect of this theme, as were to be the various agency agreements of the later 1940s and the 1950s. When the voluntary sector, in particular, gained a new momentum in the 1960s and 1970s, it did so within a broad acceptance of the Welfare State—to which it looked for continuing support. When, in the 1980s, there was an attempt to give a more clearly defined role to voluntary-sector initiatives, this was resisted; indeed, some of the strongest opponents of the New Right came from charitable organizations and the churches. In March 1983 Robert Heasman, Appeals director of the Shaftesbury Society, said that there was 'no way we could take over the role of the Welfare State. We could not even begin . . .' Later the same year Hinton, in describing the role of the voluntary sector as director of the National Council for Voluntary Organisations, wrote that 'this is not to suggest that the voluntary sector should, or could, substitute for the statutory social services'.

This kind of interpretation would cast doubt on whether the

voluntary sector had an effective 'voice'; if it was so close to government, how could it act as a watchdog or a critic of government? Again—to adapt the terms used by Hirschman—it is difficult to see how the voluntary sector can be an effective means of 'Exit' from the Welfare State when it is so closely bound up with it. This line of argument would, then, suggest that there is something to be said for the 'Whig' interpretation of the development of the Welfare State. The political and cultural norms since the late 1880s seemed to dictate a growth of state welfare—to which voluntarism itself, and particularly the voluntary sector, accommodated itself, either unwillingly or willingly.

Yet, if some of the material in this book can be used to come to that conclusion—and it was earlier admitted that the Whig road to welfare had its attractions—by no means all of it can. The linear development *from* voluntarism *to* state reduces the contribution of voluntarism to welfare to insignificance, or sees it as a positive hindrance; it concentrates on all the demerits of voluntarism as stated above. It distorts the role of voluntarism by seeing it through collectivist spectacles. Equally, it ignores the ways in which voluntarism itself changed, and does not take into account the complex relationship between voluntarism and the state which ran through all the periods covered by this book—and fails to see how collectivist developments were themselves shadowed—and indeed often permeated—by voluntarist ideas.

This was clearly true of the period from 1830 to 1880; and the collectivism of the period from 1880 to 1914 took place in the context of strong voluntarist assumptions, such as those of Loch, Bosanquet, and Dicey—and of Margaret Loane, who, as a district nurse with great familiarity with the lives of poor families, wrote a number of pamphlets which put forward traditional voluntarist solutions to social issues and was totally out of sympathy with the legislation of the 'New Liberals'. It may be said that these were extreme libertarian points of view which were becoming marginalized; but there were others who, while seeing their limitations, did not wish to depart too far from them. Thus Sir Oliver Lodge, writing in 1912, acknowledged that 'the environment . . . is by no means faultless and free from blame', and admitted that charity organization was 'not the last words on the social problem', adding that 'there is a better kind of organization open to statesmen and social reformers'. Yet he supported the methods used by the Charity Organisation Society in preventing the demoralization of the poor and the defrauding of the rich by excessive charity; 'all our help', he wrote, 'is to be given in a personal manner, and as long as the Society works on these lines it deserves generous support.' Even the 'New Liberals' themselves may have been 'new', but they remained 'liberals'; and, as Vincent has put it, 'ambiguity was written into the innovations of the period'. They could be regarded as 'stepping-stones to something better', as Labour members tended to see them; but to look at the legislation in this light can be tantamount to embarking on what has been described as the collective train journey into the future; and many Liberals regarded the purpose of the reforms as making that particular venture as unnecessary as it was undesirable. If collectivism challenged voluntarism, voluntarism intersected collectivism.

The period from 1914 to 1939 was also noted for its ambiguities in social policy. Voluntarist ideas coexisted with collectivist thinking, and very often influenced it; boundaries may have been becoming somewhat clearer, but often remained fluid and ill-defined. The state displayed a reluctance to extend its boundaries very far. Cronin points out that, despite repeated calls for policies to deal with the effects of the depression, the role of central government remained largely unaltered from the early 1920s through the 1930s. The years from 1939 to 1948 may be seen as representing a hardening of the boundaries and a greater definition of the frontiers, as, with the advent of the Labour government, the need for social planning under the vicissitudes of war and social fairness advanced the state. And yet, if the Beveridge Report of 1942 put forward universalist, statutory solutions to social problems, voluntarist assumptions about the desirability of individual effort in building on the still fairly minimal state provision permeated Beveridge's thinking. As Harris has put it:

In the course of cross-examination of witnesses before the Social Insurance Committee, [Beveridge] scathingly invoked the image of 'the Santa Claus state' as the epitome of the kind of welfare system that he was determined to avoid . . . 'Benefits in return for contributions, rather than free allowances from the State is what the people of Britain desire' was perhaps the key sentiment in the whole of the Beveridge report, and the one most often quoted by contemporary commentators.

To regard Beveridge as an arch-collectivist, responsible for sponsoring massive Welfare State provision—as Correlli Barnett has done—is to misrepresent him, and to ignore the plea for a continuing role for voluntary social action which Beveridge made in 1948 in *Voluntary Action*.

It is true that the legislation of the Attlee government after 1945 went rather further than Beveridge would have liked in divorcing voluntary-sector agencies from National Insurance—and absorbed the voluntary hospitals into the statutory system of health care. Beveridge's *Voluntary Action* might be regarded as a despairing plea for the continuation of principles which had been overtaken by events. Certainly, as the Wolfenden Committee stated, the voluntary sector was thereafter 'dominated by the problems of adaptation to the new role of government'; and when it underwent a certain revival in the 1960s and 1970s, it did not seek to set itself up as an alternative to the Welfare State, but acted within in. Nevertheless, it remained conscious of its potential to encourage a degree of participation not offered by the state and to draw attention to needs not met by the state; and the widespread acceptance of a pluralist system of social welfare afforded it a role within the mixed economy. It is also true to say that, even in a period often characterized as one of consensus, in which the pre-eminence of the statutory sector was widely accepted, there was room for ideologies which were anti-collectivist and retained some libertarian traditions. Thus Titmuss in 1962 noted the existence of hostility to the Welfare State on the grounds that it undermined thrift and family responsibility, and that it was a cause of social decadence among the working classes. Marshall's optimistic views of the Welfare State are open to criticism, and he himself failed to reconcile the continuing existence of the market, which he saw to be necessary to create the wealth which would uphold the citizenship of entitlement, with that citizenship of entitlement itself. The market was the means to inequality and, as such, was dubiously reconcilable with the social rights of citizenship which were held to be the means to equality. This left room for the view that such social rights, delivered by the state, hindered and hampered the market; and that what was required was a dismantling of the state and a greater role for the market.

Such ideas may have been unfashionable in the 1960s and

1970s—but they were present. However, they came into prominence after 1979, to a degree which gave that period a different character in social policy. Voluntarist ideology was then again clearly present both within the state, seen in the greater degree of participation and local control envisaged in opting-out schemes; and outside it, in the encouragement given to the voluntary and informal sectors—and notably to the market-led commercial sector, which, especially in certain areas such as provision for the elderly, made great strides.

If, then, it would be wrong to ignore the continuing strains of voluntarist ideology and the ways in which they often penetrated the state, it would also be greatly mistaken to overlook the continuing activity of voluntarist agencies themselves, even when their role changed in the context of a greater statutory presence. Even when their role converged with the state, thus endangering the separate identity and independence of the voluntary sector in particular, there remained a desire to protect and preserve that identity as far as was possible. The convergent role of the voluntary sector was always shot through with an awareness of the tensions which this involved: tensions between control and independence, undue direction and freedom of movement. A long-standing issue was simply restated in 1990, when government proposals suggested that the £2 billion of taxpayers' money annually spent on voluntary bodies should be more closely linked to the achievement of government policies. The National Council for Voluntary Organisations stated that attempts to make funding reflect government policy more closely could compromise the independence of the voluntary sector, which was, it said, 'its great strength'. Prashar noted that there was a danger that the sector 'could become a simple extension of government policy'; and that, while organizations 'sub-contracted' to deliver government services had clearly to reflect departmental policy, other voluntary groups acted as the 'conscience of the Government'. The voluntary sector was also well aware of the danger of too close an identification with the commercial sector. This was evident in the disappointment of the mutual-aid friendly societies at the arrangement for Approved Societies in the National Insurance Act of 1911; it was also evident in the 1980s, as voluntary-sector organizations felt themselves compelled to move closer to commercial-sector practice. Yet voluntary-sector provision, even 'within' the state, retained certain distinctive characteristics, implicit or explicit; it still gave scope for choice and variety, even when the state paid most of the cost.

The period since 1830 has seen a constantly changing mixture of the citizenship of contribution and the citizenship of entitlement, sometimes in harmony, sometimes in tension. It seems possible that the future may see some coming together of previously hostile positions. Whereas at the beginning of the twentieth century the general opinion was that the voluntary sector neither *could* nor *should* cope with the range of social needs and deprivation, by 1990, despite a proliferating and increasingly costly Welfare State, there was in many quarters a growing conviction that the state *could not* cope alone, and needed the collaboration of the voluntary sector and of charitable funds; and furthermore that it *should not* undertake the extensive role it had assumed in the decades since the 1940s. The New Right was much concerned to identify and specify entitlements within the statutory services, through the Citizen's Charter and other means, and to harness the voluntary sector as agent of the state. Its overt aim was ultimately to reduce the role of the state, which would fill the gaps in non-statutory provision only: a return to the notion of the minimal state. As has been suggested, there was little that was new in New Right thinking, and any change it effected tended to be in rhetoric rather than in fact. Yet it would be wrong to deny the changes in balance and emphasis—part of the continual process of experimentation that reflects the concerns and aspirations of successive generations. While the Left rejected the New Right ideology, it did come to accept the need for a certain amount of choice, and to realize that expenditure on state services could not increase forever unchecked.

The result of the growth of the Welfare State is that the voluntary sector is increasingly influenced by the state, and often functions within or as an agent of the statutory sector, although not always willingly. This change epitomizes the reversal of emphasis that this book has traced, but also oversimplifies the process and the result. By putting the evolution of social policies into historical perspective and context, this book has sought to dispel the idea of a logical progression from 1830 to 1990, and to show how, as Titmuss suggested, welfare systems arise from and reflect the cultural and political norms and assumptions of the time. These have changed and will change continually, as the debate about the role of government veers over the generations. 'The notion of a settled equilibrium is, as every student of history must affirm, simple nonsense.'

Bibliography

1. PRIMARY SOURCES

(a) Archive Material

Edinburgh University Library
  Oral and written evidence presented to the Wolfenden Committee on the future of voluntary organisations.
National Council for Voluntary Organisations, London
  Information reports and sheets.
Nuffield College, Oxford
  Nuffield MSS.

(b) Reports, Lectures, Speeches, Pamphlets

Annual Charities Register and Digest.
Board of Guardians and Trustees for the Relief of the Jewish Poor Registered: Annual Report, 1958.
Charities Aid Foundation: Annual Charity Statistics.
Charities Digest.
Charity Law and Voluntary Organisations: Report of the Goodman Committee (London: Bedford Square Press, 1976).
Conference on War Relief and Personal Service (London: Longmans, Green, 1915).
50 Million Volunteers: A Report on the Role of Voluntary Organisations and Youth in the Environment (London: HMSO, 1972).
The Future of Voluntary Organisations: Report of the Wolfenden Committee (London: Croom Helm, 1978).
GILMOUR, SIR IAN, Speech to Child Poverty Action Group, NN, 1988.
HARRISON, BRIAN, and DEACON, NICHOLAS, *Voluntary Organisations and Democracy*, Sir George Haynes Lecture, 1987 (London: National Council for Voluntary Organisations, 1988).
HESELTINE, MICHAEL, 'Re-Building the Cities', Speech at Knowsley (Apr. 1986).
—— 'Congestion in the South: The Subsidised Market', Speech at Blackpool (Apr. 1988).
—— 'On Solid Ground', Twelfth Duke of Edinburgh Lecture, London (Oct. 1989).
LOW, SAMPSON, *The Charities of London: Comprehending the Benevolent, Educational and Religious Institutions; their Origin and Design, Progress, and Present Position* (London, 1850).

—— *The Charities of London in 1852–3 ... With an Introductory Analysis* (London, 1854).

—— *The Charities of London in 1861. Comprising an Account of the Operations ... of the Charitable, Educational, and Religious Institutions of London* (London, 1862).

Men without Work: A Report Made to the Pilgrim Trust, with an Introduction by the Archbishop of York and a Preface by Lord Macmillan (Cambridge: Cambridge University Press, 1938).

MENCHER, S., 'The Relationship of Voluntary and Statutory Agencies in the Welfare Services', Loch Memorial Lecture, 1954 (London: Family Welfare Association, 1954).

PILGRIM TRUST: Annual Reports.

PLANT, R., *Citizenship, Rights and Socialism* (London: Fabian Society, 1988).

Report of the Committee on Public Participation in Planning (London: HMSO, 1969).

Report of Industrial Tribunal RE 74767/2 IM 3/80 TBL, 17 Jan. 1989.

Report of the Working Party on Social Workers in the Local Authority Health and Welfare Services (London: HMSO, 1959).

Report on the British Social Services: A Survey of the Existing Public Social Services in Great Britain with Proposals for Future Development (London: Political and Economic Planning, 1937).

Shaftesbury Society and Ragged School Union: Annual Reports and Minutes (using Harvester Microform for Minutes).

Social Workers, their Role and Tasks, Report of a Working Party set up in October 1980 at the request of the Secretary of State for Social Services by the National Institute for Social Work under the chairmanship of Mr Peter M. Barclay (London: Bedford Square Press, 1982).

Voluntary Social Services: Handbook of Information and Directory of Organisations (London: The National Council of Social Service, 1948).

Working Together: Partnerships in Local Social Service (London: Bedford Square Press, 1981).

(c) Journals and Periodicals

The Charity Organisation Quarterly (using Harvester Microform)
The Charity Organisation Reporter (using Harvester Microform)
The Charity Organisation Review (using Harvester Microform)
The Charity Record and Philanthropic News
The Charity Record, Hospital Times and Philanthropist
Community Care
Contemporary Review
The Economist
The Graduate
Health and Social Service Journal
Marxism Today

New Socialist
New Society
The Nineteenth Century
Political Quarterly
Quarterly Review
The Spectator
The Times Education Supplement, Scotland
Voluntary Action (from Oct. 1985, published as part of *New Society*)
Westminster Review
Whitaker's Almanack

(d) Newspapers

The Church Times
The Daily Telegraph
Financial Times
The Glasgow Herald
The Guardian
The Independent
The Independent on Sunday
The Observer
Scotland on Sunday
The Scotsman
The Sunday Correspondent
The Sunday Times
The Times

(e) Parliamentary Papers

(i) Series

Annual Reports of the Chief Registrar of Friendly Societies.
Annual Reports of the Charity Commissioners for England and Wales.
Hansard: House of Commons and House of Lords Debates, third, fourth, and fifth series.

(ii) Special Reports and Returns

Report on the Administration and Practical Operation of the Poor Laws (PP 1834).
Royal Commission on Friendly and Benefit Building Societies (PP 1874, Pt. 1; C. 961).
First Report of the Royal Commission for inquiring into the Housing of the Working Classes, with Evidence, Appendix and Indices (PP 1884–5; C. 4402).
Report of the Inter-Departmental Committee on Physical Deterioration (PP 1904; Cd. 2175).

Minutes of Evidence Taken Before the Inter-Departmental Committee on Physical Deterioration (PP 1904; Cd. 2210).

Report of the Royal Commission on the Poor Laws and Relief of Distress (PP 1909; Cd. 4499).

Report on the Special Work of the Local Government Board Arising out of the War (PP 1915; Cd. 7763).

Report of the Committee on War Charities (PP 1916; Cd. 8287).

Report on the Administration of the National Relief Fund (PP 1917; Cd. 8449).

Voluntary Hospitals Committee (PP 1921; Cmd. 1335).

Report of the Committee on the Co-ordination of Administrative and Executive Arrangements for the Grant of Assistance from Public Funds on Account of Sickness, Destitution and Unemployment (PP 1923; Cmd. 2011).

Report of the Home Office Department Committee on the Supervision of Charities (PP 1927; Cmd. 2823).

First Report of the Commissioner for the Special Areas (England and Wales) (PP 1935; Cmd. 4957).

Social Insurance and Allied Services Report by Sir William Beveridge (PP 1942–3, 2 vols.; Cmd. 6404, 6405).

Report of the Committee on the Law and Practice relating to Charitable Trusts (PP 1952–3; Cmd. 8710).

Report of the Committee on Local Authority and Allied Personal Social Services (PP 1969; Cmnd. 3703).

Report of the Royal Commission on the National Health Service (PP 1979; Cmnd. 7615).

Caring for People: Community Care in the Next Decade and Beyond (PP 1989; Cm. 849).

Charities: A Framework for the Future (PP 1989; Cm. 984).

2. SECONDARY SOURCES

(a) Articles

ASHLEY, LORD, 'Infant Labour', *Quarterly Review*, LXVIII (1840).

BARNETT, REVD SAMUEL, 'Sensationalism in Social Reform', *The Nineteenth Century*, XIX (Jan.–June 1886).

BARTRIP, P. W. J., 'State Intervention in Mid-Nineteenth Century Britain: Fact or Fiction?', *Journal of British Studies*, XXIII, no. 1 (1983).

BELL, COLIN, 'A Volunteer Spectrum', *New Society*, 32, no. 663 (19 June 1975).

BRIGGS, ASA, 'The Welfare State in Historical Perspective', *European Archives of Sociology*, II, no. 2 (1961).

BROWN, JOHN, 'Charles Booth and the Labour Colonies, 1889–1905', *Economic History Review*, 2nd ser., XXI (1968).

—— 'The Appointment of the 1905 Poor Law Commission', *Bulletin of the Institute of Historical Research*, XLII, no. 106 (Nov. 1969).

—— 'Social Judgements and Social Policy', *Economic History Review*, 2nd ser., XXXIV (1971).

BUGLER, JEREMY, 'The Volunteer Upsurge', *New Society*, 6, no. 159 (14 Oct. 1965).

CAHILL, MICHAEL, and JOWITT, TONY, 'The New Philanthropy: The Emergence of the Bradford Guild of Help', *Journal of Social Policy*, 9 (1980).

CROSSICK, GEOFFREY, 'The Labour Aristocracy and its Values: A Study of Mid-Victorian Kentish London', *Victorian Studies*, XIX, no. 3 (Mar. 1976).

DUTTON, H. I., and KING, J. E., 'The Limits of Paternalism: The Cotton Tyrants of North Lancashire, 1836–54', *Social History*, 7 (1982).

EASTWOOD, DAVID, 'Robert Southey and the Intellectual Origins of Romantic Conservatism', *English Historical Review*, CIV, no. 411 (Apr. 1989).

ELLIS, L. F., 'The Respective Spheres of Public Authorities and Voluntary Organisations in the Administration of Social Services', *Public Administration*, V, no. 4 (Oct. 1927).

EVANS, NEIL, 'Urbanisation, Elite Attitudes and Philanthropy: Cardiff, 1850–1914', *International Review of Social History*, XXVII (1982).

FIELDEN, KENNETH, 'Samuel Smiles and Self-Help', *Victorian Studies*, XII, no. 2 (Dec. 1968).

FISHLOW, ALBERT, 'Trustee Savings Banks, 1817–1861', *Journal of Economic History*, XXI, no. 1 (Mar. 1961).

GERARD, JESSICA, 'Lady Bountiful: Women of the Landed Classes and Rural Philanthropy', *Victorian Studies*, XXX, no. 2 (1987).

GILBERT, B. B., 'The Decay of Provident Institutions and the Coming of Old Age Pensions in Great Britain', *Economic History Review*, 2nd ser., no. 3, XVII (Apr. 1965).

GRAYCAR, A., 'Informal, Voluntary and Statutory Services: The Complex Relationship', *British Journal of Social Work*, 13, no. 4 (1983).

HARRISON, BRIAN, 'Victorian Philanthropy', *Victorian Studies*, IX, no. 4 (June 1966).

HARRISON, J. F. C., 'The Victorian Gospel of Success', *Victorian Studies*, I, no. 2 (Dec. 1957).

HATCH, STEPHEN, and MOCROFT, IAN, 'Voluntary Workers', (*New Society*, 40, no. 757 (7 Apr. 1977).

HAYBURN, RALPH H. C., 'The Voluntary Occupational Centre Movement 1932–39', *Journal of Contemporary History*, 6, no. 3 (1971).

HENNOCK, E. P., 'Poverty and Social Theory in England: The Experience of the Eighteen-Eighties', *Social History*, 1 (1976).

HENRIQUES, U., 'How Cruel was the Victorian Poor Law?', *Historical Journal*, XI, pt. 2 (1968).

HONIGSBAUM, FRANK, 'The Interwar Health Insurance Scheme: A Rejoinder', *Journal of Social Policy*, 12 (1983).

IGNATIEFF, M., 'Citizenship and Moral Narcissism', *Political Quarterly*, 60, no. 1 (Jan. 1989).

JEFFERYS, KEVIN, 'British Politics and Social Policy during the Second World War', *Historical Journal*, XXX (1987).

JOHNSON, PAUL, 'Conspicuous Consumption and Working-Class Culture in Late Victorian and Edwardian Britain', *Transactions of the Royal Historical Society*, 5th ser. 38 (1988).

KAMERMAN, S., 'The New Mixed Economy of Welfare: Public and Private', *Social Work* (Jan.–Feb. 1983).

KRAMER, R., 'Voluntary Agencies in the Welfare State: An Analysis of the Vanguard Role', *Journal of Social Policy*, 8, pt. 4 (Oct. 1979).

LEADBEATER, CHARLIE, 'New Times Back to the Future', *Marxism Today* (May 1989).

LEECH, KEN, 'Caesar's Religion?', *New Socialist*, no. 66 (Apr.–May 1990).

LUMMIS, TREVOR, 'Charles Booth: Moralist or Social Scientist?', *Economic History Review*, 2nd ser., XXIV (1971).

MACDONAGH, OLIVER, 'The Nineteenth-Century Revolution in Government: A Re-Appraisal', *Historical Journal*, I (1958).

MACNICOL, JOHN, 'In Pursuit of the Underclass', *Journal of Social Policy*, 16 (1987).

MARWICK, ARTHUR, 'Middle Opinion in the Thirties: Planning, Progress and "Political Agreement"', *English Historical Review*, LXXIX (Apr. 1964).

MILLER, FREDERIC M., 'The Unemployment Policy of the National Government, 1936', *Historical Journal*, XIX (1976).

MOORE, M. J., 'Social Work and Social Welfare: The Organisation of Philanthropic Resources in Britain, 1900–1914', *Journal of British Studies*, XVI (1977).

MORRIS, R. J., 'Samuel Smiles and the Genesis of *Self-Help*: The Retreat to a Petit Bourgeois Utopia', *Historical Journal*, XXIV, pt. 1 (1981).

—— 'Voluntary Societies and British Urban Elites', *Historical Journal*, XXVI (1983).

PARRIS, HENRY, 'The Nineteenth-Century Revolution in Government: A Re-Appraisal Re-Appraised', *Historical Journal*, III (1960).

PRICE, L. L., Review of B. Seebohm Rowntree, *Poverty: A Study in Town Life*, *Economic Journal*, XII (1902).

PROCHASKA, F., 'A Mother's Country: Mothers' Meetings and Family Welfare in Britain, 1850–1950', *History*, 74, no. 242 (Oct. 1989).

PRUGER, R., 'Social Policy: Unilateral Transfer or Reciprocal Exchange', *Journal of Social Policy*, 2, pt. 4 (1973).

ROBERTS, DAVID, 'Jeremy Bentham and the Victorian Administrative State', *Victorian Studies*, II, no. 3 (Mar. 1959).

—— 'How Cruel was the Victorian Poor Law?', *Historical Journal*, XI, pt. 2 (1968).

RODGER, RICHARD, 'Political Economy, Ideology and the Persistence of Working Class Housing Problems in Britain', *International Review of Social History*, XXXII (1987).

ROWNTREE, B. S., Review of A. L. Bowley and A. R. Barnett-Hurst, *Livelihood and Poverty*, *Economic Journal*, XXV (1915).

THANE, PAT, 'The Historiography of the British Welfare State', *Social History Society Newsletter*, 15, no. 1 (Spring 1990).

—— 'The Working Class and State "Welfare" in Britain, 1880–1914', *Historical Journal*, 274 (1984).

TRAINOR, RICHARD, 'Urban Elites in Victorian Britain', *Urban History Yearbook* (1985).

TREBLE, JAMES H., 'The Attitudes of Friendly Societies Towards the Movement in Great Britain for State Pensions, 1878–1908', *International Review of Social History*, XV, pt. 2 (1970).

UTTLEY, STEPHEN, 'The Welfare Exchange Reconsidered', *Journal of Social Policy*, 9, pt. 2 (1980).

VINCENT, A. W., 'The Poor Law Report and the Social Theory of the Charity Organisation Society', *Victorian Studies*, XXVII, no. 3 (Spring 1984).

WEST, PATRICK, 'The Family, the Welfare State and Community Care: Political Rhetoric and Public Attitudes', *Journal of Social Policy*, 13 (1984).

WHITESIDE, NOELLE, 'Private Agencies for Public Purposes: Some New Perspectives on Policy Making in Health Insurance Between the Wars', *Journal of Social Policy*, 12 (1983).

—— and KRAFCHIK, MAX, 'Interwar Health Insurance Revisited: A Reply to Frank Honigsbaum', *Journal of Social Policy*, 12 (1983).

WORPLE, KEN, 'Volunteers for Socialism', *New Society*, 55, no. 950 (29 Jan. 1981).

(b) Books

ABEL-SMITH, BRIAN, *The Hospitals, 1800–1948: A Study in Social Administration in England and Wales* (London: Heinemann Educational Books Ltd., 1964).

—— and TITMUSS, KAY (eds.), *The Philosophy of Welfare: Selected Writings of Richard M. Titmuss* (London: Allen & Unwin, 1987).

—— and TOWNSEND, PETER, *The Poor and the Poorest* (London: Bell, 1965).

ADDISON, PAUL, *The Road to 1945* (London: first publ. by Jonathan Cape, 1977; Quartet Books, 1977).

ALCOCK, PETER, *Poverty and State Support* (London: Longman, 1987).

ANDERSON, MICHAEL, *Family Structure in Nineteenth Century Lancashire* (Cambridge: Cambridge University Press, 1971).

ANDERSON, OLIVE, *Suicide in Victorian and Edwardian England* (London: Routledge & Kegan Paul, 1981).

ANDREWS, KAY, and JACOBS, JOHN, *Punishing the Poor: Poverty under Thatcher* (London: Macmillan, 1990).

ASHFORD, DOUGLAS E., *The Emergence of the Welfare State* (Oxford: Basil Blackwell, 1986).

AVES, G. M., *The Voluntary Worker in the Social Services* (London: Allen & Unwin, 1969).

BANTING, KEITH G., *Poverty, Politics and Policy: Britain in the 1960s* (London: Macmillan, 1979).

BARBALET, J. M., *Citizenship: Rights, Struggle and Class Inequality* (Milton Keynes: Open University Press, 1988).

BARKER, RODNEY, *Political Ideas in Modern Britain* (London: Methuen, 1978).

BARNETT, CORRELLI, *The Audit of War: The Illusion and Reality of Britain as a Great Nation* (London: Macmillan, 1986).

BARRY, N. P., *The New Right* (London: Croom Helm, 1987).

BARRY, NORMAN, *Welfare* (Milton Keynes: Open University Press, 1990).

BATTISCOMBE, GEORGINA, *Shaftesbury: A Biography of the Seventh Earl, 1801–1885* (London: Constable, 1974).

BEAN, PHILIP, FERRIS, JOHN, and WHYNES, DAVID (eds.), *In Defence of Welfare* (London: Tavistock Publications, 1985).

BEHLMER, GEORGE K., *Child Abuse and Moral Reform in England, 1870–1908* (Stanford, Calif.: Stanford University Press, 1982).

BENTLEY, MICHAEL, *The Climax of Liberal Politics: British Liberalism in Theory and Practice 1868–1918* (London: Edward Arnold, 1987).

—— and STEVENSON, JOHN (eds.), *High and Low Politics in Modern Britain* (Oxford: Clarendon Press, 1983).

BERTHOUD, RICHARD, and BROWN, JOAN C., with COOPER, STEPHEN, *Poverty and the Development of Anti-Poverty Policy in the UK* (London: Heinemann, 1981).

BEST, G. F. A., *Mid-Victorian Britain, 1851–1875* (London: Weidenfeld & Nicolson, 1971).

—— *Shaftesbury* (London: Batsford, 1964).

BEVERIDGE, LORD, *Voluntary Action: A Report on Methods of Social Advance* (London: Allen & Unwin, 1948).

—— and WELLS, A. F., *The Evidence for Voluntary Action* (London: Allen & Unwin, 1949).

BIRCH, R. C., *The Shaping of the Welfare State* (London: Longman, 1974).

BLACK, EUGENE C., *The Social Politics of Anglo-Jewry, 1880–1980* (Oxford: Basil Blackwell, 1988).

BLAKE, LORD, and CECIL, HUGH (eds.), *Salisbury: The Man and his Policies* (London: Macmillan, 1987).

BONFIELD, LLOYD, SMITH, RICHARD M., and WRIGHTSON, KEITH, *The World We Have Gained: Histories of Population and Social Structure* (Oxford: Basil Blackwell, 1986).

432 *Bibliography*

BOOTH, CHARLES, *Life and Labour of the People in London*, 17 vols., 3rd edn. (London: Macmillan, 1902–3).

BOOTH, GENERAL WILLIAM, *In Darkest England and the Way Out* (first publ. by the Salvation Army, 1890; 6th edn. London: Charles Knight, repr. from the edn. of 1890 with the addition of an Introduction by General Erik Wickberg, 1970).

BOURDILLON, A. F. C. (ed.), *Voluntary Social Services: Their Place in the Modern State* (London: Methuen, 1945).

BOURNE, J. M., *Patronage and Society in Nineteenth-Century England* (London: Edward Arnold, 1986).

BOWLEY, A. L., *Livelihood and Poverty: A Study in the Economic Conditions of Working-Class Households in Northampton, Warrington, Stanley and Reading* (London: Bell, 1915).

BOYD, NANCY, *Josephine Butler, Octavia Hill, Florence Nightingale: Three Victorian Women who Changed their World* (London: Macmillan, 1982).

BRADLEY, IAN, *The Strange Rebirth of Liberal Britain* (London: Chatto & Windus, 1985).

BRAITHWAITE, CONSTANCE, *The Voluntary Citizen: An Enquiry into the Place of Philanthropy in the Community* (London: Methuen, 1938).

BRASNETT, MARGARET, *Voluntary Social Action: A History of The National Council of Social Service, 1919–1969* (London: National Council of Social Service, 1969).

BRENTON, MARIA, *The Voluntary Sector in British Social Services* (London: Longman, 1985).

—— and UNGERSON, CLARE, *Year Book of Social Policy, 1987–8* (London: Longman, 1988).

BRIGGS, ASA, *A Study of the Work of Seebohm Rowntree, 1871–1954* (London: Longman, 1961).

—— *Victorian People: A Reassessment of Persons and Themes, 1851–67* (first publ. 1954; publ. with minor revisions, Harmondsworth: Penguin Books, 1965).

—— and MACARTNEY, ANNE, *Toynbee Hall: The First Hundred Years* (London: Routledge & Kegan Paul, 1984).

BROWN, KENNETH D., *The English Labour Movement 1700–1951* (London: Gill and Macmillan, 1982).

BROWN, MURIEL, and BALDWIN, SALLY (eds.), *The Year Book of Social Policy in Britain, 1979* (London: Routledge & Kegan Paul, 1980).

BRUCE, MAURICE, *The Coming of the Welfare State* (London: Batsford, first publ. 1961, 4th edn. 1968).

—— (ed.), *The Rise of the Welfare State: English Social Policy, 1601–1971* (London: Weidenfeld & Nicolson, 1973).

BRUNDAGE, ANTHONY, *The Making of the New Poor Law: The Politics of Inquiry, Enactment and Implementation, 1832–39* (London: Hutchinson, 1978).

BUCK, PHILIP W., *How Conservatives Think* (Harmondsworth: Penguin Books, 1975).

BULL, DAVID (ed.), *Family Poverty: Programme for the Seventies* (London: Duckworth, 1971).

BULLOCK, A., and SHOCK, M., (eds.), *The Liberal Tradition: From Fox to Keynes* (Oxford: Oxford University Press, 1956).

BURNETT, JOHN, *Destiny Obscure: Autobiographies of Childhood, Education and Family from the 1820s to the 1920s* (Harmondsworth: Penguin Books, 1984).

CAMPBELL, JOHN, *Nye Bevan and the Mirage of British Socialism* (London: Weidenfeld & Nicolson, 1987).

CANNADINE, DAVID, *The Pleasures of the Past* (London: Fontana Press, 1990).

CHECKLAND, OLIVE, *Philanthropy in Victorian Scotland: Social Welfare and the Voluntary Principle* (Edinburgh: John Donald Publishers, 1980).

CHECKLAND, SYDNEY, *British Public Policy, 1776–1939: An Economic, Social and Political Perspective* (Cambridge: Cambridge University Press, 1983).

CHURCH, R. A. *The Great Victorian Boom, 1850–1873* (London: Macmillan, 1975).

CHURCHILL, W. S. *Liberalism and the Social Problem* (London: Hodder & Stoughton, 1909).

CLARK, G. KITSON, *Churchmen and the Condition of England, 1832–1885* (London: Methuen, 1973).

CLARKE, JOHN, COCHRANE, ALLEN, and SMART, CAROL, *Ideologies of Welfare: From Dreams to Disillusion* (London: Hutchinson, 1987).

CLARKE, P. F., *Lancashire and the New Liberalism* (Cambridge: Cambridge University Press, 1971).

COATES, KEN, and SILBURN, RICHARD, *Poverty: The Forgotten Englishmen* (Harmondsworth: Penguin Books, 1970).

COLE, TONY, *Whose Welfare?* (London: Tavistock Publications, 1986).

COLEMAN, B. I. (ed.), *The Idea of the City in Nineteenth Century Britain* (London: Routledge & Kegan Paul, 1973).

CONSTANTINE, STEPHEN, *Unemployment in Britain between the Wars* (London: Longman, 1980).

COOPER, JOAN, *The Creation of the British Personal Social Services, 1962–74* (London: Heinemann Educational, 1983).

CROMWELL, VALERIE, *Revolution or Evolution? British Government in the Nineteenth Century* (London: Longman, 1977).

CROSSICK, GEOFFREY, *An Artisan Elite in Victorian Society: Kentish London 1840–1880* (London: Croom Helm, 1978).

CROWLEY, BRIAN LEE, *The Self, the Individual and the Community: Liberalism in the Political Thought of F. A. Hayek and Sidney and Beatrice Webb* (Oxford: Clarendon Press, 1987).

434 *Bibliography*

CROWTHER, M. A., *The Workhouse System, 1834–1929: The History of an English Social Institution* (London: Methuen, University Paperback, 1983).
—— *Social Policy in Britain, 1914–1939* (Basingstoke: Macmillan Education, 1988).

DALTROP, ANNE, *Charities* (London: Batsford, 1978).

DEACON, ALAN, *In Search of the Scrounger: The Administration of Unemployment Insurance in Britain 1920–1931* (London: Bell, 1976).
—— and BRADSHAW, JONATHAN, *Reserved for the Poor: The Means Test in British Social Policy* (Oxford: Basil Blackwell & Martin Robertson, 1983).

DICEY, A. V., *Lectures on the Relation between Law and Public Opinion in England during the Nineteenth Century* (London: Macmillan, 1905; 2nd edn. 1914; reissued with a Preface by E. C. S. Wade, 1962).

DICKENS, CHARLES, *Our Mutual Friend* (London: Chapman & Hall, Popular Edition, 1907).
—— *The Uncommercial Traveller* (London: Chapman & Hall, Popular Edition, 1907).

DIGBY, ANNE, *British Welfare Policy: Workhouse to Workfare* (London: Faber & Faber, 1989).

DONNISON, DAVID, *The Politics of Poverty* (Oxford: Martin Robertson, 1982).

DRIVER, C., *Tory Radical: The Life of Richard Oastler* (Oxford: Oxford University Press, 1946).

DURBIN, ELIZABETH, *New Jerusalems: The Labour Party and the Economics of Democratic Socialism* (London: Routledge & Kegan Paul, 1985).

DWORK, DEBORAH, *War is Good for Babies and other Young Children: A History of the Infant and Child Welfare Movement in England, 1898–1918* (London: Tavistock Publications, 1987).

DYHOUSE, CAROL, *Girls Growing Up in Late Victorian and Edwardian England* (London: Routledge & Kegan Paul, 1981).

EDSALL, NICHOLAS C., *The Anti-Poor Law Movement, 1834–44* (Manchester: Manchester University Press, 1971).

EMY, H. V., *Liberals, Radicals and Social Politics 1892–1914* (London: Cambridge University Press, 1973).

EVANS, ERIC J. (ed.), *Social Policy, 1830–1914: Individualism, Collectivism and the Origins of the Welfare State* (London: Routledge & Kegan Paul, 1978).

EWING, K. D., and GEARTY, C. A., *Freedom under Thatcher: Civil Liberties in Modern Britain* (Oxford: Clarendon Press, 1990).

FIELD, FRANK, *Unequal Britain: A Report on the Cycle of Inequality* (London: Arrow Books, 1973).

FINLAYSON, GEOFFREY B. A. M., *The Seventh Earl of Shaftesbury* (London: Eyre Methuen, 1981).

FISHMAN, WILLIAM J., *East End 1888: A Year in a London Borough among the Labouring Poor* (London: Duckworth, 1988).

FITZGERALD, MIKE, HALMOS, PAUL, MUNCIE, JOHN, and ZELDIN, DAVID, *Welfare in Action* (London: Routledge & Kegan Paul in association with The Open University Press, 1977).

FITZGERALD, ROBERT, *British Labour Management and Industrial Welfare, 1846–1939* (London: Croom Helm, 1988).

FLOUD, RODERICK, and MCCLOSKEY, DONALD (eds.), *The Economic History of Britain since 1700*, 2 vols. (Cambridge: Cambridge University Press, 1981).

FOOT, MICHAEL, *Aneurin Bevan*, 2 vols. (London: Granada Publishing, 1975).

FORD, COLIN, and HARRISON, BRIAN, *A Hundred Years Ago: Britain in the 1880s in Words and Photographs* (London: Allen Lane, Penguin Books, 1983).

FRASER, DEREK, *The Evolution of the British Welfare State* (London: Macmillan, 1973; 2nd edn. 1984).

—— (ed.), *The New Poor Law in the Nineteenth Century* (London: Macmillan, 1976).

FREEDEN, MICHAEL, *The New Liberalism: An Ideology of Social Reform* (Oxford: Clarendon Press, 1978).

FRIED, ALBERT, and ELMAN, RICHARD M. (eds.), *Charles Booth's London: A Portrait of the Poor at the Turn of the Century, Drawn from his 'Life and Labour of the People in London'* (London: Hutchinson, 1969).

FRIEDMAN, MILTON, *Capitalism and Freedom* (Chicago: University of Chicago Press, 1962).

—— and FRIEDMAN, ROSE, *Free to Choose* (Harmondsworth: Penguin Books, 1980).

GALLAGHER, J. P., *The Price of Charity* (London: Robert Hale, 1975).

GEORGE, VIC, and WILDING, PAUL, *Ideology and Social Welfare* (London: Routledge & Kegan Paul, 1985).

GERARD, DAVID, *Charities in Britain: Conservation or Change?* (London: Bedford Square Press, 1983).

GILBERT, BENTLEY B., *The Evolution of National Insurance in Great Britain: The Origins of the Welfare State* (London: Michael Joseph, 1966).

—— *British Social Policy, 1914–1939* (London: Batsford, 1970).

—— *David Lloyd George: The Architect of Change* (London: Batsford, 1987).

GILMOUR, IAN, *Britain Can Work* (Oxford: Martin Robertson, 1983).

GILSON, MARGARET BARNETT, *Unemployment Insurance in Great Britain: The National System and Additional Benefit Plans* (London: Allen & Unwin, 1931).

GINSBERG, MORRIS (ed.), *Law and Opinion in England in the 20th Century* (London: Stevens & Sons, 1959).

GLADSTONE, FRANCIS, *Charity Law and Social Justice* (London: Bedford Square Press, 1982).

GLENNERSTER, HOWARD (ed.), *The Future of the Welfare State: Re-Making Social Policy* (London: Heinemann, 1983).

—— *Paying for Welfare* (Oxford: Basil Blackwell, 1985).

GOLDING, PETER, and MIDDLETON, SUE, *Images of Welfare: Press and Public Attitudes to Poverty* (Oxford: Basil Blackwell, 1982).

GOODIN, ROBERT E., LE GRAND, JULIAN, with DRYZEK, JOHN, GIBSON, D. M., HANSON, RUSSELL L., HAVEMAN, ROBERT H. and WINTER, DAVID, *Not Only the Poor* (London: Allen & Unwin, 1987).

GOSDEN, P. H. J. H., *The Friendly Societies in England, 1815–1875* (Manchester: Manchester University Press, 1961).

—— *Self-Help: Voluntary Associations in Nineteenth-Century Britain* (London: Batsford, 1973).

GRAY, B. KIRKMAN, and HUTCHINS, B. L., *Philanthropy and the State, or Social Politics* (London: P. S. King, 1908).

GRAY, ROBERT Q., *The Labour Aristocracy in Victorian Edinburgh* (Oxford: Clarendon Press, 1976).

GREEN, D., *The New Right* (Brighton: Wheatsheaf, 1987).

GREENLEAF, W. H., *The British Political Tradition*, 2 vols. (London: Methuen, 1983).

HADLEY, ROGER, and HATCH, STEPHEN, *Social Welfare and the Failure of the State: Centralised Social Services and Participatory Alternatives* (London: Allen & Unwin, 1981).

—— WEBB, ADRIAN, and FARRELL, CHRISTINE, *Across the Generations: Old People and Young Volunteers* (London: Allen & Unwin, 1975).

HALL, PHOEBE, *Reforming the Welfare State: The Politics of Change in the Personal Social Services* (London: Heinemann Educational, 1976).

—— LAND, HILARY, PARKER, ROY, and WEBB, ADRIAN, *Change, Choice and Conflict in Social Policy* (London: Heinemann, 1975).

HALSEY, A. H., (ed.), *Traditions of Social Policy: Essays in Honour of Violet Butler* (Oxford: Basil Blackwell, 1976).

HANNAH, LESLIE, *Inventing Retirement: The Development of Occupational Pensions in Britain* (Cambridge: Cambridge University Press, 1986).

HARRIS, DAVID, *Justifying State Welfare: The New Right Versus the Old Left* (Oxford: Basil Blackwell, 1987).

HARRIS, JOSÉ, *Unemployment and Politics: A Study in English Social Policy, 1886–1914* (Oxford: Oxford University Press, 1972).

—— *William Beveridge: A Biography* (Oxford: Clarendon Press, 1977).

HARRIS, RALPH, and SELDON, ARTHUR, *Welfare without the State: A Quarter Century of Suppressed Public Choice* (London: London Institute of Economic Affairs, 1987).

HARRISON, BRIAN, *Drink and the Victorians: The Temperance Question in England, 1815–1872* (London: Faber & Faber, 1973).

—— *Peaceable Kingdom: Stability and Change in Modern Britain* (Oxford: Clarendon Press, 1983).

HARRISON, J. F. C., *The Common People: A History from the Norman Conquest to the Present* (London: Fontana, 1984).

HATCH, STEPHEN, *Outside the State: Voluntary Organisations in Three English Towns* (London: Croom Helm, 1980).

—— and MOCROFT, I., *Components of Welfare: Voluntary Organisations, Social Services and Politics in Two Local Authorities* (London: Bedford Square Press, 1983).

HAY, J. R., *The Origins of the Liberal Welfare Reforms, 1906–1914* (London: Macmillan, 1975).

—— (ed.), *The Development of the British Welfare State 1880–1975* (London: Edward Arnold, 1978).

HAYEK, F. A., *The Constitution of Liberty* (London: Routledge & Kegan Paul, 1960).

—— *Law, Legislation and Liberty*, 2 vols. (London: Routledge & Kegan Paul, 1976).

HEASMAN, KATHLEEN, *Evangelicals in Action: An Appraisal of their Social Work in the Victorian Era* (London: Geoffrey Bles, 1962).

HENNOCK, E. P., *British Social Reform and German Precedents: The Case of Social Insurance, 1880–1914* (Oxford: Clarendon Press, 1987).

HENRIQUES, URSULA R. Q., *Before the Welfare State: Social Administration in Early Industrial Britain* (London: Longman, 1979).

HIGGINS, JOAN, DEAKIN, NICHOLAS, EDWARDS, JOAN, and WICKS, MALCOLM, *Government and Urban Poverty: Inside the Policy-Making Process* (Oxford: Basil Blackwell, 1983).

HILTON, BOYD, *The Age of Atonement: The Influence of Evangelicalism on Social and Economic Thought, 1785–1865* (Oxford: Clarendon Press, 1988).

HIMMELFARB, GERTRUDE, *The Idea of Poverty: England in the Early Victorian Age* (London: Faber & Faber, 1984).

HOBHOUSE, L. T., *Liberalism* (London: Williams & Norgate, 1911).

HODDER, EDWIN, *The Life and Work of the Seventh Earl of Shaftesbury, K. G.*, 3 vols. (London: Cassell, 1887).

HOLLIS, PATRICIA, *Ladies Elect: Women in English Local Government 1865–1914* (Oxford: Clarendon Press, 1987).

—— (ed.), *Pressure from Without in Early Victorian England* (London: Edward Arnold, 1974).

HOLMAN, BOB, with WILES, DAVID, and LEWIS, SANDIE, *Kids at the Door: A Preventive Project on a Council Estate* (Oxford: Basil Blackwell, 1981).

HOLME, R., and ELLIOTT, M. (eds.), *The British Constitution 1688–1988* (London: Macmillan, 1988).

HOWE, ANTHONY, *The Cotton Masters, 1830–1860* (Oxford: Clarendon Press, 1984).

HUNT, E. D., *British Labour History, 1815–1914* (London: Weidenfeld & Nicolson, 1981).

JEFFERYS, MARGOT, *An Anatomy of Social Welfare Services: A Survey of Social Welfare Staff and their Clients in the County of Buckinghamshire* (London: Michael Joseph, 1965).

JENKINS, PETER, *Mrs Thatcher's Revolution: The Ending of the Socialist Era* (London: Jonathan Cape, 1987).

JENNINGS, HILDA, *The Private Citizen in Public Social Work: An Account of the Voluntary Children's Care Committee System in London* (London: Allen & Unwin, 1930).

JOHNSON, NORMAN, *Voluntary Social Services* (Oxford: Basil Blackwell & Martin Robertson, 1981).

—— *The Welfare State in Transition: The Theory and Practice of Welfare Pluralism* (Brighton: Wheatsheaf Books, 1987).

JONES, C., and STEVENSON, J. (eds.), *The Year Book of Social Policy in Britain, 1980–81* (London: Routledge & Kegan Paul, 1982).

JONES, G. STEDMAN, *Outcast London: A Study in the Relationship between Classes in Victorian Society* (Oxford: Oxford University Press, 1971; Harmondsworth, Peregrine Books, 1976).

JONES, KATHLEEN, BROWN, JOHN, and BRADSHAW, JONATHAN, *Issues in Social Policy* (London: Routledge & Kegan Paul, 1978).

JORDAN, BILL, *The Common Good: Citizenship, Morality and Self-Interest* (Oxford: Basil Blackwell, 1989).

JOSEPH, RT. HON. SIR KEITH, *Stranded on the Middle Ground: Reflections on Circumstances and Policies* (London: Centre for Policy Studies, 1976).

JOYCE, PATRICK, *Work, Society and Politics: The Culture of the Factory in Later Victorian England* (London: Methuen, 1980).

KAVANAGH, DENNIS, *Thatcherism and British Politics: The End of Consensus?* (Oxford: Oxford University Press, 1987).

KIDD, A. J., and ROBERTS, K. W. (eds.), *City, Class and Culture: Studies of Social Policy and Cultural Production in Victorian Manchester* (Manchester: Manchester University Press, 1985).

KINCAID, J. C., *Poverty and Equality in Britain: A Study of Social Security and Taxation* (Harmondsworth: Penguin Books, first publ. 1973, rev. edn. 1975).

KING, DESMOND S., *The New Right: Politics, Markets and Citizenship* (London: Macmillan, 1987).

KIRK, NEVILLE, *The Growth of Working Class Reformism in Mid Victorian England* (London: Croom Helm, 1985).

KLEIN, RUDOLPH, and O'HIGGINS, MICHAEL (eds.), *The Future of Welfare* (Oxford: Basil Blackwell, 1985).

KRAMER, R., *Voluntary Agencies in the Welfare State* (Berkeley: University of California Press, 1981).

KRIEGER, JOEL, *Reagan, Thatcher and the Politics of Decline* (Oxford: Basil Blackwell, 1986).

LANGAN, MARY, and SCHWARTZ, BILL (eds.), *Crises in the British State* (London: Hutchinson, in association with the Centre for Contemporary Cultural Studies, University of Birmingham, 1985).

LANSLEY, JOHN, *Voluntary Organisations Facing Change: The Report of a Project to Help Councils for Voluntary Service Respond to Local Government Reorganisation* (London: Calouste Gulbenkian Foundation UK and British Commonwealth Branch in association with the Joseph Rowntree Memorial Trust, 1976).

LAYBOURN, KEITH, *The Rise of Labour: The British Labour Party 1890–1979* (London: Edward Arnold, 1988).

—— *Britain on the Breadline: A Social and Political History of Britain between the Wars* (Gloucester: Sutton, 1990).

LEVITT, IAN, *Poverty and Welfare in Scotland 1890–1948* (Edinburgh: Edinburgh University Press, 1988).

LEWIS, JANE, *Women in England, 1870–1950* (Brighton: Wheatsheaf Books, 1984).

The Life of Thomas Cooper, with an Introduction by John Saville (Leicester: Leicester University Press, 1971).

LIPMAN, V. D., *A Century of Social Service, 1859–1959: The Jewish Board of Guardians* (London: Routledge & Kegan Paul, 1959).

LISTER, RUTH, *The Exclusive Society: Citizenship and the Poor* (London: Child Poverty Action Group, undated, but assumed to be 1990).

LOCHHEAD, A. V. S., *A Reader in Social Administration* (London: Constable, 1968).

LONEY, MARTIN, *The Politics of Greed: The New Right and the Welfare State* (London: Pluto Press, 1986).

—— BOSWELL, DAVID, and CLARRE, JOHN, *Social Policy and Social Welfare* (Milton Keynes: Open University Press, 1983).

The Long Debate on Poverty (London: The Institute of Economic Affairs, 1972; 2nd impression, 1974).

LOWNDES, G. A. N., *The Silent Social Revolution: An Account of the Expansion of Public Education in England and Wales, 1895–1965* (Oxford: Oxford University Press, 1st edn. 1937, 2nd edn. 1969, repr. 1970).

LUBENOW, WILLIAM C., *The Politics of Government Growth: Early Victorian Attitudes towards State Intervention 1833–1848* (Newton Abbot: David & Charles, 1971).

MACADAM, ELIZABETH, *The New Philanthropy: A Study of the Relations betweeen the Statutory and Voluntary Services* (London: Allen & Unwin, 1934).

McBRIAR, A. M., *An Edwardian Mixed Doubles: The Bosanquets versus the Webbs: A Study in British Social Policy, 1890–1929* (Oxford: Clarendon Press, 1987).

MACDONAGH, OLIVER, *A Pattern of Government Growth, 1800–1860: The Passenger Acts and their Enforcement* (London: Macgibbon & Kee, 1961).

—— *Early Victorian Government 1830–1870* (London: Weidenfeld & Nicolson, 1977).

MACFARLANE, L. J., *Issues in British Politics since 1945* (London: Longman, 3rd edn. 1986).

MACGREGOR, SUSANNE, *The Politics of Poverty* (London: Longman, 1981).

MCKENDRICK, NEIL (ed.), *Historical Perspectives: Studies in English Thought and Society in honour of J. H. Plumb* (London: Europa Publications, 1974).

MACKENZIE, NORMAN, and MACKENZIE, JEANNE, *The Diary of Beatrice Webb*, 4 vols. (London: Virago Press, in association with the London School of Economics and Political Science, 1982–5).

MCKIBBIN, ROSS, *The Ideologies of Class: Social Relations in Britain, 1880–1950* (Oxford: Clarendon Press, 1990).

MACMILLAN, HAROLD, *The Middle Way* (London: Macmillan, 1938).

MACMILLAN, LORD, *A Man of Law's Tale: The Reminiscences of Rt. Hon. Lord Macmillan* (London: Macmillan, 1952).

MACNICOL, JOHN, *The Movement for Family Allowances, 1918–45: A Study in Social Policy Development* (London: Heinemann, 1980).

MARQUAND, DAVID, *Ramsay MacDonald* (London: Jonathan Cape, 1977).

MARSDEN, GORDON (ed.), *Victorian Values: Personalities and Perspectives in Nineteenth Century Society* (London: Longman, 1990).

MARSHALL, T. H., *Citizenship and Social Class* (Cambridge: Cambridge University Press, 1950).

—— *Social Policy* (London: Hutchinson, 1st edn. 1965).

MARTIN, DAVID E., and RUBENSTEIN, DAVID (eds.), *Ideology and the Labour Movement: Essays Presented to John Saville* (London: Croom Helm, 1979).

MARTIN, E. W. (ed.), *Comparative Developments in Social Welfare* (London: Allen & Unwin, 1972).

MARWICK, ARTHUR, *The Deluge: British Society and the First World War* (London: Bodley Head, 1965).

—— *Britain in the Century of Total War: War, Peace and Social Change, 1900–1967* (Harmondsworth: Pelican Books, 1970).

—— *The Home Front: The British and the Second World War* (London: Thames & Hudson, 1976).

—— *Women at War, 1914–1918* (London: Fontana for the Imperial War Museum, 1977).

—— *Total War and Social Change* (Basingstoke: Macmillan, 1988).

MASTERMAN, C. F. G. (ed.), *The Heart of the Empire: Discussions of Problems of Modern City Life in England* (London: Fisher Unwin, 1901), ed. with an Introduction by Bentley B. Gilbert (Brighton: Harvester Press, 1973).

MATHER, F. C. (ed.), *Chartism and Society: An Anthology of Documents* (London: Bell & Hyman, 1980).

MEAD, L., *Beyond Entitlement: The Social Obligations of Citizenship* (New York: The Free Press, 1986).

MEARNS, ANDREW, *The Bitter Cry of Outcast London*, with leading articles from the *Pall Mall Gazette* of October 1883 and articles by Lord Salisbury, Joseph Chamberlain, and Forster Crozier. Edited with an

Introduction by Anthony S. Wohl (Leicester: Leicester University Press, 1970).

MELLER, H. E., *Leisure and the Changing City, 1870–1914* (London: Routledge & Kegan Paul, 1976).

MELLING, J. (ed.), *Housing: Social Policy and the State* (London: Croom Helm, 1980).

MESS, HENRY A., *Voluntary Social Services since 1918* (London: Kegan Paul, Trench, Trubner, 1947).

MILL, J. S., *Principles of Political Economy with some of their Applications to Social Philosophy*, 2 vols. (London: Longmans, Green, Reader & Dyer, 1878).

MILIBAND, RALPH, *The State in Capitalist Society* (London: Weidenfeld & Nicolson, 1969; Quartet Books, 1973).

MISHRA, RAMESH, *Society and Social Policy: Theories and Practice of Welfare* (London: Macmillan, 1st edn. 1977, 2nd edn. 1981).

—— *The Welfare State in Crisis: Social Thought and Social Change* (Brighton: Wheatsheaf Books, first publ. 1984).

MOMMSEN, W. J., in collaboration with MOCK, WOLFGANG, *The Emergence of the Welfare State in Britain and Germany, 1850–1950* (London: Croom Helm, on behalf of the German Historical Institute, 1981).

MORRAH, DERMOT, *A History of Industrial Life Assurance* (London: Allen & Unwin, 1955).

MORRIS, MARY, *Voluntary Work in the Welfare State* (London: Routledge & Kegan Paul, 1969).

MOWAT, CHARLES LOCH, *Britain Between the Wars, 1918–1940* (London: Methuen, 1955).

—— *The Charity Organisation Society, 1869–1913: Its Ideas and Work* (London: Methuen, 1961).

MUGGERIDGE, MALCOLM, *The Thirties* (London: Hamish Hamilton, 1940).

MUSSON, A. E., *British Trade Unions, 1800–1875* (London: Macmillan, 1972).

NICHOLAS, KATE, *The Social Effects of Unemployment in Teesside, 1919–35* (Manchester: Manchester University Press, 1986).

NIGHTINGALE, BENEDICT, *Charities* (London: Allen Lane, 1973).

NOVAK, TONY, *Poverty and the State: An Historical Sociology* (Milton Keynes: Open University Press, 1988).

NOZICK, R., *Anarchy, State and Utopia* (Oxford: Basil Blackwell, 1974).

ORTON, DIANA, *Made of Gold: A Biography of Angela Burdett Coutts* (London: Hamish Hamilton, 1980).

OWEN, DAVID, *English Philanthropy, 1660–1960* (Cambridge, Mass.: Harvard University Press, 1965).

PAPADAKIS, ELIM, and TAYLOR-GOOBY, PETER, *The Private Provision of Public Welfare: State, Market and Community* (Brighton: Wheatsheaf Books, 1987).

PARRIS, HENRY, *Government and the Railways in Nineteenth Century Britain* (London: Routledge & Kegan Paul, 1965).

PARRY, J. P., *Democracy and Religion: Gladstone and the Liberal Party* (Cambridge: Cambridge University Press, 1986).

PARRY, NOEL, RUSTIN, MICHAEL, and SATYAMURTI, CAROLE, *Social Work, Welfare and the State* (London: Edward Arnold, 1979).

PAUL, ELLEN FRANKEL, MILLER, FRED D., JR., PAUL, JEFFREY, and AHRENS, JOHN (eds.), *Beneficence, Philanthropy and the Public Good* (Oxford: Basil Blackwell for the Social Philosophy and Policy Center, Bowling Green State University, 1987).

PAYNE, PETER L. (ed.), *Studies in Scottish Business History* (London: Frank Cass, 1967).

PEDEN, G. C., *British Economic and Social Policy: Lloyd George to Margaret Thatcher* (Deddington: Philip Alan Publishers, 1985).

PERKIN, HAROLD, *The Rise of Professional Society: England since 1880* (London: Routledge, 1989).

PINDER, JOHN (ed.), *Fifty Years of Political and Economic Planning: Looking Forward, 1931–1981* (London: Heinemann, 1981).

PINKER, R., *Social Theory and Social Policy* (London: Heinemann Educational Books, 1971).

POOLE, H. R., *The Liverpool Council of Social Service 1909–1959* (Liverpool: The Liverpool Council of Social Service (Inc.), 1960).

POPE, REX, PRATT, ALAN, and HOYLE, BERNARD (eds.), *Social Welfare in Britain, 1885–1985* (London: Croom Helm, 1986).

Poverty and Social Policy, 1870–1950 (Milton Keynes: Open University Press, 1974).

Poverty in the Victorian Age: Debates on the Issue from 19th Century Critical Journals, with an Introduction by A. W. Coates, 4 vols. (Westmead, Farnborough: Gregg International, 1973).

PREST, JOHN, *Liberty and Locality: Parliament, Permissive Legislation and Rate-payers' Democracies in the Mid-Nineteenth Century* (Oxford: Clarendon Press, 1990).

PRIESTLEY, J. B., *English Journey* (London: William Heinemann in association with Victor Gollancz, 1934).

PROCHASKA, FRANK, *Women and Philanthropy in Nineteenth Century England* (Oxford: Clarendon Press, 1980).

—— *The Voluntary Impulse: Philanthropy in Modern Britain* (London: Faber & Faber, 1988).

PROUTY, ROGER, *The Transformation of the Board of Trade, 1830–1855: A Study of Administrative Reorganisation in the Heyday of Laissez Faire* (London: Heinemann, 1987).

PYM, FRANCIS, *The Politics of Consent* (London: Hamish Hamilton, 1984).

QUINN, VINCENT, and PREST, JOHN (eds.), *Dear Miss Nightingale: A Selection of Benjamin Jowett's Letters to Florence Nightingale 1860–1893* (Oxford: Clarendon Press, 1987).

RAWLS, JOHN, *A Theory of Justice* (Oxford: Basil Blackwell, 1972).

READ, DONALD (ed.), *Edwardian England* (London: Croom Helm, in association with the Historical Association, 1982).

REES, A. M. (ed.), *T. H. Marshall's Social Policy in the Twentieth Century* (London: Hutchinson, 1985).

REEVES, MAUD PEMBER, *Round About a Pound a Week* (London: Virago, 1979).

REYNOLDS, JACK, *The Great Paternalist: Titus Salt and the Growth of Nineteenth Century Bradford* (London: Maurice Temple Smith, in association with the University of Bradford, 1983).

RICHARDSON, ANN, *Participation* (London: Routledge & Kegan Paul, 1983).

RIDDELL, PETER, *The Thatcher Government* (Oxford: Basil Blackwell, 1985).

RITTER, G., *Social Welfare in Germany and Britain: Origins and Development*, trans. from German (Leamington Spa: Berg, 1986).

ROACH, JOAN, *Social Reform in England 1780–1880* (London: Batsford, 1978).

ROBBINS, KEITH (ed.), *The Blackwell Biographical Dictionary of British Political Life in the Twentieth Century* (Oxford: Blackwell Reference, 1990).

ROBERTS, DAVID, *Victorian Origins of the British Welfare State* (New Haven, Conn.: Yale University Press, 1960).

—— *Paternalism in Early Victorian England* (London: Croom Helm, 1979).

ROBERTS, ROBERT, *The Classic Slum* (Harmondsworth: Penguin Books, 1973).

ROOFF, MADELEINE, *Voluntary Societies and Social Policy* (London: Routledge & Kegan Paul, 1957).

—— *A Hundred Years of Family Welfare* (London: Michael Joseph, 1972).

ROSE, MICHAEL E., *The Relief of Poverty, 1834–1914* (London: Macmillan, 1st edn. 1972, 2nd edn. 1986).

—— (ed.), *The Poor and the City: The English Poor Law in its Urban Context, 1834–1914* (Leicester: Leicester University Press, 1985).

ROSE, RICHARD, and SHIRATORI, REI, *The Welfare State East and West* (Oxford: Oxford University Press, 1986).

ROWNTREE, B. SEEBOHM, *Poverty: A Study in Town Life* (London: Macmillan, 1st edn. 1901, 2nd edn. 1902).

—— *The Human Needs of Labour* (London: Nelson, 1918).

—— *Poverty and Progress: A Second Social Survey of York* (London: Longmans, Green, 1941).

—— and LAVERS, G. R., *Poverty and the Welfare State* (London: Longmans, Green, 1951).

SAUL, S. B., *The Myth of the Great Depression, 1873–1896* (London: Macmillan, 1969).

SCHWEINITZ, KARL DE, *England's Road to Social Security: From the Statute of Laborers in 1349 to the Beveridge Report of 1942* (New York: A. S. Barnes & The University of Pennsylvania Press, 1943).

SEARLE, G. R., *The Quest for National Efficiency: A Study in British Politics and Political Thought, 1899–1914* (Oxford: Basil Blackwell, 1971).

SHOTWELL, JAMES T. (ed.), *Economic and Social History of the World War* (London: Oxford University Press, 1927).

SHRAGGE, ERIC, *Pensions Policy in Britain: A Socialist Analysis* (London: Routledge & Kegan Paul, 1984).

SIMEY, MARGARET B., *Charitable Effort in Liverpool in the Nineteenth Century* (Liverpool: Liverpool University Press, 1951).

SIMEY, T. S., *Principles of Social Administration* (Oxford: Oxford University Press, 1937).

SKIDELSKY, ROBERT (ed.), *Thatcherism* (Oxford: Basil Blackwell, 1988).

SLACK, KATHLEEN M., *Social Administration and the Citizen* (London: Michael Joseph, 1966).

SLATER, S. D., and DOW, D. A. (eds.), *The Victoria Infirmary of Glasgow, 1890–1990: A Centenary History* (Glasgow: The Victoria Infirmary Centenary Committee, 1990).

SLEEMAN, J. F., *The Welfare State: Its Aims, Benefits and Costs* (London: Allen & Unwin, 1973).

SMILES, SAMUEL, *Character* (London: John Murray, 1872).

—— *Thrift* (London: John Murray, 1882).

—— *Self Help: With Illustrations of Conduct and Perseverance* (London: John Murray, first publ. 1859, 68th impression 1936).

—— *Self Help with Illustrations of Conduct and Perseverance*, abridged by George Bull, with an Introduction by Sir Keith Joseph, Bt. (Harmondsworth: Penguin Books, 1986).

SMITH, HAROLD L. (ed.), *War and Social Change: British Society in the Second World War* (Manchester: Manchester University Press, 1980).

SNAITH, ROY (ed.), *Neighbourhood Care and Social Policy* (London: Her Majesty's Stationery Office, 1989).

Speeches of the Seventh Earl of Shaftesbury upon Subjects Relating to the Claims and Interests of the Labouring Class (Shannon: Irish University Press, 1971).

SPICKER, PAUL, *Principles of Social Welfare: An Introduction to Thinking about the Welfare State* (London: Routledge, 1988).

STEVENSON, JOHN, *British Society, 1914–45* (Harmondsworth: Penguin Books, 1984).

STRAIN, R. W. M., *Belfast and its Charitable Society* (London: Oxford University Press, 1961).

SULLIVAN, MICHAEL, *Sociology and Social Welfare* (London: Allen & Unwin, 1987).

SWENARTON, MARK, *Houses Fit for Heroes: The Politics and Architecture of Early State Housing in Britain* (London: Heinemann Educational, 1981).

TAYLOR, A. J. P., *English History, 1914–1945* (Oxford: Clarendon Press, 1965).

TAYLOR, ARTHUR J., *Laissez-Faire and State Intervention in Nineteenth Century Britain* (London: Macmillan, 1972).

TAYLOR-GOOBY, Peter, *Public Opinion, Ideology and State Welfare* (London: Routledge & Kegan Paul, 1985).

TEBUTT, MELANIE, *Making Ends Meet: Pawnbroking and Working Class Credit* (London: Methuen, University Paperback, 1984).

THANE, PAT, *The Foundations of the Welfare State* (London: Longman, 1982).

—— (ed.), *The Origins of British Social Policy* (London: Croom Helm, 1978).

THOLFSEN, TRYGVE, *Working Class Radicalism in Mid-Victorian England* (London: Croom Helm, 1976).

THOMPSON, DOROTHY, *The Chartists* (London: Temple Smith, 1984).

THOMPSON, F. M. L. (ed.), *The Cambridge Social History of Britain, 1750–1950*, vol. 3, *Social Agencies and Institutions* (Cambridge: Cambridge University Press, 1990).

TINKER, ANTHEA, *The Elderly in Modern Society* (London: Longman, 1981).

TITMUSS, RICHARD M., *Problems of Social Policy* (London: HMSO and Longmans, Green, 1950).

—— *The Gift Relationship* (London: Allen & Unwin, 1971).

TIVEY, LEONARD, and WRIGHT, ANTHONY (eds.), *Party Ideology in Britain* (London: Routledge, 1989).

TOMPSON, RICHARD, *The Charity Commission and the Age of Reform* (London and Henley: Routledge & Kegan Paul, 1979).

TOWNSEND, PETER, *Sociology and Social Policy* (Harmondsworth: Penguin Books, 1976).

TREVELYAN, J., *Voluntary Service and the State* (London: George Barker & Son, for the National Council of Social Service Inc. and King Edward's Hospital Fund for London, 1952).

TURNER, BRYAN S., *Citizenship and Capitalism: The Debate over Reformism* (London: Allen & Unwin, 1986).

TYRRELL, ALEX, *Joseph Sturge and the Moral Radical Party in Early Victorian Britain* (London: Croom Helm, 1987).

VINCENT, ANDREW, and PLANT, RAYMOND, *Philosophy, Politics and Citizenship: The Life and Thought of the British Idealists* (Oxford: Basil Blackwell, 1984).

VINCENT, DAVID, *Bread, Knowledge and Freedom: A Study of Nineteenth Century Working Class Autobiography* (London: Methuen, University Paperback, 1982).

WADDILOVE, LEWIS E., *Private Philanthropy and Public Welfare: The Joseph Rowntree Memorial Trust, 1954–1979* (London: Allen & Unwin, 1983).

WAGNER, GILLIAN, *Barnardo* (London: first publ. Weidenfeld & Nicolson, 1979; pbk. edn. Eyre & Spottiswoode, 1980).

—— *The Chocolate Conscience* (London: Chatto & Windus, 1987).

WALTON, R. G., *Women in Social Work* (London: Routledge & Kegan Paul, 1975).

WALVIN, JAMES, *Victorian Values* (London: Sphere Books, 1988).

WARE, ALAN (ed.), *Charities and Government* (Manchester: Manchester University Press, 1989).

WEBB, A., DAY, L., and WELLER, D., *Voluntary Social Services: Manpower Resources* (London: Personal Social Services Council, 1976).

WEBB, ADRIAN, and WISTOW, GERALD, *Whither State Welfare? Policy and Implementation in the Personal Social Services, 1979–80* (London: Royal Institute of Public Administration, 1982).

—— and —— *Social Work, Social Care and Social Planning: The Personal Social Services since Seebohm* (London: Longman, 1987).

WEBB, BEATRICE, *Our Partnership*, ed. Barbara Drake and Margaret I. Cole (London: Longmans, Green, 1948).

WEBB, SIDNEY, and WEBB, BEATRICE, *The History of Trade Unionism* (London: Longmans, Green, 1920).

WEBSTER, CHARLES, *The Health Services since the War*, vol. 1, *Problems of Health Care: The National Health Service before 1957* (London: HMSO, 1988).

WESTALL, OLIVER M. (ed.), *The Historian and the Business of Insurance* (Manchester: Manchester University Press, 1984).

WHITAKER, B., *The Foundations* (London: Eyre Methuen, 1974).

WHITE, ARNOLD, *Efficiency and Empire* (1901), ed. G. R. Searle (Brighton: Harvester Press, 1972).

WICKS, MALCOLM, *A Future for All: Do We Need the Welfare State?* (Harmondsworth: Penguin Books, 1987).

WILDING, PAUL (ed.), *In Defence of the Welfare State* (Manchester: Manchester University Press, 1986).

WILENSKY, HAROLD L., *The Welfare State and Equality: Structural and Ideological Roots of Public Expenditures* (Berkeley: University of California Press, 1975).

WILLIAMS, GERTRUDE, *The Coming of the Welfare State* (London: Allen & Unwin, 1967).

WILLIAMS, IAN, *The Alms Trade: Charities, Past, Present and Future* (London: Unwin Hyman, 1989).

WILLIAMS, KAREL, *From Pauperism to Poverty* (London: Routledge & Kegan Paul, 1981).

WILSON, SIR ARNOLD, and LEVY, PROFESSOR HERMAN, *Industrial Assurance: An Historical and Critical Study* (Oxford: Oxford University Press, 1937).

WILSON, ELIZABETH, *Women and the Welfare State* (London: Tavistock Publications, 1977).

WINTER, J. M., *The Great War and the British People* (Basingstoke: Macmillan, 1985).

WOHL, ANTHONY S., *Endangered Lives: Public Health in Victorian Britain* (London: J. M. Dent, 1983).

WOODROOFE, KATHLEEN, *From Charity to Social Work* (London: Routledge & Kegan Paul, 1966).

WOOTTON, GRAHAM, *The Official History of the British Legion* (London: Macdonald & Evans, 1956).

YEO, Stephen, *Religion and Voluntary Organisations in Crisis* (London: Croom Helm, 1976).

YOUNG, A. F., and ASHTON, E. T., *British Social Work in the Nineteenth Century* (London: Routledge & Kegan Paul, 1956).

YOUNG, G. M., and HANDCOCK, W. D. (eds.), *English Historical Documents, 1833–1874* (London: Eyre & Spottiswoode, 1956).

YOUNG, HUGO, *One of Us: A Biography of Margaret Thatcher* (London: Macmillan, 1989).

YOUNGHUSBAND, EILEEN, *Social Work in Britain 1950–1975: A Follow-Up Study* (London: Allen & Unwin, 1978).

Index

Abbeyfield Society 404
Abel-Smith, Brian (with Peter Townsend), *The Poor and the Poorest* 312–13, 328
Aberdeen, 4th Earl, *see* Gordon, George Hamilton, 4th Earl of Aberdeen
Aberdeen Savings Bank 34
Academic Assistance Council, later Society for the Protection of Science and Learning 229
Ackroyds of Halifax 56
'Action for Cities' campaign 375
Action on Smoking and Health (ASH) 405
actuarial tables 25
Addison, Paul 254, 258
adoption of deprived by prosperous areas (1920s) 224, 240
affinity credit cards 381
Age Concern (1971) 328, 336, 342, 348, 350, 386, 410
agency arrangements 280, 292, 293, 298, 301, 417
Ainsworth, J. H. 57
Ainsworths of Bolton 56
Alanon 328
Alcohol Concern 405
Alcoholics Anonymous 328, 405
Allied Dunbar Assurance, work for charity 384, 388
Allotments for the Unemployed scheme 225
Althorp, Viscount, *see* Spencer, John Charles, Viscount Althorp, later 3rd Earl Spencer
Amalgamated Society of Carpenters and Joiners 29
Amalgamated Society of Engineers 29
Amnesty International 350, 405
Ancient Order of Foresters 27, 40, 127, 138, 166, 207
Anderson, Digby 376
Anderson, Olive 100
Anglo-Turkish Relief Fund 228
Anne, Princess 412

Annual Charities Register 134
Anti-Corn Law League 81, 406
Approved Societies under National Health Insurance Act (1911) 167, 185, 191, 205, 207–8, 210–11, 238, 248, 266, 268–70, 301, 303, 421
Argyll, 8th Duke, *see* Campbell, George Douglas, 8th Duke of Argyll
Arnold, John 31
Arundel and Surrey, Earl of, *see* Howard, Henry Granville Fitzalan, Earl of Arundel and Surrey, later 14th Duke of Norfolk
ASH, *see* Action on Smoking and Health
Ashley, Lord, *see* Cooper, Anthony Ashley, 7th Earl of Shaftesbury
Ashtons of Hyde 56, 58
Ashworth, Henry 56, 97
Ashworths of Bolton 56, 58
Asquith, H. H., 1st Earl of Oxford and Asquith 164, 189, 198, 415
Assistance Board, *see* Unemployment Assistance Board
Assisted Places Scheme, *see* education
Astbury, Benjamin 246, 277, 278, 279
Attlee, Clement, 1st Earl Attlee 3, 258, 280–1, 297, 321, 420
Attwood, Thomas 95
Aves Committee Report 1969, *The Voluntary Worker in the Social Services* 307, 316, 326, 328, 329, 332, 333–4, 335, 337, 384, 410

Baden-Powell, Robert Stephenson Smyth, 1st Baron Baden-Powell 192, 250
Bailward, W. A. 174, 192
Baldwin, Stanley, 1st Earl Baldwin of Bewdley 261
Balfour, Arthur James, 1st Earl of Balfour 165, 185, 187
Ball, Colin 346
Ball, Stuart 332, 335

Band Aid Appeal and Trust 378–9, 402
Bands of Hope 39
Banting, Keith 314
Barclay Committee Report on the role of social workers (1982) 398
Barnardo, Dr Thomas John 129–30, 135, 139–40, 412
Barnardo's 323, 331–2, 335, 343–4, 345, 403, 411
Barnett, Correlli 420
Barnett, Revd Samuel Augustus 131–2, 133, 140–2, 171, 179, 195
Barnett, William, of Macclesfield 41
Barry, Norman 17, 407
Bartley, Sir George Christopher Trout 194
Bates, John 39–40, 41
BBC 202, 224, 227–8, 314, 378, 402
Beaconsfield, 1st Earl, *see* Disraeli, Benjamin, 1st Earl of Beaconsfield
Bedford, 7th Duke, *see* Russell, Francis, 7th Duke of Bedford
Behlmer, George 168
Bermondsey workhouse 148
Best, Geoffrey 98
Bethnal Green, poverty in 202, 311
Bevan, Aneurin 271, 272, 282
Beveridge, William Henry, 1st Baron Beveridge 8, 67, 151, 164, 182, 184, 189, 208, 211, 228, 229, 278, 305, 308, 328, 402, 403, 420
   Beveridge Report (1942) 256–7, 262, 267–70, 278, 419
   Voluntary Action (1948) 217, 259–60, 268, 283, 285, 290, 299, 420
Beveridge, W. H., and A. F. Wells, *The Evidence for Voluntary Action* 301, 302, 411
Biffen, John 367
Birch, Nigel 393
Birmingham 139, 168
Bishop, Henry, of Uley, Glos. 82
Bismarck, Otto von 164
Bitter Cry of Outcast Children, The (Barnardo) 130
Bitter Cry of Outcast London, The (London Congregational Union) 108, 116, 118, 130, 132, 167, 191, 405

blind people 228–9, 292, 403
   local authority responsible for 280, 298, 344
Blind Persons Act (1920) 280
Blomfield, Revd Charles James, Bp. of London 55
Blunkett, David 374
Bochel, Hugh Main 394, 397, 413
Bondfield, Margaret 263
Boone, Revd James Shergold 48–9
Booth, Charles, author of statistical surveys of London (1889–1903) 109–11, 115, 116, 119, 128, 131, 154, 158, 177–8, 179, 201
Booth, 'General' William, *In Darkest England and the Way Out* (1890) 109, 115, 131, 140, 179, 180, 412
Booth, William Bramwell 168
Bosanquet, Bernard 173, 418
Bosanquet, Helen 159, 173
Bournville factory village 139
Boy Scouts (1908) 134, 135, 192, 221, 250
Boys' Brigade (1883) 134, 135, 225
Boyson, Rhodes, *Down with the Poor* (1971) 356
Brabazon, Reginald, 12th Earl of Meath 157
Bradley, Ian, *The Strange Rebirth of Liberal Britain* (1985) 362, 368
Braithwaite, Constance, *The Voluntary Citizen* (1938) 215, 226, 233, 279, 300
Braithwaite, W. J. 184, 185, 189
Bray, John Francis 95
Brebner, J. B. 80
Brelsford, Anthony 41
Brenton, Maria 292, 293, 297, 304, 321, 325
Briggs, Asa 4–5, 10, 17, 20, 394, 395
Bristol, *see* statistical social surveys, Bristol
British Association for the Promotion of Temperance, later British Temperance League 39
British Association of Social Sciences, Bradford meeting (1859, 1874) 58
British Broadcasting Corporation, *see* BBC
British and Foreign School Society 87
British Heart Foundation 381
British Hospitals Association 236, 240, 271, 272

British Legion 222–3, 226, 239, 241, 406
British Red Cross Society 220, 221, 227, 337, 381
British Temperance League, *see* British Association for the Promotion of Temperance
Brophy, Michael 377, 378, 387, 388
Brougham, Henry Peter, Baron Brougham and Vaux 86
Brown, Gordon 369, 386
Brown, John 173, 178
Buchanan, Archibald, of Catrine 56
Bugler, Jeremy 338
building societies 31–3, 38, 69, 295
burial societies 30–1
Burke, Edmund, *Reflections on the Revolution in France* (1790) 51, 52
Burn, W. L. 104, 105, 106
Burnett, Maud 175
Butler, R. A. 256
Buxton, C. R. 161

Cadbury, George 138–9, 412
Callaghan, James 320
Campaign for Homosexual Equality (1969) 328
Campbell, George Douglas, 8th Duke of Argyll 55
Campbell-Bannerman, Sir Henry 189
Canterbury, Archbishop of, *see* Runcie, Rt. Revd Dr Robert
Caring for People: Community Care in the Next Decade and Beyond (1989 White Paper) 364, 365, 387
Carlisle, *see* Howard, Rosalind Frances, Countess of Carlisle
Carlyle, Thomas 106, 108
Carnegie United Kingdom Trust (1913) 223, 240
Carter, Charles 394
Carter, Eyre 286
casework, pioneered by Charity Organisation Society 71, 103, 145, 151
Cave Committee on Voluntary Hospitals (1921) 237, 240, 267
Cavendish, William George Spencer, 6th Duke of Devonshire 55
Cecil, Lord Hugh Gascoyne-, later 1st Baron Quickswood 163
Cecil, Lady Maud, Countess of Selborne 122

Cecil, Robert Arthur Talbot Gascoyne-, 3rd Marquess of Salisbury 133, 146
Central British Fund 229, 235
see also Jewish Refugees Committee
Central Bureau of Hospital Information 215
Chadwick, Sir Edwin 83, 108
Chalmers, Revd Thomas 77
Chamberlain, Joseph 162, 165, 188
Poor Law minute 150
tariff reform 124
'unauthorized programme' 124
Chambers' Edinburgh Journal 21
Champion, H. H. 117
Champneys, Revd William Weldon 55
Chapman, Gordon 380
charitable law and status 8, 86, 87, 169, 289, 291, 349–51
charitable trusts 288–91
charitable trusts, Nathan Committee, *see* Nathan Committee on the law and practice relating to charitable trusts, report (1952)
Charitable Trusts Act (1853) 86
Charitable Trusts Act (1860) 86, 289
charities:
finances of 215–16, 233–8, 279–80, 298–300, 365–6, 379–83, 386–8, 402, 411–12
numbers and extent of 62–3, 91, 133–4, 215–17, 219–29, 402
professionalization and commercialization of 176, 379–82
revival of 304–8, 316–29, 358, 421
war-related 218–21, 239, 264–5
see also under voluntarism; volunteers, availability and adequacy of
Charities: A Framework for the Future (1989 White Paper) 360, 365–6
Charities Act (1960) 290, 291
Charities Act (1985) 291
Charities Aid Foundation 349, 377, 378, 383–4, 387
Charities of London, Sampson Low (1850) 62–3, 91
Charity Commissions 86–7, 133–4, 169, 215, 219, 265, 289, 291, 366, 402
charity law and voluntary organisations, Goodman Committee Report on (1976) 350

Charity Organisation Quarterly 233–4
Charity Organisation Review 174, 192, 193, 194, 196, 205, 231
Charity Organisation Society (from 1946 Family Welfare Association, *q.v.*) 140, 142, 148–51, 171–2, 180, 215, 227, 332, 333, 338, 354, 409–10, 414
  attitude to state 173, 174, 192–5, 199, 277–8
  co-ordinating role 71, 79, 92, 106, 134, 135–6, 239, 241, 404, 412
  criticism of 135, 141, 156, 158, 179
  finances 235
  ideology 77, 92, 105, 147, 192, 245–6
  methods 103, 145, 405, 419
  and poor law 147, 148–51, 158–9, 170, 172, 196
Charity Record, Hospital Times and Philanthropist 267
Charity Record, Hospital Times, Philanthropic News and Official Advertiser 143
Charity Record and Philanthropic News 129
Charles, Prince of Wales 374
Chartists 96, 121
Chauhan, Neena 332, 335
Checkland, Olive 63
Cherry, Mary 382
Chew, Ada 160
Chichester, 3rd Earl, *see* Pelham, Henry Thomas, 3rd Earl of Chichester
Child Poverty Action Group (1965) 328, 340, 342, 350
children 31, 36, 48, 116, 129–30, 146, 168–9, 204, 219, 222, 227, 237, 275–6, 313, 343
  legislation concerning 164, 182–3, 192–3, 296
  see also specific charities
'Children in Need' campaign 378, 402
Children's Act (1908) 168, 183
Children's Act (1948) 296
Children's Aid Society 219
Children's Society, *see* Church of England Children's Society
China Inland Mission 139
Christian Aid 350
Christian Revival Association (1865) 131

Christian Social Council 241
Chronically Sick and Disabled Act (1971) 317
Church Army 227
Church of England Children's Society 331–2, 339, 342–3
Church of Scotland, General Assembly's Committee on Social Responsibility 331
  Mrs Thatcher's speech to (1988) 358, 360, 369, 372, 397
Churches:
  and education 96, 277
  as critics of 'New Right' 371–3
  and voluntarism 48–9, 55, 60, 132, 219, 225, 227, 330–2, 378
Churchill, Winston 117–18, 124–5, 164, 184, 186, 198–9, 256, 260–1
Circle Trust (for ex-prisoners) 328
Citizen's Charter 422
Citizens' Advice Bureaux 276, 337, 406
Citizens' Advice Centre 274
Citizens' Aid Society, *see* Guilds of Help
citizenship 4–5, 8–9, 12–13, 416
  of contribution 9, 12–13, 15–16, 68, 92, 101, 176, 182, 191–2, 273, 275, 283, 306–8, 370, 373–4, 377, 384, 401–2, 415, 422
  of political and social entitlement 12–13, 68, 92, 101, 121–4, 162, 165, 182, 191–2, 198, 253, 259, 273, 275, 370–1, 396, 413, 415–16, 420, 422
citizenship, lectureship in, *see* Stevenson Lectureship in Citizenship, University of Glasgow
Citizenship, Report of the Commission on (1990) 13, 374
City companies and charitable funds 59, 72
Clark, George Kitson 2–3
Clynder, Mark 386
Cohen Committee on Life Assurance, report (1932) 214, 248
Coke, Thomas William, 2nd Earl of Leicester 55, 133
Cole, G. D. H. 255
Coleridge, Samuel Taylor 51
collectivism 2, 163, 165, 182, 186, 198, 250, 255, 417, 419
  opposition to 355–8, 394–400

Colwell, Maria 354
Comic Relief appeal 402
Commission on Citizenship, *see*
Citizenship, Report of the
Commission on (1990)
Commissioners of the Royal
Hospital for Soldiers at Chelsea
218
community charge 368, 390
Community Development
Programme 322
Community Health Councils 306
Community Service Volunteers 339,
374
Comrades of the Great War 220
Conference on War Relief (1915) 219,
239, 241, 245
Congregational Church 41, 108
Conservative Party 14–16, 124, 163,
256, 295, 313, 317–18, 352–68,
393
'New Right' policies 14, 15,
352–66, 408, 417, 422
opponents within party 366–8
other opponents 368–91, 417
and voluntarism 14, 358–62, 365–6,
371–91, 417
Constantine, Stephen 261
Cooper, Anthony Ashley, 7th Earl
of Shaftesbury 49, 52–3, 55, 56,
61–2, 71–2, 76, 89, 90–1, 93, 97,
106, 118–19, 124, 129, 130, 143,
405, 412
Cooper, Joan, 332, 333
co-operative movement 28–30, 35, 38,
126, 188
see also voluntarism
Corn Laws, repeal of 81–2
covenanted payments to charity 236,
298–9
Craik, George, *The Pursuit of
Knowledge under Difficulties* (1830)
21
credit arrangements, *see* pawnbrokers
and moneylenders
Cronin, James, *The Politics of State
Expansion* 11, 419
Crosland, C. A. R., *The Future of
Socialism* 310, 313, 314
Crossleys of Halifax 56, 74
Crossman, R. H. S. 249–50, 255, 272,
318–19
Crowther, M. A. 253–4

Crozier, Forster, *Methodism and the
Bitter Cry of Outcast London*
(1885) 191–2
Cruse (for needy widows) 403
Cunningham, William 113, 114
Currie, Edwina 371
Curtis Report on the care of deprived
children 296
cy pres, doctrine of 86, 87, 169, 289,
291

D'Aeth, F. G. 239, 275
Dahrendorf, Ralf 5
Daily Mail 354
Daily News trust 139
Daily Telegraph 380
Dalton, Hugh 255
dame schools, *see* schools
Darwin, Charles, *Origin of Species*
(1859) 92
Davis-Smith, Justin 249, 384
Day, L., *see* Webb, A. (with L. Day
and D. Weller)
Deacon, Alan 211, 406
Dearnley, Prebendary Patrick 378
Deevey, Derek, of Liverpool,
fraudulent social security claims
by 354
Department of the Environment, *see*
Environment, Department of the
deposit societies 213
depression:
after 1880: 107, 112–13, 136, 146
after 1914–18: 203–4, 210, 213–14,
222–6, 233
Devonshire, 6th Duke, *see* Cavendish,
William George Spencer, 6th
Duke of Devonshire
Dicey, Albert Venn 2, 165, 194, 418
Dickens, Charles 106
Dickson, Alec 339, 373–4
Digby, Anne 17, 251
Disability Alliance 404
disabled people 220, 223, 226, 317, 387
Disablement Income Group 328
Disraeli, Benjamin, 1st Earl of
Beaconsfield 51, 94, 124
Donnison, David 314–15, 341, 342,
344, 392, 409, 416
Douglas-Mann, Bruce 320
Dr Barnardo's Homes, *see* Barnardo's
Drapers' Company and charitable
funds 59

Duncan, Revd Henry, pioneer of savings bank movement 33
Durbin, Evan 255
Durnford, Revd Richard, sen. 55

Earl Haig Fund 223, 226
Earle, A. B. 236
Eden, Sir Frederick Morton 67
education:
  Assisted Places Scheme (1980) 363
  reports on (1960s) 253, 313–14
  self-improvement through 22, 35–7
  state intervention in 87, 96, 276–7
  teacher training 96
  see also schools
Education Act (1870) 87, 95, 97, 169
Education Act (Scotland: 1871) 87
Education Act (1902) 165, 187
Education Act (1944) 257, 276–7
Education (Provision of Meals) Act (1906) 192
educational charitable trusts 289
educational reform 253, 313
Edward, Prince of Wales (later Edward VIII) 222, 225, 226
Edwards Rees, Revd, W. G. 192
efficiency scrutiny of government funding of the voluntary sector (1989) 407
Eichholz, Dr Alfred 116
Elberfeld system, Germany 170
Elderly Contact (1965) 328
elderly people, care of 292, 361, 389–90
Ellis, L. F. 242
Embankment Fellowship (1932) 241
Emergency Hospital Service (World War II) 240
Emergency Powers Act (1920) 249
emigration 75, 130, 168, 219, 223
employer paternalism, *see* paternalism and philanthropy
employment exchanges 223
Environment, Department of the 306, 348, 368
Equal Opportunities Commission, government grants to 322
Escott, T. H. S. 112
Ethiopia, famine relief for 379
evacuees 226–7
evangelicalism and philanthropy 47, 129, 131, 330

Fabian Society 128, 158, 162, 180, 305, 311
Factory Acts 97, 116
factory owners as paternalists, *see* paternalism and philanthropy
family, as unit of mutual aid 7, 13, 64, 127, 192, 229–30, 296–7, 361–2, 365, 389–90, 407
Family Allowances Act 1945: 257
family expenditure surveys 377
Family Policy Studies Centre 405
Family Welfare Association (formerly Charity Organisation Society, *q.v.*) 235, 279, 341
famine relief 379, 404
Farnell, H. B. 105
Ferrers, Mary Jane, Countess (wife of 11th Earl Ferrers) 245
Ferris, John 371
Field, Frank, *Unequal Britain: a report on the cycle of inequality* (1974) 312
Fielden, John 97
Fieldens of Todmorden 56, 57
Fielding, Nick 381
Finance Act 1946, effect on covenants 298–9
Finland Fund 228
Finlay, James, of Deanston 56
Fishman, William J. 179
Fitzroy, Sir Almeric, Clerk of the Privy Council 111–12
Fitzroy, Augustus Charles Lennox, 7th Duke of Grafton 133
Fitzwilliam, Charles William Wentworth, 3rd Earl Fitzwiliam 55
Flockhart, Ross 381
Ford, Isabella, *On the Threshold* 157
Ford Foundation 342
Foresters, *see* Ancient Order of Foresters
Fowler, Norman 319–20
Fox, J. C. 40
Friedman, Milton 355, 371
Friendly Societies 24–8, 67, 69, 73, 83, 84, 125–6, 127, 137, 301
  finances and membership 137–8, 206, 212–13, 301
  and National Health Insurance Act (1911) 185–6, 194; *see also* Approved Societies under National Health Insurance Act (1911)

relations to state 83–4, 95, 166, 167, 187–91, 268
Friendly Societies, National Conference of 301
Friendly Societies, Royal Commission on (1871–4) 25, 28, 32, 84, 95, 284
Friends, *see* Society of Friends

Gaitskell, Hugh 255, 416
Gay Switchboard (1974) 328
'Geddes Axe' 260
Geldof, Bob, Band Aid appeal 378
General Board of Health (1848–58) 94–5
General Strike (1926) 249
George, David Lloyd 124, 165, 184, 186, 189–90, 191, 273
Germany 113, 117, 164, 168, 170, 185
refugees from 229, 231
Gilbert, Bentley B. 137, 253, 254, 269
Gilmour, Sir Ian 366, 390
Gingerbread (1970), 327, 336, 338–9
Gladstone, Francis 351
Gladstone, William Ewart 38, 176
Glasgow 34, 75, 219, 220, 239, 245, 385
University, Stevenson Lectureship in Citizenship 13, 416
Victoria Infirmary 9, 133, 144, 145, 146, 283n.
Glasgow and West of Scotland Institute for the Deaf 380
Glen, William 245
Golding, Peter (with Sue Middleton) 263
Goodman Committee on Charity Law and Voluntary Organisations (1976) 350
Gordon, George Hamilton, 4th Earl of Aberdeen 55
Gordon-Lennox, *see* Lennox, Charles Gordon-, 6th Duke of Richmond
Goschen Minute (1869) 92, 105, 147, 148, 150, 152, 196, 414
Gosden, P. H. J. H. 69
Grafton, 7th Duke, *see* Fitzroy, Augustus Charles Lennox, 7th Duke of Grafton
Gray, Benjamin Kirkman, *Philanthropy and the State, or Social Politics* (1908) 175–6, 415
Gray, John 396
Graycar, A. 13–14

Green, John Richard 131, 132
Green, Thomas Hill 161
Greenwood, Arthur 249
Greenwood, Walter, *Love on the Dole* 202
Greg, Samuel, sen. 56, 97
Gregs of Bollington 56, 58
Greville, Frances Evelyn, Countess of Warwick 159
Greville, Lady Violet 53–4
Griffins Society (for ex-prisoners) 328
Grinling, C. H. 173
Groundwork Trust 402
Guardian, The 387–8
Guilds of Help 170, 171–2, 195, 239
Gulbenkian Trust 342

Hadley, Roger (with Stephen Hatch) 296, 303
Hadow Report on education (1926) 253
Hampstead Council of Social Welfare 174
handicapped, charities for 168, 169, 307, 403
Hannah, Leslie 295
Harcourt, Sir William 125
Hardwick, Charles 83
Harris, John Henry, Baron Harris of Greenwich 319, 321
Harris, José 121, 136, 172, 179, 254, 264, 305, 413, 416, 419
Harrison, Brian 49, 81
Harrowby, 2nd Earl, *see* Ryder, Dudley, 2nd Earl of Harrowby
Harvey, Audrey, *Casualties of the Welfare State* (1960) 311
Hatch, Stephen 328, 331, 340
(with Roger Hadley) 296, 303
(with I. Mocroft) 330, 333
Hattersley, Roy 369
Hay, J. R. 187
Hayday formula 263
Hayek, Friedrich August von 355, 371
Health, Ministry of 251, 265, 266, 276, 280, 293, 296
'Hearing the Cry of the Poor' (1989) 373
Heasman, Robert 417
Heath, Edward 318, 366–7, 343, 393
Help the Aged (1961) 328

Hennessy, David James George, 3rd Baron Windlesham 319, 325, 343–4

Hennock, E. P. 164, 185, 186

Heseltine, Michael 367–8

High Churchmanship and philanthropy 132

Hill, Octavia 74, 140, 158

Hilton, Boyd 47

Hinks, V. E. 174

Hinton, Nicholas 8, 339, 387, 417

Hirschfeld, Gerhard 231

Hirschman, Albert 406, 418

Hobhouse, Arthur, Baron Hobhouse of Hadspen 50

Hobhouse, Leonard Trelawny 155, 181, 182

Hobman, David 348

Hobson, John Atkinson 155, 156, 161, 181

Hollis, Patricia 159

Holloway, Thomas 50

Holt, Alderman, of Manchester 219, 245

Home Office, Committee on Charities (1927) 221, 266

Home Office, Voluntary Services Unit 321–2, 346

Hopkins, Sir Richard 259

Horrockses of Preston 56

Horrockses & Miller 57

Horsfall, T. C. 117

hospice movement 403

Hospital Saturday Fund 145

Hospital Sunday movement 60, 145

Hospital Trusts within NHS 363

hospitals:
  municipal 240
  National Health Service 288; voluntary help organisations in 282, 329
  voluntary 9, 60–1, 144–6, 219, 236–8, 240, 248, 270–3, 420; financial problems and charges to patients 144–6, 236–8, 248, 272; Cave Committee Report on Voluntary Hospitals (1921) 237, 240, 267

House to House Collections Act 1939 266

houses, sale of council 363

housing 31–3, 55, 57, 112, 118–19, 164, 167, 186–7, 295, 296, 306, 314, 343, 363

housing (England and Wales), survey (1967) 314

housing (Greater London), Milner Holland Committee on 314

Housing Associations, government grants to 322

housing review by Dept. of the Environment (1977) 306

Howard, Henry Granville Fitzalan, Earl of Arundel and Surrey, later 14th Duke of Norfolk 55, 72

Howard, Rosalind Frances, Countess of Carlisle 159

Howe, Anthony 57

Huntley & Palmer, attack on 158

Hurd, Douglas 360, 370

Hurry, J. B., *Poverty and its vicious circle* 232

Hyndman, Henry Mayers 109

IBM, donations to charity 380–1

ICI, donations to charity 380–1

Ignatieff, Michael 402

Illustrated London News 134

Imperial Cancer Research Fund 381

Import Duties, Report of the Select Committee on (1840) 81

In Darkest England and the Way Out, William Booth (1890) 109, 115, 131

Independent Labour Party 176

Independent Order of Rechabites, *see* Rechabites, Independent Order of

independent schools, *see* schools

inner cities, regeneration of 402

insurance and commercial assurance societies 7, 64, 126–8, 135, 167, 207–11, 213–14, 268–70, 294–5, 303, 363–4

insurance, national 166–7, 184–5, 189, 194, 253, 258, 262, 268, 282, 294, 352, 363, 420; *see also* National Health Insurance Act (1911), National Insurance Acts (1920, 1946)

Inter-Departmental Committee on Physical Deterioration, report (1904) 111–12, 113, 115–17, 147, 178

Invalid Children's Aid Association 276

ITV, Telethon appeals 378, 387, 402, 404

Jacobs, Brian D. 375
Jay, Douglas 255, 305
Jebb, Eglantyne 222
Jefferys, Kevin 258, 264, 281
Jellicoe, George Patrick John
  Rushworthy, 2nd Earl Jellicoe
  317
Jenkin, Patrick 358, 359, 361
Jewish Board of Guardians 234,
  293–4, 299–300
Jewish community, response to New
  Right 373
Jewish philanthropic tradition 47
Jewish refugees 220, 229, 231, 235
Jewish Refugees Committee 229; *see
  also* Central British Fund
Job Creation programme 322
Johnson, Norman 362
Johnson, Paul 137, 212, 213, 214, 232,
  362
Jones, Gareth Stedman 121
Jones, Sir Henry, Professor of Moral
  Philosophy, University of
  Glasgow 13, 415
Jones, Revd Richard, President of
  Methodist Conference 372
Jordanhill College School, Glasgow
  385
Joseph, Sir Keith 356–7, 394
Joseph Rowntree Memorial Trust
  (1959) 294, 342
Jowett, Benjamin 49
Jowitt, Sir William Allen, attorney
  general 263
Joyce, Patrick 58, 74
Justice, journal of the Social
  Democratic Federation 115

Keble, John 49, 52
Kelling sanatoria, Norfolk, Friends of
  283
Kentish London 26, 31, 40, 43
Keynes, John Maynard, *General
  Theory of Employment, Interest and
  Money* (1936) 223, 261
King, Desmond S. 16
King Edward's Hospital Fund for
  London 215, 240, 271, 272
King George's Fund for Sailors 228
King George VI Social Service
  Scheme for Old People, training
  courses 410
Kinnear, Sir Walter 210
Kirk, Neville 37

Kirkman Gray, *see* Gray, Benjamin
  Kirkman
Kochan, Nick 379

'Labour aristocracy' 42, 44, 45, 112,
  315
labour colonies 180–1
labour exchanges 164, 167, 184, 223
Labour movement 122–4
Labour Party policies 254–6, 257,
  259, 261, 263–4, 277, 295, 303,
  309, 313, 419–20
  attitude to voluntarism 248–50,
  260, 272, 281, 282, 291, 297–8,
  317, 318, 320–1, 335, 358, 369–70,
  374
  'Immediate Programme' (1937) 255
  'The Old World and the New
  Society' (1942) 256
  and Welfare State 3, 258, 264, 268,
  272–3, 281, 321, 369, 393–4,
  419–20
Labour Representation Committee 124
Laing, Sir Hector, founder of Percent
  Club 387
'*laissez-faire*' system 90, 181, 369
Lambert, Royston 312
Land, Hilary 391
Lang, Ian 365
Lansbury, George 157, 248, 254
Laski, Harold 272
Lavers, G. R. (with Seebohm
  Rowntree), survey of York (1951)
  309, 310
Lawson, Nigel 378
legal advice centres 406
Leicester, 2nd Earl, *see* Coke, Thomas
  William, 2nd Earl of Leicester
Leicester, unemployment in 244
Lennox, Charles Gordon-, 6th Duke
  of Richmond 72, 133
Liberal Party policies 124, 256, 368
  legislation on social reform after
  1906: 164, 183–7
  neo-liberalism of Mrs Thatcher 362,
  366
  'New Liberalism' 124, 155–6, 161,
  165, 181–2, 185–7, 262, 415, 416,
  418, 419
  and Tory 'New Right' 368
Liberty and Property Defence League
  194
Lichfield, charities in 72–3
  poor law guardians 251

Life Assurance, *see* Cohen Committee on Life Assurance, report (1932) *see also* insurance and commercial assurance societies
Lincoln, John A. 301
Lincoln People's Service Club 225 n.
Lipman, V. D. 234
Lister, Ruth 370–1
Liverpool 105, 132, 226
  Council of Voluntary Aid 175, 239
  Council for Social Service 215, 235–6, 265, 297–8
Loane, Margaret 418
local authorities and welfare 150, 252, 283, 292, 293, 296, 298, 301, 317, 322–4, 364
Local Authority Social Services Act (1970) 323
Local Government Act (1929) 240, 252
Local Government Board 152, 273
Loch, Sir Charles Stewart, Secretary, Charity Organisation Society 77, 79, 111, 135 141, 142, 174, 194, 199, 213, 246, 287, 346, 417, 418
  opposition to state intervention 101–2, 195, 279
Lodge, Sir Oliver 418
London:
  charities 62–3, 72, 91, 134, 149, 216, 226, 233, 237; *see also* City companies and charitable funds
  riots in 121
  surveys of, *see* statistical social surveys, London
  War Relief, Conference on (1915) 219, 239, 241, 245
London, Greater, housing in (Milner Holland Committee report) 314
London Congregational Union 108
London Council for Social Service 276, 281
London Missionary Society 139
Longford, 7th Earl, *see* Pakenham, Francis Aungier, Baron Pakenham, later 7th Earl of Longford
Lord Mayor's National Air Raid Distress Fund 228
Low, Sampson, *Charities of London* (1850) 62–3, 91
Low, Sir Sidney 163
Lowndes, G. A. N. 277

Loyal Order of Ancient Shepherds Friendly Society 27–8, 382–3
Lynes, Tony 312
Lyon, Alexander 320, 325

Macadam, Elizabeth, *The New Philanthropy* (1934) 279, 285, 417
McCord, Norman 93
MacDonald, James Ramsay 157, 263
McIntosh, Neil, 348
Mackay, Thomas 194
Macmillan, Hugh Pattison, Baron Macmillan of Aberfeldy 231, 247, 277, 284, 356
Macnicol, John 262
Major, John 368, 417
Manchester, charities in 61, 237, 245, 300
Manchester Guardian 37
Manchester Statistical Society 103
Mann, *see* Douglas-Mann, Bruce
Manning, Cardinal Henry Edward 135
Mansion House Committees 141, 149
Markham, Violet 174
Marsden, Richard 75–6
Marshall, Mary Paley, Mrs Alfred Marshall 132
Marshall, Thomas Humphrey 3, 4, 5, 283–4, 285, 289, 304, 308, 416, 420
Marten, Rosemary 316–17
Marwick, Arthur 257
Mason, Hugh, of Ashton 57
Mass Observation 212, 302
Masterman, Charles 106, 156
Mayhew, Henry 78
Mead, Larry 408
Meath, 12th Earl, *see* Brabazon, Reginald, 12th Earl of Meath
Mechanics' Institutes 36
Men without Work, report on unemployment to Pilgrim Trust (1938) 201, 204, 243–4, 264
Mencap 381
Mencher, S., Loch Memorial Lecturer (1954) 5, 12
Mercers' Company and charitable funds 59
Merseyside, Social Survey of (1928) 201
Mess, Henry A., *Voluntary Social Services since 1918* (1947) 215, 231

Methodism and the Bitter Cry of Outcast London, Forster Crozier (1885) 191–2
Methodist Church 40, 372
Middleton, Sue (with Peter Golding) 263
Milan, Audrey, organizer, Scottish Charities Effectiveness Review Trust 380
Mill, John Stuart 88, 92, 161
Millar, Frederick 194
Miller, Frederic M. 203
Milliband, Ralph 3–4, 5
Milner, Alfred, Viscount Milner 163
Milner Holland Committee on housing in Greater London 314
Ministry of Health, *see* Health, Ministry of
Ministry of Pensions and National Insurance, *see* Pensions and National Insurance, Ministry of
Ministry of Social Security, *see* Social Security, Ministry of
Minto, Dr James 381
Mocroft, I. (with Stephen Hatch) 330, 333
Molesworth, William Nassau 35
Montagu, Samuel, 1st Baron Swaythling 157
Morgan, Kenneth O. 394
Morgan, William, compiler of Southwell Tables 25
MORI poll on volunteers (1990) 389
Morris, R. J. 60, 102
Morris, William 157
Morris, William Richard, Viscount Nuffield 247
Morrison, Herbert 255, 281, 297
Mortimer, John 371
Mothers-in-Action (1967) 327
Mothers' Union (1876) 74
Mowat, Charles L. 229, 231, 254
Muggeridge, Malcolm 201–2
Municipal Review 348
Murray, Charles 408
mutual aid and co-operation, *see* building societies; burial societies; co-operative movement; Friendly Societies; penny banks; savings banks; teetotalism and temperance; trade union and co-operative movement; voluntarism

Nathan, Harry Louis, 1st Baron Nathan 290
Nathan Committee on the law and practice relating to charitable trusts, report (1952) 9, 288–91, 292, 294, 299, 300
National Assistance Act (1948) 258, 280, 293
National Assistance benefit 311, 312–13
National Assistance Board (formerly Unemployment Assistance Board, *q.v.*; Assistance Board; later Supplementary Benefits Commission) 312
National Association for the Care and Resettlement of Offenders 328, 348
National Association of Boys' Clubs 241
National Association of Discharged Prisoners Aid Societies 241
National Association of Discharged Sailors and Soldiers 220
National Association of Girls' Clubs 227
National Association of Guilds of Help 239
National Council on Alcoholism (1963) 328
National Council for One Parent Families (formerly National Council for the Unmarried Mother and her Child) 338–9, 390
National Council of Social Service (later National Council for Voluntary Organisations) 217, 225, 229, 239–40, 241, 242, 265, 274–5, 276, 318
  Report on Voluntary Services (1947) 302
National Council for Voluntary Organisations 339, 386, 389, 401, 404, 417, 421
National Council for Voluntary Youth Services 404
National Debt Office 85
National Deposit Friendly Society 213, 268
National Federation of Discharged and Demobilised Sailors and Soldiers (1917) 220

National Federation of Housing Associations 404

National government 261

National Health Insurance, Royal Commission on (1925) 238, 248

National Health Insurance Act (1911) 166, 176, 184–5, 194, 205, 207, 269, 421

National Health Service 9, 257, 270–3, 280, 282, 363, 369, 397

National Institute for the Blind 280

National Insurance 184–5, 189, 194, 253, 258, 262, 282, 294, 420

National Insurance Act (1920) 209, 211

National Insurance Act (1946) 257, 268

National League of Hospital Friends 283

National Milk Hostels Committee 221

National Organising Committee for War Savings (later National War Savings Committee) 209

National Relief Fund (1914) 218, 220

National Society 87, 96

National Society for Autistic Children (1962) 328

National Society of Discharged Prisoners' Aid Societies 328

National Society for the Prevention of Cruelty to Children 146, 168, 176, 193, 381

National Temperance Society (later National Temperance League) 39

National Women's Aid Federation (1975) 327

Natran, Mrs 224

neighbourhood as unit of mutual aid 7, 65–6, 128, 230, 296, 361

Neil, Sir Edward 210

Neuberger, Julia 329

New Lanark 58

New Right, *see* Conservative Party, 'New Right' policies

New Society 307, 325, 333, 338, 347, 348

New Survey of London Life and Labour (1934), *see* statistical social surveys, London

New Unionism 122

Newcastle upon Tyne, philanthropy in 60–1, 129, 136, 149

Newsome Report on Secondary Education (1963) 313–14

Next Five Years Group (1934) 254

Nichol, Francie 230

Nichols, Beverley, *News of England* 202

Nightingale, Florence 49

Nineteenth Century 141

Nonconformist Churches and voluntarism 40, 96, 187

Norfolk, 14th Duke, *see* Howard, Henry Granville Fitzalan, Earl of Arundel and Surrey, later 14th Duke of Norfolk

Normal School (for teacher training) 96

Norris, Arthur 175

Northumberland, 4th Duke, *see* Percy, Algernon, 4th Duke of Northumberland

Nottingham, survey of voluntary workers 334

Novak, Tony 184–5

Nozick, Robert 355

Nuffield, Viscount, *see* Morris, William Richard, Viscount Nuffield

Nuffield Foundation 294, 342, 375

Nuffield Provincial Hospitals Trust 240, 272

Nuffield Trust 224

Nunn, Hancock 159, 174

Oastler, Richard 69, 97

Observer, The 368

Oddfellows, *see* Friendly Societies

Old Age Pension Act (1908) 183–4, 189

Orkney inquiry on child abuse (1991) 410

Orwell, George, *The Road to Wigan Pier* 202

Osborne, Revd Lord Sidney Godolphin, of Durweston 55

Owen, A. D. K., 1938 Stevenson Lecturer in Citizenship, Glasgow University, 416

Owen, David, *English Philanthropy, 1660–1960* 63, 70, 293

Owen, Dr David 319

Owenism 28–9

Oxfam 382

Oxford, voluntary organizations in 340

Oxford University, settlement
movement 131, 132

Pakenham, Francis Aungier, Baron
Pakenham, later 7th Earl of
Longford (1961) 259, 260, 281,
283, 291, 297
Pall Mall Gazette 80, 89, 108, 109,
115 n.
Palmers of Reading 145
Palmerston, 3rd Viscount, *see* Temple,
Henry John, 3rd Viscount
Palmerston
panel doctors 191
Parker, Roy 390
Parmoor Committee (1920) 248
paternalism and philanthropy 6,
45–63, 129–33, 288–91, 302–28,
358–60
criticism of 155–60
examples 54–9, 71–4, 294–5, 327–9
extent 62–3, 133–4, 215–18, 327–9
finances 143–5, 233
limitations 58, 78–80, 139–47
motivation 46–54, 129–33, 218
relations to state 74, 97, 175–6,
279–81, 284, 302
war and want, effect on 214–29
see also voluntarism
Paterson, Alexander 165
Patten, John 366, 370
pawnbrokers and moneylenders 65,
66, 78, 128, 230
pay beds in NHS hospitals 288
Peden, G. C. 261
Peek, Francis 121
Peel, Sir Robert, 2nd Bt. 81–2
Pelham, Henry Thomas, 3rd Earl of
Chichester 54
Penlee Life Boat disaster appeal
(1981) 379, 404
penny banks 34–5
Penny Magazine, The 21
pensions:
contributory 188–9, 209, 262
state old age 164, 166, 183–4,
187–8, 193
Pensions and National Insurance,
Ministry of 311
Percent Club 388
Percy, Algernon, 4th Duke of
Northumberland 55, 133
Percy, Lord Eustace 284

Perkin, Harold 395–6
permissive legislation 88, 183
Personal Service League 224, 227
Phelps, Lancelot Ridley 196
Philanthropist, The 134, 143, 144
Phillips Committee 311
Philpot, Terry 348
Picture Post 202, 255
Pilgrim Trust (1930) 210, 223–4,
225–6, 230, 231, 240, 245, 247,
405
Pinker, Robert 395
Pitt, William 52
Plant, Raymond 182, 409
Plowden Report on Primary
Education (1967) 314
Political and Economic Planning
(1931) 254, 310
Report on the British Social Services
(1937) 216, 242–3, 285
Pollit, Tim 40
Poole, H. R. 297, 298, 299
Poor Law, Royal Commission on
(1834) 82, 94
Poor Law, Royal Commission on
(1905–9), Majority Report 153–4,
172–3, 194, 196, 197–8
Poor Law, Royal Commission on
(1905–9), Minority Report 158,
180, 197–8
Poor Law Act (1834) 82–3, 413
Poor Law Board, Goschen Minute
(1869) 92, 105, 147, 152, 196
Poor Law minute (1886) 150, 151
poor law system 82, 92, 93, 98, 136,
147–55, 158, 176, 196–7, 198,
251
principle of 'less eligibility' 98–100,
147, 151, 251–2, 254
Poplar:
poor law union 148, 252
poverty in 202
Porter, George, *Progress of the Nation*
(1851) 45
Portsmouth, survey of voluntary
workers 334
poverty 104, 108–21, 134, 177–8, 191,
196, 201–4, 309–11
rediscovery of 311–13, 314–17
Poverty and Progress, Seebohm
Rowntree (1941) 202–3
Powell, Enoch 355, 393
Prashar, Usha 386, 421

Pratt, John Tidd, Registrar of
    Friendly Societies 84, 85
Pre-School Playgroups Association
    (1961) 327, 340
pressure groups 306, 328, 349–50,
    353, 406
Prest, John 88
Prevention and Relief of Distress,
    government committee on 273
Price, Dr Richard, compiler of
    Northampton Tables 25
Priestley, J. B., *English Journey* 202,
    243–4
Pringle, Revd J. C., *The Nation's
    Appeal to the Housewife and her
    Response* 246
Privy Council, Committee on
    Education 96
probation service, voluntary help in
    329
Prochaska, Frank K. 48, 54, 63, 71,
    102, 279
professionalization of welfare 145,
    146, 152, 235
Project Fullemploy 402
Public Assistance Committees 252
Pym, Francis 366

Quarrier, William 75
Quarrier's Homes in Scotland 381
Queen Mary's Needlework Guild 218
Quickswood, 1st Baron, *see* Cecil,
    Lord Hugh Gascoyne-, later 1st
    Baron Quickswood

'Rachmanism' 314
Ragged School Union 74, 90, 169–70,
    205
ragged schools 48, 74–5, 87, 97, 169
Raison, Timothy 376
Rathbone, Eleanor 175
Reading:
    philanthropy in 135, 144–5, 146,
        158, 340
    public assistance in 265
Rechabites, Independent Order of 26,
    37–8
Red Cross, *see* British Red Cross
    Society
Rees, Merlyn 320
Reeves, Maud Pember, *Round About a
    Pound a Week* 128
reformatory schools 87

refugees 220–1, 229, 231, 235
Registrar of Friendly Societies (later
    Chief Registrar, with Assistant
    Registrars for Scotland and
    Ireland) 84, 95
Release (1967) 328
relief organizations (after 1918) 221,
    404
religion and philanthropy 47–9,
    129–32, 330–2
Rentoul, Dr Robert Reid 144, 154
Richardson, Ann 305
Riches, Wendy 379
Richmond, 6th Duke of, *see* Lennox,
    Charles Gordon-, 6th Duke of
    Richmond
Rifkind, Malcolm 360
Ritchie, D. G. 156, 161
Robbins Report on Higher Education
    (1963) 313
Roberts, David 58
Roberts, Robert, *A Ragged Schooling,
    The Classic Slum*, 128
Robertson, J. M., *The Fallacy of Saving*
    (1892) 155
Robertson, William 146
Rochdale Pioneers 29–30, 31, 38, 41
Rockliffe, Percy 270
Rose, Hilary 391
Rowntree, Joseph, Memorial Trust
    294, 342
Rowntree, Seebohm 254
    Progress and Poverty (1941) 202–3
    statistical survey of York (1901)
        109–10, 111, 115, 119–21, 125–7,
        128, 137, 138, 154, 178
    statistical survey of York (1935–6)
        201, 202, 214
    statistical survey of York (with
        G. R. Lavers, 1951) 309–10
Royal Air Force Benevolent Fund 228
Royal Commission on the Aged Poor
    (1893–5) 183
Royal Commission on Depression in
    Trade and Industry, report
    (1886) 111, 113
Royal Commission on Friendly
    Societies, report (1871–4) 25, 28,
    32, 84, 85, 95, 284
Royal Commission on the Housing of
    the Poor (1884–) 118–19
Royal Commission on Labour (1892)
    122

Royal Commission on National Health Insurance, majority report (1925) 238; minority report 248
Royal Commission on the National Health Service, report (1979) 307
Royal Commission on the Poor Law, report (1834) 82, 94, 354
Royal Commission on the Poor Law, report (1905–9), majority report 153–4, 172–3, 194, 196, 197–8; minority report 158, 180, 197–8
Royal National Institute for the Blind 344, 411
royal patronage of charities 412
Runcie, Rt. Revd Dr Robert, Archbishop of Canterbury 372–3
Ruskin, John 106
Russell, Charles 175
Russell, Francis, 7th Duke of Bedford 55, 133
Ruthwell, Dumfriesshire, first savings bank at 33
Ryder, Dudley, 2nd Earl of Harrowby 47

Saatchi & Saatchi 381
Sadler, Michael 89
St George's-in-the-East poor law union 147
St John Ambulance Brigade 337
Salisbury, 3rd Marquess, *see* Cecil, Robert Arthur Talbot Gascoyne-, 3rd Marquess of Salisbury
Salt, Titus 57
Saltaire, model factory town 57–8
Salts of Saltaire 56, 97
Salvation Army (1878) 109, 131, 168, 179, 180, 181, 219, 225, 403
Samaritans 331, 336, 381, 405
Sanitary Commission (1869) 94–5
Sankey, John, Viscount Sankey 240
Save the Children Fund (1919) 222, 276, 379, 380, 381, 412
savings banks 33–4, 38, 95, 213
see also penny banks; thrift
School Boards of Governors 384–5
school inspectorate 96
schools:
 Church 187, 276–7
 dame 36, 95
 independent 277, 288, 296
 state 306
 voluntary 277
see also education
Scotland, philanthropy in 33, 34, 63, 75, 77, 133, 144, 145, 146, 219, 220, 239, 323, 380, 381
Scotsman, The 75
Scottish Charities Effectiveness Review Trust (1989) 380
Scottish Council for Voluntary Organizations 381
Searle, G. R. 116
Seebohm Committee on Local Authority and Allied Personal Social Services in England and Wales, report (1969) 292, 305–6, 316, 323, 344, 398
Selborne, Countess of, *see* Cecil, Lady Maud, Countess of Selborne
self-help 19–21
SERPS, *see* State Earnings-Related Pension Scheme
settlement house movement 131–3, 141, 159, 225, 227
Shaftesbury, 7th Earl, *see* Cooper, Anthony Ashley, 7th Earl of Shaftesbury
Shaftesbury Society 331, 417
Sheffield:
 poor law guardians in 251
 voluntary organizations in 340
Shelter (1966) 328, 342, 348, 406
Sheppard, Rt. Revd David, Bishop of Liverpool 371–2
Simey, T. S. 242, 249
Simon, Sir John, 242
Skeffington Committee on Public Participation in Planning, report (1969) 306
Slack, Revd Kenneth 350
slumming 131, 132, 158
Smiles, Samuel 19–24, 35, 40, 41, 43, 45, 75, 76, 92, 357, 414
Smith, James, of Deanston 56
Smith, Joshua Toulmin 94
Smith, Justin Davis, *see* Davis-Smith
Social Affairs Unit 376
Social Darwinism 92, 180
Social Democratic Federation 115, 157, 158
Social Fund (1988) 369, 386–7
Social Security, Ministry of 313
Social Services Departments (England and Wales) 323, 354

social survey of Merseyside (1928)
    201
Social Welfare, councils of 239
Social Work (Scotland) Act 1968 and
    Social Work Departments 323,
    354
social workers, Barclay Committee
    Report on (1982) 398
socialism and socialists 122–3, 133,
    157, 162, 175–6, 193–4, 415
Socialist, The 157
Society of Friends 220, 224, 227, 229,
    276
Society for the Improvement of the
    Working Population in the
    County of Glamorgan 73
Society for the Protection of Science
    and Learning (formerly
    Academic Assistance Council)
    229
Soldiers and Comrades of the Great
    War 220
Soldiers' and Sailors' Families
    Association 218–19, 239, 246, 274
Soldiers', Sailors' and Airmen's
    Families Association 226, 227,
    406
Soldiers and Sailors Help Society 220
Southey, Robert 52, 89
Spastics Society 336, 380, 386
Spectator, The 316
Spencer, Herbert 355
Spencer, John Charles, Viscount
    Althorp, later 3rd Earl Spencer
    87
Spens Report on education (1938)
    253
Spinal Injuries Association (1974) 327
Sproat, Ian 354
Standing Committee of Voluntary
    Organizations in War Time 241
state:
    distrust of 95, 96–8, 123, 182, 187,
        192–5, 199, 266–7, 336
    enabling 81–9, 95–6, 182, 365
    in co-operation with local and
        voluntary bodies 105, 147–51,
        166–71, 173, 175–6, 181–2,
        185–6, 264–81, 281–6, 291–8,
        304–29, 341–2, 344–5, 358–66
    inadequacy 147–55, 307–8, 311–16,
        408
    increased role 160–6, 198, 204,
        250–64, 287

    in mixed economy 80–100, 101,
        147–55, 160–6, 182–7, 198–200,
        250–64, 287–8, 288–93, 304–29,
        412–23
    New Right policies 352–66, 392,
        396–400
    paternalist 89–91, 93, 305
    regulatory 89–98, 264–6
    'social service' 198, 254, 256
    see also Welfare State
State Children's Association 168
State Earnings-Related Pension
    Scheme (SERPS) 363
statistical social surveys:
    Bristol: Tout (1938) 201, 214
    London: Mayhew (1851–4) 78;
        Booth (1889–1903) 109–11, 115;
        *New Survey of London Life and
        Labour* (1929–30, pub. 1934) 201,
        202
    Merseyside (1928) 201
    York: Rowntree (1901) 109, 115,
        119–21; Rowntree (1935–6) 201,
        214; Rowntree and Lavers (1951)
        309–10
Stead, J. Lister 138
Stead, W. T. 108
Stedman Jones, *see* Jones, Gareth
    Stedman
Steel, David 368
Steeel-Maitland, Arthur 163
Steen, Anthony 336, 339
Stephen, Caroline Emilia 79
Stepney 131, 149
Stern, Vivien 348
Stevenson, John 217
Stevenson Lectureship in Citizenship,
    University of Glasgow 13, 416
Sturge, Joseph 76, 93
Sugden, Robert 408
Sunderland 147, 340
Supple, Barry 67
Supplementary Benefits Commission
    (formerly National Assistance
    Board) 312
Swaythling, 1st Baron, *see* Montagu,
    Samuel, 1st Baron Swaythling
*Sweet Herbs for the Bitter Cry, or
    Remedies for Horrible Outcast
    London* 191
Switzerland 164

Task Force 328, 336–8, 339, 402, 409
tax relief 236, 296, 298–9, 364

taxation, effects on social services 165, 288, 295, 296, 298–9, 322, 349, 352
Taylor, A. J. P. 231
Taylor, J. S. 168
Taylor Committee report (1977) 306
Taylor-Gooby, Peter 394, 397, 413
teetotalism and temperance 37–9, 43
see also Bands of Hope; British Association for the Promotion of Temperance; National Temperance Society; Rechabites, Independent Order of; United Kingdom Alliance
Temple, Henry John, 3rd Viscount Palmerston 58
Temple, William, *Christianity and the Social Order* 255
Ten Hours movement 69, 89, 97, 406
Tesco, donations to charity 380–1
Thane, Pat 191
Thatcher, Margaret 14, 357–8, 359, 361, 399
address to General Assembly of Church of Scotland (1988) 358, 360, 369, 372, 397
New Right policies 14, 357–400, 417
see also Conservative Party, New Right policies
Tholfsen, Trygve 44
Thomas, Mike 329
Thomson, David 13, 16, 398
Thorneycroft, Peter 393
thrift 112, 120, 155, 209, 212–13, 214, 232, 294
Times, The 62, 115, 310, 410
Titmuss, Richard 1, 100, 312, 315, 391, 413, 420, 422
Tompson, Richard 86
Tory Party, see Conservative Party
Toulmin Smith, see Smith, Joshua Toulmin
Tout, Herbert, survey of Bristol 201, 214
Townsend, Peter 294, 305, 310–11
(with Brian Abel-Smith), *The Poor and the Poorest* 312–13
Toynbee, Arnold 132, 133
Toynbee Hall (1884) 132, 133, 142, 281
Trade Boards Act (1909) 165

trade union and co-operative movement 28–30, 38, 44, 122–3, 126, 244, 248, 249, 263
financial problems 211–12
and National Health Insurance Act (1911) 166–7, 185, 189, 269
relations with state 85, 166, 353
training, provision of 130, 169, 223, 402
Treasury, payments to voluntary sector 87, 208, 236, 237, 276, 279, 300, 322, 325, 341, 374–6
Trevor, John 175
Tyrrell, Alex 76

'Unauthorized Programme' (1885) 124
Unell, Judith 344–5
Unemployed Workmen Act (1905) 150–1, 153, 154
unemployment 114, 179, 203–4, 211
insurance against 208–9, 210–13, 257
state relief of 104, 136, 148, 168–9, 197, 251–3, 263–4
and voluntarism 29, 222–6, 229–31, 240, 243–6
Unemployment Act (1934) 252
Unemployment Assistance Board (later Assistance Board, from 1948 National Assistance Board) 252
see also National Assistance Board; Supplementary Benefits Commission
Unionist Social Reform Committee 163
United Kingdom Alliance 39
United Nations Organization 229, 357
United States of America 305
universities 285, 305, 383
see also settlement house movement
unmarried wives and mothers 245, 292, 338–9, 390
Upholland Experiment, near Wigan 224
Urban Programme (1968–78) 322, 323, 325

Varah, Revd Chad 331
Vincent, Andrew W. 172, 182, 416, 419

voluntarism 6–8, 24–45, 45–63,
    125–36, 205–31, 286–305
  characteristics 66–80
  collaboration with state 81–100,
    149–51, 166–76, 264–6, 273–86,
    291–7, 302–3, 342–4, 365–6,
    392–400
  could it cope? 136–47, 231–43,
    369–70
  criticism of 77–80, 155–60, 231–50,
    338–51, 408–12, 414–15
  distrust of state 187–9, 191–8,
    266–7, 413, 420
  divergence from state 267–73,
    297–8, 347
  effects of war and want on 205–31
  finances 206, 210, 232, 293,
    298–300, 301, 324–5, 341–2,
    344–5, 346–8, 349, 374–83,
    411–12, 421
  ideology 73–7, 103–6, 263–4,
    330–51
  influence on collectivism 181–7,
    263–4, 418–19
  merits of 102, 260, 289, 347, 351,
    401–8
  and New Right 371–92
  relations with state 81–100, 166–76,
    198–200, 259–60
  revival as alternative to state
    304–8, 316–29, 358–62, 417, 421
  should it cope? 155–60, 231,
    243–50, 369–70
  see also Approved Societies;
    building societies; burial
    societies; charities; co-operative
    movement; deposit societies;
    Friendly Societies; hospitals,
    voluntary; insurance and
    commercial assurance societies;
    paternalism and philanthropy;
    penny banks; savings banks;
    teetotalism and temperance;
    trade union and co-operative
    movement; and under specific
    voluntary organizations
voluntary hospitals, *see* hospitals,
    voluntary
voluntary occupational centre
    movement 225
voluntary organizations:
  special conference on (1915) 219,
    239, 241, 245
  surveys of 326–7, 332–3

Wolfenden Committee, *see*
    Wolfenden Committee on the
    Future of Voluntary
    Organizations, report (1978)
voluntary schools, *see* schools,
    voluntary
Voluntary Service Overseas 339, 373
Voluntary Services, report on (1947)
    215
Voluntary Services Unit, Home Office
    321–2, 346
Volunteer Bureaux 329
Volunteer Centre 327, 329
Volunteer Service Committees 249
Volunteers:
  availability and adequacy of 146,
    205, 214, 216, 220–1, 299, 323,
    329, 383–4
  training of 337, 338, 410

Waddilove, Lewis 342
Waifs and Strays Society 276
Wakely, Thomas, 94
Waldron, Sheona, convenor, Board of
    Governors of Jordanhill College
    School 385
Wales, Prince of, *see* Charles, Prince
    of Wales
Wales, Prince of, *see* Edward, Prince
    of Wales (later Edward VIII)
Walley, Sir John, Ministry of
    Pensions and National Insurance
    256
Walzer, Michael 9
War Charities Act (1916) 265
War Office, payments to voluntary
    hospitals 236
War Refugees Committee 220
Ware, Alan 14–15, 379
Warnock, Dame Mary 383
wars, *see* World War I; World War II
Warwick, Countess of, *see* Greville,
    Frances Evelyn, Countess of
    Warwick
Watson, A. W., Chief Government
    Actuary 208, 210
Watson Report (1930) 210
Weatherill, Bernard, Speaker of the
    House of Commons 374
Webb, A. (with L. Day and D.
    Weller) survey of voluntary
    organizations 326
Webb, Beatrice 157, 158–9, 162, 173,
    174, 179, 180

Webb, Sidney 122, 123, 157, 162, 173, 180, 181, 297
Webster, Charles 272
Wedderburn, Dorothy 312
Weinberg, Sir Mark 388
welfare, mixed economy of 1–3, 6–8, 9–10, 12, 80–106, 166–76, 187–8, 191–200, 250–4, 259–60, 263–86, 287–97, 304, 317–21, 330, 344, 347–52, 358–66, 391–400, 401–3, 413–23
Welfare State 254, 258, 264, 281, 301, 371, 392–400
    criticism of 307–8, 312–13, 314–17, 394, 420
    and New Right 14, 352–8, 362–6, 376, 392, 394–400
    voluntarism in 288–97, 301–4, 305–8, 317–25, 347–8, 359–62, 376, 403, 417, 420–2
Welfare State escalator 1–6, 10, 17–18, 81, 198, 250, 413, 418
Westbourne School for Girls, Glasgow 385
Westminster Review 69, 78, 108
Whig Party, *see* Liberal Party
Whitaker's Almanack 215, 216
Whitechapel 131, 140, 147, 149
Whiteheads of Hollymount 56
Whiteside, Noelle 269
Whittaker, Ben 350, 351
Whittaker, Thomas 38, 41
Whyte, Rt. Revd Professor James, Moderator, General Assembly of Church of Scotland 372
Wigan Subsistence Production Society 225 n.
Williams, H. R. 169
Willink, H. U. 276
Wilson, Sir Arnold 202
Wilson, Des 342
Wilson, Roger 299, 300
Windlesham, 3rd Baron, *see* Hennessy, David James George, 3rd Baron Windlesham
Wolfenden Committee on the Future of Voluntary Organizations, Report (1978) 296, 302, 307, 308, 316, 322, 323–4, 325, 330, 339–40, 341, 345–6, 393, 402, 420
    evidence to 323, 331–2, 334, 336, 338–9, 341, 343, 344, 345
    reactions to 320, 348–9

survey of voluntary work 326–7, 332–3
women:
    effects of depression on 210, 229–30
    in philanthropic work 48, 68, 159, 175, 205, 334, 361, 391
    in settlement house movement 132–3, 159
    and war service 205–6, 207–8, 220–1
    see also under specific charities for women
Women's Army Auxiliary Corps 205
Women's Defence Relief Corps 221
Women's Emergency Corps 221
Women's Hospital Corps 221
Women's International League 222
Women's Legion 221
Women's Royal Voluntary Service 359
Women's Voluntary Service 275
Women's Volunteer Reserve 221
Wordsworth, William 89
workhouses, conditions in 99–100, 151–3
World War I 205, 218
World War II 226–8, 237–8, 243, 255
Worpole, Ken 334–5
Would, Marian 337
Wright, Thomas 42–3, 44–5

Yeo, Stephen 144
York, statistical surveys, *see* statistical social surveys, York
    voluntary organizations in 125–7, 138
Yorkshire Miners' Association 212
Yorkshire Penny Savings Bank 35
Young, Ken 380
Young Men's Christian Association 139, 225, 227, 404
Young Volunteer Force Foundation 336
Young Women's Christian Association 225, 227
Younghusband, Eileen, *Social Work in Britain* 301
Younghusband Committee on Social Workers in the Local Authority Health and Welfare Services, report (1959) 291–2, 298, 301, 405, 408–9, 410
Youth Clubs 329, 333–5, 341
Youthful Offenders Act (1854) 87